CHEMISTRY

For B.Sc. Students

Fundamentals of Chemistry | Quantitative Analysis

About the Author

Dr R L Madan has over 35 years experience of teaching Chemistry at different levels. He has done extensive research work in the areas of adsorption, catalysis and surface chemistry at the Indian Institute of Technology, New Delhi. He has to his credit 15 research papers in the areas of adsorption, catalysis, polymers and superconductivity published in different national and international journals.

He started his teaching career at Government Postgraduate College, Gurgaon. He has held positions of Head of the Chemistry Department, Government Postgraduate College, Faridabad and Principal, Government College, Panchkula and Tigaon (Faridabad). He is a recipient of UNESCO and Swedish Institute Fellowships and has authored a number of books on Chemistry and Environmental Education.

CHEMISTRY

For B.Sc. Students

Fundamentals of Chemistry | Quantitative Analysis

Theory | Practical

RL MADAN
M.Sc., Ph.D.
Former Head of the Chemistry Department
Government Postgraduate College, Faridabad
and *Principal*, Government College, Panchkula

S Chand And Company Limited
(ISO 9001 Certified Company)

S Chand And Company Limited
(ISO 9001 Certified Company)
Head Office: Block B-1, House No. D-1, Ground Floor, Mohan Co-operative Industrial Estate, New Delhi – 110 044 | Phone: 011-66672000
Registered Office: A-27, 2nd Floor, Mohan Co-operative Industrial Estate, New Delhi – 110 044 | Phone: 011-49731800
www.**schandpublishing.com**; e-mail: **info@schandpublishing.com**

Branches

Chennai	:	Ph: 23632120; chennai@schandpublishing.com
Guwahati	:	Ph: 2738811, 2735640; guwahati@schandpublishing.com
Hyderabad	:	Ph: 40186018; hyderabad@schandpublishing.com
Jalandhar	:	Ph: 4645630; jalandhar@schandpublishing.com
Kolkata	:	Ph: 23357458, 23353914; kolkata@schandpublishing.com
Lucknow	:	Ph: 4003633; lucknow@schandpublishing.com
Mumbai	:	Ph: 25000297; mumbai@schandpublishing.com
Patna	:	Ph: 2260011; patna@schandpublishing.com

First Edition 2022
Reprint 2022 (Twice)

ISBN: 978-93-550-1162-6 **Product Code:** H6CBSCHEM6810ENAA21O

PRINTED IN INDIA

By Vikas Publishing House Private Limited, Plot 20/4, Site-IV, Industrial Area Sahibabad, Ghaziabad – 201 010 and Published by S Chand And Company Limited, A-27, 2nd Floor, Mohan Co-operative Industrial Estate, New Delhi – 110 044.

Preface

It gives me immense pleasure to present this textbook to the Undergraduate students and teachers fraternity of Chemistry. This textbook has been specifically developed as per the Common Minimum Syllabus prescribed for all Uttar Pradesh State Universities and Colleges under the recommended National Education Policy 2020.

Designed strictly as per B.Sc. Chemistry first semester syllabus, this textbook comprehensively covers two Papers, namely, Fundamentals of Chemistry and Quantitative Analysis.

A long span of interaction with students has guided me to give special attention to dark areas which students find difficult to grasp. Keeping that in view, this textbook has been written in a simple and lucid language with following special features to aid student's understanding of the subject matter:

- Well drawn illustrations and examples have been provided to make the reading interesting and engaging
- A large number of solved problems have been provided for effective understanding of the theoretical concepts
- Questions for practice have been provided at the end of each chapter

I am thankful to the management and editorial team of S. Chand Publishing for the help and support in the publication of this textbook.

I believe that the textbook contains all that is needed to understand the subject in a systematic manner. However, I also believe that no work is perfect and there is always scope for improvement. I would welcome suggestions from the teaching fraternity and students for further improvement of the book.

R L Madan
Mob. 9971775666

Contents

PAPER I: FUNDAMENTALS OF CHEMISTRY

PAPER II: QUANTITATIVE ANALYSIS

Paper I

Fundamentals of Chemistry

1

Introduction to Indian Ancient Chemistry and Contribution of Indian Chemists

1.1 INDIAN ANCIENT CHEMISTRY

Early Indian philosophers believed that matter exists in the form of five basic elements called *Panch Tatva* namely air, earth, fire, sky and water. In their view, everything living and non-living was made up of these *pancha tatvas*. The idea of divisibility of matter caught the attention of thinkers around 500 B.C. Maharishi Kanad, an Indian philosopher gave out the postulate that if we go on crushing and dividing matter, we shall get smaller and smaller particles till a stage reaches when further division cannot be carried out. He named these smallest particles as *Parmanu* (now called atom). Another Indian philosopher Pakudha Katyayama further advanced this theory by saying that these *parmanus* existed in combined state to give us various forms of matter.

Indians were pioneers in various metallurgical operations. High quality steel was produced in India about 2000 years back and we were much superior to the west in this area. A seamless celestial globe was made in Kashmir for the first time and it is still there for display. It was a task which was considered as impossible at that time. A glaring example of technological superiority in India is an iron pillar near Qutab Minar in Delhi which was built more than 1600 years ago by Indian metallurgists. They had developed a wonderful process which could prevent iron from rusting. Scientists from all over the world have been visiting the site from time to time to investigate resistance towards rusting in the pillar. The pillar is 8 metre in height and weighs 6000 kilogram.

1.2 MODERN INDIAN CHEMISTS

A large number of chemists have made valuable contribution to different branches and fields of chemistry. We give below the contribution of some of them.

Acharya Prafulla Chandra Ray

Acharya Prafulla Chandra Ray was an eminent Bengali chemist, educationist and industrialist. He established the first modern Indian research school in chemistry and is regarded as father of chemical science in India. He founded Bengal chemicals and pharmaceutical and Government P.C. College Bagerhat. Prafulla Chandra started his work in the field of discovering nitrite chemistry and published a paper on preparation of new stable chemical compound mercurous nitrite.

Acharya Prafulla Chandra Ray (1861–1944)

Shanti Swaroop Bhatnagar

Sir Shanti Swaroop Bhatnagar was a colloid chemist, academic and scientific administrator. The first Director-General of Council of Scientific and Industrial Research, he is revered as father of research laboratories in India. In 1928, he and K.N. Mathur jointly developed the Bhatnagar-Mathur interference balance which was one of the most accurate and sensitive instruments at the time for measuring magnetic properties.

Shanti Swaroop Bhatnagar (1894–1955)

Asima Chatterjee

Asima Chatterjee was a brilliant organic chemist and is known for her work in the field of organic chemistry. Her most notable work includes research on vince alkaloids, the development of anti-epilectic drugs Ayush-56 and development of antimalarial drugs.

Asima Chatterjee (1917–2006)

Har Gobind Khorana

Har Gobind Khorana was an Indian-American biochemist. While working at the university of Wisconsin Madison, he shared the Nobel Prize in Physiology and Medicine with Marshall W. Nirenberg. He made important contributions to this field by building different RNA chains with the help of enzymes. He could produce proteins by using these enzymes. The amino acid sequence of these proteins then solved the rest of the puzzle.

Har Gobind Khorana (1922–2011)

C.N.R. Rao

C.N.R. Rao worked in solid state and structural chemistry. He has honorary doctorates from 83 universities from around the world and has authored 1770 research papers and 53 books. He was Director of Indian Institute of Science, Bangalore from 1984 to 1994. During 1985–89 and 2005–2014, he served as chairman of the Scientific Advisory Council to the Prime Minister of India. He was awarded Bharat Ratna, the highest Indian Civil Award in 2014.

C.N.R Rao

R.A. Mashelkar

R.A. Mashelkar served as the Director General of Council of Scientific Research— a network of 38 laboratories for over 11 years. Prior to that, he was Director of National Chemical Laboratory, Pune for 6 years. He is known for his work on transport phenomenon, particularly in thermodynamics of swelling, superswelling and shrinking polymers and modelling of polymerisation reactors.

R.A. Mashelkar

1.3 RESONANCE AND RESONANCE ENERGY

Sometimes it is not possible to describe the properties of a substance on the basis of a single structure. We explain it by saying that the substance exists in a number of structures called **resonating** structures. The actual substance is then hybrid of these resonating structures. This phenomenon is called resonance. Each resonating structure makes a definite contribution, big or small, to the actual structure of the substance. This is explained with the help of resonating structures I, II, III of H_2.

$$\underset{\text{I}}{\underset{\text{(covalent)}}{H:H}} \leftrightarrow \underset{\text{II}}{\underset{\text{(ionic)}}{H^{+}:H^{-}}} \leftrightarrow \underset{\text{III}}{\underset{\text{(ionic)}}{H^{-}:H^{+}}}$$

The double pointing arrows (↔) between these structures indicate that they are in resonance with one another. However it is not to be inferred that H_2 exhibits all of these three structures, now can it be said that hydrogen exists for a certain fraction of time in one form and for another fraction of time in some other form. The molecules have single structures which cannot be described in terms of electron dot diagram on the paper. The difficulty lies in the description and not in the molecule. The real structure is a resonance hybrid of these three structures. A resonance hybrid can be equated to a mule which exhibits the characteristics of both the donkey and the horse, but at no moment it is either of these. The resonance hybrid is more stable than any one of the contributing structures. This extra stability of the resonance hybrid as compared with the most stable of the resonating structures is known as resonance energy. It is the greatest when all the resonating structures are of the same energy.

Resonance energy = Actual bond energy – Energy of the pure covalent bond

It may be pointed out that if a molecule or ions cannot be represented by a single structure, then the real structure is expressed in terms of resonance hybrid of all possible structures.

Necessary Conditions for Writing Resonating Structures

The necessary conditions for writing resonating structures are as follows :

(*i*) The nuclei of the atoms is each structure must remain in fixed positions. Only the arrangement of electrons may change. The bond angles and bond lengths should be closer to the real structure. Only then the contribution of that structure to the hybrid will be significant. For example, the Dewar structures of benzene are less important than the Kekule structures because in Dewar structures there is one very long bond across the ring.

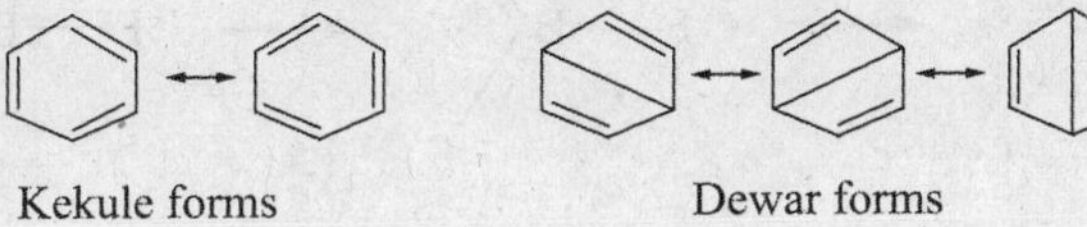

Kekule forms　　　　Dewar forms

The following two structures of phosphorus acid (H_3PO_3) are not resonance structures because of the displacement in the position of atoms.

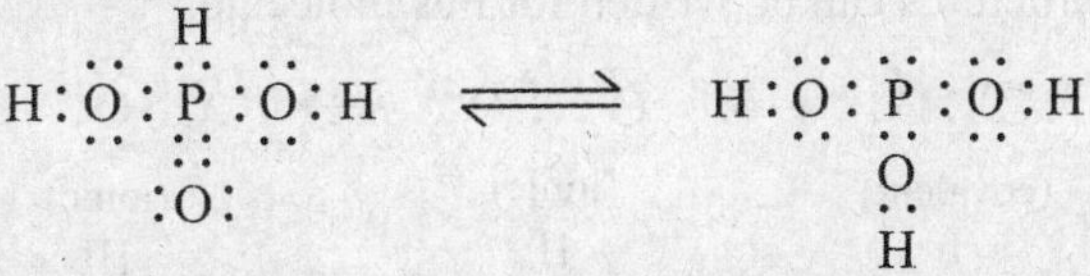

$$H:\ddot{\underset{..}{O}}:\underset{:O:}{\overset{H}{P}}:\ddot{\underset{..}{O}}:H \rightleftharpoons H:\ddot{\underset{..}{O}}:\underset{\underset{H}{O}}{\ddot{P}}:\ddot{\underset{..}{O}}:H$$

The two structures represent two different chemical species (tautomers) which are in equilibrium, but are not resonance structures.

(*ii*) Each structure must have the same number of unpaired electrons. We should not draw structures in which one form contains a single unpaired electron and another contains two unpaired electrons. For example:

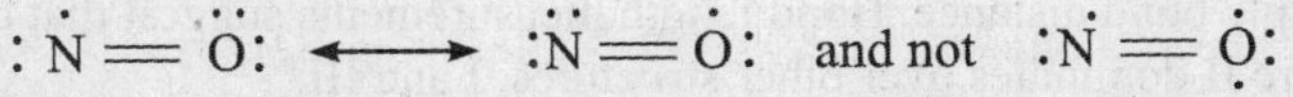

$$:\dot{N}=\ddot{O}: \longleftrightarrow :\ddot{N}=\dot{O}: \quad \text{and not} \quad :\dot{N}=\dot{O}:$$

(*iii*) The contributing structures should all have similar energies. This rule may be illustrated by taking the example of benzene. The Dewar structures have higher energy and are, therefore, less important than the more stable Kekule forms in the combination that represents the true structure of benzene.

(*iv*) Those structures in which negative charge resides on the most electronegative atoms and positive charge on the most electropositive atom will be closest to the true structure. For example, we may write the following resonating structures of HCl.

$$\underset{\text{I}}{\underset{\text{(covalent)}}{H : \ddot{\underset{..}{Cl}} :}} \longleftrightarrow \underset{\text{II}}{\underset{\text{(ionic)}}{H^+ \; :\ddot{\underset{..}{Cl}}:^-}} \longleftrightarrow \underset{\text{III}}{\underset{\text{(ionic)}}{\bar{H}: \; \overset{+}{\underset{..}{Cl}}:}}$$

There is significant contribution from structure II (because of greater electronegative of chlorine). However, any contribution by structure III is not possible.

(*v*) The contributing structures should be so written that unlike charges reside on neighbouring atoms. Consider the resonance structures of HNO_3. The last structure does not contribute because of +ve charge on adjacent N atoms and double –ve charge on the third nitrogen atom.

$$H-\ddot{N}=\overset{+}{N}=\ddot{N}:$$
$$H-\overset{-}{\ddot{N}}-\overset{+}{N}\equiv N:$$
$$H-\overset{+}{N}=\overset{+}{N}-\ddot{\underset{..}{N}}:^{2-}$$

(*vi*) The greater the number of covalent bonds, greater is the contribution of the resonating structures. For example, the double bonded structures of BF_3 are important because of the formation of an additional covalent bond.

$$\overset{(+)}{F}=\overset{(-)}{B}\langle^{F}_{F} \longleftrightarrow F-\overset{(-)}{B}\langle^{\overset{(+)}{F}\,(=)}_{F} \longleftrightarrow F-\overset{(-)}{B}\langle^{F}_{\underset{(+)}{F}\,(=)}$$

Resonating Structures for CO

Following resonance structures can be written for this molecule.

$$\underset{\text{I}}{\underset{\text{(covalent)}}{:C::\ddot{O}:}} \longleftrightarrow \underset{\text{II}}{\underset{\text{(ionic)}}{:\overset{-}{C}:::\overset{+}{O}:}} \longleftrightarrow \underset{\text{III}}{\underset{\text{(ionic)}}{:\overset{+}{C}:\overset{-}{\underset{..}{\ddot{O}}}:}}$$

(*i*) **Bond length.** The observed bond length between carbon and oxygen in CO is 113 pm. The bond length of a normal carbon to oxygen double bond as in ketone is 122 pm and that observed for carbon to oxygen triple bond is 110 pm. It is, therefore, obvious that the bond length in carbon monoxide is shorter that that of for a carbon to oxygen double bond but slightly longer than that for a triple bond. However, bond length in carbon monoxide is closer to carbon oxygen triple bond distance. Bond length measurements suggest that contribution from resonance structure II dominates over other structures, I and III.

(*ii*) **Dipole moment.** On the basis of bond length, we may say that structure II makes the maximum contribution. However, we may note that this structure suggest a partial positive charge on oxygen and partial negative change on carbon. If the electronegativities of carbon and oxygen were the same, carbon monoxide would have an appreciable dipole moment in the direction shown.

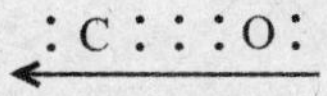

$$:C:::O: \quad (\longleftarrow)$$

But since oxygen is more electronegative than carbon it, therefore, draws electron density back from carbon to the oxygen atom. This force works in the opposite direction and hence carbon monoxide has very low dipole moment (0.12 D).

Resonating Structures for Carbon Dioxide

It may be represented as a resonance hybrid of the following three structures:

(*i*) **Bond length.** On the basis of structure I the bond length in CO_2 should be equal to

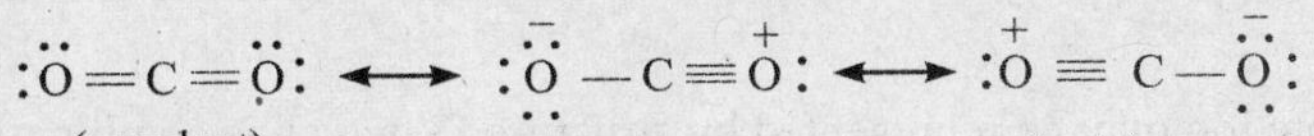

$$:\ddot{O}=C=\ddot{O}: \longleftrightarrow :\overset{-}{\ddot{\underset{..}{O}}}-C\equiv\overset{+}{O}: \longleftrightarrow :\overset{+}{O}\equiv C-\overset{-}{\ddot{\underset{..}{O}}}:$$

(covalent) I (ionic) II (ionic) III

carbon-oxygen double bond distance of 122 pm. The observed bond distance is shorter than this value and is 115 pm. Therefore, there must be some contribution from structures II and III.

(*ii*) **Dipole moment.** Contributions from structures II and III must be equal. If their contributions are unequal, the molecule will have dipole moment. But CO_2 has zero dipole moment.

(*iii*) **Bond energy.** The energy of a carbon - oxygen double bond is 731.5 kJ/mole. Therefore, heat of formation of the molecule O = C = O (structure I) should be about 1463.0 kJ/mole. The experimental value of heat of formation is 1601 kJ/mole. The difference between these two values, *i.e.*, 138 kJ/mole suggests the extra stability acquired due to contribution by structures II and III. It may be noted here that structure I is most dominant form due to its symmetrical nature.

Resonance Structures of N_2O

The molecule is isoelectronic with CO_2 and hence has the same linear structure. It can be

$$:\overset{-}{\underset{..}{\ddot{N}}}=\overset{+}{N}=\ddot{O}: \longleftrightarrow :N\equiv\overset{+}{N}-\overset{-}{\ddot{\underset{..}{O}}}:$$

(I) (II)

represented as resonance hybrid of two resonance structures I and II.

Each of the structures I and II separately predicts a sizeable dipole moment for the molecule N_2O. The low value (0.12 D) is explained on the cancelling effect of dipole moments in opposite directions in structures I and II.

Resonance Structures of Carbonate ion

The Lewis dot representation of carbonate ion contains a double bond and two single bonds between central C and oxygen atoms as shown below. This structure indicates that one of the carbon oxygen bonds (C = O) should be shorter than the other two bonds. Also the angle α should be greater than the angle β. But this is contrary to observations.

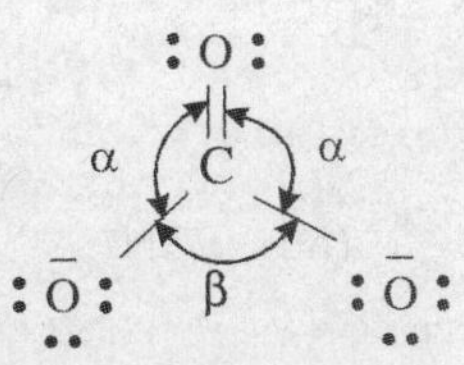

:O: α C α $:\overset{-}{\underset{..}{O}}:$ β $:\overset{-}{\underset{..}{O}}:$

X-ray studies show that all the three bonds have the same bond length and each angle is 120°.

I ⟷ II ⟷ III

IV

This has been explained by a combination of resonance structures I, II and III for carbon dioxide.

Thus carbonate ion may be represented by structure IV which is combination of these three structures.

Solved Examples

Example 1: Write down the resonance structures of

(*i*) Cl_2O
(*ii*) N_3^-
(*iii*) HNO_2
(*iv*) SCN^-
(*v*) NO_2^-

Solution:

(*i*) Cl_2O

(*ii*) N_3^-

The three structures are equally important and result in the same bond order (≅ 2) for each bond in N_3^-.

$$\overset{(-)}{:N}=\overset{(+)}{N}=\overset{(-)}{N:} \longleftrightarrow \overset{(2-)}{:N}-\overset{(+)}{N}\equiv N: \longleftrightarrow :N\equiv\overset{(+)}{N}-\overset{(2-)}{N:}$$

(*iii*) HNO_2

(*iv*) SCN^-

$$:\bar{S}\equiv C-N: \longleftrightarrow :S=C=\bar{N}:$$

S — C bond order is between 1.5 and 2 and C—N bond order is between 2 and 3.

(*v*) NO_2^-

$$:\ddot{O}=\ddot{N}-\ddot{O}:^- \longleftrightarrow {}^-:\ddot{O}-\ddot{N}=\ddot{O}:$$

1.4 FORMAL CHARGE

Lewis dot structures do not, in many cases, give the actual shape of molecules. In polyatomic ions, the net charge is possessed by the ion as a whole and not by a particular atom. But, it is possible to find a charge (called as formal charge) on each atom.

The formal charge of an atom in a polyatomic molecule or ion is defined as the difference between the number of valence electrons of that atom in an isolated or free state and the number of electrons assigned to that atom in the Lewis structure.

Mathematically it amy written as:

Formal charge of an atom = [No. of valence electrons on the atom in free state]

– [Total number of non-bonding electrons]

$-\frac{1}{2}$ [Total number of shared electrons]

It is based on the assumption that the atom in the molecule owns one electron of each shared pair and both the electrons of lone pair.

Formal Charge in the Molecule of CO_2

The structure of CO_2 may be sketched as

$$:\ddot{O}::C::\ddot{O}:$$

Applying the above criteria, we have

Formal charge on C = 4 – 0 – 2 = 0

Formal charge on L.H.S. O = 6 – 4 – 2 = 0

Similary the formal charge on the R.H.S O = 0

Formal Charge in the Molecule of O_3

The structure of O_3 may be written as

$$\overset{2}{:\ddot{O}}=\overset{1}{\ddot{O}}-\overset{3}{\ddot{O}:}$$

The three O atoms marked 1, 2, and 3 are bonded as under:

$$\text{Formal charge on O atom } 1 = 6 - 2 - \left(\frac{1}{2} \times 6\right) = +1$$

$$\text{Formal charge on O atom } 2 = 6 - 4 - \left(\frac{1}{2} \times 4\right) = 0$$

Formal charge on O atom 3 $= 6 - 6 - \left(\frac{1}{2} \times 2\right) = -1$

We can represent O_3 showing formal charges as under:

$$O{=}\overset{+}{O}{-}O^{-}$$

Formal charges help in the selection of the lowest energy structure from a number of possible Lewis structures for a given species. Generally the lowest energy structure is the one with the smallest formal charges on the atoms.

1.5 VAN DER WAALS' FORCES

Forces of attraction exist between *neutral molecules* as well. The magnitude of these forces is maximum in case of solids and decreases on passing from solid to liquid and from liquid to gaseous states. The forces existing between the molecules of a substance are known as **intermolecular forces**. These are also designated as **Van der Waals' forces**. The attractive forces which keep the molecules in position in a molecular crystal are van der Waals' forces.

The question arises, how can there be electrical attraction between neutral molecules lying close to one another? The existence of electrical repulsion between such molecules, on the other hand, can be more readily understood as these may arise from the interaction of the electron clouds of the molecules when they are in close proximity to each other.

Thus, what could be the cause of **physical forces or molecular attraction?** The answer is as follows:

Dipole-Dipole Interaction. In the case of **polar molecules** which have permanent dipoles, the van der Waals' forces are mainly due to electrical interaction between the dipoles known as **dipole-dipole interaction**. For instance, gases such as ammonia, sulphur dioxide, hydrogen fluoride, hydrogen chloride, etc., have permanent dipoles, as a result of which there is appreciable dipole-dipole interaction between the molecules of these gases. The magnitude of this type of interaction depends upon the dipole moment of the molecule concerned. The greater the dipole moment, the greater is the dipole-dipole interaction. Because of the attractive interaction, these gases can be easily liquefied.

Ion-Dipole Interaction. If an ionic solid is to dissolve, some energy is needed to overcome the force of inter-ionic attraction. If water is the solvent, this energy is supplied by the *interaction of water molecules with the ions*. This is known as **ion-dipole interaction**. The positive pole of the water molecules reacts with the negative ion while the negative pole reacts with the positive ion. The ion-dipole interaction results in the release of a considerable amount of energy which becomes available for the separation of the oppositely charged ions. This results in the dissolution of the solute.

London Forces. But van der Waals' forces exist even in non-polar molecules such as F_2, O_2 and N_2 and even in non-polar mono-atomic molecules such as He, Ne, Ar, etc. This attraction is evident from the condensation of these gases into liquids at sufficiently high pressures and low temperatures. This is explained by London forces.

In 1930, F. London provided an explanation for the existence of forces of attraction between non-polar molecules, based on quantum mechanics. According to this view, *electrons of a neutral molecule keep on oscillating with respect to the nuclei of the atoms. As a result of this, at a given instant, positive charge may be concentrated in one region and negative charge in another region of the same molecule. Thus, a non-polar molecule may become momentarily self-polarised.* This polarised molecule may induce a dipole moment in a neighbouring molecule, as shown in Fig. 1.1.

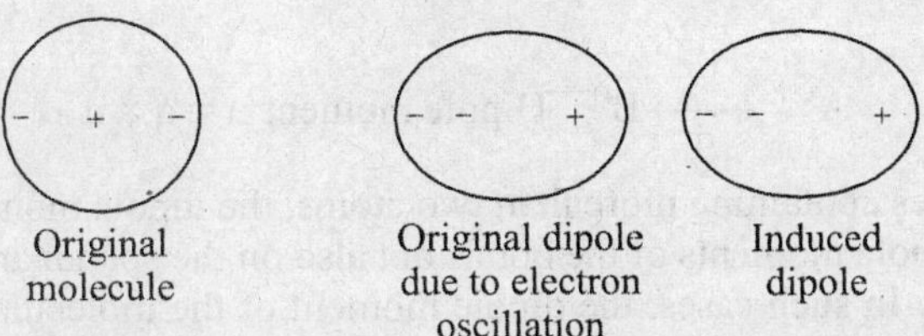

***Fig. 1.1:** Origin of cohesive forces in non-polar molecules.*

The electrostatic forces of attraction between induced dipoles and the original dipoles (due to electron oscillation) are known as **London forces**. These forces are also called **dispersive forces** because the well known phenomenon of dispersion of light is also connected with these dipoles. For a pair of adjacent molecules, London forces vary inversely as the *seventh power* of the distance between them, *i.e.*, $F \propto 1/r^7$. The magnitude of these forces, evidently, would be very small.

The Van der Waals' attraction in *non-polar molecules* is thus *exclusively* due to London forces. In the case of polar molecules having permanent dipoles, however, other electrostatic forces due to dipole-dipole interaction also contribute towards the Van der Waals' attraction.

Factors Determining Van der Waals' Forces

Van der Waals' forces depend largely on the following factors:

1. The Number of Electrons Present in a Molecule. Van der Waals' forces increase with increase in the number of electrons in the molecule. Thus, boiling points (T_b) of the halogens increase as we move from fluorine to chlorine, bromine and iodine. Similarly, boiling points of noble gases increase as we move from helium to radon, as shown below:

Noble gas	He	Ne	Ar	Kr	Xe	Rn
Boiling pt. (K)	4.1	27	67.2	121	165	211.2

2. Molecular Size. The larger the molecular size (or roughly the larger the molar mass), the stronger the van der Waals' forces. Thus, the boiling point of ethane, C_2H_6 (185 K) is higher than that of methane, CH_4 (112 K). In compounds having similar structures, viz. CH_4, SiH_4, GeH_4, the boiling points increase with increase in the number of electrons and size of the molecule, as shown below:

Substance	CH_4	SiH_4	GeH_4
No. of electrons	10	18	36
Boiling point (K)	112	161	183

1.6 DIPOLE MOMENT AND STRUCTURE OF MOLECULES

Dipole moment is a physical property of polar molecules. Let us suppose there is a molecule. $\overset{\delta+}{A} - \overset{\delta-}{B}$ in which one atom A carries a partial charge δ+ and the second atom B carries an equal but opposite charge δ–. Such a molecule carries a moment called **dipole moment**. It is an electrical property of the molecules. Dipole moment which is represented by μ is given by

$\mu = e \times d$

where e = charge on either atom and d is the bond length or bond length of the molecule A – B. e is measured in e.s.u. and d is measured in angstrom unit.The unit of dipole moment, μ is D.

$$A^{\delta+} \underset{d}{\longleftrightarrow} B^{\delta-} \quad \text{Dipole moment } \mu = q \times d$$

In case of molecules containing more than two atoms, the dipole moment not only depends upon the individual dipole moments of the bonds but also on the spatial arrangement of various bonds in the molecule. In such cases, the dipole moment of the molecule is the vector sum of the dipole moments of the various bonds. Obviously, the polar or non-polar nature of molecule will depend upon the spatial arrangement of atoms in the molecule. The bonds may be polar yet the molecule could be non-polar.

For example, carbon dioxide (CO_2) and water (H_2O) molecules are both triatomic molecules but the dipole moment of carbon dioxide is zero while that of water is 1.84 D. This can be easily explained on the basis of their structures.

In *carbon dioxide* molecule, both the carbon-oxygen bonds are polar. Since the molecule is linear, the dipole moment of C = O bond on one side of the molecule is cancelled by that on the other side of the molecule giving net zero dipole moment. On the other hand, *water* molecule is not linear, it has a *bent structure* as shown. Therefore, the dipole moment of water molecule is not zero. It is the resultant of the dipole moments of the two O — H bonds inclined at an angle of 104.5°. It has been found to be 1.84 D.

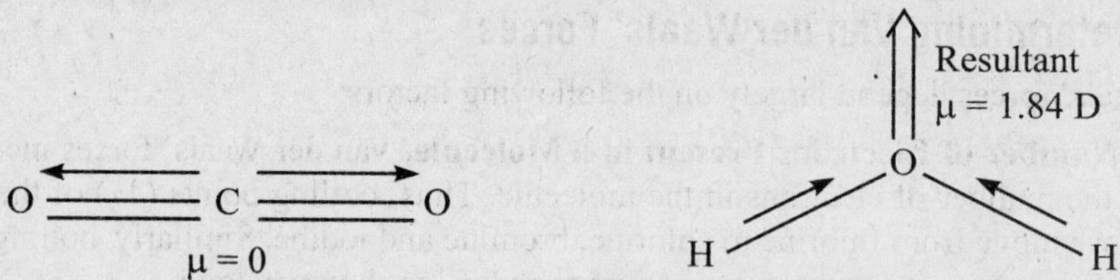

Similarly, the dipole moment of BH_3 is zero while that of NH_3 is 1.49 D, although both the molecules are tetra-atomic. This is because BH_3 has symmetrical structure in which the three B — H bonds are oriented at an angle of 120° to one another. The three bonds lie in one plane and the dipole moments of these bonds cancel one another giving net dipole moment equal to zero. On the other hand, the ammonia molecule has pyramidal structure. The dipole moments of three N — H bonds do not cancel each other (as they are in different planes). The molecule of ammonia shows a net value of dipole moment.

Example 2: Describe Fajan's rules. How does it explain relative covalent/ionic nature of the following pairs of compounds?

(*i*) $FeCl_2$, $FeCl_3$

(*ii*) Li I, Cs I

(*iii*) Cucl, NaCl

Solution: The Fajan's rule may be stated as

(*i*) Induced covalent character on ionic compound increases with decrease in size of the cation or increase in charge on the cation.

(*ii*) Covalent character induced in ionic compounds due to polarization of anion increases with an increase in size and charge of the anion.

(*iii*) Cations with pseudo noble gas configuration (*i.e.*, 18 e^- in outer shell) have higher polarizing power than cation with noble gas configuration.

Covalent/ionic nature of the pairs of compounds may be compared as under:

(*i*) $FeCl_2$, $FeCl_3$

As both Fe^{2+} and Fe^{3+} have almost same ionic radii but Fe^{3+} has more charge, so according to Fajan's rule $FeCl_3$ will be more covalent or less ionic than $FeCl_2$.

(*ii*) LiI, CsI

As both Li and Cs have some charge but radius of Cs is much greater than that of Li so according to Fajans' rule LiI will be more covalent.

(*iii*) CuCl, NaCl

As Cu and Na have some charge but Na is much smaller than Cu in radius, so according to Fajan's rule NaCl will be more covalent.

1.7 PERCENTAGE IONIC CHARACTER

(*i*) **Electronegativity Difference and Per Cent Ionic Character.** A pure covalent bond is formed between atoms *A* and *B* when the electronegativities of the two atoms are the same. If *A* and *B* have different electronegativities, the resulting bond would be a polar covalent bond because the bonding electron-pair is pulled towards the more electronegative atom causing some excess negative charge on it. As a result, some excess positive charge is developed on the less electronegative atom. If *A* is more electronegative than *B,* a polar covalent bond $\overset{-\delta}{A} \bullet \overset{+\delta}{B}$ would be formed between *A* and *B*. Larger the difference in the electronegativities *of A* and *B,* greater would be the magnitude of δ and the higher would be the polarity of the bond.

Pauling plotted a graph between the electronegativity difference and the % ionic character and showed that the bond becomes more and more ionic as the difference in electronegativity increased (Fig. 1.2)

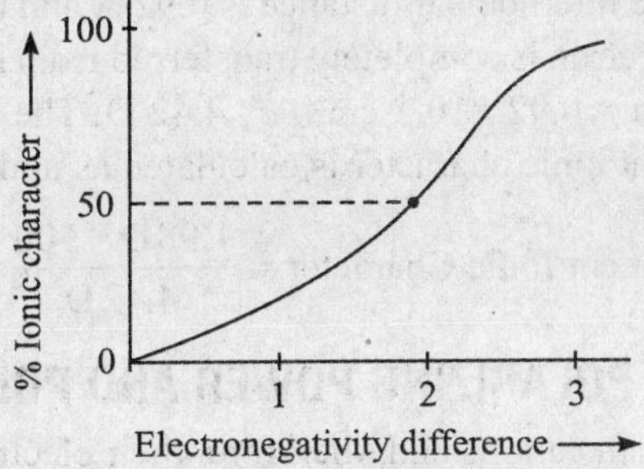

***Fig. 1.2:** Relation between% ionic character and electronegativity difference*

Pauling gave an empirical relationship to derive the % ionic character from electronegativity difference. This is given as under:

% ionic character of a bond between *A* and *B* = $18\ [X_A - X_B]^{1.4}$

where $X_A - X_B$ denote the electronegativities of the atoms *A* and *B* ($X_A > X_B$). A simplified version for % ionic character was provided by Hannay and Smith which is given as

% ionic character = $16(X_A - X_B) + 3.5\ (X_A - X_B)^2$

Example 3: Given the electronegativities of H, Cl, Br and I as 2.1, 3.0, 2.8 and 2.4 respectively, calculate the % ionic character of HCl, HBr and HI and arrange them in increasing order of % ionic character. Use Hannay-Smith relation.

Solution:

(*i*) % Ionic character of HCl $= 16[X_A - X_B] + 3.5\,[X_A - X_B]^2$

$= 16\,[3.0 - 2.1] + 3.5\,[3.0 - 2.1]^2$

$= 17.23$

(*ii*) % Ionic character of HBr $= 16\,[2.8 - 2.1] + 3.5[2.8 - 2.1]^2$

$= 12.93$

(*iii*) % Ionic character of HI $= 16\,[\,2.4 - 2.1] + 3.5\,[2.4 - 2.1]^2$

$= 5.11$

Increasing order of ionic character HI < HBr < HCl

***(ii)* Per cent Ionic Character and Dipole Moment.** Consider the bond H – X where X is a halogen atom. If the bond is purely covalent, its dipole moment would be zero. If the bond is ionic, *viz.*, H^+X^-, it implies that complete transfer of an electron has taken place from H to X and the bond would have a high value of dipole moment which is obtained by the product of the electronic charge and the internuclear distance between H and X. For a polar covalent bond which is intermediate between a pure covalent and a pure ionic bond, the dipole moment would be given by the product of the actual charge (δ) caused by polarisation and the internuclear distance. The magnitude of δ will depend upon the extent of the ionic character developed in the bond.

Thus,

$$\text{Per cent Ionic Character} = \frac{\text{Actual dipole moment of the bond}}{\text{Dipole moment of pure ionic bond}} \times 100$$

For example, in **HF,** the internuclear distance is 0.92 Å and the dipole moment for the ionic structure $\mathbf{H^+F^-}$ when an electron is completely transferred from hydrogen atom to fluorine atom is given by 4.8×10^{-10} esu $\times\ 0.92 \times 10^{-8}$ cm, *i.e.*, 4.42 D. The actual dipole moment of HF is found to be 1.98 D. Per cent ionic character is calculated as under:

$$\text{Per cent Ionic Character} = \frac{1.98\,\text{D} \times 100}{4.42\,\text{D}} = 44.8$$

1.8 POLARIZATION, POLARIZING POWER AND POLARIZABILITY

Anions are larger in size than cations and, therefore, their electron clouds are less lightly held. A small highly charged cation shall, therefore, distort the electron cloud of the large anions in a manner that it increases the electron density between the nuclei. For example, the large iodide ion by itself is perfectly symmetrical. However when a small positively charged lithium ion comes close to the iodide ion, the electron cloud on the anion is pulled towards the positive lithium ion. The iodide ion is said to be polarized and the process is called polarization. The polarization effect produces covalence in LiI molecule because there is some electron density in between the nuclei as in the sharing of electrons in a covalent bond. The power of an ion to distort the other ion is known as its **polarizing power** and the tendency of the anion to distort is known as its **polarizability**. The polarizing power of a cation is proportional to its charge/radius ratio. This is illustrated in Fig. 1.3. When a large and soft anion comes under the influence of a small cation, the cation is able to polarize the anion (Fig. 1.3 (*b*)).

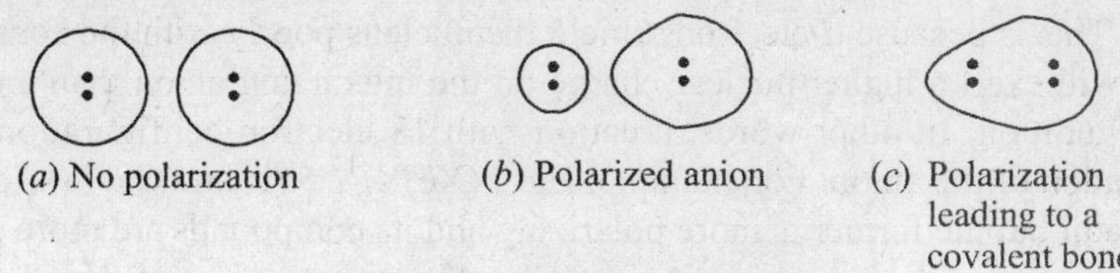

(*a*) No polarization (*b*) Polarized anion (*c*) Polarization leading to a covalent bond

***Fig. 1.3:** Interaction of + ve and – ve ions.*

This results in deformation of electron cloud on anion, called the polarization of anion. Due to small size of the cation, polarization of the cation is not much. Extensive polarization would be witnessed when cation penetrates the anionic electron cloud giving a covalent bond (Fig. 1.3). In compound consisting of large negative ions and small positive ions, the polarization leads to partial covalent character in ionic compounds. Examples of such ionic covalent compounds are $FeCl_3$, $AlCl_3$, LiBr etc.

1.9 FAJAN'S RULES AND COVALENT CHARACTER IN IONIC COMPOUNDS

Fajans explained the variation of nonpolar character in ionic compounds in terms of polarization effects. He gave qualitative ideas to offer simple approach to the problem of partial covalent character in ionic compounds. Fajans proposed the following rules to determine the extent of polarization of an anion by a cation, that is, the extent of covalent character induced in an ionic compound.

Kasimir Fajans (1887–1975)

Kashmir Fajans was an American physical chemist of Polish origin and a pioneer in the field of radioactivity. He also developed Fajans rules on the covalent character in ionic compounds

(*i*) **Small, highly charged cations.** Small, highly charged cations have higher polarizing effects on anions than large, lowly charged cations. In other words, induced covalent character in ionic compounds increases with decrease in size of the cation or increase in charge on the cation. This is because very small cations or cations with higher charge have higher charge density which tends to distort or polarize the electron cloud around the anion. The greater the polarization, the higher the induced covalency. For example, Na^+ and Ca^{2+} have almost similar ionic radii but $CaCl_2$ (m.p. = 772° C) has higher covalent character than NaCl (m.p. = 800° C) because of higher charge on Ca^{2+}. With identical charges on cations, $BeCl_2$ (m.p. = 405° C) is relatively more covalent than $CaCl_2$ (m.p. = 772° C) because of smaller size of Be^{2+} as compared to Ca^{2+}.

(*ii*) **Large, highly charged anions.** Covalent character induced in ionic compound due to polarization of the anion increases with an increase in size and charge on the anion. The electron cloud on the large-sized anion is less strongly held by its nucleus and hence it is easily polarized by the approaching cation. In other words, the larger is the anion charge, the higher is its polarizability. For example, anions like Br^-, I^-, S^{2-}, Te^{2-}, As^{3-}, Sb^{3-} etc., are easily polarizable and have tendency to induce covalent character in ionic compounds. For a given cation, say Li^+, as the size of the anion increases from F^- to I^-, the covalent character increases and consequently melting point decreases: LiF = 870° C, LiCl = 613° C, LiBr = 574 °C, LiI = 446 °C.

(*iii*) **Cation configuration.** Cations with pseudo noble gas configuration (*i.e.*, 18 electron outer-shell) have higher polarizing power than cations with noble gas configurations. In other words, cations with $ns^2\ np^6$ configuration cause less distortion than those with $ns^2\ np^6\ nd^{10}$

configuration. This is because *d*-electrons shield the nucleus poorly with the consequence that such a cation will exert a higher nuclear charge on the interacting anion than a cation with 8 electron configuration. In other words, a cation with 18 electron configuration will lead to higher polarization of the anion. For example, Hg^{2+} (Xe) $4f^{14}\ 5d^{10}$ and Ca^{2+} (.... $3s^2\ 3p^6$) have similar ionic radii but the former is more polarizing and its compounds are more covalent than those of Ca^{2+}. For example, for a given anion (Cl^-), the melting point of $HgCl_2$ = 276°C and that of $CaCl_2$ = 772°C. Also Cu^+ (..... $3s^2\ 3p^6\ 3d^{10}$) and Na^+ (..... $2s^2\ 2p^6$) have similar ionic radii but the former is more polarizing and induces higher covalent character than the latter. This is supported by their melting points : CuCl : 430°C; NaCl= 800°C.

Example 4: Silver halides are least soluble in water, though their lattice energy is almost the same as that of highly soluble alkali metal halides. Explain.

OR

Ag I is covalent while NaI is covalent. Explain.

Solution: Ag^+ can cause greater polarization of the halide because of its electronic configuration. There are *d*-electrons which cannot screen the nucleus effectively and thus pull the electrons of halide more than expected. This brings about çovalency leading to the substance being insoluble in water.

Example 5: Give the trends of thermostability of alkaline earth metal carbonates.

Solution: The thermal stability increases in the order

$$BeCO_3 < MgCO_3 < CaCO_3 < SrCO_3 < BaCO_3$$

This can be explained on the basis of decreasing polarizing power of the cation as we move from L.H.S. to R.H.S. making the substance more and more ionic or thermally stable.

Example 6: Explain the sequence of solubility of lithium halide in ethyl alcohol.

Solution: The halides to be considered are: LiF, LiCl, LiBr, LiI

The cation is same in all the cases. Hence the nature of the anion will decide solubility. Larger the anion, greater the polarizability hence greater the covalent character. And greater the covalent character, greater the solubility in ethyl alcohol. On this basis solubility increases from LiF to LiI.

Example 7: State, giving reasons, which cation will have greater polarizing power in the following:

(*i*) Na^+ or Mg^{2+} (*ii*) Cu^{2+} or Ca^{2+} (*iii*) Pb^{2+} or Pb^{4+}

Solution: (*i*) Mg^{2+} has greater polarizing power because of greater charge.

(*ii*) Ca^{2+} has greater polarizing power because of smaller size.

(*iii*) Pb^{4+} has greater polarizing power because of greater charge.

Example 8: $AlCl_3$ anhydrous is covalent but $AlCl_3 . 6H_2O$ is ionic in nature. How would you account for this behaviour?

Solution: $AlCl_3$ is covalent in nature because of small and highly charged Al^{3+} ion. This polarizes the chloride ion causing covalency.

In the hydrated sample, the Al^{3+} ion get surrounding by water molecules. A lot of energy called hydration energy is released and thus Al^{3+} lose their polarizing power and remain in ionic state.

Example 9: Give reasons why $ZnCl_2$ is soluble in organic solvents while $MgCl_2$ is insoluble.

Solution: Zn^{2+} ions have greater polarizing power, because of the presence of low shielding *d*-orbitals, as compared to Mg^{2+} ions. Thus Zn^{2+} polarizes the chloride ion and brings about covalent character and therefore $ZnCl_2$ is soluble in organic solvents.

Example 10: Highly charged cations are rare. Explain.

Solution: Highly charged cations strongly polarize the anion and bring about covalent character in the molecule. Thus the charge on the cation is neutralized and a covalent bond involving sharing of electrons or overlapping of orbitals is formed.

Example 11: Explain the following:

(*i*) $SnCl_4$ is more covalent than $SnCl_2$

(*ii*) NaCl is more ionic than CuCl

Solution: (*i*) $SnCl_4$ is more covalent because Sn^{4+} has greater polarizing power than Sn^{2+}.

(*ii*) NaCl is more ionic than CuCl because Cu^+ has greater polarizing power than Na^+. This is because there are *d*-electrons which poorly shield the nucleus.

The cation thus can polarize the anion more powerfully.

Example 12: The inter-nuclear distance in HI is 1.62 Å. Assuming complete transfer of electron from H to I, calculate % ionic character and fractional charge on each ion. If the measured dipole moment is 0.38 D, also calculate the % ionic character of HI.
Given e = (electronic charge) = 4.8×10^{-10} e.s.u.

Solution: Assuming complete transfer of electron from H to I, the charge on H and I would be $+e$ and $-e$ respectively.

The dipole moment of HI in such case,

$$= q \times r$$
$$= e \times r$$
$$= (4.8 \times 10^{-10} \text{ e.s.u.})(1.62 \times 10^{-8} \text{ cm})$$
$$= 7.776 \text{ D}$$

$$\text{Observed dipole moment} = 0.38 \text{ D}$$

$$\% \text{ ionic character} = \frac{0.38}{7.776} \times 100 = 4.88.$$

1.10 HYDROGEN BOND

1. Hydrogen Bond. When hydrogen is joined to a highly electronegative element, it can form an additional bond to another electronegative element. This additional bond is known as hydrogen bond. For example, in the compound KHF_2, the anion HF_2^- is believed to have structure $(FHF)^-$ in which hydrogen acts as bridge between the two fluorine atoms. The hydrogen bond is considerably less stable than the usual valence bond. In order to distinguish a hydrogen bond from other valence bond, it is written as dotted line so that HF_2^- ion becomes (F.......H — F)$^-$. In general, when a hydrogen bond links two electronegative atoms A and B as a resonance hybrid between A – H.....B and A.....H – B, the more electronegative the atom to which hydrogen is joined , and the smaller it is, the stronger is the hydrogen bond. Hydrogen bonds are formed only between highly electronegative atoms like F, O and N. The energy of the hydrogen bond varies depending on the state and the nature of the species to which hydrogen is joined. The energy of the hydrogen bond H ..... F is about 40 kJ while the energies of the O.....H and N.....H bonds are about 20 and 8 kJ respectively. Evidence in support of the existence of hydrogen bonding is obtained, if we compare some of the physical properties of compounds containing hydrogen bonds.

1.10.1 Intermolecular Hydrogen Bond

We find that the boiling points of HF and H_2O are abnormally high as compared with other members of each series (Fig. 1.4). In the series HF, HCl, HBr and HI boiling points are expected to rise due to increasing number of electrons (because of increased Van der Waals forces). The unexpectedly high boiling point of H_2O in the series H_2O, H_2S, H_2Se and H_2Te is also attributed to hydrogen boiling.

Hydrogen fluoride consists of $(HF)_n$ molecules which have the following structure.

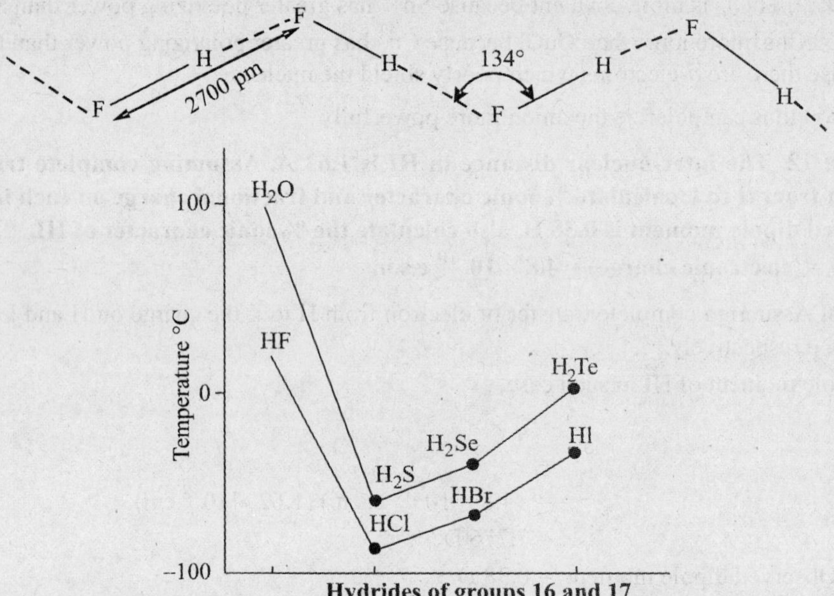

Fig. 1.4: Comparison of boiling points of hydrides of 6th and 7th group elements.

1.10.2 Intramolecular Hydrogen Bonding

In many organic compounds, often the hydrogen bond joins part of a single molecule (*i.e.*, within the molecule) and in such cases intramolecular hydrogen bonding is favoured (Fig. 1.5). Substances which are intramolecularly hydrogen bonded are more soluble. In non-polar solvents (such as CCl_4, C_6H_6 etc.) and have lower melting and boiling points than their other isomers which are intermolecularly hydrogen bonded.

The hydrogen bond plays important part in many processes. For example, the solubility of an uncharged organic compound in water depends mainly on the ability of a substance to form hydrogen bonds with the solvent. Thus dimethyl ether is completely miscible with water whereas dimethyl sulphide has slight solubility; sugar, an organic compound, is water soluble due to hydrogen bonding with water. Hydrogen bonding is of importance in explaining some physical properties of certain liquids. For example, the high dielectric constant, high boiling point, high density and viscosity of water is explained on the basis of hydrogen bonding.

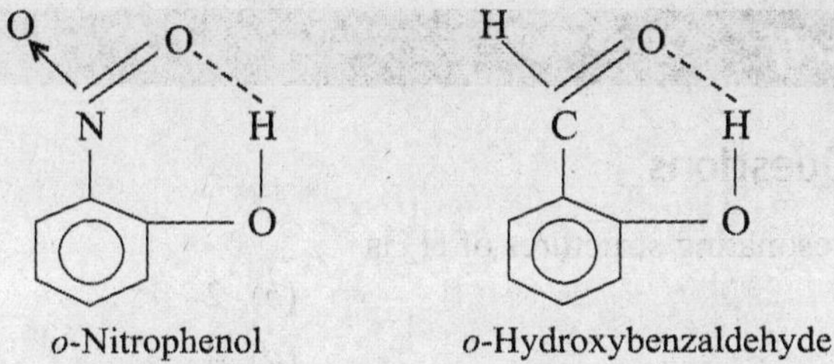

Fig. 1.5: Intramolecular hydrogen bonding

Example 13: Explain the following:

'H_2O has a higher boiling point while H_2S and H_2Te are gases'.

Solution: Oxygen is more electronegative than sulphur, selenium and tellurium. Therefore oxygen forms hydrogen bond more effectively. The hydrogen bonding in water may be depicted as follows.

$$\ldots.H-\underset{\displaystyle H}{\underset{|}{O}}\ldots.H-\underset{\displaystyle H}{\underset{|}{O}}\ldots.H-\underset{\displaystyle H}{\underset{|}{O}}\ldots.$$

Substances having hydrogen bonding boil at higher temperature.

Example 14: Which of the following will have higher boiling point or melting point? Justify your answer:

(*i*) H_2O or H_2S

(*ii*) Nitrophenol or nitrobenzene

Solution: (*i*) H_2O boils at a high temperature. It has effective hydrogen bonding than H_2S because oxygen is more electronegative than sulphur.

(*ii*) *Nitrophenol* has a higher boiling point compared to nitrobenzene.

Example 15: Methane is very slightly soluble in water, but methanol is highly soluble. Explain.

Solution: Methanol forms hydrogen bond with water. No such bonding takes place between methane and water.

Example 16: Why is boiling point of NH_3 higher than that of PH_3 ?

Solution: There is greater electronegativity difference between N and H than between P and H. Thus due to hydrogen bonding, although small, NH_3 molecule is associated and boils at a higher temperature.

Example 17: Explain the following :

(*i*) Alcohol is a better drying agent than acetone.

(*ii*) Density of ice is less than that of water.

Solution: (*i*) **Alcohol can combine with water more than with acetone due to hydrogen bonding. Therefore, alcohol is a better drying agent.**

(*ii*) Ice has a cage like structure comprising hydrogen bonds. There is a lot of empty space in the structure due to which its density is much less than that of water.

Evaluate Yourself

Multiple Choice Questions

1. The number of resonating structures of H_2 is
   (*a*) 1 (*b*) 2
   (*c*) 3 (*d*) 4
2. Choose the wrong option with regard to necessary conditions for resonating structures.
   (*a*) Nuclei of atoms in each structure must remain in fixed position.
   (*b*) Each structure must have the same number of unpaired electrons.
   (*c*) The contributing structures should all have similar energies.
   (*d*) The contributing structures should be so written that like charges reside on neighbouring atoms.
3. The attractive forces which keep the molecules in position in a molecular crystals are called
   (*a*) Newton forces (*b*) Fajan's forces
   (*c*) Van der Waals forces (*d*) Pauling forces
4. Dipole moment of a linear molecule is given by the relation
   (*a*) $\mu = q \times d$ (*b*) $\mu = q/d$
   (*c*) $\mu = q \times d^2$ (*d*) $\mu = q^2 \times d$
5. Which of the following molecules has a zero value of dipole moment?
   (*a*) CO_2 (*b*) CO
   (*c*) NH_3 (*d*) H_2O
6. The variation of non-polar character in ionic compounds in terms of polarization effect was given by
   (*a*) Faraday (*b*) Van der Walls
   (*c*) Fajan (*d*) Avogadro
7. Internuclear distance in HI is 1.62 Å. If the observed dipole moment of HI is 0.38 D, the percentage of ionic character in HI is
   (*a*) 2.88 (*b*) 3.88
   (*c*) 4.88 (*d*) 5.88
8. Methanol is highly soluble in water because of
   (*a*) low density (*b*) high viscosity
   (*c*) low surface tension (*d*) hydrogen bonding
9. Which of the following has the highest boiling point
   (*a*) H_2O (*b*) H_2S
   (*c*) H_2 Se (*d*) H_2 Te
10. Which Indian scientist worked on the amino acid sequence of proteins?
    (*a*) Asima Chatterjee (*b*) Har Gobind Khorana
    (*c*) Acharya P.C. Roy (*d*) Shanti Swaroop Bhatnagar

Short Answer Questions

1. Which scientist is known as Father of Chemical science in India? Give one of his discoveries.
2. Which Nobel Prize was awarded to Har Gobind Khorana? What was his achievement?
3. State any two conditions for writing resonating structures of a molecule.
4. Write the resonating structures of carbon monoxide. Justify your answer on the basis of bond length.
5. Write the resonating structures of carbonate ion.
6. Calculate the formal charges on the three oxygen atoms in the molecule of ozone.
7. What are London faces? How do they vary with the distance between the molecules?
8. State two factors that determine Van der Waals forces.
9. Predict the shape of H_2O molecule on the basis of its dipole moment value as 1.84 D.
10. Why are highly charged cations rare?

Long Answer Questions

1. Give a brief description of the contribution of ancient Indian scientists and philosophers towards development of science and technology.
2. Describe the contribution to the development of scientific knowledge by the following:
   (*a*) Acharya Prafulla Chandra Ray
   (*b*) Har Gobind Khorana
   (*c*) Asima Chatterjee
3. Discuss necessary conditions for writing resonating structures of a compound.
4. Write the resonating structures for carbon dioxide. Justify them on the basis of
   (*a*) Bond length
   (*b*) Dipole moment
5. Write notes on
   (*a*) Dipole-dipole interactions
   (*b*) Ion-dipole interactions
   (*c*) London forces
6. How do we arrive at the structures of the following molecules on the basis of dipole moment studies?
   (*a*) CO_2
   (*b*) H_2O
   (*c*) BF_3
7. How do we determine the percentage of ionic character in a molecule based on dipole moment?
8. Write notes on
   (*a*) Polarization
   (*b*) Ploarizing power
   (*c*) Ploarizability

9. How do Fajan's rules help to determine covalent character in ionic compounds?

10. (*a*) What is meant by hydrogen bond?

(*b*) Name a compound which shows intramolecular hydrogen bonding. Show the formation of hydrogen bond in the molecule.

(*c*) Explain why ice is higher than water although the former is a solid.

Answers

Multiple Choice Questions

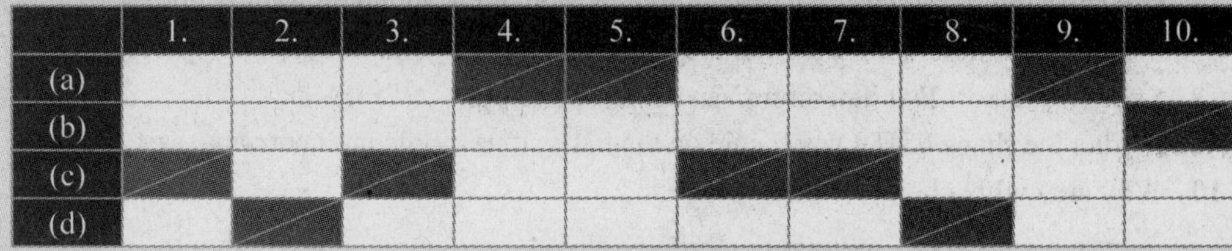

	1.	2.	3.	4.	5.	6.	7.	8.	9.	10.
(a)				■	■				■	
(b)										■
(c)	■		■			■	■			
(d)		■						■		

2

Simple Bonding Theories of Molecules

2.1 VALENCE BOND THEORY

The main points of valence bond approach are as under:

- Atoms retain their individuality in the molecule.
- The bond is formed due to the interaction of valence electrons as the atoms approach each other, *i.e.,* the inner atomic orbits from each atom forming the bond are undisturbed.
- When they form a bond, only valence electrons from each bonded atom lose their identity.
- The stability of the bond is explained by the fact that electrons forming the bond between two atoms undergo exchange between them.

This method is based on two **theorems** which are stated as:

(*i*) If Ψ_A and Ψ_B are the wave functions for two isolated independent atoms, with energies E_A and E_B, respectively, then the total wave function ψ of the system can be written as a product of the wave functions of the two atoms

$$\Psi = \Psi_A \Psi_B \qquad ...(1)$$

and energy of the system by

$$E = E_A \pm E_B \qquad ...(2)$$

(*ii*) If a system can be represented by a number of wave functions such as Ψ_1, Ψ_2, Ψ_3, ..., then the true wave function Ψ can be obtained by taking a linear combination of all these wave functions.

$$\Psi = N(C_1 \Psi_1 + C_2\Psi_2 + C_3\Psi_3 + ...) \qquad ...(3)$$

where N is the normalization constant and C_1, C_2, C_3 ......, are the coefficients indicating the weight of each of the Ψ_n's. They are so adjusted as to give a state of lowest energy. The squares of the coefficients may the taken as a measure of the weights of each wave function to the total wave function.

2.1.1 Formation of the Hydrogen Molecule

Let us now apply the concept of valence bond theory of the formation of hydrogen molecule from hydrogen atoms and consider the various forces of attraction and repulsions which may come into play.

For two hydrogen atoms which are infinitely apart when there is no interaction between them the wave function of system is:

$$\Psi = \Psi_a \Psi_b \qquad ...(4)$$

where Ψ_a and Ψ_b represent the wave functions for two hydrogen atoms H_a and H_b respectively. Now if we bring them close together, *i.e.*, distance close enough for interaction, the wave function for the system I, $H_a^{\,1} .. H_b^{\,2}$ can be written as :

$$\Psi_1 = \Psi_a\,(1) \cdot \Psi_b(2) \qquad ...(5)$$

where the hydrogen nuclei are represented as H_a and H_b and the electrons as 1 and 2 (Fig. 2.1).

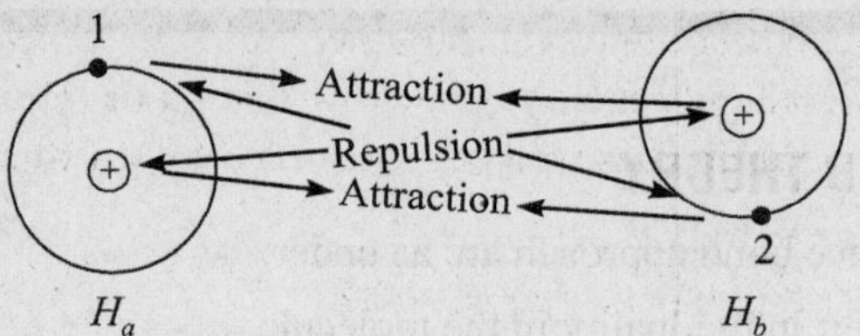

***Fig. 2.1:** Various interactions between two H atoms.*

With the help of wave function Ψ_1, as given by eq. (5), the energy of the system consisting of two hydrogen atoms may be calculated as a function of internuclear distance r_{ab} by applying Schrodinger wave equation. The energy changes as a function of distance r_{ab} may be shown graphically in Fig. 2.2 (curve I).

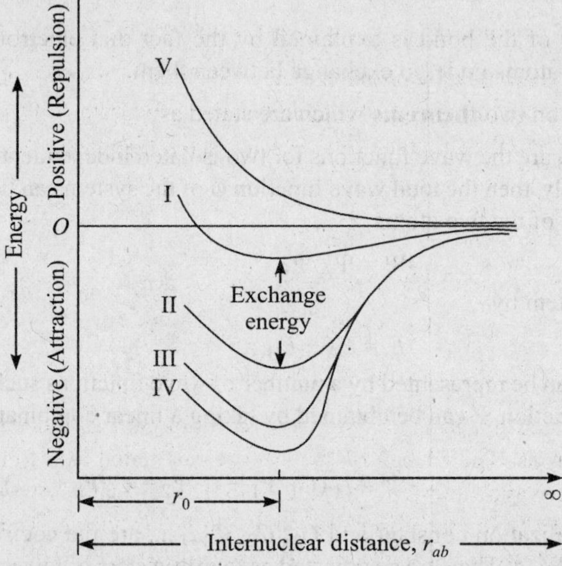

***Fig. 2.2:** Potential energy curves for hydrogen molecule.*

It may be noted that the total energy of the two isolated hydrogen atoms is taken as zero. As the two atoms approach one another [without exchange of electrons, eq. (5)], the electron 1 of H_a is attracted by the nucleus of H_b and electron 2 of H_b is similarly attracted to the nucleus of H_2. As a result there is weak attraction and consequently energy of the system starts decreasing. With decrease in distance between the two atoms, forces of attraction increase rapidly. Ultimately an equilibrium internuclear distance (r_0) is reached where the system has lowest energy. At distances closer than this, stronger repulsion due to close proximity between the two nuclei sets in and consequently the energy of the system becomes positive (curve I). The minima in curve I represents that a molecule is formed but the bond energy represented by wave function Ψ_1 (about 25.2 kJ/mole) compares very poorly with the experimental value of 431.4 kJ/mole (curve IV). One may thus conclude that the wave function Ψ_1 representing structure I is not correct. Certain improvements are therefore necessary to match the theoretical and observed values.

***(a)* First Improvement: Exchange Energy.** A careful examination of the wave function Ψ_1 reveals that electron 1 is associated with atom H_a and electron 2 is associated with atom H_b. When a molecule is formed the two atoms come close together, their atomic orbitals overlap and we are no longer definite that the atoms retain their individual electrons. We cannot trace any one electron in a system according to uncertainty principle. It clearly states that we cannot exactly locate an electron but only the probability of finding the electron is given. Hence the system of two hydrogen atoms may as well be represented by structure II.

II $\quad H_a{}^2 \cdot H_b{}^1$

The wave function for this may be represented as

$$\Psi_{II} = \Psi_a(2) \cdot \Psi_b(1)$$

So if both wave functions Ψ_I and Ψ_{II} are equally probable representations then the real wave function is likely to be a linear combination of these two wave functions.

$$\Psi = C_1 \Psi_I + C_2 \Psi_{II}$$

or
$$\Psi = C_1 \Psi_a(1) \Psi_b(2) + C_2 \Psi_a(2) \Psi_b(1) \qquad ...(6)$$

Since structures I and II are equally probable, the contribution of wave functions, Ψ_I and Ψ_{II} to the true wave function must be equal. As stated earlier in theorem II, the weight of each wave function is proportional to the squares of its coefficients. So we have

$$C_1{}^2 = C_2{}^2 \text{ or } C_I = \pm C_2$$

and if for simplicity we assume $C_1 = 1$, then $C_2 = \pm 1$.

Equation (2.6) may be represented by two equations

$$\Psi_+ = \Psi_a(1) \Psi_b(2) + \Psi_a(2) \Psi_b(1) \qquad ...(7)$$

$$\Psi_- = \Psi_a(1) \Psi_b(2) - \Psi_a(2) \Psi_b(1) \qquad ...(8)$$

Equation (7) represented by Ψ_+ is a symmetric combination as there is no change of sign on exchange of electrons. The energy of the system calculated as a function of internuclear distance, $r_{ab}$by using wave function Ψ_+ results in a significant lowering of energy and is represented by curve II. The bonding energy is shown in curve II and is approximately 302.4 kJ/mole and compares well with the experimental curve IV. The additional lowering in energy *i.e.*, 302.4 – 25.2 = 277.2 kJ/mole has been obtained by virtue of exchange of electrons between the two hydrogen atoms and is known as **exchange energy.** If we plot the energy of the system using Ψ_- eq. (8) as function of distance r_{ab} we obtain curve V which shows that the energy curve represented by Ψ_- is an antisymmetric combination since there is a change of sign on electron interchange. In this case the two atoms approach each other with their electrons having parallel spins, Fig. 2.3 (*b*). It is clear that Ψ_+ is the wave function which represents the H_2 molecule, *i.e.*, electrons approach each other with opposite spins, Fig. 2.3 (*a*). Ψ_+ is also referred to as Ψ_{cov} as each nuclei is always in possession of one electron at all times.

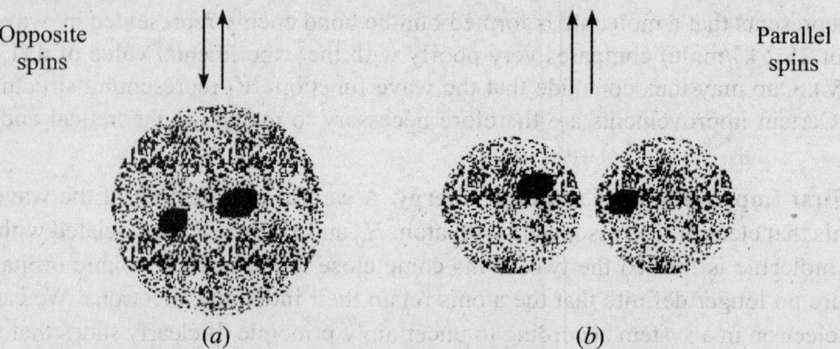

Fig. 2.3: Electrons approaching each other.

(b) Second Improvement: Shielding Effect. The wave function can be improved by considering the screening effect of electrons. Since electrons shield one another by varying extents from the nuclear charge, so we must use, Z_{eff} (effective nuclear charge) rather than Z. When Z_{eff} is used, bonding energy of 339.4 kJ/mole is obtained.

(c) Third Improvement: Ionicity. By the use of wave function Ψ_+ (or Ψ_{cov}) in eq. (7), we have made a significant improvement in the choice of our wave function. But so far we have assumed that one electron is always associated with one atom. Such a situation may not always be true. There is the possibility that both electrons 1 and 2 are either on atom H_a or H_b. The wave function describing such a state would be a combination of eqs. (9) and (10).

III $\quad H_a^{1,2}$..........H_b

Its wave function may be written as

$$\Psi_{III} = \Psi_a(1).\Psi_a(2) \qquad ...(9)$$

and $\quad$ IV $\quad H_b^{1,2}$ ....H_a

is represented as

$$\Psi_{IV} = \Psi_b(1)\,\Psi_b(2) \qquad ...(10)$$

The resulting wave function representing both electrons on one nucleus may be summed as

$$\Psi_{ion} = \Psi_a(1)\Psi_a(2) + \Psi_b(1)\,\Psi_b(2) \qquad ...(11)$$

and is called Ψ_{ion}. Since it represents a state in which ionic forms also contribute to the structure. If we take wave function Ψ_{cov} and Ψ_{ion} together then the real wave function may be written as

$$\Psi = \Psi_{cov} + \lambda\,\Psi_{ion}$$

or

$$\Psi = \Psi_a(1)\,\Psi_b(2) + \Psi_a(2)\,\Psi_b(1) + \lambda[\Psi_a(1)\,\Psi_a(2) + \Psi_b(1)\,\Psi_b(2)] \quad ...(12)$$

where λ represents the mixing coefficient. It tells us how much Ψ_{ion} wave function is to be introduced in the real wave function Ψ. By applying the variation method, we can adjust the value of λ so as to obtain the lowest energy. This way we can measure the extent of ionic character in the covalent bond. For H_2, the value of λ is about 0.17, and the ionic contribution to the bonding energy is about 23.0 kJ/mole. If we now calculate the energy of the system using wave function as given by eq. (12) we get a new energy wave which is marked III. The energy associated with curve III is 362.4 kJ/mol and is an improvement over our earlier results and is quite close to the experimental value.

This treatment which we have discussed for the formation of H_2 is essentially the pairing of two electrons, one from each bonded atom. The valence bond method is also referred to as method of electron pairing. It is obvious even from eq. (7) that the atoms must approach one another with the spins of their electrons in opposite collection. It follows that the formation of covalent bond is explained by the lowering of the potential energy of the electrons, resulting from the increased electron density in the internuclear space.

2.1.2 σ (sigma) and π (pi) Bonds

σ-covalent bond. Sigma bond is formed by end-to-end overlap of any one of these combinations of atomic orbitals. This type of overlapping results in a strong covalent bond. In these cases, bond is formed by electron cloud having maximum density on the line connecting the centres of atoms.

(*a*) *s*—*s* overlap (*b*) s—p_z overlap (*c*) p_z—p_z overlap

Bond formation between two hydrogen atoms to give H_2 results due to overlap of two 1*s* atomic orbitals. The covalent bond formed by the *s*-orbital electron cloud below is called a σ-bond.

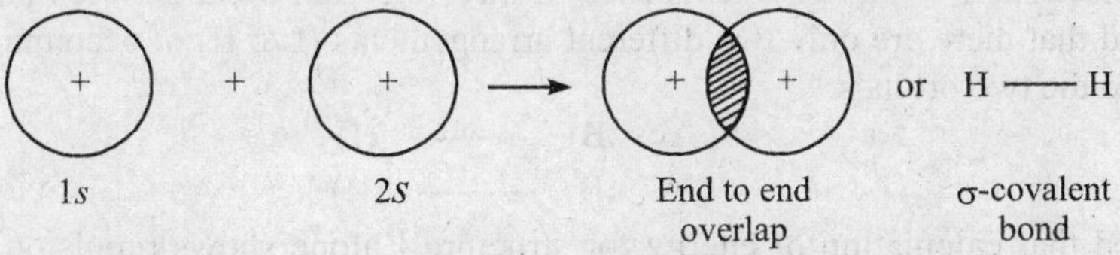

1*s* 2*s* End to end overlap σ-covalent bond

or H — H

Formation of H_2 molecule.

The formation of the HF may be visualized as an example of the overlap between 1*s* and $2p_z$ atomic orbitals as shown below.

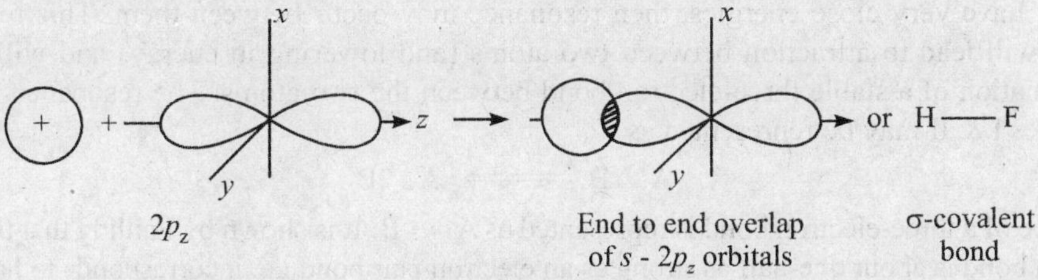

$2p_z$ End to end overlap of *s* - $2p_z$ orbitals σ-covalent bond

or H — F

Formation of HF.

The formation of F_2 molecule results by the overlap of $2p_z$ atomic orbitals of fluorine atoms. This is shown in the figure below.

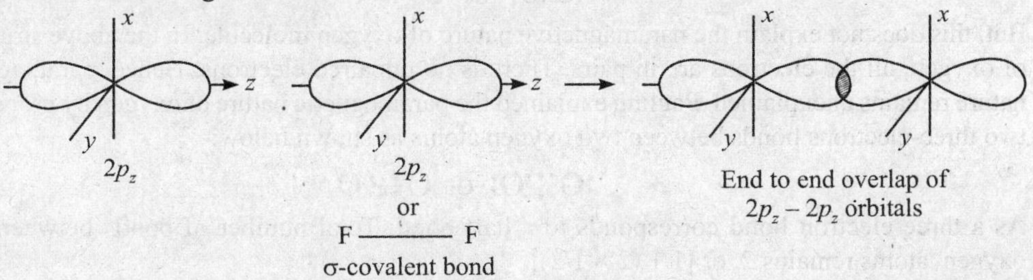

$2p_z$ $2p_z$ End to end overlap of $2p_z - 2p_z$ orbitals

or

F — F

σ-covalent bond

Formation of F_2

π bond. π bond is formed by sideways or lateral overlap between two *p*-orbitals which have their lobes perpendicular to the molecular axis.

The sidewise overlap is not efficient and results in a weak bond. Sigma bond is always stronger than a pi-bond.

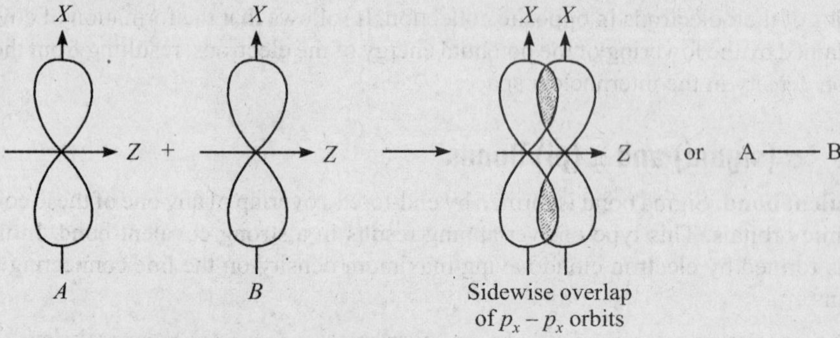

Sidewise overlap of $p_x - p_x$ orbits

2.1.3 Three-electron (Odd-electron) Bond

Pauling in 1931 explained stability of all odd molecules such as NO (nitric oxide) having odd no. of electrons 5 + 6 = 11 to existence of three-electron bond between pairs of atoms. He suggested that there are only two different arrangements (I & II) of accommodating three electrons into the two orbitals.

A: .B --------- (I)

A. :B --------- (II)

He suggested that calculation of energy for structure I alone shows repulsion between the two atoms (+ve potential energy) and so structure (I) does not correspond to the formation of a stable bond. Similarly, structure (II) alone also leads to an unstable arrangement. Pauling suggested that if two atoms A and B are identical or are very similar, so that the two structures I and II have very close energies, then resonance may occur between them. This resonance energy will lead to attraction between two atoms (and lowering in energy) and will lead to the formation of a stable three-electron bond between the two atoms. The resonance between structures I & II may be represented as

$$\text{A:}\ .\text{B} \rightleftharpoons \text{A}.\ :\text{B}$$

This type of a three-electron bond is represented as A· · · B. It is shown by Pauling that the three-electron bond is about one-half as strong as an electron pair bond i.e. it corresponds to half bond.

Paramagnetic nature of oxygen molecule can be explained with the help of three-electron bond. Normally, we represent the bond between two oxygen atoms as

:Ö::Ö: or O═O

But, this does not explain the paramagnetive nature of oxygen molecule. In the above structure of oxygen, all the electrons are in pairs. There is no unpaired electrons. Hence, paramagnetic nature remains unexplained. Pauling explained the paramagnetic nature of oxygen by proposing two three-electrons bonds between two oxygen atoms as shown below:

:O⁝⁝O: or O⩨O

As a three-electron bond corresponds to a half bond. Total number of bonds between two oxygen atoms remains 2, or [1 + (2 × 1/2)].

This structure accounts for the presence of two unpaired electrons, one from each three-electron bond, hence the molecule of oxygen is paramagnetic.

Conditions for the formation of a three-electron bond

Pauling suggested the following conditions for the existence of a three-electron bond between atoms A and B.

(*i*) Atoms A and B must be identical or very similar.

A: .B ---------- (I)

A. :B ---------- (II)

(*ii*) Structures (I) and (II) between atoms A and B must have nearly the same energy, so that resonance stabilization is provided to the system.

(*iii*) Three-electron bond is formed between two different atoms A and B if the electronegativity difference between A and B does not exceed by 0.5. Thus, three-electron bonds have been found to exist between oxygen and fluorine, nitrogen and oxygen and chlorine and oxygen.

Some examples of molecules containing three-electron bond

(*i*) Nitric oxide is the most stable of various odd molecules. The valence bond representation of NO is given below. Structure (II) is expected to be less stable than structure (I) because of distribution of unfavourable charges, *i.e.*, we are placing positive charge on electronegative oxygen atom.

:N̈ = Ö: ------ (I)

:N̈⁻ = Ö⁺: ------ (II)

However, structures I and (II) are nearly of equal stability and thus there is complete resonance between the two structures.

:N̈ = Ö: ⟷ :N̈⁻ = Ö⁺:

The molecule can thus be assigned the following structure consisting of a double bond and

:N ≡ O:

a three-electron bond. This structure is more stable than either of the two structures I and II.

Thus molecule is described as having $2\frac{1}{2}$ bond. It is expected to show bond length between that for a double and a triple bond. The experimental value for bond length for NO is 115 pm, somewhat larger than the triple bond value of 106 pm for NO^+.

(*ii*) Nitrogen dioxide (NO_2). It may be assigned the following resonance structures.

O=N–O ⟷ O–N=O

The NO bond distance was predicted to be 118 pm which agrees well with the experimentally determined value of 119 pm by infrared spectroscopy.

2.1.4 Bond Energy

For a diatomic molecule, say AB, the bond dissociation energy is defined as the energy needed (absorbed) to break the molecule AB into its atoms A & B. The process of bond rupture in a molecule is called **dissociation.** Therefore, the bond energy of a diatomic molecule which is identical with bond dissociation energy (D) may also be defined as the enthalpy change for dissociation of gaseous molecule at 25°C into gaseous atoms at the same temperature. As for example,

$$H_2\,(g) \longrightarrow 2H\,(g) \qquad \Delta\,(H-H) = \Delta\,H = 435.9\ \text{kJ/mole}^{-1}.$$

It is observed that there is a definite trend in bond energy among successive numbers in a group. The heavier analogs generally show lower values of dissociation energy (F_2 is an exception). As far as range of dissociation energies is concerned, the diatomic alkali metals have low values and hydrogen halides have comparatively large values of dissociation energy. There is no trend along a period. It is found that for similar molecules the dissociation energy decreases as bond order decreases. In other words, for related molecules, the bond dissociation energy decreases as bond length increases. Bond dissociation energy of F_2 is exceptionally low because of high repulsion between the non-bonding electrons on the similar fluorine atoms (other halogens have longer bonds).

For polyatomic molecules, the bond dissociation energy and bond energy terms are not identical and should not be used synonymously. Bond dissociation energy (D) of a polyatomic molecule AB_n is defined as the energy required to break just one bond to form atom B and a group of atoms (radical) AB_{n-1}. Bond dissociation energies for a given bond are different for different structural and electronic arrangements in the radical.

Although the bond dissociation energy of a given bond is not independent of the environments but the variation is not very large. The bond dissociation energies may not change significantly with change in environments around a given bond. Thus, it should be possible to characterise a bond by an average bond energy (E) which is defined as the approximate energy required for breaking of the bond in any gaseous molecule. It does not include energies necessary for vaporization or sublimation.

The distinction between bond dissociation energy (D) and average bond energy (E) shall be clear from the following examples showing stepwise dissociation of gaseous water.

$$H_2O\ (g) \longrightarrow H\ (g) + OH\ (g) \qquad D_1\ (H-OH) = 500\ kJ$$

$$OH\ (g) \longrightarrow H\ (g) + O\ (g) \qquad D_2\ (H-O) = 424\ kJ$$

The average bond energy (E) for O – H bond is the mean of the two separate bond dissociation energies $(D_1 + D_2)/2$, that is, $(500 + 424)/2 = 462$ kJ. The enthalpy change for the formation of water molecule by the reaction is –926 kJ mol^{-1}.

$$2H\ (g) + O\ (g) \longrightarrow H_2O\ (g)$$

It is negative because heat is evolved in the formation of gaseous water. As expected, it is almost twice the average bond energy (E = 462) for an O–H bond and hence in close agreement with the presence of two O–H bonds in H_2O. However, the average bond energy (E) is quite different from the bond dissociation energy D_1 or D_2.

Solved Examples

Example 1: The bond energy of Li_2 (113 kJ mol^{-1}) is less than that of H_2 (431 kJ mol^{-1}) though both contain a σ-bond.

Solution: The bond energy of a bond depends upon the bond length. Greater the bond length, smaller the bond energy. Li—Li bond is larger than H—H bond. Hence bond energy of Li_2 is smaller than that of H_2.

2.2 HYBRIDIZATION OF ORBITALS

Ground state of configuration of carbon is

$$1s^2\ 2s^2\ 2p_x^1\ 2p_y^1$$

To account for tetravalency of carbon it is assumed that one electron from 2*s* orbital is excited to $2p_z$ orbital so that the configuration in excited state is

$$1s^2\ 2s^1\ 2p_x^1\ 2p_y^1\ 2p_z^1$$

The structure of methane consists of four equivalent bonds arranged about the carbon atom at the centre in a manner that all the angles between carbon and hydrogen are equal, its value is 109° 28'. The geometric arrangement which fulfils these requirements is a tetrahedron. In such a structure, carbon atom occupies a position at the centre of the tetrahedron and four hydrogen atoms occupy the corner positions. This arrangement is shown in Fig. 2.4.

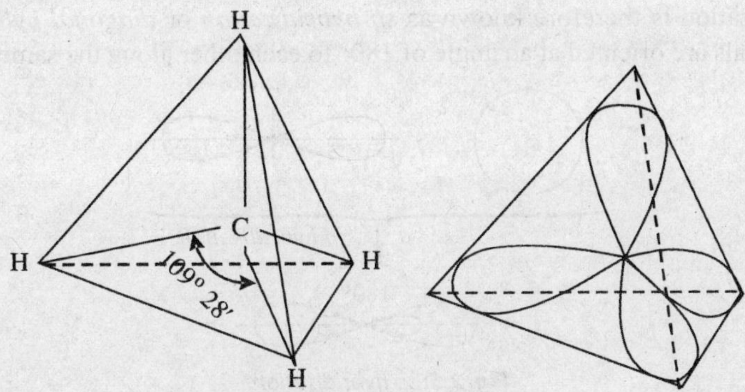

Fig. 2.4: *Structure of methane.*

The equivalence of four bonds can be explained by assuming that the available orbitals of carbon, the 2*s* and three 2*p* orbitals are intermixed or hybridized in a manner as to result in four equivalent orbitals which are oriented towards the four corners of regular tetrahedron. *This mixing of atomic orbitals to give equal number of symmetrically oriented orbitals of equal energy is referred to as hybridization.*

The carbon in this case is said to be sp^3 hybridized and carbon hydrogen bonds are referred to as hybrid bonds.

Different types of hybridization are:

(*i*) sp^3 type (*ii*) sp^2 type
(*iii*) sp type (*iv*) sp^3d type
(*v*) sp^3d^2 or d^2sp^3 type (*vi*) sp^3d^3 type

2.2.1 *sp* Hybridization or Diagonal Hybridization and the Shape of Beryllium Fluoride

Electronic configuration of beryllium in ground state is $1s^2\ 2s^2$. One of the 2*s* electrons gets promoted to next available empty orbital (*i.e.*, $2p_x$) and therefore electronic configuration of beryllium in excited state is $1s^2, 2s^1, 2p_x^1$.

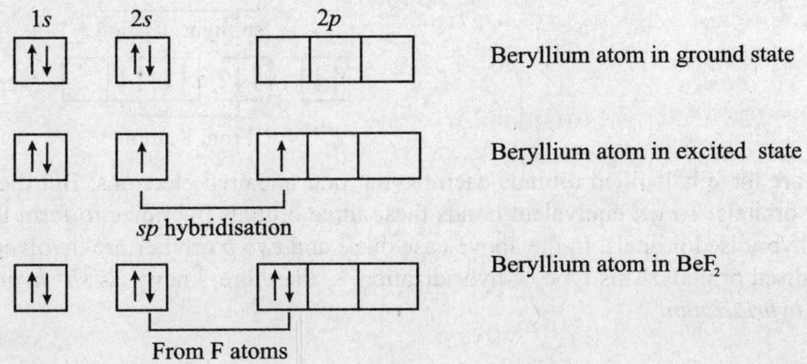

Now there are two half-filled orbitals, each having single unpaired electron. But they belong to two different orbitals. One belongs to *s* and the other two *p*-orbital. Therefore, to get equivalent bonds, these two orbitals hybridise or get mixed up to form two new equivalent orbitals each of which has half *s* and half *p* character.

In the above case one *s* and one *p*-orbitals are involved to form hybridized orbitals. This type of hybridization is therefore known as *sp hybridization* or *diagonal hybridization.* The hybridized orbitals are oriented at an angle of 180° to each other along the same axis (Fig. 2.5).

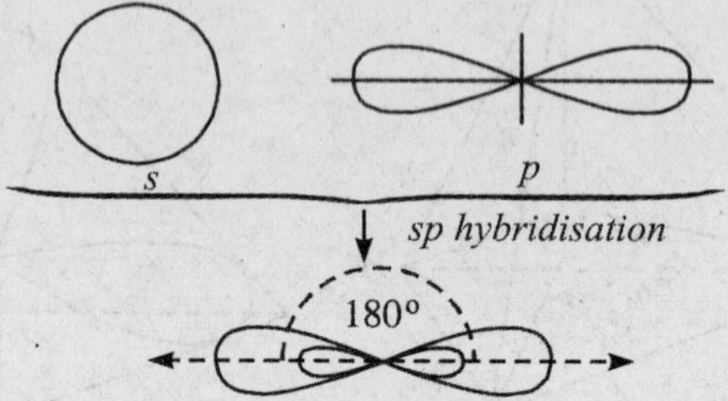

Fig. 2.5: *sp hybridisation.*

These two hybridized orbitals overlap separately with the *p*-orbitals of fluorine to form two Be-F bonds. Shape of BeF_2 molecule can be represented as shown in Fig. 2.6. There are two bonded electron pairs. Therefore molecule is linear with two orbitals at an angle of 180° to each other.

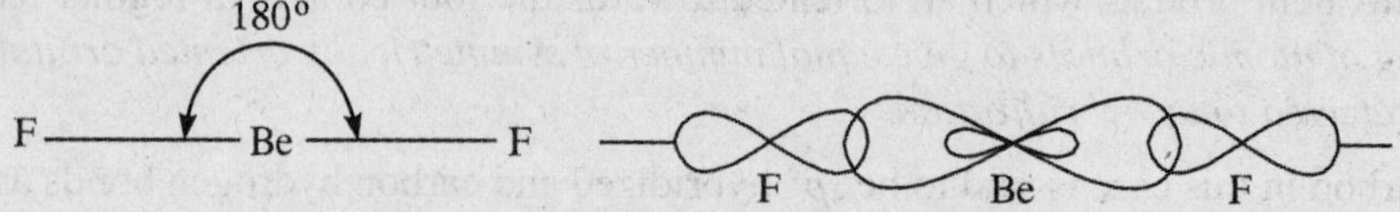

Fig. 2.6: *Pictorial representation of BeF_2.*

2.2.2 sp^2 Hybridization or Trigonal Hybridization and the Shape of BF_3 Molecule

Electronic configuration of boron in ground state is $1s^2\ 2s^2\ 2p_x^1$. One of the two 2*s* electrons gets promoted to next available vacant orbital ($2p_y$). The electronic configuration of boron in the excited state is $1s^2\ 2s^1\ 2p_x^1\ 2p_y^1$.

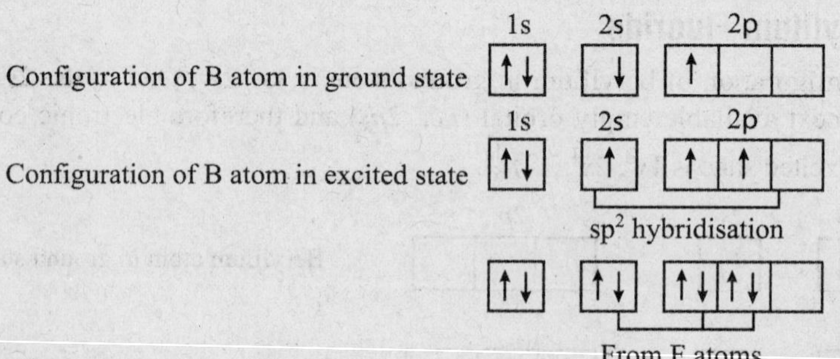

Now there are three half-filled orbitals each having odd unpaired electrons. But they belong to different orbitals. To get equivalent bonds these three orbitals hybridize to form three new equivalent hybridised orbitals. In the above case one *s* and two *p* orbitals are involved to form three hybridised orbitals. This type of hybridization is, therefore, known as *sp^2 hybridization or trigonal hybridization.*

Boron forms sp^2 hybridised orbitals. These three orbitals lie in one plane (*i.e.*, boron atom is planar) and are directed towards the three corners of an equivalent triangle, so that the angle between them is 120°. (Fig. 2.7)

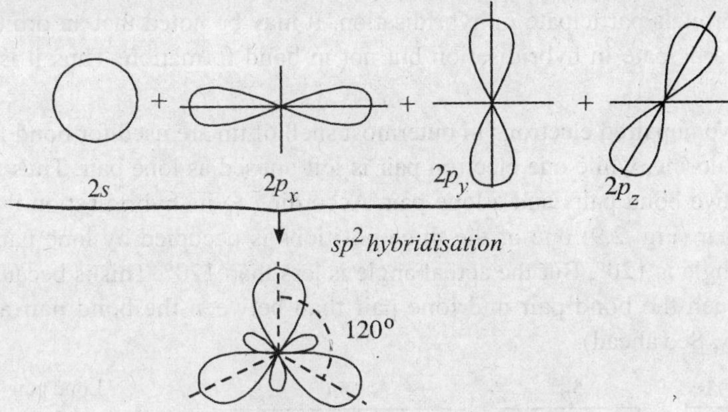

Fig. 2.7: Orientation of sp^2 hybrid orbitals.

Boron atom has now three sp^2 hybridised orbitals each having an odd unpaired electron. They are capable of forming three bonds by overlapping with, three half-filled orbitals of other atoms.

Bonding capacity of boron, therefore, is three. Boron forms compounds of type X — B(X)(X) where X = H or Cl

Shape of BF_3

Shape of BF_3 molecule can be represented as shown in Fig. 2.8. There are three bonded electron pairs. The three bonds are equivalent and 120° apart. The molecule is, therefore, triangular and planar in shape.

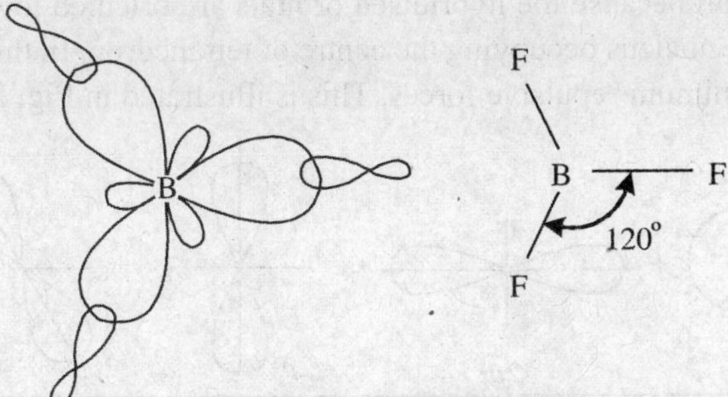

Fig. 2.8: Shape of BF_3.

Example 2: Explain why BF_3 is triangular in shape while BeF_2 is linear.

Solution: In BeF_2, Be atom is *sp* hybridized. The *sp* hybrid orbitals are linearly oriented. That is why the molecule of BeF_2 is linear.

In BeF_3, B atom is sp^2 hybridized. The sp^2 hybrid orbitals are oriented at an angle of 120° towards the corners of a triangle. That is why the shape of BF_3 is triangular.

Example 3: Discuss the shape of Stannous chloride Molecule ($SnCl_2$)

Solution: Atomic no. of Sn is 50. In stannous chloride the tin (Sn) atom has electronic configuration of outermost shell as : $5s^2\ 5p_x^{\ 1}\ p_y^{\ 1}$. Two electrons in the 5*s* orbital and two electrons in *p*-orbitals participate in hybridisation. It may be noted that an orbital with paired electrons can participate in hybridisation but not in bond formation. Thus it is a case of sp^2 hybridisation.

In $SnCl_2$, two unpaired electrons in outermost shell of tin are used for bond formation with two atoms of chlorine, while one electron pair is left unused as lone pair. Thus there are three electron pairs, two bond pairs and a lone pair. According to its hybridisation it is expected to be trigonal planar (Fig. 2.9) one of the three positions is occupied by lone pair of electrons. The expected angle is 120°. But the actual angle is less than 120°. This is because of a greater repulsion between the bond pair and lone pair than between the bond pair and bond pair. (VSEPR Theory, See ahead).

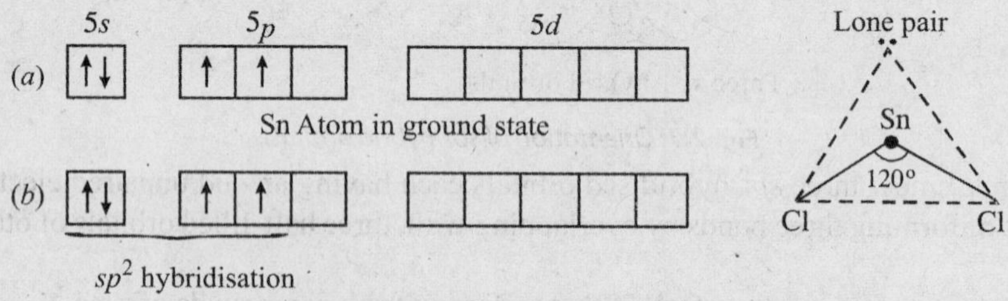

Fig. 2.9: Formation of stannous chloride.

2.2.3 sp^3 Hybridisation or Tetrahedral Hybridisation

When one *s* orbital and three *p* orbitals combine together to produce equivalent type of orbitals, sp^3 hybridisation takes place. Four sp^3 hybridised orbitals are produced which have the same energy and shape and are oriented at an angle of 109°28' to one another. This is also known as tetrahedral hybridisation because the hybridised orbitals are oriented towards the four corners of tetrahedron with the nucleus occupying the centre of tetrahedron. In this position, hybridised orbitals experience minimum repulsive forces. This is illustrated in Fig. 2.10.

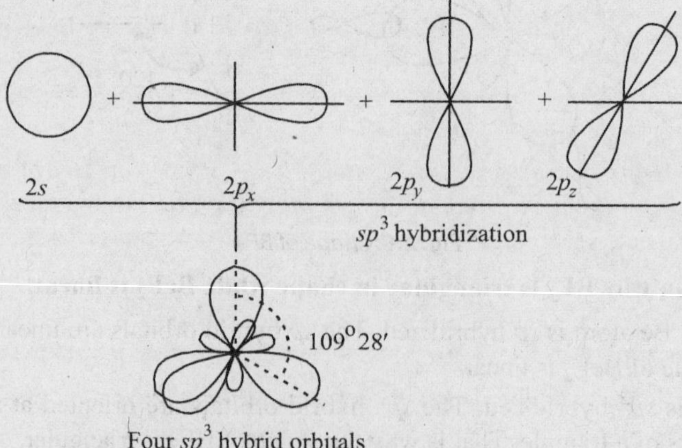

Fig. 2.10: sp^3 hybridisation.

Shape of methane molecule

At no. of carbon = 6

Electronic configuration of C in ground state = $1s^2\ 2s^2\ 2p_x^1\ 2p_y^1$

Electronic configuration of C in excited state = $1s^2\ 2s^1\ 2p_x^1\ 2p_y^1\ 2p_z^1$

There are four orbitals having unpaired electrons. These $2s$, $2p_x$, $2p_y$ and $2p_z$ orbitals will first hybridise. So it is a case of sp^3 hybridisation. Four hybridised orbitals tetrahedrally are shown in Fig. 2.11.

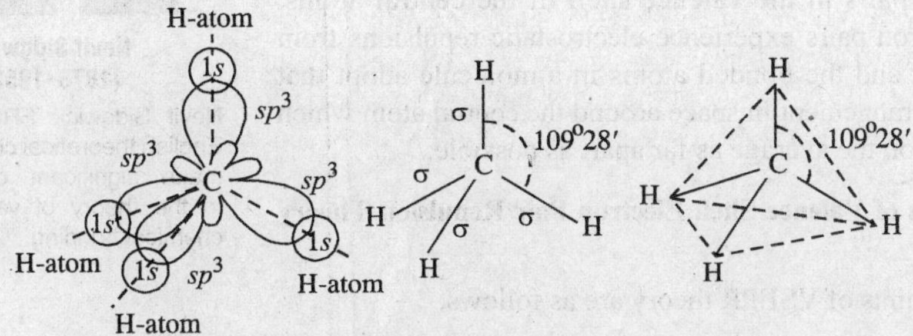

Fig. 2.11: Shape of methane molecule.

All the four hybridised orbitals overlap with the $1s$ orbital of four hydrogen atoms. All these overlappings take place along the internuclear axes. Hence four carbon-hydrogen σ bonds are formed. The angle ∠ HCH is 109° 28'.

2.2.4 Factors that Determine the Shape of Molecules

The shapes of molecules depend upon the following factors:

1. Types of hybridisation. Type of hybridisation decides the shape of molecules. If sp hybridisation takes place and the molecule is of the type AB_2 where the atom A is central and surrounded by two B atoms then molecule will have a linear shape B — A — B with the ∠ BAB equal to 180°.

Similarly if the molecule is of the type AB_3 with sp^2 hybridisation the atom A lies in the centre of an equilateral traingle and three B atoms occupy the vertices of the triangle. If however the molecule is of type AB_4 with sp^3 hybridisation taking place the atom A occupies the centre of tetrahedral and vertices of tetrahedron being occupied by B. This is based on the fact that the hybridised orbitals repel each other due to similar charge and occupy positions in which there are minimum repulsive forces.

2. Lone pair of electrons. Another factor which decides the geometry of a molecule is the lone pair of electrons on the central atom. Certain elements like nitrogen and oxygen contain lone pair or pairs of electrons on them which repel the shared pair of electron away from them. In such a case bond angle changes from expected angle. Repulsion between the electrons is in the following order:

Lone pair, lone pair > lone pair, shared pair > shared pair, shared pair.

Repulsion between the two lone pairs is maximum followed by that between a lone pair and a shared pair followed by the repulsion between two shared pairs of electrons.

Greater the number of lone pairs of electrons on the central atom, greater is the distortion produced in the normal angle or shape.

2.2.5 Valence Shell Electron Pair Repulsion (VSEPR) Theory

Valence shell electron pair repulsion theory (in short VSEPR theory) is the simplest theory for predicting the geometries of molecules. It is based on the repulsive interactions between the electron pairs in the valence shell. This theory was proposed by Sidgwick and Powell in 1940 and given the final shape by Gillespie and Nyholm (1957). According to this theory, the shapes of molecules can be determined by the number of electron pairs in the valence shell of the central atoms. These electron pairs experience electrostatic repulsions from one another and the bonded atoms in a molecule adopt that particular arrangement in space around the central atom which keeps them on the average as far apart as possible.

Nevil Sidgwick (1873–1952)

Nevil Sidgwick FRS was an English theoretical chemist who made significant contribution to the theory of valency and chemical bonding.

Main Points of Valence Shell Electron Pair Repulsion Theory (VSEPR)

The main points of VSEPR theory are as follows:

(*i*) Geometry of a molecule depends upon the total number of valence shell electron pairs (bonded or non-bonded) around the central atom in the molecule.

(*ii*) Repulsion between valence shell electron pairs determines molecular shape. In order to minimise electron-electron repulsion or to acquire a state of minimum energy or maximum stability the valence shell electron pairs keep as far apart as possible.

(*iii*) In case more than one geometrical arrangement is possible for a given number of bonded and non-bonded pairs, then the most stable arrangement is in accordance with the following:

(*a*) Lone pair-lone pair (*lp-lp*) repulsion is greater than lone pair-bond pair (*lp-bp*) repulsion which in turn is greater than bond pair-bond pair (*bp-bp*) repulsion. That is

lp-lp > *lp-bp* > *bp-bp*

(*b*) Repulsion between electron pairs at vertices greater than 115° apart can be neglected.

In the formation of a bond, the central atoms shares its valence electrons with the surrounding atoms. However, in certain cases, all the valence shell electrons may not take part in the blood formation. The electrons left in the valence shell without forming bonds exist as lone pairs. For example, in methane, CH_4, carbon uses all the four valence electrons in forming four bond pairs. In water, H_2O, the central oxygen atoms has ($1s^2$, $2s^2$ $2p^4$) six valence electrons. The hydrogen atom shares two of these six valence electrons in bond formation leaving four electrons as two lone pairs.

·C· (Four valence electrons)

:Ö· (Six valence electrons)

H×C×H with H above and below (Four bond pairs)

:Ö×H with H below (Two bond pairs and two lone pairs)

Thus, in methane, there are four pairs around carbon, while oxygen in water has two bond pairs and two lone pairs around it. According to VSEPR theory, it is the total number of electron pairs (bonded as well as lone pairs) that determines the geometry of molecule.

Regular and irregular geometries

The molecules in which the central atom is surrounded only by similar bonded electron pairs have ***regular geometries*** *while those in which the central atom is surrounded by bond pairs as well as lone pairs have* ***irregular geometries.***

Molecules such as CH_4, BF_3, PF_5, SF_6, etc., have regular geometries because the central atom in these molecules are bonded to similar atoms and there are no lone pairs in these molecules.

Molecules such as CH_2Cl_2, $CHCl_3$ etc., in which the central atom is bonded to different atoms and the molecules such as NH_3 and H_2O which have lone pairs as well as bond pairs, have irregular geometries.

VSEPR theory provides a simple approach to predict the shapes of molecues. The results obtained on the basis of this theory are quite in agreement with those obtained from hybridisation concept.

This theory is very simple to use. We make no distinction between *s* and *p*-electrons. We take into account only the number of electron pairs present in the valence shell of the central atom. The basic point is that the electron pairs (bonded or lone pairs) try to remain as far apart as possible to get a state of stability.

Limitations of VSEPR theory

Important limitations of VSEPR theory are:

(*i*) The theory is applicable to covalent compounds only and cannot be applied to ionic compounds.

(*ii*) The theory does not make any distinction between *s*, *p*, *d* and *f* orbitals.

(*iii*) The theory does not help in the prediction of shapes of coordination compounds.

(*iv*) The theory simply predicts that molecules such as NH_3, H_2O, $CHCl_3$, etc. have distinction from the regular geometrical shapes but does not quantify the extent of distortion.

Shape of ammonia molecule

Atomic no. of nitrogen = 7

Electronic configuration of nitrogen, $1s^2\ 2s^2\ 2p_x^1\ 2p_y^1\ 2p_z^1$

Here, there is no possibility of shifting of electron from 2*s* level to 2*p* level as there is no empty 2*p* orbital. 2*s* orbital, although incapable of overlapping or forming the bond or forming the bond, participates in hybridisation. This will give rise to tetrahedral shape. Hybridised orbitals are oriented towards the corners of a tetrahedron with one corner occupied by the lone pair of electrons from 2*s* orbital. Three sp^3 hybridised orbitals overlap with the 1*s* orbitals of three hydrogen atoms (Fig. 2.12.). We expect an angle of 109° 28' between H — N — H in tetrahedral geometry. Actually this angle is 107°. This contraction in angle takes place because the lone pair of electrons repels the shared pair of electrons or bonded pair of electrons with a greater force (Fig. 2.12.) thereby reducing the angle. (Valence Shell Electron Pair Repulsion, VSEPR Theory).

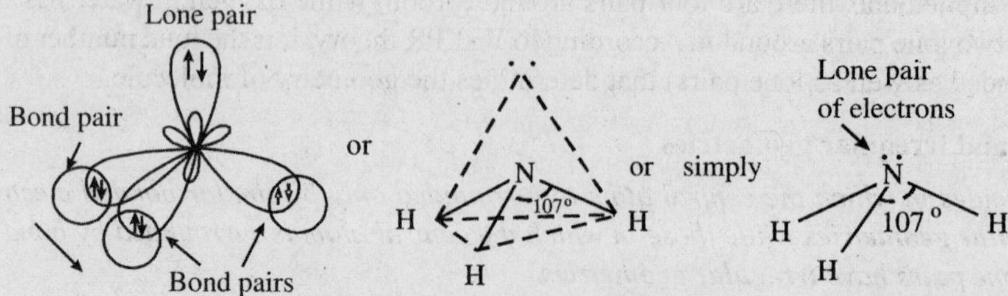

Fig. 2.12: Shape of ammonia molecule.

Thus it has pyramidal shape.

Shape of water molecule

At. no. of oxygen = 8

Electronic configuration = $1s^2\ 2s^2\ 2p_x^2\ 2p_y^1\ p_z^1$

In the 2nd orbit there are four orbitals : 2*s*, $2p_x$ $2p_y$ and $2p_z$. Out of these 2*s* and $2p_x$ cannot form the bonds as they are paired. But they can participate in hybridisation. Hence it is case of sp^3 hybridisation. The hybridised orbitals are oriented along the corners of a tetrahedron. Two of the positions on the tetrahedron are occupied by lone pair of electrons from 2*s* and $2p_x$ orbitals. The other two hybridised orbitals will overlap with the 1*s* orbital of two hydrogen atoms to form a water molecule as shown in Fig. 2.13. We expect an angle of 109°28' in HOH. Actually the angle is 105°. This is due to stronger repulsion of two lone pairs of electrons with shared pair of electrons (VSEPR Theory). Thus water is a V-shaped molecule.

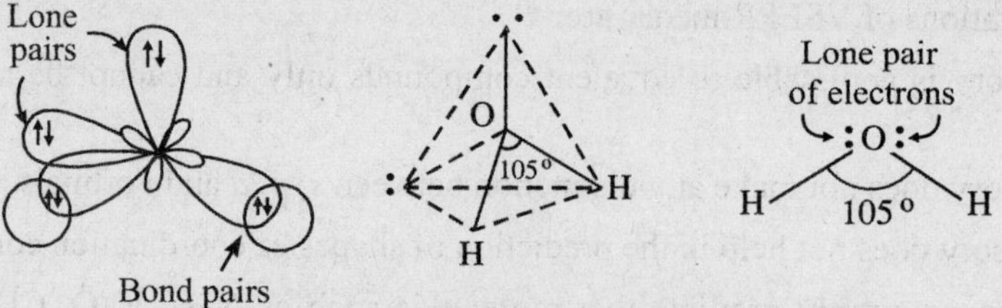

Fig. 2.13: Shape of water molecule.

Structure of hydronium ion $[H_3O]^+$

In the formation of hydronium ion, coordinate, bond is involved. Here, oxygen atom in the water molecule is the donour while hydrogen ion is the acceptor. The formation of coordinate bond in H_3O^+ may be represented as below pointing from the donor to the acceptor, as shown below in the formation of hydronium ion.

$$H_2\ddot{O}: + H^+ \longrightarrow [H_3O]^+ \quad \text{OR} \quad \left[H_2O \rightarrow H\right]^+$$

It is important to note that the coordinate covalent bond once formed is indistinguishable from a covalent bond.

According to the atomic orbital overlap concept of covalency, a coördinate covalent bond results when an empty orbital present in the other atom. The central atom, oxygen, in water molecule has four orbitals. Two of these orbitals contain bond pairs of electrons while the other two (shaded ones) contain lone pairs of electrons, as shown in Fig. 2.14. The H^+ ion has an empty s orbital which overlaps with one of the orbitals of oxygen atom containing a lone pair of electrons forming hydronium ion, H_3O^+, as illustrated in Fig. 2.14.

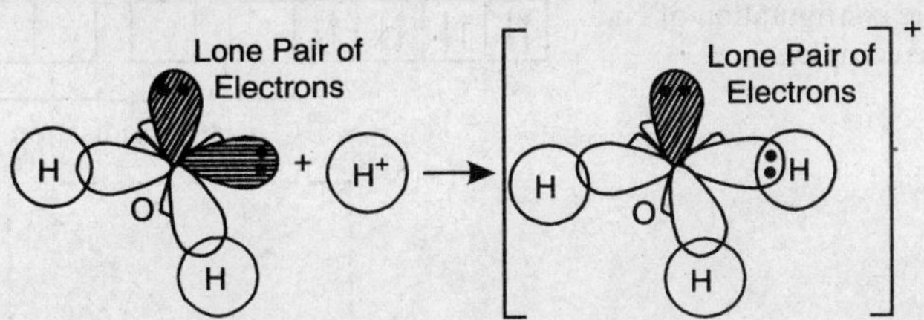

Fig. 2.14: Formation of hydronium ion.

It may be noted that the shape of $[H_3O]^+$ will continue to remain tetrahedral because the hybridisation involved remains sp^3. The difference between H_2O and H_3O^+ is: while in H_2O, two tetrahedral positions are occupied by lone pairs of electrons, it is only one tetrahedral position that is occupied by loans pair of electrons in H_3O^+.

2.2.6 *dsp*² Square Planar Hybridisation

This type of hybridisation takes place when one *s,* two *p* (p_x, p_y) and one *d*($d_{x^2-y^2}$) orbitals mix together to give four equivalent hybrid orbitals. These four hybrid orbitals keep their lobes directed towards the corners of a square in the *XY* plane, *i.e.*, these hybrid orbitals point away from the origin in the ± *X* and ± *Y* direction of *X* and *Y* axes. The angle of maximum repulsion between their orbitals is 90° as shown in Fig. 2.15.

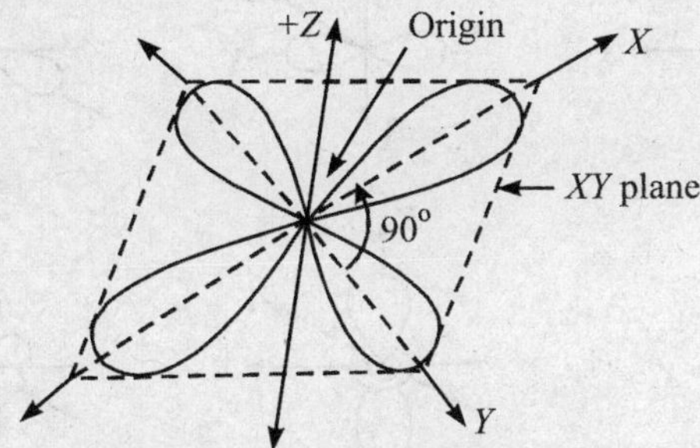

Fig. 2.15: dsp² hybridisation.

Shape of $[Ni(CN)_4]^{2-}$

Pairing of single electrons in 3*d* orbitals in Ni^{2+} takes place thereby creating one vacant 3*d* orbital.

Electron pairs from four CN^- ions are filled up in four hybrid orbitals obtained as a result of dsp^2 hybridisation as shown in Fig. 2.16.

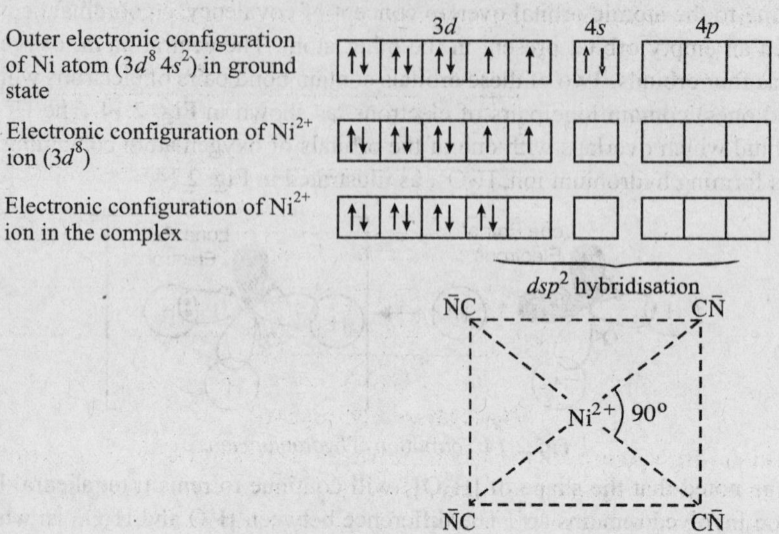

Fig. 2.16: Shape of [Ni(CN)$_4$]$^{2-}$].

2.2.7 sp³d Hybridisation (or dsp³ Hybridisation)

Mixing of one *s*, three *p* and one *d* atomic orbitals gives five sp^3d hybrid orbitals and process is called sp^3d hybridisation. These are directed towards the corners of a trigonal bipyramid as shown in figure. They form three coplanner bonds with bond angles of 120°, remaining two bonds are at right angles to this plane one above and one below.

Formation of five sp^3d hybrid orbitals is shown in Fig. 2.17.

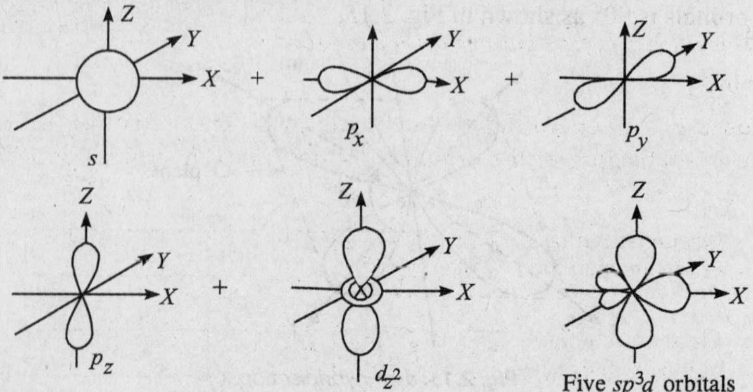

Fig. 2.17: sp³d hybridisation.

Shapes of molecules involving sp^3d hybridisation

(i) Shape of PCl_5

Here sp^3d type hybridisation is involved. At. no. of phosphorus atom is 15. Its outer electronic configuration in the ground state is $3s^2\ sp^3$ as shown in Fig. 2.18.

In order to have the requisite number of half-filled orbitals available for hybridisation purpose one of the 3*s* electrons is made to jump to one of the 3*d* empty orbitals, thereby giving

a *T*-shape. The angle F — Cl —F expected from this geometry is 90°. However actual angle is 87.6°. This is due to repulsion from lone pairs which result in contraction of angle.

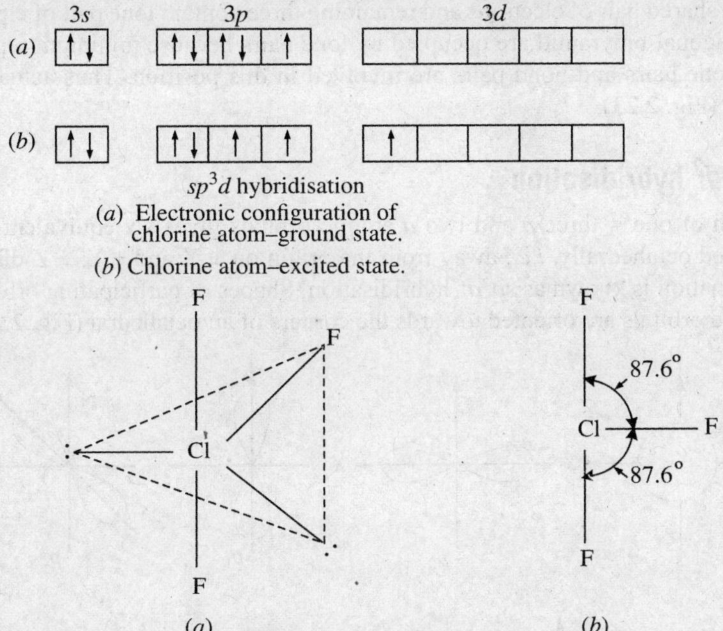

Fig. 2.22: *Shape of ClF_3 molecule.*

Example 4: In XeF_2, Xe undergoes sp^3d hybridisation but the molecule is linear. Explain.

Solution: It is a case of sp^3d hybridisation. Atomic number of Xe is 54. Its outer electronic configuration is $5s^2\ 5px^2\ 5py^2\ 5pz^2$ as shown in Fig. 2.23. In order to have the requisite number of half-filled orbitals for hybridisation one of the $5p_z$ electrons is made to jump to one of the 5*d* empty orbitals. The unpaired electrons in the 5*p* and 5*d* orbitals are used in chemical bonding, the pairing electrons being provided by two fluorine atoms.

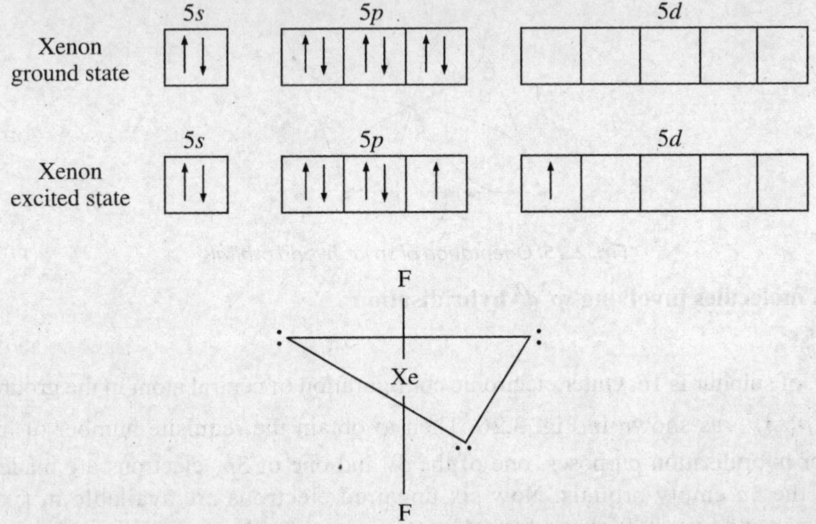

Fig. 2.23: *Shape of Xe F_2 molecule.*

The *s*, *p* and *d* orbitals hybridise to yield five sp^3d hybrid orbitals of equivalent energy. Thus in XeF_2 molecule the central atom, Xe, is surrounded by five completely filled orbitals, two of which contain shared pair of electrons and remaining three contain lone pair of electrons. Three positions in trigonal bipyramid are occupied by lone pairs because minimum repulsive forces between the lone pairs and bond pairs are involved in this position. Thus actual structure of XeF_2 is linear (Fig. 2.23).

2.2.8 sp^3d^2 hybridisation

A combination of one *s,* three *p* and two *d* atomic orbitals gives six equivalent sp^3d^2 hybrid orbitals directed octahedrally, *i.e.*, away from the origin on ± X and ± Y, ± Z directions. This type of combination is known as sp^3d^2 hybridisation. Shapes of participating orbitals is shown in 2.24. Hybrid orbitals are oriented towards the corners of an octahedral (Fig. 2.25).

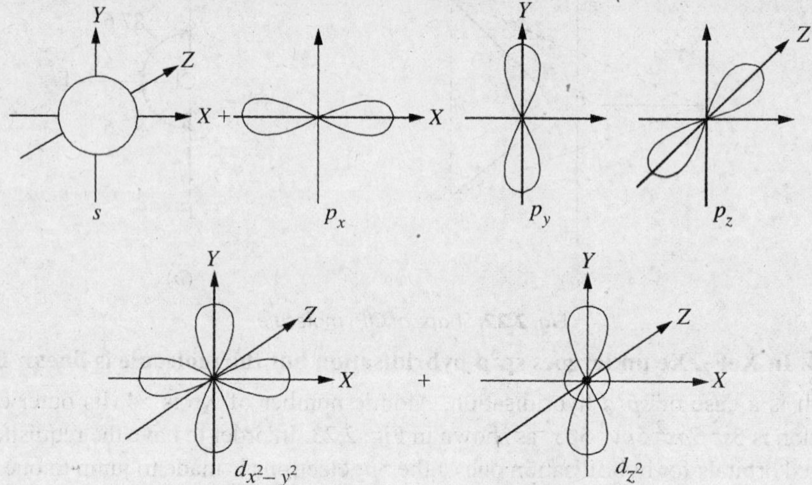

Fig. 2.24: *Shapes of participating orbitals.*

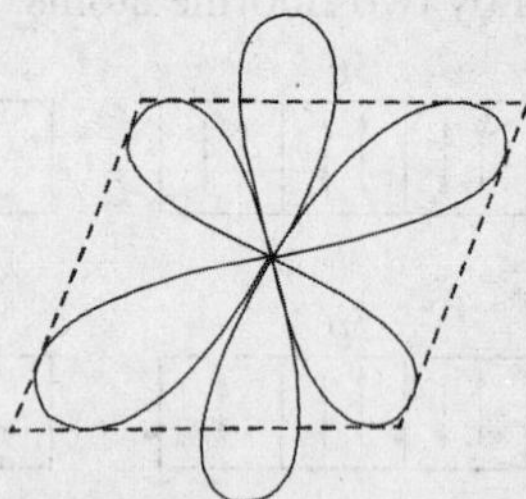

Fig. 2.25: *Orientation of sp^3d^2 hybrid orbitals.*

Shapes of molecules involving sp^3d^2 hybridisation

Shape of SF_6

At. no. of sulphur is 16. Outer electronic configuration of central atom in the ground state is $3s^2 3p_x^2\ 3p_y\ 3p_z$ as shown in Fig. 3.26. Then to obtain the requisite number of half-filled orbitals for hybridisation purposes, one of the 3*s* and one of $3p_x$ electrons are made to jump to two of the 3*d* empty orbitals. Now six unpaired electrons are available in six orbitals (one *s,* three *p* and two *d*), for bond formation to give rise to SF_6 molecule.

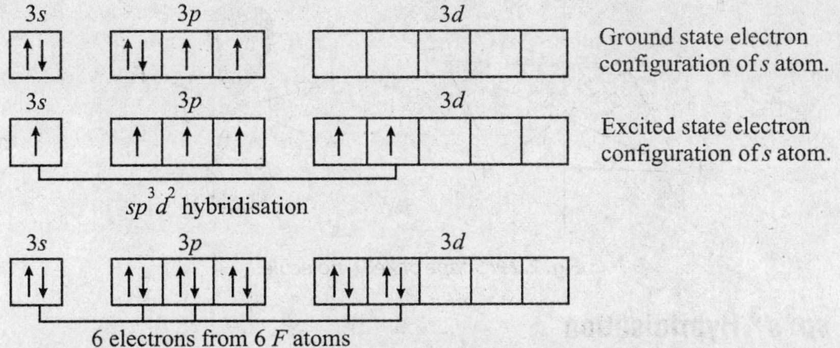

***Fig. 2.26:** Electronic configuration of S.*

These six orbitals hybridise in sp^3d^2 type. The six hybrid orbitals are now directed towards the corners of a regular octahedron. These six hybrid orbitals overlap with the *p*-orbitals of six fluorine atoms. So SF_6 molecule has an octahedral structure as shown in Fig. 3.27.

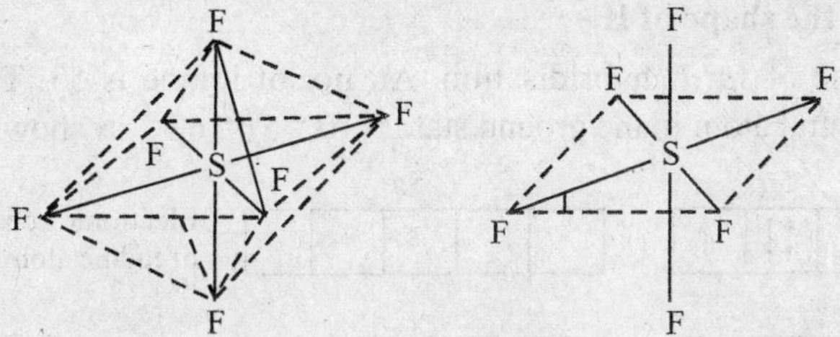

***Fig. 2.27:** Octahedral molecule of sulphur hexafluoride formed by sp^3d^2 hybridisation.*

Example 5: Discuss the Shape of XeF_4

Solution: It is a case of sp^3d^2 hybridisation. At. no. of Xe is 54. Its outer electronic configuration in the ground state is $5s^2\ sp^6$ (Fig. 2.28).

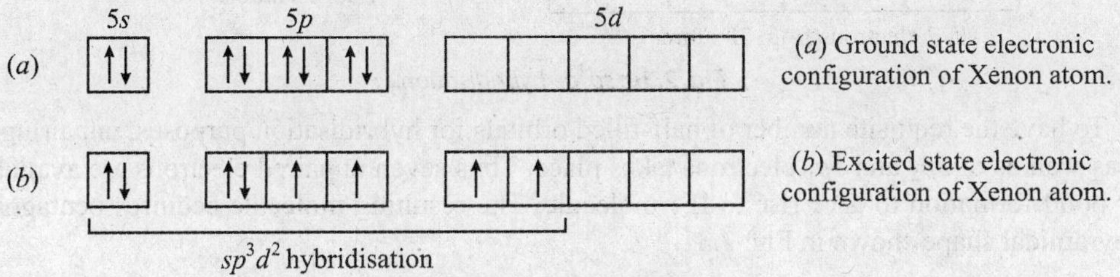

***Fig. 2.28:** sp^3d^2 hybridisation.*

In the excited state, two of the 5*p* electrons go to the 5*d*-orbitals so that there are now four unpaired electrons (two in 5*p* and two in 5*d* orbitals). These are used in bonding with four atoms of fluorine as shown in figure. The central atom, Xe, is surrounded by six orbitals resulting from sp^3d^2 hybridisation. The hybrid orbitals are oriented octahedrally. Four of these orbitals contain shared pairs while the remaining two contain lone pair of electrons.

As the vertex positions are occupied by lone pairs, the actual shape is square planar as represented in Fig. 2.29. As per VSEPR Theory, the lone pairs occupy vertex positions to have minimum repulsion and maximum stability.

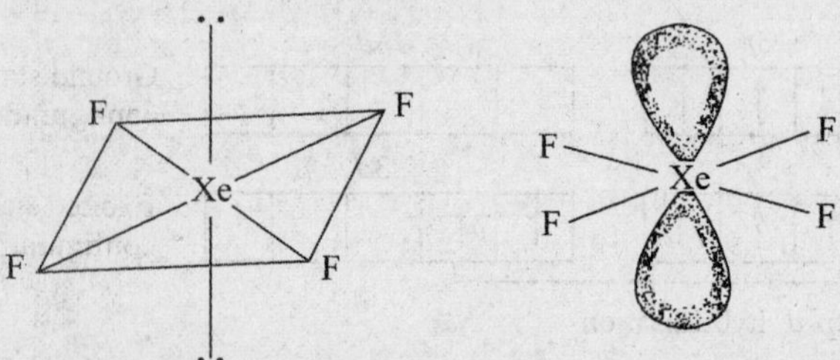

Fig. 2.29: Shape of XeF_4 molecule.

2.2.9 sp^3d^3 Hybridisation

Mixing of one *s*, three *p* and three *d* atomic orbitals gives seven sp^3d^3 hybrid orbitals which are directed towards the corners of a pentagonal bipyramid. These are not equivalent hybrid orbitals. Five of them point towards the vertices of a regular pentagon while others are perpendicular to the plane.

Example 6: Discuss the shape of IF_7

Solution: It is a case of sp^3d^3 hybridisation. At. no. of iodine is 53. The outer electronic configuration of central atom in the ground state is $5s^2\ 5p_x^2\ 6p_z^2$ as shown in Fig. 2.30.

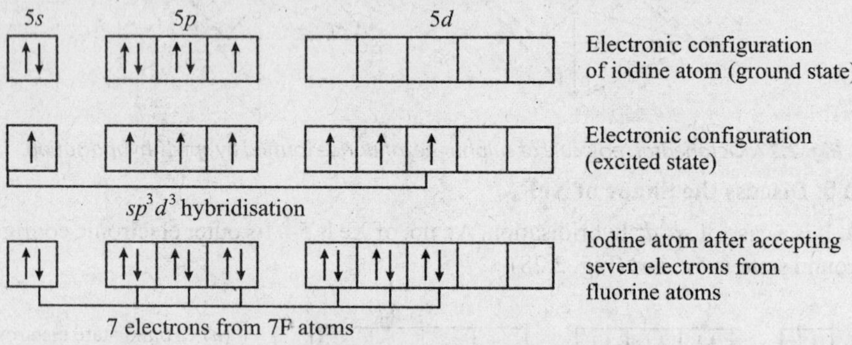

Fig. 2.30: sp^3d^3 hybridisation.

To have the requisite number of half-filled orbitals for hybridisation purposes, unpairing of 5*s* as well as of $5p_x$ and $5p_y$ electrons takes place. Thus seven unpaired electrons are available for bond formation to give rise to IF_7 molecule. The resulting molecule acquires pentagonal bipyramidal shape shown in Fig. 2.31.

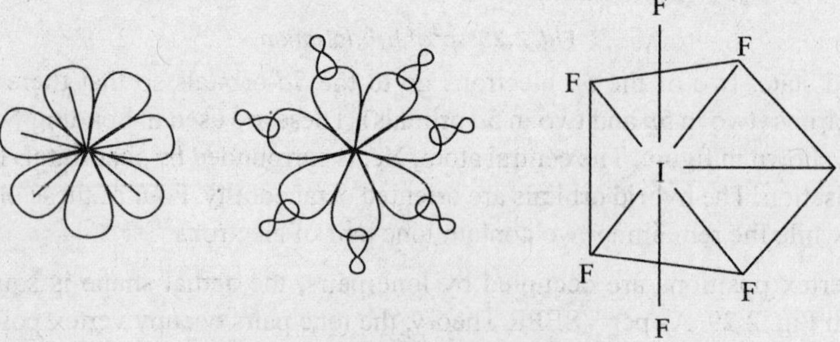

Fig. 2.31: Formation of IF_7 molecule.

In this case all the seven hybrid orbitals arenot equivalent. Five of them are directed towards the vertices of a regular pentagon giving an angle 72° with one another, the rest of two are oriented at right angle to the plane of the first set of five orbitals. Thus the bond angles in the molecule are of 72°and 90°.

Example 7: Discuss the shape of BF_4^- ion

Solution: Boron constitutes the central atom in the BF_4^- ion. The ground state electronic configuration of boron (Z = 5) is $B : 1s^2\,2s^2\,2p^1$. In order to form four bonds around boron, four hybrid orbitals are needed. This can be achieved by the combination of one 2*s* and three 2*p* orbitals of boron as shown below.

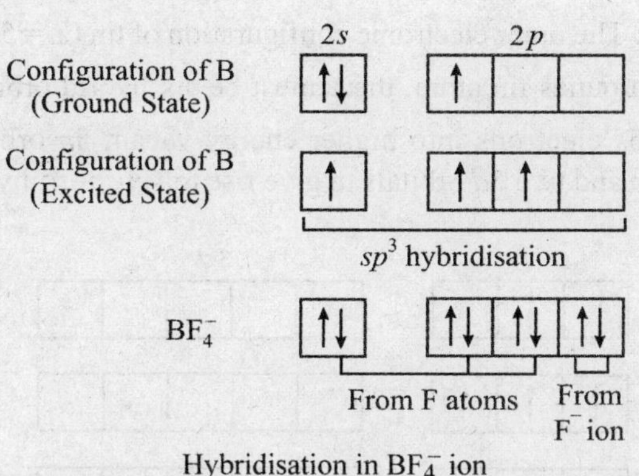

Hybridisation in BF_4^- ion

Applying Chemistry to Life

Chemistry between individuals

Structures of molecules determine the chemistry of substances. Likewise structures of genes determine the chemistry between individuals.

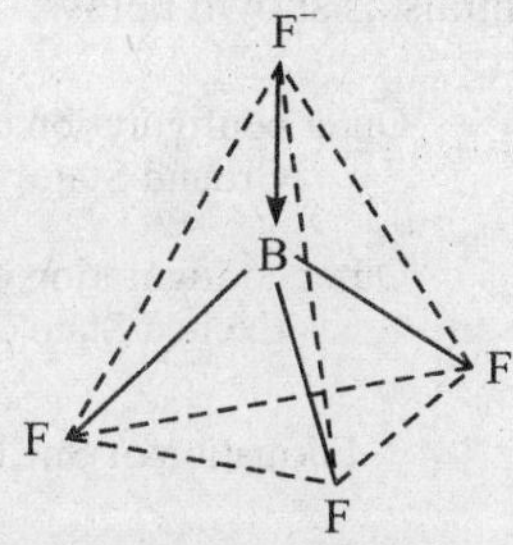

Fig. 2.32: Shape on BF_4^- ion.

This results in sp^3 hybridisation. There are four sp^3-hybrid orbitals around boron atom that are directed towards the four corners of a tetrahedron. Three of the hybrid orbitals are half-filled while the fourth orbital is vacant. The three half-filled sp^3 hybrid orbitals overlap with three 2*p* orbitals of fluorine atoms to form three B—F bonds. The vacant sp^3-hybrid orbital accepts a pair of electrons from a fluoride ion, F^- and forms a dative $^-F \longrightarrow B$ bond. It may be noted that in BF_4^- ion, boron atom completes its octet. Thus, the geometry of BF_4^- ion is tetrahedral as shown in Fig. 2.32.

Example 8: Discuss the shape of PF_6^- ion

Solution: The phosphorus atom is the central atom in phosphorus hexafluoride ion. The outer electronic configuration of phosphorus (Z = 15) is $3s^2\ 3p^3$. In order to form six bonds around phosphorus, we need six hybrid orbitals. This can be achieved by promoting the 3*s* electrons to the vacant higher energy 3*d* orbital followed by combination of one 3*s*, three 3*p* and two 3*d* orbitals to obtain six sp^3d^2 hybrid orbitals as follows:

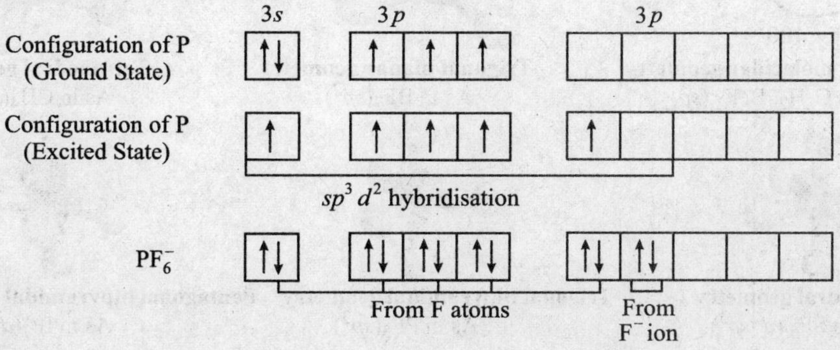

The six sp^3d^2 orbitals are directed towards the six corners of an octahedron. Five of the sp^3d^2-hybridised orbitals are half-filled while the sixth hybrid orbital is vacant. The half-filled hybrid orbitals overlap with the five $2p$ orbital of fluorine atoms to form five P—F bonds. The vacant sp^3d^2 hybrid orbital accepts a pair of electrons from the fluoride ion, F^- and forms a dative $^-F \longrightarrow P$ bond. The geometry of PF_6^- ion is octahedral as shown in Fig. 2.33.

Fig. 2.33: Shape on PF_6^- ion

Example 9: Discuss the shape of $SnCl_6^{2-}$ ion

Solution: Sn is the central atom in $SnCl_6^{2-}$. The outer electronic configuration of tin (Z = 50) is $5s^2 5p_x^1 5p_y^1$. In order to form six bonds arounds tin atom, there must be six hybrid orbitals. This can be achieved by promoting the 5*s* electrons into higher energy vacant 5*p* orbitals followed by combining the one 5*s*, three 5*p* and two 5*d* orbitals to give rise to six $sp^3 d^2$ hybrid orbitals as shown below:

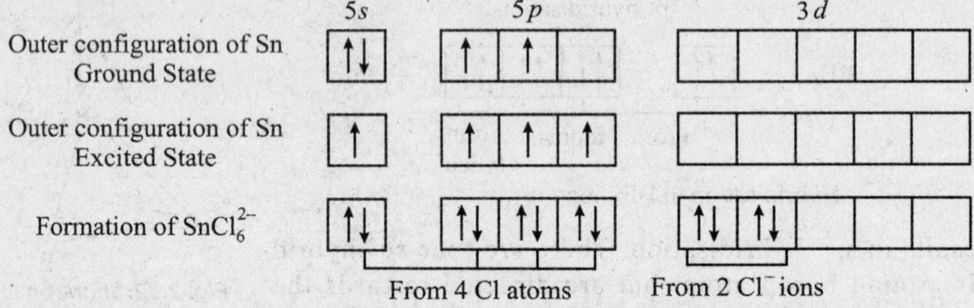

The hybrid orbitals are directed towards the six corners of a regular octahedron.

Four the sp^3d^2 hybrid orbitals are half-filled while the remaining two hybrid orbitals are vacant. The half-filled hybrid orbitals overlap with the 2*p* orbital of chlorine atom to form four Sn—Cl bonds. The vacant sp^3d^2 – orbitals accept two pairs of electrons from two chloride ions and form a pair of dative $^-Cl \longrightarrow Sn$ bonds. Thus, $SnCl_6^{2-}$ ion has a regular octahedral geometry as shown in Fig. 2.34.

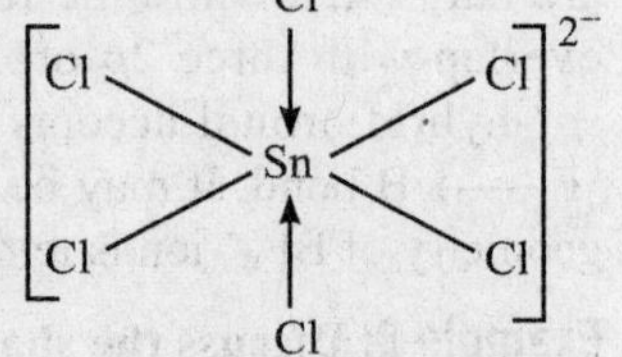

Fig. 2.34: Shape of $SnCl_6^{2-}$

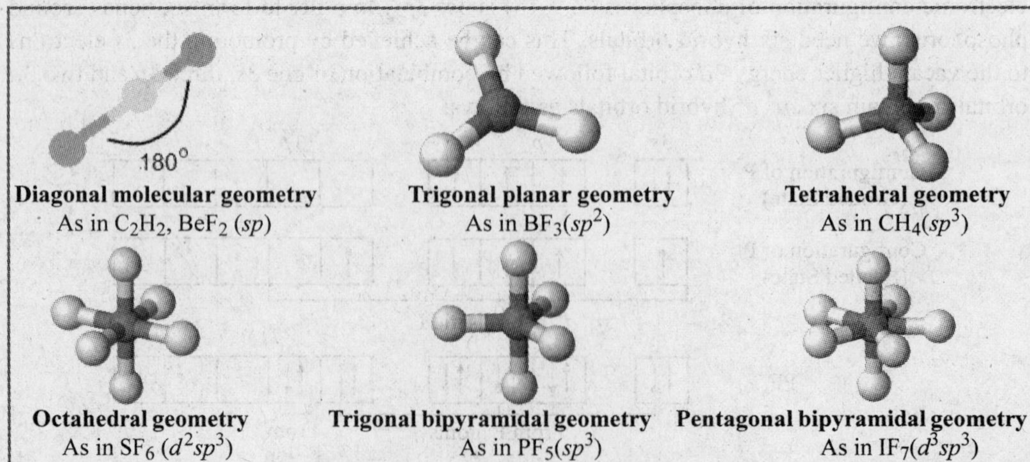

2.3 BENT'S RULE

Bent's rule was formulated by American chemist Henry Bent to explain deviations in structures provided by orbital hybridisation theory. Ammonia and water molecules involve sp^3 hybridisation and are expected to be tetrahedral in strucutre. The angle HNH is supposed to be 109°28′ but actually it is found to be 107°. Similary the angle HOH in water is supposed to be 109°28′ but actually it is 104.5°. Bent tried to explain deviations in angle through his theory.

Bent's rule states: **Atomic *s*-character tends to concentrate in orbitals that are directed towards electropositive groups and *p*-character tends to concentrate in orbitals that are directed towards electronegative groups.**

Bent's rule has been proposed as an alternative to VSEPR theroy as an explanation for observed molecular geometrics of simple molecules. It has the advantage that is supports modern theories of bonding. There is also a strong experimental support. Bent's rule is also applicable to *d*-block elements and coordination compounds. The hybrid orbitals of the central metal are arranged in such a way that orbitals with more *s*-character are directed towards ligands that form bonds with more covalent character. Similarly orbitals with more *d*-character are directed towards groups (ligands) that form bonds of greater ioinic character.

Methane forms four C—H bonds to give a tetrahedral angle of 109°28′. As all the atoms linked to carbon are the same, we find that ∠HCH is 109°28′. But the position changes when one of the atoms is different from hydrogn or three atoms are linked to carbon, the fourth position being occuped by a lone pair of electrons (for example NH_3). May be, two positions are occupied by lone pairs of electrons (example, water). These situations will give rise to polar covalent bonds.

2.3.1 Polar Covalent Bonds

Consider the molecule fluoromethane (CH_3F). Bonds between elements of different electronegativities will be polar and electron density in such bonds will be shifted towards the more electroneative element. By applying this to fluoromethane, we can demonstrate Bent's rule. Carbon is more electronegative than hydrogne, electron density in C—H bonds is closer to carbon. By increasing the amount of *s*-character in these hybrid orbitals, energy of these electrons can be reduced because *s*-orbitals are lower in eneergy than *p*-orbitals. Smaller energy systems are always more stable.

F
C — H
H H

Fluoromethane

Using the same long, we can say that electron density in the C—F bond will be close to fluorine because fluorine is more electronegative than carbon. Therefore hybrid orbitals of more *p*-character are shifted towards fluorine. We can therefore say that: **s-character on carbon atom is shifted towards electropositive hydrogen substituents and away from the electronegative fluorine.** This is another statement of Bent's rule.

2.3.2 Non-bonding Orbitals

An occupied non-bonding orbital (lone pair) can be looked as extreme case of electropositive substituent, with electron density completely polarised towards the carbon atom. As per Bent's rule, for stabilisation, the lone pair orbitals should take on high *s*-character. On the other hand, an unoccuped non-bonding orbital can be considered as an extreme case of electronegative substituent and the electron density is polarised towards the ligands. Therefore, unoccuped non-bonding orbitals should maximse *p*-character. With the help of these conclusions, we can explain the reduced bond angles in the molecules of NH_3 and H_2O.

Consider the bond angles in the following hydrocarbons:

Methane (sp^3)	Ethane (sp^2)	Ethyne (sp)
109.5°	120°	180°
p-character = 75%	*p*-character = 67%	*p*-character = 50%

The bond angles between the substituents (hydrogen in this case) are 109.5°, 120° and 180° corresponding to the hybridisation sp^3, sp^2 and sp respectively. It demostrates that hybrid orbitals with higher *p*-character will have a smaller angle between them.

Consider the following molecules and angles between the substituents with oxygen as the central atom.

Molecules ***Angle between the substituents***

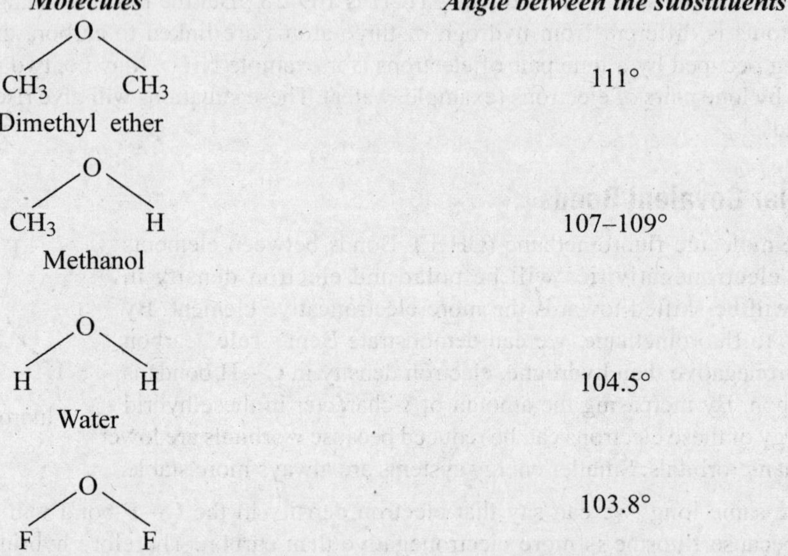

It may be noted that as we move down the table, the substituents become more electronegative and the bond angle between them decreases. This is in accordance with the Bent's rule which states that as the substituent's electronegativity increases, oribitals of greater *p*-character will be directed towards these groups.

Example 10: Molecules CH_4, NH_3 and H_2O involve the same kind of sp^3 hybridisation, yet they possess different geometry.

Solution: One of the tetrahedral positions in NH_3 is occupied by lone pair of electrons. Similarly in the case of water two positions are occupied by lone pair of electrons.

The repulsion between lone pair-bond pair is greater than that between bond pair and bond pair. As a result ∠ HNH is decreased to 107°. There are still greater repulsion in the case of water. Here the ∠ HOH is further decreased to 105°.

Example 11: Explain: *lp-lp* repulsion > *lp-bp* repulsion > *bp-bp* repulsion.

Solution: A bond pair is under the influence of two nuclei of bonding atoms whereas the lone pair is under the influence of only one nucleus. Hence lone pair is more active and mobile in causing repulsion with other orbitals. As a result, *lp-lp* repulsion is greater than *lp-bp* repulsion which in turn is greater than *bp-bp* repulsion.

Example 12: Giving reason arrange the following molecules in order of increasing bond angle.

$$H_2O, NH_3, PH_3$$

Solution: The order of increasing bond angle in

$$H_2O < PH_3 < NH_3$$

In case of water, there are two lone pair of electrons, therefore repulsion between lone pair and bond pair will be maximum and angle will be minimum.

Out of NH_3 and PH_3 repulsion between bond pair and bond pair will be smaller in case of PH_3 because of smaller electronegativity of phosphorus and larger P-H bond length and hence $\angle$HPH will be smaller than $\angle$HNH.

2.4 MOLECULAR ORBITAL THEORY

Main points of molecular orbital theory of covalent bonding.

The main points of molecular orbital theory put forward by F. Hund and R.S. Mulliken in 1930 are:

(*i*) Electrons belonging to two bonding atoms are controlled by the entire molecule. The electrons will occupy molecular orbitals that are analogous to atomic orbitals. These molecular orbitals belong to the entire molecule.

(*ii*) In an atom there are *s, p, d* .... atomic orbitals determined by various values of quantum numbers. In a molecule we have a set of molecular orbitals σ, π, δ ..... determined by various quantum numbers.

(*iii*) Just as an atomic orbital can contain a maximum of two electrons, molecular orbitals can also accommodate only a maximum of two electrons as per Pauli's exclusion principle.

R.S. Mulliken (1896 – 1986)

R.S. Mulliken was an American physicist and chemist, primarily responsible for the early development of molecular orbital theory.

(*iv*) The various electrons occupy different orbitals according to Hund's rule of maximum multiplicity as in the case of atomic orbitals.

2.4.1 Linear Combination of Atomic Orbitals (LCAO)

Molecular orbitals can be visualised as being made up of appropriate atomic orbitals provided by the atoms joined together in the molecule. A very simple, reasonable and satisfactory model is obtained if it is assumed that atomic orbitals of constituents combine in a linear additive fashion to form molecular orbitals. Consider two atoms *A* and *B* each possessing a single valence electron. Let ψ_A and ψ_B represent the wave functions of atoms *A* and *B.* Let atomic orbitals A and B accommodating valence electrons overlap. The valence electrons will be in region where the orbitals overlap and therefore, they can be associated with either nucleus. Consequently, the valence electrons have a much larger volume available for their movement as compared with that available in each isolated atom. The electrons can be thought of as moving in a molecular orbital whose total volume is approximately equal to the sum of the volume of atomic orbitals of A and B. In this fashion, the wave function of molecular orbitals can be expressed as a linear combination of atomic orbitals (LCAO). ψ_{AB} is the wave function of molecular orbital.

$$\psi_{AB} = C_A \psi_A + C_B \psi_B$$

and C_A and C_B are mixing coefficients. Value of C_A and C_B is so chosen as to get a molecular orbital of lowest energy.

In case we are considering the bonding in two similar atoms (homonuclear) then the magnitude of the coefficients C_A and C_B must be same.

In that case

$$C_A^2 = C_B^2 \text{ or } C_A = \pm C_B$$

There will be two molecular orbitals as a result of two types of combinations as given below.

$$\psi^b = \psi_A + \psi_B$$

$$\psi^* = \psi_A - \psi_B$$

Values of ψ_A and ψ_B have been taken as unity.

Thus one molecular orbital (ψ^b) can be obtained by addition of wave function of two atomic orbitals and then the other molecular orbital (ψ^*) can be obtained by the subtraction of wave function of the atomic orbitals. This is shown in Fig. 2.35.

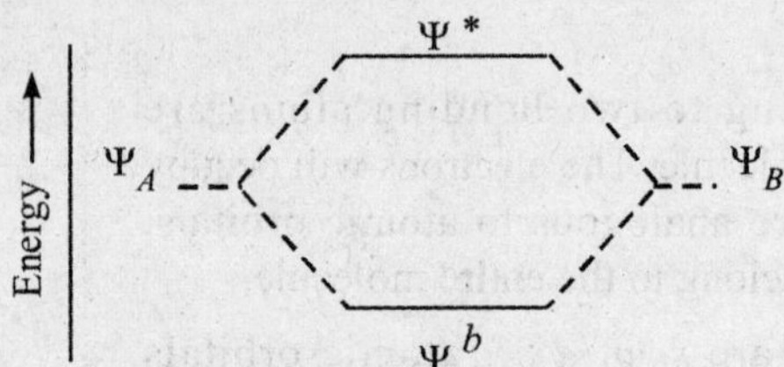

Fig. 2.35: Formation of MO.

The number of molecular orbitals is always equal to the number of atomic orbitals involved in bonding. Effective combination of atomic orbitals to give rise to stable molecular orbitals requires:

(*i*) Symmetry and relative energies of atomic orbitals ψ_A and ψ_B must be close to each other.

(*ii*) Extent of overlap between the charge clouds of ψ_A and ψ_B should be large.

(*iii*) Atomic orbitals of same sign should overlap.

2.4.2 Bonding and Antibonding Molecular Orbitals

Bonding orbitals. The molecular orbital that is obtained by the addition overlap of two atomic orbitals is termed bonding molecular and is represented as ψ^b

$$\psi^b = \psi_A + \psi_B$$

Some features of bonding molecular orbitals are:

(*i*) It possesses lower energy than the atomic orbitals from which it is formed.

(*ii*) It has high electron density in the region between the two nuclei and this accounts for stability of bond.

(*iii*) It is formed when lobes of the combining atomic orbitals have been same sign. The magnitude of ψ^b is numerically bigger than ψ_A or ψ_B.

(*iv*) Every electron in a bonding M.O. contributes to attraction between two atoms.

Antibonding M.O. The other molecular orbital which is obtained by the subtraction overlap of two atomic orbitals is termed the antibonding molecular orbital and is represented as ψ^*.

$$\psi^* = \psi_A - \psi_B$$

Some features of antibonding molecular orbitals are:

(*i*) It possesses higher energy than the atomic orbitals from which it is formed.

(*ii*) The probability of finding the electron in between the nuclei is negligible. The electron density is concentrated only on one nucleus at any particular moment.

(*iii*) It is formed when the lobes of combining atomic orbitals have opposite signs. ψ^* is numerically smaller than ψ_A or ψ_B.

(*iv*) Every electron in an antibonding molecular orbital contributes to repulsion between two atoms.

Combination of *s* orbitals to give bonding and antibonding molecular orbitals

Let us consider the combination of two 1*s* atomic orbitals belonging to say two hydrogen atoms. Using LCAO approach the two atomic orbitals will overlap to give two molecular orbitals. The first combination is obtained by the addition of two atomic orbitals. The pictorial representation is shown in Fig. 2.36.

$$\psi^b \text{ MO} = N\,(\psi_{1s_a} + \psi_{1s_b})$$ where N is a normalizing constant.

For simplicity its value may be taken as 1

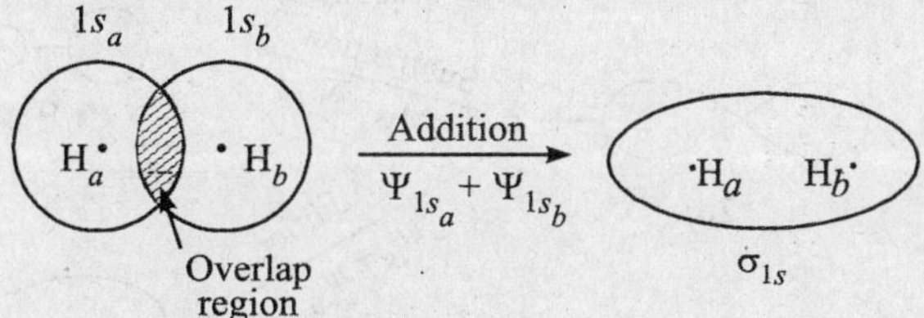

Fig. 2.36: Formation of a bonding MO obtained by the addition overlap of 1s atomic orbitals.

The electron in this MO will spend most of its time between the two nuclei H_a and H_b. The electron is now stabilized by two nuclear charges instead of one in an atomic orbital. The resulting MO is of lower energy than the 1*s* orbital. That is why it is called a bonding MO.

The other linear combination is obtained by subtracting the two atomic orbitals and is shown in Fig. 2.37.

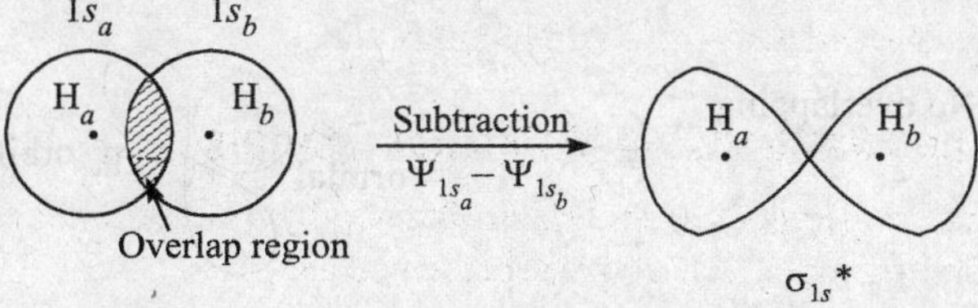

Fig. 2.37: Formation of an antibonding MO formed by the subtraction overlap of 1s atomic orbitals.

$$\Psi^*_{MO} + N^*\,(\Psi_{1sa} - \psi_{1sb})$$ where N^* is a normalizing constant.

The resulting molecular orbital has zero electron density (Nodal Plane) between the nuclei. The electron in this orbital is concentrated in regions away from each nuclei. The net effect is to push the nuclei apart rather than to hold them together. The resulting molecular orbital is of higher energy than the isolated 1*s* atomic orbital. The resulting MO is called an antibonding molecular orbital. The molecular orbitals discussed above have cylindrical symmetry and are called σ (sigma) molecular orbitals.

The combination of $2s$ atomic orbitals also gives rise to σ-molecular orbitals. The situation is exactly like the overlapping of $1s$ atomic orbitals. The only difference is that their sizes are different. Their overlap is illustrated in a diagram below (Fig. 2.38a).

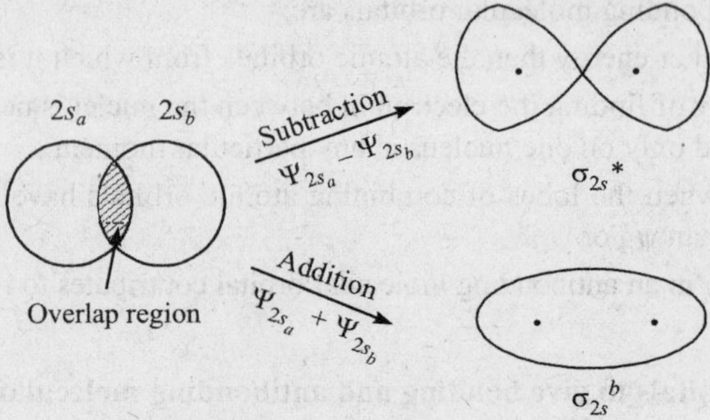

Fig. 2.38(a): Formation of bonding and antibonding MO's obtained by the overlap of 2s atomic orbitals.

Combination of s- and p-orbitals to give bonding and anti-bonding molecular orbitals. Let us consider the combination of 1s and $2p_Z$ orbitals as in the case of formation of HF molecule from H and F atoms. The p-orbital is oriented along the internuclear axis (generally taken as Z-axis). They will overlap to give σ-molecular orbitals, one bonding and the other antibonding as represented below:

Z — 1s — 2p$_Z$ — Z

Subtraction $\psi_{1S} - \psi_{2pz}$ → $\sigma^* sp_z$

Addition $\psi_{1S} + \psi_{2pz}$ → σsp_z

Fig. 2.38(b): Formation of bonding and anti-bonding MO's obtained by the overlap of s- and p-orbitals. Ψ_{1s} and Ψ_{2pz} represent functions of 1s and $2p_Z$ orbitals respectively.

It may be noted that there will be no overlapping of the s-orbital with $2p_X$ (or $2p_Y$) orbital.

X — s orbital — $2p_x$ orbital — No overlapping

Y — s orbital — p_y orbital — No overlapping

This is called non-bonding combination of orbitals.

2.4.3 Formation of σ molecular Orbitals Resulting from the Overlapping of *p*-orbitals Along the Internuclear Axis

σ-type molecular orbitals are also formed when p_z atomic orbitals of two atoms combine with each other. We are now assuming that the internuclear axis is the z-axis. This is illustrated in a diagram shown in Fig. 2.39.

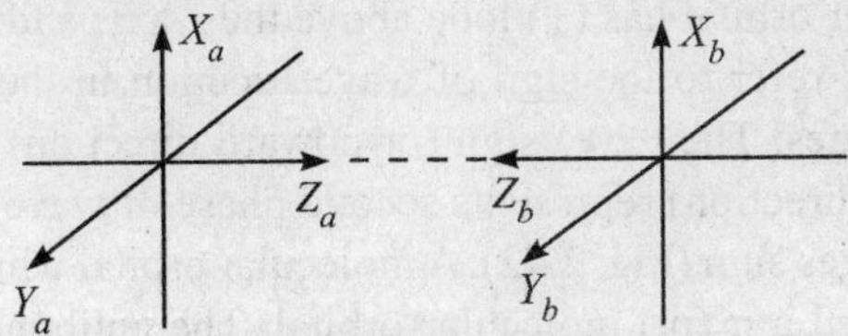

Fig. 2.39: Co-ordinate system for the overlap of 2p atomic orbitals.

The molecular orbital formed by the addition, overlap of $2p_z$ atomic orbital is designated as σ^b_{2pz} or simply as σ^b_z while the molecular orbital formed by the subtraction of $2p_z$ atomic orbitals is designated as $\sigma^*_{2p_z}$ or simply σ^*_z. These orbitals also have cylindrical symmetry around the molecular axis and hence they are also classified as σ-molecular orbitals (Fig. 2.40.)

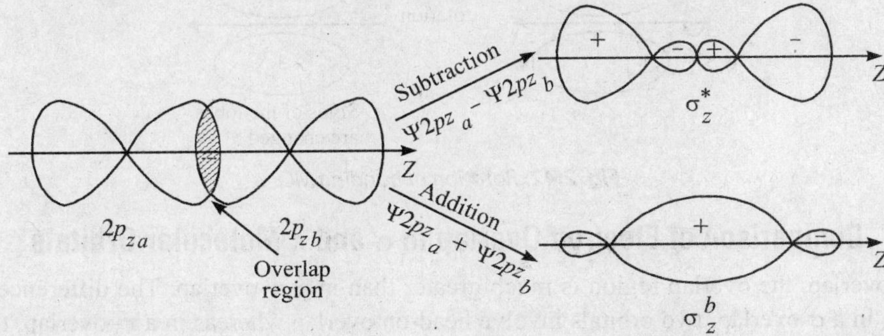

Fig. 2.40: Diagram showing the formation of bonding and antibonding MO's by the overlap of $2p_z$ atomic orbitals.

2.4.4 Formation of π orbitals by the Lateral Overlap of *p*-atomic Orbitals

Molecular orbitals which are obtained by the lateral (or sidewise) overlap of p_x or p_y orbitals are designated as π (pi) molecular orbitals. This is illustrated by showing overlap of $2p_x$ atomic orbitals.

Overlaps containing the same algebraic signs yield bonding MO and those of opposite sign give antibonding M.O. (Fig. 2.41)

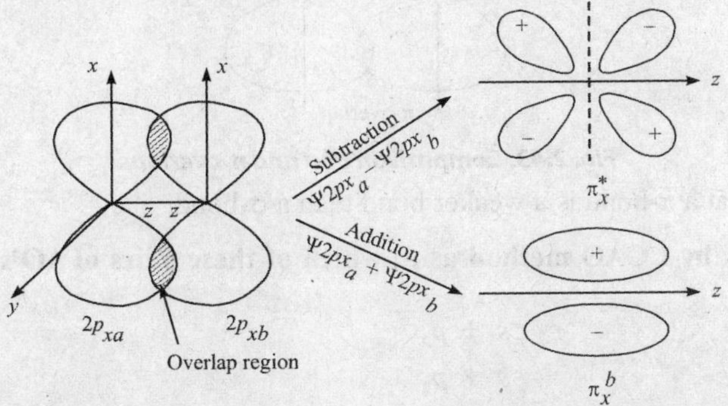

Fig. 2.41: Diagram showing the formation of bonding and antibonding MO's by the overlap of $2p_x$ atomic orbitals.

The bonding molecular orbital has (+) lobe above the z-axis and (–) lobe below the z-axis. The plus and minus signs refer to the sign of wave function in the various lobes and not to nuclear or electronic charges. The (+ve) sign (or upward direction) represents one phase and (–ve) sign (or downward direction) represents second phase of wave function. If we rotate this MO through 180°, it changes sign (Fig. 2.42). A molecular orbital which is antisymmetric about the molecular axis is called a π (pi) molecular orbital. The antibonding MO is also a π type M.O. They are labelled as π_x^b and π_x^* orbitals.

The two $2p_y$ atomic orbitals will overlap in a similar fashion to give π_y^b and π_x^*. Both π_x and π_y molecular orbitals are equivalent and have the same energy. These orbitals are said to be degenerate, *i.e.*, orbitals with same energy.

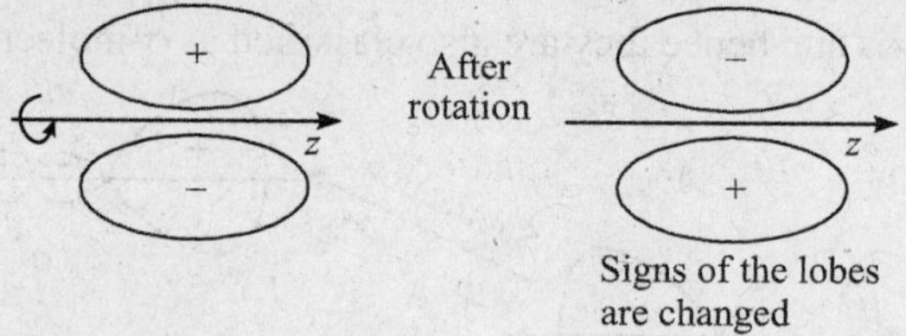

Fig. 2.42: Rotation of bonding MO.

2.4.5 Comparison of Electron Overlap in σ and π Molecular Orbitals

In a σ-overlap, the overlap region is much greater than in a π–overlap. The difference arises because in a σ-overlap, two orbitals involve head-on overlap whereas in a π–overlap, the two orbitals overlap laterally (or sideways) as shown in diagram (Fig. 2.43). It is assumed that z-axis is the molecular axis.

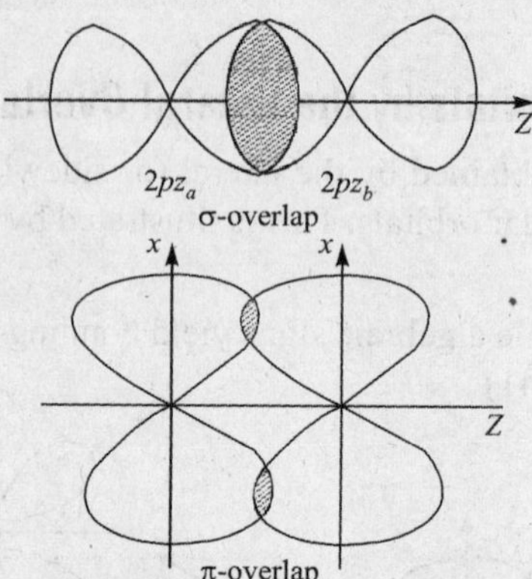

Fig. 2.43. Comparison of σ and π-overlaps.

The net result is that a π-bond is a weaker bond than a σ-bond.

Example 13: Show by LCAO method as to which of these pairs of AO's result in positive overlap

$s + p_x$

$s + p_z$

$p_x + p_z$

$p_z + p_z$

z-axis may be assumed as a molecular axis.

Solution: $s + p_z$ and $p_z + p_z$ will result in positive overlap.

2.4.6 Variation of Electronic Charge with Internuclear Distance

From the molecular orbital wave functions ψ_{MO} and ψ^*_{MO}, we can determine the distribution of electron charge in the molecule.

Writing the wave functions of molecular orbitals in terms of those of 1*s* atomic orbitals of two atoms *a* and *b*.

$$\psi_{MO} = \psi_{1s_a} + \psi_{1s_b}$$

$$\psi^*_{MO} = \psi_{1s_a} - \psi_{1s_b}$$

Taking squares of both sides of the above equations

$$\psi^2_{MO} = [\psi^2_{1s_a} + \psi^2_{1s_b} + 2\psi_{1s_a} \cdot \psi_{1s_b}]$$

$$\psi^{*2}_{MO} = [\psi^2_{1s_a} + \psi\psi^2_{1s_b} - 2\psi_{1s_a} \cdot \psi_{1s_b}]$$

It is observed that the bonding MO functions shows an increase in the electron charge density in the overlap region by an amount $2\psi_{1s_a}\ \psi_{1s_b}$ over that of the individual atoms as described by the functions $\psi^2_{1s_a}$ and $\psi^2_{1s_b}$.

This is represented graphically in Fig. 2.44. The dotted lines represent the charge densities of individual atoms and heavy lines represent the electron density for bonding MO.

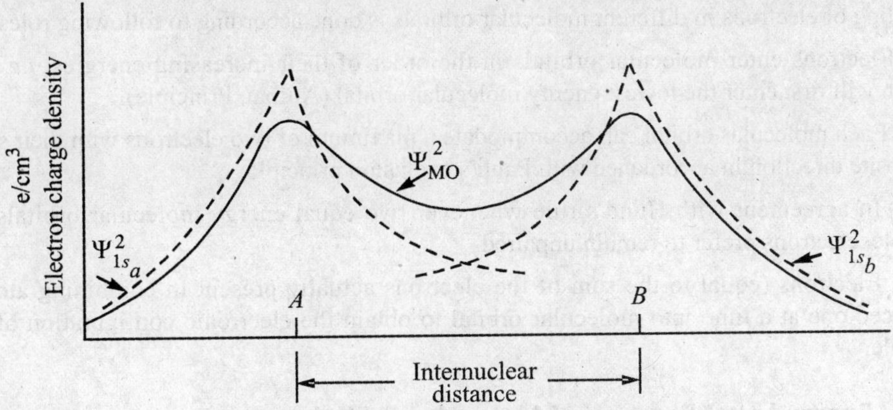

Fig. 2.44: Graph of electron density vs. distance results.

On the other hand the antibonding MO functions results in decrease in the charge density in the overlap region by an amount $\psi_{1s_a}\ \psi_{1s_b}$. This is represented in Fig. 2.45. It is also clear that bonding MO favours electron density as it is concentrated between the nuclei, whereas the antibonding MO tends to decrease the charge density between the nuclei and concentrate it in regions on the individual atoms.

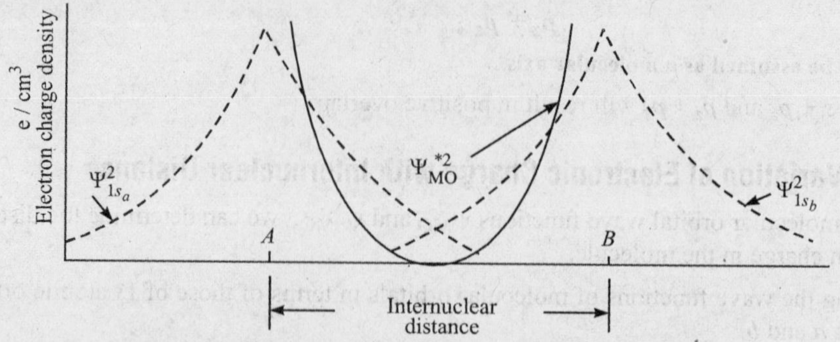

Fig. 2.45: Graph of electron density vs. internuclear density.

Electron density maps for bonding and antibonding (σ_{1s}^{b} and σ_{1s}^{*}) MO's are shown in Fig. 2.46.

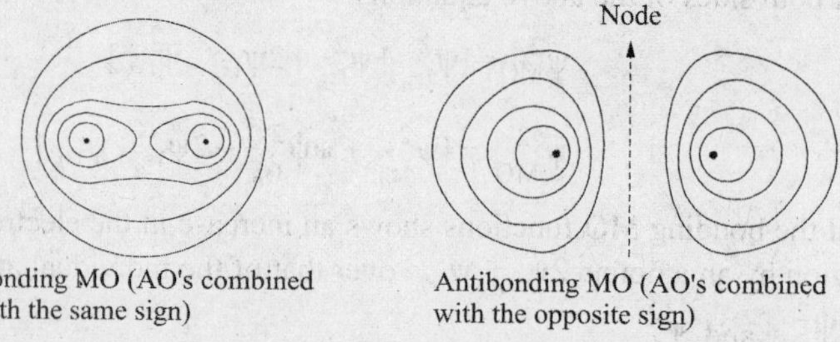

Fig. 2.46: Electron density map of σ_{1s}^{b} and σ_{1s}^{*} MO's.

2.4.7 Rules for Filling of Electrons in Molecular Orbitals

The filling of electrons in different molecular orbitals is done according to following rules:

(*i*) Electrons enter molecular orbitals in the order of their increasing energies, *i.e.*, the electron will first enter the lowest energy molecular orbital (Aufbau Principle).

(*ii*) Each molecular orbital can accommodate a maximum of two electrons with their spins in opposite direction in accordance with Pauli's exclusion principle.

(*iii*) In agreement with Hund's rule whenever two equal energy molecular orbitals are available, electrons prefer to remain unpaired.

(*iv*) Electrons (equal to the sum of the electrons actually present in combining atoms) are placed one at a time into molecular orbital to obtain the electronic configuration of the molecule.

2.4.8 Energy Level Diagram of Molecular Orbitals

Energy level diagram of MO's is shown in Fig. 2.47.

In this type of diagram the combining atomic orbitals are shown on two extremes and the resulting molecular orbitals are represented in the middle column. Atomic orbitals of same energy are shown at the same level. The difference between the energies of atomic orbitals and the bonding MO's depend upon the extent of overlap of atomic orbitals. A large overlap will result in greater lowering of bonding MO (and a corresponding large raise in the antibonding MO). Larger the overlap, greater is the overlapping and hence stronger will be resulting bond.

According to above diagram the sequence of energy levels in which they are filled up is:

$$\sigma_{1s}^{b} < \sigma_{1s}^{*} < \sigma_{2s}^{b} < \sigma_{2s}^{*} < \sigma_{z}^{b} < \pi_{x}^{b} = \pi_{y}^{b} < \pi_{x}^{*} = \pi_{y}^{*} < \sigma_{z}^{*}$$

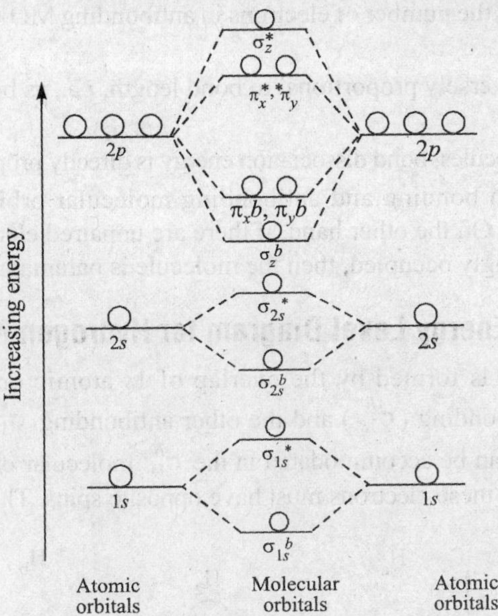

Fig. 2.47: *Energy level diagram.*

The above sequence of energies does not apply to lighter elements like B, C and N. Here $2s - 2p_z$ mixing takes place which changes the sequence of energy. The sequence in such a case is

$$\pi_{x}^{b} = \pi_{y}^{b} < \sigma_{z}^{b} < \pi_{x}^{*} = \pi_{y}^{*} < \sigma_{z}^{*}$$

Lower molecular orbitals have the same energy sequence.

2.4.9 Bond Order from Number of Electrons in Bonding and Antibonding Molecular Orbitals

The number of electrons belonging to two atoms are counted and then filled in the energy level diagram as constructed above. It is possible to predict the behaviour of molecules from their configuration. All the electrons occupying bonding molecular orbitals (N^b) and antibonding molecular orbitals (N^*) are counted separately. The following cases arise.

(a) $N^b > N^*$. If the number of electrons in bonding MO's are greater than the number of electrons in antibonding MO's, then the molecule would be stable.

(b) $N^b = N^*$. If the number of electrons in bonding MO's are equal to the number of electrons in antibonding MO's, then the molecule is unstable and it does not exist. This is because an electron in an antibonding MO cancels out the stability gained by electron in the bonding MO.

Bond order. It is defined as the number of covalent bonds present in a molecule. It is calculated as

$$\text{Bond order} = \frac{1}{2}\left\{\begin{matrix}\text{number of electrons in} \\ \text{bonding MO's}\end{matrix} - \begin{matrix}\text{Number of electrons in} \\ \text{antibonding MO's}\end{matrix}\right\}$$

Information conveyed by bond order

(*i*) The number gives nature of a bond whether it is a single, double or a triple bond.

(*ii*) When the bond order comes out to be zero (*i.e.*, when the number of electrons in bonding MO's is equal to the number of electrons in antibonding MO's), then the molecule does not exist.

(*iii*) Bond order is inversely proportional to bond length, *i.e.*, as bond order increases, bond length decreases.

(*iv*) For diatomic molecules, bond dissociation energy is directly proportional to the bond order.

(*v*) If all electrons in bonding and antibonding molecular orbitals are paired, then the molecule is diamagnetic. On the other hand, if there are unpaired electrons (or electrons), *i.e.*, molecular orbitals are singly occupied, then the molecule is paramagnetic.

2.4.10 Molecular Energy Level Diagram for Hydrogen Molecule (H_2)

The hydrogen molecule is formed by the overlap of 1*s* atomic orbitals. It shall have two molecular orbitals, one bonding (σ_{1s}^{b}) and the other antibonding σ_{1s}^{*}). The H_2 molecule has two electrons and these can be accommodated in the σ_{1s}^{b} molecular orbital. In accordance with Pauli exclusion principle, these electrons must have opposite spins. The energy level diagram of H_2 is shown in Fig. 2.48.

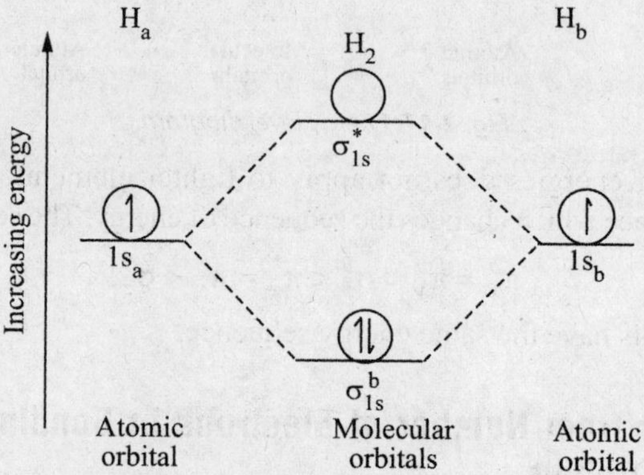

Fig. 2.48: Energy level diagram of H_2.

The ground state of H_2 is represented as [(σ_{1s}^{b})^2] and the bond order is 1/2 (2 – 0) = 1, *i.e.*, one σ-bond. Bond dissociation energy in H_2 is 431.4 kJ/mole and bond length is 77 pm.

Molecular energy level diagram for Be_2

The electronic configuration of beryllium (Z = 4) atom is $1s^2$ $2s^2$. Number of electrons per beryllium atom are four and therefore, there are a total of eight electrons in the beryllium molecule to be accomodated in the molecular orbitals. Four of the electrons that fill the σ 1s and σ* 1*s* molecular orbitals, do not infact contribute to bonding.

The other four electrons are now to be accommodated. Two of these electrons will go into σ2*s* bonding molecular orbital while the other two will go into σ*2*s* antibonding molecular orbital as shown in Fig. 2.49.

The molecular orbital electronic configuration can be written as

$$Be_2 : KK\,(\sigma 2s)^2\,(\overset{*}{\sigma}\,2s)^2$$

$$\text{Bond order} = \frac{1}{2}(2-2) = 0.$$

The bond order is zero. Therefore stable Be_2 molecule does not exist.

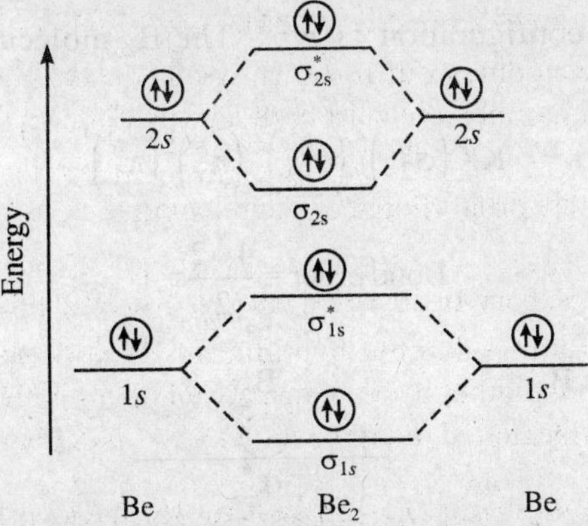

***Fig. 2.49:** Molecular orbital energy level diagram for Be_2*

2.4.11 Molecular Orbital Energy Level Diagram of C_2

Carbon has the electronic configuration $1s^2s^2p^2$. The C_2 molecule has the following M.O. configuration:

$$KK\left(\sigma_{2s}^{b}\right)^{2}\left(\sigma_{2s}^{*}\right)^{2}\left(\pi_{x}^{b}\right)^{2}\left(\pi_{y}^{b}\right)^{2}$$

$$\text{Bond order} = \frac{1}{2}(6-2) = 2$$

The molecule of C_2 is diamagnetic as there are no unpaired electrons. The M.O. diagram of C_2 is shown in Fig. 2.50.

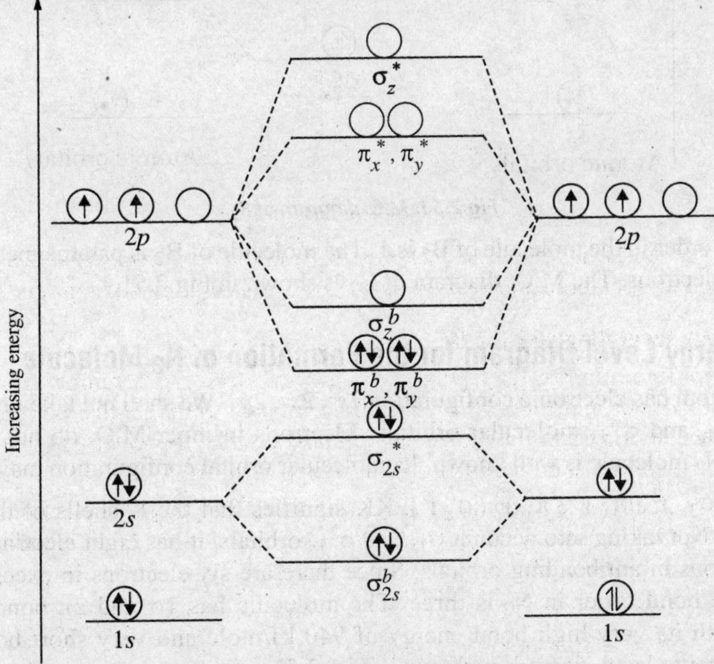

***Fig. 2.50:** M.O. energy level diagram of C_2.*

2.4.12 Molecular Orbital Energy Level Diagram of B_2

Boron has the electronic configuration $1s^2s^2p^1$. The B_2 molecule has the folowing M.O. configuration.

$$KK\left(\sigma_{2s}^{b}\right)^2\left(\sigma_{2s}^{*}\right)^2\left(\pi_x^{b}\right)^1\left(\pi_y^{b}\right)^1$$

$$\text{Bond order} = \frac{4-2}{2} = 1$$

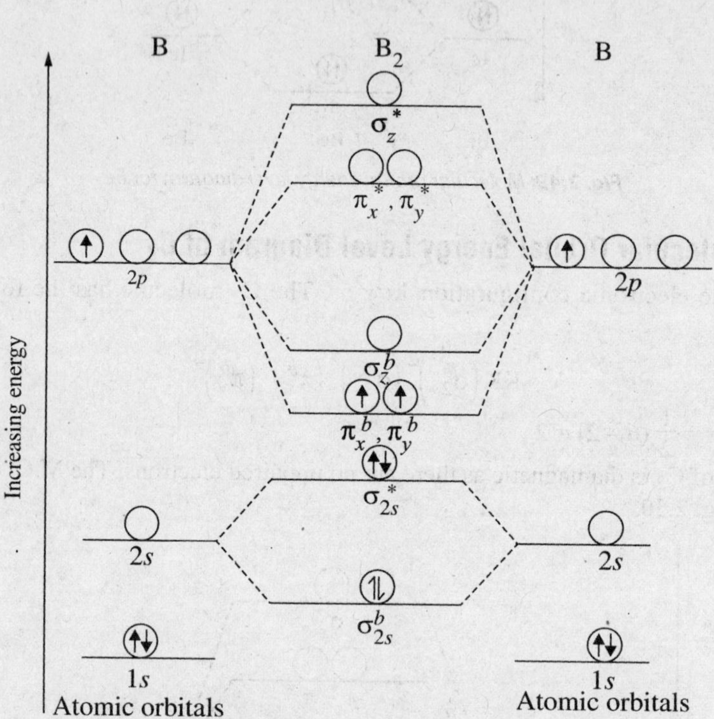

Fig 2.51: M.O. diagram of B_2.

Thus bond order in the molecule of B_2 is 1. The molecule of B_2 is paramagnetic as there are two unpaired electrons. The M.O. diagram of B_2 is shown in Fig 2.51.

2.4.13 Energy Level Diagram for the Formation of N_2 Molecule

The nitrogen atom has electronic configuration $1s^2$, $2s^2$, $2p^3$. We shall not take into account the electrons in σ_{1s} and σ^*_{1s} molecular orbitals. Electrons in inner M.O. do not contribute to bonding. The N_2 molecule is well known. Its molecular orbital configuration may be written as [KK $(\sigma_{2s}^{b})^2$ $(\sigma_{2s}^{*})^2$ $(\pi_x^{b})^2$ $(\pi_y^{b})^2$ $(\sigma_z^{b})^2$]. KK signifies that the K shells of the combining atoms are full. Not taking into account σ_{1s} and σ^*_{1s} orbitals, it has eight electrons in bonding and two electrons in antibonding orbitals. Since there are six electrons in excess in bonding orbitals so the bond order in N_2 is three. The molecule has 1σ and 2π bonds. This is in conformity with its very high bond energy of 940 kJ/mole and very short bond length of 110 pm. The energy level diagram is shown in Fig. 2.52.

N_2^+ ion

N_2^+ ion has one election less than N_2. Its molecular orbital configuration may be written as

$$[\text{KK } (\sigma_{2s}^b)^2(\sigma_{2s}^*)^2(\pi_x^b)^2(\pi_y^b)^2(\sigma_z^b)^1]$$

Thus, it has seven electrons in bonding orbitals and two electrons in antibonding orbitals.

Bond order in $N_2^+ = \frac{1}{2}(7-2) = 2.5$

Thus the ion N_2^+ is weaker than the molecule of N_2.

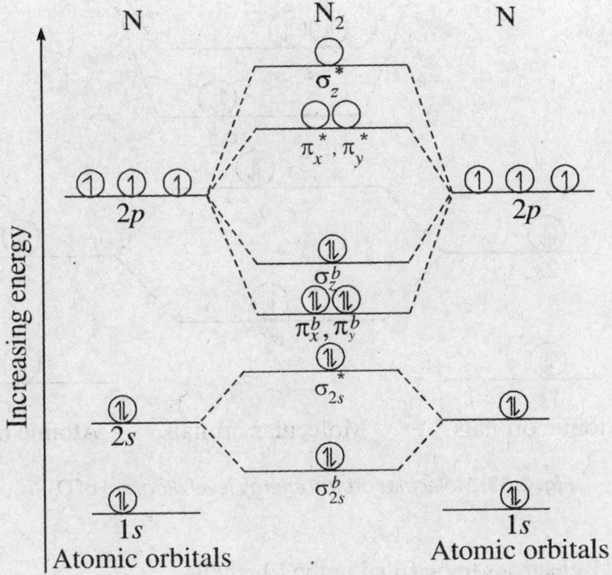

Fig. 2.52: Molecular orbital energy level diagram of hypothetical N_2 molecule.

2.4.14 Molecular Orbital Energy Level Diagram for Oxygen Molecule (O_2)

The oxygen has electronic configuration $1s^2$, $2s^2$, $2p^4$. The O_2 molecule is well known and shows paramagnetism (Fig. 2.53), equivalent to that of two unpaired electrons. The molecule has the following configuration:

$$[\text{KK } (\sigma_{2s}^b)^2(\sigma_{2s}^*)^2(\sigma_z^b)^2(\pi_x^b)^2(\pi_y^b)^2(\pi_y^*)^1(\pi_y^*)^1]$$

$$\text{Bond order} = \frac{1}{2}(8-4) = \frac{1}{2}\times 4 = 2$$

The bond order is two. In accordance with Hund's rule the two electrons in the π^* orbitals have parallel spins. The molecular orbital method explains the presence of two unpaired electrons in the molecule which accounts for its paramagnetism (Fig. 2.53). The valence bond theory had failed to predict the presence of unpaired electrons in O_2 molecule.

This is in accordance with the experimental results that O_2 consists of a double bond (one σ and one π bond).

Bond dissociation energy = 493.2 kJ/mol

Bond length = 121 pm.

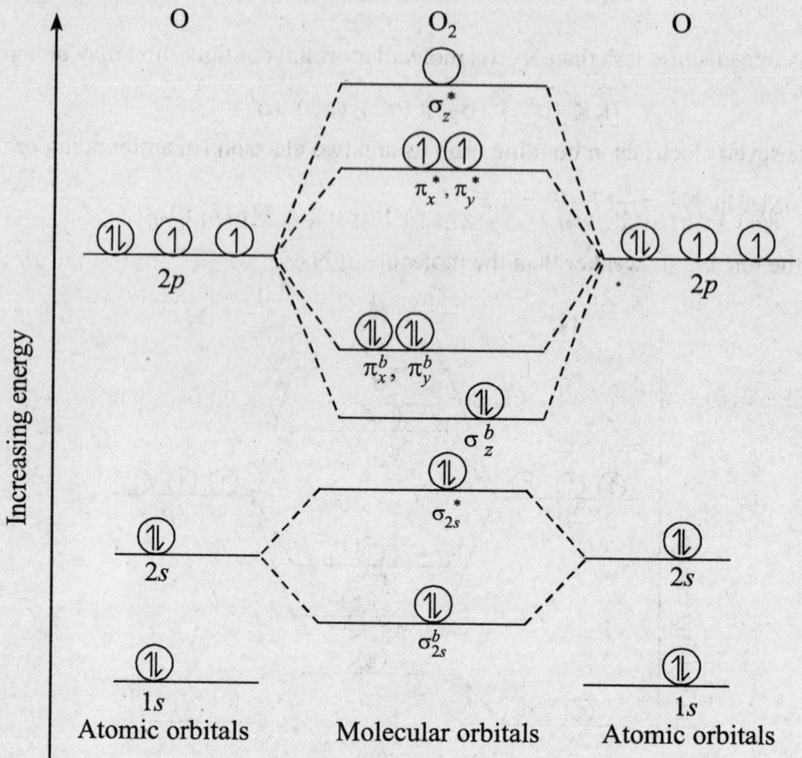

Fig. 2.53: Molecular orbital energy level diagram of O_2.

O_2^+ ion

There are 12 – 1 = 11 electrons to be filled in the LL shells.

The bond order is = 1/2 (8 – 3) = $2\frac{1}{2}$. Thus it has a stronger bond compared to oxygen. O_2^+ is paramagnetic.

The O_2^+ ion will have the configuration:

$$[KK(\sigma_{2s}^b)^2\ (\sigma_{2s}^*)^2\ (\sigma_z^b)^2\ (\pi_x^b)^2\ (\pi_y^b)^2\ (\pi_y^*)^1]$$

O_2^- ion

There are a total of (2 × 8) + 1 = 17 electrons to be filled. Out of this, four electrons are filled in KK molecular orbital. Thus 17 – 4 = 13 electrons are to be filled in LL molecular orbital. O_2^- ion will have molecular orbital configuration as :

$$KK(\sigma_{2s}^b)^2\ (\sigma_{2s}^*)^2\ (\sigma_z^b)^2\ (\pi_x^b)^2\ (\pi_y^b)^2 (\pi_x^*)^2 (\pi_y^*)^1$$

$$\text{Bond order} = \frac{1}{2}(8-5) = \frac{1}{2}\times 3 = 1.5$$

O_2^- ion is weaker than O_2 molecule and it is paramagnetic

O_2^{2-} ion

Now there are a total of 14 electrons to be filled in LL molecular orbitals. O_2^{2-} ion will have the molecular orbital configuration as:

$$KK(\sigma_{2s}^{b})^2\ (\sigma_{2s}^{*})^2\ (\sigma_{z}^{b})^2\ (\pi_{x}^{b})^2\ (\pi_{y}^{b})^2 (\pi_{x}^{*})^2 (\pi_{y}^{*})^2$$

$$\text{Bond order} = \frac{1}{2}(8-6) = \frac{1}{2}\times 2 = 1$$

Bond order in O_2^{2-} is 1, it is therefore less stable than O_2^- and O_2.

2.4.15 MO Energy Level Diagram of Fluorine Molecule

On adding two more electrons to the O_2 configuration we get configuration for fluorine molecule. This is shown in Fig. 2.54. The molecular orbital configuration of F_2 is:

$$[KK(\sigma_{2s}^{b})^2 (\sigma_{2s}^{*})^2 (\sigma_{z}^{b})^2 (\pi_{x}^{b})^2 (\pi_{y}^{b})^2 (\pi_{x}^{*})^2 (\pi_{y}^{*})^2]$$

and its bond order is 1/2 [10 – 8] = 1. It is diamagnetic since it has no unpaired electrons.

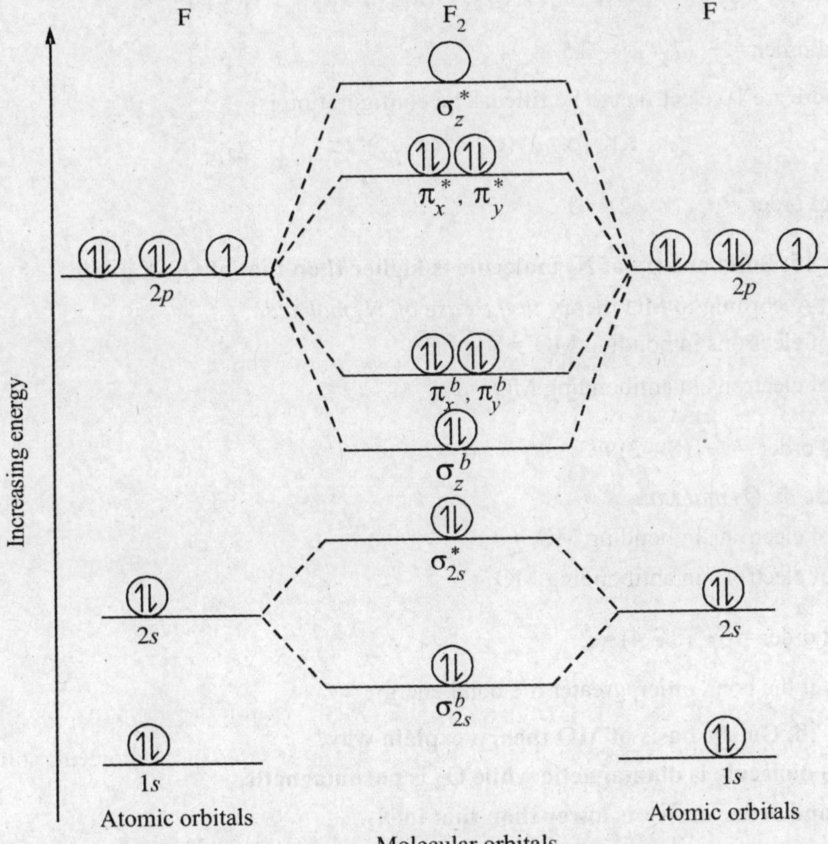

Fig. 2.54: Molecular orbital energy level diagram of F_2.

Miscellaneous Examples

Example 14: How does the MO theory account for the following?

(i) Bond order in O_2^+ is more than in O_2 while.

(ii) Bond order in N_2^+ is less than in N_2 molecule.

Solution: (*i*) In O_2^+, there are 11 valence electrons to be filled. The outer shell molecular orbital configuration is

$$(\sigma_{2s})^2\ (\sigma_{2s}^*)^2\ (\sigma_{2pz})^2\ (\pi_{2px})^2\ (\pi_{2py})^2\ (\pi_{2px}^*)^1$$

$$\text{Bond order} = \frac{1}{2}(8-3) = 2.5$$

In O_2, there are 12 valence electrons to be filled. The outer shells MO configuration is

$$(\sigma_{2s})^2(\sigma_{2s}^*)^2(\sigma_{2pz})^2(\pi_{2px})^2(\pi_{2py})^2(\pi_{2px}^*)^1(\pi_{2py}^*)^1$$

$$\text{Bond order} = \frac{1}{2}(8-4) = 2$$

(*ii*) In N_2^+, there are 9 valence electrons to be filled. The configuration is

$$KK\ (\sigma_{2s})^2(\sigma_{2s}^*)^2(\pi_{2px})^2(\pi_{2py})^2(\pi_{2pz})^1$$

$$\text{Bond order} = \frac{1}{2}(7-2) = 2.5$$

In N_2, there are 10 electrons to be filled. The configuration is

$$KK\ (\sigma_{2s})^2(\sigma_{2s}^*)^2(\pi_{2px})^2(\pi_{2py})^2(\sigma_{2pz})^2$$

$$\text{Bond order} = \frac{1}{2}(8-2) = 3$$

Example 15: Bond energy of N_2 molecule is higher than that of O_2. Explain.

Solution: According to MO theory *in the case of N_2 molecule*

No. of electrons in bonding MO = 8

No. of electrons in antibonding MO = 2

$$\text{Bond order} = \frac{1}{2}(8-2) = 3$$

In case of O_2 molecule

No. of electrons in bonding MO = 8

No. of electrons in antibonding MO = 4

$$\text{Bond order} = \frac{1}{2}(8-4) = 2$$

Greater the bond order, greater the bond energy.

Example 16: On the basis of MO theory, explain why?

(*i*) **N_2 molecule is diamagnetic while O_2 is paramagnetic.**

(*ii*) **Bond order in N_2^+ is lower than that in N_2.**

Solution: (*i*) The MO configuration of N_2 and O_2 can be written as

$$N_2:\ KK\ (\sigma_{2s})^2(\sigma_{2s}^*)^2(\pi_{2px})^2(\pi_{2py})^2(\sigma_{2pz})^2$$

$$O_2:\ KK\ (\sigma_{2s})^2(\sigma_{2s}^*)^2(\sigma_{2pz})^2(\pi_{2px})^2(\sigma_{2py})^2(\pi_{2px}^*)^1(\pi_{2py}^*)^1$$

N_2 does not contain unpaired electron, it is diamagnetic. Oxygen is paramagnetic as it contains two unpaired electrons.

(*ii*) Bond order in $N_2^+ = \frac{1}{2}$ (7 – 2) = 2.5

Bond order in $N_2 = \frac{1}{2}$ (8 – 2) = 3

2.4.16 Molecular Orbital Energy Level Diagram of Ne_2.

The electronic configuration of neon atom (Z = 10) is $1s^2\ 2s^2\ 2p^6$. The number of valence electrons per neon atom is 8. Thus, a total of 16 electrons in the neon molecule have to be placed in the LL molecular orbitals as shown in Fig. 2.55.

The molecular orbital electronic configuration of neon molecule can be written as

$$Ne_2 : KK\ (\sigma\ 2s)^2\ (\overset{*}{\sigma}\ 2s)^2\ (\sigma\ 2p_z)^2\ (\pi\ 2p_x)^2\ (\pi\ 2p_y)^2\ (\pi^*\ 2p_x)^2\ (\pi^*\ 2p_y)^2\ (\overset{*}{\sigma}\ 2p_z)^2$$

Bond order $\frac{1}{2}$ (8 – 8) = 0

Bond order value of zero in case of Ne_2 molecule suggests that the molecule does not exist.

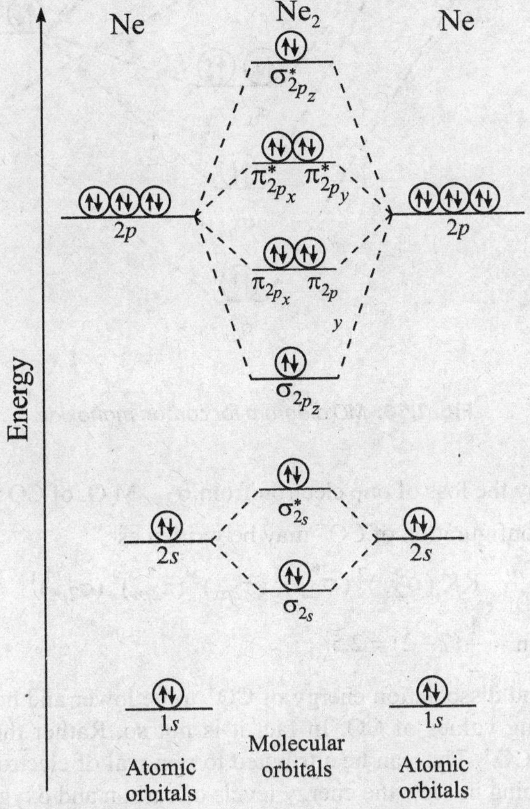

Fig. 2.55: Molecular orbital energy level diagram of Ne_2.

2.4.16 MO Energy Level Diagram for CO Molecule

In CO, the oxygen atomic orbitals are lower in energy than the carbon atomic orbitals. This is because oxygen is more electronegative than carbon. The 2*s* and 2*p* orbitals of oxygen have lower energy than the corresponding orbitals of carbon. Energy levels of different M.O. are shown in the figure. Due to this difference, the σ^*_{2s} orbital is higher in energy than the σ_{2px} orbital(Fig. 2.56). Carbon monoxide possesses 10 valence electrons and, therefore, has a valence configuration :

$$(\sigma^b_{2s})^2(\sigma^b_{2pz})^2(\pi^b_x \cdot \pi^b_y)^4(\sigma^*_{2s})^2$$

There are three net bonding pairs (one σ and one π) describing the C ≡ O molecule.

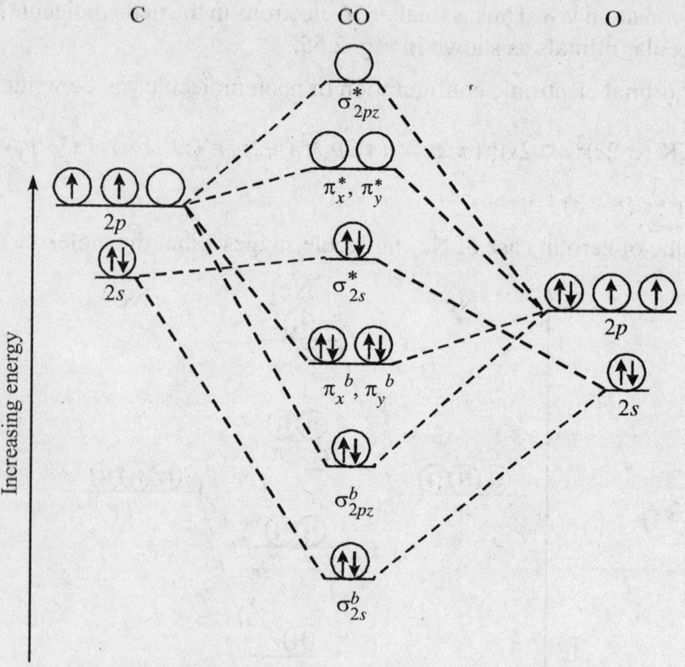

Fig. 2.56: *MO diagram for carbon monoxide.*

CO^+ ion

CO^+ ion is obtained by the loss of one electron from σ_{2pz} M.O. of CO molecule.

M.O. electronic configuration of CO^+ may be written as

$$\text{KK}\,(\sigma^b_{2s})^2\,(\sigma^*_{2s})^2\,(\pi_{2px})^2\,(\pi_{2py})^2\,(\sigma_{2pz})^1$$

Bond order of CO^+ ion $= \frac{1}{2}(7-2) = 2.5$

We expect the bond dissociation energy of CO^+ to be lower and bond length to be greater than the corresponding values of CO. In fact it is not so. Rather the bond order increases when CO changes to CO^+. This can be attributed to removal of electron from the antibonding molecular orbital keeping in view the energy levels of carbon and oxygen atoms.

2.4.17 MO Electrons Configuration for Nitrogen Oxide (NO) Molecule

The electronic configurations of N and O are

N : $1s^2\, 2s^2\, 2p^3$

O : $1s^2\, 2s^2\, 2p^4$

There are five electrons in the valence shell of N and six electrons in the valence shell of O. Thus a total of 11 electrons are to be accommodated in the M.O. of NO molecule. It may be noted that the bonding M.O. are close to oxygen atom whereas antibonding orbitals are close to nitrogen atom.

MO energy level diagram of NO is shown in Fig 2.57.

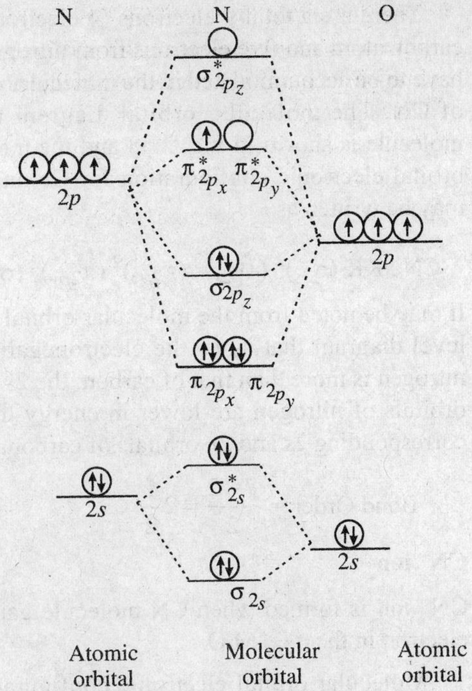

NO (11 valence electrons) has an electron configuration :

$$(\sigma^b_{2s})^2(\sigma^b_{2pz})^2(\pi^b_x.\pi^b_y)^4(\sigma^*_{2s})^2(\pi^*_x)^1$$

$$\text{Bond order in NO} = \frac{1}{2}(8-3) = 2.5$$

It is paramagnetic with a single unpaired electron. This is manifested by its easy oxidation to NO^+ (by loss of π^* electron).

Fig. 2.57: Molecular orbital energy level diagram of NO

Nitrosyl ion, NO^+

Nitrosyl ion, NO^+ can be obtained if we remove one electron from the nitric oxide molecule.

$$NO \longrightarrow NO^+ + e^-$$

The molecular electronic configuration of NO^+ can be obtained by removing one electron from nitric oxide

$$NO^+ : KK\,(\sigma^b_{2s})^2\,(\overset{*}{\sigma}_{2s})^2\,(\pi^b_{2px})^2\,(\pi^b_{2py})^2\,(\pi^b_{2pz})^2$$

$$\text{Bond order} = \frac{8-2}{2} = 3.$$

Bond order in NO^+ is 3 which represents one σ and two π-bonds.

Since the bond order of NO^+ is greater than that present in NO molecule, its bond dissociation energy is greater and bond length smaller than that of NO.

NO^- ion

NO^- conte easily generated by adding one electron to neutral nitric oxide molecule.

$$NO + e^- \longrightarrow NO^-$$

The molecular orbital electronic configuration of NO^- may written as

$$NO^- : KK\,(\sigma^b_{2s})^2\,(\overset{*}{\sigma}_{2s})^2\,(\pi^b_{2px})^2\,(\pi^b_{2py})^2\,(\sigma^b_{2pz})^2\,(\pi^*_{2px})^1\,(\pi^*_{2py})^1$$

$$\text{Bond order} = \frac{8-4}{2} = 2.$$

Since the bond order of NO^- is less than that of NO^+, its bond dissociation energy is less and bond length greater than that of NO.

CN molecule

The electronic configurations of carbon and nitrogen atoms are:

C $1s^2\ 2s^2\ 2p^2$

N $1s^2\ 2s^2\ 2p^3$

There are a total 9 electrons (4 electrons from carbon atom and five electrons from nitrogen) that have to be accommodated in the molecular orbitals of CN. The molecular orbital diagram for CN molecule is shown in Fig. 2.58 and the molecular orbital electronic configuration for CN molecule may be written as

$$CN : KK\ (\sigma_{2s})^2\ (\overset{*}{\sigma}_{2s})^2\ (\pi_{2px})^2\ (\pi_{2py})^2\ (\sigma_{2pz})^1$$

It may be noted from the molecular orbital energy level diagram that since the electronegativity of nitrogen is more than that of carbon, the 2*s* and 2*p* orbitals of nitrogen are lower in energy than the corresponding 2*s* and 2*p* orbitals of carbon.

$$\text{Bond Order} = \frac{7-2}{2} = 2\frac{1}{2}.$$

CN⁻ ion

CN^- ion is formed when CN molecule gains one electron in the σ_{2pz} M.O.

Molecular orbital electronic configuration of CN^- ion is given by

$$KK\ (\sigma^b_{2s})^2\ (\overset{*}{\sigma}_{2s})^2\ (\pi_{2px})^2\ (\pi_{2py})^2\ (\sigma_{2pz})^2$$

$$\text{Bond order} = \frac{1}{2}(8-2) = 3.$$

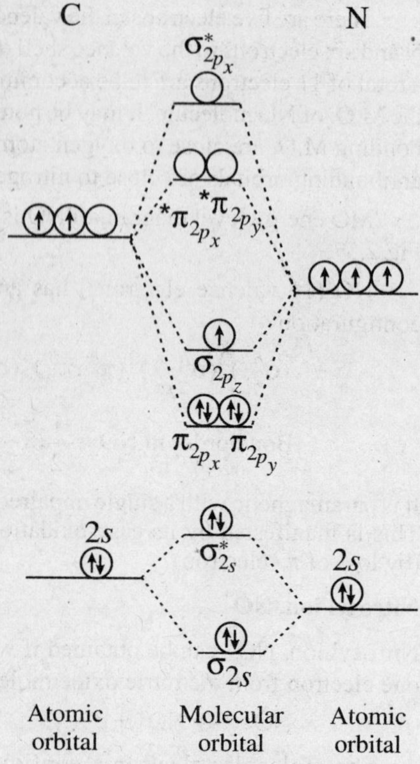

Fig. 2.58: Molecular orbital energy level diagram for CN.

It since the bond order is CN^- ion is greater than in CN molecule, it is expected that CN^- will have greater bond dissociation energy and will have a smaller bond length.

Example 17: On the basis of MO theory, explain the magnetic character of N_2, O_2, NO and CO molecules. Also give the bond order in each case.

Solution: (*i*) Molecular orbital configuration of N_2 is

$$KK\ (\sigma_{2s})^2(\sigma^*_{2s})^2(\pi_{2px})^2(\pi^*_{2py})^2(\sigma_{2pz})^2$$

As there is no unpaired electron, the molecule is diamagnetic

$$\text{Bond order} = \frac{1}{2}(n_b - n_a)$$

$$= \frac{1}{2}(8-2) = 3$$

(*ii*) Molecular orbital configuration of O_2 is

$$KK\ (\sigma_{2s})^2(\sigma^*_{2s})^2(\sigma_{2pz})^2(\pi_{2py})^2(\pi_{2py})^2(\pi^*_{2px})^1(\pi^*_{2py})^1$$

As there are two unpaired electrons, the molecule is paramagnetic.

$$\text{Bond order} = \frac{1}{2}(8-4) = 2$$

(*iii*) Molecular orbital configuration of NO is

$$KK\ (\sigma_{2s})^2(\sigma_{2pz})^2(\pi_{2px})^2(\pi_{2py})^2(\sigma^*_{2s})^2(\pi^*_{2px})^1$$

The molecule is paramagnetic due to presence of an unpaired electron

$$\text{Bond order} = \frac{1}{2}\ (8-3) = 2.5$$

(*iv*) Molecular orbital configuration of CO is

$$KK\ (\sigma_{2s})^2(\sigma_{2pz})^2(\pi_{2px})^2(\pi_{2py})^2(\sigma^*_{2s})^2$$

As there are no unpaired electrons, the molecule is diamagnetic.

$$\text{Bond order} = \frac{1}{2}\ (8-2) = 3.$$

Example 18: Draw MO diagram for O_2^+, O_2^- and O_2^{2-} and give the value of bond order in each case.

Solution: Molecular orbital configuration of O_2^+, O_2^- and O_2^{2-} are written as under:

$$O_2^+ : KK\ (\sigma_{2s})^2(\sigma^*_{2s})^2(\sigma_{2pz})^2(\pi_{2px})^2(\pi_{2py})^2(\pi^*_{2px})^1$$

$$O_2^- : KK\ (\sigma_{2s})^2(\sigma^*_{2s})^2(\sigma_{2pz})^2(\pi_{2px})^2(\pi_{2py})^2(\pi^*_{2px})^2(\pi^*_{2py})^1$$

$$O_2^{2-} : KK\ (\sigma_{2s})^2(\sigma^*_{2s})^2(\sigma_{2pz})^2(\pi_{2px})^2(\pi_{2py})^2(\pi^*_{2px})^2(\pi^*_{2py})^2$$

Bond order

(*i*) in $O_2^+ = \frac{1}{2}(8-3) = 2.5$

(*ii*) in $O_2^- = \frac{1}{2}(8-5) = 1.5$

(*iii*) in $O_2^{2-} = \frac{1}{2}(8-6) = 1.0$

Example 19: The bond energy of NO is 623 kJ/mol whereas that of NO^+ molecule ion is 1049 kJ/mol. Justify.

Solution: NO : $KK\ (\sigma_{2s})^2(\sigma_z)^2(\pi_x)^2(\pi_y)^2(\sigma^*_{2s})^2(\pi^*_x)^1$

$$\text{Bond order} = \frac{8-3}{2} = 2\frac{1}{2}$$

$$NO^+ : KK\ (\sigma_{2s})^2(\sigma_z)^2(\pi_x)^2(\pi_y)^2(\sigma^*_{2s})^2$$

$$\text{Bond order} = \frac{8-2}{2} = 3$$

Higher bond order of NO^+ justifies its higher bond energy than NO.

Example 20: Give molecular orbital configuration of O_2, O_2^+ and O_2^-. Give order of stability with appropriate reasons.

Solution: O_2 : KK $(\sigma_{2s})^2(\sigma_{2s}^*)^2(\sigma_z^b)^2(\pi_x^b)^2(\pi_y^b)^2(\pi_x^*)^1(\pi_y^*)^1$

$$\text{Bond order} = \frac{8-4}{2} = 2$$

$$O_2^+ : \text{KK } (\sigma_{2s}^b)^2(\sigma_{2s}^*)^2(\sigma_z^b)^2(\pi_x^b)^2(\pi_y^b)^2(\pi_x^*)^1$$

$$\text{Bond order} = \frac{8-3}{2} = 2\frac{1}{2}$$

$$O_2^- : \text{KK } (\sigma_{2s}^b)^2(\sigma_{2s}^*)^2(\sigma_2^b)^2(\pi_x^b)^2(\pi_y^b)^2(\pi_x^*)^2(\pi_y^*)^1$$

$$\text{Bond order} = \frac{8-5}{2} = 1.5$$

Because of decreasing bond order, the stability decreases as

$$O_2^+ > O_2 > O_2^-$$

2.4.18 Points of Similarity and Difference Between Valence-Bond and Molecular Orbital Theory

Points which are common to both theories:

(*i*) Both these theories are approximations.

(*ii*) Both interpret covalent bonds as orbitals embracing two atomic nuclei.

(*iii*) Both require that the combining atomic orbitals should be of nearly equal energy: they should be capable of overlapping and the combining orbitals must have the same symmetry.

(*iv*) Both predict the concentration of electron density between the nuclei.

(*v*) Both can account for directed valency.

(*vi*) Both predict the non-existence of helium molecule.

Some points of difference between the two theories:

Valence bond theory	*Molecular orbital theory*
(*i*) Electrons in molecules are localized as if they are in isolated atoms.	It treats the nuclei of the molecule as polycentric and then constructs one electron molecular orbital.
(*ii*) The total wave function in the valence bond treatment takes the contribution due to ionic terms.	Molecular orbital theory overlapping estimates the role of ionic terms in its total wave functions.
(*iii*) It could not explain the paramagnetism of O_2.	It can easily explain the paramagnetism of O_2.
(*iv*) Resonance is an integral part of valence bond theory.	Resonance has no role in molecular orbital theory.
(*v*) It is simple to apply.	It is more difficult to apply.

Example 21: Why a σ_{2s}^b orbital has a higher energy than σ_{1s}^* orbital? Why is the former MO called a bonding orbital while the latter is called an antibonding MO?

Solution: The relative energies of σ_{2s}^{b} and σ_{2s}^{*} are determined by the energies of the atomic orbitals from which they originate. The σ_{2s}^{b} MO is lower in energy compared to the 2*s* atomic orbital from which it is originated and is, therefore, called a bonding orbital while the σ_{1s}^{*} MO is higher in energy than the 1*s* atomic orbital from which it originates and thus called an antibonding MO.

Example 22: Draw a diagram showing the formation of a σ_{2p} bonding MO from atomic orbitals.

Solution: Formation of σ_{2p} bonding MO from atomic orbitals is shown in Fig. 2.59.

(• = nucleus) σ_{2p}^{b}

Fig. 2.59: Formation of σ2p orbital.

2.5 BOND PARAMETERS

Covalent bonds are associated with certain characteristics like bond length, bond dissociation energy, etc. These characteristics help us to arrive at certain decisions regarding their reactivities. The parameters are discussed in some detail as under.

1. Bond length. It is defined as *the distance between the centres of two bonded atoms in a molecule*. The bond lengths are experimentally determined with the help of spectroscopic methods. The value obtaine are very small. It was expressed in Angstrom units (Å) earlier. But S.I. units encouraged the use of picometers (pm). The relation between the two units can be established as under:

$$1\ \text{Å} = 10^{8}\ \text{cm}$$
$$= 10^{-10}\ \text{m}$$
$$1\ \text{pm} = 10^{-12}\ \text{m where pm stands for picometer}$$

Thus a length of 1 Å would correspond to a length of 100 pm.

Bond length is equal to the sum of the radii of atoms forming the bond. The radius of the hydrogen atom is 37 pm, therefore, the distance between the centers of the two hydrogen atoms in a hydrogen molecule.

$$37\ \text{pm} + 37\ \text{pm} = 74\ \text{pm}$$

The bond lengths of some simple bonds are given in Table 2.1. It is important to note that the triple bond is shorter than the double bond, which in turn is shorter than a single bond.

TABLE 2.1 *Single and multiple bond lengths of some common bonds (pm)*

Bond	Bond length	Bond	Bond length
H—H	74	C—C	154
H—F	92	Si—Si	234
H—Cl	127	Ge—Ge	244
H—Br	141	Sn—Sn	280
H—I	160	C=C	134
C—H	110	C=O	122

(Contd...)

Bond	**Bond length**	**Bond**	**Bond length**
N—H	98	C = N	127
O—H	94	N ≡ O	115
F—F	128	C ≡ C	120
Cl—Cl	200	C ≡ N	115
Br—Br	228	C ≡ O	113
I—I	265	N ≡ O	108

A perusal of the Table 2.1 reveals that the bond lengths in a given family increase with increase in atomic number. For example, the H—X distance in the hydrogen halides increases in the order

$$H—F < H—Cl < H—Br < H—I$$

The trend is expected because size of the atom increases down a group. As a result, the distance between the bonding atoms increases.

2. Bond order. Bond order is defined as the number of bonds between two atoms or the number of bonding electron pairs shared by two atoms in a molecule. Electron pairs are also called covalent bonds.

Thus, if the bond order is 1, it means there is only one single covalent bond between a pair of atoms. Typical examples of bond order 1 are molecules such as H_2. Cl_2 and H_2O. The bond order is 2, when two electron pairs are shared between two atoms. The O = O in oxygen molecule, C = O bond in CO_2 and C = C bond in C_2H_4 are some examples of bond order 2. The bond order is 3 when three electron pairs are shared between two atoms. The N ≡ N bond in N_2, C ≡ O bond in carbon monoxide and C ≡ C bond in carbon monoxide adn C ≡ C bond in acetylene are examples of bond order 3. There are no bonds with order greater than 3 because of the constraints of octet rule.

Bond orders can be fractional also. A fractional bond order is found in molecules or ions which cannot be completely represented by a single Lewis structure. In other words, fractional bond order is possible in molecules or ions which show the phenomenon of resonance. Consider a nitrogen dioxide, NO_2 molecule. Two resonance structures can be written for NO_2.

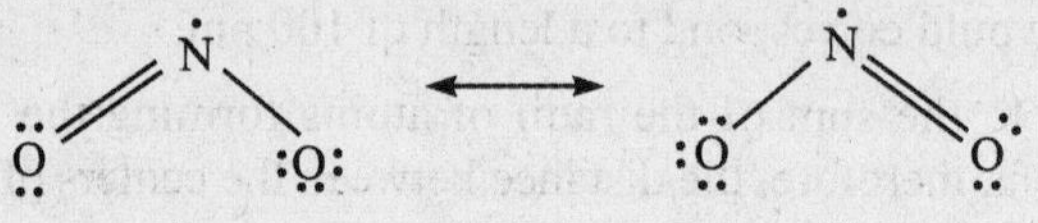

I ⟷ II

It is seen that each resonance structure has one N—O single bond and one N = O double bond. Thus, there are three shared bonding pairs of electrons for two nitrogen-oxygen links. Bond order for such molecules may be calculated as

$$\text{Bond order} = \frac{\text{number of shared pairs linking } X \text{ and } Y}{\text{number of } X - Y \text{ links in the molecule or ion}}$$

Thus, the bond order in $NO_2 = \frac{3}{2} = 1.5$.

Similarly, the bond order in ozone O_3 molecule can be calculated to be 1.5.

Molecular orbital theory also allows the existence of fractional bonds as follows:

$$\text{Bond order} = \frac{1}{2}\,[\text{No. of electrons in bonding orbitals-No. of electrons in non-bonding orbitals}]$$

The bond order values of some of the molecules are given in the Table 2.2 along with their bond lengths.

TABLE 2.2 *Bond order values of some molecules*

Molecule	*Bond*	*Bond order*	*Bond length (pm)*
H_2	H—H	1	74
Cl_2	Cl—Cl	1	200
NH_3	N—H	1	98
H_2O	O—H	1	94
O_2	O = O	2	120
CO_2	C = O	2	122
C_2H_4	C = C	2	134
N_2	N ≡ N	3	110
C_2H_2	C ≡ C	3	120

3. Bond angle. *The angle at which the two bonds in a molecular are inclined is called bond angle.* Bond angles are measured experimentally by X-ray diffraction or molecular spectroscopy. The determination of bond angles is very useful in deciding the shape of the molecules. Bond angles in some of the molecules are presented in the Table 2.3.

TABLE 2.3 *Bond angles in some molecules*

Molecule	*Bond angle*
H_2O	104.5°
H_2S	92.6°
NH_3	107°
CH_4	109.5°
BF_3	120°

These angles are determined by the kind of hybridisation that takes places in the central atom and interactions between shared pair-shared pair, shared pair-lone pair and lone pair pair-lone pair of electrons.

4. Bond dissociation energy. It is defined as the amount of energy required to break one mole of a particular bond between the atoms in the gaseous state. Bond dissociation energy measures the stability of a molecule. Higher the bond dissociation energy, the stronger is the bond in the molecule.

The bond dissociation energies of some common bonds are given in the Table 2.4.

Bond dissociation energy depends upon the following factors:

(*i*) **Size of the atoms.** Smaller the size of the bonded atoms, the larger is the value of bond dissociation energy. The bond dissociation energy of H—H bond (458 kJ mol^{-1}) is greater than the bond dissociation energy H—Cl (431 kJ mol^{-1}). H—Br (366 kJ mol^{-1}) and H—I (298 kJ mol^{-1}) because the size of the second atom (other than H) increases in the order H $\longrightarrow$ Cl $\longrightarrow$ Br $\longrightarrow$ I.

TABLE 2.4 *Bond dissociation energy of some common bonds.*

Bond	***Bond dissociation energy***	***Bond***	***Bond dissociation energy***
H—H	458	N—H	391
H—Cl	432	C—H	413
H—Br	366	O—H	463
H—I	299	C—C	346
Cl—Cl	243	C = C	602
Br—Br	193	C ≡ C	835
I—I	151	N ≡ N	945

(*ii*) **Bond length.** The bond dissociation energy is directly proportional to the bond order and inversely proportional to the bond length. The shorter the bond between two atoms, the larger is the value of bond dissociation energy. A greater value of bond order means, there is a greater overlapping of orbitals of the two participating atoms thereby increasing the strength of the bond.

5. Bond energy. It is defined as the average value of bond dissociation energies of the same type of bonds present in a molecule. The bond energy is calculated from the values of the heat of formation. For example, in the formation of methane from carbon and hydrogen in their gaseous atomic state, 1661 kJ of heat is liberated.

Thus, average value of C—H bond energy in $CH_4 = \frac{1661}{4} = 415.25$ kJ. It may be mentioned that the average bond energy of the same bond may not be the same in different molecules.

Evaluate Yourself

Multiple Choice Questions

1. A sp^3 hybrid orbital possesses

(*a*) $\frac{1}{4}$ s – character (*b*) $\frac{1}{2}$ s – character

(*c*) $\frac{2}{3}$ s – character (*d*) $\frac{3}{4}$ s – character

2. Experiment shows that H_2O has a dipole moment while CO_2 does not. Point out the structures which best illustrate these facts.

(*a*) O = C = O, O / \ H H (*b*) O = C = O H – O – H

(*c*) C //\\ O O H – H – O (*d*) O ‖ C = O H | O—H

3. The compound formed by sp^3d hybridisation will have the structure

(*a*) planar (*b*) pyramidal

(*c*) angualr (*d*) trigonal bipyramidal

4. Which of the following compounds of boron will be more covalent in nature ?
(*a*) BCl_3 (*b*) BF_3
(*c*) $B Br_3$ (*d*) BI_3
5. Bond order of a molecule is given by
(*a*) The difference between the number of electrons in bonding and antibonding orbitals
(*b*) total number of electrons in bonding and antibonding orbitals
(*c*) twice the differences between the number of electrons in bonding and anti bonding orbitals
(*d*) half the differnce between the number of electrons in bonding and non-bonding orbitals.
6. Which one of the following will have a tetrahedral disposition?
(*a*) SO_2 (*b*) SO_3
(*c*) SO_4^{2-} (*d*) SO_3^{2-}
7. Resonance structure of a molecule should have
(*a*) identical arrangement of atoms (*b*) nearly same energy contant
(*c*) the same number of paired electrons (*d*) identical bonding
8. CO_2 is isostructural with
(*a*) $Hg Cl_2$ (*b*) $SnCl_2$
(*c*) C_2H_6 (*d*) NO_2
9. Which of the following is paramagnetic?
(*a*) O_2^- (*b*) CN^-
(*c*) CO (*d*) NO^+
10. Covalant compounds generally show the following properties:
(*a*) They are soluble in water (*b*) They are insoluble in water
(*c*) They ionise in water (*d*) They hydrolyse in water

Short Answer Questions

1. State three main points of valence bond theory.
2. With the help of a diagram, indicate various forces of attraction and repulsion is a molecule of hydrogen.
3. List three necessary conditions for writing resonating structures.
4. Write the resonating structure of (*i*) N_2O and (*ii*) CO_3^{2-} ion.
5. Explain with the help of a diagram how two *p*-orbitals overlap (*i*) end-to-end and (*ii*) laterally. Which bonds are formed in the two cases.
6. Define hybridisation of orbitals. Name different kinds of hybridisation and the shapes of molecules obtained from such hybridisations.
7. Name two factors that determine the shapes of molecules. Briefly discuss one of them.
8. Which type of hybridisation is involved in the formation of a molecule of $Xe F_4$? What is the shape of this molecule ?
9. Bond energy of N_2 molecule is higher than that of O_2. Explain.
10. Draw the MO energy level diagram of hydrogen fluoride.

Long Answer Questions

1. (*a*) What is valence bond theory of bonding? How does valence bond theory account for bonding in a hydrogen molecule?
   (*b*) What do the following structure of hydrogen molecule signify:
   $$H—H \longleftrightarrow H^+ H^- \longleftrightarrow H^- H^+$$
   (*c*) Write the various resonating structures for carbon monoxide molecule.
2. (*a*) What do you understand by the terms resonance and resonance energy?
   (*b*) What are the essential conditions for writing resonating structures?
   (*c*) Draw all the resonating structures of nitrous oxide.
   (*d*) Why does nitrous acid (HNO_2) show *cis* and *trans* isomers?
3. Give the salient points of valence bond theory.
4. In the potential energy diagram, the combined wave function ψ, for two hydrogen atoms. $\psi = \psi_A(1)\,\psi_B(2)$ (where $\psi_A(1)$ and $\psi_B(2)$ represent wave functions of two hydrogen atoms H_A and H_B associated with electrons 1 and 2 respectively, results in decrease in energy of the system by 24 kJ mol^{-1}. But the experimental bond energy of H_2 is 458 kJ mol^{-1}. What improvement in the wave function of the system are made to account for this difference?
5. (*a*) Explain what is meant by the terms exchange energy of hydrogen molecule. How would you account for it?
   (*b*) What is resonance? Discuss this by taking the example of CO_3^{2-} ion.
   (*c*) Draw the various resonating structures of CO and CO_2 molecules. Justify the significance of each structure on the basis of their physical properties.
6. (*a*) What do you understand by resonance and resonance energy?
   (*b*) Discuss resonance structure of CO_3^{2-} ion.
7. Write a short note on resonance structure of CO and cause of its low dipole moment.
8. What is a three electron bond? Give examples.
9. (*a*) What do you mean by resonance? Write the resonance structures of CO and explain the cause of its low dipole moment.
10. (*a*) Write short note on:
    Resonance structure of CO and cause of its low dipole moment.
11. (*a*) Give two examples of a three electron bond.
    (*b*) N_2O is linear structure. Explain with the help of resonating stuructures.
    (*c*) Why is CO_2 linear? Explain with the help of resonating structures.
12. What is hydrogen bond? What are the essential conditions for hydrogen bond formation: Give example.
13. Use valence bond theory to explain bonding in N_2 and CO.
14. What is hybridisation? What shapes are associated with the following hybrid orbitals:
    $$sp^2,\ sp^3d \text{ and } sp^3d^2$$
15. On the basis of hybridisation, explain the shapes of the following molecules/ions:
    $$SF_6,\ NH_3,\ BF_3,\ IF_7,\ CO_3^{2-},\ NO_3^-.$$

16. (*a*) Discuss the geometry of PF_3 on the basis of VSEPR theory. Compare its bond angle with PCl_3 and PBr_3.

(*b*) Using VSEPR theory, how will you show that.

(*i*) XeF_4 is square planar

17. (*a*) Why is the use of hybrid orbitals preferred than atomic orbitals? Illustrate your answer.

(*b*) Give the hybridisation of the central atom and expected as well as actual geometry of the following molecules/ions.

NO_3^-, PF_5, NH_3, SF_4, ClO_3^-

18. What are the main postulates of VSEPR theory? How does this account for the geometries of the following molecules?

(*i*) PF_5 (*ii*) H_2O (*iii*) $SnCl_2$
(*iv*) BF_3 (*v*) SF_6 (*vi*) ClF_3

19. (*a*) Use VSEPR theory to predict the shapes of the following molecules:

(*i*) NH_3 (*ii*) SF_4 (*iii*) XeF_4
(*iv*) PF_5

(*b*) Account for the following order of bond angles:

(*i*) $PF_3 < PBr_3 < PCl_3$ (*ii*) $H_2O > H_2S > H_2Se$
(*iii*) $PF_3 > PH_3$

(*c*) What are the limitations of VSEPR theory.

20. (*a*) What is hybridisation? What are the important characteristics of hybridisation?

(*b*) Beryllium (Z = 4) has no unpaired electron in its ground state. However, in all its compounds, beryllium shows divalency. Explain.

(*c*) The central atom in the molecules of CH_4, NH_3 and H_2O involves sp^3 hybridisation. But the bond angles in these molecules are 109.5° 107° and 104.5° respectively. Account for this.

(*d*) What shapes are associated with the molecules involving sp^3d and sp^3d^2 hybridisations? Which *d*-orbitals are specifically required for each set?

21. (*a*) Boron has only one unpaired electron in its ground state and is expected to show monovalency. However, in all its compounds, boron shows trivalency. Discuss.

(*b*) The ground state electronic configuration of chlorine is $1s^2\ 2s^2\ 2p^6\ 3s^2\ 3p^5$. Account for the geometry of following molecules/ions of chlorine:

(*i*) ClF_3^- (*ii*) ClO_3^-

(*c*) In XeF_2, xenon undergoes sp^3d hybridisation but the molecule is linear. Explain.

22. Account for the following:

(*a*) All the bond lengths in SF_6 are equal but these are not equal in IF_5 molecule.

(*b*) BeF_2 molecule is linear while SF_2 is angular, though both are triatomic.

(*c*) The geometics of H_2O and H_2S are same, but their bond angles are $H_2O > H_2S$.

(*d*) BH_3 is trigonal planar while NH_3 is pyramidal.

23. (*a*) What is hybridisation? Discuss the stereochemistry of the following molecules on the basis of hybridisation:

PF_5, $SnCl_2$, NH_3, ClF_3.

(*b*) Which of the following molecules has largest bond angle?

H_2O, NH_3, CH_4, BH_3

24. (*a*) What do you understand by hybridisation? Explain with one example sp^3 hybridisation.

(*b*) What type of geometry is possible for molecules undergoing the following types of hybridisations?

(*i*) sp (*ii*) sp^2 (*iii*) sp^3
(*iv*) sp^3d (*v*) sp^3d^2 (*vi*) sp^3d^3.

(*c*) Name the four important types of hybrid orbitals which can be formed by an atom with *s*, *p* and *d*-orbitals in its valence shell.

25. One the basis of hybridisation, discuss the geometry but the molecules is linear. Explain.

SF_4, IF_5, $SnCl_2$, XeF_4, SF_6, H_2O, PCl_5 and NH_3.

26. (*a*) Give the hybridisation of the central atom of the following molecules/ions:

IF_7, ClO_3^- and SF_6.

(*b*) Giving examples explain the concept of hybidisation with reference to:

(*i*) sp^3 and (*ii*) sp^3d.

27. (*a*) What is LCAO molecular orbital approach?

(*b*) What do you understand by bonding and antibonding molecular orbitals?

(*c*) Draw the molecular ortbitals obtained by the combination of two 2*s*-atomic orbitals.

28. (*a*) Discuss the conditions necessary for the combination of atomic orbitals. Sketch and discuss the combination of *p*-atomic orbitals to form molecular orbitals.

(*b*) What is meant by bond order? Calculate the bond order in He_2^+, O_2 and N_2 molecules.

(*c*) Is B_2 molecule paramagnetic or diamagnetic? Discuss.

29. (*a*) Sketch the shapes of MO obtained by the overlap of:

(*i*) two *s*-orbitals

(*ii*) end on overlap of two *p*-orbitals

(*iii*) side wise overlap of two *p*-orbitals

(*b*) How does molecular orbital theory account for the following:

(*i*) bond order in O_2^+ is more than in O_2 molecule while bond order in N_2^+ is less than in N_2 molecule.

(*ii*) He_2 does not exist.

30. (*a*) Is it correct to say that bond energy in a diatomic molecule always increases when an electron is lost?

(*b*) Why is the bond energy of Li_2 less than that of H_2?

(*c*) Draw the molecular orbital diagram for HCl molecule.

31. (*a*) Discuss the shapes of SF_6 and NO_3^-.

(*b*) What do you understand by linear combination of atomic orbitals? Explain.

(*c*) Discuss the resonance structures of CO_3^{2-}.

32. The internuclear distance is some O—O bonds are as follows:

O_2^+	O_2	O_2^-	O_2^{2-}
1.12Å	1.21 Å	1.30Å	1.49 Å

(*a*) Draw the molecular orbital diagram for O_2 molecule and account for the gradation of the internuclear distance in the above series.

(*b*) Which of these species are paramagnetic?

33. (*a*) Write molecular orbital configurations for O_2, O_2^+, O_2^- and O_2^{2-} and arrange them in increasing order of their bond lengths.

(*b*) With the help of MO diagrams explain

(*i*) that the bond energy of NO^+ is larger than that of NO.

(*ii*) that the bond length of CO^+ is larger than that of CO.

34. (*a*) Give the postulates of molecular orbital theory and discuss the distribution of electron charge density in bonding as well as antibonding molecular orbitals.

(*b*) What is meant by dsp^2 hybridisation? How are these hybrid orbitals formed? Discuss the formation of $[Ni(CN)_4]^{2-}$ ion on the basis of hybridisation.

(*c*) PF_5 is more reactive than SF_6. How will you account for this?

35. (*a*) Distinguish two aspects of the following:

(*i*) atomic and molecular orbitals

(*ii*) bonding and antibonding orbitals

(*iii*) sigma and pi bonds.

(*b*) Do you expect bond order in superoxide ion (O_2^-) more or less than in peroxide ion (O_2^{2-})?

(*c*) Give an account of the relationship between electronic configuration and molecular behaviour.

36. (*a*) Explain the following:

(*i*) lone pair—lone pair repulsion > lone pair — bond pair repulsion > bond pair—bond pair repulsion.

(*ii*) He_2 does not exist. (Use MO theory).

37. (*a*) Bring out the differences between the valence bond and molecular orbital theories.

(*b*) Distinguish between σ and π molecular orbitals.

(*c*) (*i*) Why is the force of repulsion between lone pairs different from that of the bond pairs of electrons?

(*ii*) All P–F bonds in PF_5 are not equivalent in length. Explain.

38. (*a*) Discuss the structure of the following on the basis of hybridisation

(*i*) IF_5, (*ii*) CO_3^{2-} ion.

(*b*) Define bonding and antibonding molecular orbitals. Describe salient features of these orbitals.

39. (*a*) Which of the following combinations of orbitals are not allowed in LCAO method (consider Z-axis to be molecular axis):

(*i*) $s + p_z$ (*ii*) $p_x + p_x$ (*iii*) $p_y + p_z$

(*iv*) $s + p_x$.

(*b*) What is resonance? What are the rules which have resctricted our choice of resonating structures?

(*c*) State the geometrical arrangements possible in sp^3d and sp^3d^2 hybridisations. Name the *d*-orbitals involved in these.

40. (*a*) Explain the following:

(*i*) PF_5 is more reactive than SF_6.

(*ii*) BeF_2 molecule is linear while BF_3 molecule is trigonal.

(*iii*) Bond angle in NH_3 is 107° while in H_2O it is 104°.

(*iv*) He_2^+ ion is less stable than H_2^+ ion.

(*b*) Distinguish between molecular orbital theory and valence bond theory.

41. (*a*) How is molecular orbital wave function (ψ_{MO}) obtained from atomic orbital wave functions (ψ_A and ψ_B) for a molecule AB?

(*b*) How will you account for the fact that bond strength of nitrogen molecule is more than that of N_2^+ ion whereas bond strength of O_2 is less than that of O_2^+ ion. Explain your answer on the basis of molecular orbital theory.

(*c*) Is B_2 molecule paramagnetic or diamagnetic ? Discuss.

42. (*a*) Give the hybridisation of the central atom and expected as well as actual geometry of the following molecules/ions:

H_2O, NO_3^-, XeF_4, $SnCl_2$.

(*b*) Explain the following:

(*i*) Nitrogen molecule is diamagnetic while oxygen molecule is paramagnetic.

(*ii*) Boron molecule is stable while beryllium molecule is extremely unstable.

(*c*) Explain what is meant by the term exchange energy of hydrogen molecule. How would you account for it ?

43. (*a*) Which of the following molecules/ions have *sp*^{2} hybridized central atom and draw their structures:

(*i*) ClO^- (*ii*) NO_2 (*iii*) $SnCl_2$

(*iv*) SO_3^{2-} (*v*) CO_3^{2-}

(*b*) Draw an MO diagram of CO and show its bond order. How does this description compare with its valence bond strucuture.

44. (*a*) How does molecular orbital theory account for the following:

Bond order in O_2^+ is more than in O_2 molecule while bond order in N_2^+ is less than in N_2 molecule?

(*b*) Why is the force of repulsion between lone pairs different from that of the bond pairs of electrons.

(*c*) Distinguish the two aspects of the following:

(*i*) bonding and antibonding orbitals

(*ii*) sigma and pi bonds.

45. (*a*) Use valence bond theory to explain bonding in N_2 and CO.

(*b*) Explain on the basis of V.B.T. and hybridisation that

(*i*) BeF_2 molecule is linear while H_2O is bent.

(*ii*) Phosphorus forms two chlorides (PCl_3 and PCl_5) while nitrogen forms only one *i.e.* NCl_3.

(*c*) Chlorate and perchlorate ions have the same number of electron pairs around the chlorine atom but their geometry is different.

(*d*) Explain on the basis of M.O.T.

(*i*) N_2 molecule is diamagnetic while O_2 molecule is paramagnetic.

(*ii*) Bond order of N_2^+ is lower than that of N_2.

46. (*a*) Account for the decreasing bond angle in the order $NO_2^+ > NO_2 > NO_2^-$.

(*b*) Use VSEPR theory to predict the shapes and hybridisation of the following molecules:

NH_3, SF_4, PF_5, IF_7

(*c*) Account for the following bond angles:

(*i*) $PF_3 < PBr_3 < PCl_3$

(*ii*) $H_2O > H_2S > H_2Se$

(*iii*) $PF_3 > PH_3$.

(*d*) In XeF_2, xenon undergoes sp^3d hybridisation, but the molecule is linear. Explain.

47. Discuss M.O. theory. How does this theory differ from VB theory? Discuss the diamagnatic nature of N_2 molecule with the help of M.O. theory.

48.(*a*) On the basis of hybridisation, discuss the geometry of the following molecules:

IF_5, XeF_4, PCl_5, NH_3

(*b*) Draw the molecular orbital diagram for HCl molecule.

(*c*) Draw the M.O. energy level diagram for fluorine and predict

(*i*) bond order

(*ii*) magnetic properties, therein.

49. Explain the following:

(*i*) Oxygen molecule is paramagnetic

(*ii*) Bond order in NO^+ is 3.

(*iii*) Bond distance in O_2^+ is smaller than in O_2 molecule.

(*iv*) Bond strength of N_2 molecule is more as compared to O_2 molecule.

(*v*) Non-existence of He_2 molecule.

50. (*a*) All P-F bonds in PF_5 are not equivalent length. Explain.

(*b*) Write down the differences between valence bond and molecular orbital theory?

(*c*) Give the hybridisation of the central atom and expected as well as actual geometry of the following molecules/ions:

H_2O, NO_3^-, XeF_4, $SnCl_2$.

51. (*a*) Draw MO diagram of CO and calculate its bond order.

(*b*) Discuss the geometry shapes of molecules involving sp^3d and sp^3d^2 hybridisation with at least one example each.

(*c*) PF_5 is more reactive than SF_6, Explain.

52. What do you understand by bonding and antibonding molecular orbitals? Give the number of electrons which occupy the bonding and antibonding molecular orbitals of

(*i*) H_2^+ (*ii*) H_2 (*iii*) He_2 molecule.

53. (*a*) How will you explain that the geometries of H_2O and H_2S are the same but their bond angles are $H_2O > H_2S$.

(*b*) What is bond order? Calculate the bond order of He_2^+.

(*c*) Explain why phosphorus forms two chlorides (PCl_5 and PCl_3) while nitrogen forms only NCl_3?

(*d*) What are the postulates of VSEPR theory?

54. Discuss the shapes and types of hybridisation in the following:

$$ClO_3^-, ClO_4^-, PCl_5, SF_6, NO_3^-$$

(*a*) On the basis of M.O. theory calculate bond order in

(*i*) O_2^{2-} ion (*ii*) N_2^+ ion.

(*b*) On the basis of molecular orbital theory explain why ionisation energy of O_2 molecules is less than that of O_2^{2+} ion.

55. Explain on the basis of M.O. theory

(*i*) N_2 molecule is diamagnetic while O_2 molecule is paramagnetic.

(*ii*) Bond order of N_2^+ is lower than that of N_2.

56. (*a*) Give the structure and bonding in electron deficient diborane, B_2H_6.

(*b*) What are molecular orbitals? Sketch sigma and pi molecular orbitals that result from the combination of the *p*-orbitals. One of each atom in a diatomic molecule.

Answers

Multiple Choice Questions

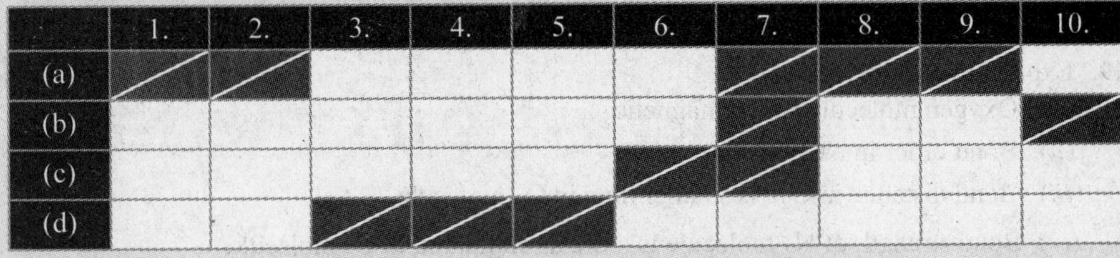

	1.	2.	3.	4.	5.	6.	7.	8.	9.	10.
(a)	■	■					■	■	■	
(b)							■			■
(c)						■	■			
(d)			■	■	■					

3

Periodic Properties of Atoms (With Reference to *s*– and *p*– Block)

3.1 INTRODUCTION

If the elements are arranged in order of increasing atomic numbers, then their properties get repeated after regular intervals. The repetition of similar properties of the element after regular intervals is called **periodicity**. It is possible to explain the cause of periodicity in the light of the structure of the atom.

It has now been established that chemical properties of the elements are governed by the number of valence electrons in their atom. Therefore it is expected that atoms having similar valence shell electronic configuration will have similar properties. This is actually true. The arrangement of elements in order of increasing atomic number results in the repetition of similar electronic configuration after regular intervals.

Consider the electronic configuration of alkali metals (Table 3.1). The alkali metals have one electron in the *s* orbital of their valence shell. In other words, their electronic configuration can be written as ns^1 where n is the number of outmost energy level. It is due to the similar electronic configuration in the outermost orbit that all the alkali metals have similar properties.

TABLE 3.1 *Electronic configuration of alkali metals*

Element	At. No.	Electronic configuration
Li	3	$1s^2;2s^1$
Na	11	$1s^2; 2s^2\ 2p^6; 3s^1$
K	19	$1s^2; 2s^2\ 2p^6; 3s^2 3p^6; 4s^1$
Rb	37	$1,s^2; 2s^2\ 2p^6; 3s^2\ 3p^6\ 3d^{10}; 4s^2\ 4p^6; 5s^1$
Cs	55	$1s^2; 2s^2\ 2p^6; 3s^2\ 3p^6\ 3d^{10}; 4s^2\ 4p^6\ 4d^{10}; 5s^2 5p^6; 6s^1$
Fr	87	$1s^2; 2s^2\ 2p^6; 3s^2\ 3p^6\ 3d^{10}; 4s^2 4p^6\ 4d^{10}\ 4f^{14}; 5s^2\ 5p^6\ 5d^{10}; 6s^2 6p^6; 7s^1$

Hence, the cause of periodicity of the properties of elements is the repetition of similar electronic configurations after certain regular intervals.

3.1.1 Features of Long Form of Periodic Table

The long form periodic table is arranged in seven horizontal rows called *periods* and eighteen vertical columns called *groups* (See Table 3.2).

TABLE 3.2 *Latest Periodic Table of the Elements*

Key: atomic number / Symbol / name / conventional atomic weight / standard atomic weight

1	2	3	4	5	6	7	8	9	10	11	12	13	14	15	16	17	18
1 H hydrogen 1.000 [1.0078, 1.0082]																	2 He helium 400.26
3 Li lithium 6.94 [6.936, 6.997]	4 Be beryllium 9.0122											5 B boron 10.01 [10.805, 10.821]	6 C carbon 12.011 [12.009, 12.012]	7 N Nitrogen 14.007 [14.006, 14.006]	8 O oxygen 15.999 [15.999, 16.000]	9 F fluorine 18.996	10 Ne neon 20.180
11 Na sodium 22.990	12 Mg magnesium 24.305 [24.304, 24.307]											13 Al aluminium 26.962	14 Si silicon 28.095 [28.084, 28.095]	15 P phosphorus 30.974	16 S sulfur 32.05 [35.069, 35.076]	17 Cl chlorine 36.45 [35.446, 35.457]	18 Ar argon 39.95 [39.792, 39.963]
19 K potassium 39.098	20 Ca calcium 40.078(4)	21 Sc scandium 44.956	22 Ti flanium 47.867	23 V vanadium 50.942	24 Cr chromium 54.936	25 Mn manganese 54.938	26 Fe iron 55.845(2)	27 Co cobalt 58.933	28 Ni nickel 58.693	29 Cu copper 63.546(3)	30 Zn zinc 65.38(2)	31 Ga galllium 69.723	32 Ge germarium 72.530(8)	33 As arsenic 74.922	34 Se selenium 78.971(8)	35 Br bromine 79.904 [79.901, 79.907]	36 Kr krypton 63.796(2)
37 Rb rubidium 85.468	38 Sr stonfium 87.62	39 Y yttrium 86.906	40 Zr zirconium 91.224(2)	41 Nb niobium 92.905	42 Mo molyodenum 95.95	43 Tc technetium	44 Ru rutherium 101.07(2)	45 Rh rhodium 102.91	46 Pd paladium 106.42	47 Ag silver 107.87	48 Cd cadmium 112.41	49 In indium 114.82	50 Sn fin 118.71	51 Sb anfimony 121.76	52 Te lellurium 127.60(3)	53 I iodine 126.90	54 Xe xenon 131.29
55 Cs caesium 132.91	56 Ba barium 137.33	57-71 lanfhanoids	72 Hf halfnium 178.49(2)	73 Ta tantaium 180.95	74 W tungsten 183.84	75 Re rhenium 186.84	76 Os osmium 190.23(3)	77 Ir iridium 192.22	78 Pt platinum 190.08	79 Au gold 196.97	80 Hg mercury 200.59	81 Tl thallium 204.38 [204.36, 204.39]	82 Pb lead 207.2	83 Bi bismuth 208.96	84 Po polnium	85 At astatine	86 Rn radon
87 Fr francium	88 Ra radium	89-103 acinoids	104 Rf rutherfordium	105 Db dubrium	106 Sg seaborgium	107 Bh bohrium	108 Hs hassium	109 Mt meinerium	110 Ds darmstadfum	111 Rg roenigerium	112 Cn coperridium	113 Nh nihonium	114 Fl ferovium	115 Mc moscovium	116 Lv livermorium	117 Ts tennessine	118 Og oganesson

57 La lanthanum 138.91	58 Ce cerium 140.12	59 Pr praseodymium 140.91	60 Nd neodymium 144.24	61 Pm promethium	62 Sm samarium 150.36(2)	63 Eu europium 151.96	64 Gd gaddinium 158.25(3)	65 Tb terbium 158.93	66 Dy dysprosium 162.50	67 Ho holmium 164.93	68 Er 167.26 168.93	69 Tm thulium 168.93	70 Yb ytterbium 173.05	71 Lu luteium 174.97
89 Ac acinium	90 Th thorium 232.04	91 Pa protactinium 231.04	92 U Uranium 238.03	93 Np neptunium	94 Pu plutonium	95 Am ameificium	96 Cm curium	97 Bk bericelium	98 Cf californium	99 Es einsleinium	100 Fm fermium	101 Md mendelevium	102 No nobelium	103 Lr lawrencium

Periods

The seven periods are numbered from 1 to 7 starting from top and going downwards. Each period begins with an alkali metal and ends with an inert gas element. The number of elements in each period is as given in Table 3.3.

The first three periods are called *short* periods because they contain small number (2 or 8) of elements. The next four periods are called *long* periods because they contain large number (18 or 32) of elements.

TABLE 3.3 *Periods with Number of Elements*

Period	*No. of elements*
1	2
2	8
3	8
4	18
5	18
6	32
7	32

Elements from atomic numbers 104 to 118 have been reported recently. But these heavy elements are highly unstable. Names of these elements as suggested by American Chemical Society and IUPAC are given in Table 3.4.

Thus this period is incomplete and requires 6 more elements to be discovered to complete $7p^{1-6}$.

TABLE 3.4 *American chemical society and IUPAC names of some elements*

Atomic number	*American chemical society names*	*IUPAC names*
104	Rutherfordium (Rf)	Unnilquadium (Unq)
105	Hahnium (Ha)	Unnilpentium (Unp)
106	Seaborgium (Sg)	Unnilhexium (Unh)
107	Bohrium (Bh)	Unnilseptium (Uns)
108	Hassium (Hs)	Unniloctium (Uno)
109	Meitnerium (Mt)	Unnilennium (Une)
110	Darmstadtium (Ds)	Ununnilium (Uun)
111	Roentgenium (Rg)	Unununilium (Uuu)
112	Copernicium (Cn)	Unundodium (Uud)
113	Nihonium (Nh)	Ununtrium (Uut)
114	Flerovium (Fl)	Ununquadium
115	Mascovium (Mc)	Ununpentium
116	Livermorium (Lv)	Ununhexium
117	Tennessine (Ts)	Ununseptium
118	Oganesson (Og)	Ununoctium

Groups

There are 18 vertical columns in the periodic table which constitute 18 groups and are numbered as 1, 2, 3, 4, 5, 6, 7, 8, 9, 10, 11, 12, 13, 14, 15, 16, 17, and 18.

The elements belonging to groups 1, 2, 13, 14, 15, 16, 17 and 18 are known as *normal or representative elements.* Elements in between groups 2 and 13 are called *transition elements* because they represent a transition (change) from electropositive elements on the left-hand side to electronegative elements on the right-hand side of the periodic table.

Two rows of elements (each containing 14 elements) are known as *lanthanides and actinides* respectively. They are placed separately in the periodic table to avoid uncontrolled sideway expansion of the periodic table. Names of elements in alphabetical order, their symbols and at. numbers are given in Table 3.5.

TABLE 3.5 *Name of Elements, their Symbols and Atomic Numbers*

Element	***Symbol***	***Atomic No.***	***Element***	***Symbol***	***Atomic No.***
Actinium	Ac	89	Iodine	I	53
Aluminium	Al	13	Iridium	Ir	77
Americium	Am	95	Iron	Fe	26
Antimony	Sb	51	Krypton	Kr	36
Argon	Ar	18	Lanthanum	La	57
Arsenic	As	33	Lawrencium	Lr	103
Astatine	At	85	Lead	Pb	82
Barium	Ba	56	Lithium	Li	3
Berkelium	Bk	97	Lutetium	Lu	71
Beryllium	Be	4	Magnesium	Mg	12
Bismuth	Bi	83	Manganese	Mn	25
Boron	B	5	Mendelevium	Md	101
Bromine	Br	35	Mercury	Hg	80
Cadmium	Cd	48	Molybdenum	Mo	42
Calcium	Ca	20	Neodymium	Nd	60
Californium	Cf	98	Neon	Ne	10
Carbon	C	6	Neptunium	Np	93
Cerium	Ce	58	Nickel	Ni	28
Cesium	Cs	55	Niobium	Nb	41
Chlorine	Cl	17	Nitrogen	N	7
Chromium	Cr	24	Nobelium	No	102
Cobalt	Co	27	Osmium	Os	76
Copper	Cu	29	Oxygen	0	8
Curium	Cm	96	Palladium	Pd	46
Dysprosium	Dy	66	Phosphorus	P	15
Einsteinium	Es	99	Platinum	Pt	78
Erbium	Er	68	Plutonium	Pu	94
Europium	Eu	63	Polonium	Po	84
Fermium	Fm	100	Potassium	K	19
Fluorine	F	9	Praseodymium	Pr	59
Francium	Fr	87	Promethium	Pm	61
Gadolinium	Gd	64	Protactinium	Pa	91

(Contd...)

Element	Symbol	Atomic No.	Element	Symbol	Atomic No.
Gallium	Ga	31	Radium	Ra	88
Germanium	Ge	32	Radon	Rn	86
Gold	Au	79	Rhenium	Re	75
Hafnium	Hf	72	Rhodium	Rh	45
Helium	He	2	Rubidium	Rb	37
Holmium	Ho	67	Ruthenium	Ru	44
Hydrogen	H	1	Samarium	Sm	62
Indium	In	49	Scandium	Sc	21
Selenium	Se	34	Thulium	Tm	69
Silicon	Si	14	Tin	Sn	50
Silver	Ag	47	Titanium	Ti	22
Sodium	Na	11	Tungsten	W	74
Strontium	Sr	38	Uranium	U	92
Sulphur	S	16	Vanadium	V	23
Tantalum	Ta	73	Xenon	Xe	54
Technetium	Tc	43	Ytterbium	Yb	70
Tellurium	Te	52	Yttrium	Y	39
Terbium	Tb	65	Zinc	Zn	30
Thallium	Tl	81	Zirconium	Zr	40
Thorium	Th	90			

3.1.2 Different Blocks Constituting the Periodic Table

To simplify the study of elements the periodic table has been divided into four blocks known as *s, p, d* and *f* blocks. The division depends upon the type of atomic orbital which receives the last electron in an atom *e.g.*, magnesium ($1s^2 2s^2 2p^6 3s^2$) which receives its last electron in *s*-orbital belongs to *s*-block. The division of periodic table into four blocks is depicted in Fig. 3.1.

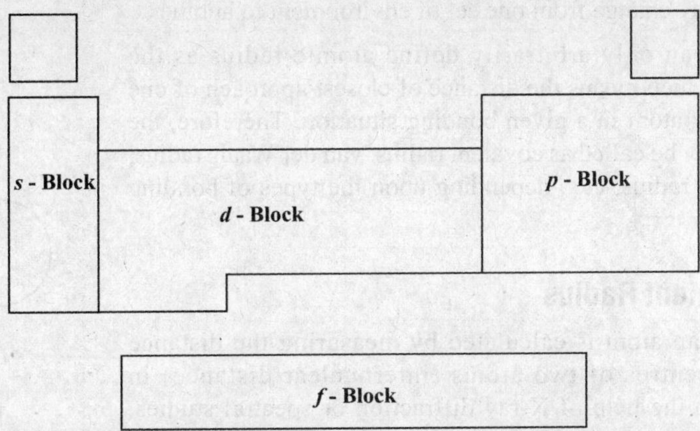

Fig. 3.1: Division of periodic table into four blocks

s-block elements are those elements whose last electron enters the *s*-orbital of the valence shell. Therefore, elements of group 1 and group 2 constitute *s*-block elements. General electronic configuration of *s*-block elements is: ns^{1-2}.

p-block elements are those elements whose last electron enters the *p*-orbital of the valence shell. Therefore, elements of groups 13, 14, 15, 16, 17 and 18 constitute *p*-block. General electronic configuration of *p*-block elements is $ns^2np^{1–6}$.

d-block elements are those elements whose last electron enters *d*-orbitals. Therefore, elements of groups 3, 4, 5, 6, 7, 8, 9, 10, 11 and 12 constitute *d*-block. These elements are called transition elements. General electronic configuration of *d*-block elements is: $(n-1)\,d^{1-10}ns^{1,\,2}$.

f-block elements are those whose last electron enters *f*-orbital. Two series of elements at the bottom of the periodic table known as lanthanides and actinides constitute *f*-block elements. These elements are also known as inner transition elements because they constitute transition series within the transition elements. General electronic configuration of *f*-block elements is: $(n-2)f^{1-14}$ $(n-1)\,d^{0-1}ns^2$.

Periodic Properties

There are many physical and chemical properties of elements which show periodic variation with atomic number. Some of these properties such as valency, atomic size, ionisation energy, electron affinity and electronegativity are directly related to the electronic configuration of the atom while some properties such as melting point, density, etc., are indirectly related to electronic configurations.

3.2 ATOMIC RADII

Generally, the term atomic radius means *the distance from the centre of the nucleus to the outermost shell of electrons*. If the atom is assumed to be spherical, it is the radius of the sphere. However, the absolute size of an atom is difficult to be defined because of the following reasons:

(*i*) According to the probability picture of electrons, an atom does not have well defined boundary. The probability of finding the electron is not zero even at large distances from the nucleus.

(*ii*) It is not possible to isolate an atom and measure its radius. The probability distribution of an atom is also affected by the presence of other atoms in its neighbourhood. Therefore, the size of atom may change from one set of environment to another.

Thus, we can only arbitrarily define atomic radius as the effective size which means the distance of closest approach of one atom to another atom in a given bonding situation. Therefore, the atomic radii may be called as covalent radius, van der Waals radius, ionic or crystal radius, etc., depending upon the types of bonding prevalent.

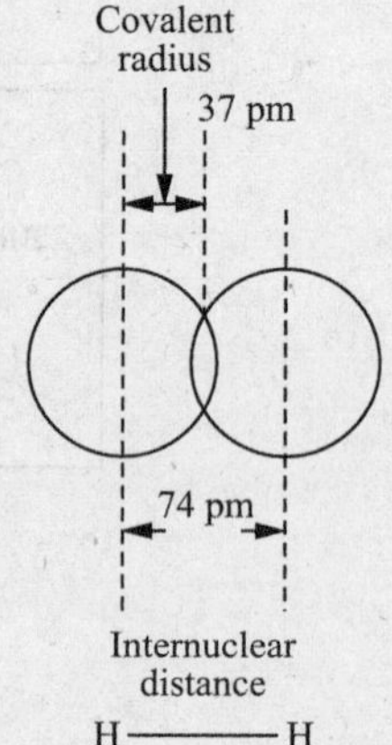

Fig. 3.2: Covalent radius of hydrogen atom

3.2.1 Covalent Radius

The radius of an atom is calculated by measuring the distance between the centres of two atoms (internuclear distance) in molecules with the help of X-ray diffraction or spectral studies. In the case of homonuclear diatomic molecules, the atomic radius is equal to one half of the distance between the centres of nuclei of two similar atoms bonded together in a molecule. The radius is also called covalent radius because the atoms in a homonuclear diatomic molecule are held together by covalent bonds. For example, the internuclear distance between the two atoms in F_2 molecule is 1.28Å or 128 pm (Fig. 3.2).

$$\text{Therefore, Atomic radius of fluorine} = \frac{128 \text{ pm}}{2} = 64 \text{ pm}.$$

It may be mentioned that 1Å = 100 pm.

Similarly, the atomic radii of chlorine and bromine are 99 pm and 114 pm respectively because the internuclear distances in Cl_2 and Br_2 are 198 pm and 228 pm respectively.

In the case of heteronuclear diatomic molecules (containing different atoms) it has been observed that when the covalent radii of different atoms are added, the resulting value agrees fairly well with the experimentally determined internuclear distance of that molecule. For example, the internuclear distance in HCl molecule can be obtained by adding the covalent radii of H and Cl.

$$r\,(\text{HCl}) = r\,(\text{H}) + r\,(\text{Cl}) = 37 + 99 = 136 \text{ pm}$$

The calculated value of internuclear distance is in fair agreement with the experimentally observed internuclear distance of 131 pm in HCl molecule. Again, the atomic radius of H atom may be calculated by subtracting the atomic radius of Cl from the internuclear distance of HCl molecule. In general, the atomic radius of an atom B in AB molecule can be calculated by measuring the internuclear distance (r_{AB}) of AB molecule and subtracting the atomic radius of atom A. Thus,

$$r_B = r_{AB} - r_A$$

The atomic radii of atoms which do not form diatomic molecules with single bonds are calculated by indirect methods. For example, the single bond radii of nitrogen and oxygen are not obtained from the bond lengths in N_2 (N≡N) and O_2 (O═O) because these molecules contain multiple bonds. One half of the internuclear distance of these molecules will correspond to multiple bond radii. The single bond atomic radius of nitrogen is obtained by indirect method. Compounds in which N atom is bonded to another atom by a single bond is selected. For example, the internuclear distance between C—N in H_3 CNH_2 has been found to be 147 pm. Since the atomic radius of carbon is 77 pm (obtained from C—C bond distance in diamond), the atomic radius of nitrogen is (147 – 77) = 70 pm.

3.2.2 Multiple Bond Radii

For multiple bonded atoms, the corresponding radii are called multiple bond radii. For example, carbon has double bonded radius of 66 pm in ethylene ($H_2C{=}CH_2$) and triple bonded radius of 60 pm in acetylene (HC≡CH). The carbon has single bond radius of 77 pm (as in ethane, CH_3—CH_3). Similarly, nitrogen has single, double and triple bond radius of 70 pm, 60 pm and 55 pm respectively. As the number of bonds increases, the attraction between the atoms also increases and, therefore, the atoms approach closer and atomic radius decreases.

Bond	Radius	Bond	Radius
C—C	77 pm	N—N	70 pm
C═C	66 pm	N═N	60 pm
C≡C	60 pm	N≡N	55 pm

3.2.3 Hybridisation and Atomic Radius

The state of hybridisation also affects the radius of an atom. For example, the carbon-hydrogen single bond distance in methane (sp^3 hybridisation), ethylene (sp^2 hybridisation) and acetylene (*sp* hybridisation) is different and therefore, the atomic radius of carbon is different. For example, C—H, internuclear distances are:

$$CH_4 = 114 \text{ pm}, H_2C{=}CH_2 = 111 \text{ pm}, HC{\equiv}CH = 107 \text{ pm}$$

Hybridisation	*s-character*	*Example*	*C – H distance*	*Radius of C*
sp^3	25%	CH_4	114 pm	77 pm
sp^2	33.3%	$H_2C{=}CH_2$	111 pm	74 pm
sp	50%	$HC{\equiv}CH$	107 pm	70 pm

Since the atomic radius of hydrogen is 37 pm, the atomic radius of carbon in CH_4, $H_2C{=}CH_2$ and $HC{\equiv}CH$ is 77 pm, 74 pm and 70 pm respectively. The decrease in atomic radius of carbon or carbon-hydrogen internuclear distance may be explained in terms of increase in *s*-character in going from sp^3 (25%) to sp^2 (33%) to *sp* (50%). With increase in *s*-character, the electron pair between C and H becomes closer to the nucleus resulting in greater attraction. Therefore, atomic radius decreases.

The atomic radii of elements of *s*- and *p*-block elements are given in Table 3.6.

TABLE 3.6 *Atomic radii (in pm) of main group (s and p-block) elements*

Li 123	Be 89	B 80	C 77	N 70	O 66	F 64	Ne* (160)
Na 157	Mg 136	Al 125	Si 117	P 110	S 104	Cl 99	Ar (191)
K 203	Ca 174	Ga 125	Ge 122	As 121	Se 117	Br 114	Kr (200)
Rb 216	Sr 191	In 150	Sn 141	Sb 137	Te 133	I (220)	Xe
Cs 237	Ba 198	Tl 155	Pb 154	Bi 152	Po 153	At —	Rn —

*The values for atomic radii of noble gas atoms are van der Waals radii rather than their covalent bonded radii.

3.2.4 Metallic or Crystal Radius

In case of metals, a large number of atoms are closely packed and are held together by means of metallic bonds. The close packing of the metal atoms is known as *crystal lattice* or *metallic lattice* and this packing is different in different metals. The **metallic radius** may be defined as: *one half of the distance between the nuclei of two adjacent atoms of a metal in a metallic lattice.*

The internuclear distance between the nearest neighbouring atoms in a metallic crystal is determined by X-ray diffraction. This is divided by 2 to obtain the metallic radius.

$$r_{\text{metallic}} = \frac{\textbf{Internuclear distance between two adjacent atoms in metallic lattice}}{2}$$

The metallic radii are larger than the corresponding single bond covalent radii. For example, the covalent radius of sodium is 154 pm, while its metallic radius is 186 pm. This is because metallic bond is weaker than a covalent bond and, therefore, the metal atoms in a metallic lattice are not drawn as close to each other as in a covalent bond.

3.2.5 van der Waals' Radius

van der Waals' radius is defined as *one half of the internuclear distance between the adjacent atoms belonging to two nearest neighbouring molecules of the same substance in the solid state.*

van der Waals (1837-1923)

van der Waals was a Dutch theoretical physicist and thermodynamicist. He is known for his work on equation of state for gases and liquids.

It has been observed that there are some weak forces of attraction between the neutral atoms of noble gas atoms and non-polar molecules of various substances. These are known as van der Waals' forces. Thus, the van der Waals' radius corresponds to the closest approach of two atoms of noble gases or non-polar molecules. The measurement of van der Waals' radius for chlorine is shown in Fig. 3.3.

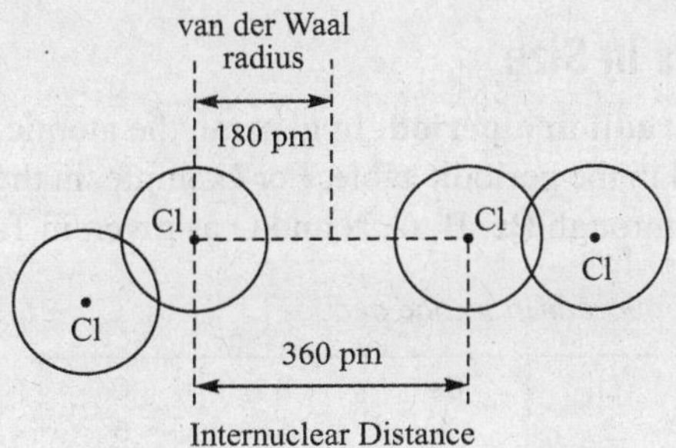

Fig. 3.3: van der Waals' radius of chlorine

Thus,

$$r_{\text{vanderWaals}} = \frac{\textbf{Internuclear distance between two non-bonded nearest neighbouring atoms}}{\textbf{2}}$$

Internuclear distance between two chlorine atoms of nearest neighbouring molecules = 360 pm.

$$\therefore \text{ van der Waals' radius of chlorine} = \frac{360}{2} = 180 \text{ pm}$$

The van der Waals' radii of some atoms are given in Table 3.7 along with their covalent radii. The van der Waals' radii are larger than the covalent radii. This is obvious because in the formation of covalent bond, the atoms come close to each other due to the overlapping of orbitals. On the other hand, van der Waals' forces existing between atoms or molecules (non-bonded) are weaker and the atoms are at larger distances. Therefore, the internuclear distances in case of atoms held by van der Waals' forces is more than that between covalently bonded atoms. Consequently, van der Waals' radii are larger than covalent radii.

TABLE 3.7 *Covalent and van der Waals' radii in pm of some atoms*

Element	N	O	F	Ne	P	S	Cl	Ar
Covalent	77	74	72	—	110	104	99	—
van der Waals'	150	140	135	131	180	190	180	174

3.2.6 Bragg Slater Radii

Bragg and Slater proposed a set of internally consistent atomic radii. These radii can be added, irrespective of the bond type involved in the interaction between two atoms to give good correlations with observed internuclear distances. In general terms, the Bragg Slater radii represent the radii of inner cores of electrons, which in turn determine how closely two atomic species can approach each other. The Bragg Slater radii of elements of second period are given in Table 3.8.

William Bragg (1862-1942)
William Bragg was a British scientist who uniquely shared a Nobel prize with his son W. Lawrence Bragg. He is known for his formulation of Bragg equation in crystallography.

TABLE 3.8 *Covalent and Bragg-Slater radii*

Element	Li	Be	B	C	N	O	F
Covalent radius (pm)	123	89	80	77	70	66	64
Bragg Slater radius (pm)	145	105	85	70	65	60	50

3.2.7 Periodic Trends in Size

1. Variation of atomic radii in a period. In general, the atomic radii decrease as we move from left to right in a period in the periodic table. For example, in the second period, the atomic radii decrease from Li to F through Be, B, C, N and O as given in Table 3.9.

TABLE 3.9 *Decrease in atomic radii in second period*

Element and its atomic no.	Li 3	Be 4	B 5	C 6	N 7	O 8	F 9
Nuclear charge	+3	+4	+5	+6	+7	+8	+9
Atomic radius (pm)	123	89	80	77	70	66	64

This may be explained on the basis of increasing nuclear charge along a period. With the increase in atomic number from lithium to flourine, the magnitude of the nuclear charge increases and the addition of electrons takes place in the same orbit (principal shell). Electrons in the same shell do not screen each other from the nucleus, therefore, increase in nuclear charge is not neutralised by the extra electrons added. The electrons are pulled closer to the nucleus by the increased effective nuclear charge. Hence, we observe a decrease in the size of the atom.

2. Variation of atomic radii in a group. The atomic radius increases from top to bottom in a group. Table 3.10 on next page gives the variation of atomic radius of alkali metals group.

TABLE 3.10 *Atomic radii of alkali metals*

Element	*Atomic No.*	*Outermost Electronic Configuration*	*Atomic radius (pm)*
Li	3	$2s^1$	123
Na	11	$3s^1$	157
K	19	$4s^1$	203
Rb	37	$5s^1$	216
Cs	55	$6s^1$	237

As we move down the group, the nuclear charge increases and it is expected that atomic size should decrease. However, we observe the reverse. This happens because the extra electrons that are added go to the next shell. The effect of increase in size is more pronounced than the effect of increased nuclear charge. Consequently, the distance of outermost electron from the nucleus gradually increases down the group. In other words, atomic size increases as we move down the group.

If we plot atomic radius *vs*. atomic number, we obtain a graph as shown in Fig. 3.4.

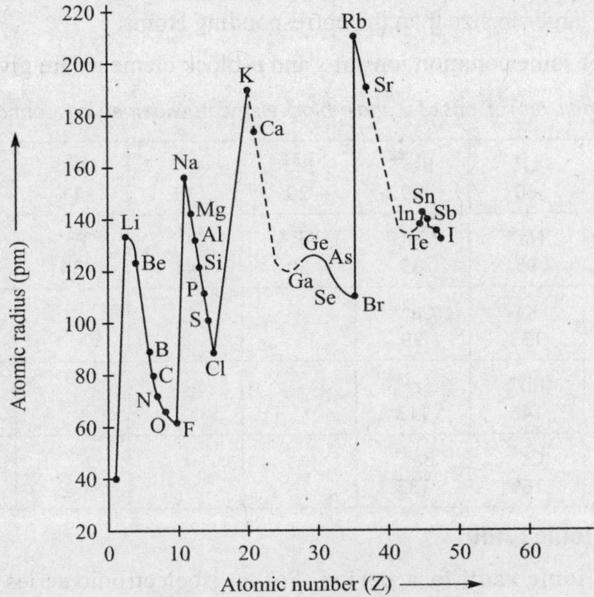

Fig. 3.4: Variation of atomic radii with atomic number

It is evident from the figure that alkali metals occupy the maxima and halogen atoms occupy the minima in the graph. We can infer that alkali metal is the largest and the halogen is the smallest atom in any period.

Noble gases have not been considered in the graph because their radii correspond to the van der Waals' radii.

3.2.8 Ionic and Crystal Radii

The ions are formed as a result of addition or removal of electrons from the outermost shells of atoms. The ions formed by the loss of electrons acquire positive charge and are called **cations** while the ions formed by the gain of electrons acquire negative charge and are called **anions. Ionic radius may be defined as the effective distance from the nucleus of the ion up to which it has an influence in the ionic bond.**

The internuclear distance between the nuclei of adjacent positive and negative ions in a crystal is obtained by X-ray studies or spectroscopic studies. By knowing the radius of one ion, that of the other ions can be calculated.

Size of the cation. Size of a cation is smaller than a neutral atom. This is due to the fact that with the removal of electrons from an atom, the magnitude of nuclear charge remains same while the number of electrons decreases. As a result, the nuclear charge now acts on lesser number of electrons. Electrons are more strongly attracted and are pulled towards the nucleus. This causes a decrease in the size of the atom.

Size of the anion. Size of the negative ion or anion is always larger than that of the corresponding atom. The negative ion is formed by the gain of one or more electrons in the neutral atom and the number of electrons increases while the magnitude of nuclear charge remains the same. As a result, the same nuclear charge acts on large number of electrons. In other words, the electron cloud is held less tightly by the nucleus. This causes an increase in size and thus, anions are larger in size than the corresponding atoms.

The ionic radii of some common ions of *s* and *p*-block elements are given in Table 3.11.

TABLE 3.11 *Ionic radii (pm) of ions of s- and p-block elements with inert gas configuration*

	H 154	Li^+ 60	Be^{2+} 39	B^{3+} 20	C^{4+} 15	N^{5+} 11	O^{6+} 9	
O^{2-} 140	F^- 136	Na^+ 95	Mg^{2+} 65	Al^{3+} 50	Si^{4+} 41	P^{5+} 34	S^{6+} 29	Cl^{7+} 26
S^{2-} 184	Cl^- 181	K^+ 133	Ca^{2+} 99					
Se^{2-} 198	Br^- 195	Rb^+ 148	Sr^{2+} 113					
Te^{2-} 221	I^- 216	Cs^+ 169	Ba^{2+} 135					

Periodic Trends in Ionic Radii

1. **Variation of ionic radii in a period.** For an isoelectronic series (ions having same number of electrons), the ionic radius decreases as the nuclear charge increases.

In an isoelectronic series, there is an increase in nuclear charge and, therefore, the attraction for the same number of electrons increases. As a result, the electrons are pulled more strongly and thus ionic radius decreases. This is given in Table 3.12.

TABLE 3.12 *Variation of ionic radii in an isoelectronic series*

Ion	N^{3-}	O^{2-}	F^-	Na^+	Mg^{2+}	Al^{3+}
Nuclear charge	+7	+8	+9	+11	+12	+13
Radius (pm)	172	140	126	95	65	50

2. **Variation of ionic radii in a group.** As we go down a group, the ionic radii increase with increase in atomic number.

This is mainly due to increase in the principal quantum levels. The effect of increase in principal quantum level is more pronounced than the effect of increased nuclear charge.

3.2.9 Determination of Ionic Radius

Pauling's method for the determination of ionic radius, which is widely accepted is discussed here. However, this method is limited to univalent isoelectronic ions.

The method is based upon the observed internuclear separation in four crystals, namely NaF, KCl, RbBr and CsI. These compounds were selected by Pauling because they have almost the same radius ratio ($r_{cation}/r_{anion} = 0.75$) and nearly equal ionic character and in each of them the cation and anion are isoelectronic (same number of electron).

Two basic assumptions were made by Pauling while assigning radii to the individual atoms.

(*a*) The cation and anion are assumed to be in contact *i.e.*, $r_{(+)} + r_{(-)} = R$(Internuclear distance)

(*b*) The radius of the ion is inversely proportional to the effective nuclear charge (z_{eff}) of the ion.

i.e., $$r_{ion} \propto \frac{1}{Z_{eff}} \qquad ...(i)$$

We know $Z_{eff} = Z - S$ (Refer to Art. 3.6.1)

where Z is the atomic number of the atom and S is the *screening or shielding constant.*

$$r_{ion} \propto \frac{1}{Z - S} \qquad ...(i)$$

$$r_{ion} = \frac{C}{Z - S} \qquad ...(ii)$$

where C is the constant of proportionality and has the same value for two isoelectronic ions.

Let us take the example of sodium fluoride to explain the concept of Pauling for calculating the ionic radii.

The internuclear distance in NaF has been experimentally determined by X-ray technique to be 3.31 Å. (Pauling used anstrom as the unit of distance)

Thus $r_{Na} + r_{F^-} = 3.31$ Å (First assumption of Pauling) ...(*iii*)

Now both Na^+ and F^- ions are isoelectronic i.e., both have 10 electrons and consequently have the same screening constant. The effective nuclear charge on Na^+ and F^- can be calculated by substracting the screening constant from the actual nuclear charge (as per slater rules).

Effective nuclear charge on $Na^+ = Z_{Na}$ – screening constant

$$= 11 - [2 \times 0.85 + 8(0.35)] = 11 - 4.5 = 6.5$$

Effective nuclear charge on $F^- = Z_F$ – screening constant

$$= 9 - 4.5 = 4.5.$$

According to Pauling, the radius of the Na^+ and F^- ion can be evaluated from equation (*ii*) as

$$r_{Na^+} = \frac{C}{6.5} \qquad ...(iv)$$

$$r_{F^-} = \frac{C}{4.5} \qquad ...(v)$$

Substituting the value of (*iv*) and (*v*) in equation (*iii*), we get

$$\frac{C}{6.5} + \frac{C}{4.5} = 2.31$$

On soling the equation, we get the value of C as under:

$$4.5\,C + 6.5\,C = 2.31 \times 6.5 \times 4.5$$

or $$11C = 70.51$$

or $$C = 6.14$$

Substituting the value of C, in equation (iv) and (v), we get

$$r_{Na^+} = 0.95 \text{ Å (or 95 pm)}$$

and $$r_{F^-} = 1.36 \text{ Å (or 136 pm)}$$

This procedure can be used to find out the radii of different cations and anions.

Solved Examples

Example 1: Explain: Increasing order of size in case of following species should be

$$\mathbf{Fe^{3+} < Fe^{2+} < Fe}$$

Solution: When two electrons are removed from Fe atom, Fe^{2+} ion is obtained. As the positive charge on the nucleus outnumbers negative charge on the electrons, the nucleus attracts the electrons with a much greater force resulting in the shrinking of size.

On removal to a further electron to convert Fe^{2+} into Fe^{3+}, difference in the positive charge on nucleus and negative charge on the electron further increases, this increases further the pull of the nucleus on the electrons. Hence the size decreases further. Increasing order of size is therefore

$$Fe^{3+} < Fe^{2+} < Fe$$

Example 2: Ionic radius of K^+ is smaller than that of Cl^-, both are isoelectronic. Explain.

Solution: Electronic configurations of K^+ and Cl^- are

$$K^+ : 1s^2, 2s^2, 2p^6, 3s^2, 3p^6 \text{ (At. No. 19)}$$

$$Cl^- : 1s^2, 2s^2, 2p^6, 3s^2, 3p^6 \text{ (At. No. 17)}$$

Thus both configurations are isoelectronic, *i.e.*, same configuration. However K^+ is smaller in size compared to Cl^-. This is because K^+ has a greater nuclear charge (No. of protons) compared to Cl^-. Therefore electron cloud in K^+ is pulled to a greater extent than in Cl^-. Thus K^+ is smaller in size compared to Cl^-.

Example 3: Radius of a cation is invariably smaller than that of an atom and that of an anion invariably lower than that of the corresponding atom. Explain.

Solution: After an electron is removed from an atom, the cation is obtained.

$$\underset{\text{Atom}}{M} \longrightarrow \underset{\text{Cation}}{M^+} + e$$

Positive charge in M^+ outweighs the negative charge on electron. The pull of the nucleus on the electron, therefore increases. That is why a cation is smaller than the atom. However, when an electron is added to an atom, an anion is obtained.

$$M + e^- \longrightarrow \underset{\text{Anion}}{M^-}$$

Now the electronic charge is greater than the nuclear charge. Moreover repulsion among the electrons will increase thereby increasing the size of the anions compared to that of the neutral atom.

3.3 IONISATION ENTHALPY OR IONISATION ENERGY AND SUCCESSIVE IONISATION ENTHALPY

The ionisation enthalpy or energy of an element is defined as amount of energy required to remove the most loosely bound electron from an isolated gaseous atom.

$$M\,(g) + \text{Ionisation Energy} \longrightarrow M^+\,(g) + e$$

The experimental values of I.E. of elements are determined from their spectra and are reported either in electron volts or in kcal or kJ (1 kJ = 4.184 kcal). Ionisation enthalpy is also known as ionisation energy.

Successive ionisation enthalpies. After the first electron has been removed from a neutral atom, it is possible to remove second, third or even more electrons. The energies required for the removal of subsequent electrons are known as second **IE_2, third IE_3, fourth IE_4 or in general successive ionisation enthalpies.** This may be expressed as

$$A\,(g) + IE_1 \longrightarrow A^+\,(g) + e^- \quad \text{(first ionisation enthalpy)}$$

$$A^+\,(g) + IE_2 \longrightarrow A^{2+}\,(g) + e^- \quad \text{(second ionisation enthalpy)}$$

$$A^{2+}\,(g) + IE_3 \longrightarrow A^{3+}\,(g) + e^- \quad \text{(third ionisation enthalpy)}$$

It is observed that successive ionisation enthalpies go on increasing progressively because it becomes increasingly difficult to remove each successive electron. This is because of the following reasons. (*i*) After the removal of first electron, the atom changes into a positive ion in which the electrons are held more tightly by the nucleus. This is because the positive ion contains smaller number of electrons while the nuclear charge remains the same. Similarly, the removal of the second electron would further increase the attractive force of the nucleus on the remaining electrons and so on. This naturally leads to increases in ionisation energies. (*ii*) Another situation that may arise in many cases is that after the removal of one, two or more electrons from the atom, the next one may be present in a lower energy level. This electron would naturally require much more energy for its removal *e.g.*, after 2 electrons have been removed from 2*s* orbital of Be to form Be^{2+}, the next electron lies in 1*s* orbital. Therefore, the third ionisation energy of beryllium which involves the removals of 1*s* electron has a much higher value than second ionisation enthalpy.

3.3.1 Factors that Govern Ionisation Enthalpy of an Element

The ionisation enthalpy depends upon the following factors:

(*i*) *Magnitude of nuclear charge.* This attractive force of the nucleus on the electron is directly proportional to the product of the nuclear and electronic charges. Therefore as the nuclear charge increases, the electron would be held more strongly by the nucleus. In other words, more energy would have to be supplied to remove the electron from the atom. Thus the ionisation enthalpy increases as the nuclear charge increases.

(*ii*) *Size of the atom.* As the size of the atom increases, the outer electrons are less strongly attracted by the nucleus, because the force of attraction is inversely proportional to the square of the distance between the charged particles. With the decrease in attractive force, the outer electron is less tightly held and is, therefore, easier to remove. Thus the ionisation enthalpy decreases as the size of the atom increases.

(*iii*) *Screening effect of the inner electrons.* The inner electronic shells act as a screen between the nucleus and outer shell. This reduces the pull of the outer shell towards the nucleus. In other words, the electrons that lie between the nucleus and outermost shell have a shielding or screening effect on the electrons of outermost shell. The larger the number of electrons in the inner shells, the greater will be the screening effect and the lesser will be nuclear attraction on the outermost electrons. Thus increase in the number of inner electrons will trend to decrease I.E. It should be carefully noted that electrons in the same or similar type of orbital do not shield each other. Thus the electrons in *s*-orbital will not shield each other. Similarly, electrons in p_x, p_y and p_z orbital of the same subshell do not shield each other. It has also been found that the screening effect of *s*-electron is more than that of *p*-electron whose effect is in turn more than that of a *d*-electron and so on.

Actual charge felt by an electron is termed as **effective nuclear charge** (Z_{eff}).

$$Z_{eff} = \text{Total nuclear charge (Z)} - \text{Screening constant (S)}$$

(*iv*) *Penetration effect of the electrons.* Electrons in the *s*-orbitals have the maximum probability of being nearer to the nucleus while this probability goes on decreasing in case of *p*, *d* and *f* electrons. In other words *s*-electrons have the greatest penetration towards the nucleus and the penetrating effect of the electron with a given principal quantum number, *n* is in the order : $s > p > d > f$. Greater the penetration of electron, greater is the ionisation energy since the electron would be bound more tightly to the nucleus in that case. Thus, for the same value of *n*, the ionisation energy would be more for *s*-electron compared to that for a *p*-electron which is turn will be greater than for *d*-electron and so on.

(*v*) *Electronic arrangement.* (*a*) Noble gases have the most stable electronic configuration having $s^2 p^6$ arrangement of the outermost shell while all the inner shells are also complete.

(*b*) The arrangement in which all the occupied orbitals are completely filled as, for instance, in the case of Be ($1s^2$, $2s^2$) and Mg ($1s^2$, $2s^2$, $2p^6$, $3s^2$).

(*c*) The configuration in which all the orbitals of the same sublevel are exactly half filled also represents a very stable arrangement such as in the case of N ($1s^2$, $2s^2$, $2p^1{}_x 2p^1{}_y$ and $2p^1{}_z$) and *P* ($1s^2$, $2s^2$, $2p^6$, $3s^2$, $3p^1{}_x 3p^1{}_y 3p^1{}_z$).

The more stable the electronic arrangement the greater is the ionisation enthalpy. That is why each noble gas has the highest ionisation enthalpy of the element in the same period.

Example 4: First ionisation enthalpy of Al is lower than that of Mg. Explain.

Solution: Electric configuration of Al is $1s^2$, $2s^2$, $2p^6$, $3s^2$, $3p^1$) and that of Mg is $1s^2$,$2s^2$, $2p^6$, $3s^2$., Although we expect the I.E. to increase as we move form left to right in the periodic table, here the situation is different. Fully filled orbitals are more stable compared to half filled orbital and therefore greater energy is needed to remove the electron. Therefore Mg has a fully filled 3s orbital and it is more difficult to remove the electron from the atom. In Al, it is the electron from half filled 3*p* orbital which is to be removed, this will require comparatively less energy.

3.3.2 Variation in Ionisation Enthalpy (*i*) Along a Period and (*ii*) Down a Group

Variation of ionisation enthalpy with atomic number is shown in Fig. 3.5.

This figure shows the variation of first ionisation enthalpy of elements with atomic number upto atomic number 60. It can be seen that in each period, the maxima are found at the noble gases while minima are found at alkali metals. Thus, the metals of group 1 with one electron in outermost *s*-orbital are easy to ionise while the noble gases (group 18) with ns^2np^6 configuration are the most difficult to ionise. The following periodic trends have been observed.

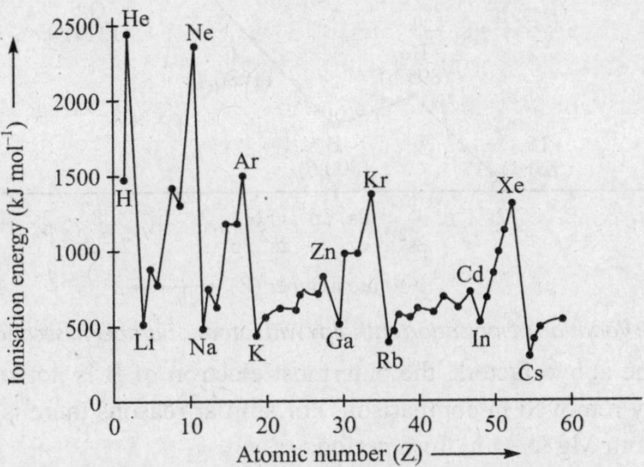

Fig. 3.5: Variation of ionisation enthalpy with atomic number

Variation along a period. In general, the ionisation enthalpy increases with increasing atomic number as we move from left to right along a period. This is because of the following reasons:

(*i*) The nuclear charge increases from left to right.

(*ii*) The number of main energy levels remains the same while the atomic size decreases. Due to the gradual increase in the nuclear charge and simultaneous decrease in the atomic size, the electrons get more and more firmly bound to the nucleus. Therefore it becomes increasingly difficult to remove an electron and hence the ionisation energy keeps on increasing. Some of the exceptional values observed within a period can be explained in terms of the role played by the other factors governing ionisation enthalpy. To illustrate this let us consider the changes in the second period.

As we move from Li to Be there is an increase in the ionisation enthalpy. This may be easily explained in terms of increased nuclear charge and smaller atomic size while other factors do not make a significant contribution.

On passing from Be to B, we observe that in spite of the increased nuclear charge and smaller atomic size, there is a slight decrease in ionisation enthalpy.

This can be explained in terms of following factors:

(*a*) The electronic arrangement of B ($1s^2$, $2s^2$, p_x^1) is less stable that than of Be ($1s^2$, $2s^2$).

(*b*) The outermost electron in B is present in $2p$ orbital which is less penetrating than $2s$ orbital which contains the outermost electron of Be.

(*c*) The outermost electron in B is shielded by 4 electrons while that in Be is shielded only by 2 electrons.

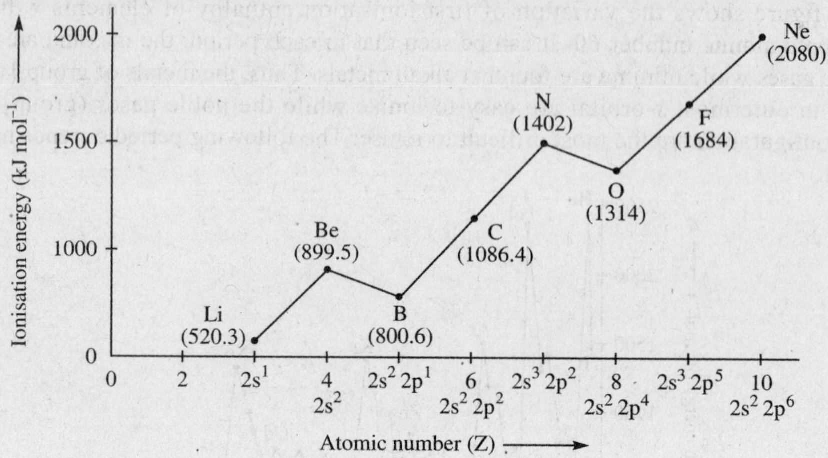

Fig. 3.6: Variation of ionisation enthalpy with atomic number in second period

As a result of the above factors, the outermost electron of B is not so firmly held by the nucleus and is easily removed in comparison. For similar reasons there is a slight decrease in energy in moving from Mg to Al in third period.

As we pass from B to C to N the ionisation enthalpy keeps on increasing primarily due to increasing nuclear charge and decreasing atomic size, the combined effect of other factors not being appreciable.

Oxygen has a slightly smaller ionisation enthalpy than N. This is primarily due to the more stable electronic arrangement of nitrogen ($1s^2$, $2s^2$, $2p_x^1\ 2p_x^1\ 2p_x^1$) in which all the *p* orbitals are half-filled while in oxygen ($1s^2\ 2s^2$, $2p_x^2\ 2p_y^1\ 2p_x^1$) all the *p* - orbitals are neither half-filled not completely filled. In the third period the ionisation energy of *S* is smaller than that of P for similar reasons.

There is increase in ionisation enthalpy in going from O to F to N as expected.

Variation along a group. The values of ionisation energies show a regular decrease in going from top to bottom in a group. This can be attributed to the following factors:

(*i*) In going from top to bottom in a group the nuclear charge increases.

(*ii*) There is a simultaneous increase in the number of energy levels and therefore, the atomic size increases.

(*iii*) There is an increase in the number of electrons that lie in between the nucleus and the outermost electron and therefore, the shielding effect in the outermost electron gradually increases.

The increase in atomic size and the shielding effect more than neutralise the effect of the increased charge. As such the electron in the higher orbital is less firmly bound to the nucleus. Consequently there is gradual decrease in the ionisation enthalpy.

Example 5: The Be and N in second period and Mg and P in the third period of the table have slightly higher ionisation enthalpies than expected. Explain.

Solution: Configurations in which there are fully filled and half filled orbitals are extraordinarily more stable than others. So more energy is needed to take out electrons from the outermost shells. In Be and Mg, there are fully filled orbitals in the outermost shell. Similarly in nitrogen and phosphorus, the outermost shells have half-filled orbitals.

$$_7N: 1s^2, 2s^2, 2p^2{}_x\, 2p_y{}^1\, 2p_z{}^1,\ _{15}P: 1s^2, 2s^2\, 2p^6\, 3s^2\, 3p_x{}^1\, 3p_y{}^1\, 3p_z{}^1$$

Therefore these atoms have higher ionisation enthalpy than expected.

Example 6: Explain: Nitrogen has higher value of I.E. than oxygen.

Solution: Nitrogen has more stable electronic configuration in which the orbitals are all half-filled.

$$_7N: 1s^2, 2s^2\, 2p_x{}^1\, 2p_y{}^1\, 2p_z{}^1$$

$$8O: 1s^2, 2s^2\, 2p_x{}^2\, 2p_y{}^1\, 2p_z{}^1$$

Half-filled configuration is more stable than others. Hence greater energy is needed to extract the electron from them.

Example 7: Calculate the amount of energy required to convert 1.5 g of potassium atoms in the gaseous state to form potassium ions. Ionisation energy of potassium is 419 kJ mole^{-1} and atomic mass of potassium is 39 a.m.u.

Solution:

$$\underset{(1\text{ mole})}{K(g)} + 419\text{ kJ (IE)} \longrightarrow \underset{(1\text{ mole})}{K^+(g)} + \underset{(1\text{ mole})}{\text{electron}}$$

Thus 39 g of potassium atoms require = 419 kJ energy for ionisation

$$\therefore\ 1.5\text{ g of potassium atoms required} = \frac{419}{39} \times 1.5.$$

$$= 16.1\text{ kJ}$$

3.3.3 Determination of Ionisation Energy

Ionisation energy of an element is measured using a discharge tube containing the gas or vapours of atom under consideration at low pressure. It is connected to a source of current. On increasing the potential difference, we reach a point where a sudden flow of current occurs. This is a stage when the gas is ionized or the first ionisation potential occurs. The applied voltage gives the ionisation energy. If we increase the voltage further, again we come to point where there is an abrupt rise of current. This corresponds to second ionisation energy. In this way, we can evaluate third, fourth, fifth etc. ionisation energy. In case of hydrogen, the first ionisation value corresponds to 13.598 eV per atom. Thus, the ionisation energy of hydrogen atom is 13.598 eV per atom.

Converting to SI units,

$$1\text{ eV} = 1.602 \times 10^{-19}\text{ J}$$

Ionisation energy of hydrogen= 13.598 eV per atom

$$= 13.598 \times 1.602 \times 10^{-19}\text{ J per atom}$$

$$= 13.598 \times 1.602 \times 10^{-19} \times 6.023 \times 10^{23}\text{ J mol}^{-1}$$

$$= 1312\text{ kJ mol}^{-1}$$

Thus, the first ionization energy of hydrogen is 1312 kJ mol^{-1}.

3.4 ELECTRON GAIN ENTHALPY (OR ELECTRON AFFINITY)

The amount of energy released when a neutral atom in the gaseous state acquires an extra electron to form a negatively charged ion is known as gain enthalpy. The process may be depicted as

$$A\,(g) + e^-\,(g) \longrightarrow A^-\,(g) + \text{Energy (Electron affinity)}$$

The electron gain enthalpy determines the tendency of an atom to add an extra electron and the firmness with which the added electron is bound to the nucleus.

If an atom has greater tendency to accept an electron, larger amount of energy will be released. Consequently, the gain enthalpy will be high. On the other hand, if an electron has less tendency to hold the electron, smaller amount of energy will be released. Consequently, electron gain enthalpy will be less.

3.4.1 Factors Determining Electron Gain Enthalpy

Electron gain enthalpy of an element depends mainly upon the following factors:

(*i*) *Nuclear charge.* More the nuclear charge of the atom, more strongly will it attract additional electron. Therefore, as electron gain enthalpy increases, the nuclear charge increases.

(*ii*) *Atomic size.* The smaller the size of atom, smaller will be the distance between the extra electron and the nucleus. Therefore, electrostatic force of attraction will be more and the electron affinity will be higher.

(*iii*) *Electronic configuration.* Atoms having stable electronic configuration (*i.e.*, those having completely filled or exactly half-filled outer orbitals) do not show much tendency to add extra electron and have either zero or very low electron affinities.

3.4.2 Variations of Electron Gain Enthalpy in the Periodic Table (*i*) Down the Group and (*ii*) Along the Period

Variation of electron affinity down the group and along a period in the periodic table is discussed as under: (also see Table 3.13)

TABLE 3.13 *Electron gain enthalpies of some elements (kJ mol^{-1})*

H 72.8							He 0
Li 59.8	Be ≈ 0	B 83.0	C 127.5	N ≈ 0	O 140.9	F 327.9	Ne 0
Na 53.1	Mg ≈ 0	Al 50.2	Si 119.6	P 74.3	S 200.7	Cl 348.3	Ar 0
K 48.4	Ca ≈ 0	Ga 35.7	Ge 115.8	As 77.2	Se 195.0	Br 324.2	Kr 0
Rb 47.0						I 295.3	Xe 0

Down a group. The atomic size as well as the nuclear charge increase on moving down the group. But the overall effect of these factors is that the effective nuclear attraction for the electron decreases. As such atom would have less tendency to attract additional electron towards itself so that its electron gain enthalpy would decrease.

Across a period. The atomic size decreases while the nuclear charge increases. Naturally, therefore, the nucleus would have increased attraction for additional electron and electron affinity would be more. But there are many exceptions to this general trend which are mostly due to the relative stabilities of electronic configurations. Electron gain enthalpies of some elements are given in Table 3.13.

3.4.3 Some Important Features of Electron Gain Enthalpies of Different Elements

(i) Electron gain enthalpy of fluorine is smaller than that of chlorine. It has been pointed out above that in general electron gain enthalpies go on decreasing in moving down a group. Therefore, amongst the halogens the electron gain enthalpy of fluorine should be higher than that of chlorine. Actually the electron gain enthalpy of fluorine is lesser than that of chlorine (Fig. 3.7).

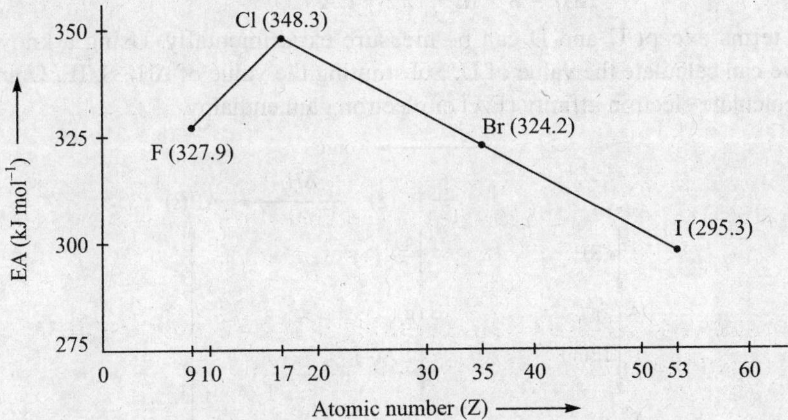

Fig. 3.7: Electron gain enthalpy values of the halogens

This is due to the small size of fluorine atom. In fluorine the second shell is the outermost shell. Due to the small volume of this shell the addition of an extra electron results in strong electron-electron repulsions. As a result, attractive interaction between the incoming electron and the nucleus of fluorine atom is considerably depressed. This result is low electron gain enthalpy of fluorine.

(ii) Electron gain enthalpies of halogens are very high. This is because halogens have the general electronic configuration $n^2\ np^5$. As such they have a strong tendency to acquire an extra electron to change into ions having the stable s^2p^6 configuration of the next noble gas. Therefore their electron gain enthalpies are very high.

(iii) Electron gain enthalpies of noble gases are zero. This can be attributed to the fact that their electronic configurations are very stable and they have absolutely no tendency to add an extra electron in the higher energy level. Similarly, the low value of electron gain enthalpies

in case of elements like Be, Mg. N and P can be explained in terms of their stable electronic arrangements marked by the presence of either only completely filled or exactly half filled orbitals of the same type. Therefore it is not easy to add an electron in their case.

3.4.4 Determination of Electron Gain Enthalpy (Electron Affinity)

There is no direct procedure for the determination of electron gain enthalpy of an element. However, we can calculate it using Born Haber Cycle.

Consider the formation of A^+B^- from the elements A and B and we are interested to find the electron affinity of B. A exists as solid and B as diatomic gas at room temperature. Formation of AB can be illustrated as under. It involves the steps: heat of sublimation (S), ionisation energy (IE), heat of dissociation (D), electron affinity (EA), lattice energy (U) to form the crystal of A^+B^-. The energy required to form the crystal lattice of A^+B^- from A and B at normal room temperature and pressure is called heat of formation ΔH_f. Thus there are two routes to obtain A^+B^- from elemental A and B in their natural state at room temperature and pressure, route I and route II. These two routes are shown below in Fig. 3.8. According the Hess's Law of constant heat summation, the total heat change along the two routes should be equal. Signs of the energy change absorption (+) and evolution (–) are given in Fig. 3.8. Thus

$$\Delta H_f = S + IE + D/2 + EA + U \qquad ...(i)$$

All the terms except U and D can be measure experimentally. Using a known crystal structure, we can calculate the value of U. Substituting the value of ΔH_f, S, IE, D and U in eq (*i*) we can calculate electron affinity (EA) or electron gain enthalpy.

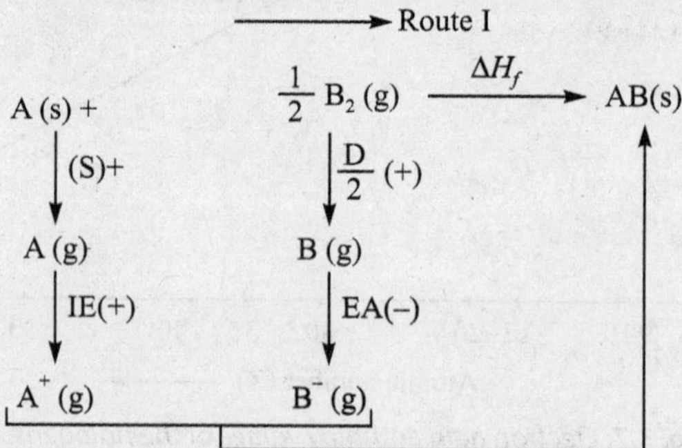

Fig. 3.8: Born-Haber cycle for the formation of A^+B^-

Example 8: Successive electron gain enthalpies have negative value. Explain.

Solution: Successive electron gain enthalpy means gain enthalpy for the addition of second, third or next electrons to the anion after one electron has been added to the neutral atom.

Actually there is a lot of resistance put up by the anions (uninegative) to the addition of more electrons because of repulsive forces. That is why successive electron gain enthalpies have negative values.

Example 9: How much energy in kJ is released when 1.0 g of chlorine atom are converted completely to Cl^- ions in the gaseous state, electron affinity of Cl (g) = 349 kJ and atomic mass of chlorine is 35.5 a.m.u.

Solution:

$$\underset{1\ \text{mole}}{Cl} + \underset{1\ \text{mole}}{\text{electron}} \longrightarrow \underset{1\ \text{mole}}{Cl^-}\ (g) + 349\ \text{kJ}$$

35.5 g of chlorine on conversion to Cl^- ions release 349 kJ of energy.

$\therefore$ 1 g of chlorine on conversion to Cl^- releases $= \frac{349}{35.5} \times 1$ kJ $= 9.83$ kJ

3.5 ELECTRONEGATIVITY

In a covalent bond between two homonuclear atoms, the shared pair of the covalent bond lies exactly midway between the nuclei of the two atoms because both the atoms may have same attraction for these electrons. For example, in molecules such as H_2,Cl_2, F_2, the electron pair remains exactly at half distance between the two nuclei. However, in the case of covalent bond between dissimilar atoms, the electron pair may be closer to one atom than to the other. This is due to the fact that different atoms have different tendencies to attract the bonded pair of electrons towards itself. *The tendency of an atom to attract the shared electron pair in a molecule towards itself is called* **electronegativity.**

Different atoms have different tendencies to attract the bonding electron pair towards themselves. Greater the ability of an atom to attract electrons in a bond, larger is the value of its electronegativity. It must be remembered that unlike other atomic properties such as ionisation energy and electron affinity which are related to the individual gaseous atoms, the electronegativity is related to the atoms in their bonded state. Various attempts have been made to derive a scale of electronegativity for the elements. Some of these are discussed below:

3.5.1 Determination of Electronegativity

Pauling's Scale of Electronegativity

In 1932 Linus Pauling proposed a scale of electronegativity. He based his scale on the difference (ΔE) between the measured bond energy of a molecule A–B [$E_{(A-B)}$] and the energy expected for the purely covalent bond A – B [$E_{(A-B)cov.}$] that is

$$\Delta E = E_{(A-B)} - E_{(A-B)cov} \quad ...(3.1)$$

Linus Pauling (1901-1994)

Linus Pauling was an American chemist. He was one of the most influential chemists in history and ranks among the most important scientists of the 20th century.

According to him if the two atoms A and B have the same electronegativity value then the molecules AB is bonded by purely covalent bonds as in homonucleur molecules A_2 or B_2. Then $E_{(A-B)cov}$ would be the mean of $E_{(A-A)}$ and $E_{(B-B)}$, that is,

$$E_{(A-B)cov} = \frac{1}{2}[E_{(A-A)} + E_{(B-B)}] \quad \text{(Arithmetical mean)}$$

or

$$E_{|A-B|cov} = [E_{(A-A)} + E_{(B-B)}]^{1/2} \quad \text{(Geometrical mean)} \quad ...(3.2)$$

Pauling used geometric mean for his calculations. Substituting from (3.2) into (3.1),

$$\Delta E = E_{A-B} - [E_{A-A} \cdot E_{B-B}]^{1/2} \quad ...(3.3)$$

When molecules AB is purely covalent then

$$E_{(A-B)} = E_{(A-B)cov} \text{ and } \Delta E = 0$$

$$\Delta E = E_{(A-B)} - E_{(A-B)cov} = 0$$

$$\Delta E = E_{(A-B)} - [E_{(A-B)} \cdot E_{B-B}]^{1/2} = 0$$

However, if the two atoms A and B have different electronegativities the bond $A - B$ will no longer be purely covalent and the energy $E_{(A-B)}$ would be greater than the mean of $E_{(A-A)}$ and $E_{(B-B)}$.

$$E_{(A-B)} > [E_{(A-A)} \cdot E_{(B-B)}]^{1/2}$$

In other words, ΔE would be greater than zero. This excess bond energy ΔE is called ionic-covalent resonance energy and arises due to the resonance stabilization of the sort

$$\underset{\text{covalent}}{A - B} \rightleftharpoons \underset{\text{ionic}}{A^{+}B^{-}} \qquad (B \text{ is more electronegative than } A)$$

Such a resonance hybrid of ionic and covalent characters gives rise to a strong bond than a purely covalent or purely ionic bond. The value of ΔE increases as the difference in electronegativity between the two atoms increases. This is clearly indicated on hydrohalides where the value of ΔE decreases as the electronegativity difference between the two atoms (H and $X = F$ to I) decreases.

Halide	HF	HCl	HBr	HI
ΔE (kJ/ mol^{-1})	268	42	46	5

This also indicates decrease in ionic character from HF to HI. In order to assign numerical values for the electronegativity of an element, Pauling proposed the following empirical expression to correlate ΔE with electronegativity difference.

$$0.18\,(\Delta E)^{1/2} = \chi_A - \chi_B \qquad \text{...(3.4)}$$

where χ_A is electronegativity of element A and χ_B is the electronegativity of element B and ΔE is expressed in kcal $mole^{-1}$.

However if ΔE is expressed in eV per molecule then the above expression becomes

$$0.208\,(\Delta E)^{1/2} = \chi_A - \chi_B \qquad \text{...(3.5)}$$

The equation valid for S.I. unit of energy is

$$0.088\,(\Delta E)^{1/2} = \chi_A - \chi_B \qquad \text{...(3.6)}$$

Assigning an arbitrary χ value of 2.1 for H, Pauling got a suitable range of numerical value for the element C to F in the range 2.5 to 4.0. This procedure allowed the evaluation of electronegativity of 14 elements H, C, N, O, F, Si, P, S, Cl, Ge, As, Se, Br and I. Values for others were then calculated from thermochemical data of compounds containing one of these 14 elements. Pauling values of electronegativity are given in Table 3.14. The determination of ΔE is subject to considerable errors and hence numerical values of electronegativity are subject to variation. This exposes the drawback of Pauling's method.

TABLE 3.14 *Electronegativities of some elements*

Element	**Revised Pauling**	**Alfred-Rochow**
H	2.2	2.20
Li.	0.98	0.97
Be	1.57	1.47

(Contd...)

Element	*Revised Pauling*	*Alfred-Rochow*
B	2.04	2.01
C	2.55	2.50
N	3.04	3.07
O	3.44	3.50
F	3.98	4.10
Na	0.93	1.01
Mg	1.31	1.23
Al	1.61	1.47
Si	1.90	1.74
P	2.19	2.06
S	2.58	2.44
Cl	3.16	2.83
Ar	......	......
K	0.82	0.91
Ca	1.00	1.04
Zn	1.65	1.66
Ga	1.81	1.82
Ge	2.01	2.02
As	2.18	2.20
Se	2.55	2.48
Br	2.96	2.74
Kr	2.9	......
Rb	0.82	0.89
Sr	0.95	0.99
Y	1.22	1.11
Cd	1.69	1.46
In	1.78	1.49
Sn	1.96	1.72
Sb	2.05	1.82
Te	2.1	2.01
I	2.66	2.21
Xe	2.6	.....
Cs	0.79	0.86
Ba	0.89	0.97
Hg	2.00	1.44
Tl	2.04	1.44
Pb	2.33	1.55
Bi	2.02	1.67

Example 10: Calculate electronegativity of C in C—H bond if $E_{C—H}$, $E_{H—H}$ and $E_{C—C}$ are 98.8, 104 and 83 kcal/mole respectively.

Solution: Pauling equation relating ΔE and electronegativity difference between the two elements

$$0.18 \times (\Delta E)^{1/2} = \chi_C - \chi_H$$

ΔE in the present case is obtained as under:

$$\Delta E = E_{C—H} - [E_{C—C} \cdot E_{H—H}]^{1/2}$$

$$= 98.8 - (83 \times 104)^{1/2}$$

$$= 98.8 - 92.9 = 5.9$$

Now

$$0.18\,(5.9)^{1/2} = X_C - 2.1$$

$$X_C = 2.1 + 0.18 \times 5.9^{1/2}$$

$$= 2.1 + 0.18 \times 2.43$$

$$= 2.1 + 0.44 = 2.54$$

Example 11: Electronegativities of hydrogen and fluorine are 2.1 and 4.0 respectively. Calculate the percentage ionic character in HF.

Solution: According to Pauling, when the electronegativity difference between two elements is 1.7 percentage of ionic character is 50.

Therefore, per cent of ionic character if the electronegativity difference is (4.0 – 2.1) or 1.9

$$= \frac{1.9}{1.7} \times 50 = 56$$

Mulliken's Scale of Electronegativity

According to Mulliken, electronegativity of an element is the arithmetic mean of its ionization potential and electron affinity.

$$\text{Thus electronegativity} = \frac{\text{Ionisation Potential + Electron affinity}}{2}$$

The physical picture of Mulliken concept is reasonable because the tendency of an atom to attract the shared electrons in a bond should be average of the tendency of the atom to hold its own electrons (IE) and the tendency to attract the additional electron (EA).

Mulliken also suggested the following empirical equation for calculating electronegativity of an element:

$$\chi = 0.374 \left[\frac{\text{IE + EA}}{2}\right] + 0.17$$

$$= 0.187\,[\text{IE + EA}] + 0.17$$

Here IE and EA values are in electron-volts.

It is possible to calculate the electronegativity of an element on Pauling scale if its electronegativity is known on Mulliken scale by using the relationship

$$\text{Electronegativity on Pauling scale (in eV)} = \frac{\text{Electronegativity on Mulliken scale (in eV)}}{2.8}$$

Disadvantage of Mulliken Scale is that IE and EA values change with the valance state of the element.

Sanderson Electron Density Ratio

Sanderson's findings are based upon the Mulliken observations that elements with large first ionisation enthalpy tend to have very negative eletron affinity and therefore gains electrons while the elements with small first ionisation enthalpy tend to lose electrons. If it is difficult to remove an electron, then the atom would naturally want electrons in its outer shell. It would more likely take the electrons from another atom than give them away.

According to Sanderson, electrons distribute themselves around the nucleus of an atom in such a way that minimises or equalises their eletronegativity, when two or more atoms of different electronegativities take part in bond formation, the charges become equalised within the molecule.

Electron loss causes an increase in electronegativity because the atom now even more strongly wants eletrons and vice-versa. Eletron gain results in decrease in electronegativity since the atom has now achieved the electron that it wanted and is now less anxious to get it. Sanderson findings convey the distribution of electrons in the molecules comprised of atoms of unequal electronegativity in such a way that their electron densities are equalised or their electronegativities are equalised.

Alfred-Rochow Electronegativity

Alfred and Rochow proposed an empirical approach to electronegativity based on electrostatic force between the nucleus and electron. They defined electronegativity as electrostatic force (F) exerted by the effective nuclear charge (Z_{eff}) on the outermost electron at a distance r from the nucleus. That is

$$F \propto \frac{Z_{eff}}{r^2}$$

where r = covalent radius of the atom in Å,

Z_{eff} is calculated according to Slater rules based on screening effect of intervening electrons. The attractive force (F) is then correlated to electronegativity value on the Pauling scale using an empirical relationship to obtain Alfred-Rochow electronegativities χ_{AR} (AR for Alfred-Rochow).

$$\chi_{AR} = 0.359 \times \frac{Z_{eff}}{r^2} + 0.744$$

The electronegativity values so obtained agree quite closely with those of Pauling's (Table 3.4).

Advantages

(*i*) Alfred-Rochow method depends on measuring covalent distance which are obtained with greater accuracy by X-ray diffraction. Therefore the X_{AR} values are quite accurate.

(*ii*) The Alfred-Rochow approach is based on the more fundamental and reasonable dependence of coulombic force on distance.

Disadvantages

(*i*) Slater rules used for calculated Z_{eff} are empirical and may not give accurate values.

(*ii*) Covalent radii are inaccurate when the bond order is not known.

Mulliken-Jaffee Electronegativity Concept

Jaffee and his co-workers revised the Mulliken definition and suggested that electronegativity of an atom is different in different environment. Some of the factors which affect electronegativity values are as follows:

(*a*) Oxidation state. Electronegativity of an atom varies from one bonding situation to another depending upon the oxidation number of the atom in the molecule, for example, Pauling electronegativity value is 1.62 for TI(I) whereas it is around 2.04 for T1(II). Similarly, electronegativity of S in SF_6 is higher than that in $SC1_2$ because the former has S in higher oxidation state. The higher the oxidation state, the greater the attraction for electron and higher the electronegativity.

(*b*) Hybridization. It affects electronegativity value considerably because *s*-orbital due to its higher penetration effect is more tightly held than other orbitals and hence has low energy. Consequently it will have greater tendency to attract electrons and hence show higher electronegativity values, for example, carbon in CH_4 is sp^3 hybridized which has 25% *s*-character. The electronegativity of C in CH_4 is 2.53. In ethylene $H_2C{=}CH_2$, carbon is sp^2 hybridized which has 33% *s*-character. The electronegativity of C in C_2H_4 is 2.75. In case of acetylene $HC{\equiv}CH$, carbon is *sp* hybridized which has 50% *s*-character. Thus electronegativity of C in C_2H_2 is raised and its value is referred to be 3.3.

(*c*) Charge. An atom with a positive charge will attract electrons more readily than a neutral atom while a negatively charged atom will attract electron less readily than a neutral atom.

(*d*) Bond order. As bond order of the atom whose electronegativity is under discussion increases, its electronegativity increases, for example, C in C_2H_2 is more electronegative than C in C_2H_4.

Periodic Variation of Electronegativity

The electronegativity generally increases on moving across a period from left to right. This is due to decrease in atomic size and increase in effective nuclear charge. As a result of increase in effective nuclear charge, the attraction for the electrons increases.

Electronegativity generally decreases from top to bottom in a group as atomic size increases and the bonding electrons become away from the nucleus.

Thus, the alkali metals of group 1 have the lowest electronegativities and the halogens of group 17 have the highest electronegativities. Further, inspection of Table 3.14 shows that the non-metals on the right-hand side of the periodic table have high electronegativities while the metals on the left-hand side have low electronegativities. As an approximation, elements with electronegativity 2.0 or greater are non-metals while those with electronegativity less than 2.0 are metals.

It is clear from Table 3.14 that the electronegativity generally increases on moving across a period from left to right and decreases on moving down a group.

Applications of Electronegativities

Some of the important applications of electronegativity values are described below:

1. Types of bonds. The type of bond formed between two atoms would depend upon the difference in their electronegativities. If this difference is zero or very small, the bond formed would be covalent and if the difference exceeds 2.5, the bond formed would be electrovalent. If, however, the electronegativity difference is less than 2.5 but otherwise quite appreciable, the bond formed would be a polar bond.

2. Explanation of diagonal relationship. The electronegativity increases as we go from Li to Be (variation of electronegativity in a period) but it decreases as we move from Be to Mg (variation of electronegativity in a group). As a result of these two opposite changes (one along the period and the other down the group), as we move diagonally, these two effects partly cancel each other and there is no appreciable change in electronegativity. This is the reason why Li (1.0) and Mg (1.2) have close values of electronegativities.

Because of similar values of electronegativities, Li and Mg have similar chemical properties.

3. Explanation for bond angles. The lesser the electronegativity of the central atom in a polyatomic molecule, the lesser would be the magnitude of the bond angle. If the electronegativity of the central atom is less, it would not be able to hold the bonding electron pairs towards itself. Therefore, the bonding electron pairs would shift more towards the other atoms attached to the central atom. This would result in a decrease in the bond pair–bond pair repulsion and hence a decrease in the bond angle will be observed.

This is illustrated by the bond angles and electronegativities of trifluorides of the fifth group elements as given below. The decrease in electronegativity of the central atom results in a decrease of the bond angle.

Compound	***Electronegativity of Central Atom***	***Bond Angle***
NF_3	3.0	102°
PF_3	2.1	97°
AsF_3	2.0	96°
SbF_3	1.9	88°

4. Calculation of bond length. If the two atoms A and B bonded together through a covalent bond differ in their electronegativities, then the covalent bond would acquire some ionic character. In other words, the bond acquires polarity. The greater the polarity, the shorter would be the length of the bond formed between A and B. Shoemaker and Stevenson proposed the following empirical equation for calculating the bond length in such cases:

$$d_{A-B} = r_A + r_B - 0.09\,(\chi_A - \chi_B)$$

where d_{A-B} is the actual bond distance between A and B; r_A and r_B are the covalent radii of A and B and $\chi_A - \chi_B$ is the electronegativity difference. The normal length of the covalent bond between A and B would have been equal to $r_A + r_B$. Evidently, the shortening of the bond between A and B due to electronegativity difference is equal to $0.09\,(\chi_A - \chi_B)$. Due to reduction in length, the bond would be more stable.

We can calculate the bond distance N—O with the help of above equation. Covalent radii of nitrogen and oxygen atoms are, respectively, 0.75 and 0.74 Å and the electronegativities of N and O are 3.0 and 3.5, respectively. Thus,

$$d_{N—O} = 0.75 + 0.74 - 0.09\,(3.5 - 3.0) = 1.445 \text{ Å}$$

The actual N—O bond length is 1.46 Å.

5. Calculation of partial ionic character of a covalent bond. The ionic character in a covalent bond between two atoms, say, A and B, is due to the difference in the electronegativities of A and B. Greater the difference in the electronegativities, greater would be the ionic character and consequently the higher would be the stability of the resulting bond.

Pauling suggested an empirical equation for calculating the per cent ionic character, according to which

$$\text{Per cent ionic character} = 18(\chi_A - \chi_B)^{1.4} \quad ...(i)$$

According to this equation, the per cent ionic character of HF comes out to be 44.12. This value is quite close to the one (*viz.* 44.8) obtained by Pauling from dipole moment of HF.

The relationship between ionic character and electronegativity difference was further improved as under:

$$\%\ \text{ionic character} = 16[\chi_A - \chi_B] + 3.5[\chi_A - \chi_B]^2 \quad ...(ii)$$

3.6 EFFECTIVE NUCLEAR CHARGE AND SCREENING EFFECT

The relation between energy and energy shell for an electron in hydrogen atom is given by expression

$$E = -R\frac{Z^2}{n^2} \quad ...(3.7)$$

For hydrogen atom ($Z = 1$, $n = 1$), the energy of the outermost electron calculated from equation (3.7) agrees with the observed I.E. 1312 kJ mole^{-1}. However the calculated and observed value for atom with $Z > 1$ do not agree fairly. The observed ionization energy of say Li is considerably lower than that calculated from equation (3.7) because of following reasons:

(*i*) The expression does not hold good for multi-electron atom because it does not take inter-electronic repulsions into account.

(*ii*) The $2s^1$ electron does not face the nuclear charge directly. There are intervening $1s^2$ electrons which not only shield the nucleus but also repel the $2s^1$ electron resulting in removal of the electron.

Thus the inner core of electrons shield or screen the nucleus from outer electron. Consequently the outer electrons experience only a part of the nuclear charge or the effective nuclear charge faced by the outer electron is lower than that expected from total nuclear charge. In case of Li, the effective nuclear charge faced by $2s^1$ electron is not 3 but between 1 and 2 (actual value is 1.59). However if we recall the radical probability distribution curve of 2*s* orbital in hydrogen like atoms, it is apparent that 2*s* electron has definite probability of finding itself near the nucleus and hence would penetrate the inner 1*s* orbital core. This means that although 2*s* electron is shielded by the 1*s* core yet 2*s* electron penetrates it to some extent and experiences somewhat higher nuclear charge. In fact the energy of outer electron is determined by the effective nuclear charge (Z_{eff}) which is less than Z (nuclear charge) by an amount shielding constant (S) of the intervening core of the electrons

$$Z_{eff} = Z - S$$

Due to greater penetration, *s*-electrons tend to shield the nucleus more effectively than *p*-electrons which in turn shield the nucleus more effectively than *d*-electrons. That is, for a given *n,* the screening or shielding effect varies as

$$s > p > d > f$$

3.6.1 Slater Rules for Determining Effective Nuclear Charge

Slater gave a set of empirical rules for calculating the effective nuclear charge (Z_{eff}) experienced by electrons in different orbitals. As stated above, the Z_{eff} acting on a given electron is calculated by subtracting the screening constant (*S*) from the atomic number *Z* (nuclear charge).

That is: $Z_{eff} = Z - S$

The 'Slater rules' for calculating screening on shielding constant (*S*) are as follows:

1. The electronic configuration of the element is first written in the following order and groupings: (1*s*); (2*s*, 2*p*); (3*s*, 3*p*); (3*d*); (4*s*, 4*p*); (4*d*); (4*f*); (5*s*, 5*p*); (5*d*); (5*f*) and so on.

2. For an electron considered in a group of *s, p* electrons the shielding constant (*S*) is the sum of the following contributions:

(*a*) No contribution for electrons in groups beyond the one considered.

(*b*) An amount of 0.35 for each electron in the group considered (except in 1*s* group where 0.30 is used instead of 0.35).

(*c*) An amount of 0.85 for each electron in the next inner shell ($n - 1$).

(*d*) An amount of 1.00 for each of all other inner shell electrons.

3. For an electron considered in *d* or *f* group, rules 2*a* and 2*b* apply as such; however rules 2*c* and 2*d* are replaced with the rule that all other electrons lying to the left of *d* or *f* group contribute 1.00 each.

Example 12: Calculate Z_{eff} faced by a 3*s* or 3*p* electron in phosphorus atom ($Z = 15$, $1s^2\ 2s^2\ 2p^6\ 3s^2\ 3p^3$)

Solution: Group configuration = ($1s^2$) ($2s^2$, $2p^6$) ($3s^2$, $3p^3$). Four other electrons in the group ($3s^2$, $3p^3$) contribute 4×0.35 and next inner shell contributes 8×0.85 and then the next 2×1.

For a 3*s* or 3*p* electron,

$$S = (2 \times 1.00) + (8 \times 0.85) + (4 \times 0.35)$$

$$S = 2.00 + 6.80 + 1.40 = 10.20$$

$$Z_{eff} = 15 - 10.20 = 4.80$$

Example 13: Calculate Z_{eff} experienced by a 2*p* electron in oxygen atom

Z (8, $1s^2$, $2s^2\ 2p^4$)

Solution: Group configuration = ($1s^2$); ($2s^2\ 2p^4$)

There are 5 other electrons in group ($2s^2$, $2p^4$) under consideration which contribute 5×0.35 towards *S*. Next inner shell contributes 2×0.85. Thus for a 2*p* electron

$$S = (2 \times 0.85) + 5 \times (0.35) = 3.45$$

$$Z_{eff} = (8 - 3.45) = 4.55$$

Example 14: Calculate Z_{eff} experienced by (*i*) 5*s* electron (*ii*) 4*d* electron in Ag atom ($Z = 47$, $1s^2$, $2s^2$, $2p^6$, $3s^2$, $3p^6$, $3d^{10}$, $4s^2$, $4p^6$, $4d^{10}$, $5s^1$).

Solution: Group configuration = ($1s^2$), ($2s^2$, $2p^6$); ($3s^2$, $3p^6$); ($3d^{10}$) ($4s^2$, $4p^6$), ($4d^{10}$) ($5s^1$)

(*i*) For 5*s* electron,

$$S = (28 \times 1.00) + (18 \times 0.85) + (0 \times 0.35)$$

$$= 43.30$$

$$Z_{eff} = 47 - 43.30 = 3.70$$

***(ii)* For 4*d* electron,** $S = (36 \times 1.00) + (9 \times 0.35) + 0$

$$= 39.15$$

$$Z_{eff} = 47 - 39.15 = 7.85$$

Example 15: Calculate Z_{eff} for *(i)* 4s and *(ii)* 3*d* electron in iron atom

$$Z = (26, 1s^2, 2s^2, 2p^6, 3s^2, 3p^6, 3d^6, 4s^2)$$

Solution: Group configuration = $(1s^2)$; $(2s^2, 2p^6)$; $(3s^2\ 3p^6)$; $(3d^6)$; $(4s^2)$

***(i)* For 4s electron,** $S = (10 \times 1.00) + (14 \times 0.85) + (1 \times 0.35) = 22.25$

$$Z_{eff} = 26 - 22.25 = 3.75$$

(ii) In case of 3*d* electron, there is no contribution from outer 4*s* group electrons inner of 3*d* contribute one each.

Example 16: Calculate the effective nuclear charge for

***(i)* an electron in 3*d* orbital, and**

***(ii)* an electron in 4s orbital of chromium (*Z* = 24) with electronic configuration = $1s^2, 2s^2, 2p^6, 3s^2, 3p^6, 3d^5, 4s^1$**

Solution: Group configuration $(1s^2)$, $(2s^2\ 2p^6)$ $(3s^2\ 3p^6)$ $(3d^5)$, $(4s^1)$

***(i)* For 3*d* electron.** There is no contribution from outer 4*s*. Remaining 4 electrons in 3*d* contribute 4 × 0.35 and all others contribute one each.

$$S = (18 \times 1) + (4 \times 0.35) + (4 \times 0)$$

$$= 18 + 1.40 + 0 = 19.40$$

$$Z_{eff} = 24 - 19.40 = 4.60$$

***(ii)* For 4*s* electron.** There are no other electron in 4*s*. Consequently there is no contribution and we have 0 × 0.35 = 0.

Next inner shell (*n* = 3) has 13 electrons contributing 13 × 0.85, others contribute each and we have

$$S = (10 \times 1) + (13 \times 0.85) + (0 \times 0.35)$$

$$= 10 + 11.45 + 0 = 21.45$$

$$Z_{eff} = 24 - 21.45 = 2.55$$

Example 17: Calculate Z_{eff} for valence electrons in Ca and Br.

Solution:

(a) Electronic configuration for Ca is

$$1s^2\ 2s^2\ 2p^6\ 3s^2\ 3p^6\ 4s^2$$

This can be grouped as

$$1s^2, (2s^2, 2p^6), (3s^2, 3p^6), 4s^2$$

Screening constant of 4*s* electron

$$= (1 \times 0.35) + (8 \times 0.85) + (10 \times 1)$$

$$= 17.15$$

Hence $Z_{eff} = 20 - 17.15 = 2.85$

(*b*) Electronic configuration for Br is

$$1s^2\ 2s^2\ 2p^6\ 3s^2\ 3p^6\ 4s^2\ 3d^{10}\ 4p^5$$

This can be grouped as

$$1s^2, (2s^2, 2p^6), (3s^2, 3p^6), 3d^{10}, (4s^2, 4p^5)$$

Screening constant of 4*p* electron

$$= (4 \times 0.35) + (10 \times 0.85) + (18 \times 1)$$
$$= 27.9$$

Hence, $Z_{eff} = 35 - 27.9 = 7.1$

3.6.2 Important Applications of Slater Rules

1. It justifies the filling of 4*s* orbitals in preference to (*n* –1) *d* orbitals. For example, potassium has electronic configuration,

$$1s^2\ 2s^2\ 2p^6\ 3s^2\ 3p^6\ 4s^1$$

Here Z_{eff} for $3d = 19 - (10 \times 1.00) + (8 \times 0.85) = 2.20$

If the electronic configuration were

$$1s^2\ 2s^2\ 2p^6\ 3p^6\ 3d^1$$

Then Z_{eff} for $3d = 19 - [(18 \times 1.00) + 0 \times 0.35)] = 1.00$

This shows that a 4*s* electron experiences a higher Z_{eff} and hence a configuration in which 4*s* is occupied in preference to 3*d* would be more stable.

2. Although Slater rules do not allow the exact calculations of the energies of electron, yet these are useful in understanding variation in size, ionization potential and electronegativity. For example, for an outer electron in elements along the 3rd period, we notice the following trend in Z_{eff} value.

Element	P	S	Cl	Ar	H
Z_{eff}	4.80	5.45	6.10	6.75	(2.2)

This shows that Z_{eff} increases along the period and attains maximum value at the noble gas which accounts for increasing ionization potential along the period with maximum at the noble gas. Ionization potential shows sudden drop after that as evidenced in Z_{eff} value of H.

Example 18: 4*s* subshell is filled first and 3*d* later on while 2*p* subshell is filled first and 3*p* later on. Explain the reason.

Solution:

(*i*) The problem can be discussed by taking the case of potassium (K).

It has an electronic configuration:

$$1s^2\ 2s^2\ 2p^6\ 3p^6\ 4s^1 \text{ and not } 1s^2\ 2s^2\ 2p^6\ 3s^2\ 3p^6\ 3d^1$$

Let us calculate effective nuclear charge on the outermost electron based on the two configurations.

Configuration I

E.N.C. for 4*s* electron $= [19 - (10 \times 1) + (8 \times 0.85)] = 2.20$

Configuration II

E.N.C. for 4*s* electron $= 19 - [(18 \times 1) + (0 \times 0.35)] = 1$

Greater E.N.C means greater stability and lower energy. Hence the configuration I is observed and 4*s* subshell has lower energy and filled first.

(*ii*) 2*p* is filled first and 3*p* later on.

This can be studied by calculating the E.A.N. of last electron in atom with atomic No. 5 *viz*., boron. The two posibilities are:

$1s^2\ 2s^2\ 2p^1$ (Configuration I)

$1s^2\ 2s^2\ 3p^1$ (Configuration II)

E.A.N. of last *i.e.*, $2p^1$ electron (Configuration I) according to Slater Rule is

$$= 5 - [(2 \times 0.35) + (2 \times 0.85)]$$
$$= 5 - [0.70 + 1.70]$$
$$= 5 - (2.40) = 2.6$$

E.A.N. of last $3p^1$ electron (Configuration II)

$$= 5 - (2 \times 0.85) + (2 \times 1)\ ]$$
$$= 5 - 3.7 = 1.3$$

Thus in configuration I, E.A.N of the $2p^1$ electron is higher indicating lower energy and greater stability of 2*p* orbital compared to 3*p* orbital.

3.6.3 Limitations of Slater Rules

(*i*) Both *s* and *p* orbitals are grouped together for calculating Z_{eff} whereas the radial probability distribution curves for a given *n* indicate a higher penetration or shielding effect of *s* as compared to *p*-orbital.

(*ii*) All electrons irrespective of *s, p, d,* or *f* orbitals at positions lower than the $(n - 1)$ shell shield the *n* shell electron with equal contribution of 1.00. This is unjustified because different orbitals cannot have the same contribution on energy consideration.

(*iii*) Penetration by higher occupied orbitals (than the one considered) into inner orbitals is well known but even then their contribution is ignored as per Slater Rule 2*a*.

Summary of variation in periodic properties

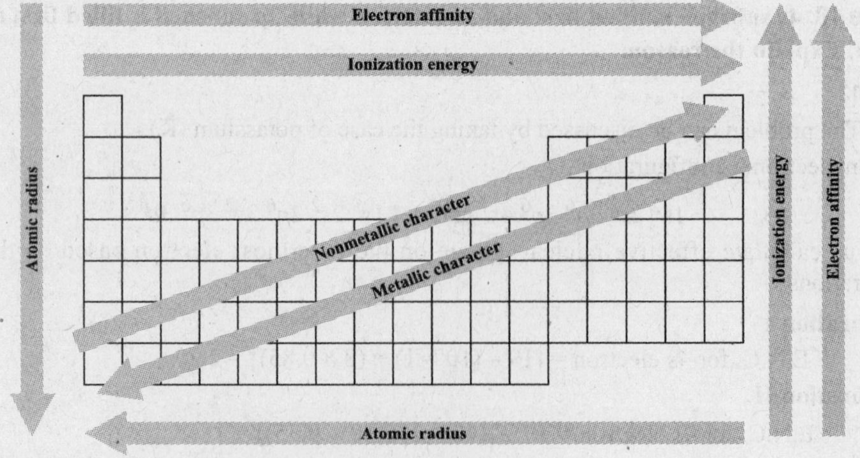

Evaluate Yourself

Multiple Choice Questions

1. The most electronegative elements have electronic configuration

(*a*) $ns^2\ np^3$ (*b*) $ns^2\ np^4$ (*c*) $ns^2\ np^5$ (*d*) $ns^2\ np^6$

2. In this order of elements: C, N, O, F the electronegativity

(*a*) decreases (*b*) increases

(*c*) remains constant (*d*) none of these

3. Highest electron affinity is of the element

(*a*) P (*b*) Cl (*c*) Br (*d*) I

4. $1s^2\ 2s^2\ 2p^6\ 3s^2$ is the electronic configuration of the element. The element is a

(*a*) metal (*b*) non-metal (*c*) inert gas (*d*) metalloid

5. Which ion is colourless ?

(*a*) Cu^+ (*b*) Co^{2+} (*c*) Ni^{2+} (*d*) Fe^{3+}

6. General electronic configuration of transition elements is

(*a*) $ns^2\ nd^{1-10}$ (*b*) $ns^2\ np^6\ nd^{1-10}$

(*c*) $(n-1)\ d^{1-10}\ np^6$ (*d*) $(n-1)\ d^{1-10}\ ns^{1-2}$

7. Increasing order of electronegativity of the elements is

(*a*) C, N, Si, P (*b*) N, Si, C, P

(*c*) Si, P, C, N (*d*) P, Si, C, N

8. Which of the *s* block elements is liquid

(*a*) Na (*b*) K (*c*) Mg (*d*) Cs

9. Lowest ionisation potential will be of

(*a*) halogens (*b*) inert gases

(*c*) *d*-block (*d*) alkali metals

10. In modern periodic table, how the elements are arranged ?

(*a*) Increasing mass (*b*) Decreasing volume

(*c*) Increasing atomic number (*d*) Alphabetically

11. Which ion has smallest size?

(*a*) N^{-3} (*b*) O^{-2} (*c*) F^- (*d*) Na^+

12. Which of the following alkaline earth metals has lowest ionisation potential?

(*a*) Mg (*b*) Ca (*c*) Sr (*d*) Ba

13. Which one of the following statement is not correct for transition elements?

(*a*) They form coloured compounds

(*b*) All compounds of them are paramagnetic

(*c*) They show variable oxidation states

(*d*) They have incomplete *d*-orbital

14. Which element is radioactive?

(*a*) Tc (*b*) Fe (*c*) Os (*d*) W

15. Most reactive element is

(*a*) Na (*b*) Fe (*c*) Hg (*d*) Cs

16. The electronic configuration of an elements is [Ar] $3d^2\ 4s^2$. The element belongs to
    (*a*) *s*-block (*b*) *p*-block (*c*) *d*-block (*d*) *f*-block
17. Magic number is
    (*a*) 3 (*b*) 54 (*c*) 20 (*d*) 19
18. Which element has lowest melting point and boiling point ?
    (*a*) Hydrogen (*b*) Helium (*c*) Neon (*d*) None
19. Elements of atomic number 10,18, 36, 54, 86 are called
    (*a*) light element (*b*) inert gases
    (*c*) halogens (*d*) rare earth elements
20. Which element has highest electron affinity ?
    (*a*) Cl (*b*) Br (*c*) N (*d*) Na

Short Answer Questions

1. Explain the cause of periodicity of properties of elements after certain regular interval giving some examples.
2. Write the American chemical society and IUPAC symbols for elements from atomic numbers 104 to 107.
3. Explain why we cannot define the absolute size of an atom.
4. Give two examples of compounds involving *sp*, sp^2 and sp^3 hybridisation.
5. Bring out the difference between metallic radius and van der Walls radius.
6. Describe the variation of atomic radii in a period and down a group.
7. What is meant by successive ionisation energies. Third ionisation energy of Be is much higher than second ionisation energy. Explain.
8. Define electron affinity. Name three factors that determine its value.
9. Write a note on Pauling scale of electronegativity.
10. Explain two applications of electronegativity value.

Long Answer Questions

1. Define atomic radius. How do the atomic radii of elements vary when we move (*i*) down a group (*ii*) across a period? How would you account for this conclusion?
2. What is ionisation energy? On what factors does it depend? How does the ionisation energy of the elements vary as we move down a group and along a period?
3. Give reasons for each of the following:
   (*a*) The size of an anion is larger than its parent atom.
   (*b*) Electron affinities of halogens are by far the highest.
   (*c*) The second ionisation energy of an atom is always than the first ionisation energy of an atom.
   (*d*) The second electron affinity of oxygen is negative.
   (*e*) The size of an atom cannot be defined precisely.
4. (*a*) Define ionisation energy and electron affinity. How do these vary in the periodic table as the atomic number increases?

(*b*) Account for the following trend in electron affinity values of halogens?

F	Cl	Br	I
332.6 kJ mol^{-1}	341.5 kJ mol^{-1}	324.7 kJ mol^{-1}	295.5 kJ mol^{-1}

(*c*) The electron affinities of noble gases are zero. Why?

5. (*a*) The radii of positive ions are always smaller than the radii of the corresponding atoms. Discuss.

(*b*) What are isoelectronic ions? Account for the decrease in size of the following isoelectronic ions:

$$O^{2-} > F^{-} > Na^{+} > Mg^{2+}$$

6. (*a*) Which of the following electronic configurations would you expect to have the lowest ionisation energy? Explain.

(*i*) $1s^2\ 2s^2\ 2p^6$ (*ii*) $1s^2\ 2s^2\ 2p^5$ (*iii*) $1s^2\ 2s^2\ 2p^6\ 3s^1$

(*b*) Mg^{2+} ion is smaller than O^{2-} ion although both have same electronic structure. Explain.

(*c*) The three ionisation energies of boron atom are 800, 2427 and 3658 kJ mol^{-1}. Explain these values.

7. (*a*) Explain the term electron affinity. Why are electron affinities of halogens so high?

(*b*) Predict which element in each of the following pairs has higher ionisation energy and why?

(*i*) Be, B (*ii*) N, C (*iii*) Ne, F (*iv*) I, Br

(*v*) Na, K

8. (*a*) What is screening effect? How does it govern the ionisation energy of an atom?

(*b*) Account for the difference in size of Fe^{2+} and Fe^{3+} as

$$Fe^{2+} = 0.076 \text{ nm}$$

$$Fe^{3+} = 0.064 \text{ nm}$$

9. (*a*) What do you understand by successive ionisation energy?

(*b*) Why is ionisation energy of B less than that of Be and of O is less than that of N?

(*c*) Among the elements Li, Na, Mg, S and Xe, which one has the lowest first ionisation energy and which has the highest first ionisation energy?

10. Give reasons for the following?

(*a*) The second ionisation energy of sodium is very high as compared to its first ionisation energy.

(*b*) Electron affinity of fluorine is less than that of chlorine.

(*c*) Ionic radius of K^+ is smaller than that of Cl^-.

(*d*) Electron affinity of N is almost zero while that of F is very high.

(*e*) Size of Cl^- is greater than that of Cl atom while that of Na^+ is less than that of Na atom.

(*f*) Electronegativity increases along a period.

(*g*) Ionisation energies of C, N and O follow the order $C < N > O$.

11. (*a*) What are isoelectronic ions? Account for the decrease in size of the following isoelectronic ions:

$$O^{2-} > F^- > Na^+ > Mg^{2+}$$

(*b*) Account for the fact that the 4th period has eighteen and not eight elements.

12. (*a*) What is electronegativity? How does it vary in period and a group in the periodic table?

(*b*) Write notes on the following scales of electronegativity:

(*i*) Pauling scale (*ii*) Mulliken's scale

(*iii*) Allred and Rochow scale

13. (*a*) For each of the following pairs, predict which one has greater ionisation energy and greater electron affinity:

(*i*) I, I^- (*ii*) Br, Cl (*iii*) Li, Li^+

(*b*) How do the following properties change on moving down a group

(*i*) ionisation energy (*ii*) electron affinity

(*iii*) ionic radius

(*c*) Distinguish between electron affinity and electronegativity.

14. (*a*) Define the following and explain their trends in a period and in a group:

(*i*) Electron affinity (*ii*) Electronegativity

(*iii*) Atomic radius (*iv*) Ionisation energy

(*b*) Answer the following with reasons:

(*i*) Which element has higher value of electron affinity, F or Cl?

(*ii*) Which element has larger atomic volume, Na or K?

(*iii*) Which element is more metallic, Na or Cl?

(*iv*) Which element has smaller size, O or F?

(*v*) Which element has larger second ionisation energy, Na or F?

15. (*a*) Explain the term electronegativity. How is it related to electron affinity and ionisation energy?

(*b*) Arrange the following species in the order of increasing size:

(*i*) Ra^{2+}, Sr^{2+}, Ca^{2+}, Ba^{2+}

(*ii*) Si, P, S, Cl

(*iii*) Ca^{2+}, Cl^-, S^{2-}, K^+

(*c*) Why is the radius of an atom not defined precisely?

16. (*a*) What do you understand by effective nuclear charge?

(*b*) Give Slater rules for calculating shielding constant.

(*c*) Calculate the effective nuclear charge for

(*i*) a 3*d*-electron in zinc (Z = 30).

(*ii*) a 4*s*-electron in zinc (Z = 30).

(*d*) The electronic configuration of Ag atom is:

$$1s^2\ 2s^2\ 2p^6\ 3s^2\ 3p^6\ 3d^{10}\ 4s^2\ 4p^6\ 4d^{10}\ 5s^1$$

Compare the effective nuclear charge experienced by

(*i*) a 5*s*-electron (*ii*) a 4*d*-electron

What conclusion do you make from this?

(*e*) Give some important applications of Slater rules.

17. Give reasons for the following:

(*a*) Electron affinity of fluorine is less than that of chlorine.

(*b*) The electron affinity of Be and N are almost zero while that of Ne is zero.

(*c*) Electron affinities of halogens are the highest.

(*d*) Ionisation potential decreases down the group but tends to increase across a period.

18. (*a*) Define electronegativity. How does it vary along a period and down the group in a periodic table?

(*b*) Explain:

(*i*) Electron affinities of halogens are very high.

(*ii*) Electron affinities of noble gases are zero.

(*iii*) Successive electron affinities have negative values.

(*c*) Calculate effective nuclear charge for an electron in 4*s* orbital of Cr (Z = 24).

19. (*a*) Define electronegativity. Give its applications.

(*b*) Name the factors upon which I.E. depend.

(*c*) (*i*) Which has the largest I.E. and why (B or Be)?

(*ii*) Which has the highest E.N. and why (F or Cl)?

(*iii*) Which has the largest size and why (N or O)?

20. (*a*) Give Slater rules for calculating shielding constant of Z_{eff}.

(*b*) Calculate Z_{eff} experienced by

(*i*) 5*s* electrons

(*ii*) 4*d* electrons in Ag atom Z = 47, $1s^2$, $2s^2\ 2p^6\ 3s^2\ 3p^6\ 3d^{10}\ 4s^2\ 4p^6\ 4d^{10}\ 5s^1$.

21. (*a*) State and explain ionisation energy.

(*b*) Discuss the various factors which govern ionisation energies of atoms.

22. (*a*) Give Slater rules for calculating shielding constant for Z effective.

(*b*) Calculate effective nuclear charge for an electron in ^{19}K.

23. Given $E(H_2) = 436\ kJ\ mol^{-1}$, $E(Cl_2) = 244\ kJ\ mol^{-1}$ and $E(HCl) = 432\ kJ\ mol^{-1}$. Calculate X_{Cl} given $X_H = 2.2$.

24. In the blank Periodic Table below, fill up at the correct place symbols of elements showing the following properties.

(*i*) used as filament in electric bulbs

(*ii*) used as a liquid element in thermometers

(*iii*) hardest cutting material

(*iv*) metal present in chlorophyll

(*v*) metal present in haemoglobin

(*vi*) an element not expected to form compounds but in recent years its compounds have been reported

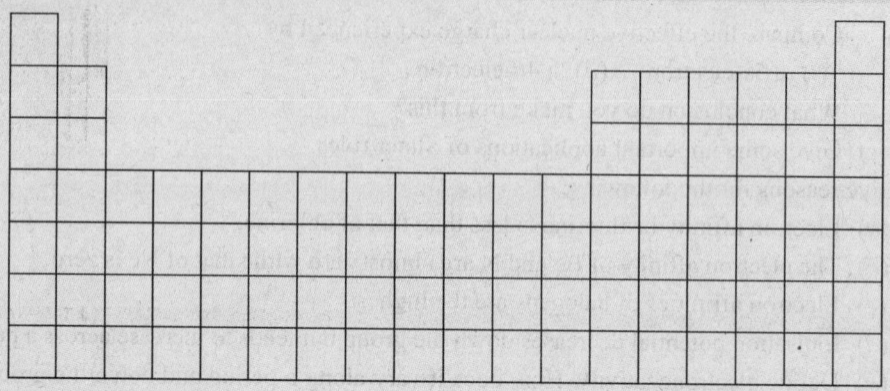

25. In the periodic table below.

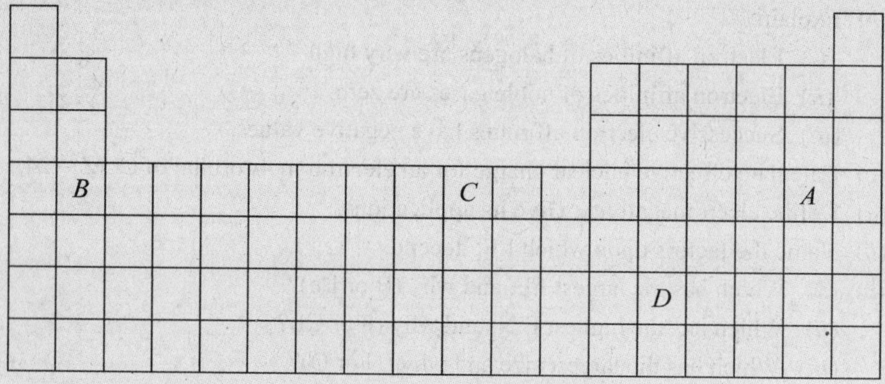

(*i*) What is the colour of element *A*

(*ii*) Write the names of two useful compounds of *B*

(*iii*) Give three uses of element *C*

(*iv*) How is the element harmful for transporting water

Answers

Multiple Choice Questions

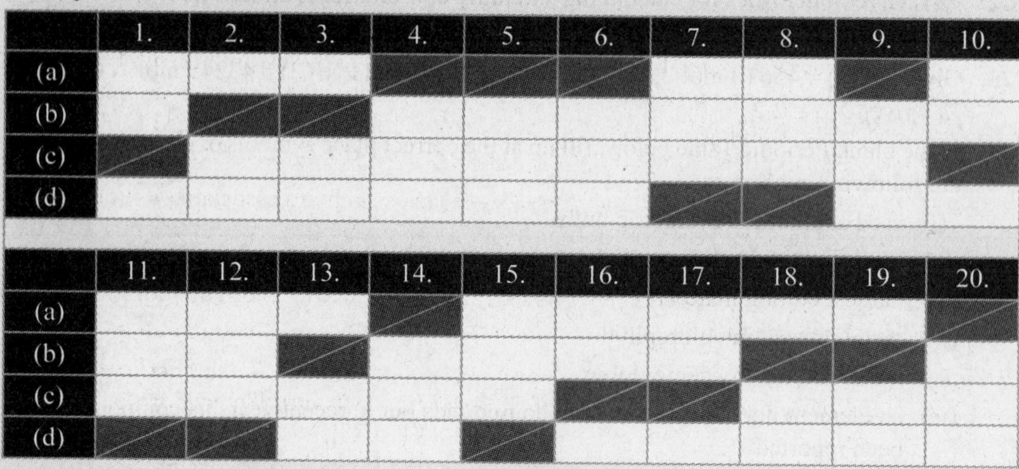

	1.	2.	3.	4.	5.	6.	7.	8.	9.	10.
(a)				■	■	■			■	
(b)		■	■							
(c)	■									■
(d)							■	■		

	11.	12.	13.	14.	15.	16.	17.	18.	19.	20.
(a)				■						■
(b)			■					■	■	
(c)						■	■			
(d)	■	■			■					

4

Basics of Organic Chemistry

4.1 HYBRIDISATION OF ORBITALS

The electronic configuration of carbon is $1s^2\ 2s^2\ 2p_x^1\ 2p_y^1$ as its At. No. is 6. As the bonds are formed by unpaired electrons, carbon should show a valency of 2. But, we observe that carbon shows tetravalency in its compounds like methane or carbon dioxide. This was explained by saying that the above-mentioned configuration is the configuration in the ground state. During the formation of bonds with other atoms, some of the electrons in lower energy levels are excited to higher levels. Thus, in the case of carbon, one electron from 2*s* level is excited to empty $2p_z$ level. (Fig. 4.1)

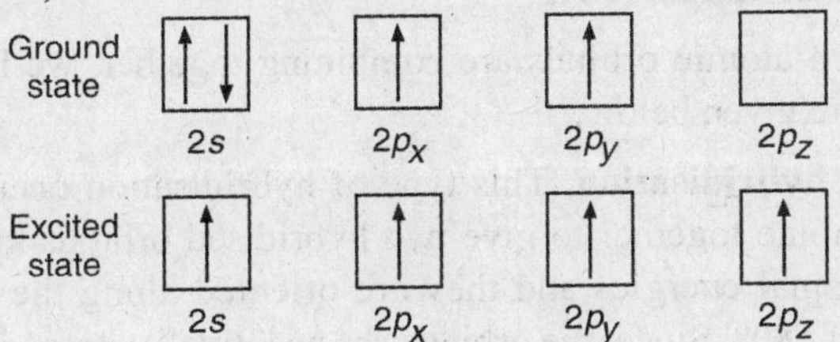

Fig. 4.1: Ground and excited state configurations of carbon.

Now, there are 4 electrons which are unpaired. These four electrons will form four bonds by overlapping with the orbitals of other atoms. For example, they combine with four hydrogen atoms to form methane (CH_4).

However, there is one thing which is surprising. We find that in methane, all the C—H bonds have the same bond energy and all the angles H—C—H are the same, *i.e.*, 109°– 28′. Looking back at the orbitals, which participate in bonding, *i.e.*, one *s*-orbital and three *p*-orbital which have different shapes and energies, we expect one of the bonds formed by *s*-orbital to be different from the three bonds formed by *p*-orbitals. Moreover, as the *p*-orbitals are inclined at an angle of 90° to each other, we expect the bond angles of 90° in methane also. But this actually is not so. To explain this anomaly, the concept of *hybridisation* was introduced.

It is assumed that the 2*s*-orbital and three 2*p*-orbitals which are associated with different shapes and energies mix with each other and produce four equivalent types of orbitals with the same shape and energy and are oriented symmetrically in space. These are called **hybrid** or **hybridised** orbitals and this phenomenon is called **hybridisation.** These hybridised orbitals then overlap with the orbitals of other atoms to form bonds.

Thus, hybridisation is the process of mixing of orbitals of different shapes and energies, to produce orbitals of equivalent shape and energy oriented symmetrically with respect to one another.

This phenomenon explains satisfactorily why the bond energies and bond angles are equal in the case of methane and many other molecules.

Necessary conditions for hybridisation

There are certain conditions which must be satisfied before the orbitals hybridise to produce equivalent type of orbitals. These are :

(*i*) The orbitals taking part in hybridisation should not differ too much in their energies. For example, 1*s* and 2*p* orbitals cannot hybridise. The participating orbitals must possess almost similar energies.

(*ii*) As many hybrid orbitals will be obtained as the number of orbitals combining together.

(*iii*) Whereas the paired orbitals do not take part in bonding, they can take part in hybridisation. In such a case, one of the positions in the geometrical shape is occupied by the lone pair of electrons. This happens in the case of ammonia and water molecules.

(*iv*) It is not essential for all the unpaired orbitals to participate in hybridisation. Those unpaired orbitals which do not take part in hybridisation form π-bonds by lateral overlapping.

4.2 TYPES OF HYBRIDISATION

Depending upon which atomic orbitals are combining together, we have different types of hybridisation, which are given below:

1. *sp* or diagonal hybridisation. This type of hybridisation occurs when one *s* orbital and one *p* orbital combine together to give two hybridised orbitals known as *sp* hybridised orbitals which have equal energies and they are oriented along the same line in opposite direction at an angle of 180°. Since, the orbitals are negatively charged, they repel each other. Hence, they orient themselves in such a way that they are maximum far apart from each other. Two orbitals can orient themselves along the same line in opposite directions to have minimum repulsive interactions. The shapes of the hybridised orbitals in *sp* hybridisation is given in Fig. 4.2.

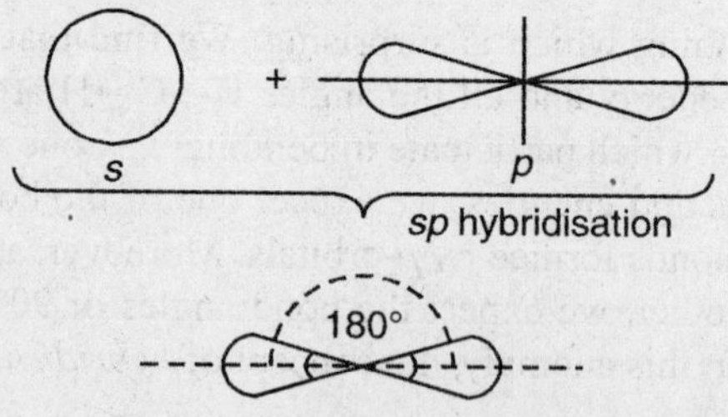

***Fig. 4.2:** sp hybridisation.*

2. sp^2 or trigonal hybridisation. This type of hybridisation takes place when one *s* orbital and two 2*p* orbitals combine together to give three sp^2 hybridised orbitals of equal energies. These hybrid orbitals are oriented at an angle of 120° in the same plane. The three orbitals point towards the corners of an equilateral triangle with the nucleus occupying the centre of the triangle. This is illustrated in Fig. 4.3.

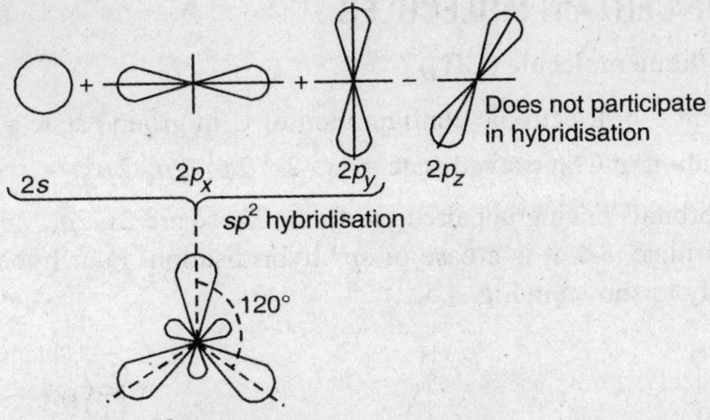

***Fig. 4.3:** sp² hybridisation.*

3. sp^3 or tetrahedral hybridisation. When one *s*-orbital and three *p*-orbitals combine together to produce equivalent type of orbitals, sp^3 hybridisation takes place. Four sp^3 hybridised orbitals are produced which have the same energy and shape and are oriented at an angle of 109°28′ to one another. This is also known as *tetrahedral* hybridisation because the hybridised orbitals are pointing towards four corners of a tetrahedron with the nucleus occupying the centre of the tetrahedron. In this position, the hybridised orbitals experience minimum repulsive forces. This is illustrated in Fig. 4.4.

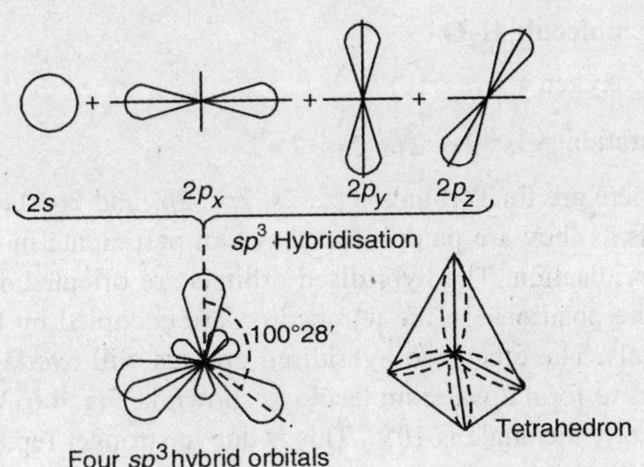

***Fig. 4.4:** sp³ hybridisation.*

The geometry and shape of molecules associated with different types of hybridisation is summarised in the table below:

S. No.	Type of Hybridisation	Combination of Orbitals	Bond Angle	Geometry
1.	sp	$s + p_x$	180°	Linear
2.	sp^2	$s + p_x + p_y$	120°	Trigonal
3.	sp^3	$s + p_x + p_y + p_z$	109°28′	Tetrahedral
4.	dsp^2	$d + s + p_x + p_y$	90°	Square planer
5.	sp^3d	$s + p_x + p_y + p_z + d$	90°, 120°	Trigonal bipyramidal
6.	sp^3d^2	$s + p_x + p_y + p_z + (2\times d)$	90°	Octahedral

4.3 SHAPES OF CERTAIN MOLECULES

1. Shape of methane molecule (CH_4)

At. No. of carbon = 6. Electronic configuration of C in ground state = $1s^2\ 2s^2\ 2p_x^1\ 2p_y^1$. Electronic configuration of C in excited state = $1s^2\ 2s^1\ 2p_x^1\ 2p_y^1\ 2p_z^1$.

There are four orbitals having unpaired electrons. These are $2s$, $2p_x$, $2p_y$, and $2p_z$ orbitals. They will first hybridise. So, it is a case of sp^3 hybridisation. Four hybridised orbitals are oriented tetrahedrally as shown in Fig. 4.5.

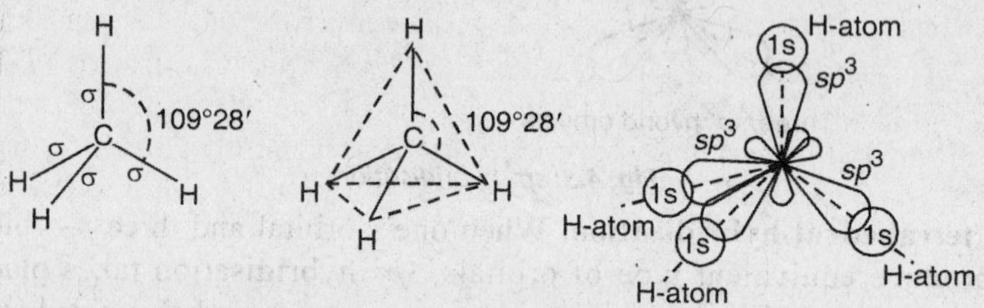

Fig. 4.5: Shape of methane molecule.

All the four hybridised orbitals overlap with the $1s$-orbital of four hydrogen atoms. All these overlappings take place along the internuclear axes. Hence, four carbon-hydrogen σ-bonds are formed. The angle ∠HCH is 109°28′.

2. Shape of water molecule H_2O

Atomic number of oxygen = 8

Electronic configuration = $1s^2\ 2s^2\ 2p_x^2\ 2p_y^1\ 2p_z^1$

In the 2nd orbit, there are four orbitals, viz., $2s$, $2p_x$, $2p_y$ and $2p_z$. Out of these $2s$ and $2p_x$ cannot form the bonds as they are paired. But they can participate in hybridisation. Hence, it is a case of sp^3 hybridisation. The hybridised orbitals are oriented along the corners of a tetrahedron. Two of the positions on the tetrahedron are occupied by lone pair of electrons from $2s$ and $2p_x$ orbitals. The other two hybridised orbitals will overlap with the $1s$-orbitals of two hydrogen atoms to form a water molecule as shown in Fig. 4.6. We expect an angle of 109°28′ in HOH. Actually the angle is 105°. This is due to stronger repulsion of two lone pair of electrons with the shared pairs of electrons. Thus, it is of V shape.

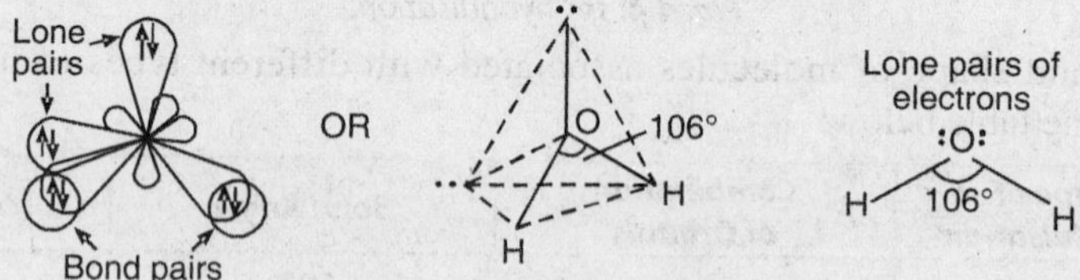

Fig. 4.6: Shape of water molecule.

3. Shape of ethane (C_2H_6) molecule

In the molecule of ethane two carbon atoms are linked to each other by a σ-bond and each carbon is linked to three hydrogens (Fig. 4.7).

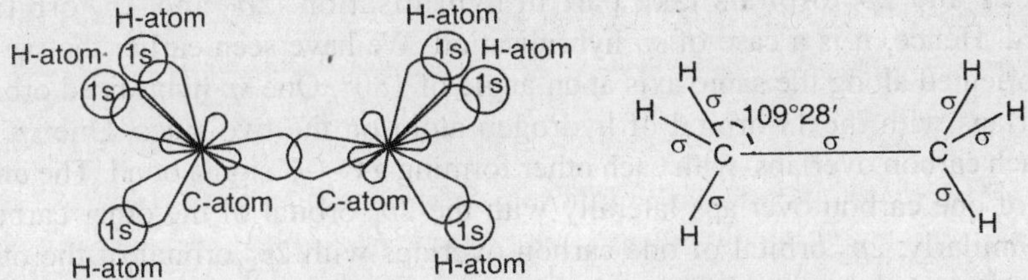

Fig. 4.7: Shape of ethane molecule.

Both the carbon atoms are sp^3 hybridised. Out of the four sp^3 hybridised orbitals of one carbon, one orbital overlaps with one of the hybridised orbitals of the second carbon making a C—C bond. The other three hybridised orbitals overlap with the 1*s*-orbitals of three hydrogen atoms. Similarly, one hybridised orbital of the second carbon overlaps with one of the orbitals of the first carbon and three orbitals overlap with three 1*s*-orbitals of three hydrogen atoms. In other words, three hybridised orbitals of each carbon overlap with three hydrogens and the fourth orbital of each overlaps with each other.

The C—C bond length in a molecule of ethane is 1.54 Å, whereas C—H bond length is 1.10 Å. The dissociation energy of C—C bond is 348 kJ/mole.

4. Shape of ethylene molecule (C_2H_4)

The electronic configuration of C in excited state is : $1s^2\ 2s^1\ 2p_x^1\ 2p_y^1\ 2p_z^1$

Here, all the four unpaired orbitals do not participate in hybridization. Out of four, only three orbitals viz. 2*s*, $2p_x$ and $2p_y$ hybridise. The fourth one $2p_z$ remains unhybridised. Hence, it is a case of sp^2 hybridisation. The hybridised orbitals are oriented in the same plane at an angle of 120°. We have two such carbons. One orbital of each carbon overlaps with each other to form a σ-bond. Two orbitals of each carbon overlap with two 1*s*-orbitals of hydrogen to form four C—H bonds. We are left with 2 unhybridised orbitals of two carbons which are oriented perpendicular to the plane of the rest of the molecule. They will overlap laterally giving rise to a weak π-bond between carbon-carbon. Hence, there will be a double bond, one σ-bond and one π-bond between carbon-carbon (Fig. 4.8)

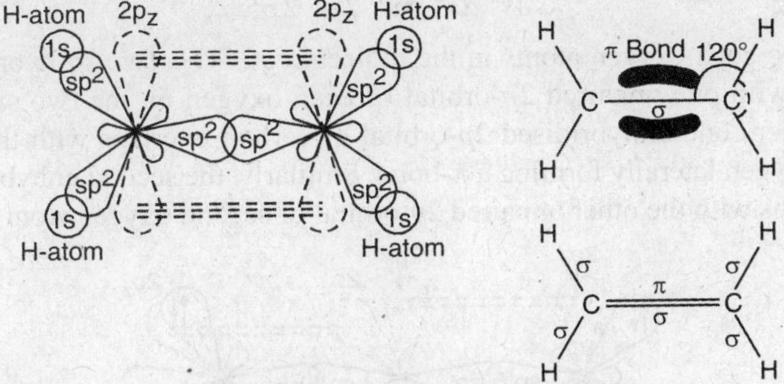

Fig. 4.8: Shape of ethylene molecule.

A double bond brings the carbon atoms together. Hence, the C = C bond length in C_2H_4 is shortened to 1.34 Å. The angle ∠HCH or ∠HCC is 120°, the trigonal angle. Bond dissociation energy of C = C bond is 614 kJ/mole.

5. Shape of acetylene molecule (C_2H_2)

Coming again to the electronic configuration of carbon:

$$1s^2\ 2s^1\ 2p_x^1\ 2p_y^1\ 2p_z^1 \quad \text{(Excited state).}$$

Here, only $2s$ and $2p_x$ orbitals take part in hybridisation. $2p_y$ and $2p_z$ orbitals remain unhybridised. Hence, it is a case of *sp* hybridisation. We have seen earlier that *sp* hybridised orbital are oriented along the same axis at an angle of 180°. One *sp* hybridised orbital of each carbon overlaps with the 1*s*-orbital of hydrogen atom on the two sides. One *sp* hybridised orbital of each carbon overlaps with each other forming a C—C sigma bond. The unhybridised $2p_y$ orbital of one carbon overlaps laterally with the $2p_y$ orbital of the other carbon forming a π-bond. Similarly, $2p_z$ orbital of one carbon overlaps with $2p_z$ orbital of the other carbon laterally forming another π-bond. The molecule of acetylene has a linear shape (Fig. 4.9). There is a cylinder of negative charge around C—C bond.

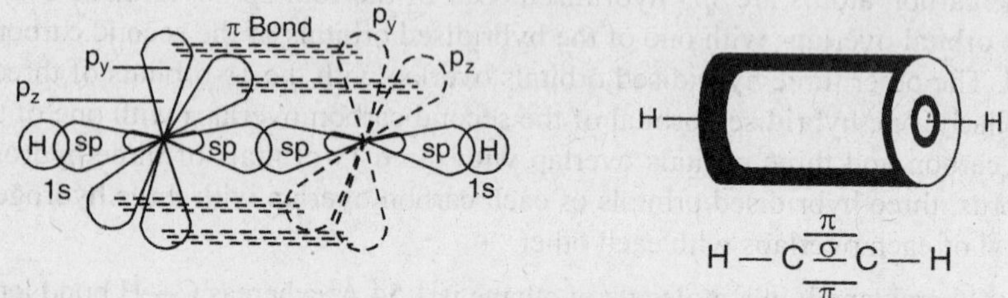

***Fig. 4.9:** Shape of acetylene molecule (Linear shape).*

A triple bond is formed between carbon-carbon. But of the three bonds, one is a σ-bond and two are π-bonds. Triple bond brings carbon atoms still nearer. The bond length C ≡ C is 1.20 Å. Acetylene being a linear molecule, angle H — C — C is 180°. Bond dissociation energy of the C ≡ C bond is 811 kJ/mole.

6. Shape of carbon dioxide molecule. At. No. of carbon is 6 and its electronic configuration in the excited state is:

$$1s^2\ 2s^1\ 2p_x^1\ 2p_y^1\ 2p_z^1$$

sp hybridisation takes place here. The hybridised orbitals are oriented along the same line at an angle of 180°. $2p_y$ and $2p_z$ orbitals do not participate in the hybridisation.

Coming to oxygen, its electronic configuration is:

$$1s^2\ 2s^2\ 2p_x^2\ 2p_y^1\ 2p_z^1$$

There are two such oxygen atoms in the molecule of CO_2. Two *sp* hybridised orbitals of carbon overlap with one unpaired 2*p*-orbital of each oxygen on the two sides forming two σ-bonds. And then, one unhybridised 2*p*-orbital of carbon overlaps with the other unpaired orbital of one oxygen laterally forming a π-bond. Similarly, the second unhybridised 2*p*-orbital of carbon overlaps with the other unpaired 2*p*-orbital of second oxygen atom (Fig. 4.10)

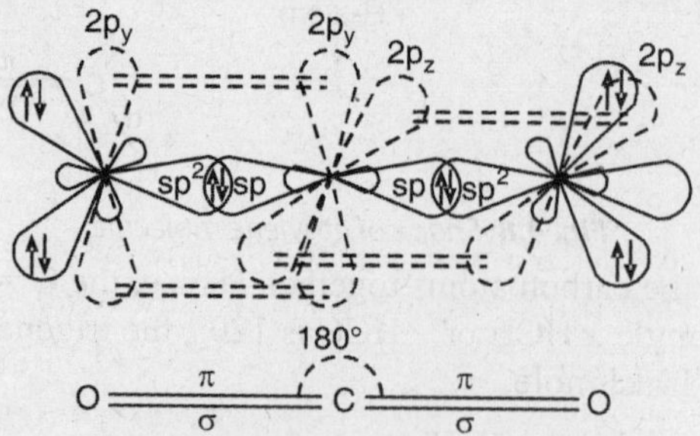

***Fig. 4.10:** Shape of CO_2 molecule.*

The molecule of carbon dioxide has a linear shape.

4.4 SOME IMPORTANT BOND PARAMETERS

1. Bond Length

When atoms are brought close to each other, attraction takes place between them and, therefore, the potential energy of the system keeps on decreasing till at a particular distance, the potential energy is minimum. If the atoms are further brought closer, the repulsion starts and the potential energy of the system begins to increase.

The average distance between the centres of the nuclei of the two bonded atoms is called its **bond length.**

Bond length is expressed in Angstrom (1Å = 10^{-10}m) or picameter (1 pm = 10^{-12} m). It is determined experimentally by X-ray diffraction methods or spectroscopic methods. In an ionic compound, the bond length is the sum of their ionic radii and in a covalent compound, it is the sum of the covalent radii of the constituent atoms.

Factors governing bond length

(*i*) *Size of the atoms*. The bond length increases with increase in the size of the atoms. For example, bond lengths of H—X are in the order : HI > HBr > HCl > HF.

(*ii*) *Multiplicity of bond*. The bond length decreases with the multiplicity of the bond. Thus, bond length of carbon-carbon bonds changes in the order : $C \equiv C < C = C < C - C$.

Multiplicity of the bond involves increasing overlapping of orbitals leading to decrease in bond length.

(*iii*) *Type of hybridisation*. An *s*-orbital is smaller in size. Greater the *s*-character, shorter is the hybrid orbital and, hence, shorter is the bond length. For example,

$$sp^3\ C - H > sp^2\ C - H > sp\ C - H$$

sp hybrid orbital has 50% *s* character (one *s* and one *p*). This percentage of *s* decreases as we move to sp^2 and sp^3.

The bond lengths of a few common bonds are given in the table below.

Some Bond Lengths

Bond	Bond length (Å)	Bond	Bond length (Å)
C – H	1.09	C – O	1.43
C – C	1.54	C = O	1.21
C = C	1.34	C – N	1.47
C ≡ C	1.20	C – Cl	1.77
O – H	0.96	C – Br	1.91

2. Bond Energy

Energy is released when atoms come close together resulting in the formation of bond between them. Conversely, the energy is required to break the bond to get the separated atoms.

The amount of energy required to break one mole of bonds of a particular type so as to separate them into gaseous atoms is called **bond dissociation energy** or simply **bond energy.**

Bond energy is expressed in kJ mol^{-1}. Greater is the bond dissociation energy, stronger is the bond.

Since, a particular type of bond present in different molecules (e.g., O – H bond in H – O – H) or even in the same molecule (*e.g.*, four C – H bonds in CH_4) do not possess the same bond energy, bond energies are usually the *average values.*

Table 4.1 gives the average bond energies of a few common bonds.

TABLE 4.1 *Some Bond Energies.*

Bond	**Bond energy (kJ/mole)**	**Bond**	**Bond energy (kJ/mole)**
C – H	414.2	C – O	359.8
C – C	347.3	C = O	748.9
C = C	610.9	C – N	305.4
C ≡ C	836.8	C – Cl	338.9
O – H	464.4	C – Br	284.5
N – H	389.1	C – I	213.4

Factors governing bond energy

(*i*) *Size of the atoms.* Greater the size of the atoms, greater is the bond length and smaller is the bond energy.

(*ii*) *Multiplicity of bonds.* Greater the multiplicity of the bond, greater is the bond dissociation energy.

(*iii*) *Number of lone pairs of electrons present.* Greater the number of lone pairs of electrons present on the bonded atoms, greater is the repulsion between the atoms and, hence, smaller is the bond dissociation energy.

Bond	C – C	N – N	O – O	F – F
Lone pairs of electrons	0	1	2	3
Bond energy (kJ mol^{-1})	348	163	146	139

3. Bond Angle

A bond is formed by the overlap of atomic orbitals of different atoms. The direction of overlap gives direction of the bond.

The angle between the lines representing the directions of the bonds is called the **bond angle.** It is expressed in degrees, minutes and seconds. H—C—H bond angle in CH_4, H—N—H bond angle in NH_3 and H—O—H bond angle in H_2O are shown in the Fig. 4.11.

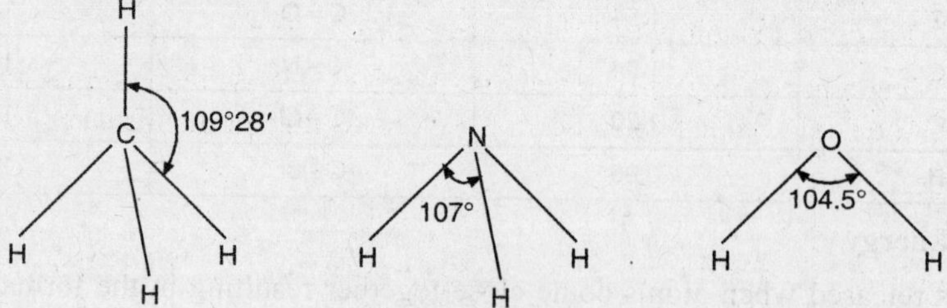

Fig. 4.11: Bond angles in CH_4, NH_3 and H_2O

4.5 LOCALIZED AND DELOCALIZED BONDS

Bonds in which the overlapping orbitals are almost in fixed positions are called localized bonds. Sigma(σ) bonds are localized bonds. Consider again the case of methane molecule. There are four carbon–hydrogen sigma bonds.

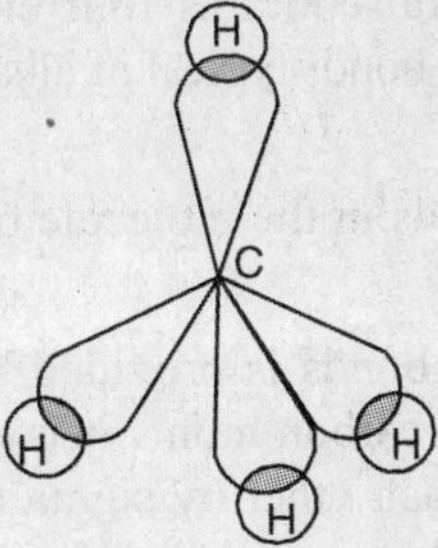

These are all localized bonds since the positions of the overlapping orbitals are fixed.

Now consider the case of 1, 3-Butadiene. This is a conjugated diene.

All four carbon atoms in 1, 3-butadiene are sp^2 hybridized. The sp^2 hybrid orbitals overlap with each other and with *s* orbitals of the hydrogen atoms to form C–C and C–H σ bonds. Since the bonds result from the overlap of trigonal sp^2 orbitals, all carbon and hydrogen atoms lie in one plane.

Also each carbon atom in 1, 3-butadiene possesses an unhybridized *p* orbital. The *p* orbitals are perpendicular to the plane of σ bonds. The *p* orbital on C-2 can overlap with the *p* orbitals on C-1 and C-3. The *p* orbital on C-3 can overlap with the *p* orbitals on C-2 and C-4. That is, all four *p* orbitals overlap to form a large π molecular orbital (Fig. 4.12). Each pair of π electrons is thus attracted, not by two, but all four carbons.

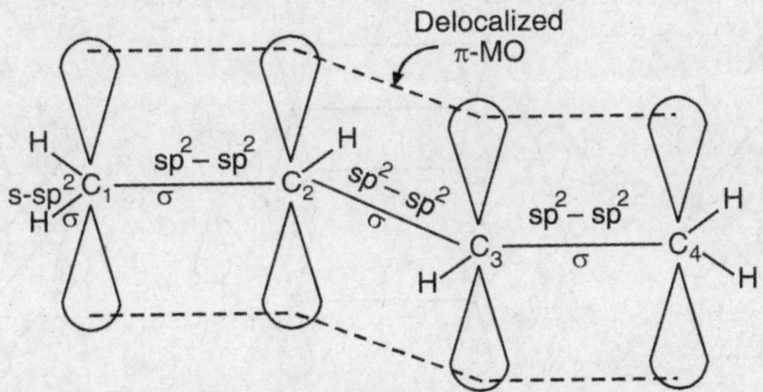

***Fig. 4.12:** Orbital structure of 1, 3-Butadiene.*

The overlap of *p* orbitals of C-2 and C-3 in both directions, which allows the π electrons to be spread over a larger area, is referred to as **delocalization**. This delocalization of π electrons is responsible for greater stability of 1, 3-butadiene.

The C–C single bonds in 1, 3-butadiene are shorter (1.48 Å) than normal carbon—carbon single bonds. The C–C double bonds are longer (1.37 Å) than normal isolated carbon—carbon double bonds.

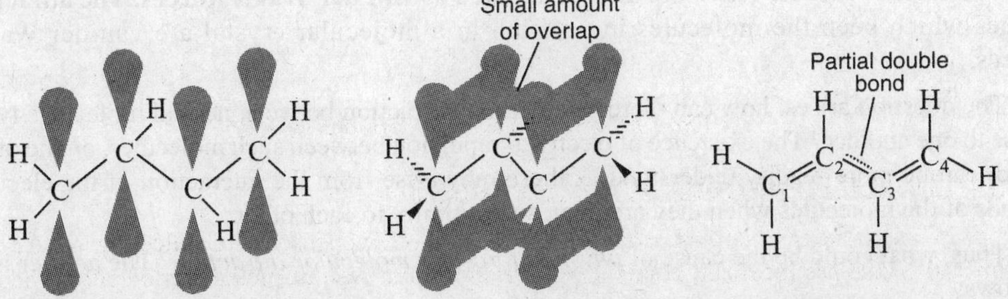

The delocalized molecular orbital contains four electrons. The central carbon-carbon single bond is shorter than the 1.54 Å bonds typical of alkanes because of its partial double bond character.

The electrons forming two π bonds in the molecule of 1, 3-butadiene are thus delocalized chemical bonds.

Another example of delocalized bonds is provided by the structure of benzene. It has a hexagonal structure in which the six carbon atoms occupy the corners of a regular hexagon. All the carbon atoms are linked to each other by sigma bonds. Also each carbon is linked to one hydrogen by sigma bond. It may be noted that carbon atoms in benzene are sp^2 hybridised. Thus, all carbons lie in the same plane. There is one orbital in each carbon, which does not participate in hybridisation.

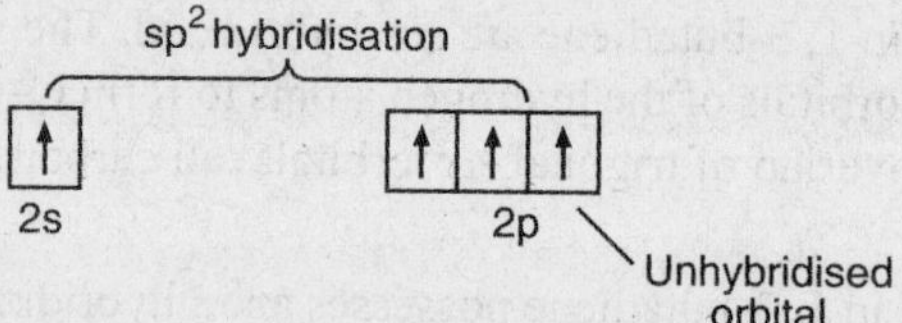

There are six such unhybridised orbitals these can overlap laterally in pairs to form three π bonds as shown in Fig. 4.13 (*a*) and (*b*). But the same situation exists as in 1, 3-butadiene. All the six orbitals overlap together forming a circular electron cloud above and below the benzene ring (Fig. 4.13)

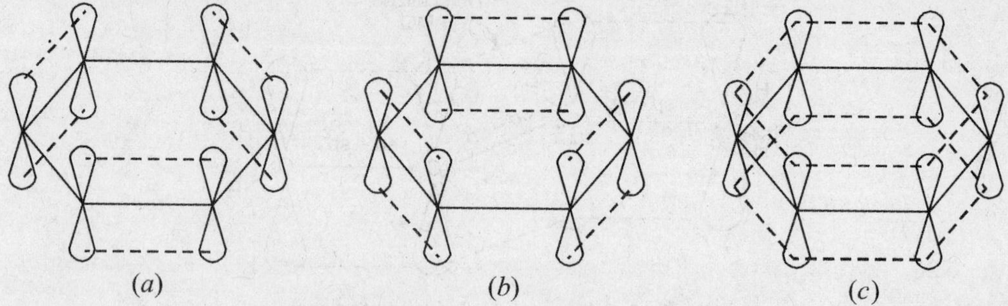

***Fig. 4.13:** Overlapping of orbitals in benzene molecule*

4.6 VAN DER WAALS' FORCES

Forces of attraction exist between *neutral molecules* as well. The magnitude of these forces is maximum in case of solids and decreases on passing from solid to liquid and from liquid to gaseous states. The forces existing between the molecules of a substance are known as **intermoleculer forces.** These are also designated as **van der Waals' forces.** The attractive forces which keep the molecules in position in a molecular crystal are van der Waals' forces.

The question arises, how can there be electrical attraction between neutral molecules lying close to one another? The existence of electrical repulsion between such molecules, on the other hand, can be more readily understood as these may arise from the interaction of the electron clouds of the molecules when they are in close proximity to each other.

Thus, what could be the cause of *physical forces* or *molecular attraction*? The answer is as follows:

Dipole-Dipole Interaction

In the case of *polar molecules* which have permanent dipoles, the van der Waals' forces are mainly due to electrical interaction between the dipoles known as *dipole-dipole interaction*. For instance, gases such as ammonia, sulphur dioxide, hydrogen fluoride, hydrogen chloride, etc., have permanent dipoles as a result of which there is appreciable dipole-dipole interaction between the molecules of these gases. The magnitude of this type of interaction depends upon the dipole moment of the molecule concerned. Greater the dipole moment, greater is the dipole-dipole interaction. Because of the attractive interaction, these gases can be easily liquefied.

Ion-Dipole Interaction

If an ionic solid is to dissolve, some energy is needed to overcome the force of inner-ionic attraction. If water is the solvent, this energy is supplied by the *interaction of water molecules with the ions*. This is known as ion-dipole interaction. The positive pole of the water molecules reacts with the negative ion while the negative pole reacts with the positive ion. The ion-dipole interaction results in the release of a considerable amount of energy which becomes available for the separation of the oppositely charged ions. This results in the dissolution of the solute.

But van der Waals' forces exist even in non-polar molecules such as F_2, O_2 and N_2 and even in non-polar mono-atomic molecules such as He, Ne, Ar, etc. This attraction is evident from the condensation of these gases into liquids at sufficiently high pressures and low temperatures. This is explained by London forces.

London Forces

In 1930, F. London provided an explanation for the existence of forces of attraction between *non-polar* molecules, based on quantum mechanics. According to his view, *electrons of a neutral molecule keep on oscillating with respect to the nuclei of the atoms. As a result of this, at a given instant, positive charge may be concentrated in one region and negative charge in another region of the same molecule. Thus, a non-polar molecule may become momentarily self-polarised.* This polarised molecule may induce a dipole moment in a neighbouring molecule, as shown in Fig. 4.14.

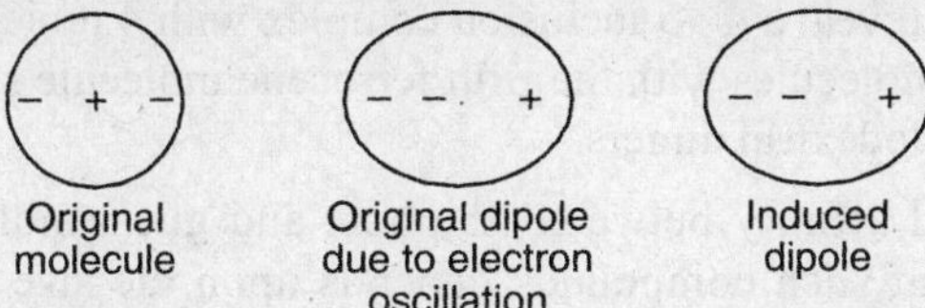

***Fig. 4.14:** Origin of cohesive forces in non-polar molecules.*

The electrostatic forces of attraction between induced dipoles and the original dipoles (due to electron oscillation) are known as **London forces.** These foreces are also called dispersive forces because the well known phenomenon of dispersion of light is also connected with these dipoles. For a pair of adjacent molecules, London forces vary inversely as the *seventh power* of the distance between them, *i.e.*, $F \propto 1 / r^7$. The magnitude of these forces, evidently, would be very small.

The van der Waals' attraction in *non-polar molecules* is thus *exclusively* due to London forces. In the case of polar molecules having permanent dipoles, however, other electrostatic forces due to dipole-dipole interaction also contribute towards the van der Waals' attraction.

Factors determining van der Waals' forces

Van der Waals' forces depend largely on the following factors:

1. The Number of Electrons present in a Molecule. van der Waals' forces increase with increase in the number of electrons in the molecule. Thus, boiling points (T_b) of the halogens increase as we move from fluorine to chlorine, bromine and iodine. Similarly, boiling points of noble gases increase as we move from helium to radon, as shown below:

Noble gas	He	Ne	Ar	Kr	Xe	Rn
Boiling pt. (K)	4.1	27	67.2	121	165	211.2

2. Molecular Size. The larger the molecular size (or roughly the larger the molar mass), the stronger the van der Waals' forces. Thus, the boiling point of ethane, C_2H_6 (185 K) is higher than that of methane, CH_4 (112 K). In compounds having similar structures, *viz.*, CH_4, SiH_4 and GeH_4, the boiling points increase with increase in the number of electrons and the size of the molecule, as shown below:

Substance	CH_4	SiH_4	GeH_4
No. of electrons	10	18	36
Boiling point (K)	112	161	183

4.7 INCLUSION COMPOUNDS

An inclusion compound is a complex in which one chemical compound (the 'host') form a cavity in which molecules of a second 'guest' compound are located. The definition of inclusion compound is very broad, extending to channels formed between molecules in a crystal lattice in which guest molecules can fit. If the spaces in the host lattice are enclosed on all sides so that the guest species is 'trapped' as in a cage, the compound is known as a **clathrate**. In molecular encapsulation, a guest molecule is actually trapped inside another molecule.

Cyclodextrin inclusion compounds

Inclusion compounds have been reported between cyclodextrins and ferrocene. When a solution of both compounds in a 2 : 1 ratio in water is boiled for 2 days and then allowed to rest for 10 hours at room temperature, orange-yellow crystals are obtained. X-ray diffraction analysis of these crystals reveal a 4 : 5 inclusion complex with 4 molecules of ferrocene in the cavity of 4 cyclodextrin molecules with the fifth ferrocene molecule sandwiched between two stacks, of ferrocene – cyclodextrin dimers.

There is no chemical affinity between the host and guest molecules in the inclusion compounds. Formation of such compounds depends upon the size and shape of the guest molecules and the size of the cavities or channels created in the host molecules.

Urea Inclusion Compounds

Urea forms an inclusion compound with straight chain alkanes. Urea crystallises in hexagonal lattice, in the presence of guest molecules and traps them in the cavity. This is represented as under:

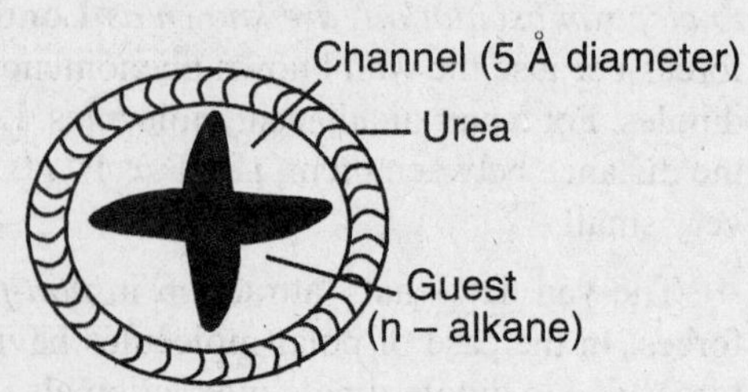

The channels in crystallised urea are of the dimensions 5 A which can trap only the straight chain hydrocarbons. Branched-chain hydrocarbons which are of bigger dimensions do not form inclusion compounds with urea. However thiourea which crystallises with bigger cavities can from inclusion compounds with branched chain hydrocharbon, the dimension of thiourea channel is appropriate in size and shape to trap the molecules of branched alkanes, cycloalkanes and chloroform etc.

4.8 CHARGE TRANSFER COMPLEXES

A charge transfer complex (or CT complex, electron-donor-acceptor-complex is a chemical association of two or more molecules, or of different parts of one very large molecule, in which attraction between the molecules (or parts) occurs due to an **electronic transition** into an excited electronic state, such that a fraction of electron charge is transferred between the molecules. The resulting **electrostatic** attraction stabilizes the moleculer complex. The source molecule from which the charge is transferred is called the **electrons donor** and the receiving molecule is called the **electron acceptor,** hence the alternate name, electron-donor-acceptor-complex.

The attraction in a charge-transfer complex is not equivalent of a stable chemical bond and is much weaker than **covalent forces**. It is better characterised as a weak electron resonance. As a result excitation energy of this resonance occurs very frequently in the visible region of the **electro-magnetic spectrum.** This produces the visually intense colours characteristic for these complexes. These optical absorption bands are referred to as **charge-transfer bands** or **CT bands**. Optical spectrocopy is a powerful technique which is used to characterise charge-transfer bands

Charge transfer complexes exist in different types of molecules, organic as well as inorganic and in all phases of matter *i.e.* in solids, liquids and even gases.

In inorganic chemistry, most charge-transfer complexes involve electron transfer between metal atoms and **ligands**. The charge-transfer band in transition metal complexes result from movement of electrons between molecular orbitals (MO) that are predominantly metal in character and those that are predominantly ligand in character.

The classic example of charge-transfer complex is that between iodine and starch to form an intense purple colour. This is widely used for screening counterfeit currency. Unlike most paper, paper used in currency is not sized with starch, thus formation of this purple colour on application of iodine solution indicates a counterfeit.

Coming to organic compounds, in 1962, the well known acceptor tetracyanoquinodimethane (TCNQ) was reported. Similarly classic donor tetrathiafulvalence (TTF) was synthesised in 1970. A CT complex composed of TTF and TCNQ was discovered in 1973. This was the first organic conductor to show almost metallic conductance.

Some electron rich organic molecules combine to give crystalline molecular addition compounds like picrates, trinitrobenzoates. In molecular addition compounds, the donor molecule is capable of donating non bonding or π electrons to the acceptor molecule. The binding force between the donor and acceptor is a kind of weak coulombic force. This is illustrated by taking the example of anthracene and picric acid and toluene and 1, 3, 5 trinitrobenzene forming charge transfer complexes as shown below:

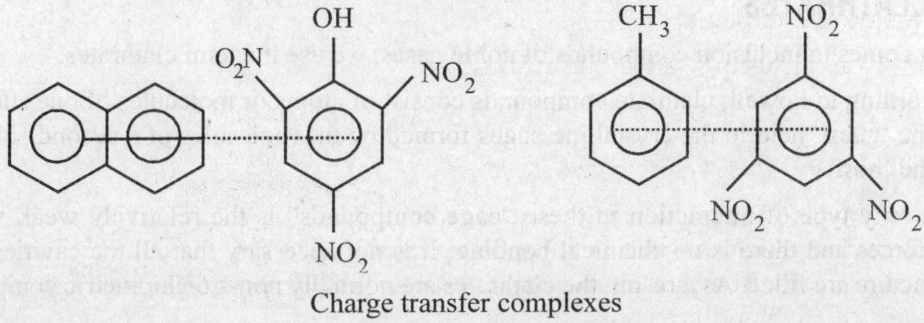

OH O_2N NO_2 NO_2 CH_3 NO_2 NO_2 NO_2

Charge transfer complexes

If we represent the donor by D and acceptor by A, then the addition compound may be represented by the resonance hybrid of the following three structures I, II and III

$$\underset{\text{I}}{(A-D)} \longleftrightarrow \underset{\text{II}}{(\overset{-}{A}-\overset{+}{D})} \longleftrightarrow \underset{\text{III}}{(\overset{+}{A}-\overset{-}{D})}$$

However form I contributes to the actual compound by the greatest extent. The forces that are involved in charge-transfer complexed are van der Waals, dipole-dipole, ion-dipole, dipole- induced dipole forces. The formation of picrate using picric acid and trimethylbenzene (mesitylene) is represented as under

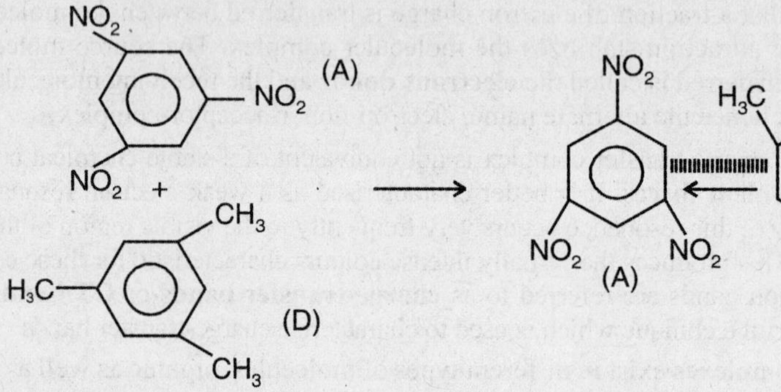

(A) + (D) ⟶ (A) ⟵ D

It may be noted that presence of strong electron donating groups in the donor molecule (D) and presence of strong electron withdrawing groups in acceptor molecule (A) favours the formation of charge transfer complexes (C.T.C). The C.T.C as given above has electron donating methyl groups in the donor molecule and electron withdrawing $-NO_2$ groups in the acceptor molecule.

The distance between donor and acceptor molecules is close to 3Å which is greater than a normal covalent bond length, indicating that the π orbitals of both rings in the complex overlap poorly. That is why the binding forces are not as strong as in a covalent bond. The resonance that occurs in the formation of the C T C is shown as under taking the examples of toluene and trinitrobenzene.

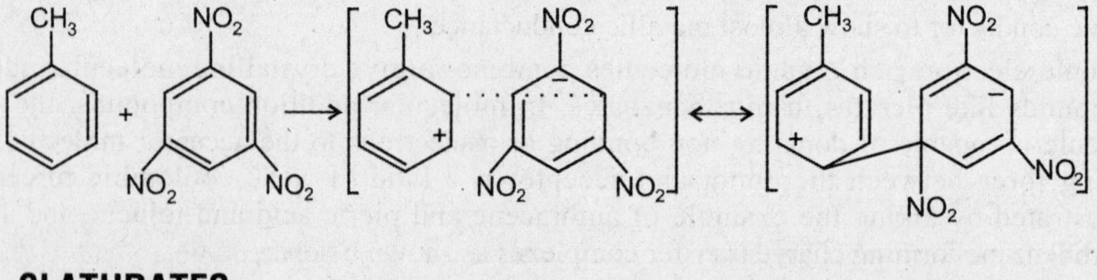

4.9 CLATHRATES

When it comes to inclusion compounds of noble gases, we use the term clathrates.

According to Powell, clathrate compounds consist of atoms or molecules of one substance called the 'guest' held in the crystalline cages formed by the molecules of a second substance called the 'host'.

The only type of interaction in these "cage compounds" is the relatively weak van der Waals' forces and there is no chemical bonding. It is not necessary that all the cavities in the host structure are filled. As a result, the clathrates are normally non-stoichiometric compounds.

Essential conditions for clathrate formation

(*a*) Presence of cavities of appropriate size in the crystal lattice of the 'host'.

(*b*) Size of the 'guest' particle should be such as to fit in the cavities of the 'host' without bringing any atoms closer together than corresponding to the van der Waals' radii of the atoms.

Stability of clathrate compounds

Clathrate compounds once formed are quite stable due to the following reasons:

(*a*) The 'guest' molecules tightly fit in the cavities of the 'host' molecules.

(*b*) The 'guest' molecules within the cages are at a minimum potential energy.

The 'guest' can escape from the 'host' only when the forces holding the molecular cages together are overcome. This can be achieved by the following two methods:

(*i*) By heating the crystals

(*ii*) By dissolving them in a suitable solvent such as alcohol.

Preparation of clathrates

Clathrate compounds of argon, krypton and xenon have been isolated by locking up these gases in the cages of water, phenol or quinol. However, clathrate compounds of helium and neon have not yet been prepared because helium atoms are thought to be too small and difficult to deform or polarize as required by van der Waals bonding to be imprisoned in the cages. The neon is borderline element and its clathrate could possibly be formed at pressures in excess of 160 atmospheres. It is predicted that in clathrate of neon, if formed, the neon atoms (being so small) will diffuse through the crystal from one cavity to another.

The other molecules to form clathrates with quinol are SO_2, O_2, H_2S and CH_3OH. During crystallisation, three molecules of quinol form a cup shaped structure due to hydrogen bonding and two such cups give rise to a cage like structure for the guest molecule. The crystals are quite stable and exist for a pretty long time.

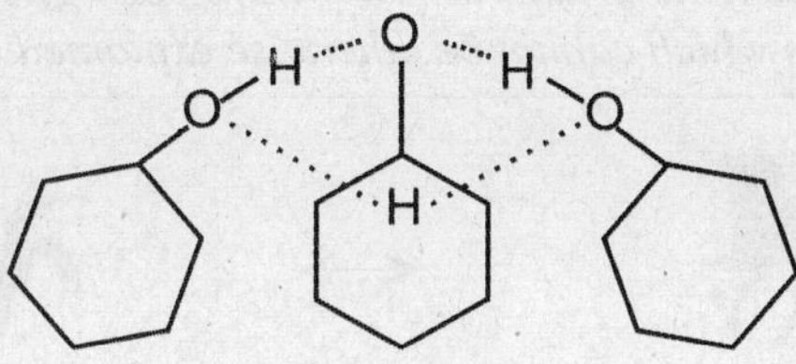

Quinol Clathrate

Uses of clathrates

(*i*) Krypton-85 clathrate provides a safe and useful source of beta radiation which are useful for measuring thickness of gauges.

(*ii*) Xenon-133 clathrate provides a compact source for gamma radiation.

(*iii*) In the separation of noble gases. For example, neon can be separated from argon, krypton and xenon because neon is the only gas that does not form clathrates with quinol.

(*iv*) Clathrates play an important role in some physiological actions, e.g., it is thought that the anaesthetic action of xenon and many other anaesthetics is due to aqueous clathrate in physiologically strategic spots. When the anaesthetic is no longer administered, the clathrate equilibrium is destroyed, the clathrate decomposes and the consciousness returns.

4.10 RESONANCE OR MESOMERIC EFFECT

If two double bonds in a molecule are separated by a single bond, they are said to be in **conjugation** and the molecule having such bonds are called conjugated molecules e.g., 1, 3-butadiene.

$$H_2C=CH-CH=CH_2 \qquad\qquad H_2C=CH-\ddot{\underset{\cdot\cdot}{Cl}}:$$

1, 3-Butadiene   Vinyl chloride

Another example of conjugation is given by benzene which is a hexagonal ring of carbon atoms with three double bonds in the alternate positions. Alternatively, a **double** bond or a **triple** bond may also be in conjugation with a lone electron pair e.g., in *vinyl chloride.*

The conjugated molecules do not exhibit the character of pure double bond or triple bond, for example, benzene is expected to be highly reactive since it has three double bonds in the ring but is actually quite stable. In order to explain the difference in the expected and the actual behaviour of the conjugated molecules, *Robinson* and *Ingold* stated that such compounds exist in two or more forms none of which can explain all the properties of the molecule under investigation. They called this concept as **mesomerism** or **mesomeric effect.** *Heisenberg* studied the same mathematically and named it as **resonance** or **resonance effect.** According to the concept,

If a compound having a certain molecular formula can be represented by different structural formulae which differ only in the arrangement of the electron pairs and not of the atoms, such like structures are called **resonating** or **contributing** or **canonical structures** *and the phenomenon is known as* **resonance.** *The compound cannot be represented completely by any of the resonating or contributing structures but by a mixture of all of them which is called* **resonance hybrid** (cannot be actually represented). Resonance is indicated by the sign ↔.

It may be noted that the various resonating or contributing structures do not actually exist i.e., they are all hypothetical structures. They have been given simply to explain certain properties of the compounds which cannot be otherwise explained.

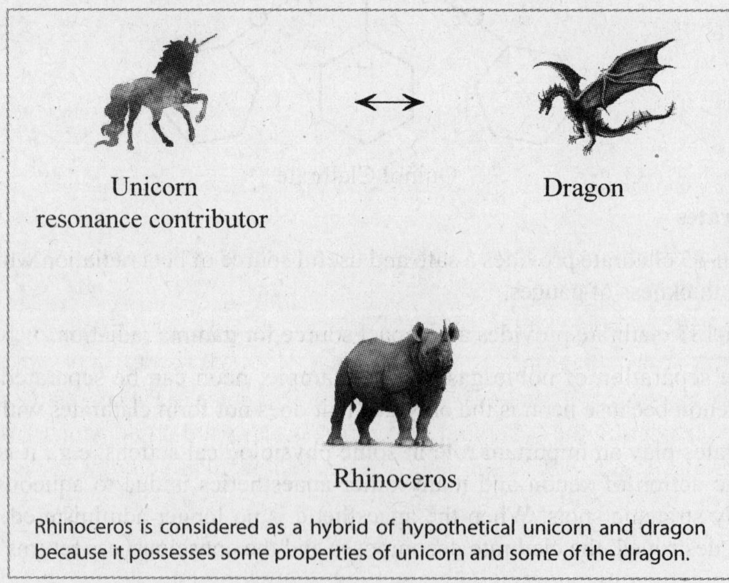

Rhinoceros is considered as a hybrid of hypothetical unicorn and dragon because it possesses some properties of unicorn and some of the dragon.

Examples of Resonance

A common analogy of a resonance hybrid is that of a mule which is a hybrid of horse and donkey.

1. Monocarboxylic acid. The acidic character of monocarboxylic acid is explained with the help of resonance. The following contributing structures for the monocarboxylic acid are possible which differ in the position of the electron pairs.

$$R-\underset{\|}{\overset{:\ddot{O}:}{}}C-\ddot{O}-H \longleftrightarrow R-\overset{:\ddot{O}:^{-}}{\overset{|}{C}}=\overset{+}{\ddot{O}}-H$$

As a result of resonance, the oxygen atom of the O — H group acquires a positive charge *i.e.*, it draws the electrons pair towards itself resulting in the release of protons.

2. Benzene. Benzene is a hybrid of two equivalent contributing structures (I and II) which differ in the position of the π-electron pairs representing double bonds. These were suggested by Kekule.

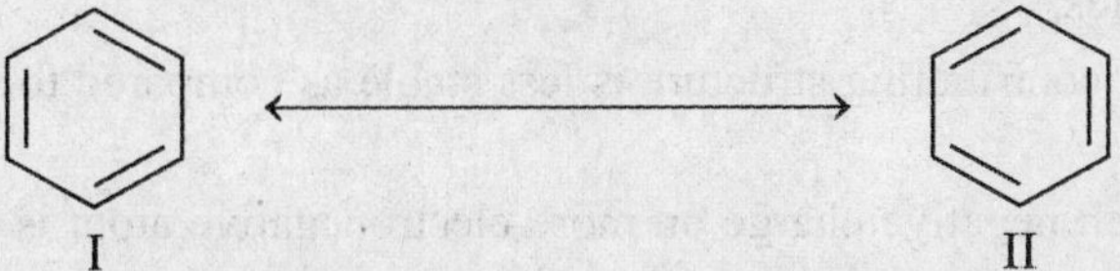

Three more contributing structures (III, IV and V) have been proposed by **Dewar**. Being less symmetrical they have small contribution (28% only) towards the hybrid. Benzene exists mainly in the form of **Kekule structures** (I and II). Benzene is, in fact, quite stable and its stability is explained

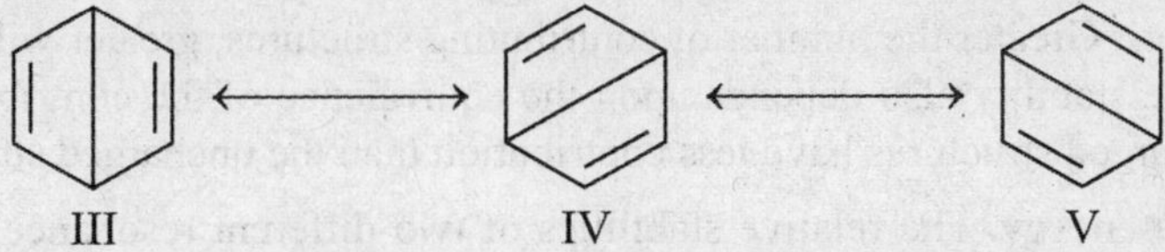

with the help of resonance. As the π-electron charge is distributed over greater area *i.e.*, it gets delocalised.

3. 1, 3- Butadiene. The diene can be regarded as the hybrid of the following contributing structures :

$$\underset{(I)}{CH_2=CH-CH=CH_2} \longleftrightarrow \underset{(II)}{\overset{\oplus}{C}H_2-CH=CH-\overset{\ominus}{C}H_2} \longleftrightarrow \underset{(III)}{\overset{\ominus}{C}H_2-CH=CH-\overset{\oplus}{C}H_2}$$

The charged structures II and III make lesser contribution towards the hybrid. However, they do explain the 1, 4-addition in the conjugated dienes.

4. Carbon dioxide. The structural formula of carbon dioxide (CO_2) molecule is O = C = O. The standard C = O bond length is 122 pm but the bond length which is obtained for the molecule from spectroscopic studies is 115 pm. The difference in the bond length values can be explained by considering the following structures for carbon dioxide which are known as the *resonating structures,* or *contributing structures* or *canonical structures.*

$$\underset{(I)}{:\ddot{O}=C=\ddot{O}:} \qquad \underset{(II)}{:\overset{-}{\ddot{O}}-C\equiv\overset{+}{O}:} \qquad \underset{(III)}{:\overset{+}{O}\equiv C-\overset{-}{\ddot{O}}:}$$

The carbon-oxygen bond length is the mean of all the bond length values. Carbon dioxide cannot be represented by any of the contributing structures but by an average of all. Carbon dioxide is said to be a resonance hybrid of these structures.

Conditions of resonance

Wheland has suggested the following conditions for resonance :

(*i*) The resonance or the contributing structures must differ only in the position of the electron pairs and not of the atomic nuclei.

(*ii*) The resonating structures must have the same number of paired and unpaired electrons.

(*iii*) The energies of the various resonating structures must be either same or nearly the same.

(*iv*) All the contributing or resonating structures do not contribute equally towards the hybrid. The equivalent structures have greater contribution. The contribution of any resonating structure towards the hybrid depends upon the following factors :

- Structures with more covalent bonds are more stable than the structures with less covalent bonds.
- The charged contributing structure is less stable as compared to the structure without any charge.
- Structure with negative charge on more electronegative atom is more stable than the structure with negative charge on less electronegative atom.

Effects of resonance

Some effects of the resonance are explained as under :

1. Stability. As a result of resonance, the energy of the hybrid decreases and its stability, therefore, increases. Greater the number of contributing structures, greater will be the stability of the hybrid. The stability also depends upon the equivalence of the contributing structures. Moreover, the charged structures have less contribution than the uncharged structures.

2. Resonance energy. The relative stabilities of two different resonance hybrids may be compared in terms of **resonance energy.** *It may be defined as the difference in the energy content of the hybrid and its most stable contributing structure.* It may be expressed either as the difference in the heat of combustion of the contributing structures and the hybrid or in terms of the difference in the heat of hydrogenation values. This is discussed as follows :

(*a*) Heat of combustion value. In benzene, the heat of combustion of the contributing structure is calculated by determining the values for different bonds mathematically.

Heat of combustion of 6 C — H bonds = 6 × 225.5 = 1355 kJ / mole

Heat of combustion of 3 C — C bonds = 3 × 206.0 = 618 kJ / mole

Heat of combustion of 3 C == C bonds = 3 × 491.0 = 1473 kJ / mole

3446 kJ / mole.

The value as determined experimentally for the hybrid is 3300 kJ / mole. Thus, the resonance energy for benzene is (3446 – 3300) kJ or **146 kJ / mole.**

Similarly, resonance energies for some typical molecules are as follows :

1, 3-Pentadiene (17.6 kJ / mole); 1, 3-Butadiene (14.6 kJ/mole) and 1, 3-Cyclohexadiene (7.5 kJ / mole).

(*b*) **Heat of hydrogenation value.** In benzene, the expected heat of hydrogenation value is 376 kJ/mole. But the value for the hybrid as determined experimentally is 230 kJ/mole *i.e.* the resonance energy is the same *i.e.* (376 – 230) kJ or (146 kJ / mole).

The relative stabilities of two hybrids can be compared in terms of the resonance energy value.

3. Bond length values. The resonance causes a change in bond length values. For example, the standard C — C bond length is 154 pm and C == C bond length is 134 pm. But the value as determined for benzene is 139 pm which does not coincide with any of the two values and is intermediate between the two values.

Types of resonance or mesomeric effect

Depending upon the nature of the functional group present adjacent to the multiple bond, the resonance effect (R) or mesomeric effect (M) are of two types :

(*i*) **Groups having electron-withdrawing resonance effect.** Groups such as — NO_2, > C == O, — C ≡ N, — COOH etc. tend to withdraw the electrons from the multiple bond through resonance and are said to have – M or – R effect. For example, in the following compound, the aldehyde group (— CH == O) has – R effect.

$$CH_3 — CH{=}CH — CH{=}\ddot{O}: \longleftrightarrow CH_3 — \overset{\oplus}{C}H — CH{=}CH — \ddot{O}:^{\ominus}$$

(*ii*) **Groups having electron-releasing resonance effect.** Groups such as — $\ddot{N}H_2$ — $\ddot{N}HR$, — $\ddot{N}R_2$ — $\ddot{O}$ — H, — $\ddot{O}$ — R etc. which can release electrons through resonance are said to have + M or + R effect. For example, the amine group (– NH_2) in the following compound has + R effect

$$CH_2{=}CH — \ddot{N}H_2 \longleftrightarrow \overset{\ominus}{C}H_2 — CH{=}\overset{\oplus}{N}H_2$$

Applications of resonance effect

Resonance effect or mesomeric effect is quite useful in explaining many observations in organic compounds. A few typical applications are being listed as follows :

1. Explanation for the acidic character of carboxylic acids. The acidic character of caboxylic acids is due to release of H^+ ion in aqueous solution.

$$R — \overset{\overset{\ddot{O}:}{\|}}{C} — \ddot{O} — H \rightleftharpoons R — \overset{\overset{\ddot{O}:}{|}}{C} — \ddot{O}:^{-} + H^+$$

This is explained with the help of resonance. Both the acid and the carboxylate ion are resonance stabilised as shown below :

$$\left[R — \overset{\overset{\ddot{O}:}{\|}}{C} — \ddot{O} — H \longleftrightarrow R — \overset{\overset{:\ddot{O}:^{\ominus}}{|}}{C} = \overset{\oplus}{\ddot{O}} — H \right] \rightleftharpoons \left[R — \overset{\overset{\ddot{O}:}{\|}}{C} — \ddot{O}:^{\ominus} \longleftrightarrow R — \overset{\overset{:\ddot{O}:^{\ominus}}{|}}{C} = \ddot{O}: \right] + H^+$$

Acid — Carboxylate ion

While the contributing structures for the carboxylate ion are exactly equivalent, they are not so for the acid. *Therefore, hybrid for the ion is more stable than hybrid for the acid. The acid changes to a more stable ion by releasing a proton and this accounts for the acidic character of carboxylic acid.*

2. Explanation for acidic character of phenols. The acidic nature of phenols is due to the release of H^+ ion in aqueous solution.

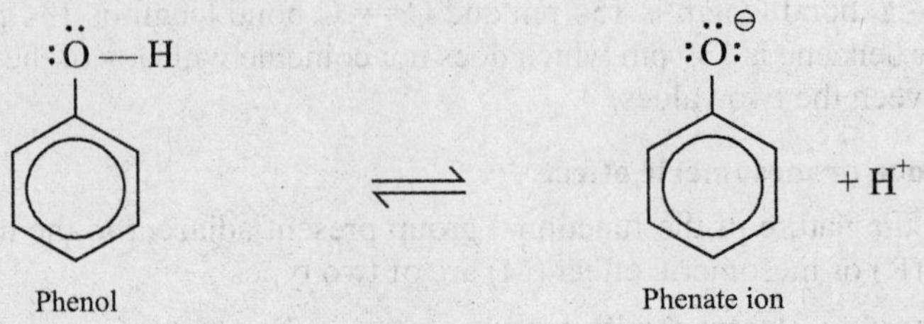

Phenol ⇌ Phenate ion + H^+

The acidic character in phenol is exhibited on the basis of resonance both in phenol and phenate ion. They exist as hybrid of a number of contributing structures as follows :

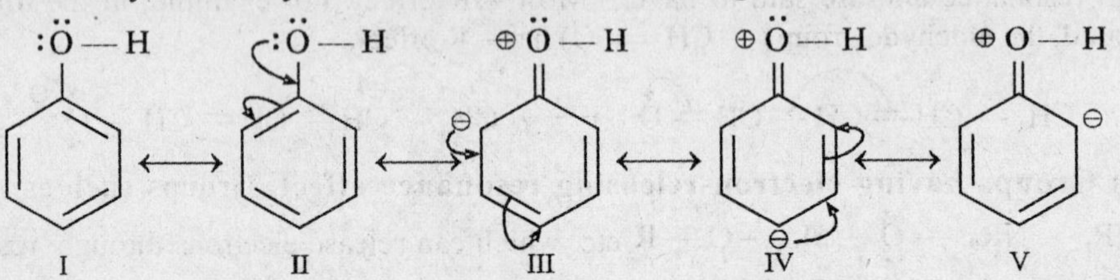

I ⟷ II ⟷ III ⟷ IV ⟷ V

Resonating structures of phenol

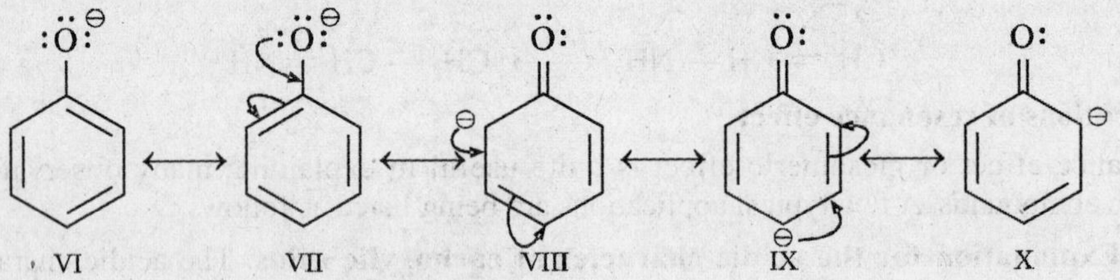

VI ⟷ VII ⟷ VIII ⟷ IX ⟷ X

Resonating structures for phenate ion

In case of phenol, contributing structures (III), (IV) and (V) involve charge separation i.e. they have both positive and negative charges. Energy is needed to separate the opposite charges. But no such structures are noticed in case of phenate ion. Therefore, the hybrid for the phenate ion is more stable and phenol changes to phenate ion by releasing proton. This accounts for the acidic character of phenol.

3. Comparison of relative basic strength of ethyl amine and acetamide. Ethyl amine is a stronger base than acetamide. In ethyl amine, the ethyl group with + I effect increases the electron density on the nitrogen atom. As a result, its electron releasing tendency is more. In acetamide the carbonyl group is an electron withdrawing group and takes away the electron pair from the nitrogen atom because of resonance as shown below :

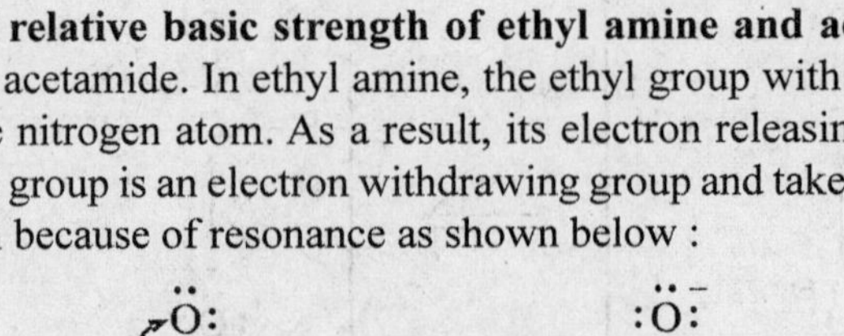

$$CH_3-\underset{}{\overset{\ddot{O}:}{\overset{\|}{C}}}-\ddot{N}H_2 \longleftrightarrow CH_3-\overset{:\ddot{O}:^-}{\overset{|}{C}}=\overset{+}{N}H_2$$

Resonance hybrids of acetamide

4. Comparison of relative basic strength of ethyl amine and aniline. Ethyl amine ($K_b = 5.6 \times 10^{-4}$) is much more basic than aniline ($K_b = 3.8 \times 10^{-10}$). In the former, the ethyl group with + I

$$H_5C_2 \rightarrow \ddot{N} - H \quad (\text{with } H \text{ on } N)$$

Ethyl amine

$$H - \ddot{N} - H \quad (\text{N bonded to benzene ring})$$

Aniline

effect increases the electron density on the nitrogen atom and, thus, increases electron releasing tendency or basic character. In the latter, the phenyl group with – I effect tends to decrease the electron density on the nitrogen atom resulting in a decreased basic strength. Aniline is a hybrid of following contributing structures :

$$\ddot{N}H_2 \longleftrightarrow \overset{\oplus}{N}H_2 \longleftrightarrow \overset{\oplus}{N}H_2 \longleftrightarrow \overset{\oplus}{N}H_2 \longleftrightarrow \ddot{N}H_2$$

The electron density on the nitrogen atom decreases, consequently, the electron releasing tendency or basic strength decreases.

Solved Examples

Example 1: Which of the following canonical forms would contribute most towards resonance? Explain.

$$\underset{(a)}{CH_2 = CH - CH = \overset{-}{C}H_2} \longleftrightarrow \underset{(b)}{CH_2 - \overset{-}{C}H = CH - \overset{+}{C}H_2} \longleftrightarrow \underset{(c)}{\overset{-}{C}H_2 - \overset{+}{C}H - CH = CH_2}$$

Solution: The resonance structures fulfilling the following conditions are more stable.

1. Greater number of covalent bonds
2. Less separation of charges
3. Negative charge on electronegative atom
4. Positive charge on electropositive atom
5. More dispersal of charges

Structure (*b*) takes care of dispersal of charge.

Hence, it is more stable and contributes more towards resonance.

Example 2: By what electronic effect can you explain the low reactivity of halogen atom in vinyl bromide.

or

On the basis of resonance, how will you explain low reactivity of vinyl bromide as compared to ethyl bromide?

Solution: Low reactivity of halogen in vinyl bromide can be explained on account of the phenomenon of resonance or mesomerism.

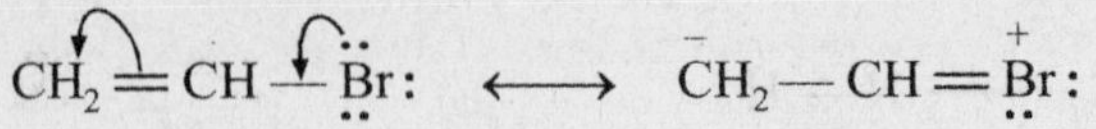

$$CH_2{=}CH{-}\ddot{\underset{..}{Br}}: \longleftrightarrow \overset{-}{C}H_2{-}CH{=}\overset{+}{\underset{..}{Br}}:$$

Halogen compounds generally give nucleophilic substitution reactions, in which the halogen is removed as halide ion.

But in the case of vinyl bromide, resonance takes place as illustrated above. This creates a double bond between carbon and bromine. Removal of bromine thus becomes difficult. Moreover, bromine, acquires a positive charge and hence cannot be substituted by a nucleophile. That is why vinyl bromide shows low reactivity.

Electron Displacement in Organic Compounds

The behaviour of an organic compound is influenced by the electron displacement taking place in its covalent bonds. These displacements may be permanent or temporary which take place in presence of another species in the molecule. The acidity and basicity of organic compounds, their stability, their reactivity towards other substances, etc. can be predicted based on such electronic displacements.

4.11 INDUCTIVE EFFECT

This is a permanent effect operating in polar covalent bonds. The induction of a permanent dipole in a covalent bond between two unlike atoms of different electronegativities is called the inductive effect. The development of partial +ve and –ve charges is due to shift of the shared pair of electrons towards the more electronegative atom. This results in small fractional charges on the constituent atoms. When a carbon atom is bonded to a hydrogen (C – H) or another carbon (C – C) atom by a covalent bond as in alkanes, the sharing of electron-pair is symmetrical between them. Thus, no charges are induced on the atoms. However, when carbon is bonded to a halogen (X), charges are created.

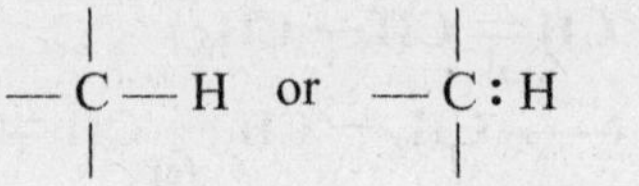

$-\overset{|}{\underset{|}{C}}-H$ or $-\overset{|}{\underset{|}{C}}:H$ (Symmetrical sharing of electron pair) Electronegativities of C and H are almost the same.

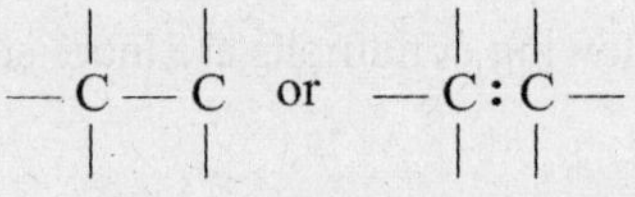

$-\overset{|}{\underset{|}{C}}-\overset{|}{\underset{|}{C}}$ or $-\overset{|}{\underset{|}{C}}:\overset{|}{\underset{|}{C}}-$ (Symmetrical sharing of electron pair)

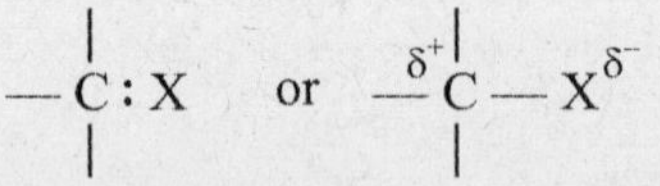

$-\overset{|}{\underset{|}{C}}:X$ or $-\overset{\delta^+}{\underset{|}{\overset{|}{C}}}-X^{\delta^-}$ (Fractional charges due to greater electronegativity of X)

The direction of displacement is shown by placing an arrow head midway along the line representing the sigma bond.

$$C_4 \rightarrow C_3 \rightarrow C_2 \rightarrow \overset{\delta^+}{C_1} \rightarrow \overset{\delta^-}{Cl}$$

The inductive effect of an atom or a group of atoms diminishes rapidly with distance. Infact, the inductive effect is almost negligible beyond two carbon atoms from the active atom or group.

Inductive effect does not involve actual transfer of electrons from one atom to another but simply helps in displacing them permanently.

Groups with –I effect:

$$NO_2 > CN > F > COOH > Cl > Br > I > OCH_3 > C_6H_5$$

Decreasing order of – I effect ⟶

Groups with + I effect :

$$(CH_3)_3C > (CH_3)_2CH > C_2H_5 > CH_3 > -H$$

Decreasing order of + I effect ⟶

Applications

(*i*) Reactivity of alkyl halides: The presence of halogen atoms in the molecule of alkyl halide creates a centre of low electron density on adjacent carbon which is readily attacked by the negatively charged reagents.

$$CH_3 \rightarrow Cl \quad \text{or} \quad \overset{\delta^+}{CH_3}\!-\!\overset{\delta^-}{Cl}$$

↑ Site for the attack of electron rich reagent

(*ii*) Dipole moment: As the inductive effect increases, the dipole moment increases. This is because the dipole moment is the product of distance and charge.

$$\underset{1.64\ D}{CH_3 \rightarrow I} \qquad \underset{1.79\ D}{CH_3 \rightarrow Br} \qquad \underset{1.83\ D}{CH_3 \rightarrow Cl}$$

Inductive effect increases ⟶

(*iii*) (*a*) Acidity of acetic acid and halogen substituted acetic acid:

$$Cl \leftarrow CH_2 \leftarrow \underset{\underset{O}{\|}}{C} \leftarrow O \leftarrow H \qquad H_3C - \underset{\underset{O}{\|}}{C} - O - H$$

Chloroacetic acid $pK_a = 2.86$ — Acetic acid $pK_a = 4.76$

$$Cl_2CH \leftarrow \overset{\overset{O}{\|}}{C} \leftarrow O \leftarrow H \qquad Cl_3C \leftarrow \overset{\overset{O}{\|}}{C} \leftarrow O \leftarrow H$$

Dichloroacetic acid $pK_a = 1.25$ — Trichloroacetic acid $pK_a = 0.65$

The decreasing order of acid strength

$$Cl_3CCOOH > Cl_2CHCOOH > ClCH_2COOH > CH_3COOH$$

On the other hand, electron withdrawing –I effect decreases electron availability on carbonyl carbon and therefore increases the rate of nucleophilic addition.

$$CCl_3-\overset{\overset{O}{\|}}{C}-H > H-\overset{\overset{O}{\|}}{C}-H > H_3C-\overset{\overset{O}{\|}}{C}-H > CH_3-\overset{\overset{O}{\|}}{C}-CH_3$$

Decreasing order of nucleophilic addition ⟶

(*b*) Relative acid strength of formic acid and acetic acid:

$$H_3C \rightarrow \underset{\underset{O}{\|}}{C} \rightarrow O \rightarrow H \qquad H - \underset{\underset{O}{\|}}{C} - O - H$$

$pK_a = 4.79$ — $pK_a = 3.77$

Methyl group has an electron-releasing inductive effect (+*I* effect). It reduces the release of protons. Therefore acetic acid is a weaker acid than formic acid.

(c) Relative acid strength of fluoroacetic acid, chloroacetic acid, bromoacetic acid and iodoacetic acid

Halogenated acids are much stronger acids than the parent acid and the acidity increases with the increase in electronegativity of the halogen present which helps in the release of protons. Thus, the strength of halogenated acids follows the order :

$$FCH_2COOH > ClCH_2COOH > BrCH_2COOH > ICH_2COOH$$

Inductive effect decreases with increase in distance of halogen atom from the carboxylic group, hence the strength of the acid is proportionally decreased. Thus,

$$\underset{\alpha\text{-Chlorobutyric acid}}{CH_3CH_2CH(Cl)COOH} > \underset{\beta\text{-Chlorobutyric acid}}{CH_3CH(Cl)CH_2COOH} > \underset{\gamma\text{-Chlorobutyric acid}}{CH_2ClCH_2CH_2COOH} > \underset{n\text{-Butyric acid}}{CH_3CH_2CH_2COOH}$$

(*iv*) (*a*) Relative reactivity of toluene and benzene in aromatic substitution reactions

Aromatic substitution reactions are electrophilic in nature. Methyl has an electron-releasing inductive effect (+*I* effect). Therefore, toluene with higher electron density than benzene has greater reactivity in electrophilic substitution reactions.

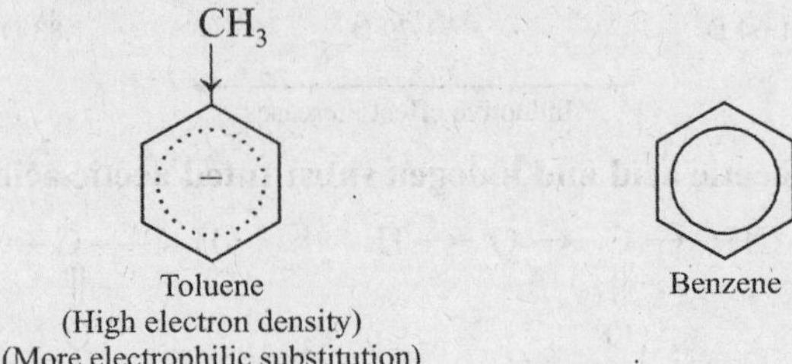

Toluene
(High electron density)
(More electrophilic substitution)

Benzene

(*b*) Relative reactivity of nitrobenzene and benzene in electrophilic aromatic substitution reactions

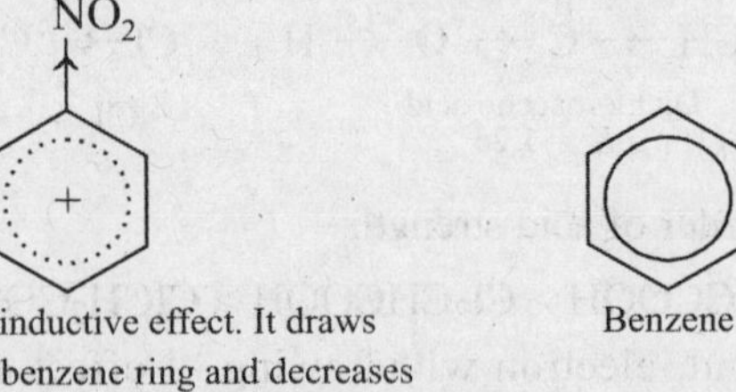

NO_2 group has –*I* inductive effect. It draws electrons from the benzene ring and decreases electron density on the ring
(Less reactive towards electrophilic substitution reactions)

Benzene

(*v*) Compared to water, phenol is more acidic (–*I* effect) but methyl alcohol is less acidic (+*I* effect)

This is because phenyl group has –*I* effect while methyl group has +*I* effect.

$$\underset{\text{Phenol}}{C_6H_5 \leftarrow OH} > \underset{\text{Water}}{H — OH} > \underset{\text{Methyl alcohol}}{CH_3 \rightarrow OH}$$

(*vi*) Inductive effect is dependent on state of hybridisation of the atoms linked by covalent bond

Relative acidity of hydrocarbons may be given as

$$\underset{sp}{HC \equiv CH} > \underset{sp^2}{CH_2 = CH_2} > \underset{sp^3}{CH_3 - CH_3}$$

Electron density on *s*-orbital is more than on, *p*-orbital. Percentage of *s* character decrease from left to right.

Relative basicity of corresponding carbanions is as :

$$CH_3-\bar{C}H_2 > CH_2=\bar{C}H > CH\equiv\bar{C}$$

(*vii*) Strength of base. Base strength is defined as the tendency to donate an electron pair for sharing. Strength of a base can be explained on the basis of inductive effect.

(*a*) As compared to ammonia, methyl amine is more basic (+*I* effect) but aniline is less basic and diphenyl amine is a still weaker base (–*I* effect).

$$CH_3NH_2 > NH_3 > C_6H_5NH_2 > (C_6H_5)_2NH$$

(*b*) The decreasing order of base strength in alcohols from tertiary to primary is due to +I effect of alkyl groups.

$$\underset{3°}{(CH_3)_3COH} > \underset{2°}{(CH_3)_2CHOH} > \underset{1°}{CH_3CH_2OH} > \underset{\text{methyl}}{CH_3OH}$$

(*c*) Greater the tendency to donate electron pair for coordination with proton, more is the basic nature, or more the negative charge on nitrogen atom (due to +*I* effect of alkyl group), higher is the basic strength.

Thus, the basic nature decreases in the order,

Alkyl group	Relative basic strength
CH_3	$R_2NH > RNH_2 > R_3N > NH_3$
C_2H_5	$R_2NH > RNH_2 > NH_3 > R_3N$
$(CH_3)_2CH$	$RNH_2 > NH_3 > R_2NH > R_3N$
$(CH_3)_3C$	$NH_3 > RNH_2 > R_2NH > R_3N$

(*viii*)Relative stabilities of carbocations :

Greater the number of alkyl groups attached to positive carbon, greater the dispersal of charge and hence greater is the stability.

$$(CH_3)_3\overset{\oplus}{C} > (CH_3)_2\overset{\oplus}{C}H > (CH_3)\overset{\oplus}{C}H_2 > \overset{\oplus}{C}H_3$$

(*ix*) +*I* group increases electron availability on carbonyl carbon :

This therefore decreases the rate of nucleophilic addition.

4.12 FIELD EFFECT

Inductive effect is a permanent effect in the ground state of the molecule and usually operates through single bonds. However, when the inductive effect is transmitted through space or solvent molecules, it is called as field effect. Consider the two isomers I and II of the following molecule

$pK_a = 5.67$
I

$pK_a = 6.07$
II

The two chlorine atoms in I and II exert the same inductive effect with respect to the position of electrons associated with the – COOH group and therefore the two compounds should exhibit the same acid strength. However, the two chlorine atoms in the molecule I are closer to the acid group as compared to II, and therefore will exert greater electron withdrawing effect in I as compared to II. Hence the isomer I is a stronger acid than II.

4.13 ELECTROMERIC EFFECT

This is a temporary effect operating in unsaturated compounds only at the demand of a reagent. As soon as this attacking reagent is removed, the original condition is restored.

It involves the complete transfer of π-electrons of multiple bond, because π-bonds are loosely held and are easily polarisable.

$$>C=\ddot{O}: \underset{\text{Reagent withdrawn}}{\overset{\text{Reagent added}}{\rightleftharpoons}} >\overset{+}{C}-\ddot{O}:^{\ominus}$$

The complete transfer of shared pair of π-electrons of a multiple bond to the more electronegative atom of the bonded atoms at the requirement of an attacking reagent is called electromeric effect (*E*-effect).

When the transfer of π-electrons takes place towards the attacking reagent (electrophile), the effect is called +*E*-effect.

For example,

$$>C=C< + H^+ \longrightarrow >\overset{+}{C}-\underset{H}{C}<$$

$$\underset{\text{Propene}}{CH_3 \rightarrow CH = CH_2} + H^+ \longrightarrow CH_3-\overset{+}{C}H-CH_3$$

When the transfer of electrons takes place away from the attacking reagent, the effect is called –*E* effect, For example,

$$>C=O + CN^- \longrightarrow >\underset{CN}{C}-O^-$$

$$\left[>C=\ddot{O}: + :CN^{\ominus} \xrightarrow[\text{slow}]{\text{step (i)}} >\underset{CN}{C}-\ddot{O}:^{\ominus} \xrightarrow[\text{step (ii) fast}]{H^{\oplus}} >\underset{CN}{C}-OH \right]$$

When the I- and E-effect occur together in a molecule, they may be supporting or opposing each other. When they are opposing, the *E*-effect generally dominates over *I*-effect.

Applications

(*i*) Electrophilic addition reactions of unsaturated compounds involve electromeric effect or the polarisation of the carbon-carbon double bond in the presence of attacking electrophiles like H^+.

(*ii*) Nucleophilic addition reactions of carbonyl compounds involve electromeric effect or polarisation through –*E* electromeric effect of the carbon-oxygen double bond in the presence of a nucleophile.

(*iii*) Electrophilic substitution reactions of benzenoids involve polarisation through electromeric effect of the benzene ring when an electrophile approaches them. For example,

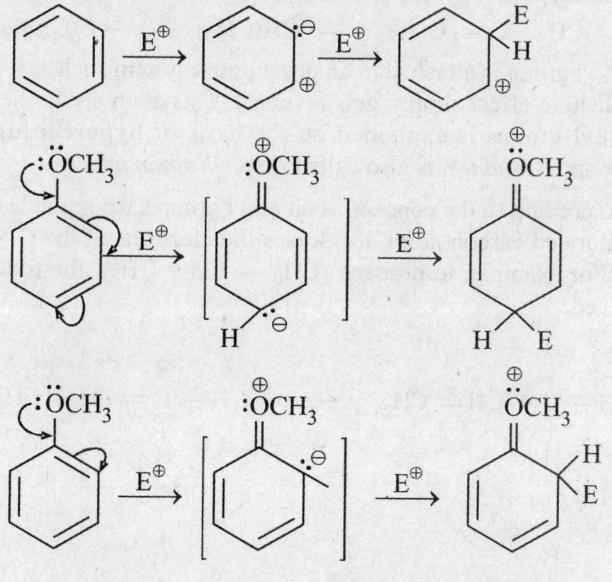

Comparison of Inductive and Electromeric Effects

Inductive Effect	Electromeric Effect
1. It involves a permanent displacement of the electron pairs in the molecule.	It involves a temporary transference of the electron pair towards more electronegative atom in the molecule.
2. The displaced electron pair does not leave its molecular orbital. There is only a distortion in shape of the molecular orbital.	The electron pair which gets transferred, completely leaves its molecular orbital and takes up a new position.
3. The presence of the outside attacking reagent is not needed	The presence of the outside attacking reagent is essential.
4. There is a partial separation of the charges.	There is a complete separation of the charges.
5. No ions are formed.	Ions are formed.
6. The presence of multiple bond is not essential.	The presence of multiple bond is essential.

Comparison of Resonance and Inductive Effects

Resonance Effect	Inductive Effect
1. It occurs in conjugated systems.	It occurs in saturated compounds.
2. It involves the transference of the π-electrons.	It involves the displacement of the σ-electrons.
3. It involves delocalisation of electrons.	It does not involve any delocalisation of electrons.
4. It does not undergo any change in charge density with distance.	It decreases as we move away from the atom involved in the initial polar bond.

4.14 HYPERCONJUGATION OR NO BOND RESONANCE

In the study of inductive effect, we have observed that the alkyl group has +I effect and the order of +I effects of different alkyl groups follow the order :

$$—CH_3 < —C_2H_5 < —CH(CH_3)_2 < —C(CH_3)_3$$

But when the alkyl group is attached to an unsaturated system such as $—CH=CH_2$ group, the order of the inductive effect simply gets reversed. This anomaly in the electron releasing tendency of the alkyl groups is explained on the basis of **hyperconjugation** which was developed by *Baker* and *Nathan.* It is also called *Baker-Nathan effect.*

Explanation. According to the concept, if an alkyl group carrying at least one hydrogen is attached to an unsaturated carbon atom, it releases the electrons of the C — H bond towards the multiple bond. For example, in propene ($CH_3 — CH = CH_2$), the following contributing structures are involved.

$$H—\overset{H}{\underset{\alpha|\,H}{C}}—CH=CH_2 \longleftrightarrow H—\overset{H^+}{\underset{H}{C}}=CH—\overset{\ominus}{C}H_2$$

$$\updownarrow$$

$$H—\overset{H}{\underset{^+H}{C}}=CH—\overset{\ominus}{C}H_2 \longleftrightarrow H^+\ \overset{H}{\underset{H}{C}}=CH—\overset{\ominus}{C}H_2$$

Since there is no bond between the α-carbon atom and one of the hydrogen atoms, the hyper conjugation is also called **no-bond resonance.** Now, hyperconjugation due to $CH_3—$ group is expected to be more than due to $CH_3CH_2—$ group since the latter has only two hydrogen atoms attached to the α-carbon atom directly linked to the double bonded carbon atom. Therefore, the number of contributing structures for ethyl group will be less. Similarly, the electron releasing tendency in $(CH_3)_2CH—$ group will be still less as it has only one hydrogen atom attached to the α-carbon atom and this tendency will be the least when the $(CH_3)_3C—$ group is attached to the $CH=CH_2$ group. Thus, the order of the electron releasing tendency or inductive effect of the alkyl groups get reversed because of the phenomenon of hyperconjugation.

Orbital concept of hyperconjugation

The orbital concept of hyperconjugation is illustrated with the help of propene ($H_3C—CH=CH_2$). As mentioned earlier the electron pair of C — H bond (σ-bond) is involved in conjugation with the π-electron pair of the double bond. This may be shown with the help of Fig. 4.15.

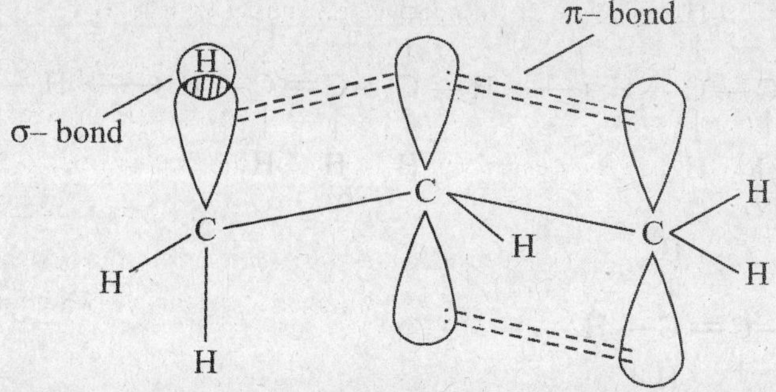

Fig. 4.15: Overlapping of orbitals in propene

The σ — π conjugation is called hyperconjugation. Though hydrogen atom of the methyl group is not forming any real bond with the double bonded carbon atom but it is not actually free to leave its original position. From the orbital structure, it is evident that there is interaction between the electrons of the C — H bond and the π-electrons of the adjoining double bond. This will bring about a change in the bond lengths of C — H and C ═ C bonds. This has been supported by the experimental determination of the bond lengths.

Applications of hyperconjugation

The concept of hyperconjugation is quite useful in explaining relative stabilities of a number of species such as alkyl free radicals, carbocations and alkenes. These are briefly discussed as follows :

1. Relative Stabilities of Alkyl Free Radicals

The order of the relative stabilities of different alkyl free radicals is :

$$\underset{\substack{\text{Tert-butyl}\\(3^\circ)}}{(CH_3)_3\dot{C}} \;>\; \underset{\substack{\text{Isopropyl}\\(2^\circ)}}{(CH_3)_2\dot{C}H} \;>\; \underset{\substack{\text{Ethyl}\\(1^\circ)}}{CH_3\dot{C}H_2} \;>\; \underset{\substack{\text{Methyl}\\(1^\circ)}}{\dot{C}H_3}$$

Ethyl free radical is regarded as a hybrid of four contributing structures.

$$\underset{(I)}{\begin{array}{ccccccc} & & H & & & & H & & \\ & & | & & \cdot & & | & & \\ H & — & C & — & C & — & C & — & H \\ & & | & & | & & | & & \\ & & H & & H & & H & & \end{array}} \longleftrightarrow \underset{(II)}{\begin{array}{ccccccc} & & \overset{}{H}\!\cdot & & & & H & & \\ & & & & & & | & & \\ H & — & C & = & C & — & C & — & H \\ & & | & & | & & | & & \\ & & H & & H & & H & & \end{array}} \longleftrightarrow \underset{(III)}{\begin{array}{ccccccc} & & H & & & & H & & \\ & & | & & & & | & & \\ H & — & C & = & C & — & C & — & H \\ & & | & & | & & | & & \\ & & \dot{H} & & H & & H & & \end{array}}$$

But there is no possibily of any hyperconjugation in methyl free radical. Therefore, ethyl free radical is more stable than the methyl free radical.

In isopropyl free radical, there are two methyl groups attached to the carbon atom which has single electron. As a result, six contributing structures in addition to normal structure are possible as shown below :

$$\underset{(I)}{\begin{array}{ccccccc} & & H & & & & H & & \\ & & | & & \cdot & & | & & \\ H & — & C & — & C & — & C & — & H \\ & & | & & | & & | & & \\ & & H & & H & & H & & \end{array}} \longleftrightarrow \underset{(II)}{\begin{array}{ccccccc} & & \underset{\cdot}{H} & & & & H & & \\ & & & & & & | & & \\ H & — & C & = & C & — & C & — & H \\ & & | & & | & & | & & \\ & & H & & H & & H & & \end{array}} \longleftrightarrow \underset{(III)}{\begin{array}{ccccccc} & & H & & & & H & & \\ & & | & & & & | & & \\ H & — & C & = & C & — & C & — & H \\ & & | & & | & & & & \\ & & \dot{H} & & H & & \underset{\cdot}{H} & & \end{array}}$$

```
          H      H                  H                     H         H
          |      |                  |          H•         |         |
⟷ H• C = C — C — H  ⟷  H — C — C = C — H  ⟷  H — C — C = C •H
      |     |     |                 |     |     |          |     |     |
      H     H     H                 H     H     H          H     H     H
            (IV)                          (V)                   (VI)

           H          H
           |          |
⟷ H — C — C = C — H
           |    |     Ḣ
           H    H
              (VII)
```

Similarly, *nine contributing structures* are possible for the tertiary butyl free radical in addition to its normal structure. Therefore, it is still more stable and thus, the order of the relative stabilities of the different alkyl free radicals can be explained.

2. Relative Stabilities of Alkyl Carbocations

The order of relative stabilities of the alkyl carbocations is

$$\underset{\text{Tert-butyl}}{(CH_3)_3C^{\oplus}} > \underset{\text{Isopropyl}}{(CH_3)_2CH^{\oplus}} > \underset{\text{Ethyl}}{CH_3CH_2^{\oplus}} > \underset{\text{Methyl}}{CH_3^{\oplus}}$$

and the order is the same as in case of free radicals. This can also be explained with the help of hyperconjugation. The ethyl carbocation (primary) has three contributing structures in addition to its normal structure based upon hyperconjugation.

```
     H    H              H⁺  H              H    H              H    H
     |    |                  |              |    |              |    |
H — C — C⁺  ⟷  H — C = C  ⟷  H — C = C  ⟷  H⁺   C = C
     |    |              |    |                  |              |    |
     H    H              H    H             ⁺H   H              H    H
      (I)                 (II)               (III)               (IV)
```

It is more stable than methyl carbocation where no resonance is possible. Similarly, the contributing structures in isopropyl carbocation and tertiary butyl carbocation are six and nine respectively in addition to the normal structure. Hence these are more stabilised and relative order of their stabilities is justified.

The order of the relative stabilities of the different alkyl carbocations can also be explained with the help of inductive effect (+*I* effect).

```
        CH₃                 CH₃                  H                 H
         ↓                   ↓                   ↓                 ↓
H₃C ⟶ C ⊕          HC ⟶ C ⊕          H₃C ⟶ C ⊕         H ⟶ C ⊕
         ↑                   ↑                   ↑                 ↑
        CH₃                  H                   H                 H
      Tertiary           Isopropyl             Ethyl             Methyl
       butyl
```

Because of the +I effect, the alkyl group will tend to increase the electron density on positively charged carbon atom neutralising its +ve charge to some extent. As the reactivity of carbocation is due to the positive charge on it, the reactivity will tend to decrease and the stability will correspondingly increase. Thus, greater the number of the alkyl groups present, greater will be the stability of carbocation and lesser will be the reactivity. Thus, the relative stabilities of different alkyl carbocations can be explained.

3. Relative Stabilities of Alkenes

The order of the relative stabilities of different alkenes is:

$$R_2C=CR_2 > R_2C=CHR > RCH=CHR > RCH=CH_2 > CH_2=CH_2$$

This can be explained on the basis of hyperconjugation. The presence of alkyl group (say methyl group) on the double bonded carbon atom is likely to increase the number of contributing structures due to hyperconjugation.

$$H-\underset{H}{\overset{H}{|}}{C}-CH=CH_2 \qquad H-\underset{H}{\overset{H}{|}}{C}-HC=CH-\underset{H}{\overset{H}{|}}{C}-H$$

Propene (Three contributing structures)

2-Butene (Six contributing structures)

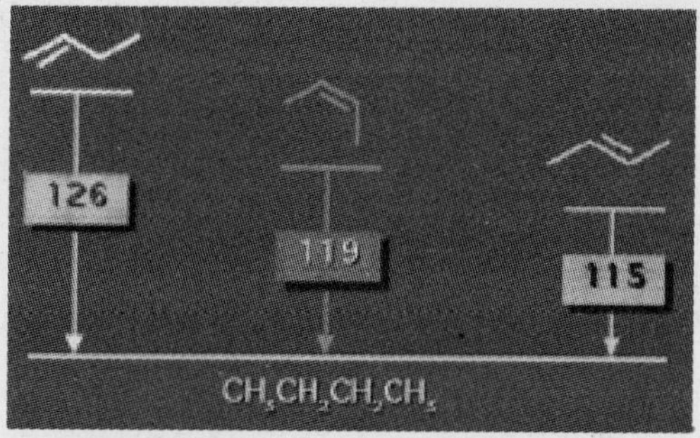

Stability of isomeric alkenes

Thus, greater the number of the contributing structures, greater will be the stability of the alkene.

4. Bond length

Hyperconjugation, like conjugation and resonance, also affects bond length.

$$H-\underset{H}{\overset{H}{|}}{C}\overset{1.46\,Å}{-}CH\underset{1.353\,Å}{=}CH_2 \longleftrightarrow H-\underset{H}{\overset{H^+}{|}}{C}=CH-\overset{\ominus}{C}H_2$$

Bond length in propene is 1.46 Å in contrast to normal 1.54 Å (in propane). It is due to the partial double bond character acquired and hence a little shorter.

5. Dipole moment

Since hyperconjugation causes the separation of charges, it also affects the dipole moment in the molecule.

$$\begin{array}{c} H \\ | \\ H-C=O \end{array} \quad \begin{array}{c} H \\ | \\ H-C-CH=O \\ | \\ H \end{array} \longleftrightarrow \begin{array}{c} H^+ \\ \\ H-C=CH-O^- \\ | \\ H \end{array}$$

$\mu = 2.27$ D $\quad\quad \mu = 2.72$ D

6. Ortho-para directing property of methyl group in toluene is partly due to +I effect and partly due to hyperconjugation.

$$\begin{array}{c} H \\ | \\ H-C-H \\ | \\ C_6H_5 \end{array} \longleftrightarrow \begin{array}{c} H \\ | \\ H-C\ H^+ \\ \| \\ \text{(ortho }\ominus) \end{array} \longleftrightarrow \begin{array}{c} H \\ | \\ H-C\ H^+ \\ | \\ \text{(para }\ominus) \end{array} \longleftrightarrow \begin{array}{c} H \\ | \\ H-C\ H^+ \\ | \\ \text{(ortho }\ominus) \end{array}$$

Types of Hyperconjugation

(*a*) Sacrafacial hyperconjugation

The essential condition is the attachment of alkyl group to double bond or triple bond.

$$\begin{array}{c} H \\ | \\ H-C-C=C\langle \\ | \\ H \end{array} \quad \text{or} \quad \begin{array}{c} H \\ | \\ H-C-C\equiv C- \\ | \\ H \end{array}$$

Carbon atom of alkyl group attached to double bond must contain atleast one hydrogen atom in hyperconjugation.

$$\begin{array}{c} H \\ | \\ H-C-C=C- \\ | \quad | \quad | \\ H \end{array} \longleftrightarrow \begin{array}{c} H \\ | \\ H-C=C-\overset{\ominus}{C}- \\ | \quad | \\ H^+ \end{array}$$

$$\updownarrow$$

$$\begin{array}{c} H^+ \\ \\ H-C=C-\overset{\ominus}{C}- \\ | \quad | \quad | \\ H \end{array} \longleftrightarrow \begin{array}{c} H \\ | \\ H^+\ \ C=C-\overset{\ominus}{C}- \\ | \quad | \quad | \\ H \end{array}$$

It involves a sort of sacrifice of bond and hence the name sacrafacial.

(*b*) Isovalent hyperconjugation

This kind of hyperconjugation involves no sacrifice of bonds. Ethyl radicals have the same number of real bonds as the classical structure.

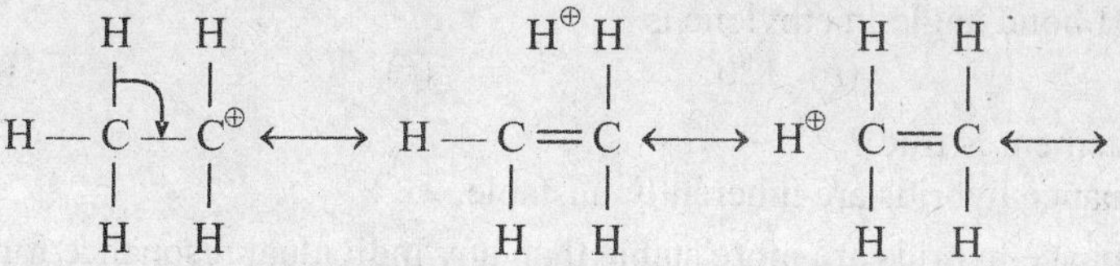

$$H-\underset{H}{\overset{H}{C}}-\underset{H}{\overset{H}{C^{\oplus}}} \longleftrightarrow H-\underset{H}{C}=\underset{H}{\overset{H}{C}} \; (H^{\oplus}) \longleftrightarrow H^{\oplus} \; \underset{H}{\overset{H}{C}}=\underset{H}{\overset{H}{C}} \longleftrightarrow$$

(I) (II) (III)

Note: For Dipole Moment studies, refer to Chapter 1, Molecular polarity and weak chemical forces.

Evaluate Yourself

Multiple Choice Questions

1. When the carbon atom is sp^2 hybridized in a compound, it is bonded to
(*a*) 2 other atoms (*b*) 4 other atoms
(*c*) 3 other atoms (*d*) 5 other atoms

2. What is bond angle between the hybrid orbitals in methane ?
(*a*) 180° (*b*) 120° (*c*) 109.5° (*d*) 115.5°

3. What is the bond length of a carbon-carbon double bond ?
(*a*) 1.20 Å (*b*) 1.34 Å (*c*) 1.54 Å (*d*) 1.68 Å

4. Which of the following is the correct order of bond lengths :
(*a*) $C-C < C=C < C\equiv C$ (*b*) $C-C > C\equiv C > C=C$
(*c*) $C\equiv C > C-C > C=C$ (*d*) $C\equiv C < C-C > C=C$

5. The carbon-carbon bond length is maximum in
(*a*) $CH_2=CH_2$ (*b*) CH_3CH_3
(*c*) $HC\equiv CH$ (*d*)

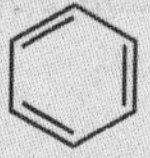

6. Compound in which carbons use only sp^2 hybrid orbitals for bond formation is
(*a*) 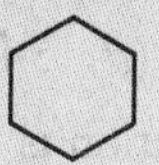 (*b*) 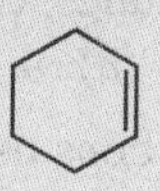
(*c*) $CH_2=CH-CH=CH_2$ (*d*) $CH_3CH=C=CH_2$

7. The H-C-C bond angle in ethane is
(*a*) 60° (*b*) 109°28′ (*c*) 120° (*d*) 118°28′

8. The carbon-carbon bond lengths in rank of increasing bond length is:
(*a*) triple, double, single (*b*) single, double, triple
(*c*) single, triple, double (*d*) triple, single, double

9. Which of the following hydrocarbons has the shortest C-C bond length?
(*a*) $CH_2=CH_2$ (*b*) CH_3CH_3
(*c*) $HC=CH$ (*d*)

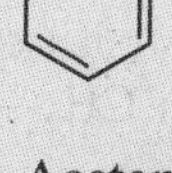

10. Which of the following is a planar molecule?
(*a*) Formaldehyde (*b*) Acetone
(*c*) Formic acid (*d*) Acetic acid

11. The H-C-H bond angle in ethylene is
(*a*) 60° (*b*) 120° (*c*) 90° (*d*) 180°

12. Which statement is true ?
(*a*) Resonance hybrids are inherently unstable.
(*b*) Resonance hybrids are more stable than any individual resonance form.
(*c*) Resonance hybrids are averages of all resonance forms resembling .the less stable forms.
(*d*) Resonance hybrids are averages of all resonance forms resembling the more stable forms.

13. The order of stability of carbonium ions is
(*a*) tertiary > secondary > primary (*b*) secondary > tertiary > primary
(*c*) primary > secondary > tertiary (*d*) primary > tertiary > secondary

14. Which of the following carbonium ions will be most stable ?
(*a*) $\overset{+}{C}H_3$ (*b*) $CH_3\overset{+}{C}H_2$
(*c*) $(CH_3)_2\overset{+}{C}H$ (*d*) $CH_2=CH\overset{+}{C}H_2$

15. Resonance structures of a molecule have
(*a*) same arrangement of atoms (*b*) different arrangement of atoms
(*c*) same number of paired electrons (*d*) different number of paired electrons

16. Which of the following compounds will show dipole moment ?
(*a*) *Cis*-l, 2-dichloroethylene (*b*) *o*-dichlorobenzene
(*c*) *trans.* l, 2-dichloroethylene (*d*) *p*-dichlorobenzene

17. The order of stability of carbanions is
(*a*) primary > secondary > tertiary (*b*) secondary > tertiary > primary
(*c*) tertiary > secondary > primary (*d*) tertiary > primary > secondary

18. Which of the following compounds have planar molecules ?
(*a*) ethyl alcohol (*b*) formaldehyde
(*c*) diethyl ether (*d*) 1,3-butadiene

19. In stable organic compounds, carbon will always form
(*a*) 2 bonds (*b*) 4 bonds (*c*) 3 bonds (*d*) 5 bonds

20. Compound in which carbons use only sp^3 hybrid orbitals for bond formation is
(*a*) $CH_3CH_2CH_3$ (*b*) $CH_3C\equiv CH$
(*c*) $CH_3CH=CH_2$ (*d*) $CH_2=CH—CH=CH_2$

Short Answer Questions

1. What are + I and – I effects ? Illustrate with two examples in each case.
2. How will you account for the polarisation of a covalent bond ?
3. Define resonance. What is the difference between resonance and isomerism ?
4. Why is phenol a stronger acid than aliphatic alcohol ?
5. Show how the carbanion $\overset{\ominus}{C}H_2—\underset{}{\overset{O}{\overset{\|}{C}}}—CH_3$ is stabilised due to resonance ?
6. Arrange the following in decreasing order of – I effect.

$$-C_6H_5, -NO_2, -COOH, -CN, -I, -F, -Br, -Cl$$

7. Compare the relative acidic strengths of the following on the basis of inductive effect.

$$HC \equiv CH, CH_3C \equiv CH, C_2H_5C \equiv CH$$

8. The electromeric effect is only temporary in nature. How will you account for this ?
9. Give the decreasing order of basicity of the following carbanions :

$$\overset{\ominus}{C_2H_5} > \overset{\ominus}{HC} = CH_2 > \overset{\ominus}{C} \equiv CH$$

10. Electromeric effect is only a temporary effect. Comment.
11. Out of ethylamine and acetamide, which is more basic and why ?
12. How will you distinguish between resonance and inductive effect ?
13. Out of $(CH_3)_3\overset{+}{C}$ and $(CH_3)_2\overset{+}{CH}$ carbocations, which is more stable and why ?
14. The dipole moment of *m*-dichlorobenzene is 1.48 D while that of the *o*-dichlorobenzene is 2.30 D. How will you account for this ?
15. How does hyperconjugation help in comparing the relative stabilities of alkenes ?
16. Why is ethylamine more basic than ammonia ?
17. Give the names and definitions of two effects involving electron displacement.

Long Answer Questions

1. Enlist the various conditions for a compound to exhibit resonance.
2. How will you account for the acidic character of phenol ?
3. Differentiate between inclusion compounds and clathrates.
4. What are charge transfer complexes ? Give an example.
5. What is meant by field effects ? Give an example.
6. What is meant by localized and delocalized chemical bond ? Explain by taking example of 1, 3-butadiene
7. What is hybridisation ? What are the distinguishing features of sp^3 and sp^2 orbitals ? Explain with examples.
8. Explain why four covalent bonds in methane are equivalent.
9. Discuss the orbital structure of methane.
10. Explain clearly (*a*) bond length (*b*) bond angle and (*c*) bond energy.
11. What is the difference between inductive and electromeric effects ?
12. In what way a covalent bond is fissioned ? What are its results ?
13. Write a short note on resonance effect.
14. Write note on electromeric effect.
15. Define inductive effect and mesomeric effect.
16. What is meant by inductive effect ? Describe with the help of inductive effect that dichloro acetic acid is a stronger acid than acetic acid.
17. (*a*) Explain what do you understand by inductive effect.

    (*b*) How does inductive effect help in explaining.

    i. Relative acidic strengths of acetic acid and formic acid ?

    ii. Relative basic strengths of primary, secondary and tertiary amines ?

18. Explain the following :
(*i*) Hyperconjugation effect. (*ii*) Electromeric effect.

19. Write notes on :
(*i*) Inductive effect (*ii*) Electromeric effect (*iii*) Hyperconjugation.

20. What is hyperconjugation ? With its help, explain which of the following free radicals is the most stable :

$$CH_3-\dot{C}H_2,\ \dot{C}H_3,\ (CH_3)_3\dot{C},\ (CH_3)_2\dot{C}H$$

21. Give the main points of difference between inductive and electromeric effects.

22. Give a brief account of :
(*i*) Resonance effect (*ii*) Inductive effect.

23. What is inductive effect ? With its help, show that dichloro acetic acid is a stronger acid than acetic acid.

24. What is inductive effect ? How does inductive effect help in explaining the relative strengths of organic acids.

25. Write a short note on resonance.

26. Indicate the type of hybridization of each carbon atom in the following structures :
(*a*) CH_3CH_3 (*b*) $CH_3C\equiv CCH_3$ (*c*) $CH_2=C=CH_2$ (*d*) $CH_3C\equiv N$

27. (*a*) Explain the relative stabilities of various alkyl free radicals on the basis of hyperconjugation.
(*b*) Describe the two types of mesomeric effects.
(*c*) Differentiate between inductive and electromeric effects.

28. Indicate the type of hybridization of each atom in the following structures :

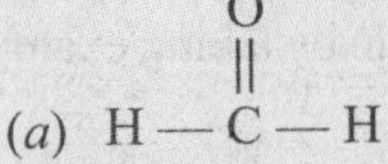

(*b*) CH_3-O-CH_3

(*c*) $H-C\equiv N$ (*d*) CH_3NH_2

Answers

Multiple Choice Questions

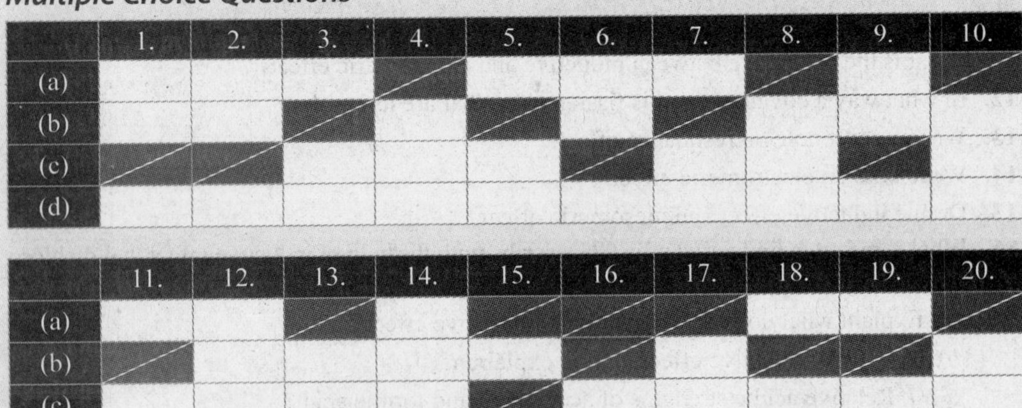

	1.	2.	3.	4.	5.	6.	7.	8.	9.	10.
(a)				■				■		■
(b)			■		■		■			
(c)	■	■				■			■	
(d)										

	11.	12.	13.	14.	15.	16.	17.	18.	19.	20.
(a)			■		■	■	■			■
(b)	■					■		■	■	
(c)					■					
(d)		■		■				■		

5

Mechanism of Organic Reactions

5.1 CURVED ARROW NOTATION

In the study of organic reaction mechanisms, we come across movement of electrons from one atom to the other. This movement of electron is represented with the help of curved arrows. This method is known as curved arrow notation. For example, when the atom B is more electronegative than atom A in the following compound, then in the presence of a reagent, the flow of electrons that takes place may be represented with the help of **curved arrows.**

$$A{=}B \xrightarrow{\text{Reagent added}} \overset{\delta+}{A}{-}\overset{\delta-}{B}$$

Electronegativity plays an important role in knowing the direction of transfer of the shared pair of electron to one of the atoms.

(*i*) In a carbonyl group, >C ═ O, present in aldehydes and ketones, the displacement is towards the oxygen atom which is represented by a curved arrow as under

$$>C{=}O \longrightarrow >\overset{+}{C}-\overset{-}{O}$$

(*ii*) In propylene, the displacement of shared pair of electrons is towards the carbon atom which is away from the methyl group due to the reason that methyl group is electron repelling.

$$CH_3{-}CH{=}CH_2 \longrightarrow CH_3{-}\overset{+}{C}H{-}\overset{-}{C}H_2$$

5.2 DRAWING ELECTRON MOVEMENTS WITH ARROWS

There are instances in organic molecules where the separation of charges (complete + ve or – ve) does not take place. But, due to the presence of electron-attracting or electron-repelling groups, some kind of polarization or movement of electrons takes place. We represent it with the help of arrows along the bonds. For example, in the molecule of ethyl chloride, the arrows would be drawn as :

$$CH_3 \rightarrow\!- CH_2 \rightarrow\!- Cl$$

Presence of a halogen group in a carboxy acid helps in the release of protons. This happens because the electron movement takes place in the direction of the halogen group. Greater the number of halogen groups, greater will be the charge movement away from the carboxylic group and towards the halogen groups. This can be illustrated as under:

$$Cl \leftarrow CH_2 \leftarrow C(=O) \leftarrow O \leftarrow H$$

Chloroacetic acid

$$Cl \leftarrow CHCl \twoheadleftarrow C(=O) \twoheadleftarrow O \twoheadleftarrow H$$

Dichloroacetic acid

$$Cl \leftarrow CCl_2 \lll C(=O) \lll O \lll H$$

Trichloracetic acid

5.3 HALF-HEADED AND DOUBLE HEADED ARROWS

The curved arrows that we use to represent electron movement from one site to another can be classified as under:

(*i*) Half-headed arrows represented as ↗ or ↖

(*ii*) Double-headed arrows represented as ↗

Half-headed or single headed arrows show the movement of a single electron. These are used in the discussion of radical chemistry mechanisms in particular. For example, we can depict the breaking of a bromine molecule into two bromine radicals as under:

$$Br - Br \longrightarrow \dot{B}r + \dot{B}r$$

Double-headed arrows show the movement of electron pair from one species to another. For example

$$H\ddot{O}^- \quad H^+ \longrightarrow H - O - H$$

The movement takes place from the tail of the arrow and goes to head.

5.4 HOMOLYTIC AND HETEROLYTIC BOND BREAKING (FISSION)

Consider a covalent bond between atoms A and B.

$$A:B \quad \text{or} \quad A - B$$

The cleavage (or breaking) of this bond can take place in three possible ways depending upon the relative electronegativities of A and B.

(*i*) $A:B \longrightarrow A\bullet + B\bullet$ (A• and B• of equal electronegativity)

(*ii*) $A:B \longrightarrow \overset{-}{A:} + \overset{+}{B}$ (A more electronegative than B)

(*iii*) $A:B \longrightarrow \overset{+}{A} + \overset{-}{:B}$ (B more electronegative than A)

The first type of cleavage is called *homolytic fission* or *homolysis* and leads to the formation of very reactive species called '*free radicals*' (atoms or groups of atoms containing odd or unpaired electrons).

In homolytic fission the covalent bond breaks in such a way that each fragment carries one unpaired electron.

The second and third types of cleavage is called *heterolytic fission* and leads to the formation of ionic species. These ionic species are also very reactive and carry charges on carbon. Cationic species carrying positive charge on a carbon atom are called *carbonium ions* or *carbocations*. Anionic species carrying negative charge on carbon atom are called *carbanions*.

In heterolytic fission the covalent bond breaks in such a way that the pair of electrons stays on the more electronegative atom.

5.5 TYPES OF ORGANIC REACTIONS

Organic reactions may be classified into four main types:

(*a*) Substitution reactions (*b*) Addition reactions

(*c*) Elimination reactions (*d*) Rearrangements.

These are separately described as under.

(*a*) Substitution reactions. A substitution reaction is one in which a part of one molecule is replaced by other atom or group without causing a change in the rest of the molecule. Following are some examples of substitution reactions.

(*i*) $\underset{\text{Methane}}{CH_4} + Cl_2 \longrightarrow \underset{\text{Methyl chloride}}{CH_3Cl} + HCl$

(*ii*) $C_2H_5Br + KOH \longrightarrow C_2H_5OH + KBr$

(*iii*) $\underset{\text{Benzene}}{C_6H_6} + Cl_2 \xrightarrow{FeCl_3} \underset{\text{Chlorobenzene}}{C_6H_5Cl} + HCl$

The substitution reactions may be brought about by free-radicals, nucleophilic or electrophilic reagents. Thus, there are free radical substitution reactions, nucleophilic substitution reactions and electrophilic substitution reactions.

(*b*) Addition reactions. When two molecules of same or different substances combine together giving rising to a new product, it is an addition reaction. Examples of addition reactions are :

$$\underset{\text{Ethane}}{CH_2 = CH_2} + Br_2 \longrightarrow \underset{\text{Ethylene dibromide}}{CH_2BrCH_2Br}$$

$$\underset{\text{Acetaldehyde}}{CH_3CHO} + HCN \longrightarrow \underset{\text{Acetaldehyde cyanohydrin}}{CH_3CH(OH)CN}$$

Addition reactions could be brought about by free-radical, electrophilic or nucleophilic reagents.

As in the case of substitution, there are free radical, electrophilic and nucleophilic substitution reactions.

***(c)* Elimination reactions.** These reactions involve the removal of atoms or groups from a molecule to form a new compounds containing multiple bonds. Dehydrohalogenation of alkyl halides is a common example of this type reaction.

$$\underset{n\text{-Propyl chloride}}{CH_3-CH_2CH_2Cl} + KOH \xrightarrow{\text{Alc.}} \underset{\text{Propene}}{CH_3CH=CH_2} + KCl + H_2O$$

Elimination reactions are of two types. Bimolecular eliminations or E_2 reactions and monomolecular or E_1 elimination reactions.

In E_2 reactions, rate determining step involves two reacting species. Dehydrohalogenation of tertiary alkyl halides with alc. KOH proceeds by E_2 mechanism. In E_1 reactions, the rate determining step involves only one reacting species. Dehydrohalogenation of primary alkyl halides with alc. KOH usually proceeds through E_1 mechanism.

***(d)* Rearrangement reactions.** Rearrangement reactions involve the migration of an atom or a group from one atom to the other within the same molecule.

It is interesting to note that the first organic compound, *i.e.*, urea synthesized in the laboratory by Wohler actually involved a rearrangement reaction.

$$\underset{\text{Amm. cyanate}}{NH_4CNO} \xrightarrow{\Delta} \underset{\text{Urea}}{NH_2-CO-NH_2}$$

Another important example of such reactions is *Hoffmann bromamide reaction.* This reaction involves the migration of an alkyl groups from the carbon to the nitrogen atom of an amide with the simultaneous elimination of CO as carbonate ion under the influence of Br_2/KOH.

$$\underset{\text{Acetamide}}{CH_3-CONH_2} + Br_2 + 4KOH \longrightarrow \underset{\text{Methylamine}}{CH_3-NH_2} + K_2CO_3 + 2KBr + 2H_2O$$

Similarly maleic acid, when heated in a sealed tube, is converted into fumaric acid.

$$\underset{\text{Maleic acid}}{\begin{array}{c} H-C-COOH \\ \| \\ H-C-COOH \end{array}} \xrightarrow{\Delta} \underset{\text{Fumaric acid}}{\begin{array}{c} H-C-COOH \\ \| \\ HOOC-C-H \end{array}}$$

5.6 TYPES OF REAGENTS—NUCLEOPHILES AND ELECTROPHILES

Nucleophilic reagents or nucleophiles

A nucleophilic reagent is a reagent with an atom having an unshared or lone pair of electrons. Such a reagent is in search of a point where it can share these electrons to form a bond. Nucleophiles are of two types:

***(i)* Neutral nucleophiles.** These are the nucleophiles which are neutral in charge. But they carry some unshared electrons which they like to share with some positive centre or electron deficient centre. Ammonia $\ddot{N}H_3$, water $H_2\ddot{O}$ and alcohols $R-\ddot{O}-H$ are examples of neutral nucleophiles.

***(ii)* Negative nucleophiles.** These are the nucleophiles which carry negative charge. Examples of this type of nucleophiles are hydroxyl ions (OH^-), halide ion (X^-), alkoxide ion (RO^-) and cyanide ion (CN^-). Carbanions also come in the category of negative nucleophiles.

Electrophilic reagents or electrophiles

An electrophile is a reagent containing electron deficient atoms. Such species have a tendency to attach themselves to centres of high electron density. There are two types of electrophiles:

***(i)* Neutral electrophiles.** These electrophile do not carry any net charge. Lewis acids like $AlCl_3$, $FeCl_3$ and BF_3 belong to this category of electrophiles. Sulphonium ion (SO_3) carries no net charge, but it acts as an electrophile for sulphonation in benzene rings. This is because of its structure.

$$\overset{-}{O}-\overset{++}{S}(=O)-\overset{-}{O}$$

As the positive charge is concentrated and the negative charge is scattered, it acts as an electrophile. Substances like $SnCl_4$ which have vacant *d*-orbitals would like to accommodate electrons in them. Thus such substances also act as electrophiles.

***(ii)* Positive electrophiles.** These electrophiles carry a net positive charge. Examples of this category of electrophiles are hydrogen ion (H^+), hydronium ion (H_3O^+), nitronium ion (NO_2^+), and chloronium ion (Cl^+). In the halogenation and nitration of aromatic systems, these electrophiles are involved.

Solved Examples

Example 1: Classify the following as nucleophiles and electrophiles: H_3O^+, NH_3, $AlCl_3$, ROH, BF_3, CN^-, SO_3.

Solution:

Nucleophiles	Electrophiles
NH_3	H_3O^+
ROH	$AlCl_3$
CN^-	BF_3
	SO_3 (Sulphonium ion)

Example 2: Pick up from the following, the electrophiles and nucleophiles:

$AlCl_3$, PH_3, HNO_3, R_3N

Solution: Electrophiles: $AlCl_3$, HNO_3.

Nucleophiles: PH_3, R_3N.

Example 3: Pick up from the following, the electrophiles and nucleophiles:

BF_3, NH_3, ROH, $SnCl_4$.

Solution: Electrophiles: BF_3, $SnCl_4$.

Nucleophiles: NH_3, ROH.

5.7 REACTIVE INTERMEDIATES

In organic reactions, reactants do not change into products in one step. The change normally takes place via an intermediate product, which is short-lived. From the intermediate product, the reaction passes on to the products. Various reaction intermediates that we come across in the study of organic reactions are:

(*i*) Carbonium ion (or carbocation) (*ii*) Carbanion

(*iii*) Free radical (*iv*) Carbene

(*v*) Nitrene (*vi*) Arynes (benzyne)

5.8 CARBOCATIONS

These are defined as the species in which the positive charge is carried by the carbon atom with six electrons in its valence shell. These are formed by the heterolytic fission in which an atom or group along with its pair of electrons leaves the carbon. In heterolytic fission, the shared pair of electrons between two atoms goes to one atom only.

$$R-CH_2-X \xrightarrow[\text{Fission}]{\text{Heterolytic}} R\overset{\oplus}{C}H_2 + \overset{\ominus}{\ddot{X}}$$

Stability of Carbocations

1. The order of stability among simple alkyl carbocations is: tertiary > secondary > primary. In most of the reactions, primary and secondary carbocations get rearranged to tertiary carbocations. Both *n*-propyl fluoride and isopropyl fluoride form the same isopropyl cation (2° carbocation). Similarly all the four butyl fluorides *viz.*, *n*-, iso-, sec. and tertiary butyl fluorides form the same tert-butyl cation. There are two factors which determine the stability:

(*i*) *Hyperconjugation or resonance.*

(*ii*) *Field effect or inductive effect of groups.*

Hyperconjugation

A large number of canonical forms can be written for tertiary carbocation compared to those for primary carbocation. Consider hyperconjugation in primary and tert-carbocation.

$$R-\underset{H}{\overset{H}{C}}-\underset{H}{\overset{H}{C}}{}^{\oplus} \longleftrightarrow R-\underset{H}{\overset{H^{\oplus}}{C}}=\underset{H}{\overset{H}{C}} \longleftrightarrow R-\underset{\underset{\oplus}{H}}{\overset{H}{C}}=\underset{H}{\overset{H}{C}}$$

Hyperconjugation in primary carbocation

$$R-\underset{H}{\overset{H}{C}}-\underset{CH_2R}{\overset{CH_2R}{C^{\oplus}}} \longleftrightarrow R-\underset{H}{\overset{H^{\oplus}}{C}}=\underset{CH_2-R}{\overset{CH_2-R}{C}} \longleftrightarrow R-\underset{H}{\overset{H^{\oplus}}{CH}}-\underset{CH_2-R}{\overset{\overset{H}{|}\;\;\;\;\;\;}{\overset{C-R}{\|}}{C}} \longleftrightarrow \text{etc.}$$

Hyperconjugation in tertiary cation

Greater the number of canonical forms, greater is the stability.

Field effect

Electron donating effect of alkyl groups increases the electron density around the +vely charged carbon. This results in reducing the magnitude of positive charge on it and thus the charge is delocalised on α-carbon. Dispersal of positive charge increases the stability. Of carbocation of all the simple cation, *tert*-butyl cation being most stable. Even *tert*-pentyl and *tert*-hexyl cations produce *tert*-butyl cation at high temperature. Lower alkanes like methane, ethane and propane when treated with super acid also yield *tert*-butyl cation as the main product. Salts of *tert*-butyl cation, like $(CH_3)_3\,C^+\,SbF_3^-$ have been prepared from super acid solutions.

2. The stability of carbocation containing a conjugated double bond is usually greater due to increased delocalisation by resonance. In such carbocations, the positive charge is dispersed on at least two carbon atoms. Consider the following carbocation.

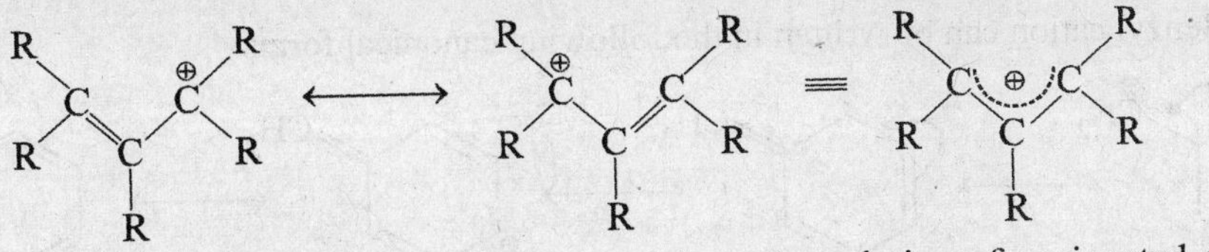

3. Allylic type cabocations have been prepared from the solution of conjugated diene in conc. sulphuric acid and are found to be most stable.

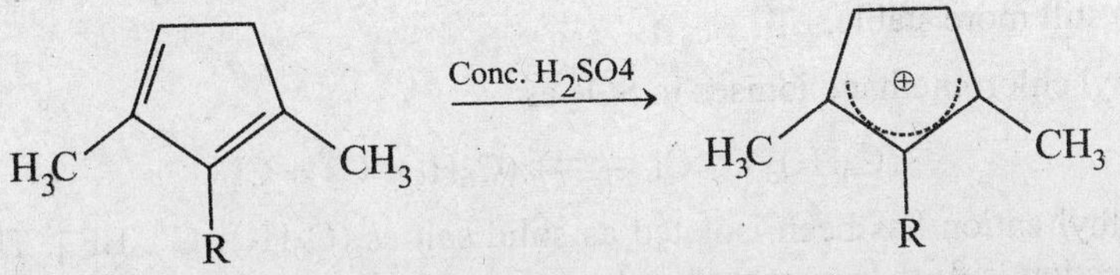

Conc. H_2SO4

4. Carbocations can be stabilised through aromatisation also. 1-Bromocyclohepta-2, 4, 6-triene tropylium bromide is a crystalline solid. It is highly soluble in water and forms bromide ions in solution. Clearly, the compound is not covalent in nature. The reason for such a behaviour is the stability of tropylium cation which follows Huckel's rule (6 π electrons) for aromaticitiy.

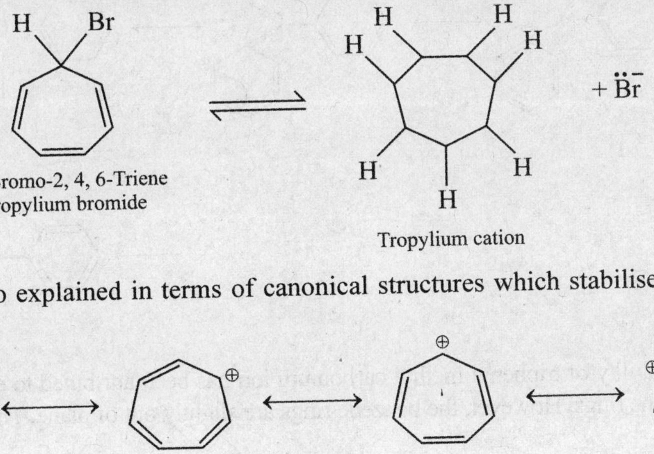

1, Bromo-2, 4, 6-Triene tropylium bromide

Tropylium cation

Its stability is also explained in terms of canonical structures which stabilise the tropylium cation.

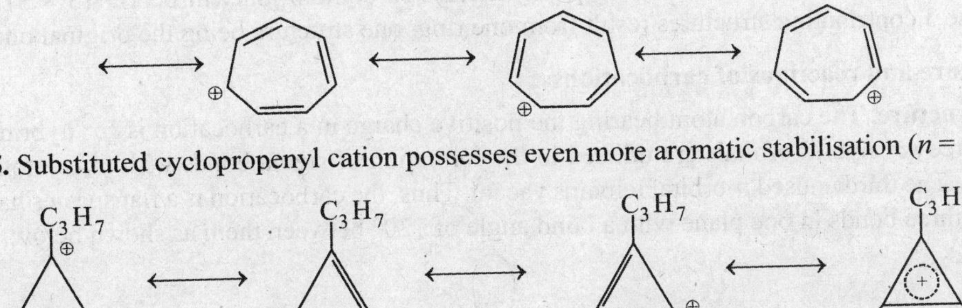

5. Substituted cyclopropenyl cation possesses even more aromatic stabilisation ($n = 0$).

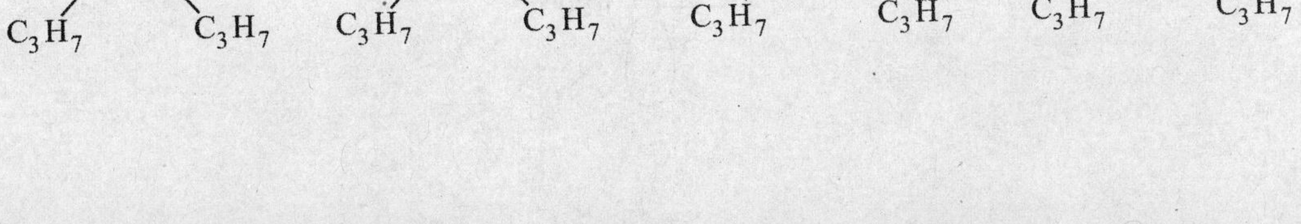

In the above tripropyl substituted cation, all the carbons are sp^2 hybridised. Thus all the *p*-orbitals including the vacant *p*-orbital of the positively charged carbon overlap forming a delocalised π molecular orbital, leading to stabilization.

6. Benzyl cation can be written in the following canonical forms:

$\overset{\oplus}{C}H_2$ ⟷ CH_2 ⟷ CH_2 ⟷ CH_2

Due to larger number of canonical forms and greater dispersal of positive change, benzyl carbocation is still more stable.

7. Triphenyl chloromethane ionises in SO_2 as

$$(C_6H_5)_3\,C \cdot Cl \rightleftharpoons (C_6H_5)_3\,C^{\oplus} + Cl^-$$

Triphenyl methyl cation has been isolated as solid salt as $(C_6H_5)_3\ C^+.\ BF_4^-$. The stability of triarylmethyl cation is further increased if the rings are substituted at *ortho* and *para* positions by electron donating groups.

C⊕ ⟷ C ⟷ C ⟶ C

The extra stability of triphenyl methyl carbonium ion has been attributed to extensive resonance with three benzene rings. However, the benzene rings are slightly out of plane. They have a propeller shape.

Total contributing structures for triphenylmethyl carbonium ion will be 1 + (3 × 3) = 10 because 3 contributing structures result from one ring, one structure being the original one.

Structure and reactions of carbocations

Structure. The carbon atom bearing the positive charge in a carbocation is sp^2 hybridised. The three sp^2 hybrid orbitals are utilised in the formation of sigma bonds with three atoms or groups. The third unused *p*-orbital remains vacant. Thus, the carbocation is a flat species having all the three bonds in one plane with a bond angle of 120° between them as shown below:

⊕ C 120°

Reactions

Carbocations, which are shortlived species and very reactive give the following reactions:

1. Proton loss. Carbocation may lose a proton to form an alkene. An ethyl carbocation loses a proton to form ethene.

$$\underset{\text{Ethyl carbocation}}{H-\underset{H}{\overset{H}{|}}C-\underset{H}{\overset{H}{|}}\overset{\oplus}{C}} \xrightarrow{-H^+} \underset{\text{Ethene}}{H-\overset{H}{\overset{|}{C}}=\overset{H}{\overset{|}{C}}-H}$$

2. Combination with nucleophiles. Carbocations combine with nucleophiles to acquire a pair of electrons. For example, a highly reactive methyl carbocation with hydroxyl ion to form methyl alcohol.

$$\underset{\text{Methyl carbocation}}{H-\underset{H}{\overset{H}{|}}\overset{\oplus}{C}} + OH^- \longrightarrow \underset{\text{Methyl alcohol}}{H-\underset{H}{\overset{H}{|}}C-OH}$$

3. Addition to alkene. A carbocation may add to an alkene to produce another carbocation possessing higher molecular weight.

$$\underset{\text{Methyl carbocation}}{\overset{\oplus}{C}H_3} + \underset{\text{Ethylene}}{H_2C=CH_2} \longrightarrow \underset{n\text{-Propyl carbocation}}{H-\underset{H}{\overset{H}{|}}C-\underset{H}{\overset{H}{|}}C-\underset{H}{\overset{H}{|}}\overset{\oplus}{C}}$$

4. Rearrangement. The migration of alkyl or aryl or hydrogen along with an electron pair to the positive centre takes place which results in the formation of more stable carbocation. Some examples are given below:

$$\underset{(1°)}{CH_3-\overset{H}{\overset{|}{C}H}-\overset{\oplus}{C}H_2} \xrightarrow{\text{Hydride shift}} \underset{(2°)}{CH_3-\overset{\oplus}{C}H-CH_3}$$

$$C_6H_5-CH_2-\overset{OH}{\overset{|}{C}}(CH_3)_2 \xrightarrow{FSO_3H} C_6H_5-\overset{H}{\overset{|}{\overset{\oplus}{C}}}H-\overset{\oplus}{C}(CH_3)_2 \xrightarrow[\text{shift}]{\text{Hydride}}$$

$$\underset{\text{(More stable)}}{C_6H_5-\overset{\oplus}{C}H-\overset{H}{\overset{|}{C}}(CH_3)_2}$$

Such a rearrangement takes place because a tertiary carbocation is more stable than secondary carbocation, which in turn is more stable then primary cabocation. Similarly, a carbocation attached to a phenyl group (benzene ring) is more stable than others.

Example 4: Arrange the following in order of decreasing stability and give suitable explanation for it.

$$\underset{\text{I}}{(CH_2)_2CH-\overset{+}{C}H_2},\quad \underset{\text{II}}{(CH_2)_2CH-\overset{+}{C}(CH(CH_2)_2)-CH(CH_2)_2}\quad \underset{\text{III}}{(CH_2)_2CH-\overset{+}{C}H-CH(CH_2)_2}$$

Solution: The stability of a carbocation depends upon two factors:

(*i*) Hyperconjugation

(*ii*) Inductive effect of groups attached.

In this problem, it is hyperconjugation or resonance which is important. Structure II can form maximum number of resonating structures and hence this is most stable. It can form resonating structures with the help of hydrogen from three sides (from three cyclopropyl groups) whereas carbocations III and I can form resonating structures from two and one side respectively. Thus the order of stability in decreasing order is:

(II) > (III) > (I)

$$\underset{\text{II}}{(CH_2)_2CH-\overset{+}{C}(C(H)(CH_2)_2)-CH(CH_2)_2} \xrightarrow{-H^+} (CH_2)_2CH-C(=C(CH_2)_2)-CH(CH_2)_2$$

Example 5: Arrange the following in order of increasing stability and explain the order on the basis of hyprconjugation.

$$\underset{\text{(I)}}{CH_3-\overset{+}{C}H_2},\ \underset{\text{(II)}}{CH_3-\overset{+}{C}(CH_3)-CH_3},\ \underset{\text{(III)}}{\overset{+}{C}H_3},\ \underset{\text{(IV)}}{CH_3-\overset{+}{C}H-CH_3}$$

Solution: Greater the number of resonating structures, greater is the stability attached to a carbocation. Carbocation (II) which is a tertiary carbocation will give the maximum number of resonating structures involving hydride shift, like

$$\overset{+}{C}H_2-CH(CH_3)-CH_3 \quad CH_3-CH(CH_3)-\overset{+}{C}H_2 \quad CH_3-CH(\overset{+}{C}H_2)-CH_3$$

Greater the number of hydrogens on carbon atoms in the immediate neighbourhood of carbocation, greater the number of resonating structures and hence greater the stability.

This is followed by secondary carbocation IV, primary carbocation I and methyl carbocation (III). Hence the order of stability in increasing order is:

$$\overset{+}{C}H_3 < CH_3-\overset{+}{C}H_2 < CH_3-\overset{+}{C}H-CH_3 < CH_3-\overset{+}{C}(CH_3)-CH_3$$

Example 6: Order of stability of carbocation is as under. Explain.

$$\underset{\text{(I)}}{(C_6H_5)_3\overset{+}{C}} > \underset{\text{(II)}}{(C_6H_5)_2\overset{+}{C}H} > \underset{\text{(III)}}{C_6H_5\overset{+}{C}H_2}$$

Solution: Carbocation (I) gives the maximum number of resonating structures, as this is linked to three benzene rings, hence this will have maximum stability.

For details, see Art. 2.8.

The order of stability in decreasing order is:

I > II > III

Example 7: Why tropyllium bromide gives precipitate with $AgNO_3$ and CH_3Br does not?

Solution: This is because tropyllium bromide behaves like an ionic compound whereas methyl bromide does not. Ionic nature of tropyllium ion is because of extra stability of tropyllium ion. For details refer to Art. 4.8.

5.9 CARBANIONS

These are defined as the species with an unshared pair of electrons and a negative charge on the central carbon atom. A carbanion may be formed in one of the following ways:

(*i*) An atom or group leaves carbon without the electron pair (Heterolytic fission).

$$R-\overset{H}{\underset{H}{C}}-Y \xrightarrow[\text{fission}]{\text{Heterolytic}} \underset{\text{Carbanion}}{R-\overset{H}{\underset{H}{C^-}}:} + Y^+$$

(*ii*) An anion adds to a carbon-carbon double or triple bond

$$-\overset{|}{C}=\overset{|}{C}- + :Y^{\ominus} \longrightarrow \underset{\text{Carbanion}}{-\overset{\ominus}{\underset{|}{C}}-\overset{|}{\underset{|}{C}}-Y}$$

Every carbanion possesses unshared pair of electrons and is therefore a base. When the carbanion accepts a proton, it gives a conjugate acid. The stability of the carbanion is directly related with the strength of the conjugated acid.

$$\underset{\text{(Base)}}{\text{Carbanion}} + H^+ \longrightarrow \text{Conjugate acid}$$

Stability of carbanions

1. It is important to note that weaker the acid, stronger is the base and hence lower is the stability of the carbanion. Clearly, the order of stability of carbanion can be determined from the order of the strength of conjugate acids. Carbanions are highly unstable in solution as compared to carbocations.

2. The order of stability of carbanions is:

Vinyl > Phenyl > Cyclopropyl > Ethyl > *n*-propyl > Isobutyl

Also it has been found that the stability of carbanions decreases in the order methyl > prim-carbanion > sec-carbanion.

$$H-\underset{H}{\overset{H}{|}}\bar{C} > CH_3 \rightarrow \bar{C}H_2 > (CH_3)_2\bar{C}H$$

This stability order can be explained simply by the field effects. The presence of electron donating alkyl groups in secondary (Isopropyl) carbanion results in greater localisation of negative charge on the central carbon atom and hence the stability falls. Cyclopropyl carbanion has greater stability due to greater *s*-character on the carbanionic carbon.

3. Vinyl and phenyl carbanions are more stable due to resonance. In cases where a double or triple bond is located at α-position to the carbanionic carbon, the ion is stabilised by resonance in which the unshared pair overlaps with π-electrons of the double bond. The stability of allylic and benzylic carbanions can be illustrated as under.

$$R-CH=CH-\overset{\ominus}{\ddot{C}H_2} \longleftrightarrow R-\overset{\ominus}{\ddot{C}H}-CH=CH_2$$

$$C_6H_5\overset{\ominus}{\ddot{C}H_2} \longleftrightarrow \longleftrightarrow \longleftrightarrow$$

4. Diphenyl methyl and triphenyl methyl carbanions are more stable then even benzylic and can be kept in solution for a longer time if water is completely excluded.

5. When the carbanionic carbon is conjugated with a carbon-oxygen or carbon-nitrogen multiple bond, then the stability of carbanion is increased. The reason is that the presence of electronegative atoms helps in the dispersal of negative charge and thus such carbanions are better capable of bearing the negative charge. Thus,

$$R-\overset{\ominus}{\ddot{C}H}-\underset{\|O}{C}-R \longleftrightarrow R-CH=\underset{|:\ddot{O}:^{\ominus}}{C}-R$$

6. The increase in the *s*-character at the central carbon increases the stability of carbon. Thus, the order of stability is expressed as:

$$R-C\equiv\overset{\ominus}{\ddot{C}} > R_2C=\overset{\ominus}{\ddot{C}H} > \overset{\ominus}{Ar} > R_3C-\overset{\ominus}{\ddot{C}H_2}$$

Acetylenic carbon contains 50% *s*-character being *sp*-hybridised.

7. Stabilisation by Sulphur or Phosphorus: The bonding of sulphur or phosphorus atom with carbanionic carbon increases the stability. It is probably due to the overlap of unshared pair with an empty *d*-orbital. Consider a carbanion containing sulphur atom:

$$R-\underset{\|O}{\overset{O\|}{S}}-\underset{R}{\overset{R}{\overset{|}{C}}}{}^{\ominus}: \longleftrightarrow R-\underset{|:\ddot{O}:}{\overset{O\|}{S}}=\underset{R}{\overset{R}{C}} \longleftrightarrow \text{etc.}$$

8. Aromatic nature. Some carbanions are stable as they are aromatic. *e.g.*, cyclopentadienyl anion is a stable carbanion.

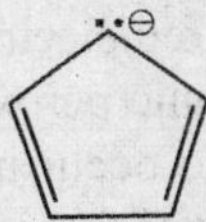

Huckel's $(4n + 2)$ rule is satisfied here with 6π electrons in the ring.

Structure and reactions of carbanions

Structure. The carbanions, being unstable have not been isolated. Therefore, their structure is not known with certainty. Most likely, the central carbon atom with an unshared pair of electrons (and negative charge) is sp^3 hybridised. The three sp^3 hybrid orbitals are used in forming three sigma bonds with the other atoms. The fourth sp^3 -orbital is occupied by a lone pair of electron. In fact, the structure of carbanion is quite similar to that of ammonia as shown in the figure.

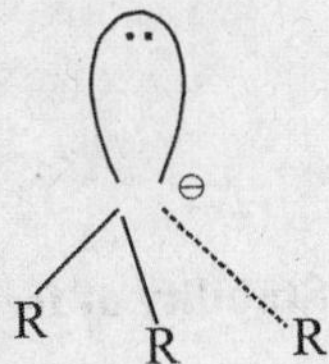

It different alkyl groups are attached to the central carbon, the carbanion will be chiral. Reactions in which such a carbanion is formed, give a product with retention of configuration. Carbanions which get stabilized by resonance involving the lone pair of electrons and the π electrons of multiple bonds, should be planar as this is the necessary condition for resonance to take place.

Reactions

Some important reactions of carbanions are described below:

1. Reaction with positive species or electrophiles. A carbanion reacts with a proton or with another action.

$$R_3C:^{\ominus} + \overset{\oplus}{Y} \longrightarrow R_3C-Y$$

2. Reactions involving the displacement of an atom or a group. Such reactions are nucleophilic substitution (SN^2) reactions observed in alkyl halides.

$$\ddot{R}^{\ominus} + {>}C{-}X \longrightarrow R{-}C{<} + \ddot{X}^{\ominus}$$

3. Addition to carbonyl compounds. Carbanions attack an electron deficient carbon in the carbonyl compounds. Such reactions are called nucleophilic addition reactions.

$$\ddot{R}^{\ominus} + {>}C{=}O \longrightarrow {>}C(R){-}\ddot{O}:^{\ominus}$$

4. Rearrangement. In some cases, carbanions may rearrange to form more stable species. Consider the rearrangement in triphenylmethyl carbanion.

$$(C_6H_5)_3\,C-\overset{\ominus}{\ddot{C}}H_2 \longrightarrow (C_6H_5)_2\,\overset{\ominus}{\ddot{C}}-CH_2-C_6H_5$$

Here the two phenyl groups directly attached to the central carbon help in dispersing the negative charge.

5.10 FREE RADICALS

Free radicals are produced by the homolytic fission of a covalent bond. These are odd electron neutral species which are formed by the homolytic fission of a covalent bond. Free radicals are paramagnetic due to the presence of unpaired electron. Formation of free radicals is favoured by the presence of UV light, heat and organic peroxides. Reactions involving radicals widely occur in the gas phase. Such reactions also occur in solutions, particularly if carried in non-polar solvents. An important characteristics of free radical reactions is that, once initiated, they proceed very fast. The free radicals can be detected by magnetic susceptibility measurements.

$$R - R \xrightarrow[\text{Fission}]{\text{Homolytic}} \underset{\text{Free radical}}{2R\bullet}$$

$$Cl - Cl \xrightarrow{h\nu} \underset{\text{Free radical}}{2Cl\bullet}$$

$$\underset{\text{Acyl peroxide}}{RCO - O - OCOR} \xrightarrow{\text{Thermal}} \underset{\text{Free radical}}{2RCOO\bullet}$$

Stability of free radicals

1. Simplest alkyl free radicals are highly reactive like carbocations and carbanions. Their life time is extremely short in solution. The relative stability of simple alkyl radicals has the order:

$$\underset{3°}{R_3\dot{C}} > \underset{2°}{R_2\dot{C}H} > \underset{1°}{R\dot{C}H_2} > \underset{\text{Methyl}}{\dot{C}H_3}$$

It can be explained on the basic of hyperconjugation similar to that in carbocations.

$$R - CH_2 - \dot{C}H_2 \longleftrightarrow R - CH = CH_2 \; (H\bullet) \longleftrightarrow R - CH = CH_2 \; (H\bullet)$$

Greater the number of the resonating structures, greater is the stability of the free radical.

2. Allylic and benzylic type of free radicals are more stable and comparatively less reactive than simple alkyl radicals. The reason is the delocalisation of the unpaired electron over the π-orbital system.

$$\underset{\text{Allylic radical}}{R - CH = CH - \dot{C}H_2} \longleftrightarrow R - \dot{C}H - CH = CH_2 \equiv R - CH \overset{\odot}{\cdots\cdots} CH \cdots CH_2$$

$$\underset{\text{Benzylic radical}}{C_6H_5 - \dot{C}HR} \longleftrightarrow (\text{ortho}\bullet)C_6H_5 = CHR \longleftrightarrow (\text{para}\bullet)C_6H_5 = CHR \longleftrightarrow (\text{ortho}'\bullet)C_6H_5 = CHR \equiv (C_6H_5\odot) \cdots CHR$$

3. Triphenyl methyl and triarylmethyl radicals are much more stable in solution at room temperature. The stability of such radicals is due to resonance.

$(C_6H_5)_3\dot{C} \longleftrightarrow$ (cyclohexadienylidene)$=C(C_6H_5)_2 \longleftrightarrow \bullet$(cyclohexadienylidene)$=C(C_6H_5)_2 \longleftrightarrow$ etc.

Steric hindrance to dimerisation is probably the major cause of their stability. If each aromatic nucleus in the radical has a bulky *p*-substitutent, then irrespective of any substitution at the *o*-positions, dimerisation will be greatly inhibited and hence radical stability increases.

Structure and reactions of free radicals

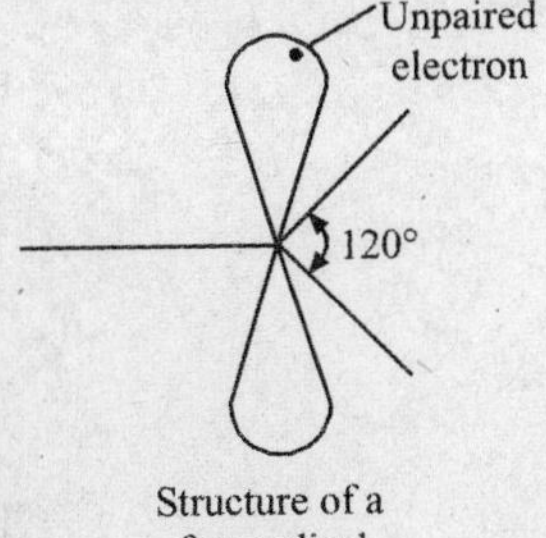

Structure of a free radical

Structure. The state of hybridisation of carbon atom having the unpaired electron is not clearly established. However, it is believed to be either pyramidal (like ammonia) or planar. But experimental evidence suggests strongly that the alkyl radicals such as methyl radical are actually planar with sp^2 hybridisation. The three coplanar hybrid orbitals are used in the formation of three sigma bonds with other atoms. The unhybridised orbital which lies in a plane at right angles to the plane of the hybrid orbitals, carries the unpaired electron. ESR spectra of $\dot{C}H_3$ and other simple alkyl radicals indicate that these radicals have planar structures. This is also in accordance with the fact that optical activity is lost when a free radical is generated at an asymmetric carbon. As a general rule we can say that simple alkyl free radicals prefer a planar or near planar shape. However, the free radicals in which the carbon is connected to atoms of high electronegativity prefer a pyramidal shape. The increase in electronegativity causes the deviation from the planar geometry.

Reactions

Some important reactions of free radicals are described below:

1. Halogenation of aliphatic hydrocarbons

$$Cl—Cl \xrightarrow{h\nu} 2Cl\bullet$$

$$CH_4 + Cl\bullet \longrightarrow CH_3\bullet + HCl$$

$$CH_3 + Cl_2 \longrightarrow CH_3Cl + Cl$$

In the presence of sunlight, chlorination of methane gives chloromethane, dichloromethane, chloroform and carbon tetrachloride.

2. Addition. Halogen addition to alkenes takes place with free radical mechanism. The addition of chlorine to tetrachloroethene is photochemically catalysed. A molecule of chlorine undergoes homolytic fission giving two chlorine radicals. Each radical is capable of initiating a reaction chain.

$$Cl—Cl \xrightleftharpoons{h\nu} C\bullet—Cl\bullet$$

$$Cl_2C = C.Cl_2 + Cl\bullet \longrightarrow Cl_2\dot{C}—CCl_3 \xrightarrow{Cl—Cl} \dot{C}l + Cl_3C—CCl_3$$

$\dot{C}l$ radical further adds to tetrachloroethene. This continues till the whole of tetrachloroethene has been converted into hexachloroethane. Chain termination occurs through radical-radical collision. The radical reactions are inhibited by the presence of oxygen. The reason is that the molecule of oxygen has two unpaired electrons and behaves as a biradical. This biradical combines with highly reactive radical intermediate and converts it to less reactive peroxy radical which is unable to propagate the chain reaction.

3. Consider the addition of chlorine to benzne in the presence of light. The reaction proceeds by radical intermediates and gives benzene hexachloride. But the attack of chlorine radical on toluene results in preferential hydrogen abstraction giving substitution in CH_2 group. Clearly, it is because of the greater stability of benzyl radical due to delocalisation.

$$\text{Benzene} + 3Cl_2 \xrightarrow[h\nu]{\text{Sunlight}} \text{Benzene hexachloride}$$

Toluene (CH_3) + $\dot{Cl}$ → [$\dot{C}H_2$ benzyl radical] More stable $\xrightarrow{Cl-Cl}$ CH_2Cl Benzyl chloride (Major)

Toluene (CH_3) + $\dot{Cl}$ → cyclohexadienyl radical (CH_3, Cl, H) Less stable, no longer aromatic

4. The addition of HBr to propene in presence of peroxides yields 1-Bromopropane. The reaction involves the formation of radical intermediates giving anti-Markownikoff addition. In this reaction, radical attacks propene to form a more stable secondary free radical.

$$ROOR \longrightarrow 2R\dot{O}$$

$$R\dot{O} + H-Br \longrightarrow RO-H + \dot{Br}$$

$$CH_3CH{=}CH_2 + \dot{Br} \longrightarrow CH_3\dot{C}H-CH_2BR$$

$$\downarrow HBr$$

$$\dot{Br} + CH_3-CH_2-CHBR_2$$

1-Bromopropane

5. Vinyl polymerisation. Radical reactions also produce polymers of great importance. Like other radical reactions, polymerisation reactions also constitute three step viz.; initiation, propagation and termination. In initiation step, a free radical is formed under the influence of peroxide. The radical formed then propagates the chain reaction.

$\dot{R} + CH_2 = CH \longrightarrow RCH_2 - \dot{C}H_2 \xrightarrow{CH_2 = CH_2} RCH_2 - CH_2 - CH_2 - \dot{C}H_2$ and so on.

In the final step, the collisions between the radicals terminate the reaction

$$R(CH_2)_n^{\bullet} + \overset{\bullet}{R} \longrightarrow R(CH_2)_n R$$

$$R(CH_2^{\bullet})_n + R(\overset{\bullet}{C}H_2)_n \longrightarrow R(CH_2)_{2n} R$$

Polythene, PVC, teflon etc. are the polymers which are formed from the respective monomers by radical pathways.

Example 8: Arrange the following free-radicals in increasing order of stability and explain your answer.

$$\overset{\bullet}{C_2H_5}, (C_2H_5)_2\overset{\bullet}{C}(C_2H_5), (C_2H_5)_2\overset{\bullet}{C}H, \overset{\bullet}{C}H_3$$

Solution: The order of stability can be given considering the hyperconjugation phenomenon.

(*i*) Ethyl radical is a hybrid of four resonating structures.

$$\underset{\text{I}}{H-\underset{H}{\overset{H}{C}}-\underset{H}{\overset{\bullet}{C}}-H} \longleftrightarrow \underset{\text{II}}{H-\underset{H}{\overset{\overset{\bullet}{H}}{C}}=\underset{H}{C}-H} \longleftrightarrow \underset{\text{III}}{\overset{\bullet}{H}\ \ \underset{H}{\overset{H}{C}}=\underset{H}{C}-H}$$

$$\longleftrightarrow \underset{\text{IV}}{H-\underset{\underset{\bullet}{H}}{\overset{H}{C}}=\underset{H}{C}-H}$$

5.11 CARBENES

These are defined as the neutral organic species containing a divalent carbon atom having a sextet of electrons but no charge on it. For example,

(*a*) : CH_2 — Methyl carbene (*b*) : CCl_2 — Dichlorocarbene

Formation of carbenes

They can be generated by the following methods:

(*b*) **By the action of UV light on diazomethane**

$$CH_2N_2 \longrightarrow \underset{\substack{\text{Methylene}\\\text{(Carbene)}}}{:CH_2} + N_2$$

(*ii*) **By the action of sodium ethoxide on chloroform**

$$\underset{\text{Chloroform}}{CHCl_3} + C_2H_5ONa \longrightarrow \underset{\substack{\text{Dichloro}\\\text{carbene}}}{:CCl_2} + C_2H_5OH + NaCl$$

These are highly reactive species.

Stability

1. The two unbonded electrons of a carbene may be either paired or unpaired. When the two electrons on the carbon atom are paired, then it is called *singlet* carbene. In the *triplet* state, it is called a biradical as the two electrons on carbon atom are unpaired.

$$H-\ddot{C}-H \quad \text{or} \uparrow\downarrow CH_2 \qquad H-\dot{C}-H \quad \text{or} \uparrow\uparrow CH_2$$

Singlet methylene — Triplet methylene

In the triplet state, carbene is relatively more stable as it has lower energy content.

2. The singlet and the triplet species can be distinguished by the common addition reaction of carbene to double bond to form cyclopropane derivatives. The addition of singlet species to *cis*-Butene forms a *cis* product. The reason is that the movement of two pairs of electrons occur either simultaneously or with one rapidly succeeding the other.

$$:CH_2 + (H)(H_3C)C{=}C(H)(CH_3) \longrightarrow (H)(H_3C)C{-}C(H)(CH_3) \text{ bridged by } CH_2$$

2-Butene (Cis) — Cis-product

3. In case of triplet carbene, the two unpaired electrons cannot form a new covalent bond simultaneously as they have parallel spins. Thus, one of the unpaired electrons will form a bond with the electron from the double bond that has opposite spin. Now, two unpaired electrons with the same spin are left and thus no bond is formed. The bond formation is possible by collision process when one of the electrons can reverse its spin. This is illustrated in the diagram below:

$$\uparrow\uparrow CH_2 + (H)(H_3C)\overset{\downarrow}{C}{-}\overset{\uparrow}{C}(H)(CH_3) \longrightarrow (H)(H_3C)C{-}C(H)(CH_3)\text{ with } \overset{\uparrow}{C}H_2 \text{ and } \uparrow \xrightarrow{\text{Collision}} (H)(H_3C)C{-}CHCH_2 \text{ with } \overset{\uparrow}{C}H_2\downarrow \longrightarrow (H)(H_3C)C{-}CH(CH_3) \text{ bridged by } CH_2$$

During this time of collision, there is a free rotation around C—C single bond and the product formed is a mixture of *cis* and *trans* isomers. It has been found that the difference in energy between the singlet and the triplet methylene is about 37–46 kJ/mole.

Structure and reactions of carbenes

Structure

The structure of two types of carbenes are different. : Singlet carbenes have their carbon in sp^2 hybridised state. Of the three sp^2 hybrid orbitals, two are used in forming two single bonds with monovalent atoms or groups attached to carbon. The unshared pair of electrons is present in the third sp^2 hybrid orbital and the unhybridised *p*-orbital is empty.

Singlet methylene

Triplet carbene has its carbon in *sp* hybridised state. The two *sp* hybrid orbitals form two bonds with monovalent atoms or groups attached to carbon. The two unhybridised p-orbitals contain one electron each.

Triplet methylene

The structure of triplet methylene is revealed by ESR measurements since these species are biradicals. Its geometry is found to be bent with bond angle of about 136°. The electronic spectra of singlet methylene formed in flash photolysis of diazomethane tell that it is also bent and the bond angle is about 103°.

Singlet methylene   Triplet methylene

The bond angles in CCl_2 and CBr_2 are 100°and 114° respectively.

Reactions

Some important types of reactions of carbenes are described below:

1. Addition to carbon-carbon double bonds. The reactions of singlet and triplet methylene to 2-Butene has been discussed above. Carbenes also add to aromatic systems and the intermediate products rearrange with ring enlargement reaction. Carbenes also show addition reactions to C = N bonds.

$$\text{Benzene} + :CH_2 \longrightarrow \text{Cycloheptatriene}$$

2. Addition reactions to alkanes. Methylene ($:CH_2$) reacts with ethane to form propane. Propane adds methylene to yield *n*-butane and isobutane. This shows the greater reactivity of carbene.

$$\underset{\text{Propane}}{CH_3-CH_2-CH_3} \xrightarrow{:CH_2} \underset{n\text{-Butane}}{CH_3-CH_2-CH_2-CH_3} + \underset{\text{Isobutane}}{CH_3-\underset{\substack{|\\CH_3}}{CH}-CH_3}$$

The reaction of carbenes with higher alkanes yield a number of possible products. It shows that the addition of carbenes is not all selective. Dichlorocarbenes do not give reactions involving insertion.

3. An important reaction of carbenes is dimerisation.

$$R_2\ddot{C} + R'_2\ddot{C} \qquad R_2C = CR'_2$$

As the carbenes are highly reactive, the dimer formed carries so much energy that it dissociates again.

4. We also come across rearrangement reactions in carbenes with the migration of alkyl group or hydrogen atom. These rearrangments are much more rapid. Thus, the addition and insertion reactions of carbenes are seldom encountered with alkyl or dialkyl carbenes. Many rearrangements of carbenes directly give stable molecules. Some rearrangements involved in carbenes are:

$$\underset{\text{Carbene}}{CH_3 - CH_2 - CH(H) - \ddot{C}H} \longleftrightarrow \underset{\text{1-Butene}}{CH_3 - CH_2 - CH = CH_2}$$

$$\underset{\text{Acyl Carbene}}{R - \underset{\underset{O}{\parallel}}{C} - \ddot{C}H} \longrightarrow \underset{\text{Ketene}}{O = C = CHR} \text{ (Wolff/rearrangement)}$$

$$\triangleright - \ddot{C}H \longrightarrow \square$$

5.12 NITRENES

Organic species having general formula as R — N : are called nitrenes. These are analogous to carbenes and are sometimes referred to as azocarbenes. The structure R — N : shows that nitrogen is bonded to one atom or group only and there are two non-bonded electron pairs. Thus, there is only a sextet of electrons around nitrogen. This explains why nitrenes are electron deficient and reactive species.

The most common method of nitrene generation involves photolytic or thermolytic decomposition of azides, acyl azides and isocyanates

$$HN_3 \xrightarrow[\text{or}\Delta]{h\nu} H - \ddot{N}: + N_2\uparrow$$

$$CH_3 - N_3 \xrightarrow{h\nu} CH_3 - \ddot{N}: + N_2\uparrow$$

$$C_6H_5 - N_3 \xrightarrow{h\nu} C_6H_5 - \ddot{N}: + N_2\uparrow$$

$$RCON_3 \xrightarrow{h\nu} N_2 + \underset{\text{Alkyl nitrene}}{RCO\ddot{N}}$$

$$R - N = C = O \xrightarrow{h\nu} CO + R - \ddot{N}$$

Stability of nitrenes

Nitrenes are highly reactive species and cannot be isolated under ordinary conditions. Alkyl nitrenes have been isolated by trapping in matrices at 4K while aryl nitrenes (less reactive) can be trapped at 77 K. Nitrenes can be generated both in the singlet and the triple states but its ground state is probably the triplet state.

$$R-\ddot{N}: \qquad R-\dot{N}\cdot$$

Singlet Triplet

Reactions of Nitrenes

Nitrenes show the following reaction:

1. Addition to C = C bonds. Nitrenes add to alkenes to form cyclic product. Such reactions are common for acyl nitrenes.

$$R-\ddot{N} + R_2C=CR_2 \longrightarrow R_2C\text{—}CR_2 \text{ (ring with N–R)}$$

Cycloaddition of nitrenes to alkenes produces acridines.

$$H-\ddot{N} + CH_2=CH_2 \longrightarrow \text{(three-membered ring with N–H)}$$

Ethylenimine

$$CH_3CH=CHCH_3 + :\ddot{N}-H \longrightarrow \text{(H}_3\text{C)HC—CH(CH}_3\text{) ring with N–H}$$

2-Butene

Acridine

2. Insertion. Nitrenes, especially acyl and sulphonyl nitrenes can insert into C — H and certain other bonds.

$$R'-\overset{O}{\overset{\|}{C}}-\ddot{N}: + R_3C-H \longrightarrow R'\overset{O}{\overset{\|}{C}}-\overset{H}{\overset{|}{N}}-CR_3$$

3. Abstraction. Nitrenes are also capable of extracting hydrogen atom form an alkane to form an alkyl radical.

$$R-\ddot{N} + R-H \longrightarrow R\dot{N}-H + \dot{R}$$

4. Rearrangements. Nitrenes undergo rearrangements also due to the migration of a group from adjacent atom to the electron deficient nitrogen. Insertion and addition to C = C bond reactions do not proceed in alkyl nitrenes as the rearrangement is much more faster.

$$R-\underset{H}{CH}-\ddot{N} \longrightarrow RCH=NH$$

5. Dimerisation. Nitrenes also dimerise to form a di-imide. Aryl nitrenes yield azobenzenes.

$$2C_6H_5-\ddot{N} \longrightarrow C_6H_5-N=N-C_6H_5$$

6. Ring enlargement. Azepines are prepared by the ring enlargement of phenyl azide.

$$C_6H_5-N=\overset{+}{N}=\overset{-}{N}+(C_2H_5)NH_2 \xrightarrow{hv} \text{N}(C_2H_5)\text{-azepine}$$

5.13 ARYNES

These are highly reactive species which contain an additional bond between two carbon atoms of the benzene rings. Taking benzyne as an example of aryne, the new bond of benzyne is formed by the sideways overlap of sp^2 orbitals belonging to two neighbouring carbon atoms. It is depicted as:

Representation of benzyne

It is evident that the new extra bond orbital lies along the side of the benzene ring and it has little interaction with the π-electron cloud of the benzene ring. Since the sideways overlapping is not very effective, the new bond is a weak one and hence benzyne is highly reactive molecule.

Aryne (Benzyne) Mechanism

It has been found that electron-withdrawing groups activate the aryl halides towards bimolecular nucleophilic substitution reactions. In the absence of such activation, aryl halides can also be made to undergo nucleophilic substitution in the presence of strong nucleophiles. Thus, when chlorobenzene is treated with very strong nucleophile, viz. amide ion, it is converted into aniline.

$$C_6H_5Cl + \overset{+}{Na}\overset{-}{NH_2} \xrightarrow{\text{Liquid } NH_3} C_6H_5NH_2 + \overset{+}{Na}\overset{-}{Cl}$$

Chlorobenzene Aniline

The above type of nucleophilic substitution reaction occurs by benzyne mechanism. It involves both **elimination** and **addition** as represented below:

(*i*) **Elimination.** In the elimination step, the amide ion abstracts a proton from one of the ortho-positions with respect to the halogen. The resulting carbanion loses the halides ion to form the benzyne, as illustrated below:

$$C_6H_5Cl \text{ (ortho H)} + :\overset{-}{N}H_2 \longrightarrow \text{Carbanion} + NH_3$$

Carbanion

$$\text{Carbanion} \longrightarrow \text{Benzyne} + :\overset{-}{Cl}:$$

Benzyne

(ii) **Addition.** In the addition step, the amide ion attacks the benzyne molecule to form the carbanion which abstracts a proton from solvent ammonia to yield the final substituted product. These reactions are given below:

Carbanion

Aniline

Evidence in support of benzyne mechanism

There is ample experimental evidence to prove the truth of benzyne mechanism of aromatic substitution.

(i) **Isotope effect.** The amination of *o*-deuteriobromobezene is slower than that of bromobenzene. This observation indicates that the cleavage of *ortho* hydrogen is involved in the rate determining step during the elimination stage. This can further be illustrated as follows:

o-Deuteriobromobenzene

Bromobenzene

$\bar{N}H_2/NH_3$

Relatively slow

Relatively fast

Benzyne

(ii) **Absence of ortho hydrogen.** Aryl halides containing two groups ortho to hydrogen, like 2-bromo-3-methylanisol, do not react at all. This is because benzyne intermediate cannot be formed due to the absence of ortho hydrogens with respect to the halogen.

$\xrightarrow{\bar{N}H_2/NH_3}$ No reaction

2-Bromo-3-methylanisol

(iii) **Tracer studies.** When labelled chlorobenzene in which chlorine is linked to C^{14} isotope (C^*) is allowed to react with amide ion, two types of aniline are formed. In one type, the —NH_2 group is bonded to C^{14} while in the other it is attached to carbon *ortho* to the labelled carbon. This can be explained as follows:

Chlorobenzene (labelled) $\xrightarrow{\bar{N}H_2 / NH_3}$ Benzyne $\xrightarrow{\bar{N}H_2 / NH_3}$ (aniline, labelled NH_2 at * carbon) + (aniline, NH_2 adjacent to * carbon)

(*iv*) **Identical product from different aryl halides.** When *o*-bromo-anisol and *m*-bromo-anisol are allowed to react separately with $\bar{N}H_2$ ion in liquid NH_3, the same product, *i.e.*, *m*-anisidine is formed. The formation of the same product is due to the formation of the same intermediate benzyne as shown below. The amide ion attacks the benzyne species at *meta* position and not *ortho* position probably because of steric factor.

o-Bromoanisole $\xrightarrow{\bar{N}H_2 / NH_3}$ Benzyne (OCH_3) $\xrightarrow{\bar{N}H_2 / NH_3}$ *m*-Anisidine (OCH_3, NH_2)

m-Bromoanisole (OCH_3, Br) $\xrightarrow{\bar{N}H_2 / NH_3}$ Benzyne

5.14 METHODS OF DETERMINATION OF REACTION MECHANISM

The stoichiometry of a reaction consists of chemical formulas and relative molecular proportions of starting materials and products. Obviously, these have a bearing on the mechanism of the reaction, for the overall reaction course must proceed from the starting materials to the products. Stoichiometry of the reaction may be misleading, however, because the participants in the overall reaction may not be involved directly in the rate determining step.

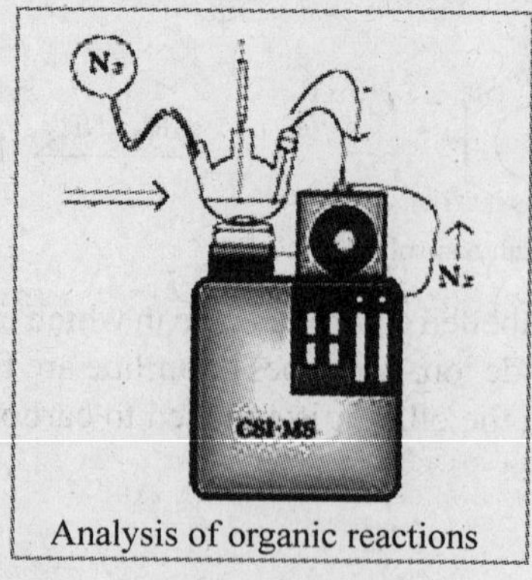

Analysis of organic reactions

Mechanism of a reaction can be determined by the following methods/techniques.

1. Product analysis
2. Intermediates
3. Isotope effects
4. Kinetic studies
5. Stereochemical studies
6. Crossover experiments

These are being described separately.

1. *Product anlysis.* In this method, we identify and determine the quantities of product and by products (if any). The following reactions are being discussed.

***(i)* Hydrolysis of isomeric allyl chlorides.** The isomeric allyl chlorides A and B as given below on hydrolysis give 85% of tertiary alcohol and 15% primary alcohol

$$\underset{(A)}{(CH_3)_2C = CH - CH_2Cl} \xrightarrow{H_2O} \underset{85\%}{(CH_3)_2-\overset{OH}{\overset{|}{C}} - CH = CH_2} + \underset{15\%}{(CH_3)_2C = CH - CH_2OH}$$

$$\underset{(B)}{(CH_3)_2-\overset{Cl}{\overset{|}{C}} - CH = CH_2} \xrightarrow{H_2O} \underset{85\%}{(CH_3)_2 - \overset{OH}{\overset{|}{C}} - CH = CH_2} + \underset{15\%}{(CH_3)_2- C = CH - CH_2OH}$$

It is intriguing that two different allyl chlorides (A and B) on hyrolysis give the same two products in same percentage. This is explained by the following mechanism.

$$\underset{(A)}{(CH_3)_2- C = CH - CH_2Cl} \xrightarrow{H^+} \underset{(C)}{(CH_3)_2- C = CH - \overset{+}{C}H_2} \longleftrightarrow \underset{(D)}{(CH_3)_2\overset{+}{C} - CH = CH_2}$$

$$(C) \xrightarrow{OH^-} \underset{15\%\ (Primary)}{(CH_3)_2C = CH - CH_2OH} \qquad (D) \xrightarrow{OH^-} \underset{85\%\ (Tertiary)}{(CH_3)_2\underset{OH}{\underset{|}{C}} - CH = CH_2}$$

$$\underset{(B)}{(CH_3)_2\overset{OH}{\overset{|}{C}} - CH = CH_2} \xrightarrow{H^+} (CH_3)_2\overset{+}{C} - CH = CH_2 \longleftrightarrow (CH_3)_2C = CH - \overset{+}{C}H_2$$

$$(CH_3)_2\overset{+}{C} - CH = CH_2 \xrightarrow{OH^-} \underset{85\%\ (Tertiary)}{(CH_3)_2\overset{OH}{\overset{|}{C}} - CH = CH_2} \qquad (CH_3)_2C = CH - \overset{+}{C}H_2 \xrightarrow{OH^-} \underset{15\%\ (Primary)}{(CH_3)_2C = CH - CH_2OH}$$

***(ii)* Beckmann reaction.** It is observed that out of cis - 2 bromo - 5 nitroacetophenone (A) and trans - 2 - bromo - 5 - nitroacetophenone (B), only the former undergoes ring closure. The latter oxime (B) does not undergo ring closure. It rather gives Beckmann reaction forming substituted amide. This difference in behaviour of the two oximes explains the mechnism by which the reaction takes place with the two compounds cis-oxime (A) and trans-oxime (B). The latter compound does not undergo rign closure because of trans geometry.

(A) (Ring closure)

(B) Substituted amide

2. *Determination of presence of intermediates.* The detection and isolation of the intermediate can provide information regarding the mechanism of the reaction.

Stable intermediates can be isolated by interrupting the reaction before it is completed. Take for example, Hofmann bromamide reaction. In this reaction, three intermediates viz. RCONHBr, $RCONBr^-$ and RNCO have been isolated. This reaction gives the conversion of an amide into an amine.

$$RCONH_2 \xrightarrow{Br_2|KOH} R-NH_2$$

Thus the mechanism which will take into account the formation of the above intermediate would be the valid mechanism for the reaction. A sure short proof for the existence fo an intermediate would be to trap it with an appropriate trapping agent. For example, in reactions with diazomethane, nitrogen gas is evolved and a carbene is produced. This carbene can be trapped as cyclopropane dérivative using cyclohaxene.

$$:\overset{-}{C}H_2 - \overset{+}{N}\equiv N \xrightarrow[-N_2]{hv} H_2C: \longrightarrow$$

Cyclopropane

Similarly mechanisms involving benzyne can be confirmed by trapping benzyne with anthracene and furan.

Benzyne Anthracene

Furan

3. *Isotope effect.* Radioisotopes like deuterium , tritium and are extensively used in the determination of mechanism of organic reactions. The principle of the method is that one of the reactants contains an isotopic atom. We can establish the mechanism of the reaction by locating the position of that isotope. We shall consider the following reactions using the radioisotopes.

I. Photosynthesis. The photosynthesis reaction may be written as under

$$6\ CO_2 + 6\ H_2O \rightarrow C_6H_{12}O_6 + 6\ O_2$$

In order to determine whether the released oxygen comes from CO_2 or H_2O, we use labelled water (i.e. water containing O_{18}). We find that oxygen evolved contains radiosotopic oxygen O_{18} thus proving that oxygen released in photosynthesis of plants comes from water.

$$6\ CO_2 + 6H_2O^{18} \rightarrow C_6H_{12}O_6 + 6\ O_2^{18}$$

II. Hydrolysis of an ester. Hydrolysis reactions may be written as:

$$R{-}\overset{O}{\overset{\|}{C}}{-}O{-}R' + H_2O \xrightarrow{NaOH} R{-}\overset{O}{\overset{\|}{C}}{-}O{-}H + R'OH$$

We want to know whether it is the alkyl (R′) oxygen or acyl oxygen which is fissioned. We perform the reaction with labelled water i.e. H_2O^{18}.

$$R{-}\overset{O}{\overset{\|}{C}}{-}O{-}R' + H_2O^{18} \longrightarrow R{-}\overset{O}{\overset{\|}{C}}{-}O{-}H + R'{-}\overset{18}{O}{-}H$$

We obtain the carboxy acid which does not contain radioactive oxygen (O^{18}), but the alcohol obtained contains redioactive oxygen O^{18}. Thus, we can say that it is the fission of alkyl oxygen and not the acyl oxygen that takes place in the mechanism of the reaction.

The rate of a reaction changes when an atom is replaced with a radioisotope. Variation in the rate of a reaction due to the presence of an isotope in the molecule is called **isotope effect**. Normally the magnitude of isotope effect is small. However, when the cleavage of the bond involving the isotope is the rate determining stap, the magnitude of isotope effect may be quite significant.

This is called **primary isotope effect**. The difference will be quite large when H is replaced by deuterium (D) and still larger when H is replaced by tritium (T). Thus the values of K_H/K_D and K_H/K_T with be greater than unity. This is because the smaller H atom reacts much faster than D or T. Also C–D and C–T bonds are associated with greater dissociation energies. Hence the activation energy required in case H is replaced by D or T will be much higher.

4. *Kinetic studies.* Information reagarding order of the reaction provides us the clue to the mechanism of the reaction. For example the rate law for acid hydrolysis of $(CH_3)_3$ CBr is as follows.

$$\frac{-d\left[(CH_3)_3\ CBr\right]}{dt} = k\left[(CH_3)_3\ CBr\right]$$

This shows that the rate of reaction is not dependent on the concentration of H_2O or H^+ amd therefore the following mechanism justifies the kinetic studies

First Step $(CH_3)_3\ C\ Br \rightarrow (CH_3)_3\ \overset{+}{C} + B\overset{-}{r}$ (Slow and rate determining step)

Second Step $(CH_3)_3\ \overset{+}{C} + O\overset{-}{H} \rightarrow (CH_3)_3\ C\ OH$ (Fast)

The rate low obtained in the kinetic studies of hydrolysis of CH_3Br in the alkaline hydrolysis is as follows.

$$-\frac{d[CH_3Br]}{dt} = k[CH_3Br]\ [O\overset{-}{H}]$$

That means both the halide and hydroxl ions participate in the rate determining step. Hence, the following mechanism is formulated.

(*i*) $CH_3\ Br + O\bar{H} \rightarrow [OH\ .....\ CH_3.....Br]^-$ (Slow and rate detemining step)

(*ii*) $[OH\ ....CH_3....Br]^- \rightarrow CH_3 - OH + Br^-$ (Fast)

5. *Sterochemical studies* Stereochemical evidance is of great importance in estabilishing the mechanism of reactions. Mechanism of nucleophilic substitution may be arrived at by performing experiments with optically active molecules. We check the optical activity of the products and then proceed to establish the mechanism. For example, if a racemic mixture is obtained after the nucleophilic substitution of an optically active compound, we can say that the reaction involves the formation of a planar intermediate as the first step.

In the second step, the nucleophide attaches itself to the planar intermediate. Since there is an equal opportunity of the nucleophile attaching from the two sides of the intermediate, we obtain a racemic mixture.

These steps indicate that the mechanism of the reaction in SN^1. However, if the product is optically active but the configuration of the product is opposite of the configuration of the reactant, it points to SN^2 mechanism. For example, we observe an inversion of configuration on alkaline hydrolysis of $C_6H_{13}(CH_3)$ CHBr. We therefore sketch the mechanism as follows.

$$OH^- + H-\underset{CH_3}{\overset{C_6H_{13}}{C}}-Br \longrightarrow \left[H-\underset{CH_3}{\overset{C_6H_{13}}{C}}-Br\right]^- \longrightarrow OH-\underset{CH_3}{\overset{C_6H_{13}}{C}}-H$$

(With inversion of configuration)

The reaction is known as **Walden inversion**

6. *Crossover experiment.* This technique is employed if we want to know whether the rearrangment takes place in one step or two steps. The reaction is carried out by taking two similar but different reactants. Analysis of the products leads to the mechanism. If the reaction involes two steps, the migrating group becomes free. In such a case, the migrating group has the possibility to attach to the intermediates of both the reactants. As we have taken two reactants, two migrating group becoms free. In such a case, the migrating group has the possibility to attach to the intermediates of both the reactants. As we have taken two reactants, two migrating groups will be formed, each of which has the possibility of attaching to the two intermediates, thus yielding a total of four products. The mechanism of **Fries rearrangement** was established by this method.

$$p\text{-}CH_3C_6H_4\text{-}OCOC_6H_5 \xrightarrow{AlCl_3} \text{(OH, } COC_6H_5\text{, } CH_3\text{)}C_6H_3 \quad \text{(Fries Rearragement)}$$

The following mechanism has been suggested for this rearrangement

O COC$_6$H$_5$ (p-methylphenyl) ⟶ O$^-$ (phenoxide) + $\overset{+}{C}OC_6H_5$ (Free migrating group)

CH$_3$

(Resonance: phenoxide ⟷ carbanion; attack of $\overset{+}{C}OC_6H_5$ to give cyclohexadienone with COC$_6$H$_5$ and H)

⟶ O$^-$ with COC$_6$H$_5$ $\xrightarrow{H^+}$ OH with COC$_6$H$_5$

To confirm this mechanism, we take a mixture of the two compounds (A) and (B) as shown below.

(A): O COC$_6$H$_5$, CH$_3$ ⟶ O$^-$, CH$_3$ (Intermediate) + $\overset{+}{C}OC_6H_5$ Migrating group

(B): O COC$_6$H$_5$, Cl, CH$_3$ ⟶ O$^-$, Cl, CH$_3$ (Intermediate) + $\overset{+}{C}OCH_3$ Migrating group

Now the migrating group from the compound A has the possibilities of attaching to the intermediates of both (A) and (B). Similarly the migrating group from the compound (B) has the possibility of attaching to the intermediates of both (A) and (B). Thus, we expect to obtain four products if this really happens. The four products as listed below have actually been isolated

I: OH, COCH$_3$, CH$_3$

II: OH, COC$_6$H$_5$, CH$_3$

III: OH, Cl, COCH$_3$, CH$_3$

IV: OH, Cl, COC$_6$H$_5$, CH$_3$

This lends support to the proposed mechanism

Example 9: Write down possible products in the following reactions:

1. $CH_2(COOEt)_2 \xrightarrow[C_2H_5I]{NaOMe}$ 2. $CH_3-CH_2-CH_2^+ \xrightarrow{OH^-}$

Solution:

1. $CH_2(COOEt)_2 \xrightarrow[-MeOH]{NaOMe} \overset{-}{C}H(COOEt)_2$ (Carbanion)

$$\xrightarrow{C_2H_5I} \underset{C_2H_5}{\underset{|}{CH(COOEt)_2}} \xrightarrow{Hydrolysis} C_2H_5CH_2COOH$$

Butanoic acid

2. $CH-CH_2-\overset{+}{C}H_2 \rightarrow CH_3-\overset{+}{C}H-CH_3 \xrightarrow{OH^-} CH_3-CH(OH)CH_3$

(*n*-Propyl carbocation) (more stable carbocation) Propanol-2

Example 10: How do you explain that

(*i*) **Benzyl carbocation is much more stable than phenylethyl carbocation?**

(*ii*) **Triphenyl methyl carbocation is a very stable carbocation?**

Solution:

(*i*) $C_6H_5-\overset{\oplus}{C}H_2$ (Benzyl carbocation) $C_6H_5-CH_2-\overset{\oplus}{C}H_2$ (Phenylethyl carbocation)

Benzyl carbocation exists in a number of canonical forms and hence is more stable than phenyl ethyl carbocation in which there is no possibility of resonance.

$C_6H_5-\overset{+}{C}H_2 \longleftrightarrow$ (ortho $\oplus$)$=CH_2 \longleftrightarrow$ (para +)$=CH_2 \longleftrightarrow$ (ortho $\oplus$)$=CH_2$

(*ii*) Triphenylmethyl carbocation is a very stable carbocation. See Art. 2.8.

Example 11: What happens when 2, 3-Dimethyl butan-2, 3-diol is treated with dil. H_2SO_4?

Solution:

$$CH_3-\underset{CH_3}{\overset{OH}{C}}-\underset{CH_3}{\overset{OH}{C}}-CH_3 \xrightarrow[Step\ I]{H_2SO_4} CH_3-\underset{CH_3}{\overset{+}{C}}-\underset{CH_3}{\overset{O-H}{C}}-CH_3$$

2, 3-Dimethyl butan-2, 3 diol (Pinacol) Carbocation

$$\xrightarrow{Step\ II} \left[CH_3-\underset{CH_3}{\overset{CH_3}{C}}-\overset{:O-H}{\underset{+}{C}}-CH_3 \rightleftharpoons CH_3-\underset{CH_3}{\overset{CH_3}{C}}-\overset{\overset{+}{O}H}{\overset{\|}{C}}-CH_3 \right]$$

$$\xrightarrow{\text{Step III}} CH_3-\underset{CH_3}{\overset{CH_3}{\underset{|}{\overset{|}{C}}}}-\underset{O}{\underset{\|}{C}}-CH_3$$

Pinacolone

Migration of methyl group in step II is facilitated by the resonance possible in the product.

Example 12: Arrange the following carbocations in the order of increasing stability:

$$C_6H_5CH_2^+, (C_6H_5)_2\ CH^+, (CH_3)_3\ C^+, (CH_3)_3\ CH^+$$

Solution: $(C_6H_5CH_2^+ < (C_6H_5)_2\ CH^+ < (CH_3)_2\overset{+}{C}H < (CH_3)\overset{+}{C}$

Example 13: Which of the two, single and triplet carbene is more stable and why?

Solution: Triplet carbenes are more stable than singlet carbenes because two unhybridised p-orbitals contain one electron each while unshared pair of electrons is present in the third sp^2 hybrid orbital and the unhydridised *p*-orbital is empty.

Example 14: Mention the methods by which you can infer that a particular reaction involves a free radical intermediate or not.

Solution: Methods:

1. Formation of free radicals is favoured by the presence of u.v. light, heat and organic peroxides.
2. Free radicals are paramagnetic due to the presence of unpaired electrons.
3. Reactions involving free radicals widely occur in the gas phase.

Example 15: Explain why benzyl carbocation is more stable than cyclohexyl carbocation.

Solution: Benzyl carbocation is able to stabilise itself through resonance as shown below:

$\overset{\oplus}{C}H_2$ ⟷ CH_2 + ⟷ CH_2 + ⟷ CH_2 +

There is no such possibility in cyclohexyl carbocation

$\overset{+}{C}H$, CH_2, CH_2, CH_2, CH_2, CH_2

Cyclohexyl carbocation

Example 16: Give the orbital structure of $\bar{C}H_3$. Mention its hybridisation and its shape.

Solution: The central carbon atom in CH_3 with a pair of unshared electrons is sp^3 hybridised. The three sp^3 hybrid orbitals are used in forming three sigma bonds with hydrogen. The fourth sp^3 hybrid orbital is occupied by a lone pair of electrons. The structure is similar to that of ammonia in which one hybrid orbital of nitrogen is occupied by a lone pair of electrons. The structure may be depicted as:

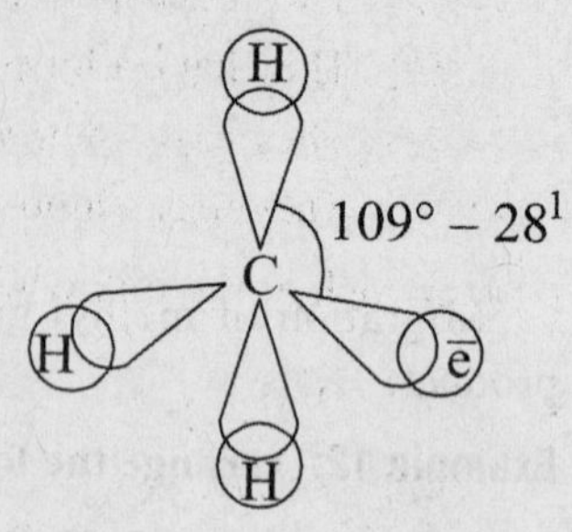

Thus it has a tetrahedral geometry. Three hydrogens are directed towards three corners of the tetrahedron. The fourth position is occupied by unshared pair of electrons.

Applying Chemistry to Life

Most common form of free radicals comes from oxygen. When an oxygen molecule becomes electrically charged, it causes damage to your DNA and other molecules. Over time this damage may become irreversible and lead to disease like cancer.

Antioxidants are our friends, they protect the cells from damage caused by free radicals. Antioxidants can be found in foods containing beta-carotene (carrots) lycopene (tomatoes) and foods with high amounts of vitamin C (kiwi, berries, dark leafy greens) and vitamin E (seeds, nuts and apricots).

Greatest enemy to our health is free radical

Evaluate Yourself

Multiple Choice Questions

1. The least stable carbanion is :

(*a*) $C_6H_5\bar{C}H_2$ (*b*) $(CH_3)_3\bar{C}$

(*c*) $\bar{C}Cl_3$ (*d*) $\bar{C}H_3$

2. Which of the following is an electrophile ?

(*a*) CH_3O^- (*b*) $CH_3\overset{+}{C}H_2$

(*c*) NH_3 (*d*) $CH_3\bar{C}H_2$

3. Which of the following statements is correct regarding nucleophiles ?
   (*a*) They have an over-all positive charge
   (*b*) They have a lone-pair of electrons
   (*c*) They have an unpaired electron
   (*d*) They have empty orbitals

4. Which of the following is not a nucleophile ?
   (*a*) NH_3 (*b*) HSO_3^-
   (*c*) $AlCl_3$ (*d*) HO^-

5. Which of the following is a Lewis acid?
   (*a*) $AlCl_3$ (*b*) CH_3OH
   (*c*) NH_3 (*d*) CH_3OCH_3

6. Homolytic fission of C-C bond leads to the formation of:
   (*a*) free radicals (*b*) carbonium ions
   (*c*) carbanions (*d*) none of these

7. Which of the following is not an electrophile ?
   (*a*) NH_3 (*b*) Br^+
   (*c*) $AlCl_3$ (*d*) NO_2^+

8. Which alkyl free radical is the most stable ?
   (*a*) Methyl (*b*) Primary
   (*c*) Secondary (*d*) Tertiary

9. Which of the following is a nucleophile ? '
   (*a*) $AlCl_3$ (*b*) H_3O^+
   (*c*) BF_3 (*d*) CN^-

10. Which of the following is not a nucleophile?
    (*a*) $\bar{C}N$ (*b*) BF_3
    (*c*) $CH_3\bar{O}$ (*d*) NH_3

11. Which of the following ranges best represents the strength of a hydrogen bond ?
    (*a*) 5 – 10 kcals
    (*b*) 60-80 kcals
    (*c*) 80-100 kcals
    (*d*) 100-120 kcals

12. Homolytic fission of covalent bond between carbon atoms will produce :
    (*a*) two carbonium ions
    (*b*) two molecules
    (*c*) free radicals
    (*d*) carbonium ion and carbanion

13. The average charge on carbon in $\overset{+}{C}H_3$ is
    (*a*) 1 (*b*) 2
    (*c*) 3 (*d*) 4

14. Which of the following free radicals is most stable ?

(*a*) $R_3\dot{C}$ (*b*) $R_2\dot{C}H$

(*c*) $R\dot{C}H_2$ (*d*) $\dot{C}H_3$

15. Which of the following is the least stable carbanion ?

(*a*) cyclopropyl (*b*) vinyl

(*c*) isobutyl (*d*) ethyl

Short Answer Questions

1. Why is dichloroacetic acid stronger than mono chloroacetic acid?
2. How shall we represent the breaking of chlorine molecule into chlorine radicals with the help of arrows?
3. Give two examples of organic substitution reactions.
4. What is meant by a nucleiphile? Give one example.
5. Name two factors that determine the stability of carboration.
6. Write the following carbanious in increasing order of stability.
7. Write the structure of a free radical.
8. Why does trophyllium bromide give a precipitate with carbon increase its stability?
9. Why does the bonding of sulphur with carbanionic carbon increase its stability?
10. Give a method for the formation of carbone.

Long Answer Questions

1. What is meant by curved arrow notation for showing movement of electrons? Explain with an example.
2. Write notes on

   (*i*) half-headed arrows

   (*ii*) double headed arrows
3. Classify the following into electrophiles and nucleophiles and give reasons?

   (*i*) Water

   (*ii*) Silver cation

   (*iii*) Methylene carbene
4. In what way a covalent bond is fissioned? What are its results?
5. Which of the following will generate the most stable carbocation and why?

   CH_3CH_2OH, $CH_3CHOHCH_3$, $C_6H_5CHOHCH_3$
6. What do you understand by electrophilic and nucleophilic reagents. Which of the two will readily attack a carbocation and why?
7. In how many ways can fission of covalent bonds take place? Illustrate with examples.
8. Discuss the structure and shape of carbocations and carbanion.

9. Discuss the relative stabilities of carbocations and free radicals.
10. Define electrophile and nucleophile.
11. Explain the structure and stability of carbenes.
12. What are carbanions? How are they formed?
13. What is a free radical? Discuss its stability
14. What are arynes? How can you represent benzyne is different ways?
15. What are the different types of organic reactions? Explain any one of them
16. What are E_1 and E_2 reactions? Explain with the help of examples.
17. SO_3 (sulphonium ion) appears to the neutral, but still it acts as an electrophile, why?
18. What is meant by reactive intermediate? Make a list of all of them.
19. List the factors that determine the stability of a carbocation. Give an example where field effect controls the stability.
20. Draw the structure of carbocation. Give a reaction where the carbocation reacts with an alkene.
21. What are carbanions? Give a reaction where the rearrangement of a carbanion takes place to give another stable carbanion.
22. Explain vinyl polymerisation showing different steps.
23. What is meant by singlet and triplet carbenes? How are then represented?
24. How can we convert benzene into cycloheptatriene using a reaction intermediate?
25. Draw the structures of singlet and triplet carbene.
26. Give three methods of generation of nitrenes. Give any three properties of nitrenes.
27. Explain why ethyl carbocation $(CH_3-\overset{+}{C}H_2)$ is more stable than *n*-propyl carbocation $(CH_3-CH_2-\overset{+}{C}H_2)$?

Hint: Greater the number of hyperconjugative structures of a carbocation, greater is the stability.

$$\underset{(I)}{H-\overset{\displaystyle H}{\underset{\displaystyle H}{\overset{|}{\underset{|}{C}}}}-\overset{+}{C}H_2} \longleftrightarrow \underset{(II)}{H-\overset{\displaystyle H^+}{\underset{\displaystyle H}{\underset{|}{C}}}=CH_2} \longleftrightarrow \underset{(III)}{\overset{+}{H}\;\overset{\displaystyle H}{\underset{\displaystyle H}{\overset{|}{\underset{|}{C}}}}=CH_2} \longleftrightarrow \underset{(IV)}{H-\overset{\displaystyle H}{\underset{\displaystyle H^+}{\overset{|}{C}}}=CH_2}$$

$$\underset{(I)}{CH_3-\overset{\displaystyle H}{\underset{\displaystyle H}{\overset{|}{\underset{|}{C}}}}-\overset{+}{C}H_2} \longleftrightarrow \underset{(II)}{CH_3-\overset{\displaystyle H^+}{\underset{\displaystyle H}{\underset{|}{C}}}=CH_2} \longleftrightarrow \underset{(III)}{CH_3-\overset{\displaystyle H}{\underset{\displaystyle H^+}{\overset{|}{C}}}=CH_2}$$

We find the ethyl carbocation has four hyperconjugation structures while n-propyl carbocation has three. Thus, ethyl carbocation is more stable.

Answers

Multiple Choice Questions

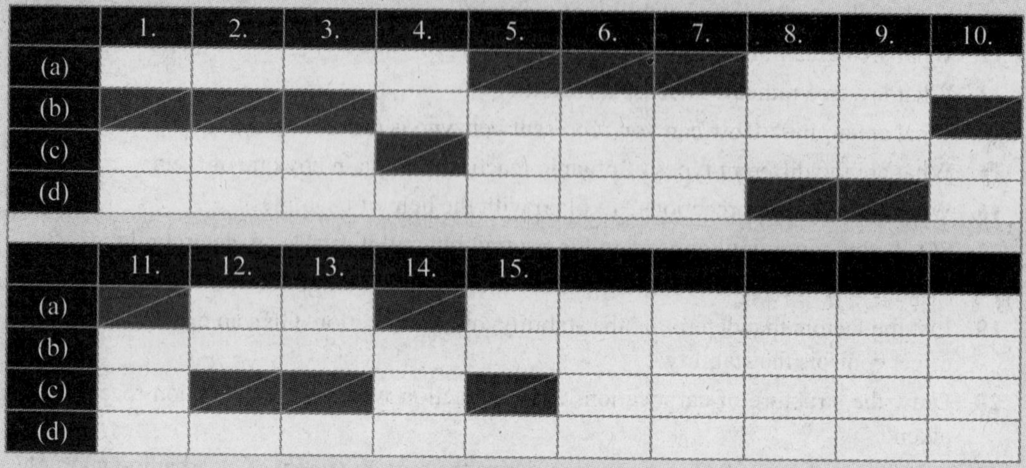

	1.	2.	3.	4.	5.	6.	7.	8.	9.	10.
(a)					■	■	■			
(b)	■	■	■							■
(c)				■						
(d)								■	■	

	11.	12.	13.	14.	15.					
(a)	■			■						
(b)										
(c)		■	■		■					
(d)										

6

Stereochemistry

6.1 INTRODUCTION

One of the striking features of organic compounds is that they exhibit isomerism. Compounds having the same molecular formula and molecular mass but having different characteristics are called isomers. This phenomenon is called isomerism. The relative position of different atoms or groups in these isomers is different and that causes the difference in properties. Isomerism may be classified into two types:

1. **Structural isomerism.** In this type of isomerism, the molecules differ in the structural arrangement of the atoms or groups.

2. **Stereoisomerism.** Here the isomers possess the same structural arrangement but differ with respect to the arrangement of atoms or groups in space.

The two types of isomerisms are discussed in detail as under:

6.2 STRUCTURAL ISOMERISM

If two or more compounds differ in the relative arrangement of atoms in the molecule, they are said to be structural isomers and this phenomenon is known as **structural isomerism.** There are different kinds of structural isomerisms as under:

(*i*) Chain isomerism or Nuclear isomerism.
(*ii*) Position isomerism.
(*iii*) Functional isomerism.
(*iv*) Metamerism.
(*v*) Tautomerism.

Each one of these is discussed as under.

Chain Isomerism or Nuclear Isomerism

If different compounds of the same class of organic compounds, having the same molecular formula, differ in the structure of carbon chain, they are called chain isomers. Examples of this type of isomerism are:

(*a*) *n-Butane and Isobutane (Mol Formula = C_4H_{10})*

```
    H   H   H   H                          H         H         H
    |   |   |   |                          |         |         |
 H— C — C — C — C — H        and       H — C ——————— C ——————— C — H
    |   |   |   |                          |         |         |
    H   H   H   H                          H    H —  C — H     H
                                                     |
                                                     H
       n-Butane                                  Isobutane
```

(*b*) *n-Pentane, isopentane and neo pentane (Mol. Formula = C_5H_{12})*

```
 H   H   H   H   H                          H        H        H   H
 |   |   |   |   |                          |        |        |   |
H—C—C—C—C—C—H          ;              H—C———C———C—C—H
 |   |   |   |   |                          |        |        |   |
 H   H   H   H   H                          H   H—C—H   H   H
                                                     |
                                                     H
```

n-Pentane

Isopentane

```
              H
              |
      H   H—C—H   H
      |       |       |
   H—C———C———C—H
      |       |       |
      H   H—C—H   H
              |
              H
```

Neo-pentane

Position Isomerism

If different compounds, belonging to some homologous series, with same molecular formula have same carbon skeleton but differ in the position of substituent or functional group; these are known as *position isomers*. Examples of this type of isomers are:

(*a*) 1-Propanol and 2-propanol (Mol. Formula = C_3H_8O)

$CH_3—CH_2—CH_2OH$ and $CH_3—CH(OH)—CH_3$

1-Propanol; 2-Propanol

(*b*) 1-Butene and 2-Butene (Mol. Formula = C_4H_8)

$CH_2=CH_2—CH_2—CH_3$ and $CH_3—CH=CH—CH_3$

1–Butene; 2–Butene

Functional Isomerism

Different compounds, with same molecular formula but different functional groups are known as *functional isomers*. For example:

(*a*) Ethyl alcohol and Dimethyl ether (Mol. Formula = C_2H_6O)

CH_3CH_2OH and $CH_3—O—CH_3$

Ethyl alcohol; Dimethyl ether

(*b*) Propionaldehyde and acetone (Mol. Formula = C_3H_6O)

CH_3CH_2CHO and $CH_3—CO—CH_3$

Propionaldehyde; Acetone

Metamerism

This is a special kind of structural isomerism in which different compounds, with same molecular formula, belong to same homologous series but differ in the distribution of alkyl groups around a central atom. Examples are:

(*a*) Diethyl ether and methyl propyl ether (Mol. Formula = $C_4H_{10}O$)

$$\underset{\text{Diethyl ether}}{C_2H_5-O-C_2H_5} \quad \text{and} \quad \underset{\text{Methyl propyl ether}}{CH_3-O-C_3H_7}$$

(*b*) Diethyl ketone and methyl propyl ketone (Mol. Formula = $C_5H_{10}O$)

$$\underset{\text{Diethyl ketone}}{C_2H_5-CO-C_2H_5} \quad \text{and} \quad \underset{\text{Methyl propyl ketone}}{CH_3-CO-C_3H_7}$$

This type of isomers are known as *metamers* and the phenomenon is known as *metamerism.*

Tautomerism

Compounds whose structures differ in the arrangement of atoms but which exist simultaneously in dynamic equilibrium with each other, are called *tautomers*. This phenomenon is called *tautomerism*.

In most of the cases tautomerism is due to shifting of a hydrogen atoms from one carbon (or oxygen or nitrogen) to another with the rearrangement of single or double bonds. For example,

$$\underset{\text{Ethyl acetoacetate (keto form)}}{CH_3-\overset{\overset{O}{\|}}{C}-CH_2-COOC_2H_5} \rightleftharpoons \underset{\text{Ethyl acetoacetate (Enolic form)}}{CH_3-\overset{\overset{OH}{|}}{C}=CH-COOC_2H_5}$$

$$\underset{\text{Nitroethane}}{CH_3-CH_2-N\begin{smallmatrix}\nearrow O \\ \searrow O\end{smallmatrix}} \rightleftharpoons \underset{\text{Isonitroethane}}{CH_3-CH=N\begin{smallmatrix}\nearrow OH \\ \searrow O\end{smallmatrix}}$$

Solved Examples

Example1: Write the structures of all possible isomers of C_3H_8O giving their IUPAC names.

Solution: Position isomers

$$\underset{\text{Propanol–1}}{CH_3CH_2CH_2OH} \qquad \underset{\text{Propanol–2}}{CH_3-CHOHCH_3}$$

Functional Isomers

$$\underset{\text{Propanol–1}}{CH_3CH_2CH_2OH} \qquad \underset{\text{Methoxyethane}}{CH_3OCH_2CH_3}$$

Stereoisomerism

Compounds having different three-dimensional relative arrangement of atoms in space are called stereoisomers. This phenomenon is called *stereoisomerism*. These compounds are said to have different configurations. Stereoisomerism is of the following different kinds:

(*i*) Optical isomerism

(*ii*) Geometrical isomerism

(*iii*) Conformational isomerism.

6.3 OPTICAL ISOMERISM OR ENANTIOMERISM

Before taking up optical isomerism, let us understand the terms: plane polarised light, optical activity and specific rotation.

Plane polarised light

Ordinary light has vibrations taking place at right angles to the direction of propagation of light spread in all the possible planes. If we pass ordinary light through **nicol**. prism vibrations in all planes except one are cut off. Thus light coming out of nicol prism has vibrations only in one plane. Such a light is called *plane polarised light.*

Optical activity

Behaviour of certain substances is strange. When a plane polarised light is passed through the solution of such substances, the light coming out of the solution is found to be in a different plane. The plane of polarised light is rotated. *Such substances, which rotate the plane of plane polarised light when placed in its path are known as optically active substances* and the phenomenon is known as *optical activity*. The angle of rotation (α) of plane polarised light is known as *Optical rotation.* The substances which rotate the plane of polarised light to the clockwise or right direction are known as dextrorotatory or having positive (+) rotation and those which rotate the plane polarised light to the anticlockwise or left direction are known as *laevorotatory* or having negative (–) rotation. Substances which do not rotate the plane of polarised light are said to be optically inactive.

The instrument used for measuring optical rotation is called polarimeter. It consists of a light source, two nicol prisms and in between a tube to hold the solution of organic substance. The schematic representation of a polarimeter is given in Fig. 6.1.

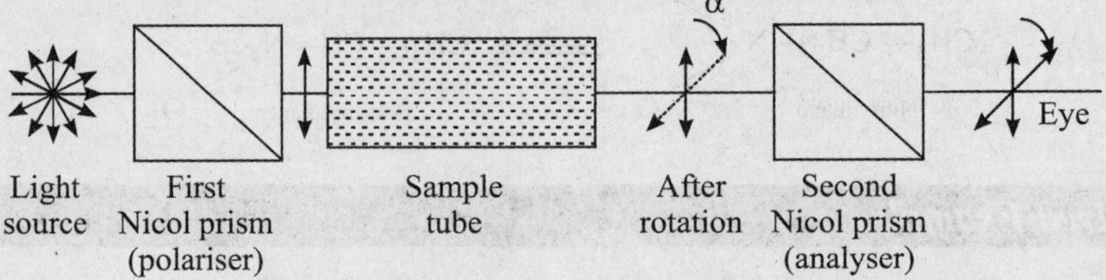

***Fig. 6.1:** Measurement of optical rotation*

Specific rotation. The angle of rotation of plane-polarised light or optical rotation (α) of an organic substance depends not only on the kind of molecules but also varies considerably with the number of molecules that light encounters in its path which in turn depends on the concentration of the solution used and the length of polarimeter tube containing it. Besides this, it depends on temperature, wavelength of light and nature of solvent used.

The optical activity of a substance is expressed in terms of *specific rotation.* $[\alpha]_\lambda^t$ which is a constant quantity, characteristic of a particular substance,

$$[\alpha]_\lambda^t = \frac{\alpha}{l \times c}$$

where, α = observed rotation in degrees

l = length of polarimeter tube in decimeter

c = concentration of substance in gm per ml of solution

t and λ signify the temperature and wavelength of light used.

When $l = 1$ and $c = 1$, $[\alpha]_\lambda^t = \alpha$

Specific rotation is thus defined as the optical rotation produced by a compound when plane polarised light passes through one decimeter length of the solution having concentration one gram per millilitre. Usually the monochromatic light used is D line of sodium (λ = 589 nm). Thus specific rotation of cane sugar can be expressed as

$$[\alpha]_D^{20°C} = +66.5° \text{ (water)}$$

In this expression D stands for D line of sodium, 20°C is temperature of measurement, + sign shows the dextrorotation and water is the solvent used.

Louis Pasteur, while studying the crystallography of salts of tartaric acid made a peculiar observation. He observed that optically inactive sodium ammonium tartarate existed as a mixture of two different types of crystals which were mirror images of each other. With the help of a hand lens and a pair of forceps, he carefully separated the mixture into two different types of crystals. These crystals were mirror images of each other and were called enantiomorphs and the phenomenon as *enantiomorphism*. Although the original mixture was optically inactive; each type of crystals when dissolved in water, were found to be optically active. Moreover the specific rotations of the two solutions were exactly equal but of opposite sign *i.e.* one solution rotated the plane polarised light to the right or clockwise while the other to the left or anticlockwise and to the same extent. Two types of crystals or solutions were identical in all other physical and chemical properties. *Isomers which are non-superimposable mirror images of each other are called enantiomers*.

According to La Bell and van't Hoff the four valencies of a carbon atom are directed towards the four corners of a regular tetrahedron at the centre of which lies the carbon atom. Consider a

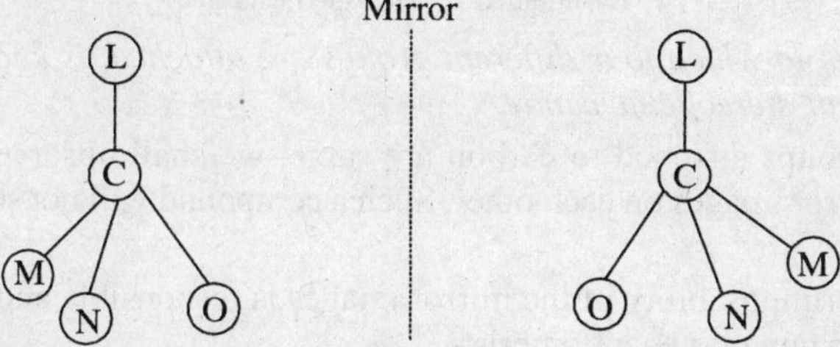

compound of formula C_{LMNO} having four different groups L, M, N and O attached to a carbon atom. This compound can be represented by two models which look like mirror images of each other.

Enantiomerism in real life

van't Hoff (1852-1911)

van't Hoff was a Dutch Chemist. His work on three dimensional molecular properties is widely acclaimed. He received the first Nobel prize in chemistry in 1901 for his work on rates of reactions, chemical equilibrium and osmotic pressure.

It is important to note here that these two molecules cannot be superimposed on each other *i.e.* they will not coincide in all their parts. We may turn them in as many ways as we like but we find that though two groups of each may coincide, the other two do not. Hence these must represent two isomers of formula C_{LMNO}. Lactic acid $CH_3CHOHCOOH$ and sec-Butyl chloride $C_2H_5CHClCH_3$, exist as two optically active isomers which are enantiomers *i.e.* mirror images of each other. Mirror images of the two compounds are represented as above.

Enantiomers of Lactic Acid

Enantiomers of Sec. Butyl Chloride

The carbon atom to which four different groups are attached, is known as asymmetric or chiral carbon atom or stereogenic centre.

If two of the groups attached to carbon are same, we shall observe that it is possible to superimpose the mirror images on each other. Such a compound will not show optical isomerism or *enantiomerism.*

Hence non-superimposability of the mirror images is responsible and essential for the type of stereoisomerism known as enantiomerism.

The term optical isomerism is used for the existence of stereoisomers which differ in their behaviour towards the plane polarised light. Thus enantiomeric molecules are always non-superimposable mirror images of each other. The non-superimposability of mirror images arises due to **chiral** or **asymmetric** nature of molecule. A molecule is said to be chiral if it has no plane of symmetry and is therefore non-superimposable on its mirror image.

It may be concluded with the remarks that chirality is the fundamental condition of enantiomerism or optical isomerism.

Elements of symmetry

(*i*) Plane of symmetry. It is defined as an imaginary plane which divides the molecule into two equal halves such that one half is the mirror image of the other half. It may pass through atoms, between the atoms or both. Chiral objects or molecules (having chiral carbons) do not have a plane of symmetry. On the other hand, achiral objects or molecules have at least one or more elements of symmetry. Thus a sphere has a plane of symmetry which passes through the centre of the sphere. It divides the sphere into two halves which are mirror images of each other. Meso tartaric acid has a plane of symmetry which passes throught the mid point of C_2 and C_3.

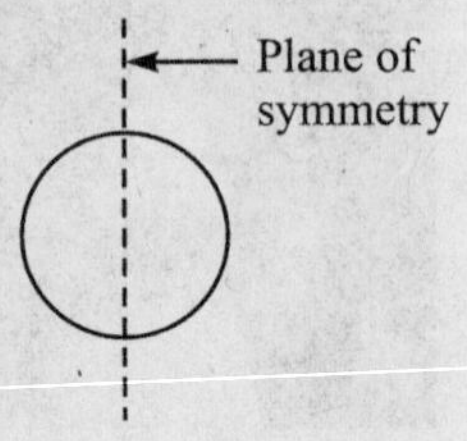

```
        1
       COOH                         CH3
        |2                           |
   H — C — OH                   H — C — OH
  ------|3-------                    |
   H — C — OH                      COOH
        |4                      Lactic acid
       C OOH
  Meso tartaric acid
```

Therefore one half of the meso tartaric acid is mirror image of the other half. Lactic acid, $CH_3CH(OH)\ COOH$ on the other hand has no plane of symmetry which can divide into two equal halves.

(ii) Centre of symmetry. *A centre of symmetry is defined as a point from which lines when drawn on one side and extended an equal distance on the other side will meet identical points (or atoms or groups).* For example *trans* –1, 3-dimethylcyclobutane has a centre of symmetry. Three dimensional (and not two dimensional) models need to be drawn to understand this point.

Centre of symmetry; CH_3, H, H, CH_3

1, 3-Dimethylcyclobutane

(iii) Alternating axis of symmetry. *A molecule is said to possess an n-fold alternating axis of symmetry if rotation through an angle of 360/n about this axis and then followed by reflection in a plane perpendicular to the axis gives a molecule which is indistinguishable from the original molecule.* Consider Z^+ and Z^- as chiral group (+) – CH (CH_3) C_2H_5 and (–) –CH(CH_3) C_2H_5 respectively. Rotation of molecule (*a*) through 90° about AB which passes through the centre of the ring and perpendicular to the plane gives (*b*). Reflection of (*b*) gives the original molecule (*a*). Thus it has 4-fold 360/90=4 alternating axis of symmetry and hence is achiral (Fig 6.2)

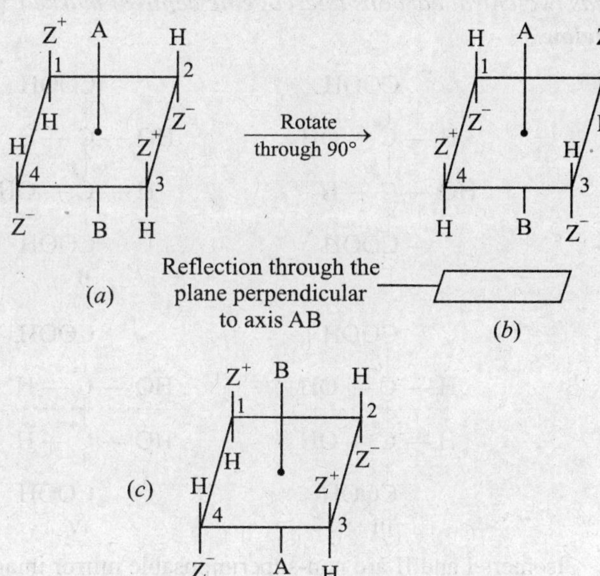

***Fig. 6.2:** Four-fold alternating axis of symmetry*

Therefore, absence of an alternating axis of symmetry is the necessary and sufficient condition for a molecule to exhibit optical activity.

Chirality and dissymetry

*An object which is non-superimposable on its mirror image is called **chiral** object. And an object which is superimposable on its mirror image is called **achiral** object.* Examples of chiral objects including letters from English alphabets are: A pair of hands, shoes, gloves, letters P, F, J etc.

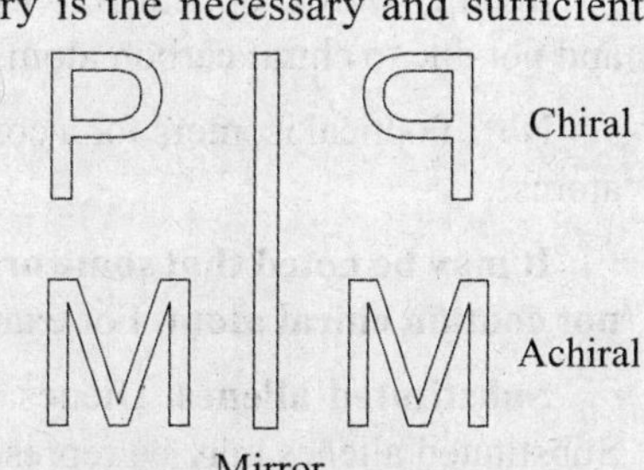

Chiral and achiral objects

Examples of achiral objects and letters are: Ball, sphere, letters A, O, M, etc.

Achiral objects or molecules possess a plane of symmetry that can divide the molecule into two identical halves. Chiral objects or molecules do not possess a plane of symmetry that can divide the molecule into two identical halves. The **chirality** is also known as **dissymetry** while **achirality** is also known as **symmetry**.

Thus chirality or dissymmetry is the property associated with certain compounds which do not have a plane of symmetry and are thus non-superimposable on their mirror images. Dissymmetry is an essential condition for optical activity. In the study of enantiomers containing one chiral carbon atom, we find that they do not have a plane of symmetry and hence are dissymmetric in nature, for example, lactic acid, sec-butyl chloride etc. We can thus say that compounds with a chiral carbon atom are optically active in nature.

This is not true, however, for compounds with two or more chiral carbon atoms. Here, one or more isomers may be optically inactive in spite of the presence of chiral carbon atoms. Consider *for example, the case of tartaric acid, CH(OH) COOHCH (OH) COOH. It has two chiral carbons (stereogenic centres) marked * and thus has four isomers as shown below:*

```
     COOH                  COOH
      |                     |
  H — C* — OH         HO — C* — H
      |                     |
 HO — C* — H           H — C* — OH
      |                     |
     COOH                  COOH
      I                     II
```

I and II are optically active due to the absence of plane of symmetry

```
     COOH                  COOH
      |                     |
  H — C* — OH         HO — C* — H
 .....|........       ......|......
  H — C* — OH         HO — C* — H
      |                     |
     COOH                  COOH
      III                   IV
```

III and IV are optically inactive due to the presence of plane of symmetry (shown by dotted line)

Isomers I and II are non-superimposable mirror images of each other, they are dissymetric and optically active. But III and IV have a plane of symmetry. Therefore, they are symmetric and optically inactive in nature.

In other words, optical activity in organic compounds is due to the presence of dissymetry and not due to chiral carbon atoms alone.

No. of optical isomers for a compound is given by 2^n where n is the number of chiral carbon atoms.

It may be noted that some organic compounds are optically active even though they do not contain chiral atom. For example,

Substituted allenes. Dienes with double bonds in adjacent positions are called allenes. Substituted allenes may be represented as RCH = C = CHR. Pentane –2, 3-diene exists in two optically active forms. This is because the groups linked to one end carbon are in different plane than those linked to the other end carbon.

$$\underset{H_3C}{\overset{H}{\diagdown}}C=C=C\underset{CH_3}{\overset{H}{\diagup}} \qquad \underset{CH_3}{\overset{H}{\diagdown}}C=C=C\underset{CH_3}{\overset{H}{\diagup}}$$

In allenes, the central carbon is *sp* hybridized, and the terminal carbons are sp^2 hybridized. The central carbon forms two sp-sp^2 σ bonds. The central carbon also has two *p* orbitals which are mutually perpendicular. These forms π bonds with the *p* orbitals on the other carbon atoms. As a result, the substituent at one end of the molecule are in a plane which is perpendicular to that of the substituents at the other end, so that the compound exists in two forms which are non-superimposable mirror images and are optically active.

Substituted biphenyl. Benzene rings in substituted biphenyl lie in different planes. Hence the compound exhibits optical activity.

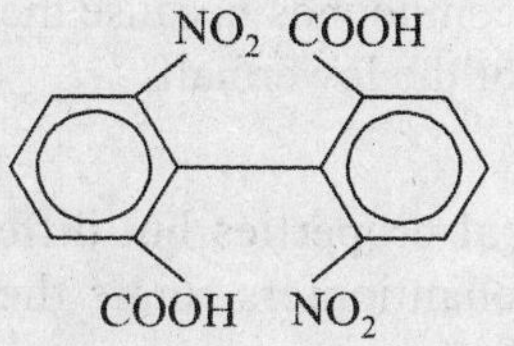

NO_2 COOH

COOH NO_2

We can conclude from the above discussion that the most essential condition for a compound to show optical activity is the presence of dissymmetry and not chirality. However, compounds containing only one chiral carbon are always dissymmetric since they do not have a plane of symmetry.

The compounds, with two or more similar chiral carbon atoms which are optically inactive due to the presence of plane of symmetry, are called **meso** compounds.

Consider the following isomer of tartaric acid

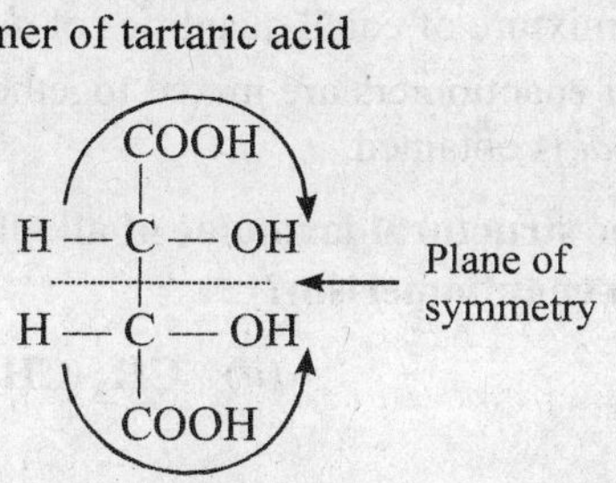

COOH
H — C — OH
H — C — OH
COOH

Plane of symmetry

It has a plane of symmetry denoted by the denoted line. The optical rotation of upper half of the molecule is neutralized by that of the lower half as the two rotations are in opposite directions. The net result is that the molecule is optically inactive. Such compounds are known as meso compounds.

Similarly, we come across meso structures in 2, 3-Dichlorobutane. This compound also possesses two asymmetric carbon atoms (stereogenic centres) marked with *.

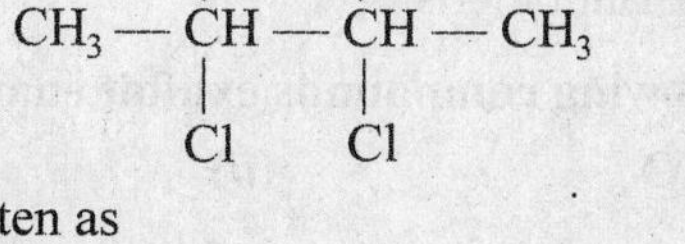

$$CH_3 - \overset{*}{C}H(Cl) - \overset{*}{C}H(Cl) - CH_3$$

The different isomers can be written as

$$\begin{array}{c} CH_3 \\ | \\ H-\overset{*}{C}-Cl \\ | \\ Cl-\overset{*}{C}-H \\ | \\ CH_3 \\ \text{I} \end{array} \qquad \begin{array}{c} CH_3 \\ | \\ Cl-\overset{*}{C}-H \\ | \\ H-\overset{*}{C}-Cl \\ | \\ CH_3 \\ \text{II} \end{array}$$

I and II show optical activity due to absence of plane of symmetry (Dissymmetry)

$$\begin{array}{c} CH_3 \\ | \\ H-\overset{*}{C}-Cl \\ | \\ H-\overset{*}{C}-Cl \\ | \\ CH_3 \\ \text{III} \end{array} \qquad \begin{array}{c} CH_3 \\ | \\ Cl-\overset{*}{C}-H \\ | \\ Cl-\overset{*}{C}-H \\ | \\ CH_3 \\ \text{IV} \end{array}$$

III and IV are optically inactive because of the presence of plane of symmetry

Structures III and IV are meso compounds because the optical activity of the upper half of the molecule is neutralised by that of the lower half.

Properties of enantiomers

(*i*) They have identical physical properties but differ in direction of rotation of plane polarised light. Though the two enantiomers rotate the plane polarised light in opposite direction, the extent of rotation is the same.

(*ii*) They have identical chemical properties except towards optically active reagents. The rates of reaction of optically active reagents with two enantiomers differ and sometimes one of the enantiomers does not react at all.

(*iii*) In biological system (–) or *l*-glucose is neither metabolised by animals nor fermented by yeast whereas (+) or *d*-glucose undergoes both these processes and plays an important role in animal metabolism and fermentation. Similarly mould *penicillium glaucum* consumes only *d*-tartaric acid when fed with a mixture of equal quantities of *d*- and *l*-tartaric acid.

(*iv*) When equal amounts of enantiomers are mixed together an optically inactive racemic modification denoted by (±) or *dl* is obtained.

Example 2: Given below are the structural formulae of all alkanes with molecular formula C_6H_{14}. Which of these exhibit enantiomerism?

(*i*) $CH_3(CH_2)_4CH_3$

(*ii*) $CH_3(CH_2)_2-\underset{\displaystyle CH_3}{\underset{|}{C}}H-CH_3$

(*iii*) $CH_3\underset{\displaystyle CH_3}{\underset{|}{C}}H-\underset{\displaystyle CH_3}{\underset{|}{C}}H-CH_3$

(*iv*) $(CH_3)_3C-CH_2CH_3$

Solution: There is no carbon in any of the compounds above which is chiral *i.e.* attached to four different groups.

Chirality is the necessary condition for a molecule to exhibit enantiomerism. Hence none of the compounds above shows enantiomerism.

Example 3: Which of the following compounds exhibit enantiomerism?

(*i*) $CH_2OH\ CHOH\ CHO$

(*ii*) $CH_3-\overset{\displaystyle CH_3}{\overset{|}{C}}H-CHCl-CH_3$

(*iii*) $CH_3-CH_2-CH-CH_3$ with CH_3 attached to CH

(*iv*) $CH_3CHOHCH_3$

(*v*) CH_2NH_2COOH

Solution: Compounds (*i*) and (*ii*) have chiral carbons marked with asterisks and hence these two compounds show enantiomerism.

$$CH_2OH\overset{*}{C}HOHCHO$$

$$CH_3-\underset{|}{\overset{CH_3}{CH}}-\overset{*}{C}HCl-CH_3$$

Compounds (*iii*), (*iv*) and (*v*) have no chiral carbon atom in the molecule.

Hence they do not show enantiomerism.

Example 4: Point out the optically active compounds out of the following:

(*i*) $CH_2OH-CHOH-CHO$

(*ii*) $CH_3-CHOH-CH_2OH$

(*iii*)

```
      CHOH
       |
   H — C — OH
       |
  HO — C — H
       |
      COOH
```

Solution: Compounds (*i*) and (*ii*) have one chiral carbon (the middle one) and hence both these compounds are optically active compounds. (*iii*) has two chiral carbons (the middle ones) and therefore this compound is also optically active.

Flying Wedge representation

Spatial arrangement of atoms or groups in a molecule is called its configuration. The three dimensional (3D) structure of an organic molecule may be represented by flying wedge model. We use three types of lines in this model. A solid wedge (━) represents a bond lying above the plane of the paper projecting towards the observer, an ordinary line (—) represents a bond lying in the plane of the paper and a dotted wedge (||||||) represents a bond lying below the plane of paper projecting away from observer. For convenience, we can use a dotted line (----) in place of dotted wedge. For example the flying wedge representation of CHPQR is given alongside

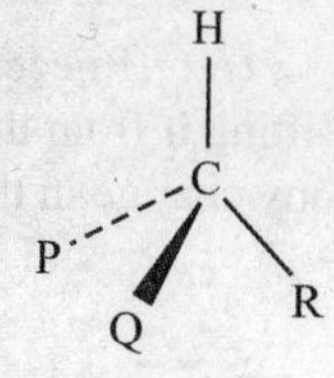

Fischer's projection formula for planar representation of three dimensional molecules.

Emil Fischer in 1891 introduced a simple method for representing three dimensional molecules in one plane. It is known as *Fischer projection formula.* Following points are to be observed for this purpose:

(*i*) The chiral molecule is imagined in such a way that two groups point towards the observer and two away from the observer. The groups pointing towards the observer are written along the horizontal line (shown by thick wedge-like bonds) and those pointing away are written along the vertical line. The central carbon is present at the crossing of the horizontal and vertical lines.

```
        x                          x
        |                          |
b ▬▬▬▬ C ▬▬▬▬ a          b ——— C ——— a
        |                          |
        y                          y
```

Flying wedge representation   Normal representation

Emil Fischer (1852-1919)
Emil Fischer was a German Chemist and recipient of 1902 Nobel Prize in chemistry. He developed the Fischer Projection, a symbolic way of drawing asymmetric compounds.

Thus if *a*, *b*, *x* and *y* are four groups attached to a carbon, the molecule will be represented by the projection formula as above. Here *a* and *b* groups point towards the observer (or above the plane) and groups *x* and *y* are away from the observer (or below the plane).

(*ii*) The longest chain of carbon atoms in the molecule (with the most oxidised carbon) should be represented along the vertical line. Lactic acid, therefore, according to the above conventions will be represented as

```
     COOH                      COOH
      |                         |
H — C — OH       or      H ————+———— OH
      |                         |
     CH3                       CH3
```

– COOH, – CHO, – CH_2OH, etc. groups should be located on the vertical line.

(*iii*) We can avoid writing carbon at the crossing of the vertical and horizontal lines. A crossing automatically means the presence of a carbon.

(*iv*) If necessary, planar formula may be imagined to be rotated from end to end without lifting it from the plane of the paper. Rotation by 180° in the plane of the paper does not create any change in the configuration of the molecule.

```
     COOH                                CH3
      |                                   |
H ————+———— OH   ——Rotation——>    HO ————+———— H
      |          through 180°             |
     CH3                                COOH
I (–) lactic acid                  II (–) lactic acid
```

In the above rotation by 180°, II has been obtained from I. There has been no change in configuration of the molecule. I and II are in fact the same thing.

(*v*) Rotation by 90° or 270° brings about a change in configuration of the molecule. Consider the following rotation.

```
     COOH                                 H
      |                                   |
H ————+———— OH   ——Rotation——>    CH3 ————+———— COOH
      |              90°                  |
     CH3                                 OH
(–) lactic acid                    (+) lactic acid
```

(*vi*) If the positions of two groups across the chiral atom are interchanged, it leads to inversion of configuration. Two consecutive such changes neutralise the effect.

COOH; H—C—OH; CH_3 — (–) lactic acid (I) —First Interchange H and OH→ COOH; HO—C—H; CH_3 — (+) lactic acid (II) —Second Interchange CH_3 and COOH→ CH_3; HO—C—H; COOH — (–) lactic acid (III)

Structures III and I are the same because as per rule (iv) above, III on rotation through 180° will give I.

Absolute configuration of optical isomers

In the earlier days, as the modern techniques of finding out configuration were not available, Fischer assigned the following configurations to the (+) and (–) enantiomers of glyceraldehyde arbitrarily and denoted them by capital letters D and L respectively. Small letters *d* and *l* represent sign of rotation, while capital letters D and L represent configuration.

MIRROR

CHO; H—C—OH; CH_2OH — D (+) glyceraldehyde | CHO; HO—C—H; CH_2OH — L (–) glyceraldehyde

The relative configurations of a number of other optically active compounds have been established by correlating them with D(+) or L(–) glyceraldehyde. All those optically active compounds, which are obtained from D(+) glyceraldehyde through a sequence of reactions *without breaking the bonds of asymmetric carbon atom*, are designated as D configuration irrespective of their sign of rotation and the other enantiomer as L configuration.

For example,

CHO; H—C—OH; CH_2OH — D(+) Glyceraldehyde —Br_2/H_2O→ COOH; H—C—OH; CH_2OH — D (–) Glyceric acid

—PBr_3→ COOH; H—C—OH; CH_2Br — D (–) 3-Bromo-2-hydroxypropanoic acid

—Zn, H^+→ COOH; H—C—OH; CH_3 — D(–) Lactic acid

In all the D configurations, —OH attached to asymmetric carbon atom is written on the right hand side of Fischer projection formula. Similarly, in all the L-configurations, –OH attached to the lowest asymmetric carbon atom is written on the left hand side in the Fisher's projection formula.

R and S specification for the configuration of an optically active compound

Cahn, Ingold and Prelog developed a method which can be used to designate the configuration of all the molecules containing asymmetric carbon atom (chiral centre). This system is known as *Cahn-Ingold-Prelog system* or R and S system and involves two steps.

Step I. The four different atoms or groups of atoms attached to chiral carbon atom are assigned a sequence of priority according to the following set of sequence rules.

Sequence Rule 1. *If the four atoms, directly attached to asymmetric carbon atom, are all different, the priority depends on their atomic number. The atom of higher atomic number gets higher priority.* For example, in chloroiodomethane sulphonic acid the priority sequence is I, Cl, SO_3H, H

$$\begin{array}{ccccc} & & SO_3H\ (3) & & \\ & & | & & \\ I & — & C & — & Cl \\ (1) & & | & & (2) \\ & & H & & \\ & & (4) & & \end{array}$$

We consider the atom of the group which is directly linked to the central carbon.

Sequence Rule 2. *If Rule 1 fails to decide the relative priority of two groups it is determined by similar comparison of next atoms in the group and so on.* In other words, if two atoms directly attached to chiral centre are same, the next atoms attached to each of these atoms, are compared. For example in 2-butanol two of the atoms directly attached to chiral centre are carbon themselves. To decide the priority between the two groups $—CH_3$ and $—CH_2CH_3$, we proceed like this. Methyl carbon is further linked to H, H and H. The sum of atomic numbers of three H is 3. The methylene carbon of the ethyl group is linked to two hydrogens and one carbon directly. The sum of at. no. of two H and one C is 8. Thus ethyl group gets the priority over methyl. Hence the priority sequence is OH, C_2H_5, CH_3, H.

$$\begin{array}{ccccccc} & & & & OH\ (1) & & \\ & & & & | & & \\ CH_3 & — & CH_2 & — & C & — & CH_3 \\ & & (2) & & | & & (3) \\ & & & & H\ (4) & & \end{array}$$

2-Butanol

In 2-methyl-3-pentanol, the C, C, H of isopropyl gets priority over the C, H, H of ethyl, so the priority sequence is OH, isopropyl, ethyl, H.

$$\begin{array}{ccccccccc} & & CH_3 & & H\ (4) & & & & \\ & & | & & | & & & & \\ CH_3 & — & CH & — & C & — & CH_2 & — & CH_3 \\ & & (2) & & | & & (3) & & \\ & & & & OH & & & & \\ & & & & (1) & & & & \end{array}$$

2-Methyl-3-pentanol

In 1, 2-dichloro-3-methylbutane the Cl, H, H of CH_2 Cl gets priority over the C, C, H of isopropyl due to atomic number of Cl being higher than that of C. So the priority sequence is Cl, CH_2Cl, isopropyl, H.

$$\begin{array}{ccccc} & CH_3 & & H\,(4) & \\ & | & & | & \\ CH_3 - & CH & - & C & - CH_2Cl \\ & (3) & & | & (2) \\ & & & Cl & \\ & & & (1) & \end{array}$$

1, 2-dichloro-3-methylbutane

Sequence Rule 3. *A doubly or triply bonded atom is considered equivalent to two or three such atoms; but two or three atoms, if attached actually, get priority over doubly or triply bonded atom.* In glyceraldehyde, O, O, H of — CHO gets priority over the O, H, H of — CH_2OH; so the priority sequence is — OH, — CHO — CH_2OH — H.

$$\begin{array}{c} (2)\ CHO \\ | \\ (4)\ H - C - OH\ (1) \\ | \\ CH_2OH \\ (3) \end{array}$$

Glyceraldehyde

Step II. After deciding the sequence of priority for four atoms or groups attached to asymmetric carbon atom; the molecule is visualised in such a way that the atom or group of lowest or last (*i.e.* fourth) priority is directed away from us, while the remaining three atoms or groups are pointing towards us. Now if on looking at these three groups (pointing towards us) in the order of their decreasing priority, our eye moves in clockwise direction, the configuration is specified as R (from Latin word *rectus* meaning right) and on the other hand if our eye moves in anticlockwise direction the configuration is specified as S (from Latin word *sinister* meaning left).

The following examples illustrate the above method for specification of configuration as R and S to molecules of compounds containing an asymmetric or chiral carbon atom.

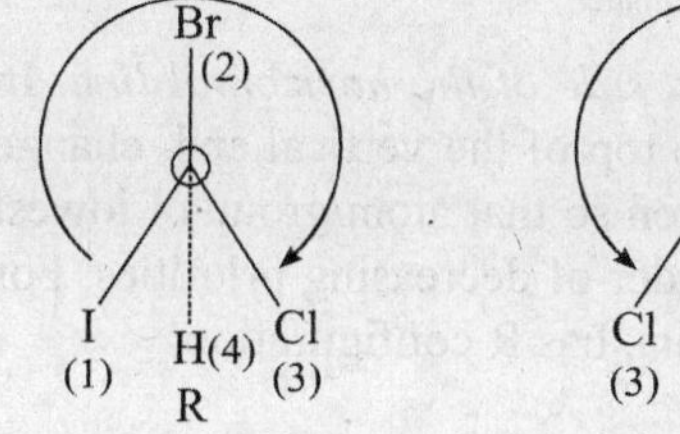

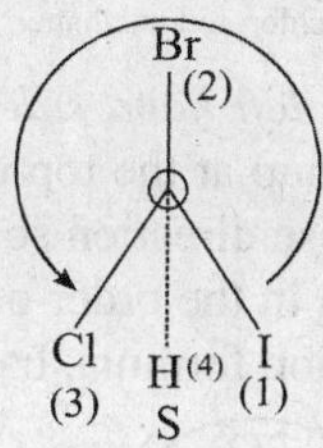

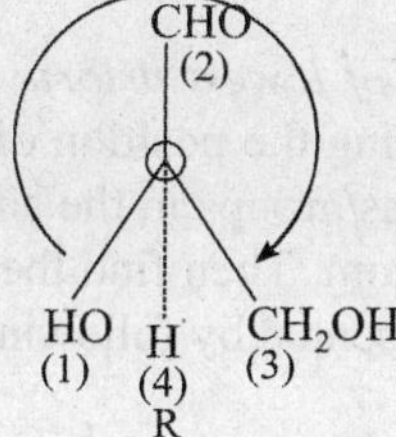

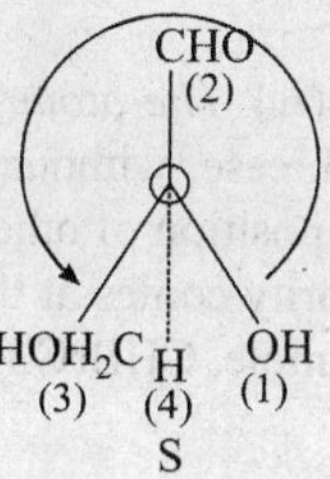

Configuration on the basis of projection formula

When a compound is represented by the Fischer projection formula, the configuration can be easily determined without constructing the model. To determine whether the eye travels clockwise or anticlockwise, we have to place the group or atom of the lowest priority at the bottom of the Fischer projection formula. The following four situations arise:

(*i*) *The atom/group of lowest priority is at the bottom.* In such a case, simply rotate the eye in the order of decreasing priorities. The configuration is R if the eye travels in clockwise direction and S if the eye travels in *anticlockwise* direction.

For example, Glyceraldehyde, represented by the following projection formula has R configuration:

(1) OH
(3) | (2)
$HOH_2C — C — CHO$
|
H

R—Glyceraldehyde

(*ii*) *The atom/group of lowest priority is at the top*. In such case, rotate the molecule by 180° so as to bring atom/group of lowest priority at the bottom. This can be done by reversing the position of all the atoms or groups. Then find the direction in the order of decreasing priorities. For example, the compound CHBrClI, represented by following projection formula, has S configuration:

H | I — C — Cl | Br ≡ (2) Br (3) | (1) Cl — C — I | H

S-Bromochloroiodomethane

(*iii*) *The atom/group of lowest priority is at the right hand side of the horizontal line.* In such case, change the position of atoms or groups in clockwise direction so that atom/group of the lowest priority comes at the bottom but do not change the position of the atom/group at the top of the vertical end. Then find the direction in the order of decreasing priorities. For example, CHBrClI, represented by following projection formula, has S configuration.

Br | I — C — H | Cl ≡ (2) Br (3) | (1) Cl — C — I | H

S-Bromochloroiodomethane

(*iv*) *The atom/group of lowest priority is at the left hand side of the horizontal line.* In such case, without changing the position of atom/group at the top of the vertical end, change the position of other atoms/groups in the anticlockwise direction so that atom/group of lowest priority comes at the bottom. Then find the direction in the order of decreasing priorities. For example, CHBrClI, represented by following projection formula, has R configuration.

Br | H — C — I | Cl ≡ (2) Br (1) | (3) I — C — Cl | H

R-Bromochloroiodomethane

Example 5: Assign R and S configuration to the following:

(*i*) Cl CH_3 | | H — C — C — H | | CH_3 H

(*ii*) NH_2 | HO — C — CH_3 | Cl

(*iii*) $HO-\overset{\displaystyle H}{\underset{\displaystyle COOH}{C}}-CH_3$ (*iv*) $CH_3-\overset{\displaystyle C_2H_5}{\underset{\displaystyle CHO}{C}}-COOH$

Solution:

(*i*) $H-\overset{\displaystyle Cl}{\underset{\displaystyle CH_3}{C}}-\overset{\displaystyle CH_3}{\underset{\displaystyle H}{C}}-H \longrightarrow H-\overset{\displaystyle CH_3}{\underset{\displaystyle H}{C}}-\overset{\displaystyle Cl}{\underset{\displaystyle H}{C}}-CH_3$ [S]

(*ii*) $HO-\overset{\displaystyle NH_2}{\underset{\displaystyle Cl}{C}}-CH_3 \longrightarrow Cl-\overset{\displaystyle NH_2}{\underset{\displaystyle CH_3}{C}}-OH$ [S]

(*iii*) $OH-\overset{\displaystyle H}{\underset{\displaystyle COOH}{C}}-CH_3 \xrightarrow[\text{Through } 180^\circ]{\text{Rotate}} CH_3-\overset{\displaystyle COOH}{\underset{\displaystyle H}{C}}-OH$ [S]

(*iv*) $CH_3-\overset{\displaystyle C_2H_5}{\underset{\displaystyle CHO}{C}}-COOH \longrightarrow HOOC-\overset{\displaystyle C_2H_5}{\underset{\displaystyle CH_3}{C}}-CHO$ [S]

Example 6: Assign R and S configuration to the following:

(*i*) $C_2H_5-\overset{\displaystyle Br}{\underset{\displaystyle OH}{C}}-H$ (*ii*) $H-\overset{\displaystyle CH_3}{\underset{\displaystyle C_2H_5}{C}}-NH_2$

(*iii*) $C_2H_5-\overset{\displaystyle CHO}{\underset{\displaystyle NH_2}{C}}-H$

Solution:

(*i*) $C_2H_5-\overset{\displaystyle Br}{\underset{\displaystyle OH}{C}}-H \longrightarrow HO-\overset{\displaystyle Br}{\underset{\displaystyle H}{C}}-C_2H_5$ [S] (*ii*) $H-C(CH_3)(C_2H_5)-NH_2 \longrightarrow H_2N-C(CH_3)(H)-C_2H_5$ [S]

(*iii*) $C_2H_5-C(CHO)(NH_2)-H \longrightarrow H_2N-C(CHO)(H)-C_2H_5$ [R]

Example 7: Assign R and S configuration to the following compounds:

(*i*) $CH_3-C(C_2H_5)(CH_2OH)-H$ (*ii*) $HO-C(H)(COOH)-CH_3$

Solution:

(*i*) $CH_3-C(C_2H_5)(CH_2OH)-H \longrightarrow HOH_2C-C(C_2H_5)(H)-CH_3$ [R]

(*ii*) $CH_3-C(C_2H_5)(CH_2OH)-H \longrightarrow HOH_2C-C(C_2H_5)(H)-CH_3$ [R]

Example 8: Assign R and S configuration to the following:

(*i*) $H-C(COOH)(CH_3)-NH_2$ (*ii*) $OH-C(CHO)(CH_2OH)-H$

Solution:

(*i*) $H-C(COOH)(CH_3)-NH_2 \longrightarrow H_2N-C(COOH)(H)-CH_3$ [R]

(*ii*) $HO-C(CHO)(CH_2OH)-H \longrightarrow HOH_2C-C(CHO)(H)-OH$ [S]

Example 9: A carboxy acid of the formula $C_3H_5O_2$ Br is optically active. What is its structure?

Solution: Two structures are possible for a carboxy acid with the above molecular formula

$$\underset{\text{I}}{CH_3-\underset{\underset{Br}{|}}{\overset{\overset{H}{|}}{C}}-COOH} \qquad \underset{\text{II}}{BrCH_2-\underset{\underset{H}{|}}{\overset{\overset{H}{|}}{C}}-COOH}$$

Of the two structures, structure I has a chiral (or asymmetric) carbon atom whereas structure II has none. Therefore the structure showing optical activity is I.

Configuration of compounds containing more than one chiral carbon

In such a case, firstly the configuration about each of the chiral carbon is specified and then with the help of numbers, the specification pertaining to the carbon atom of that number is written. Thus the configurations of isomers of 2, 3, 4-Trihydroxybutanal are:

$$\begin{array}{c} {}^{1}CHO \\ | \\ H-{}^{2}C-OH \\ | \\ H-{}^{3}C-OH \\ | \\ {}^{4}CH_2OH \end{array} \qquad \begin{array}{c} {}^{1}CHO \\ | \\ HO-{}^{2}C-H \\ | \\ HO-{}^{3}C-H \\ | \\ {}^{4}CH_2OH \end{array}$$

(2R, 3R) -2, 3, 4-Trihydroxy butanal (A)   (2S, 3S) -2, 3, 4-Trihydroxy butanal (B)

The configurations are explained as follows:

In the compound A above, sequence of groups attached to C_2 is OH, CHO, CHOH — CH_2OH and H.

Now in order to fix specification, first we consider C_2 and ignore C_3

$$\begin{array}{c} CHO \\ | \\ H-C_2-OH \\ | \\ CHOHCH_2OH \end{array} \xrightarrow{\text{Interchanges}} \begin{array}{c} \overset{(2)}{CHO} \\ | \\ \overset{(1)}{HO}-C_2-\overset{(3)}{CHOHCH_2OH} \\ | \\ H \end{array}$$

Ignoring (C_3)   (2R)

Similarly we consider C_3 and we ignore C_2. Thus

$$\begin{array}{c} CHOHCHO \\ | \\ H-C_3-OH \\ | \\ CH_2OH \end{array} \xrightarrow{\text{Interchanges}} \begin{array}{c} \overset{(2)}{CHOHCHO} \\ | \\ \overset{(1)}{HO}-C_3-\overset{(3)}{CH_2OH} \\ | \\ H \end{array}$$

Ignoring (C_2)   (3R)

(Here the sequence of groups attached to C_3 is OH, CHOHCHO, CH_2OH and H)

Hence the configuration of compound A is (2R, 3R) – 2, 3, 4-Trihydroxy butanal. Similarly the configuration of compund B can be derived as explained below:

For C_2:

CHO
HO — C_2 — H
CHOHCH_2OH
Ignoring (C_3)

Interchanges

(2) CHO
(3) HOH_2CHOHC — C_2 — OH (1)
H
(2S)

For C_3:

CHOHCHO
HO — C_3 — H
CH_2OH
Ignoring (C_2)

Interchanges

(2) CHOHCHO
(3) HOH_2C — C — OH (1)
H
(3S)

Hence configuration of compund B is (2S, 3S) – 2, 3, 4-Trihydroxybutanal.

Number of stereoisomers (optical forms and meso forms)

Different cases are discussed as under:

1. When the molecule is unsymmetrical and contains *n* stereogenic or chiral carbon atoms.

Number of optical isomers (OI) or *d*/*l* or (+)/(–) forms = 2^n

Number of meso isomers (MI) = 0

Total No. of isomers (OI + MI) = $2^n + 0 = 2^n$

Consider for example the molecule $CH_3 - \overset{*}{C}HBr - \overset{*}{C}HBr - COOH$. This molecule is unsymmetrical and has two dissimilar chiral carbon atoms. Total no. of isomers for this compound is 2^2 as shown below (structure I, II, III, & IV)

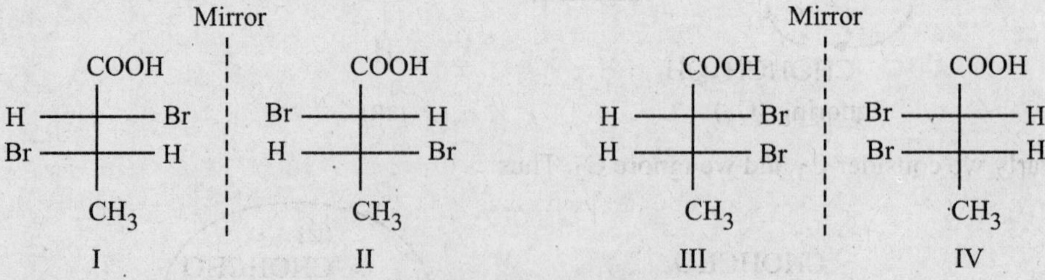

2. When the molecule is symmetrical and has even no. of stereogenic centres or chiral carbon atoms.

Number of optical isomers (OI) = 2^{n-1}

No. of meso isomers (MI) = $2^{(n/2-1)}$

Total No. of isomers (OI + MI) = $2^{(n-1)} + 2^{(n/2-1)}$

Consider for example tortaric acid HOOC – $\overset{*}{C}$HOH – $\overset{*}{C}$HOH – COOH. It is symmetrical and has two chiral carbon atoms shown by asterisks. It has a total of 3 isomers

No. of optical isomers (OI) = $2^{2-1} = 2$

Number of meso isomers (MI) = $2^{(2/2-1)} = 2^{\circ} = 1$

Total number of isomers (OI + MI) = 2 + 1 = 3

3. When the molecule is symmetrical and has odd number of chiral atoms.

No of optical isomers (OI) = $2^{(n-1)} - 2^{(n/2-1/2)}$

No. of meso isomers (MI) = $2^{(n/2-1/2)}$

Total No. of isomers (OI + MI) = $2^{n-1} - 2^{(n/2-1/2)} + 2^{(n/2-1/2)} = 2^{n-1}$

Consider the molecule HOOC–$\overset{*}{C}$HOH–$\overset{*}{C}$HOH–$\overset{*}{C}$HOH–COOH. It has three chiral carbon atoms.

I	Mirror	II	III	IV
COOH		COOH	COOH	COOH
HO — H		H — OH	H — OH	H — OH
H — OH		HO — H	H — OH	HO — H
H — OH		HO — H	H — OH	H — OH
COOH		COOH	COOH	COOH

Plane of symmetry (III, IV)

No. of optical isomers = 2

No. of meso isomers = 2

Total no. of isomers = 2 + 2 = 4

Example 10: Prove that the presence or absence of chiral carbon atom in a molecule is not the necessary and sufficient criterion for existence of optical activity.

Solution: Optical activity is a property which is related to dissymmetry in the molecule. Dissymmetry occurs normally in compounds with chiral carbon atoms. But sometimes there are deviations. For example,

(*i*) Consider the case of meso tartaric acid

$$\begin{array}{c} COOH \\ | \\ H-\overset{*}{C}-OH \\ | \\ H-\overset{*}{C}-OH \\ | \\ COOH \end{array}$$

Although there are two chiral carbons marked with asterisks, still the compound does not show optical activity. This is because the molecule has a plane of symmetry and is thus non-dissymmetric.

(*ii*) There are molecules which do not contain a chiral carbon but still show optical activity. Consider the optically active substance

$$RCH = C = CHR$$

Optical activity of this molecule is explained on the basis of dissymmetry in the molecule. Thus it can be remarked that presence or absence of chiral C-atom is not the necessary and sufficient criterion from the existence of optical activity.

In fact it is the dissymmetry criterion which is responsible for the same.

A dissymmetric molecule is that which has no plane of symmetry.

Example 11: Assign R and S configuration to the following:

(*i*)

```
       COOH
        |
HO  —  C²  —  H
        |
H   —  C³  —  OH
        |
       COOH
```

(*ii*)

```
       NH₂
        |
H  —   C   —  COOH
        |
      COOC₂H₅
```

(*iii*)

```
           Cl
           |
ClCH₂  —   C  —  CH(CH₃)₂
           |
          CH₃
```

Solution: (*i*) **First consider C_2.** The groups in order of priority attached to C_2 are —OH, —COOH, —CH(OH) COOH, H

```
       COOH                              COOH
        |                                 |
HO  —  C²  —  H     ≡    HOOC(OH)CH  —   C  —  OH
        |                                 |
    CH(OH)COOH                            H
```

Thus the configuration around C_2 is S

Now consider C_3. The groups in order of priority attached to C_3 are —OH, —COOH, —CH(OH)COOH, H

```
   CH(OH)COOH              CH(OH)COOH
        |                       |
H  —   C³  —  OH    ≡    HO —  C³  —  COOH
        |                       |
      COOH                      H
```

Thus the configuration around C_3 is S

Thus this structure has the configuration 2S, 3S

(*ii*)

```
       NH₂
        |
H  —   C   —  COOH
        |
      COOC₂H₅
```

The groups attached to central carbon, in order of priority are —NH_2, —$COOC_2H_5$, —COOH and H

```
       NH₂                        NH₂
        |                          |
H  —   C   —  COOH    ≡    HOOC — C — COOC₂H₅
        |                          |
      COOC₂H₅                      H
```

It has R configuration

(*iii*)

```
           Cl
           |
ClCH₂  —   C  —  CH(CH₃)₂
           |
          CH₃
```

The groups attached, in order of priority, to the central carbon are —Cl, —CH_2Cl, —$CH(CH_3)_2$ and CH_3.

$$ClCH_2-\overset{Cl}{\underset{CH_3}{C}}-CH(CH_3)_2$$

The compound has thus S configuration

Example 12: Assign R and S configuration to the following Fischer projection.

(*i*) Fischer projection: top Cl; H—C—OH; H—C—OH; bottom Cl

(*ii*) Fischer projection: top C_2H_5; H_3C—C—OH; H—C—CH_3; bottom OH

Solution: (*i*) The groups attached to C-2, in order of priority are —Cl, —OH, —CH(OH) Cl and —H

$$H-\overset{Cl}{\underset{CH(OH)Cl}{C^2}}-OH \equiv HO-\overset{Cl}{\underset{H}{C^2}}-CH(OH)Cl$$

Configuration around C-2 is S

Now consider configuration around C-3.

The groups around C-3 in order of priority are —Cl, —OH, —CH(OH)Cl and H

$$H-\overset{CH(OH)Cl}{\underset{Cl}{C^3}}-OH \equiv HO-\overset{CH(OH)Cl}{\underset{H}{C^3}}-Cl$$

The configuration around C-2 is *R*

Thus complete configuration of the compound is 2S, 3R

(*ii*) Fischer projection: top C_2H_5; H_3C—C—OH; H—C—CH_3; bottom OH

The groups around C_2, in order of priority are —OH, —CH(OH) CH_3, C_2H_5 and CH_3

$$H_3C-\overset{C_2H_5}{\underset{CH(OH)CH_3}{C^2}}-OH \equiv HO-\overset{C_2H_5}{\underset{CH_3}{C}}-CH(OH)CH_3$$

The configuration around C-2 is S

Configuration around C-3

$$H-\overset{C(OH)(CH_3)C_2H_5}{\underset{OH}{C^3}}-CH_3$$

The groups around C-3, in order of priority are —OH, —C(OH) (CH_3) C_2H_5, —CH_3 and —H

$$H-\overset{C(OH)(CH_3)C_2H_5}{\underset{OH}{\overset{|}{\underset{|}{C^3}}}}-CH_3 \equiv H_3C-\overset{C(OH)(CH_3)C_2H_5}{\underset{H}{\overset{|}{\underset{|}{C^3}}}}-OH$$

The configuration around C-3 is S

Thus complete configuration of the compound is 2S, 3S.

Example 13: A compound $C_4H_{10}O$ shows optical activity. Identify the compound and write the possible stereoisomers.

Solution: With the molecular formula $C_4H_{10}O$, a no. of alcohols and ethers are possible. But we are interested in a compound with a chiral carbon atom so as to give optical activity. Such a compound with the formula $C_4H_{10}O$ is 2-Butanol. It exists in two enantiomeric forms.

$$HO-\overset{CH_3}{\underset{H}{\overset{|}{\underset{|}{C}}}}-C_2H_5 \qquad C_2H_5-\overset{CH_3}{\underset{H}{\overset{|}{\underset{|}{C}}}}-OH$$

S-2-Butanol R-2-Butanol

Racemic modifications

Racemic modification is the term used for a mixture of equal amounts of enantiomers. A racemic mixture is optically inactive because of external compensation. The optical activity caused by one enantiomer is neutralised by the activity of the other enantiomer. The notation for a racemic modification or mixture is ± or *dl*. A racemic mixture may also be denoted by the letters R and S. For examples RS-sec. butyl chloride.

When a chiral compound is synthesised from an achiral reactant, a racemic variety of products is obtained. For example, when propionic acid is borminated, α-bromo propionic acid (a chiral product) is obtained. The two enantiomers (+) and (–) α-bromopropionic acids are formed in equal quantities and the product is a racemic mixture. It is optically inactive.

Optical isomerism (enantiomerism) in compounds having two dissimilar chiral carbon atoms

Two asymmetric carbon atoms are said to be dissimilar when atoms or groups attached to one asymmetric carbon atom are different from those attached to the other. Compounds of this type exist in 2^2 i.e., 4 stereoisomers. For example 3-chloro-2-butanol is a compound with two dissimilar chiral carbons marked 1 and 2 and exists in the following four forms:

(I)	(II)	(III)	(IV)
CH_3	CH_3	CH_3	CH_3
$H-\overset{1}{C}-OH$	$HO-C-H$	$H-C-OH$	$HO-C-H$
$Cl-\overset{2}{C}-H$	$H-C-Cl$	$H-C-Cl$	$Cl-C-H$
CH_3	CH_3	CH_3	CH_3

The structures I and II are non-superimposable mirror images, so these are a pair of enantiomers. Similarly structures III and IV are another pair of enantiomers. These two pairs of enantiomers give rise to two racemic modifications.

The structures I and III are neither enantiomers nor superimposable. Such type of stereoisomers are called *diastereomers*. Similarly I and IV, II and III, and II and IV, are the other pairs of diastereomers. *Diastereomers can be defined as those stereoisomers which are not mirror images of each other*.

Unlike enantiomers, diastereomers have different physical properties and may rotate the plane of polarised light in the same or different directions and to different extent.

Another example of this type is 2, 3-dichloropentane.

(I)	(II)	(III)	(IV)
C_2H_5	C_2H_5	C_2H_5	C_2H_5
H — C — Cl	Cl — C — H	H — C — Cl	Cl — C — H
Cl — C — H	H — C — Cl	H — C — Cl	Cl — C — H
CH_3	CH_3	CH_3	CH_3

A pair of enantiomers (I and II); Second pair of enantiomers (III and IV)

Properties of Diastereomers

1. They show similar, but not identical, chemical properties (as they contain the same functional groups). Rates of reactions of diastereomers with a given reagent are generally different.

2. They have different physical properties like m.p. and b.p., densities, refractive indices, specific rotations, solubilities etc. in a given solvent.

3. They can be separated by techniques like fractional crystallisation, fractional distillation and chromatography.

Example 14: Write four configurations of tartaric acid and select the pairs forming (i) Enantiomers, (*ii*) Diastereomers. Which of them are optically active and which of them are not. Why?

Solution: Tartaric acid is an example of compounds with two similar chiral carbon atoms. Here the four groups attached to both carbons (C-2 and C-3) are the same. Various configurations of tartaric acid are:

(I)	(II)	(III)	(IV)
COOH	COOH	COOH	COOH
H — C — OH	HO — C — H	H — C — OH	HO — C — H
OH — C — H	H — C — OH	H — C — OH	HO — C — H
COOH	COOH	COOH	COOH

If we rotate configuration IV by an angle of 180°, we get configuration III. Hence structures III and IV represent the same configuration. Thus there are only three configurations of tartaric acid viz., I, II & III.

(*i*) Structures I and II are enantiomers, they are mirror images of each other. There is no plane of symmetry in either of them. Therefore both I and II are optically active but display the optical activity in opposite directions.

(*ii*) Structures I and III are not mirror images of each other. Hence they are not enantiomers. Such pairs of compounds having the identical molecular formula and identical groups are called diastereomers.

Similarly structures II and III also form a pair of diastereomers.

Compound III has two chiral carbons, but still it optically inactive. This is because there is a plane of symmetry as indicated by dotted line. There being no dissymmetry, the compound is not optically active. Such a compound is caused meso comp. Thus III and IV represent meso tartaric acid.

Retention and inversion of configuration

A reactant with a chiral molecule in a reaction gives a product which may have the same configuration as the reactant or an opposite configuration. *If the configuration of the reactant and product is the same, the reaction is said to proceed with retention of configuration*-And *if the reactant and the product have opposite configurations, the reaction is said to occur with inversion of configuration consider the following examples.*

S_N^2 *reaction of alkyl halide with OH⁻ ions*. This reaction takes place with *inversion* of configuration as shown below

$$H_3C{-}Cl \xrightarrow{OH^-} HO{-}CH_3$$

Reaction of a secondary alcohol with tosyl chloride (p-toluenesulphonyl chloride) in the presence of pyridine.

This reaction takes place with retention of configuration and the product is alkyl tosylate

$$R(R')(H)C{-}O{-}H + Cl{-}Ts \xrightarrow{-HCl} R(R')(H)C{-}O\,Ts$$

Alcohol — Alkyl tosylate

Racemisation

Under suitable conditions, most of the optically active compounds can lose their optical activity without undergoing any change in their structure *i.e.*, the two enantiomers forms are convertible into each so that the final result is racemic modification. The transformation of an optically active enantiomer into the optically inactive racemic modification under the influence of heat, light or chemical reagents is known as racemisation. Thus if the starting material is the (+) form, then after treatment, half will be converted into (–) form. If the starting material is (–) form, half will be converted into (+) form. For example, (+) or (–) lactic acid on warming with sodium hydroxide gets converted into (±) lactic acid.

Though different mechanisms have been presented for the racemisation of different types of compounds in most of the cases it occurs via the formation of an intermediate which is no longer dissymmetric or chiral. For example, a ketone in which chiral carbon atom is joined to a hydrogen atom can undergo racemisation via the formation of enolic form by tautomeric change.

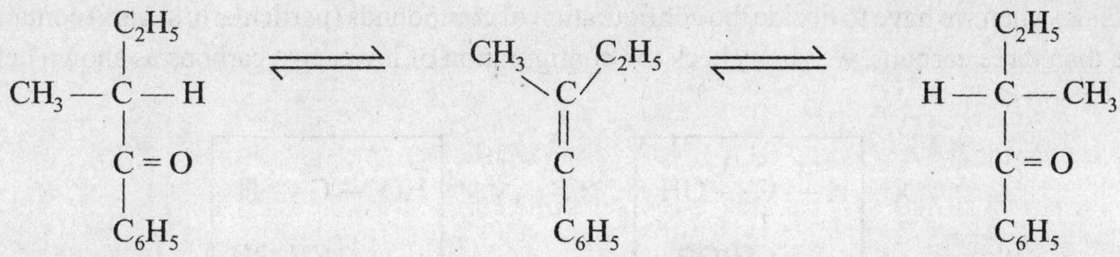

$$\underset{\text{(+) form}}{CH_3-\underset{\underset{C_6H_5}{|}}{\underset{C=O}{|}}{\overset{C_2H_5}{\overset{|}{C}}}-H} \rightleftharpoons \underset{\text{loss of chirality}}{\begin{matrix} CH_3 \quad C_2H_5 \\ \diagdown C \diagup \\ \| \\ C \\ | \\ C_6H_5 \end{matrix}} \rightleftharpoons \underset{\text{(–) form}}{H-\underset{\underset{C_6H_5}{|}}{\underset{C=O}{|}}{\overset{C_2H_5}{\overset{|}{C}}}-CH_3}$$

The intermediate enolic form, which is no longer chiral when reverts to the stable keto form, it is equally likely to produce (+) or (–) forms and thus racemisation takes place.

Example15: Giving examples distinguish between the following: Meso and Racemic forms.

Solution: Meso form of a compound is optically inactive form, in spite of the presence of asymmetric carbon atoms in it. This is because there is a plane of symmetry in the molecule. The activity of one part is neutralised by the activity of the other part. An example is meso tartaric acid.

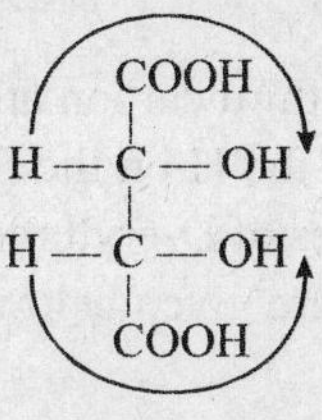

$$\begin{matrix} COOH \\ | \\ H-C-OH \\ | \\ H-C-OH \\ | \\ COOH \end{matrix}$$

meso tartaric acid

Racemic form means a mixture of equal amounts of *d* and *l* forms of a compound, like mixture of equal amounts of *d* and *l* lactic acid or ± tartaric acid.

Such a mixture does not show any optical activity.

It may be mentioned that optical inactivity of the meso form is due to **internal compensation** as the activity of one part of the molecule is neutralised by that of the other part.

Optical inactivity of the racemic form is due to external compensation as the two forms *d*- and *l*-neutralise the optical activity of each other.

Threo and Erythro Notations

Diastereomers are optical isomers of a compound which are not mirror images of each other and hence are not enantiomers. For example *d*-tartaric acid is a diastereomer of mesotartaric acid. But the two are not enantiomers.

As for as the absolute configuration of a compound is concerned we derive it from the configuration of glyceraldehyde which has been taken as arbitrary standard.

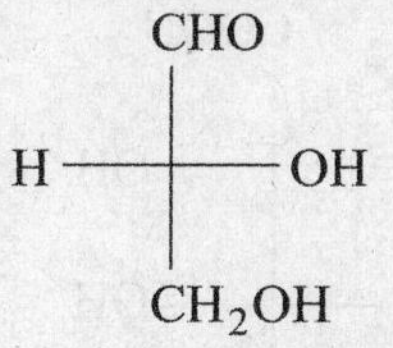

$$\underset{\text{D (+) glyceraldehyde}}{\begin{matrix} CHO \\ | \\ H-\!\!\!-\!\!\!+\!\!\!-\!\!\!-OH \\ | \\ CH_2OH \end{matrix}} \qquad \underset{\text{L (–) glyceraldehyde}}{\begin{matrix} CHO \\ | \\ HO-\!\!\!-\!\!\!+\!\!\!-\!\!\!-H \\ | \\ CH_2OH \end{matrix}}$$

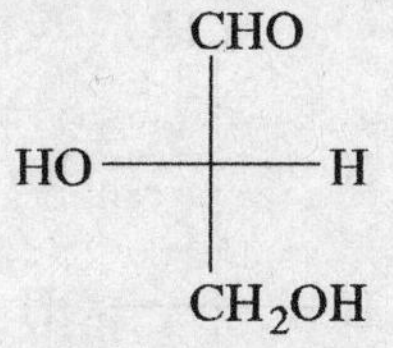

D and L stand for the configuration while (+) and (–) signs denote the actual direction of rotation of plane polarised light. If H and OH are on the LHS and RHS of central carbon, it donates D configuration. If OH and H are on the LHS and RHS of central carbon it denotes L configuration.

Any compound that can be obtained from or converted into D (+) glyceraldehyde has D configuration. Similarly any compound that can be obtained from or converted into L (–) glyceraldehyde has L configuration.

Thus, when we have to decide the configuration of compounds (particularly sugars) containing more than three carbons, we shall check the configuration of lower two carbons as shown below.

X | H — C — OH / | / CH_2OH | Y | HO — C — H / | / CH_2OH

D-series L-series

If the arrangement corresponds to X, the compound has D configuration. If the arrangement corresponds to Y, the compound belongs to L configuration.

Let us take the example of $CHO\ \overset{*}{C}H\ OH\ \overset{*}{C}HOH\ CH_2OH$. This contains two asymmetric carbon atoms marked with asterisks. There are four optical isomers possible, all of which are known.

If the H on the third carbon atom (from the bottom) is on the left hand side, the compound is *erythro*, while if the H on the third carbon atom is on the right hand side, the compound is *threo*. The structures of D-erythrose and D-threose which may be assumed to be obtained from D-glyceraldehyde are given below

CHO
H — OH
H — OH
CH_2OH
D (–) erythrose
I

← CHO
H — OH
CH_2OH
D (+) Glyceraldehyde →

CHO
HO — H
H — OH
CH_2OH
D (–) Threose
II

Compounds I and II are diastereomers of each other from the D-series. Similarly there will be another pair of diastereomers from the L-series. It must be noted that erythro compound (I) on oxidation gives mesotartaric acid.

CHO
H — OH
H — OH
CH_2OH
I

$\xrightarrow{[O]}$

COOH
H — OH
H — OH
COOH
meso tartaric acid

Similarly the erythro compound from L-series on oxidation will also produce meso tartaric acid.

Example 16: Predict whether 3-chlorohexane will be optically active or not? Give reasons for your answer.

Solution:

$$CH_3CH_2CH_2-\overset{\displaystyle H}{\underset{\displaystyle Cl}{\overset{|}{\underset{|}{C^*}}}}-CH_2-CH_3$$

3-chlorohexane

The compound contains are asymmetric carbon atom (marked with *). The four different groups attached are

1. $-H$
2. $-Cl$
3. $-CH_2-CH_3$
4. $-CH_3-CH_2-CH_3$

Hence the compund shows optical activity.

Methods for the resolution of racemic mixtures

The separation of racemic modification into enantiomers is called resolution. Since the two enantiomers in a racemic mixture have identical physical and chemical properties, these cannot be separated by usual methods of fractional distillation or fractional crystallisation. Special methods are adopted for their separation as given below:

***(i)* Mechanical separation.** This method was first adopted by Pasteur for separating the enantiomers of ammonium tartarate. When racemic modification is crytallized from a solution, two types of crystals are obained. These are mirror images of each other consisting of (+) and (–) forms which can be separated by hand picking with the help of a pair of tweezers and a powerful lens. This is a very laborious method and can be applied only to those compounds which give well defined distinguishable crystals of enantiomers.

***(ii)* Biochemical method.** Certain micro-organisms grow in a racemic mixture, consuming only one of the enantiomers while leaving the other unaffected. Thus *penicillium glaucum* when placed in (±) tartaric acid, consumes only (+) tartaric acid and leaves (–) tartaric acid unused. The major disadvantage of this method is that one of the enantiomers get destroyed.

***(iii)* Chemical method.** This method is mostly used for the resolution of racemic modification. In this method the racemic modification is treated with an optically active reagent to get a pair of *diastereomers*. Since diastereomers differ in their physical properties, it is possible to separate them by physical methods such as fractional crystallisation, fractional distillation etc. The pure diastereomers are then decomposed, into a mixture of optically active reagent and corresponding enantiomer, which can be separated.

Suppose the racemic modification is an (±) acid. When it is treated with an optically acitve, say (–) base, it gives a mixture of two salts, one of (+) acid (–) base, the other of (–) acid (–) base.

These salts are neither superimposable nor mirror images; so these are diastereomers having different physical properties and can be separated by fractional crystallisation. After separation the optically active acids can be recovered in pure forms by adding a mineral acid.

$$\left.\begin{array}{l}(+)\text{ acid}\\ \\ (-)\text{ acid}\end{array}\right] + (-)\text{ base} \longrightarrow \begin{cases}\left[\begin{array}{c}\text{Salt of}\\ (+)\text{ acid }(-)\text{ base}\end{array}\right] \xrightarrow{H^+} (+)\text{ acid}\\ \\ \left[\begin{array}{c}\text{Salt of}\\ (-)\text{ acid }(-)\text{ base}\end{array}\right] \xrightarrow{H^+} (-)\text{ acid}\end{cases}$$

Racemic modification — Diastereomers easily separable — Enantiomers in pure form

The commonly used optically active bases for the purpose are naturally occurring alkaloids such as (–) brucine, (–) quinine, (–) strychnine and (+) cinchonine.

Similarly, the resolution of racemic bases can be carried out using a naturally occurring optically active acid such as (–) malic acid. Alcohols can be resolved in a similar way by ester formation using an optically active acid.

Asymmetric Synthesis

The preparation of an optically active dissymmetric (chiral) compound from non-dissymmetric molecules under the influence of an optically active substance is known as asymmetric synthesis.

Whenever a dissymmetric product is synthesised from a non-dissymmetric reactants, it is always an optically inactive racemic modification (as described earlier). However, by the use of an optically active reagent, one of the enantiomers can be obtained in excess so that the resulting product is optically active.

For example pyruvic acid on direct reduction yields the optically inactive racemic lactic acid, but pyruvic acid, pre-esterified with an optically active alcohol say (–) menthol, on reduction and subsequent hydrolysis yields predominantly (–) lactic acid.

$$\underset{\text{Pyruvic acid}}{CH_3-\overset{\overset{\large O}{\|}}{C}-COOH} \xrightarrow[\text{reduction}]{2H} \underset{(\pm)\text{ Lactic acid}}{CH_3-CHOH-COOH}$$

$$\underset{\text{Pyruvic acid}}{CH_3-\overset{\overset{\large O}{\|}}{C}-COOH} + \underset{(-)\text{ Menthol}}{C_{10}H_{19}OH} \longrightarrow \underset{(-)\text{ Menthyl pyruvate}}{CH_3-\overset{\overset{\large O}{\|}}{C}-COOC_{10}H_{19}}$$

$$\Big\downarrow \text{reduction, } 2H$$

$$\underset{(-)\text{ Menthol}}{C_{10}H_{19}OH} + \underset{\substack{(-)\text{ Lactic acid}\\ \text{(predominantly)}}}{CH_3-CHOH-COOH} \xleftarrow{H_2O,\ H^+} \underset{(-)\text{ Menthyl lactate}}{CH_3-CHOH-COOC_{10}H_{19}}$$

Walden Inversion

In 1893, Walden was able to convert an optically active compound into its enantiomer by a series of replacement reactions. For example, conversion of (–) malic acid into (+) malic acid and vice-versa can be achieved as under :

$$\begin{array}{ccc} \underset{\text{(I)}}{\underset{\text{(–) Malic acid}}{\begin{array}{l} CHOH - CO_2H \\ | \\ CH_2 - CO_2H \end{array}}} & \underset{KOH}{\overset{PCl_5}{\rightleftharpoons}} & \underset{\text{(II)}}{\underset{\text{(+)-Chlorosuccinic acid}}{\begin{array}{l} CHCl - CO_2H \\ | \\ CH_2 - CO_2H \end{array}}} \\ \uparrow AgOH & & \downarrow AgOH \\ \underset{\text{(IV)}}{\underset{\text{(–) chlorosuccinic acid}}{\begin{array}{l} CHCl - CO_2H \\ | \\ CH_2 - CO_2H \end{array}}} & \underset{KOH}{\overset{PCl_5}{\rightleftharpoons}} & \underset{\text{(V)}}{\underset{\text{(+)- malic acid}}{\begin{array}{l} CHOH - CO_2H \\ | \\ CH_2 - CO_2H \end{array}}} \end{array}$$

During the change of (–) malic acid (I) or (+) malic acid (III) there must be a change in configuration in one of the two steps. If the configuration of II and III is same, the change must have taken place between I and II. Any single reaction in which change of configuration takes place, is termed as Walden Inversion.

In other words if an atom or group of atoms directly attached to chiral carbon atoms is replaced by another atom or group of atoms the configuration of product is sometimes found to be different from that of starting compound. Such phenomenon which involves inversion of configuration during a reaction is called *Walden Inversion or Optical Inversion.*

For example, in SN^2 hydrolysis of 2-bromooctane inversion of configuration takes place.

$$\underset{\text{(–) 2-Bromooctane}}{\begin{array}{c} C_6H_{13} \\ | \\ H - C - Br \\ | \\ CH_3 \end{array}} \xrightarrow{OH^-} \underset{\text{(+) 2-Octanol}}{\begin{array}{c} C_6H_{13} \\ | \\ HO - C - H \\ | \\ CH_3 \end{array}}$$

It must be kept in mind here that inversion of configuration may or may not lead to a change in direction of rotation. The change, if any, is only a matter of chance as in the example given above.

6.4 GEOMETRICAL ISOMERISM

Two carbon atoms joined by a single bond (σ bond) are capable of free rotation around each other, but this rotation is hindered in case of compounds containing carbon-carbon double bond. According to molecular orbital theory, carbon atoms involved in double bond formation are sp^2 hybridised so that each carbon atom has three planar sp^2 hybridised orbitals and fourth p orbital having its lobes at right angles to the plane of sp^2 orbitals. The formation of π bond involves the overlapping of p orbitals. With the formation of a π bond between C — C along with a σ bond which is already existing, there remains no possibility of rotation along C — C axis. Neither of the two doubly bonded carbon atoms can be rotated about double bond without destroying π orbital which requires large amount of energy. Thus at ordinary temperature, the rotation about a carbon-carbon double bond is restricted or hindered and gives rise to a kind of stereoisomerism known as *Geometrical Isomerism.*

Geometrical Isomerism, also known as *cis-trans* isomerism takes place in compounds containing carbon-carbon double bond in which each of the two doubly bonded carbon atoms is attached to two different atoms or groups. All the compound with general formula of the type $C_{AB} = C_{DE}$ or $C_{AB} = C_{AB}$ show geometric isomerism. If either of the two carbon atoms carries two identical groups as in $C_{AB} = C_{AA}$ or $C_{AB} = C_{DD}$, the isomerism does not exist. *This isomerism is due to difference in the relative spatial arrangement of the atoms or groups about the doubly bonded carbon atoms.*

Conditions to be fulfilled by a compound to exhibit geometrical isomerism

For a compound to show geometrical isomerism the following conditions are necessary:

(*i*) The molecule must contain a carbon-carbon double bond about which there is no free rotation.

(*ii*) Each of the fouble bonded carbon atoms must be attached to two different atoms or groups.

In case of compounds with formula of the type $C_{AB} = C_{AB}$; if two similar groups are on the same side of double bond, the isomer is known a *cis*- and if two similar groups are on the opposite sides of the double bond the isomer is known as *trans*- such as:

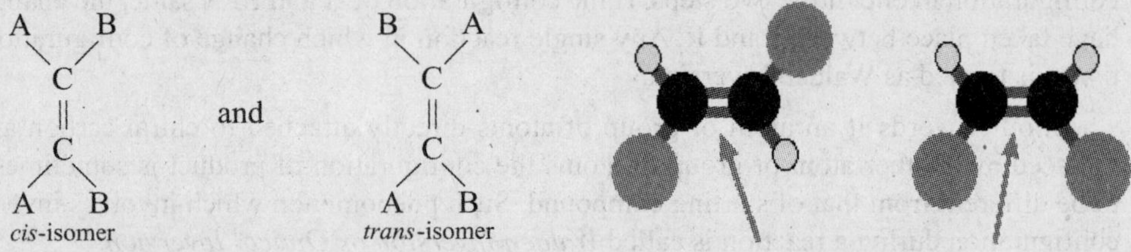

No rotation about the double bond

For example,

2-butene exists in two isomeric forms.

$$\begin{array}{c} H \quad CH_3 \\ C \\ \| \\ C \\ H \quad CH_3 \end{array} \quad \text{and} \quad \begin{array}{c} CH_3 \quad H \\ C \\ \| \\ C \\ H \quad CH_3 \end{array}$$

cis-2-butene — *trans*-2-butene

Similarly butene-dioic acid exists in two isomeric forms; *cis*- form is called maleic acid and *trans*- form is called fumaric acid.

$$\begin{array}{c} H \quad CO_2H \\ C \\ \| \\ C \\ H \quad CO_2H \end{array} \quad \text{and} \quad \begin{array}{c} H \quad CO_2H \\ C \\ \| \\ C \\ HO_2C \quad H \end{array}$$

Maleic acid (*cis*-isomer) — Fumaric acid (*trans*-isomer)

Determination of configuration of a geometrical isomer

Different methods available for determination of configuration of a geometrical isomers are described below:

(i) **From Dipole moments.** Generally *cis*-isomer has greater dipole moment as compared to *trans*-isomer. In case of cis- the similar groups being on the same side, the electronic effects are additive; while in case of *trans*-isomer, the similar groups being on opposite side, the electronic effects cancel each other.

H, CH_3 / C=C / H, CH_3
cis-2-butene
$\mu = 0.4$

H_3C, H / C=C / H, CH_3
trans-2-butene
$\mu = 0$

H, Cl / C=C / H, Cl
cis-2-Dichlorethene
$\mu = 1.85$

H, Cl / C=C / H, H
trans-1, 2-dichloroethen
$\mu = 0$

(ii) **From boiling point.** Generally speaking, a *cis* isomer has a higher boiling point compared to the *trans* isomer. This is because of higher dipole moment and higher polarity in the molecule which acts as the binding force and is responsible for higher b.p. of the *cis* isomer. Boiling point of *cis*-2-butene is 277 K while the *trans*-2-butene boils at 274 K.

CH_3, H / C=C / CH_3, H
cis-2-butene
b.p. 277 K

CH_3, H / C=C / H, CH_3
trans-2-butene
b.p. 274 K

(iii) **From melting point.** The isomers show a reverse trand here. A *cis* isomer has a lower melting point compared to the *trans* isomer. Here the factor that is important is the size of the molecule. It can be realised that a *cis* isomer will occupy a smaller volume compared to the *trans* isomer as illustrated by dotted lines. Thus maleic acid melts at 403 K whereas fumaric acid melts at 575 K.

H, COOH / C=C / H, COOH
Maleic acid (*cis*)
m.p. 403 K

H, COOH / C=C / HOOC, H
Fumaric acid (*trans*)
m.p. 575 K

(iv) **From the formation of cyclic compounds.** Two geometric isomers (*cis* and *trans*) can be distinguished through reactions that lead to formation of ring. *Cis*-isomer undergoes ring closure more readily than the *trans*-isomer. For example maleic acid readily loses water when heated to about 423 K, to give an anhydride; while fumaric acid does not give anhydride at this temperature. Rather it must be heated to 573 K to get the same anhydride. Hydrolysis of anhydride yields only maleic acid.

$$\underset{\substack{\text{Maleic acid}\\(cis\text{-2-isomer})}}{\begin{array}{c}H\quad CO_2H\\ C\\ \|\\ C\\ H\quad CO_2H\end{array}} \xrightarrow{423\ K} \underset{\text{Maleic anhyride}}{\begin{array}{c}H\quad CO\\ C\qquad\quad \\ \|\qquad O\\ C\qquad\quad \\ H\quad CO\end{array}} \xleftarrow{573\ K} \underset{\substack{\text{Fumaric acid}\\(trans\text{-2-isomer})}}{\begin{array}{c}H\quad CO_2H\\ C\\ \|\\ C\\ HO_2C\quad H\end{array}}$$

$$\downarrow \text{hydrolysis}$$

$$\underset{\substack{\text{only maleic acid and}\\\text{not fumaric acid}}}{\begin{array}{c}H\quad CO_2H\\ C\\ \|\\ C\\ H\quad CO_2H\end{array}}$$

(*v*) From the formation of the type of optical isomer. Maleic acid and fumaric acid, both on treatment with $KMnO_4$ or OsO_4 yield optically inactive variety of tartaric acid. Maleic acid yields meso tartaric acid while fumaric acid yields racemic (± or *dl*) tartaric acid.

$$\underset{\substack{\text{Maleic acid}\\(cis\text{-2-isomer})}}{\begin{array}{c}H\quad CO_2H\\ C\\ \|\\ C\\ H\quad CO_2H\end{array}} \xrightarrow[\text{or } OsO_4]{KMnO_4} \underset{\text{Meso-tartaric acid}}{\begin{array}{c}OH\\ |\\ H-C-CO_2H\\ |\\ H-C-CO_2H\\ |\\ OH\end{array}}$$

$$\underset{\substack{\text{Fumaric acid}\\(trans\text{-isomer})}}{\begin{array}{c}H\quad CO_2H\\ C\\ \|\\ C\\ HO_2C\quad H\end{array}} \xrightarrow[\text{or } OsO_4]{KMnO_4} \underset{\pm \text{ or } dl\text{-tartaric acid}}{\begin{array}{c}OH\\ |\\ H-C-CO_2H\\ |\\ HO_2C-C-H\\ |\\ OH\end{array} \quad \text{and} \quad \begin{array}{c}OH\\ |\\ HO_2C-C-H\\ |\\ H-C-CO_2H\\ |\\ OH\end{array}}$$

(*vi*) From the method of preparation. Method of preparation of a compound sometimes leads to its configuration. The isomer obtained by the rapture of a ring must be the *cis*-isomer, *e.g.*, maleic acid can be prepared by the oxidation of benzene or quinone, so it must be a *cis*-isomer.

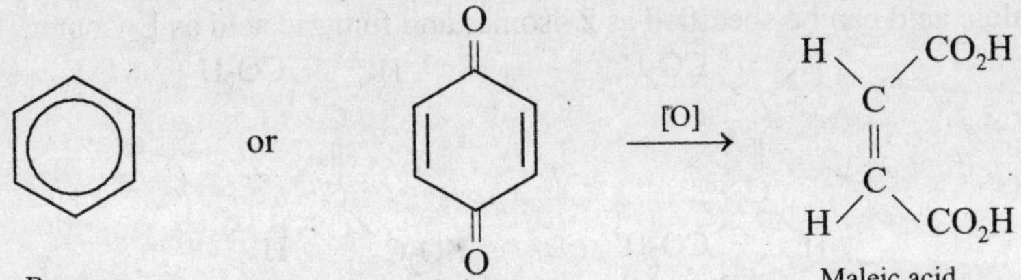

Benzene or Quinone $\xrightarrow{[O]}$ Maleic acid (*cis*-2-isomer)

$$\begin{array}{c} H\diagdown\ \ \diagup CO_2H \\ C \\ \| \\ C \\ H\diagup\ \ \diagdown CO_2H \end{array}$$

Benzene

Quinone

Maleic acid
(*cis*-2-isomer)

E and Z designations of geometrical isomers

The *cis* and *trans*- designated can be used only for the compounds in which two doubly bonded carbon atoms are having similar atoms or groups *e.g.*, of the type $C_{AB} = C_{AB}$. But, when the two doubly bonded carbon atoms are having different atoms or groups attached to them *e.g.*, of the type $C_{AB} = C_{DE}$; it is not possible to assign them *cis* or *trans* configurations. To overcome this difficulty, a more general system for designating the configuration of geometric isomers has been adopted. This system developed by *Cahn*, Ingold and Prelog originally for the absolute configuration of optical isomers is known as *E* and *Z system* and is based on priority of attached groups. The atoms or groups attached to each carbon of the double bond, are assigned first and second priority. If the atoms or groups having higher priority attached to two carbons are on the same side of double bond the configuration is designated as Z (derived from German word *Zusammen* meaning together) and if the atoms or groups of higher priority are on the opposite side of the double bond, the configuration is designated as E (derived from German word -*entgegen* meaning across or opposite).

Priorities of atoms or groups are determined in the same way as for R & S configurations of optical isomers. At. weights or atomic numbers of atoms directly linked with ethylenic carbon atoms are taken into consideration.

Let us consider an example in which two doubly bonded atoms are attached to four different halogens such as $C_{BrF} = C_{ICl}$. Since Br is having higher priority over F and I is having priority over Cl (due to their higher atomic numbers). The isomer in which Br and I are on the same side of double bond will be called Z and the isomer in which Br and I are on the opposite sides of double bond will be called E.

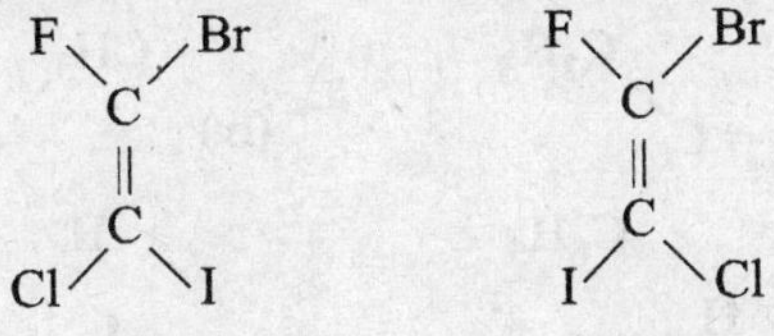

$$\begin{array}{c} F\diagdown\ \ \diagup Br \\ C \\ \| \\ C \\ Cl\diagup\ \ \diagdown I \end{array} \qquad \begin{array}{c} F\diagdown\ \ \diagup Br \\ C \\ \| \\ C \\ I\diagup\ \ \diagdown Cl \end{array}$$

Z-isomer *E*-isomer

In the same way *cis* and *trans* isomers of 2-butene can be called Z and E-2-butenes respectively.

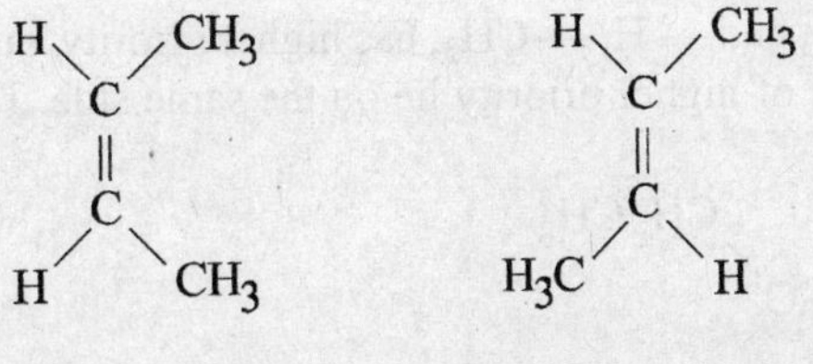

$$\begin{array}{c} H\diagdown\ \ \diagup CH_3 \\ C \\ \| \\ C \\ H\diagup\ \ \diagdown CH_3 \end{array} \qquad \begin{array}{c} H\diagdown\ \ \diagup CH_3 \\ C \\ \| \\ C \\ H_3C\diagup\ \ \diagdown H \end{array}$$

Similarly maleic acid can be specified as Z-isomer and fumaric acid as E-isomer.

$$\begin{array}{c} H \quad CO_2H \\ \diagdown \; \diagup \\ C \\ \| \\ C \\ \diagup \; \diagdown \\ H \quad CO_2H \end{array} \qquad \begin{array}{c} H \quad CO_2H \\ \diagdown \; \diagup \\ C \\ \| \\ C \\ \diagup \; \diagdown \\ HO_2C \quad H \end{array}$$

Maleic acid (*Z*-isomer) — Fumaric acid (*E*-isomer)

In determining the configuration, we have to select the group of higher priority on one carbon. Similarly we select the group of higher priority on the other carbon atom. If these two groups are on the same side of double bond, the configuration is Z, otherwise it is E.

Some more examples are:

$$\begin{array}{c} CH_3CH_2 \quad CH_2CH_2CH_3 \\ \diagdown \; \diagup \\ C \\ \| \\ C \\ \diagup \; \diagdown \\ H \quad CH_3 \end{array} \quad \text{and} \quad \begin{array}{c} CH_3CH_2CH_2 \quad CH_2CH_3 \\ \diagdown \; \diagup \\ C \\ \| \\ C \\ \diagup \; \diagdown \\ H \quad CH_3 \end{array}$$

Z-3-Ethyl-2-hexene — E-3-Ethyl-2hexene

$$\begin{array}{c} Cl \quad F \\ \diagdown \; \diagup \\ C \\ \| \\ C \\ \diagup \; \diagdown \\ I \quad Br \end{array} \quad \text{and} \quad \begin{array}{c} Cl \quad F \\ \diagdown \; \diagup \\ C \\ \| \\ C \\ \diagup \; \diagdown \\ Br \quad I \end{array}$$

Z-1-Bromo-2-chloro 2-fluoro-1-iodoethene — *E*-1-Bromo-2-chloro 2-fluoro-1-iodoethene

Example 17: Assign E and Z configurations to the following compounds.

(*i*) $\begin{array}{c} CH_3 \quad\quad Br \\ C=C \\ H \quad\quad Cl \end{array}$ (*ii*) $\begin{array}{c} CH_3 \quad\quad CH_2CH_3 \\ C=C \\ H \quad\quad CH(CH_3)_2 \end{array}$

(*iii*) $\begin{array}{c} H \quad\quad C_2H_5 \\ C=C \\ (CH_3)_2CH \quad\quad C_6H_5 \end{array}$ (*iv*) $\begin{array}{c} CH_3 \quad\quad H \\ C=C \\ H \quad\quad CHO \end{array}$

(*v*) $\begin{array}{c} CH_3 \quad\quad H \\ C=C \\ H \quad\quad COOH \end{array}$ (*vi*) $\begin{array}{c} I \quad\quad C_6H_5 \\ C=C \\ Br \quad\quad NHCH_3 \end{array}$

Solution: (*i*) Out of — CH_3 and — H, — CH_3, has higher priority, out of — Br and — Cl, — Br has higher priority. Groups of higher priority lie on the same side. Therefore the configuration is Z.

(*ii*) $\begin{array}{c} CH_3 \quad\quad CH_2CH_3 \\ C=C \\ H \quad\quad CH(CH_3)_2 \end{array}$

Out of — CH_3 and — H, — CH_3 has higher priority. Out of two groups on the second carbon, — $CH(CH_3)_2$ has higher priority. The groups of higher priority lie on opposite sides of the double bond. Therefore the configuration is E.

Following the same analogy, the students can see the configurations of compounds (*iii*), (*iv*), (*v*) and (*vi*) are Z, E, E and E respectively.

Example 18: Assign E and Z configurations to the following:

I: $CH_3(H)C{=}C(Cl)C_2H_5$ — CH_3 and Cl on the same side; H and C_2H_5 below.

II: $CH_3(H)C{=}C(H)D$ — CH_3 and H above; H and D below.

Solution: In compound I, the groups of higher priority on the two carbons linking double bond are CH_3— and Cl. Since these are on the same side of the double bond it has Z configuration. In compound II, the groups of higher priority on the two carbons linking the double bond are CH_3— and D-(Deuterium) since these are on opposite sides of the double bond, it has E configuration.

Example 19: Assign E and Z configuration to the following:

(*i*) **Maleic acid** (*ii*) **trans-But-2-enoic acid.**

Maleic acid: H(COOH)C=C(COOH)H, with both COOH groups on the same side.

Trans-But-2-enoic acid: CH_3(H)C=C(H)COOH, with CH_3 and COOH on opposite sides.

Solution: In maleic acid, groups of higher priority on the two carbon atoms are — COOH and — COOH. These two groups are on the same side of the double bond. Hence configuration is Z.

In *trans*-but-2-enoic acid, the groups of higher priority on the two carbons are — CH_3 and — COOH, since these are on the opposite sides of the double bond, it has E configuration.

Geometrical isomerism in oximes

Oximes of aldehydes having the general formula R — CH ═ N — OH are capable of exhibiting geometrical isomerism as — H and — OH groups may be present on the same side or opposite sides of the double bond. The two stereoisomers thus obtained are named as *syn* (equivalent of *cis*) and *anti* (equivalent of *trans*). Two geometrical isomers of an aldoxime may be represented as :

R(H)C=N–OH, with H and OH on the same side: *syn*-aldoxime

R(H)C=N–OH, with R and HO on the same side: *anti*-aldoxime

Geometrical isomers of benzaldoxime have been actually isolated.

syn-banzaldoxime has m.p. 35°C while *anti*-benzaldoxime has m.p. 130°C. The two compounds may be shown as under :

C_6H_5, H / C = N / OH — *syn*-benzaldoxime

C_6H_5, H / C = N / HO — *anti*-benzaldoxime

Oximes of ketones (RR′C = NOH) can also show geometrical isomerism provide R and R′ are not the same. Thus benzophenone oxime does not exhibit geometrical isomerism because the two groups attached to carbonyl carbon are the same. Phenyl tolyl ketoxime is known to exist in two geometrical forms

$CH_3C_6H_4$, C_6H_5 / C = N / OH — *syn*-phenyl tolyl oxime

$CH_3C_6H_4$, C_6H_5 / C = N / HO — *anti*-phenyl tolyl oxime

Stereochemistry (geometrical and optical isomerism) of alicyclic compounds

The discussion can be made under two headings

Even-membered rings (containing 4, 6 carbon atoms)

If the substituents are across the ring from each other, the molecule possesses a plane of symmetry. Therefore, no optical forms exist. However geometrical isomerism is possible. *Cis* and *trans* isomers of 3-methylcyclobutane carboxylic acid and cyclobutane-1, 2-dicarboxylic acid are shown below

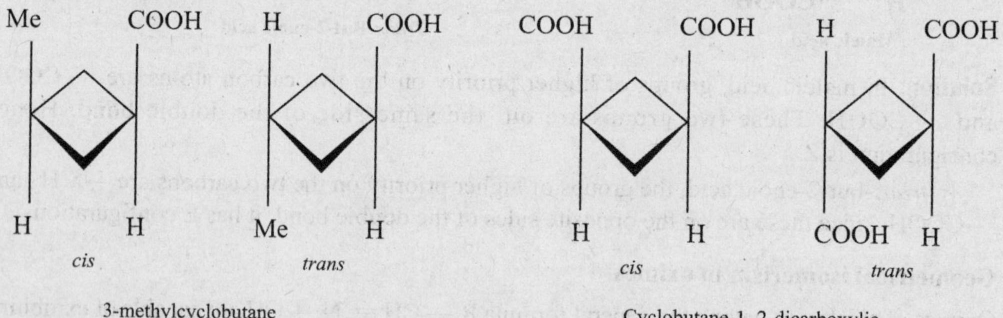

3-methylcyclobutane carboxylic acids

Cyclobutane-1, 2-dicarboxylic acids

Odd membered rings (containing 3, 5 carbon atoms)

A disubstituted (on different carbons) odd membered ring has two asymmetric carbon atoms. Therefore two diastereomeric pairs of enantiomers are possible. Take the case of 2-methylcyclopropanecarboxylic acid. Geometrical and optical isomers have been represented as under

CH_2; HOOC, Me; H, H — *cis* form | Mirror | CH_2; Me, COOH; H, H — *cis* form

One pair of enantiomers

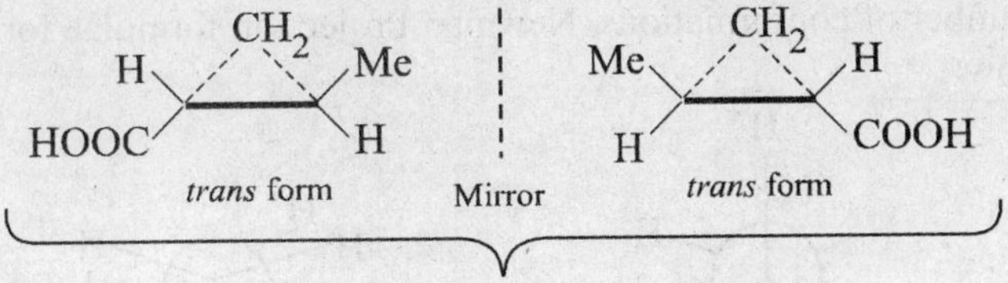

$$\underset{\text{trans form}}{\text{H, Me, HOOC, H on } CH_2 \text{ ring}} \quad \vdots \text{ Mirror} \quad \underset{\text{trans form}}{\text{Me, H, H, COOH on } CH_2 \text{ ring}}$$

Second pair of enantiomers

If however, the two substituents are the same, there will be one pair of enantiomers and a meso form. Take the case of cyclopropane-1, 2-dicarboxylic acid. *trans* form exists as a pair of enantiomers while the *cis* form as meso compound

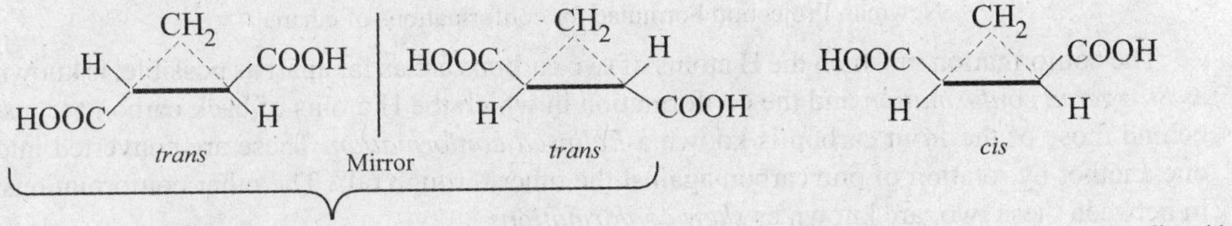

CH_2 (H, COOH / HOOC, H) *trans* | Mirror | CH_2 (HOOC, H / H, COOH) *trans* — Pair of enantiomers

CH_2 (HOOC, COOH / H, H) *cis* — Meso cyclopropane-1, 2-dicarboxylic acid

6.5 CONFORMATIONAL ISOMERISM

Carbon-carbon single bond in alkanes is a sigma bond formed by the overlapping of sp^3 hybrid atomic orbitals along the inter-nuclear axis. The electron distribution in such a bond is symmetrical around internuclear axis; so that free rotation of one carbon against the other is possible without breaking sigma or single covalent bond. Consequently such compound can have different arrangements of atoms in space, which can be converted into one another simply by rotation around single bond, without breaking it. These different arrangements are known as *Conformational Isomers or Rotational Isomers or Conformers.* Since the potential energy barrier for their inter-coversion is very low, it is not possible to isolate them at room temperature. At least 60-85 kJ/mole must be the energy difference between two conformers to make them isolatable at room temperature.

Hence, conformations can be defined as different arrangements of the atoms which can be converted into one another by rotation around single bonds.

Newman and Sawhorse representations for the conformations of ethane

Alkanes can have an infinite number of conformations by rotation around carbon-carbon single bonds. In ethane two carbon atoms are linked by a single bond and each carbon atom is further linked with three hydrogen atoms. If one of the carbon atoms is allowed to rotate about carbon-carbon single bond keeping the other carbon stationary, an infinite number of arrangements of the hydrogens of one carbon, with respect to those of the other, are obtained. All these arrangements are called conformations (Bond angles and bond lengths remain the same).

Newman representation

This can be easily understood with the help of Newman Projection formulae. The molecule is viewed from front to back in the direction of carbon-carbon single bond. The carbon nearer to the eye is represented by a point and three hydrogen attached to it are shown by three lines at an angle of 120° to one another. The carbon atom away from the eye is represented by a circle and three hydrogens attached to it are shown by shorter lines at an angle of 120° to each other.

Out of infinite number of conformations, Newman Projection formulae for two extreme cases are as shown below:

Staggered Eclipsed

Newman Projection Formulae for conformations of ethane.

The conformation in which the H atoms of two carbons are as far apart as possible, is known as *Staggered conformation* and the conformation in which the H atoms of back carbon are just behind those of the front carbon is known a *Eclipsed conformation.* These are converted into one another by rotation of one carbon against the other through 60°. The other conformations, in between these two, are known as *skew conformations.*

Sawhorse representation

In this representation, the molecule is visualised slightly from above and from the right and then projected on the paper. The bond between two carbons is drawn diagonally and is a bit longer for the sake of clarity. The lower left hand carbon is taken as front carbon and the upper right hand carbon is taken as back carbon. The Sawhorse representation of staggered and eclipsed conformations of ethane are given below :

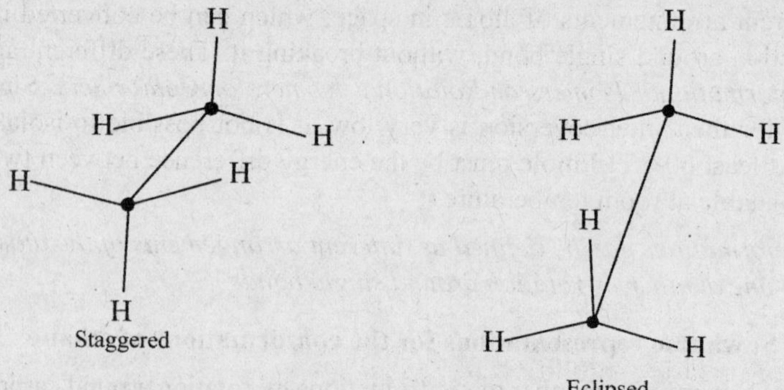

Staggered Eclipsed

Sawhorse representation for conformations of ehtane

Flying wedge representation

In this representation, the bonds connecting the two carbon atoms are drawn horizontally in the plane of paper. Wedges (—) represent the bonds lying above the plane of the paper. Ordinary lines denote the bonds lying in the plane of the planar and dotted lines (----) represent bonds lying below the plane of the paper. Flying edge representation for staggered and eclipsed conformations of ethane are shown in Fig.

Staggered Eclipsed

***Fig.**: Flying wedge representations for ethane*

Pitzer in 1936 found that the rotation is not completely free. Rather there exists a potential energy barrier which restricts the free rotations. It means that the molecule spends most of its time in the most stable staggered conformation and it spends least time in the least stable eclipsed conformation; the energy difference being 12 kJ/mole in the case of ethane.

The energy required to rotate the molecule about carbon-carbon bond is called rotational or torsional energy.

Difference between conformation and configuration

Conformation

Structures containing different arrangement of atoms of a molecule in space which can arise by rotation about a single bond are called conformers. For example ethane exists in different conformations called staggered, eclipsed and skew conformations. The energy difference between different conformers is rather small. This phenomenon is called conformation. The property of conformation is also exhibited by *n*-butane, cyclohexane, stilbene dichloride etc.

Configuration

Structures of a compound differing in the arrangement of atoms or groups around a particular atom in space are called *configurations.* Enantiomers, distereomers and geometrical isomers come under this category. For example *d*-and *l*-lactic acids are configurations of lactic acid.

```
      CH3                  CH3
      |                    |
  HO — C — H           H — C — OH
      |                    |
     COOH                 COOH
  d-lactic acid        l-lactic acid
```

cis and *trans* butenes are configuration of butene

```
CH3          CH3        H           CH3
    >C = C<                >C = C<
H            H          CH3         H
   cis-2-butene           trans-2-butene
```

Factors affecting relative stability of conformations

The following factors play a vital role in the stability of conformations.

1. Angle strain. Every atom has the tendency to have the bond angles that match those of its bonding orbitals. If there is any deviation from this normal bond angle, the molecule suffers from *angle strain.* Conformations suffering from angle strain are found to be less stable.

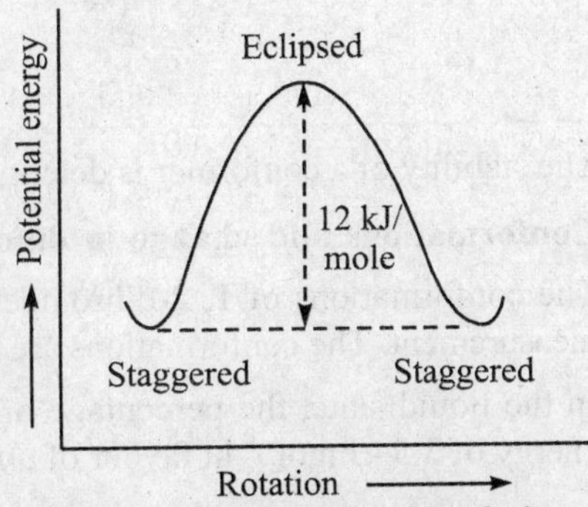

Rotational or torsional energy of ethane

2. Torsional strain. There is a tendency on the part of two carbons linked to each other to have their bonds staggered. That is why the staggered form of any molecule like ethane, *n*-butane is most stable. As the bonds of two connected carbons move towards eclipsed state, a *torsional strain* is set up in the molecule thus raising its energy. Thus the staggered conformations have the least and eclipsed the highest torsional strain. The energy required to rotate the molecule around the carbon-carbon bond is called *torsional energy.*

3. Steric strain (van der Waals' Strain). Groups attached to two linked carbons can interact in different ways depending upon their size and polarity. These interactions can be attractive or repulsive. If the distance between the groups or atoms is just equal to the sum of their van der Waals' radii, there will be attractive interactions between them. And if these atom or groups are brought closer than this distance, there will be repulsions leading to *van der Waals' strain or steric strain* in the molecule.

4. Dipole-dipole Interactions. Atoms or groups attached to bonded carbons orient or position themselves to have favourable dipole-dipole interactions. It will be their tendency to have maximum dipole-dipole attractions. Hydrogen bond is a particular case of powerful dipole-dipole attractions.

To differentiate between conformation and configuration, we are taking an analogy from real life. Two conformations and two configurations of a dog are considered here.

- Conformations are different spatial arrangements of the same compound (for example, anti and gauche conformers; They cannot be separated. Some conformations are more stable than others.

Different Conformations

- Compounds with different configurations are different compounds. They can be separated from each other. Bonds have to be broken to interconvert compound with different configurations.

Different Configurations

Stable Unstable

The stability of a conformer is determined by the net effect of all the above factors.

Conformations and change in dipole-moment of 1, 2-dibromoethane with temperature

The conformations of 1, 2-dibromoethane have been extensively studied by dipole-moment measurement. The conformations are depicted as under :

In the liquid state, the percentage of anti forms is 65 corresponding to conformational free energy of 3.5 kJ mol^{-1} in favour of *anti.*

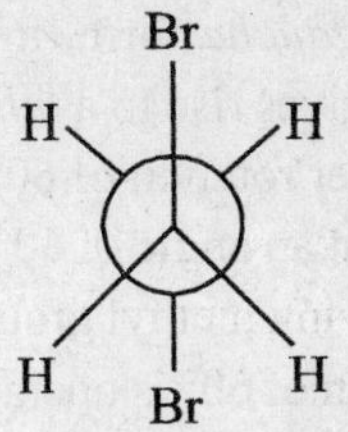

Br / H H / H H / Br — anti; Br / H Br / H H / H — gauche; Br / Br H / H H / H — gauche

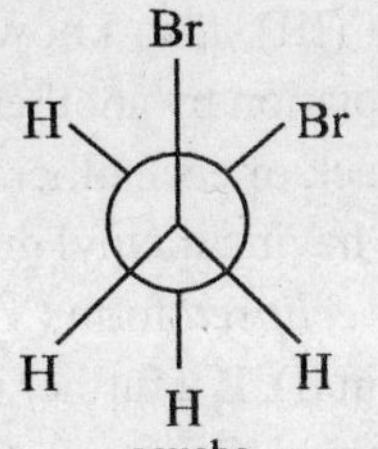

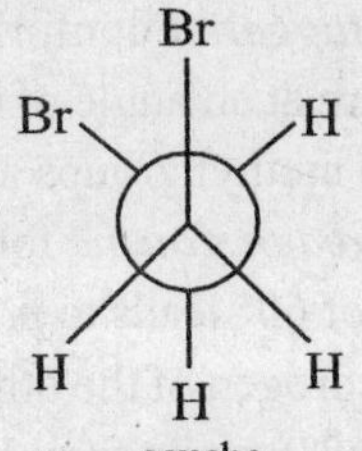

stability of *anti*-form is due to combined effects of steric factor and dipole-dipole interactions. It goes in favour of formation of *anti*- conformer. Dipole movement increases with increase of temperature.

Conformations of butane

n-butane is an alkane with four carbon atoms, which can be considered to be derived from ethane by replacing one hydrogen on each carbon with a methyl group. If we consider the rotation about the central carbon-carbon bond ($C_2 — C_2$), the situation is somewhat similar to ethane; but *n*-butane has more than one staggered and eclipsed conformations (unlike ethane which has only one staggered and one eclipsed conformation). Newman Projection formulae for various staggered and eclipsed conformations of *n*-butane are as given below :

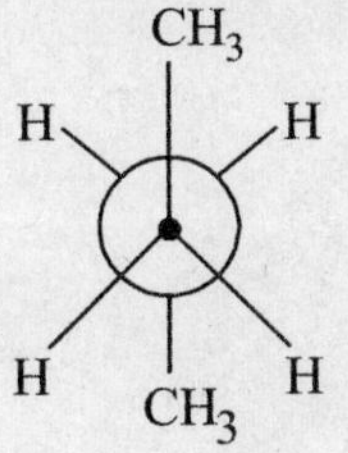

Completely staggered or anti form
I

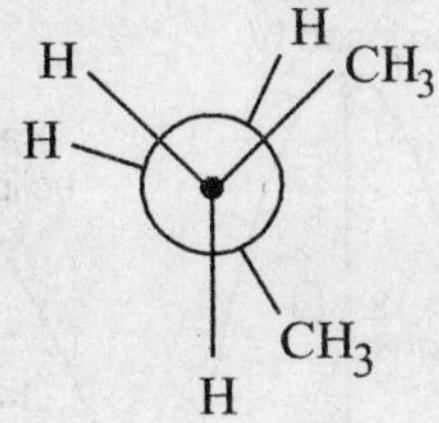

Partially eclipsed form
II

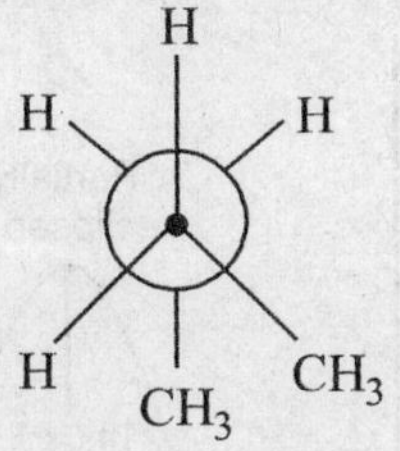

Partially staggered or gauche form or skew form
III

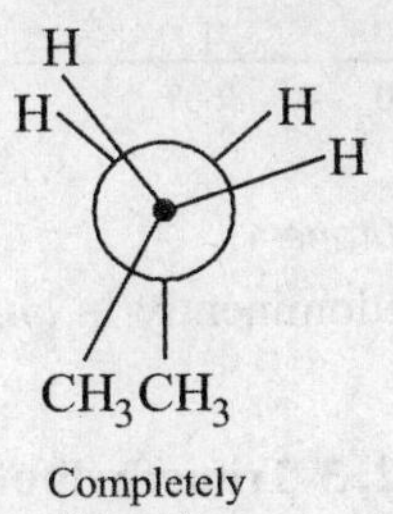

Completely eclipsed form
IV

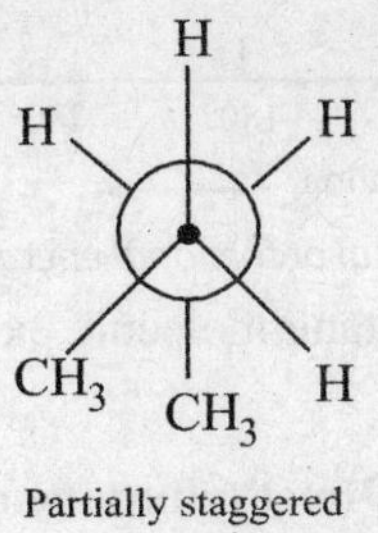

Partially staggered or gauche
V

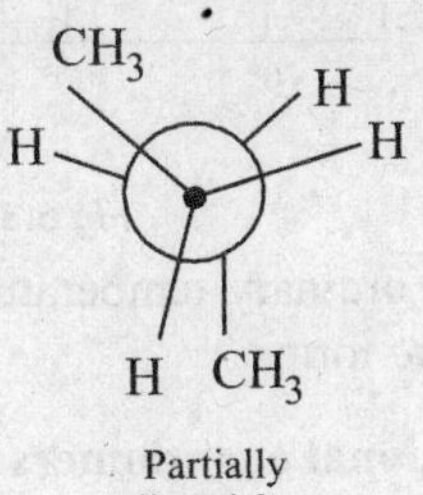

Partially eclipsed form
VI

The *completely staggered* conformation, (I) also known as *anti* form, is having the methyl goups as far apart at possible. Let us see how these forms have been obtained. Let us start from structure I. Holding the back carbon (represented by circle) fixed along with its groups, — H, — H and — CH_3, rotate the front carbon (shown by a dot) in clockwise direction by an angle of 60°. Groups attached to it will also move. *Partially eclipsed* form (II) is obtained. In this conformation (II), methyl group of one carbon is at the back of hydrogen of the other carbon. Further rotation of 60° leads of a *partially staggered* conformation (III), also known as *gauche* form, in which the two methyl groups are at an angle of 60°. Rotation by another 60° gives rise to a *fully eclipsed* form (IV) having two methyl groups at the back of each other. Further rotation of 60°, again leads to *partially staggered or gauche* form (V) having methyl groups at an angle of 60° (as in III). Still further rotation of 60° leads to *partially eclipsed* form (VI), having methyl group of one carbon at the back of hydrogen of the other (as in II). If a further rotation of 60° is operated (completing the rotation of 360°), again form I is obtained. Of course, there will be an infinite number of other conformations in between these six conformations (I to VI). (*Gauche* form is also known as skew form).

Out of these six conformations, the *completely staggered* or *anti conformation* (I) is most stable and *partially staggered* or *gauche* conformation (III or V) is slightly less stable: the energy difference being only 3.8 kJ/mole. On the other hand the *completely eclipsed* conformation (IV) is least stable and *partially eclipsed* conformation (II or VI) is slightly more stable, again the energy difference being 3.8 kJ/mole. (This is due to presence of steric strain between two methyl groups). The energy difference between most stable conformation (I) and least stable conformation (IV) is about 18.4 kJ/mole while that between I and II (or VI) is about 14.6 kJ/mole. (Fig 6.3)

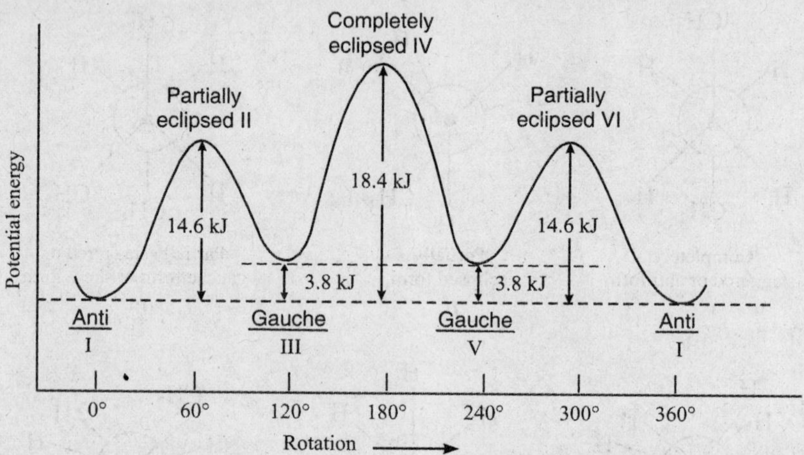

Fig 6.3: Rotational or torsional energy of n-butane.

Thus at ordinary temperature, *n*-butane molecule exists predominently in *anti* form with some *guache* forms.

Conformational enantiomers of 2, 3-Dimethylbutane and 2, 2, 3-Trimethylbutane

Conformational isomers of 2, 3-Dimethylbutane

Me, H, Me, Me, H, Me — I

Me, Me, Me, Me, H, H — II

Me, Me, H, Me, H, Me — III

Structure I is supposed to have maximum stability out of these three isomers, II and III are conformational enantiomers (mirror-images) also. This can be visualized after rotation of III as a whole.

Conformational isomers of 2, 2, 3-Trimethylbutane

I II III

All these structures have the same stability and the compound may be assumed to occur in one conformation only.

Conformations of cyclohexane

Chair conformation

Chair conformation of cyclohexane is represented below :

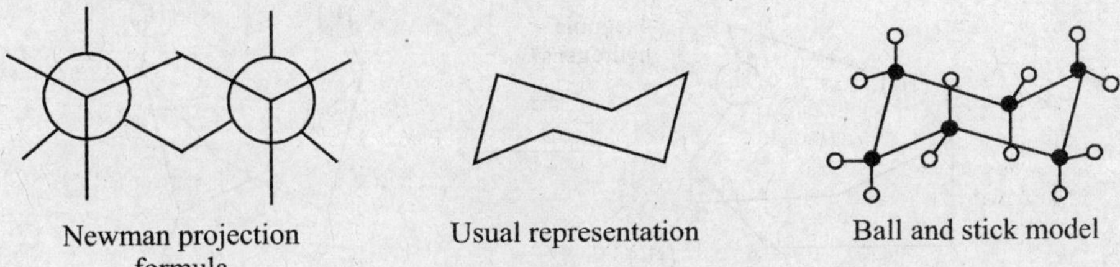

Chair conformation of *n*-butane.

This is the most stable conformation of cyclohexane. In this conformation, all the bond angles are tetrahedral and the C — H bonds on adjacent carbons are in a staggered position. This conformation has no strain and has minimum energy.

Boat Conformation

There is no angle strain in the molecule as all the angles are tetrahedral. But hydrogens on four carbon atoms (C_2 and C_3, C_5 and C_6) are eclipsed. As a result, there is considerable torsional strain. Also, two hydrogens pointing towards each other at C_1 and C_4 (called flagpole hydrogens) are very close to each other. This brings in van der Waals strain in the molecule. Due to these reasons boat conformation is less stable than chair conformation by an amount 28.8 kJ/mole.

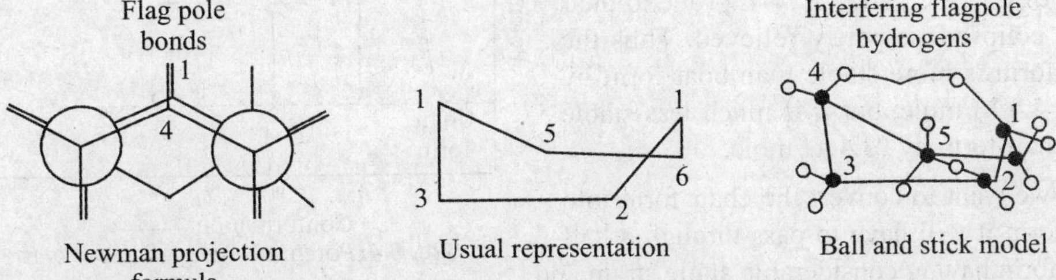

Boat conformation of cyclohexane

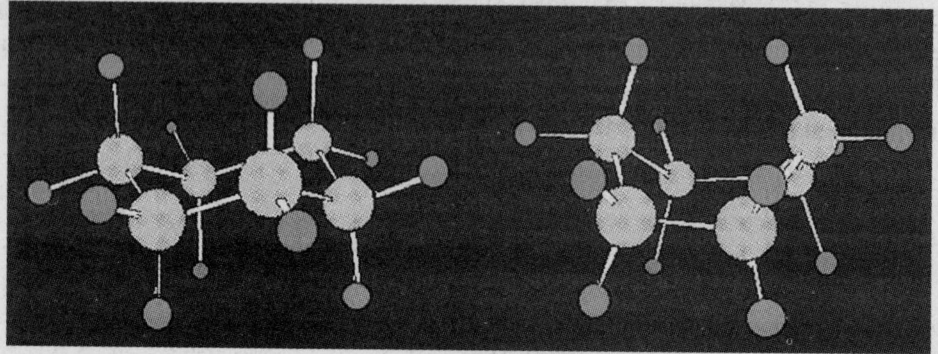

Conformations of cycloalkanes

Twist conformation of cyclohexane. Sequence of changes in going from chair form to boat form

Besides chair and boat conformation, cyclohexane can have several other possible conformations. Consider model of boat conformation of cyclohexane. Hold C_2 — C_3 bond in one hand and C_5 — C_6 in the other and twist the model so that C_2 and C_5 come upwards and C_3 and C_6 go downwards. We will get another conformation known as *twist form* or *skew boat* form.

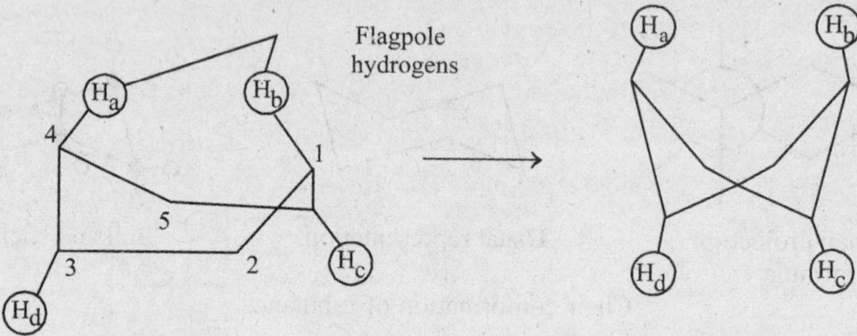

During this twisting, the flagpole hydrogens (H_a and H_b) move apart while the hydrogens H_c and H_d move closer. If this motion is continued another boat form will be obtained in which H_c and H_d become the *flagpole hydrogens*.

In twist forms the distance between H_a and H_b is equal to that of H_c and H_d and the steric strain is minimum; also the torsional strain of C_2 — C_3 and C_2 — C_6 (due to their being eclipsed) is partly relieved. Thus the twist form is more stable than boat form by about 5.4 kJ/mole, but it is much less stable than chair form by 23.4 kJ/mole.

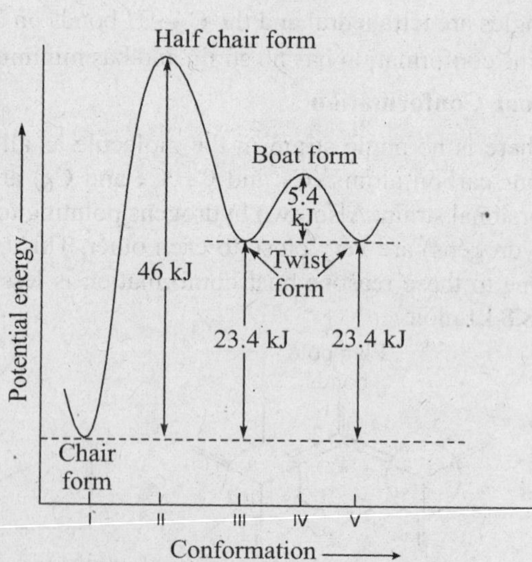

Fig. 6.4: Potential energy diagram of the conformers of cyclohexane

If we want to convert the chair form into boat form it will have to pass through a half chair form having considerable angle strain and

Solution: In structure (*b*) two Br groups are close to each other. This will result in repulsion between them leading to separation of charge and thus creation of higher dipole moment.

Example 21: Convert the Fischer's projection of D (–) erythrose sugar (*a*) to the following:

(*a*) Fischer projection: CHO at top; H—C—OH; —C—OH; CH_2OH at bottom.

D (–) Erythrose → Swahorse eclipsed form (*b*)

→ Newmann staggered form (*e*)

→ Newmann eclipsed form (*d*)

→ Sawhorse staggered form (*c*)

Solution:

D (–) Erythrose (Fischer projection: CHO; H—OH; —OH; CH_2OH)

Newmann staggered form (*e*): CH_2OH, OH, H (front); H, CHO, OH (back)

Sawhorse eclipsed form (*b*): CHO, CH_2OH, H, OH, H, OH

Newmann eclipsed form (*d*): CH_2OH, CHO, H, H, OH, OH

Sawhorse staggered form (*c*): CH_2OH, H, OH, CHO

Exmple 22: Draw the Newmann projections (eclipsed and staggered) of meso dichlorobutane. Which is more stable ?

Solution: Meso dichlorobutane may be written as :

$$CH_3-\underset{Cl}{\overset{H}{C}}-\underset{Cl}{\overset{H}{C}}-CH_3$$

Eclipsed and staggered Newmann projections may be written as :

(Staggered) (Eclipsed)

Example 23: Assign E or Z configuration to each of the following compounds:

(A) Me(Et)C=C(H)(Cl)   (B) Br(I)C=C(Cl)(H)

Solution: In compound (A), groups of higher priority on the doubly bonded carbon atoms are Et and Cl, which lie on the same side of the double bond. Hence, it is Z isomer

In compound (B), groups of higher priority on the doubly bonded carbon atoms are I and Cl, which lie on the opposite sides of the double bond. Hence, it is E isomer.

Example 24: Indicate which of the following compounds has E or Z designation

(*i*) CH_3(H)C=C(Cl)(Br)   (*ii*) CH_3(H)C=C(Cl)(Br)

(*iii*)   (*iv*) H(HOOC)C=C(COOH)(H)

Solution:

(*i*) CH_3(H)C=C(Cl)(Br)
E-isomer

(*ii*) CH_3(H)C=C(C_3H_7)(C_2H_5)
Z-isomer

(*iii*)
E-isomer

(*iv*) H(HOOC)C=C(COOH)(H)
E-isomer

Example 25: Assign E or Z configuration to the following:

(*a*) CH_3(CH_3—CH_2)C=C(H)(CH_2—C(=O)—H)

(*b*) HC≡C(H)C=C(D)(CH=CH_2)

Solution:

(*a*) Groups of higher priority on the two doubly bonded carbon atoms are on the same side of the double bond. Hence, its configuration is Z.

(*b*) Groups of higher priority on the two doubly bonded carbon atoms are on the opposite sides of the double bond (D stands for heavy hydrogen). Hence, its configuration is E.

Example 26: Assign R or S configuration to the following :

(*a*) Fischer projection: H (top), HO (left), CH_2OH (right), CHO (bottom)

(*b*) OH (wedge), H (hashed), CHO, CH_2OH

(*c*) Cl (hashed, top), OH (wedge), CH_3 (wedge), CH_2CH_3 (hashed, bottom) on C

Solution: We need to bring the group of lowest priority *i.e.* H at the bottom.
(Follow the rules given in the chapter)

(*a*) HO—C(H)(CHO)—CH_2OH ≡ HOH_2C (3), CHO (2), OH (1), H at the bottom — [S]

We move in the anticlockwise direction in moving from group of highest priority to the group of lowest priority (1 → 2 → 3). Hence it has S configuration.

(*b*) OH, CHO, H, CH_2OH ≡ H—C(CHO)(CH_2OH)—OH ≡ HO (1), CHO (2), CH_2OH (3), H at the bottom

We move in the clockwise direction in moving from group of highest priority to the group of lowest priority, (leaving H). Hence, it has R-configuration.

(*c*) OH, H, CH_3, CH_2CH_3 on C ≡ HO—C(H)(CH_2CH_3)—CH_3 ≡ CH_3 (3), CH_2CH_3 (2), OH (1), H at the bottom

We follow anticlockwise direction in moving from group of highest priority to the group of lowest priority. Hence, it has S configuration.

Example 27: Assign A or Z rotations to the following compounds showing priorities for various groups :

(i) $(CH_3)_3C$ and $CH_2=CH$ on one carbon, $COCH_3$ and CHO on the other: $(CH_3)_3C(CH_2=CH)C=C(COCH_3)(CHO)$

(ii) D and H on one carbon, NH_2 and Br on the other: $D(H)C=C(NH_2)(Br)$

Solution:

(i) $(CH_3)_3C$ ①, $CH_2=CH$ ②; $COCH_3$ ①, CHO ②

Groups of higher priority on the two doubly bonded carbon atoms are on the same side of the double bond. Hence it has Z configuration.

(ii) D ①, H ②; NH_2 ②, Br ①

Here, D stands for deuterium *i.e.* heavy hydrogen. Groups of higher priorities on the two doubly bonded carbon atoms are on the opposite sides of the double bond. Hence, it is E configuration.

Example 28: Assign R or S configuration to the following compounds showing priorities for various groups.

(i) Fischer projection: top H, left H_3COC, right CO_2H, bottom CH_2OH

(ii) Fischer projection: top $C\equiv CH$, left H_3C, right H, bottom $CH=CH_2$

Solution: To assign the configuration to the compounds, we need to bring the group of lowest priority *i.e.* H at the bottom as per the rules explained in the chapter

(i) CH_3OC—C(H)(CH_2OH)—CO_2H $\equiv$ top CH_2OH ③, left HO_2C ①, right $COCH_3$ ②, bottom H ④

We have to trace anti-chlockwise direction in moving from the group of lowest priority to the group of highest priority. Hence, it has S configuration.

(ii) H_3C—C($C\equiv CH$)($CH=CH_2$)—H $\equiv$ top $C\equiv CH$ ①, left $CH_2=CH$ ②, right CH_3 ③, bottom H ④

We have to trace anti-clockwise direction in moving from group of highest priority to group of lowest priority (leaving H). Hence, it has S configuration.

Example 29: Discuss the optical isomerism exhibited by diphenyl compounds.

Solution: Substituted biphenyls show optical isomerism when substituents in the 2-positions are large enough to prevent rotation about the bond joining the two benzene rings. For example, biphenyl-2, 2′-disulphonic acid exists in two forms.

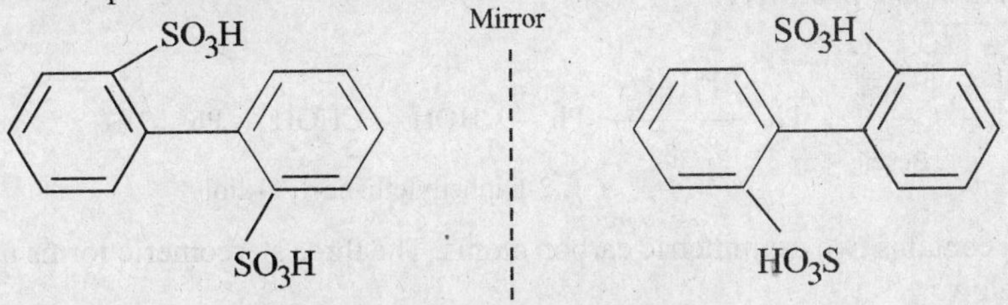

Mirror

SO_3H SO_3H SO_3H HO_3S

Biphenyl-2, 2′-disulphonic acid
(a biphenyl)

These two forms are non-superimposable mirror images. They do not interconvert at room temperature because the energy required to twist one ring through 180° relative to the other is too high. This is because, during the twisting process, the two-SO_3H group must come into very close proximity when the two benzene rings become coplaner and strong repulsive forces are introduced.

Example 30: Draw the Fischer projection formulas for all possible stereoisomers of 2, 3, 4- trihydroxyglutaric acid. Comment on the stereogenicity of C-3 centre in the active and the meso isomers.

Solution: Following are the stereoisomers of 2, 3, 4-trihydroxyglutaric acid :

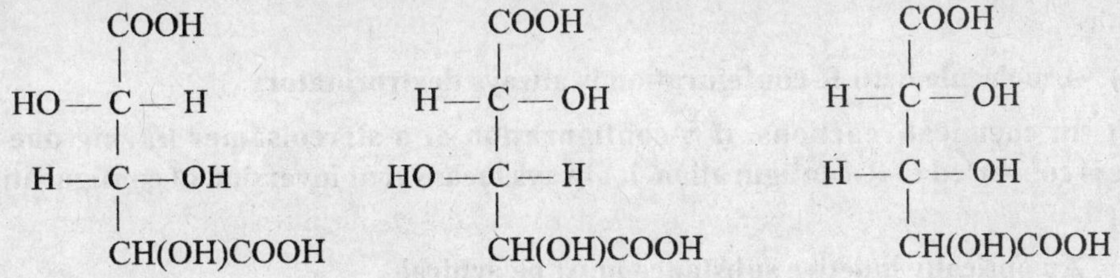

I	II	III
COOH	COOH	COOH
HO—C—H	H—C—OH	H—C—OH
H—C—OH	HO—C—H	H—C—OH
CH(OH)COOH	CH(OH)COOH	CH(OH)COOH

The Fischer projection formula of compound I is :

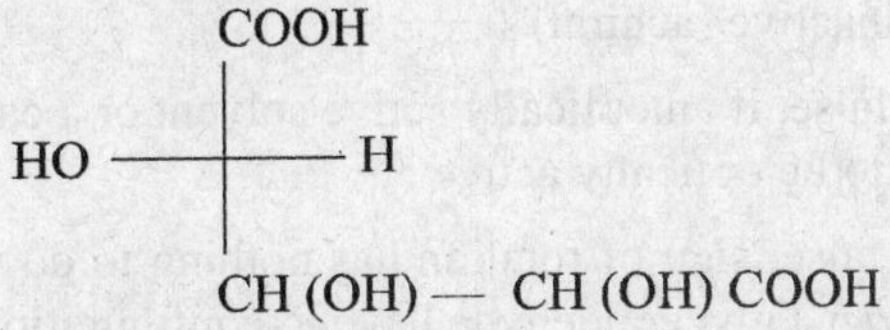

COOH
HO —+— H
CH (OH)— CH (OH) COOH

The Fischer projection formula of compound II is :

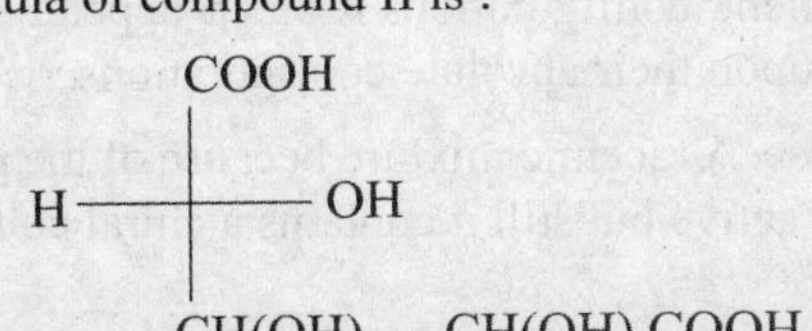

COOH
H —+— OH
CH(OH) — CH(OH) COOH

The following points are to be observed :

(*i*) The central carbon is present at the crossing of horizontal and vertical lines.

(*ii*) The longest chain of carbon atoms is present along the vertical line.

Example 31: How many asymmetric carbon atoms are created during the complete reduction of benzil PhCOCOPh with $LiAlH_4$? Also write the number of possible stereoisomers of the product?

Solution:

$$\underset{\text{Benzil}}{Ph-\overset{O}{\overset{\|}{C}}-\overset{O}{\overset{\|}{C}}-Ph} \xrightarrow{LiAlH_4} \underset{\text{1, 2-Diphenylethane-1, 2-diol}}{Ph-\underset{1}{\overset{*}{C}HOH}-\underset{2}{\overset{*}{C}HOH}-Ph}$$

The product contains two asymmetric carbon atoms. The three stereomeric forms of the product are given below.

Mirror

I		II		III
Ph		Ph		Ph
H — OH	¦	HO — H		H — OH
HO — H	¦	H — OH		H — OH
Ph		Ph		Ph

Enantiomers — *meso*-form

Example 32: Give proper resons, state whether the following statements are true or false.

(*a*) An achiral compound can have chiral centres

(*b*) When an achiral molecule reacts to give a chiral molecule, the product is always racemic

(*c*) A molecule with R-configuration is always dextrorotatory

(*d*) In chemical reactions, if S-configuration of a stereoisomer having one chiral centre is converted to R-configuration, it always means that inversion of configuration has occured.

(*e*) An optically inactive substance must be achiral

Solution:

(*a*) The statement is true. Consider the molecule of *meso*-tartaric acid. It has two chiral centres, yet it is optically inactive (achiral)

(*b*) This statement is false, if an optically active solvent or a catalyst such as an enzyme is used, the product is likely to be optically active

(*c*) This statement is false, sign of rotation has nothing to do with the configuration. For example both *dextro* and *laevo* glyceraldehyde have R-configuration

(*d*) This is a false statement, configurations R and S depend upon the priority sequence of the groups attached and not upon their absolute configurations.

(*e*) This statement is false. A racemic mixture because of the presence of equal amounts of two enantiomers is optically active but still it contains a chiral compound.

Evaluate Yourself

Multiple Choice Questions

1. The isomers of a substance must have
   (*a*) same chemical properties
   (*b*) same molecular weight
   (*c*) same structural formula
   (*d*) same functional groups
2. Ethanol (CH_3CH_2OH) and dimethyl ether (CH_3OCH_3) are best considered as
   (*a*) structural isomers
   (*b*) stereoisomers
   (*c*) enantiomers
   (*d*) diastereomers
3. Which of the following statements is false about tautomers ?
   (*a*) Tautomers are structural isomers
   (*b*) Tautomers are structural isomers which exist in dynamic equilibrium
   (*c*) Tautomerism involves movement of atoms
   (*d*) Tautomers have independent existence
4. How many structural isomers are possible for C_4H_9Br ?
   (*a*) 2
   (*b*) 3
   (*c*) 4
   (*d*) 5
5. Alkenes show geometrical isomerism due to :
   (*a*) asymmetry
   (*b*) rotation around a single bond
   (*c*) resonance
   (*d*) restricted rotation around a double bond
6. Two compounds have the same composition and also have the same atoms attached to the same atoms, although with different orientations in space. These compounds are
   (*a*) identical
   (*b*) position isomers
   (*c*) structural isomers
   (*d*) stereoisomers
7. Compounds with the same molecular formula but different structural formulas are called
   (*a*) alkoxides
   (*b*) iso compounds
   (*c*) isomers
   (*d*) ortho compounds
8. How many isomeric aromatic hydrocarbons are possible for C_8H_{10} ?
   (*a*) 3
   (*b*) 4
   (*c*) 5
   (*d*) 6
9. How many isomers are possible for the compound with molecular formula C_4H_8 ?
   (*a*) 2
   (*b*) 4
   (*c*) 6
   (*d*) 8
10. The compounds $CH_3CH_2OCH_2CH_3$ and $CH_3OCH_2CH_2CH_3$ are
    (*a*) enantiomers
    (*b*) conformational isomers
    (*c*) metamers
    (*d*) optical isomers

Short Answer Questions

1. Name different types of stereoisomerism. What is the necessary condition for a compound to exhibit enantiomerism?

2. Draw a diagram of nicol prism and show how a plane polarised light is obtained from it
3. Who postulated that the four valencies of carbon are directed towards the four corners of a regular tetrahedron? Draw the mirror images of lactic acid and sec butyl chloride
4. Name different elements of symmetry. Describe briefly one of them
5. Define chirality. Write the optically active and optically inactive forms of tartaric acid.
6. Pentene –2, 3 – diene is optically active although it does not contain chiral carbon atoms. Explain
7. How will you give flying edge representation of the molecule CHClBrI?
8. Give the configurations of R and S glyceraldehyde
9. What are distereomers? Give its three properties
10. What is meant by inversion and retention of configuration?

Long Answer Questions

1. Discuss the optical isomerism in 3, 4-dichlorohexane.
2. What are enantiomers? Write their characteristics?
3. What is chiral carbon atom?
4. What is the most essential condition of compound to be optically active in nature?
5. Assign R and S configurations to the following Fischer projection formulae :

6. Assign R and S configurations to the following :

7. Which of the following can exhibit geometrical isomerism :
   (*i*) 2-Hexene (*ii*) 2, 3-Dimethyl-2-butene
   (*iii*) 4-Methyl-2-pentene (*iv*) 2, 3-Dimethyl-1-butene.
8. Draw the structures of each of the following compounds showing its stereochemistry :
   (*i*) (2Z, 4Z)-2, 4-hexadiene (*ii*) (2R, 3S)-Tartaric acid.
9. Explain the racemisation of optical isomers with suitable examples.
10. Glucose contains four chiral carbon atoms in its molecule. What is the number of the optical isomers possible ?
11. What is resolution ? How will you resolve a racemic mixture by a chemical method?
12. Explain the difference between
    (*i*) Diastereoisomers and (*ii*) Enantiomers.
13. What do you understand by the E and Z notations for representing geometrical isomers?

Assign E and Z configurations to the following :

$$\underset{H}{\overset{CH_3CH_2CH_2}{}}\!\!C=C\!\!\underset{CH_3}{\overset{CH_2CH_3}{}} \qquad \underset{I}{\overset{F}{}}\!\!C=C\!\!\underset{Cl}{\overset{Br}{}}$$

14. What are the essential differences between enantiomers and diastereoisomers?
15. Explain the term 'meso' form with suitable examples.
16. Assign R and S configurations to the following compounds :

(i) CHO at top; HO — C — H; HO — C — H; CH_2OH at bottom

(ii) H at top; I — C — Cl; Br at bottom

(iii) NH_2 at top; HO — C — H; CH_3 at bottom

(iv) NH_2 at top; H — C — CH_3; COOH at bottom

17. What is Walden Inversion ? Give one example.
18. What do you understand by the *Rectus* and *Sinister* system for specifying a configuration?
19. Discuss the method of resolution of a racemic mixture which illustrates the formation of diastereomers.
20. Distinguish between meso and racemic forms of tartaric acid.
21. Explain with one example in each case
   (i) R and S configurations
   (ii) E and Z notations
   (iii) Racemisation.
22. Assign R and S configurations to the following :

(i) COOH at top; H — C — NH_2; CH_3 at bottom

(ii) CHO at top; HO — C — H; CH_2OH at bottom

23. What is functional isomerism ? Illustrate with an example.
24. Write down the configuration of $\overset{CHCOOH}{\underset{CHCOOH}{\|}}$ according to E and Z sequence rules.
25. Assign R and S configuration to the following :

(i) CH_3 at top; D — C — OH; H at bottom

(ii) Br at top; C_2H_5 — C — OH; OH at bottom

26. Explain biological method for the resolution of the racemic modification.

27. How will you prepare (–) Lactic acid from pyruvic acid?

28. Write a note on optical inversion.

29. Name the instrument to measure the angle of optical rotation.

30. Predict whether 3-chlorohexane will be optically active or not. Give reasons for your answer.

31. What are *cis-trans* isomers ? Give two examples of each.

32. What are diastereomers ? Write their main characteristics.

33. Give two methods of resolution of a racemic mixture.

34. Which of the following compounds exhibit geometrical isomerism ? Write *cis* and *trans* isomers :

(*i*) 2-Butene (*ii*) 2-Pentene

(*iii*) 1, 1-Dibromo-1-butene (*iv*) 1, 1-Dichloro-1-propene

(*v*) 1-Pentene (*vi*) 2-Methyl-2-butene.

35. What is geometrical isomerism ? How will you determine the configuration of geometrical isomers by

(*i*) Formation of cyclic compounds (*ii*) Dipole moment?

36. What do you understand by the E and Z notations for representing geometrical isomers. Assign E and Z configurations to the following :

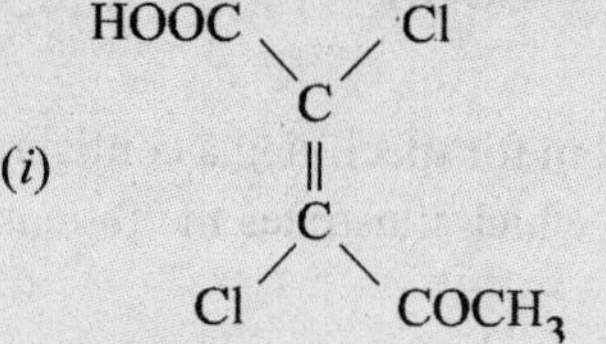

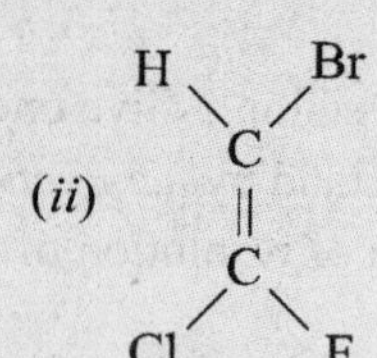

37. What are R and S configurations ? State sequence rules with examples.

38. Give a brief account of the following :

(*a*) Fischer's projection formula (*b*) Asymmetric synthesis.

39. Show that the presence or absence of chiral carbon atom in a molecule is not the necessary and sufficient condition for the existence of optical activity.

40. Optical activity is linked with the presence of asymmetric carbon atom. Justify the statement with a suitable example.

41. Define optical activity. Discuss the various methods for the resolution of a racemic mixture.

42. Explain the following terms :

(*i*) Specific rotation (*ii*) Chiral centre (*iii*) Meso compounds.

43. Write a note on E and Z method of the configuration designation of a geometrical isomer.

44. Assign R and S configurations to the following compounds :

(*i*)
```
        NH2
        |
    H — C — CH3
        |
        COOH
```

(*ii*)
```
        NH2
        |
   HO — C — H
        |
        CH3
```

(*iii*) $H_3C-C(OH)(H)-C_6H_5$ (*iv*) $H_3C-C(H)(NH_2)-C_6H_5$

45. (*a*) What do the symbols E and Z stand for ? Illustrate briefly the E and Z system of naming a pair geometrical isomers. What are the advantages of E and Z system over conventional *cis-trans* system.

(*b*) Using E and Z notations write the IUPAC names of

(*i*) $(Br)(I)C=C(Cl)(Br)$

(*ii*) $(H_3C)(H)C=C(H)-C(H)=C(CH_3)(H)$

46. How will you resolve racemic lactic acid with optically active forms ? Give two methods for this purpose.

47. What is resolution ? How will you resolve a racemic mixture by chemical method?

48. What makes a compound optically active ? How do you allot the configuration to a chiral centre. Distinguish between enantiomers and diastereoisomers.

49. (*a*) Will trichloroethane exhibit geometrical isomerism ? Give reasons for your answer.

(*b*) Assign R and S configuration to the following compounds :

(*i*) Fischer projection: top CH_3, left Br, right H, bottom COOH

(*ii*) Fischer projection: top CH_3; upper carbon: left HO, right H; lower carbon: left Cl, right H; bottom CH_3

(*c*) Denote E and Z notations and write IUPAC names of the following compounds :

(*i*) $(Br)(I)C=C(OH)(Cl)$ $(H_3C)(H)C=C(CH_2CH_3)(CH_3)$

50. (*a*) What is sequence rule ? How is it used for assigning configuration ? Discuss with suitable example.

(*b*) When a compound is expected to be optically active and why?

51. What are the requirements for a compound to be optically active ? Comment on the observation that presence of a chiral carbon is not always essential for a compound to be optically active.

52. Write four isomers of tartaric acid and select the pairs forming :

(*i*) Enantiomers (*ii*) Diastereoisomers.

53. (*a*) Discuss how geometrical isomers affect melting points and boiling points.

(*b*) Write short notes on :

(*i*) Sequence rule

(*ii*) Absolute configurations in terms of D and L notations.

(*c*) Assign R and S configurations to the following compounds.

(*i*) $HOHC_2-\underset{CH_3}{\overset{CHO}{C}}-H$

(*ii*) CHO–C(H)(Cl)–C(Cl)(H)–C_2H_5 (top carbon: H — C — Cl; lower carbon: Cl — C — H)

(*d*) Compare external compensation and Internal compensation.

54. Assign R and S to the following :

(*i*) H — C(Cl)(CH₃) — C(CH₃)(H) — H, i.e. $H-\underset{CH_3}{\overset{Cl}{C}}-\underset{H}{\overset{CH_3}{C}}-H$

(*ii*) $HO-\underset{Cl}{\overset{NH_2}{C}}-CH_3$

(*iii*) $HO-\underset{COOH}{\overset{H}{C}}-CH_3$

(*iv*) $CH_3-\underset{CHO}{\overset{C_2H_5}{C}}-COOH$

55. (*a*) Define optical isomerism. Mention the conditions and selecting lactic acid as example, explain how many isomers are possible in it.

(*b*) Giving examples, distinguish between the following :

(*i*) Enantiomers and Diastereoisomers

(*ii*) Meso and Racemic forms.

56. Represent the different conformations of ethane with the help of space models. Which out of them is more stable and why ?

57. Discuss the effect of temperature on the dipole moment of a conformation by taking a suitable example.

58. What do you understand by the following :

(*i*) Chair conformation

(*ii*) Boat conformation

(*iii*) Twist boat conformation?

59. What do you understand by the term conformation ? How are the conformations formed?

60. How will you differentiate between the conformations and configurations?

61. The rotation about the C — C bond is almost free and not completely free. Justify.

62. Why is chair conformation of cyclohexane more stable than the boat conformation?

63. Which are two main conformations of cyclohexane ? How will you represent them?

64. How do angle strain and steric strains influence the stability of a conformation?

65. The eclipsed conformation of ethane is less stable than the staggered conformation. Explain.

66. Name the different factors which influence the relative stabilities of the conformation of a molecule.

67. Normally *anti*-conformation of a molecule is more stable as compared to the *gauche* conformation. But the same is not true in case of ethylene glycol. Explain.

68. With the help of suitable example discuss the following :

(*i*) Axial hydrogen atoms

(*ii*) Flag pole hydrogen atoms.

69. Draw the structure of the chair form of cyclohexane depicting the axial and equatorial bonds.

70. There is no strain in either the chair or boat form of cyclohexane. Why then the chair conformation is more stable than the boat conformation?

71. Give a brief account of 1, 3-diaxial interactions.

72. How will you account for the energy difference in the various conformations of cyclohexane.

73. Write a note an axial and equatorial bonds in cyclohexane.

74. (*a*)Why is chair conformation of cyclohexane more stable than the boat conformation?

(*b*)Differentiate between conformation and configuration.

75. (*a*)Sketch the Newman's projection formulae of important conformations of *n*-butane with reference to central C — C bond. Arrange them in order of increasing stability and assign reason.

(*b*)Explain the difference between the terms conformation and configuration by taking suitable examles.

(*c*)Which conformation of cyclohexane is more stable and why?

(*d*)Explain the chair and boat conformations of cyclohexane.

76. Explain the term conformation and configuration. How will you differentiate between them?

77. What is conformational analysis? Draw the various conformations of *n*-butane and arrange them on the energy level diagram.

78. Discuss the brief the factors which influence the relative stabilities of the conformations.

79. Explain the following terms with suitable examples.

(*a*) Torsional strain (*b*) Steric strain (*c*) Dipole-dipole interactions.

80. Discuss the different conformations of *n*-butane by taking into account the rotation about C — C bond. Arrange them in increasing order of stability and assign suitable reason for the same.

81. Discuss the various factors which influence the relative stabilities of the conformation of a molecule.

Answers

Multiple Choice Questions

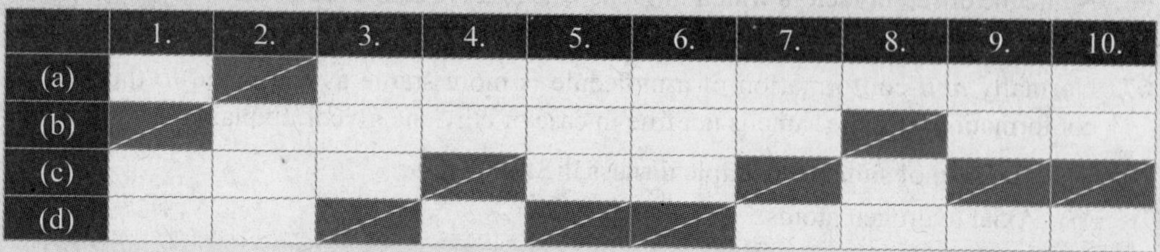

	1.	2.	3.	4.	5.	6.	7.	8.	9.	10.
(a)		■								
(b)	■							■		
(c)				■			■		■	■
(d)			■		■	■				

7

Basic Computer System

7.1 INTRODUCTION

Definition: Computer is an electronic device which is able to process unmeaningful raw data into meaningful information.

This raw data is called **Input** and the generated information is called **Output** in computer terminology.

Analog Vs Digital

An **Analog** device deals with the continuous measurement, recording or processing of information.

A speedometer is an analog device which measures the speed of the vehicle continuously. Similarly a slide-rule is an analog computing device.

A **Digital** device deals with discrete samples of information.

Both types of information can be converted to another with sufficient accuracy using either ADC (Analog to Digital converter) or DAC (Digital to Analog converter).

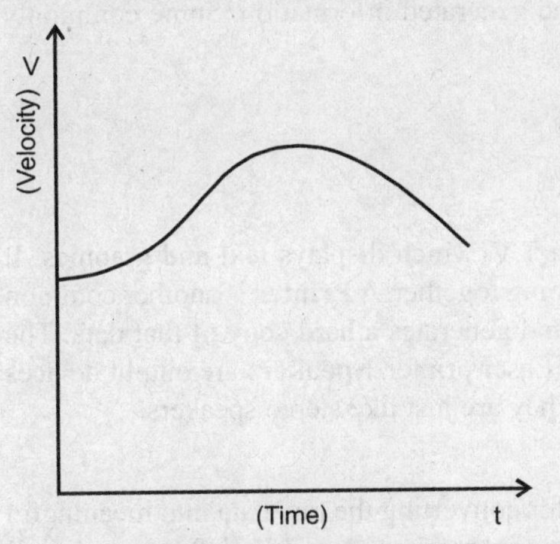

Analog Measurement

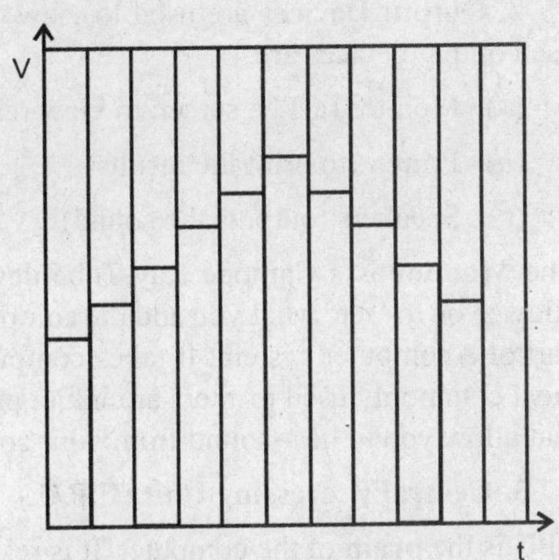

Digital Measurement

All modern computers are Digital in nature. They require Digital Output and can only generate Digital Output. Any interfacing with an Analog Input device requires use of ADC circuits.

Similarly to produce an Analog output, DAC circuits are required.

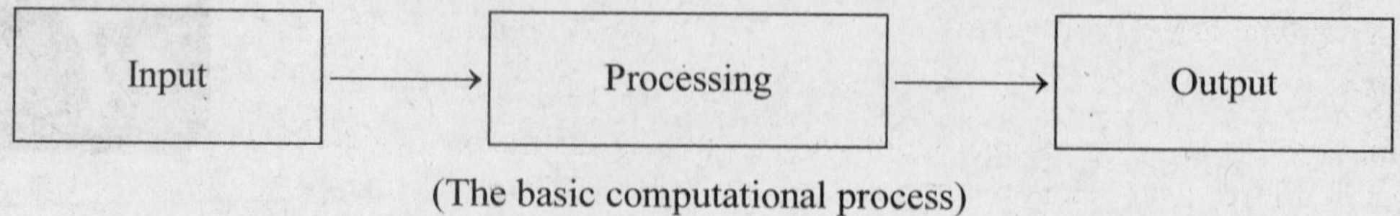

(The basic computational process)

7.2 COMPONENTS OF A COMPUTER

A computer system is made up of three basic components.

1. Input Devices
2. Output Devices
3. Central Processing Unit (CPU)

1. Input Devices provide data for the computer to operate upon. Some commonly used input devices are

(*a*) Keyboard (to enter data manually)

(*b*) Mouse (to re-position the cursor on the screen)

The **Keyboard** allows the entry of textual information. It has keys for characters (letters, numbers and punctuation marks) and special commands. Pressing the keys tells the computer what to do or what to write. The **Mouse** has a special ball that allows the selection of a point on the screen by moving a screen cursor to the point and pressing a mouse button. Alternative devices to the mouse are tracker balls, light pens and touch sensitive screens. Other types of input devices allow you to put images into the computer like **Scanner** and **Digital Camera**.

Besides these, there could be other specialised input devices, providing information about Industrial Automation System, Control Systems to the Computer, etc.

2. Output Devices are used to view or store the generated information. Some commonly used output devices are:

(*a*) Monitor (a T.V. screen to view results)

(*b*) Printer (to print the results)

(*c*) Speakers (outputs the sound)

The **Monitor** is a Cathode Ray Tube device like a T.V. which displays text and graphics. It allows you to 'see' what you and the computer are doing together. A **Printer** is another common part of a computer system. It takes computer data and generates a hard copy of that data. The most commonly used printers are inkjet printer and Laser printer. **Speakers** are output devices that allow you to hear sound from your computer. They are just like stereo speakers.

3. Central Processing Unit (C.P.U.)

CPU is the **brain** of the computer. It is responsible for converting the raw data into meaningful information based on certain instructions. These instructions are called **Programs**. All processing and calculations take place here. This is further divided into 3 parts.

(*a*) Arithmetic Logical Unit (A.L.U.):

It performs all the mathematical functions of addition, subtraction, division and multiplication. Besides this, it performs logical operations like **greater than, less than** and **equal to**.

A combination of these basic functions makes it possible for A.L.U. to solve any kind of computer numerical problems.

(*b*) Memory:

Computer requires a set of instructions and input data to produce results. In this computational process, it may also generate temporary data. A memory unit is required to store this data as well as the generated result until it can be passed on to the output device.

Memory is further classified into 2 types.

Primary Memory. The memory which resides inside the computer system (CPU) is known as primary memory. It is further classified into 2 types.

RAM (Random Access Memory). It is a dynamic memory, which can store temporary data created during the processing of a computer program. The data can be erased and re-written any number of times. RAM is volatile in nature. As soon as the power supply of the computer is turned off, the content stored in this type of memory will be erased. Essentially, more RAM in a computer system means faster processing.

ROM (Read Only Memory) – This type of memory is used to store data, which is permanent in nature. This includes configuration data used to start a computer (BIOS—Basic Input Output System). Such information is related to hardware present in the system and does not change. Data stored in ROM cannot be erased or re-written.

Secondary Memory – Secondary memory resides outside the computer system (CPU). It is used to permanently store large amounts of data. Large amount of input data and the programs/instruction required to process this data into information, both reside on the secondary memory and can be accessed any time later. Data on secondary memory has to be transferred to primary memory (RAM), for the computer to utilize it.

The various types of secondary memory are: — Floppy Disk, Hard Disk, Compact Disk (CD). Some of the devices which were earlier in use were — punched cards, magnetic tape and magnetic drums.

(*c*) Control Unit. It controls the functioning of the CPU. The flow of data between the ALU and Memory is controlled by the Control Unit.

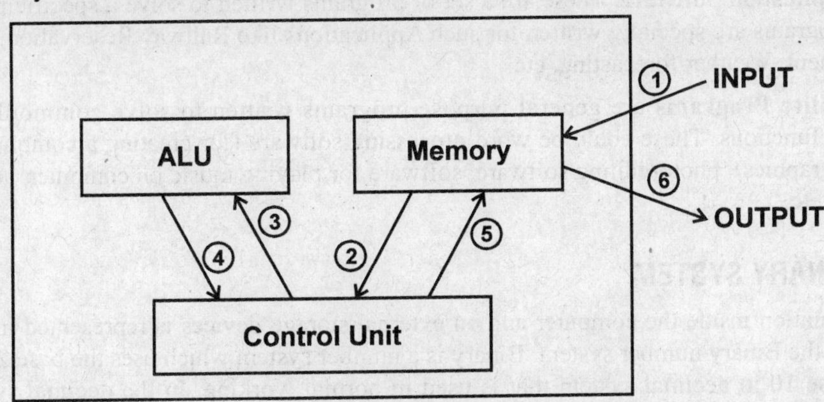

Central Processing Unit

It passes the input data present in the memory to ALU for processing. Once the data is processed, it sends the generated information to the memory so that it can be passed on to the output devices.

7.3 HARDWARE AND SOFTWARE

Hardware is a collective term used for all the physical parts of a computer which we can see and touch. Hardware consists of the monitor, keyboard, mouse, internal parts of the computer like Processor Chips, Memory Chips and other Integrated Circuits (I.Cs).

Software is a set of programs/instructions required by the hardware of the computer to perform the desired data-processing function. Software can be classified further into:

1. System Software
2. Application Software
3. Utility Programs

1. System Software consists of programs that are required for the functioning of the computer system. The following can be the examples of system software.

***(a)* Operating System.** This software controls the loading of instructions stored in the Disk (Secondary memory) into the primary memory. The other components of O.S. help in controlling the overall flow of data to various parts of the computer. It also helps in the proper functioning of various peripheral devices like Printers, Modems, etc. Most popular operating systems are: Windows, Unix, Linux and MS-DOS.

***(b)* Instruction Interpreters (Languages):** These sets of programs understand instructions written in English like language and convert them into Machine Language (Binary language) which the computer understands.

If they convert programs written in English like languages (called High Level Languages) into machine language, line by line, they are called **Interpreters**. If they convert the whole program together and then execute it, they are called **Compilers**. Some of the Interpreted Languages are Basic, Java. Some of the Compiled Languages are C, C^{++}, Pascal.

Internally, all the programs are converted to an intermediate Language called **Assembly Language** before getting converted to machine language. The program that converts Assembly Language programs to machine language are called **Assembler**.

2. Application Software. These are a set of programs written to solve a specific problem. These programs are specially written for such Applications like Railway Reservation, Library Management, Weather forecasting, etc.

3. Utility Programs are general purpose programs written to solve commonly faced problems/functions. These could be word processing software (for creating a combination of text and graphics), photo-editing software, software for playing music on computer, anti-virus software, etc.

7.4 BINARY SYSTEM

All information inside the computer and on external storage devices is represented in a form related to the Binary number system. Binary is a number system which uses the base 2 instead of the base 10 in decimal system that is used in normal working. In the decimal system, a positional number system is used which allows all numbers to be expressed using only the digits 0 – 9. Successive digits from the right represent the number of the corresponding power of 10. Thus 123 in decimal is

$$1 \times 10^2 + 2 \times 10^1 + 3 \times 10^0$$

that is, one hundred, plus two tens, plus three units.

But the binary number system builds all numbers from the bits 0 and 1, and power of 2.

101 in the binary number system represents the number

$$1 \times 2^2 + 0 \times 2^1 + 1 \times 2^0.$$

having value equal to 5 in the decimal system. Binary system allows all computation inside the computer to take place using cheap two-state electronic devices.

Modern computers organise information into small units called **bytes** which hold eight **bits**, each bit representing a 0 or 1. Each byte may hold a single character of text or a small integer. Larger numbers, computer instructions and character strings occupy several bytes.

All digital computers represent data as a collection of bits. A bit is the smallest possible unit of information. It can be in one of two states—**off** or **on, 0** or **1.**

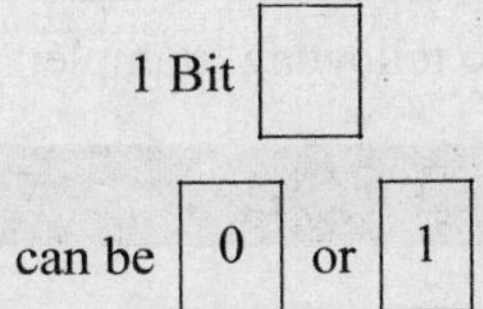

If one bit has two different states, how many states do two bits have? The answer is four. Likewise, three bits have eight states as represented below.

2 Bits = 4 States

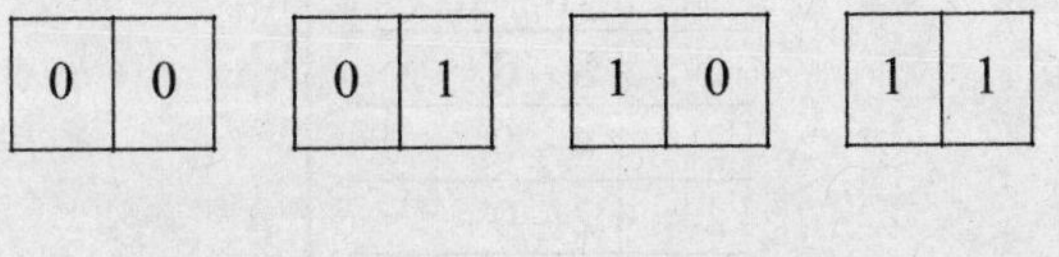

3 Bits = 8 States

0	0	0

0	0	1

0	1	0

0	1	1

1	0	0

1	0	1

1	1	0

1	1	1

A common and convenient grouping of bits is the **byte** or **Octet**, composed of eight bits. If two bits have four combinations, and three bits have eight combinations, how many combinations do eight bits have? If you don't want to write out all possible byte patterns, just multiply eight twos together – one two for each bit, *i.e.*,

$$2^8 = 256$$

So, a byte has 256 possible states.

1 Byte = 8 Bits

If a byte has 256 possible states, its exact state can be represented by a number from 1 to 256. However, since zero is a very important number, a byte is more typically represented by a number from 0 to 255. This is very common with bit pattern 00000000 representing zero, and bit pattern 11111111 representing 255. The numbers matching these two patterns, and everything in between, can be computed by assigning a weight to each bit, multiplying each bit's value (0 or 1) by its weight, and then adding the totals.

7.5 BINARY ARITHMETIC

Binary Addition. We perform binary addition in the same way as we perform addition with Decimal numbers. The following examples will illustrate.

Conversion of a decimal integer to a binary number

The following steps are involved in the conversion:

(*i*) Divide the decimal number by the base 2

(*ii*) Write down the remainder and divide the quotient by 2 again.

(*iii*) Again, write down the remainder and divide the remainder by 2.

(*iv*) Repeat till the quotient obtained is zero.

(*v*) Write down the sequence of remainders obtained from bottom to top.

This is illustrated with the help of the following example:

Solved Examples

Example 1: Write the binary equivalent of the number $(66)_{10}$.

Solution:

2	66
2	33 – 0
2	16 – 1
2	8 – 0
2	4 – 0
2	2 – 0
2	1 – 0
	0 – 1

Thus, the binary equivalent of the decimal number $(66)_{10}$ is $(1000010)_2$

Conversion of decimal number (having an integer and fraction) to binary number

The following steps are involved in the process:

(*i*) The integer part is converted to binary equivalent as explained above.

(*ii*) The fraction part of the decimal number is multiplied by two to obtain the integer part

(*iii*) Continue multiplying the fraction part by 2 until the fraction part becomes zero. The carries generated form the binary number.

(*iv*) Write the sequence of carries from bottom to top. The example given below will illustrate.

Example 2: Determine the binary equivalent of $(15.0625)_{10}$

Solution:

Step I Conversion of integer part

2	15
2	7 – 1
2	3 – 1
2	1 – 1
	0 – 1

Integer part = $(1111)_2$

Step II Conversion of fraction part

	Carry
$0.0625 \times 2 = 0.1250$	0
$0.1250 \times 2 = 0.2500$	0
$0.2500 \times 2 = 0.5000$	0
$0.5000 \times 2 = 1.0000$	1

The fractional binary part is $(0001)_2$

Hence the binary equivalent of $(15.0625)_{10}$ is $(1111.0001)_2$

Example 3: Determine the decimal equivalent of the binary number $(1100.0110)_2$

Solution: It can be obtained as under:

$$\text{Number} = (1 \times 2^3) + (1 \times 2^2) + (0 \times 2^1) + (0 \times 2^0) + (0 \times 2^{-1}) + (1 \times 2^{-2}) + (1 \times 2^{-3}) + (0 \times 2^{-4})$$

$$= 8 + 4 + 0 + 0 + 0 + \frac{1}{4} + \frac{1}{8} + 0$$

$$= 12 + 0.25 + 0.125$$

$$= (12.375)_{10}$$

7.6 OCTAL NUMBER SYSTEM

In this system, there are 8 digits from 0 to 7. The base of this number system is 8. The counting in this system is similar to decimal system. However, the digits 8 and 9 are not considered. As in the case of decimal or binary system, the octal number consists of two parts, the integral part and the fractional part. The octal number system finds use in microcomputers for direct input or output operation.

Conversion of octal to decimal numbers

The following steps are involved in the conversion.

(*i*) Multiply the extreme right digit of the given octal number with 8 having the power 0 ($8^0 = 1$)

(*ii*) Repeat the above step for all octal digits, increasing the power of 8, one by one, keeping the base fixed at 8.

(*iii*) Take the sum of all the products to obtain the decimal number.

This is illustrated with the help of the following example

Example 4: Determine the octal number $(2\,3\,4\,5)_8$ to decimal number

Solution: $(2\,3\,4\,5)_8 = (2 \times 8^3) + (3 \times 8^2) + (4 \times 8^1) + (5 \times 8^0)$

$= 1024 + 192 + 32 + 5$

$= 1253$

Conversion of octal fractional number to decimal number

The integral part of the octal number is converted to decimal number as explained above. To convert the fractional part, we multiple the first digit after the decimal point by 8^{-1} and the next successive digits by 8^{-2}, 8^{-3}, 8^{-4}, etc. Finally, we add up all the products obtained to convert the fractional octal number to the decimal number.

This is explained with help of the following example:

Example 5: Convert the number $(63.43)_8$ to decimal number.

Solution: $(63.43)_8 = (6 \times 8^1) + (3 \times 8^0) + (4 \times 8^{-1}) + (3 \times 8^{-2})$

$= 48 + 3 + (4 \times 0.125) + (3 \times 0.0156)$

$= 51 + 0.5 + 0.0468$

$= 51.5468$

Conversion of decimal to octal system

The following steps are involved in the conversion:

(*i*) Divide the given decimal number with the base 8.

(*ii*) Write down the quotient and the remainder separately.

(*iii*) Divide the quotient again by 8 and write the quotient and remainder for this step.

(*iv*) Repeat division by 8 till the quotient obtained is zero.

(*v*) Write down the sequence of the remainders obtained in the division starting from bottom to top.

This is explained with the help of the following example.

Example 6: Convert the decimal number $(470)_{10}$ to octal equivalent.

Solution:

8	470
8	58 – 6
8	7 – 2
	0 – 7

Remainders in the above division from the bottom are 7,2 and 6. Therefore the corresponding octal number is $(726)_8$

Conversion of fractional decimal number to octal number

The following steps are involved in the conversion:

(*i*) Multiply the fraction part by 8 to obtain the integer part

(*ii*) Multiply the fraction part obtained in this step by 8 to obtain the integral part again.

(*iii*) Repeat the above steps and record the sequence of integer parts starting from top to bottom.

The following example with illustrate

Example 7: Convert the decimal fractional number $(0.545)_{10}$ to octal number.

Solution: $0.575 \times 8 = 4.600$

$0.600 \times 8 = 4.800$

$0.800 \times 8 = 6.400$

$0.400 \times 8 = 3.200$

$0.200 \times 8 = 1.600$

Octal number $= (0.44631)_8$

Conversion of octal number of binary number

For the conversion of an octal number into a binary number, each octal digit is converted into its equivalent binary solution. Binary equivalents of the numbers 0 to 7 are given in Table 7.1.

TABLE 7.1 *Binary equivalents of octal numbers*

Octal number	*Binary equivalent*
0	000
1	001
2	010
3	011
4	100
5	101
6	110
7	111

To convert an octal number to an equivalent binary number, we simply replace each octal digit by its binary bits. The following example will illustrate:

Example 8: Write the binary equivalent of $(32.2741)_8$

Solution:

$(32.2741)_8$ = 3 2 • 2 7 4 1

↓ ↓ ↓ ↓ ↓ ↓

Binary equivalents 011 010 010 111 100 001

Thus, the binary number is: $(011010.010111100001)_2$

Conversion of binary to octal numbers

The following steps are involved in this conversion:

(*i*) Divide the binary number into groups of three bits each.

(*ii*) Separate the integer part of the binary number in groups of three bits starting from the binary point and proceeding to the left.

(*iii*) Separate the fractional part in groups of three bits, starting from the binary point and moving to the right.

(*iv*) Express each groups as octal equivalent according to the conversion Table 7.1

Example 9: Determine the octal equivalent of binary number

Solution:

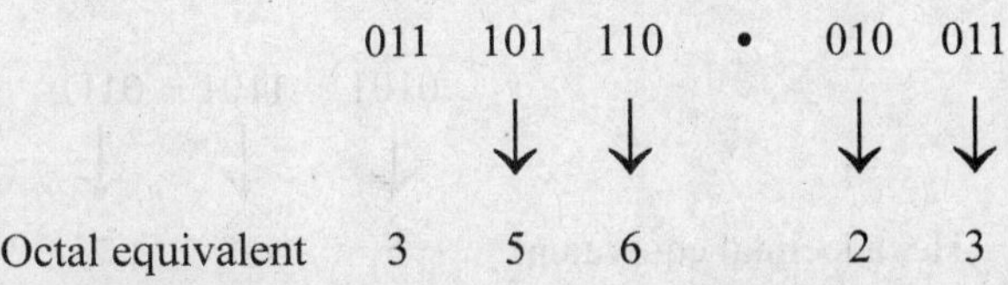

The octal number is: $(356.23)_8$

7.7 HEXADECIMAL NUMBER SYSTEM

Popular microprocessors like INTEL 8085 and 8088 use this system. This system consists of 16 symbols namely ten digits from 0 to 9 and six alphabets A, B, C, D, E, F with base 16.

Relationship between binary, decimal, octal and hexadecimal number systems which can be used for conversion from one system to the other is given in the table below.

TABLE 7.2 *Relationship between different number systems*

Binary	Decimal	Octal	Hexadecimal
0000	0	0	0
0001	1	1	1
0010	2	2	2
0011	3	3	3
0100	4	4	4
0101	5	5	5
0110	6	6	6
0111	7	7	7
1000	8	10	8
1001	9	11	9
1010	10	12	A
1011	11	13	B
1100	12	14	C
1101	13	15	D
1110	14	16	E
1111	15	17	F

Conversion of binary to hexadecimal number system

The following steps are involved in the conversion:

(*i*) Divide the binary number to groups of four bits each.

(*ii*) Separate the integer part of the binary number in groups of four bits each starting from the binary point (equivalent of decimal point) and moving to the left.

(*iii*) Separate the fractional part in groups of four bits, starting from the binary point and moving to the right.

(*iv*) Express each binary group into the hexadecimal equivalent as per the Table 7.2

The following example illustrates

Example 10: Determine the hexadecimal equivalent of $(010111010111)_2$

Solution:

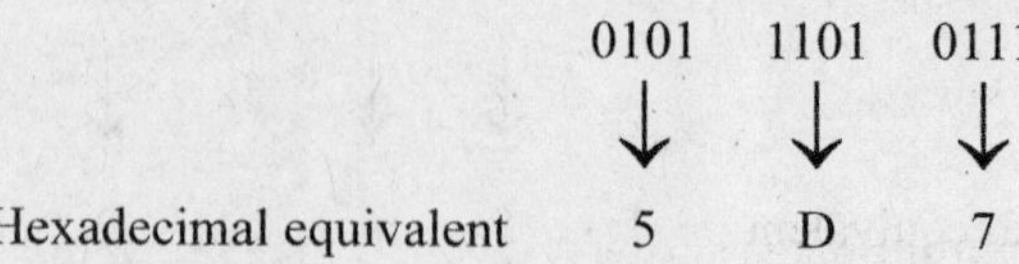

Hexadecimal number = $(5D7)_{16}$

Example 11: Determine the hexadecimal equivalent of the binary number $(10001111.10011010)_2$

Solution:

1000 1111 • 1001 1010

↓ ↓ ↓ ↓

8 F 9 A

Number is hexadecimal system = $(8F.9A)_{16}$

Conversion of hexadecimal to binary system

The following steps are involved in the conversion:

(*i*) Convert each hexadecimal digit in the integer part equivalent as given in Table 7.2.

(*ii*) Similarly convert each hexadecimal digit in the fraction part into binary equivalent.

(*iii*) Combine the integer and fractional parts to represent the binary number.

Example 12: Determine the binary equivalent of $(E3A.51)_{16}$

Solution:

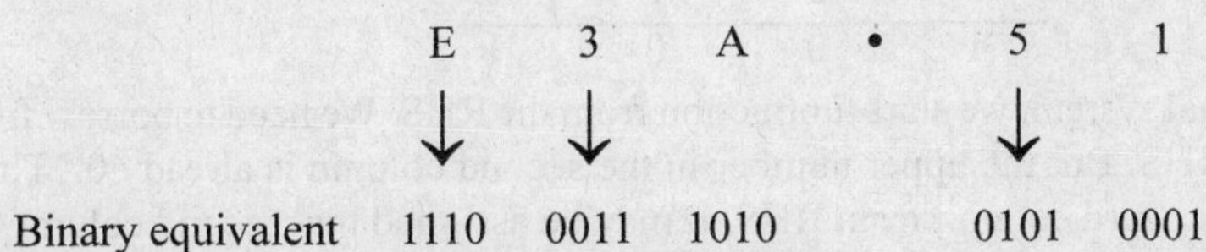

Hexadecimal number = $(111000111010.01010001)_2$

Conversion of hexadecimal number to decimal number

The following steps are involved in the conversion:

(*i*) Multiply extreme right digit before the hexadecimal point (equivalent of decimal point) with 16 raised to the power 0 i.e $16^{\circ} = 1$.

(*ii*) Repeat the above step for all hexadecimal digits increasing the power progressively by 1 i.e. multiplying by 16^1, 16^2, 16^3….etc

(*iii*) Similarly multiply the digits in the fraction part. Start with the first digit after hexadecimal point. Multiply it by 16^{-1}, next digit on the right by 16^{-2} and so on.

(*iv*) Find the sum of all these products

Example 13: Determine the decimal equivalent of $(B2.4C)_{16}$

Solution: $(B \times 16^1) + (2 \times 16^0) + (4 \times 16^{-1}) + (C \times 16^{-2})$

Substituting the decimal equivalents of hexadecimal digits from the Table 7.2, we have

$(11 \times 16^1) + (2 \times 16^0) + (4 \times 16^{-1}) + (12 \times 16^{-2})$

$= 176 + 2 + 0.25 + 0.046875$

$= 178.296875$

BINARY ARITHMETIC

Binary addition. We perform binary addition in the same way as we perform addition with decimal numbers. The following examples will illustrate

Example 14: Compute $(1010)_2 + (1111)_2$

Solution:

$$(1010)_2 + (1111)_2 = (?)_2$$

	1	1	1			→ carry
Augend		1	0	1	0	
Addend	+	1	1	1	1	
	1	1	0	0	1	

We start the addition from the RHS as we do in Decimal system. As soon as the sum becomes two or more, we carry 1 to the next position on the left and continue addition.

Binary Subtraction. This is also performed in the same way as we do in Decimal system. While subtracting, a borrow is required when subtracting 1 from 0. In such a case, when 1 is borrowed from the higher column on LHS, the difference is also 1. The following example will illustrate.

Example 15: Compute $(1100)_2 - (11)_2$

Solution:

$$(1100)_2 - (11)_2 = (?)_2$$

1	1	0	0
– 0	0	1	1
1	0	0	1

As in the decimal system, we start subtraction from the RHS. We need to borrow from the second column from RHS. But the upper number in the second column is already 0. Thus, it needs to borrow from the third column from RHS. It may be assumed that second column borrows from third column. The number in the third column becomes 0. In the seond column, it becomes 2, out of which 1 is borrowed by the number in the first column. The difference in the first column will be (2 – 1), *i.e.*, 1. Now 1 is left in the second column. The difference in the second column will be (1 – 1), *i.e.*, 0. The upper number in the third column is now 0. Therefore the difference in third column will be (0 – 0), *i.e.*, 0.

Binary Multiplication

Binary multiplication is also similar to multiplication in decimal system. The following example will illustrate.

Example 16: Compute $(1101)_2 \times (101)_2$

Solution:

			1	1	0	1
			×	1	0	1
			1	1	0	1
		0	0	0	0	×
	1	1	0	1	×	×
1	0	0	0	0	0	1

Binary Division. Binary division is performed by successive subtraction of the divisor from the dividend. The quotient bits are thus framed. The following rules are obeyed :

$$0 \div 1 = 0$$
$$1 \div 1 = 1$$

Division by 0 has no meaning.

The following example will illustrate.

Example 17: Compute $(110)_2 \div (10)_2$

Solution.

```
                 11    ←Quotient
Divisor → 10 ) 1 1 0   ←Dividend
               1 0
               ---
                 1 0
                 1 0
                 ---
                 0 0   Remainder
```

Thus, $(110)_2 \div (10)_2 = (11)_2$

7.8 OPERATING SYSTEM

An operating system is a layer of software which takes care of technical aspects of a computer's operation. It shields the user of the machine from the low-level details of the machines operation and provides frequently needed facilities. There is no universal definition of what an operating system is. You can think of it as being the software which is already installed on a machine, before you add anything of your own. Normally the operating system has a number of key elements:-

(i) A technical layer of software for driving the hardware of the computer, like disk drives, the keyboard and the screen.

(ii) A file system which provides a way of organising files logically.

(iii) A simple command language which enables users to run their own programs and to manipulate their files in a simple way.

(iv) Some operating systems also provide text editors, compilers, debuggers and a variety of other tools. Since the Operating System (OS) is in charge of a computer, all requests to use its resources and devices need to go through the OS. An OS therefore provides legal entry points into its code for performing basic operations like writing to devices.

Operating systems may be classified by how many tasks they can perform 'simultaneously' and by how many users can be using the system 'simultaneously'. That is: Single-user or multi-user and single-tasking or multi-tasking.

Single-user operating system: We are all familiar with the concept of sitting down at a computer system and writing documents or performing some task. Operating systems such as Windows 95, Windows NT Workstation and Windows 2000 Professional are essentially single user operating systems. They provide you the capability to perform tasks on the computer system such as writing programs and documents, printing and accessing files. In essence, a single-user operating system provides access to the computer system by a single user at a time. If another user needs access to the computer system, he must wait till the current user finishes what he is doing and leaves.

Students in Computer Labs at Colleges or University often experience this. You might also have experienced this at home, where you want to use the computer but some one else is currently using it. You have to wait for them to finish before you can use the computer system.

Multi-user operating system: A multi-user operating system lets more than one user access the computer system at one time. Access to the computer system is normally provided *via* a network, so that users access the computer remotely using a terminal or other computer.

In the early days of large multi-user computers, multiple terminals (keyboards and associated monitors) were provided. These terminals send their commands to the main multi-user computer for processing, and the results were then displayed on the associated terminal monitor screen. Terminals were hand-wired directly to the multi-user computer system.

Today, these terminals are generally personal computers and use a network to send and receive information to the multi-user computer system. Examples of multi-user operating systems are Unix, Linux (A Unix clone) and main frames such as the IBM A5400.

The Operating System for a large multi-user computer system with many terminals is much more complex than a single-user operating system. It must manage and run all user requests, ensuring they do not interfere with each other.

Advantages and Disadvantages of Multi-user Operating Systems. The advantage of having a multi-user operating system is that it lets a number of users share the very expensive hardware resource. This means the cost is divided amongst the users. It also makes better use of the resources. Since the resources are shared, they are more likely to be in use than sitting idle and being unproductive.

One problem with multi-user computer systems is that as more people access it, the performance becomes slower and slower. Another disadvantage is the increased cost of memory devices, as a multi-user operating system requires a lot of disk space and memory. In addition, the actual software for multi-user operating systems tend to cost more than single-user operating systems.

Multi-tasking Operating System. A multi-tasking operating system provides the ability to run more than one Program at a time. For example, a user could be running a word processing package, printing a document, copying files to the floppy disk and backing up selected files to a tape unit. Each of these tasks the user is doing appears to be running at the same time.

A multi-tasking operating system has the advantage of letting the user do more than one task at a time, so this leads to increased productivity. The disadvantage is that more the programs that are run by the user, more the memory that is required.

7.9 COMPUTER PROGRAMMING

Writing software or computer programs, is a lot like writing down the steps it takes to do something. But, if what you need to do is not obvious, programming will challenge you like when you are solving puzzles.

A computer is very dumb. It does exactly what you tell it to do, which is not necessarily what you wanted. Programming will help you to learn the importance of clarity of expression.

These days, most people don't need to know how a computer works. Most people can simply turn on a computer and point the mouse at some little graphical image on the display, double-click the left mouse button, and a computer program starts up (like a Web browser); and, this is all they need to know about their computer.

To learn how to write computer programs, you need to know a little bit about how a computer works. Your job will be to instruct the computer to do things. These lists of instructions that you will write are computer programs, and the stuff that these instructions manipulate are different types of objects.

Basically, computer perform operations on objects. A microprocessor, which is the heart of a computer, is really primitive but very fast. It takes group of binary numbers representing parts of objects and moves them around, adds pairs together, subtracts one from another, compares a pair, etc.

Computers manipulate numbers, symbolic information (think characters), visual things (images), sound (MP3), and sets of instruction (the computer's native language). As an example, computer displays consist of a bunch of coloured points called pixels. A pixel is an object. It has a position which consists of the row and column it is in. Its colour is specified as three numbers—called RGB (Red, Green, Blue) values. So, like pixels are used to compose graphics and images, there are also standard representations for the other things: numbers, characters, sound, and the computer's instructions. At the lowest level, everything is a bunch of ones and zeros (binary number).

Programming Languages (The Microprocessor's Language)

Just like we have many different languages in use throughout the world for us humans to communicate with, there are different languages that we use to communicate with a computer. Computer languages are used to tell the computer what to do, you instruct it.

If you instructed a computer in its native language (machine language), you would have to write instructions in the form of binary numbers. This is very, very hard to do. Although the pioneers of computers did this, no one does this these days.

One step above machine language is assembler language. In assembler, the operations that the microprocessor knows how to do are given names. Address in memory can also be given meaningful names. This is a big step over binary, but still very tedious to do any large software program with. It still has its place for little pieces of software that need to interact directly with the microprocessor and/or those that are executed many times. Here is an example of DEC system–10 assembler language that:

1. adds two numbers together,
2. adds in a third number if it is greater than zero, and
3. stores the results in a third location.

Op. Code	Accumulator	Operand
Move	T_1	Number 1
Add	T_1	Number 2
Skiple		Number 3
Add	T_1	Number 3
Move	T_1	Result

Programming Languages (High-Level Languages)

Most software written today is in high-level languages. There are many and some are quite old. COBOL, FORTRAN, and Lisp were written in the 1950s. Higher-level languages make it easier to describe the pieces of the Program you are creating. They abstract away the specifics of the microprocessor in your computer. Most come with large sets of common stuff you need to do.

High Level Language Programming doesn't require an intimate knowledge of the internal structure of the computer and can be ported over different computer architectures. High level language programs are processed by a program, known as a **Compiler**, which translates the high level language program into an equivalent machine language program. Thus, if a compiler was available for each machine architecture, then a program could be run on any computer without change.

At the moment there are several internationally standardised languages as given in the table below which are popular.

Language	Application Area
COBOL	Business Applications
FORTRAN	Engineering & Scientific Calculations
C	General Purpose Language
Prolog	Artificial Intelligence
Lisp	Artificial Intelligence
C++	Object Oriented version of C
Java	Object Oriented Language widely used on Web

Most popular high-level languages have been standardised by one or the other international body. Thus if Programs are written to conform strictly to the standard then they should execute correctly on any architecture for which there is a standard conforming compiler.

7.10 LOW LEVEL AND HIGH LEVEL LANGUAGES

Till now you have read about the basics of computer programming. Now let's start with low level and high level languages.

Low Level Language:

- It is a programming language that is closer to the machine language rather than the human language.
- The programs written in a low-level programming language are also called Machine codes.
- A low level language interacts with the hardware of the computer.
- Low level language can be divided into machine language and assembly language.
- Machine language is one of the most basic low level language. Codes written in machine language only comprise of 0 and 1.
- Assembly language is a development on machine language. Here instead of 0 and 1 we use English words, symbols.
- Examples of low level languages include FORTRAN, COBOL etc.

High Level Languages:

- Any programming language that enables us to write a program in a user friendly manner is called a high level language.
- A high level language is easy to understand and debug.
- It is more like a human language rather than a machine language.
- It is a complete opposite of low level language.
- High level languages were introduced to us in 1950's.
- Examples of high level languages include Java, Python, PHP

```
# This program prints Hello, world!

print('Hello, world!')
```

The output of the above code is Hello, world! This code is written in python language

```
// Your First Program

class HelloWorld {
    public static void main(String[] args) {
        System.out.println("Hello, World!");
    }
}
```

The output of the above code is Hello, World! This code is written in java language.

The output of the above code is HELLO WORLD! This code is written in QBASIC language.

7.11 SOFTWARE PRODUCTS

MS OFFICE:

- The full form of MS OFFICE is Microsoft Office.
- Microsoft office is a collection of desktop productivity applications that is designed for office or business use.
- It was first announced by Bill Gates on 1 August 1988 and was released on 19 November 1990.

Following are the most used applications that are a part of MS OFFICE:

1. MS WORD
2. MS EXCEL
3. MS POWERPOINT

MS WORD: Microsoft word is a word processor that is extensively used to write and edit documents.MS word offers a variety of features to write and edit a document like Bold, Italic font, Underline, Colour change, merge, align etc.

MS EXCEL: Microsoft excel is a spreadsheet that is extensively used to calculate numbers, maintain records of various organisations.MS excel offers a variety of features to maintain records neatly and efficiently. Some of the features are cell spacing, cell padding, merge cells, font colour, align data etc.

MS POWERPOINT: Microsoft powerpoint is a presentation program created by Robert Gaskins. MS powerpoint is widely used at organisations. Using MS powerpoint one can easily present his/her thoughts to the required person. MS powerpoint offers various features like slideshow, image and voice insertion etc.

CHEMSKETCH: It is a software that is used to create and modify chemical structures. Using chemsketch one can view chemical structures in 2D and 3D for better understanding.

Chemsketch also offers features to rotate the molecule and colour it for a better understanding. Chemsketch can be downloaded from the website of acdlabs.

MATLAB: It is a software that is used for matrix manipulation, plotting of functions and implementation of algorithms. As of now MATLAB has more than 4 million users. Users of MATLAB come from backgrounds of engineering, science and economics.

HYPERCHEM: This software is similar to Chemsketch that we discussed above. Using hyperchem we can model chemical structures.

7.12 INTERNET APPLICATIONS

Before starting the topic Internet Applications we must know the meaning of internet. In most simple terms Internet is a network that connects all the computers of the world. Using internet users can communicate or interact with the world.

Below are the applications of internet that we will discuss in this topic:

1. Communication
2. Online Shopping
3. Online Payments
4. Social Networking
5. Video Conferencing

Communication:

- Gone are the days when letters were used as a means of communication. These days computer users widely use the E-mail service to communicate with each other. The full form of E-mail is Electronic Mail. E-mail can be thought of an online letter that is sent to the E-mail address of another computer user. Every computer user has a unique e-mail address which only belongs to him in this world. All the E-mails are received on the E-mail address of the user. Example of E-mail address:xyz@gmail.com
- E-mails are mostly used for formal conversations.

Online Shopping:

- Using Internet computer users can buy or gather information about a product.
- Online shopping is an convenient way to shop.
- Using internet users get a variety of choices of the product they are looking for.
- Users can do shopping on sites like Amazon,Flipkart etc.

Online payments:

- Shopping using cash is an inconvenient method to shop as many times we do not have the required denomination note.
- This problem has been solved by online payments.
- Using online payments users can transfer funds hassle free directly from their bank account to another person's bank account.
- Online payment can be either done directly from banks website or through payment wallets like Paytm, PhonePe etc.

Social Networking:

- Social networking is the use of internet based social media platforms to connect with friends, family etc.
- Using social media we can connect with people online without the hassle of going out.
- There are many social media platforms available in our country and are very popular among internet users.
- Example of social media platforms are Facebook, Instagram, Whatsapp, Snapchat etc.

Video Conferencing:

- Internet users can now interact/communicate face to face using web camera and microphone.
- Video conferencing enables internet users in distant locations to communicate online.
- Video conferencing is widely used these days. It is used in the field of education so that teacher and students who are living kilometers apart from each other can interact easily.
- A lot of office meetings are held online where video conferencing is used as means of communication. Most used video conferencing applications are Zoom, Microsoft Teams, Skype, Hangout etc.

Evaluate Yourself

Multiple Choice Questions

1. The decimal equivalent of $(11001)_2$ is

(*a*) 25

(*b*) 50

(*c*) 35

(*d*) 15

2. General purpose computer language is

(*a*) Prolog

(*b*) COBOL

(*c*) C

(*d*) FORTRAN

3. Binary representation of the decimal number 141 is
(*a*) 10110001
(*b*) 11110001
(*c*) 10001111
(*d*) 10001101

4. General purpose programs written to solve commonly faced problems are called
(*a*) system software
(*b*) application software
(*c*) utility program
(*d*) none

5. The unit that performs the mathematical functions is
(*a*) ALU
(*b*) CPU
(*c*) RAM
(*d*) ROM

6. Which of the following is a popular social networking platform?
(*a*) Paytm
(*b*) Snapchat
(*c*) Phone Pe
(*d*) Amazon

7. Which of the following is a low-level language?
(*a*) Java
(*b*) Python
(*c*) Fortran
(*d*) Java Script

8. Low Level language is close to ________
(*a*) Human language
(*b*) Machine language
(*c*) Both A & B
(*d*) None of these

9. When were High Level Languages introduced?
(*a*) 1970's
(*b*) 1960's
(*c*) 1950's
(*d*) 1940's

10. Which of the following software is used to create and modify chemical structure?
(*a*) Chemsketch
(*b*) Hyperchem
(*c*) Both A and B
(*d*) Matlab

Short Answer Questions

1. Define a computer. Give the terms used for raw data and the information generated by the computer.

2. Differentiate clearly between analog and digital divices. Give one example of each.

3. What are the components of a computer. Classify the following into input device and output device:

(*i*) keyboard

(*ii*) printer

(*iii*) mouse

(*iv*) monitor

4. (*a*) What do you mean by 'program'?

(*b*) Explain the function of arithmetical logical unit.

5. Give the classification and sub-classification of memory.

6. Give a schematic diagram for the flow of data between the ALU and Memory.

7. Explain the following terms :

(*i*) Hardware

(*ii*) Software

Give examples of three operating systems.

8. What are utility programs ? Explain giving examples.

9. What is binary system used in computers ? Differentiate between byte and bit.

10. What are the advantages and disadvantages of multi-user operating system.

11. Give the application areas of the following programming languages :

(*i*) COBOL

(*ii*) LISP

(*iii*) C^{++}

(*iv*) FORTRAN

12. Find the binary equivalent of $(72)_{10}$

[**Ans.** $(1001000)_2$]

13. Find the decimal equivalent of $(11001)_2$ [**Ans.** 25]

14. Compute $(1010)_2 + (1101)_2$ [**Ans.** $(10111)_2$]

15. Compute $(1111)_2 - (1010)_2$ [**Ans.** $(0101)_2$]

16. Compute $(1111)_2 \times (101)_2$ [**Ans.** $(1001011)_2$]

17. Compute $(10000111)_2 \div (1001)_2$ [**Ans.** $[01111)_2$]

18. Write short note on

(*a*) Low Level language

(*b*) High Level Language

19. Who created MS PowerPoint? Write three features of MS Powerpoint.

20. State three differences between MS word and MS Excel.

21. Write short note on

  (*a*) Video Conferenceing

  (*b*) Online Payments

22. What does chemsketch do?

Answers

Multiple Choice Questions

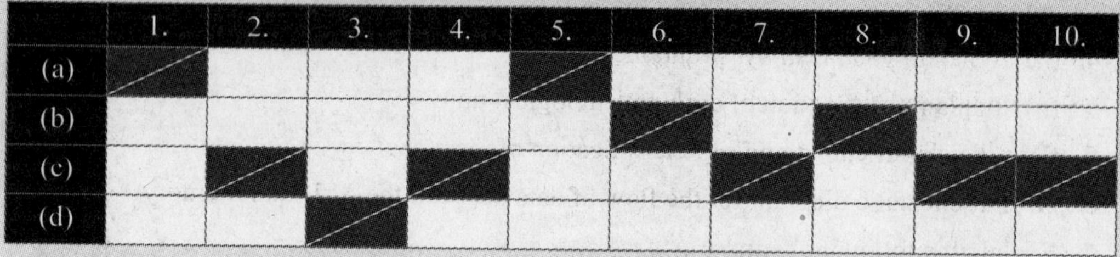

	1.	2.	3.	4.	5.	6.	7.	8.	9.	10.
(a)	■				■					
(b)						■		■		
(c)		■		■			■		■	■
(d)			■							

8

Mathematical Concepts for Chemistry

8.1 LOGARITHMIC RELATIONS

Definition of Logarithm. Logarithm of a number with respect to a given base is the power to which base must be raised to represent the number.

For example

$$1000 = 10^3$$
$$\log_{10}1000 = 3$$
$$\text{In general } N = a^x$$
$$\text{then } \log_a N = x$$

As $a^0 = 1$ It follows that $\log_a 1 = 0$

$a^1 = a$ It follows that $\log_a a = 1$.

Four standard formulae of logarithm. These four formulae are commonly used. We are mentioning them without proof.

$$\log_a mn = \log_a m + \log_a n \quad \text{(Product formula)}$$
$$\log_a \frac{m}{n} = \log_a m - \log_a n \quad \text{(Quotient formula)}$$
$$\log_a m^n = n\log_a m \quad \text{(Power formula)}$$
$$\log_a m = \log_b m \times \log_a b \quad \text{(Base changing formula)}$$

Solved Examples

Example 1: Express $\log_a \frac{x^3\sqrt[5]{y^2}}{\sqrt{z^3}}$ in terms of $\log_a x$, $\log_a y$ and $\log_a z$.

Solution:

$$\log_a \frac{x^3\sqrt[5]{y^2}}{\sqrt{z^3}} = \log_a \frac{x^3 y^{2/5}}{z^{3/2}}$$
$$= \log_a \left(x^3 y^{2/5}\right) - \log_a z^{3/2} \quad \text{(Quotient formula)}$$
$$= \log_a x^3 + \log_a y^{2/5} - \log_a z^{3/2} \quad \text{(Product formula)}$$
$$= 3\log_a x + \frac{2}{5}\log_a y - \frac{3}{2}\log_a z \quad \text{(Power formula)}$$

which is the result.

Example 2: If a, b, c, d are four positive numbers, prove that $\log_b a \times \log_c b \times \log_d c = \log_d a$

Solution:

$$\begin{aligned} \text{L.H.S.} &= \log_b a \times \log_c b \times \log_d c \\ &= \frac{\log_m a}{\log_m b} \times \frac{\log_m b}{\log_m c} \times \frac{\log_m c}{\log_m d} \quad \text{(by Base changing formula)} \\ &= \frac{\log_m a}{\log_m d} \\ &= \log_d a \\ &= \text{R.H.S.} \end{aligned}$$

Hence the result.

Solve These

1. Express in terms of log x, log y and log z.

(i) $\log_a \frac{x^3}{y^2 z^4}$ (ii) $\log_a \frac{\sqrt[n]{x^m}\, y^r}{3\sqrt{z}}$

2. Prove that $\log\frac{a^2}{bc}\ \log\frac{b^2}{ca}\ \log\frac{c^2}{ab} = 0$.

3. Prove that $\log_a mnp = \log_a m + \log_a n + \log_a p$.

4. $\log\frac{42}{55} = \log 2 + \log 3 + \log 7 - \log 11 - \log 5$. Prove it.

Answers

1. (i) $3 \log_a x - 2 \log_a y - 4 \log_a z$

(ii) $\frac{m}{n}\log_a x + r\log_a y - \frac{1}{3}\log_a z$

8.2 TWO SYSTEMS OF LOGARITHM

The two systems of logarithm in common use are:

***(i)* Neperian log or Natural log.** Here the base is e, where $e = 1 + \frac{1}{1!} + \frac{1}{2!} + \frac{1}{3!} + ...$ In all theoretical calculations, we use natural logarithm.

***(ii)* Common logarithm.** Here, the base of the log is 10. In all numerical calculations, we use common log. We can convert natural log into common log as follows.

$$\log_e m = \log_{10} m \times \log_e 10$$

and $$\log e10 = 2.3026 \times \log 1010$$

$$= 2.3026 \times 1 = 2.3026 \qquad \because \log_{10} 10 = 1$$

$\therefore$ $$\log_e m = 2.3026 \log_{10} m$$

Log tables. Log tables are the standard common log tables which are available to us for calculations. There are usually four digit tables and are given at the end of the book. The logarithm of any given number can be read from these tables. The logarithm of a number consists of two parts :

(*i*) Integral part called *Characteristic*

(*ii*) Decimal part called *Mantissa.*

(*i*) Characteristic. It can be zero, positive or negative, we use the following two rules for finding the characteristic.

Rule I : If the given number > 1, its characteristic is +ve. Count the number of digits to the left of the decimal point. Subtract one from this number. This is the characteristic of the log of given number.

For example,
Characteristic of log of 1798.3 is 4 – 1 = 3

Characteristic of log of 28.78 is 2 – 1 = 1

Characteristic of log of 1.923 is 1 – 1 = 0

Rule II : If the given number is less than one, its characteristic is negative. It is put under the bar. Count the number of zeros immediately after the decimal point. Add 1 to this number. It gives us the characteristic of the log of the given number.

For example,

Characteristic of log 0.5828 = – (0 + 1) = $\bar{1}$

Characteristic of log 0.0628 = – (1 + 1) = $\bar{2}$

Characteristic of log 0.0008 = – (3 + 1) = $\bar{4}$

(*ii*) Mantissa. As mentioned above, it is the decimal part of log of a given number. It is always positive, and can be read from the log tables as follows.

(*i*) In the given number, omit the decimal point and zeros in the beginning and at the end.

For example in the log of 0.001175, we have to look up the mantissa of 1175.

(*ii*) Take first two digits *i.e.*, 11 and locate it in the first vertical column of the four figure log table.

(*iii*) Go through the horizontal row beginning with 11 and look up the value under the column headed by the third digit *i.e.* 7. From the log tables, we find this number as 0682.

(*iv*) Continue moving in the same horizontal line and note the number in the small differences column headed by the fourth digit, i.e., 5. This number is 18.

(*v*) Add 18 to 0682, we got 0700. ∴ The mantissa is 0.0700.

Note: If the number consists of a single digit, put zeros at the end of the number to complete four digits. Read mantissa as explained above.

For example log 7 = log 7.000 = 0.8451

Mantissa for 7, 70, 700, 0.7 etc. is the same.

Anti-logarithm: Antilogarithm is the reverse process of logarithm. Thus antilogarithm to logarithm is as division to multiplication.

For example, if log 7 = 0.8451 then Antilog 0.8451 = 7.

Standard Antilog tables are also given at the end of the book for calculations. We follow the rules given below for reading antilog tables.

(*i*) Read the antilog of mantissa only (i.e. of decimal part). Locate the four digits the way we did in reading mantissa from log tables.

(*ii*) If the characteristic is positive say n, the decimal is placed after $(n + 1)$ digits in the value read.

(*iii*) If the characteristic is –ve, say $\bar{n}$, then $(n - 1)$ zeros are placed before the left side of the number read; then decimal point is placed.

For example antilog of $\bar{2}.3478 = 0.02227$

antilog of $1.7192 = 52.38$

antilog of $0 = 1.000$

Use of logarithm. Logarithm is practically very useful in simplifying the complicated calculations. Logarithm means a rule to shorten arithmetic. It was invented by John Napier in 1614.

Following examples will enable the students to use the log tables for that purpose.

Example 3: Find the fifth root of 0.0076.

Solution:

Let $x = (0.0076)^{1/5}$

Taking log on both sides, we get

$$\log x = \frac{1}{5} \log (0.0076)$$

$$= \frac{1}{5}(\bar{3}.8808) \qquad \text{(From log tables)}$$

$$= \frac{1}{5}(\bar{3}.8808 + 2 - 2)$$

$$= \frac{1}{5}(\bar{5}.8808 + 2)$$

$$= \frac{1}{5}(\bar{5} + 2.8808)$$

$$\log x = \bar{1}.5762$$

Taking antilog on both sides, we get

$$x = 0.3769$$

Example 4: Simplify $\dfrac{\mathbf{1.792 \times 77.4}}{\mathbf{(129.7)^{2/3}}}$

Solution:

Let $x = \dfrac{1.792 \times 77.4}{(129.7)^{2/3}}$

Taking log on both sides, we get

$$\log x = \log 1.792 + \log 77.4 - \frac{2}{3} \log (129.7)$$

$$= 0.2534 + 1.8887 - \frac{2}{3}(2.1130)$$

$= 0.2534 + 1.887 - 1.4087$

$= 2.1421 - 1.4087$

$= 0.7334$

$x = \text{Antilog } 0.7334$

$= 1.5413$ which is the result.

Solve These

1. Simplify the following
   (*i*) $(0.0036)^{1/5}$ (*ii*) $(0.056)^{2/3}$
   (*iii*) 10–1/5
2. Simplify the following
   (*i*) (0.05246)1/8 – 2.6055 (*ii*) $\frac{3.142 \times (80.2)^{1/2}}{(9.8)^{1/2}}$
3. Find the antilog of
   (*i*) –2.6674 **[Hint.** $(-2.6674 = \bar{3}.3326)$**]**
   (*ii*) –3.01

Answers

1. (*i*) 0.3245 (*ii*) 0.1464
   (*iii*) 0.6310
2. (*i*) –1.9137 (*ii*) 8.989
3. (*i*) 0.002151 (*ii*) 0.0009772

8.3 CURVE SKETCHING

When a variable point *P*(*x*, *y*) moves under a given set of conditions, then the path traced by *P* is called graph or locus of *P*. The equation which relates the variables *x* and *y* is called the equation of the graph of *P*.

Every point which is on the graph satisfies the given set of conditions and any point satisfying the given set of conditions lies on the graph.

To draw the graph or to sketch the curve we take *y* as the dependent variable and *x* is the independent variable. To draw the graph the following points are followed:

(*i*) Write the given equation equal to *y*.

(*ii*) Now give three, four values of *x* and find the corresponding values of *y*.

(*iii*) Plot these points in the graph by taking two perpendicular lines. Horizontal line as *x*-axis and vertical line as *y*-axis, we get the required curve.

Example 5: Sketch the curve $y = x^2 + 2x - 3$.

Solution: First of all, we get table of values for $y = x^2 + 2x - 3$ as under.

x	–2	–1	0	2	–4
y	–3	–4	–3	5	5

Plot these points in the graph and join it with free hand as illustrated below.

1.

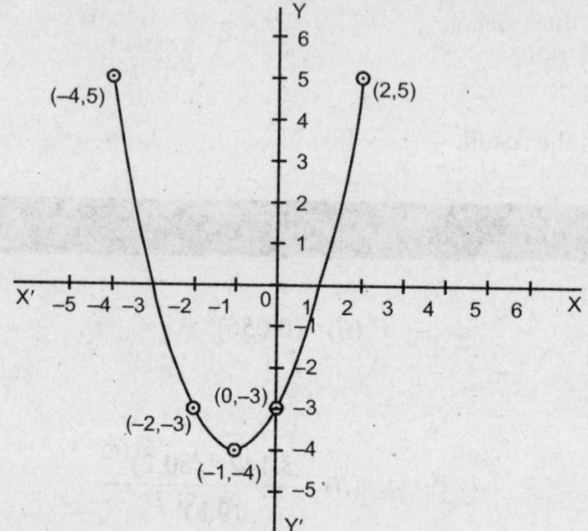

Example 6: Sketch the curve $y = x^2 - 9$.

Solution: First of all we get table of values for $y = x^2 - 9$ by taking x as independent and y as dependent variable. We get the table of values as under.

x	−3	−2	−1	0	1	2	3
y	0	−5	−8	9	−8	−5	0

Plot these points in the graph and join it with free hand as shown below.

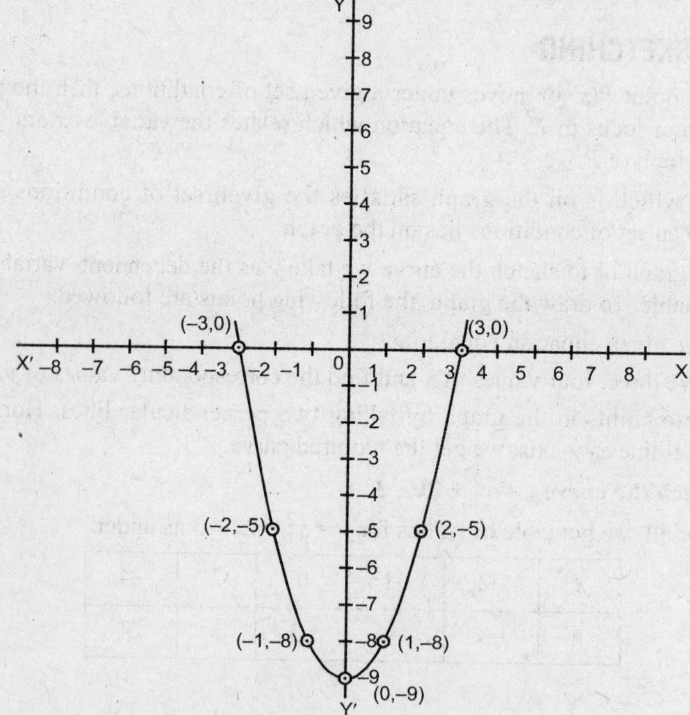

Example 7: Sketch the curve $y = x^3 + 1$.

Solution: First of all we get table of values for $y = x^3 + 1$ by taking x as independent variable and y as dependent variable, we get the table of values as under.

x	–2	–1	0	1	2
y	–7	0	1	2	9

Plot these points in the graph and join it with the free hand as shown below.

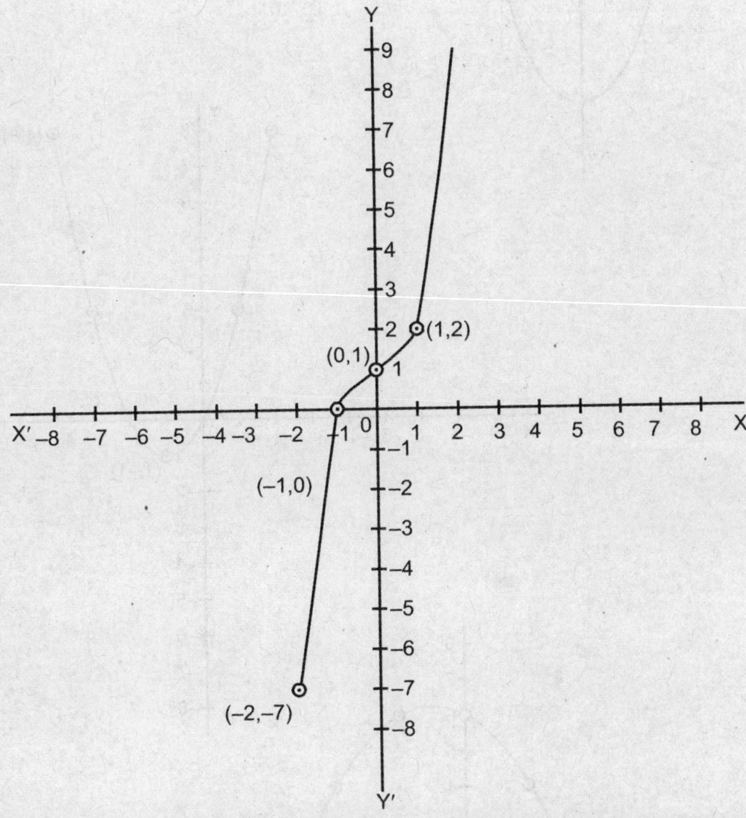

Solve These

1. Sketch the graph $y = x^4 - 1$.
2. Sketch the curve $y = x^2 - 2x$.
3. Sketch the curve $y = x^2 + x + 6$.

Answers

1.

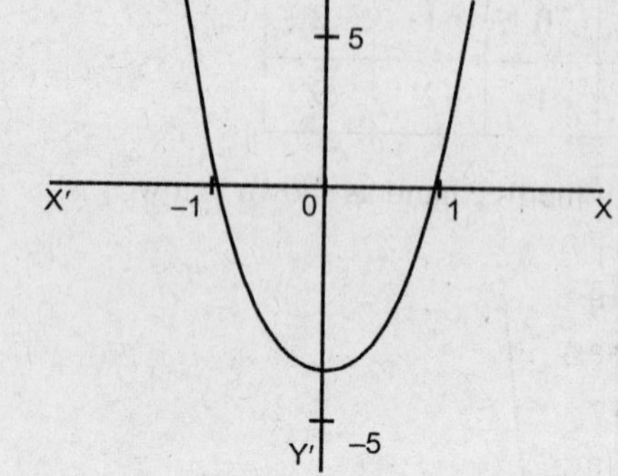

2.

(4,8)

(1,–1)

3.

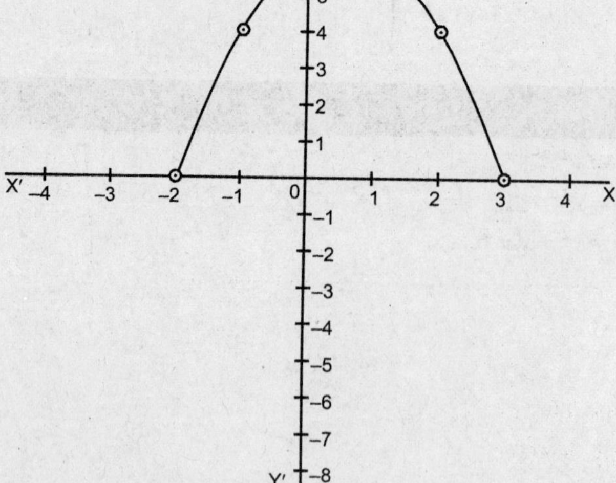

8.4 LINEAR GRAPHS AND CALCULATIONS OF SLOPES

Linear graph. The graph of a linear equation is called the linear graph.

Linear Equation. An equation of the form $ax + by + c = 0$, where a, b, c are constants and x and y are two variables, is called a linear equation of two variables. Every linear equation in x and y represents a straight line. The various cases are discussed below one by one.

(i) The equation $x = a$ represents a straight line parallel to y-axis and at a distance a from it.

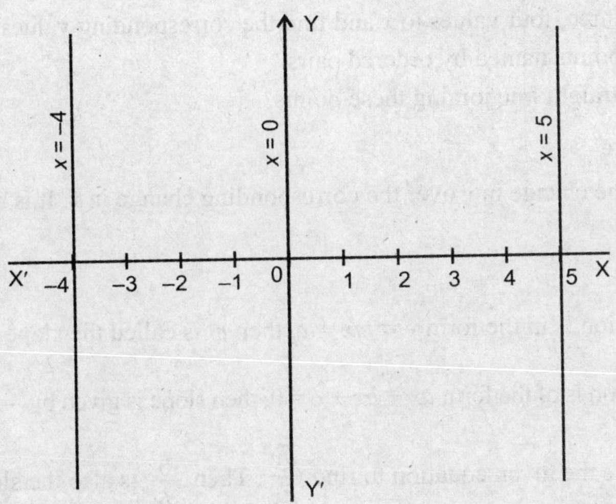

If the line is to the right of y-axis, a is +ve.

If the line is to the left of y-axis, a is –ve.

If the line coincides with y-axis, $a = 0$, the equation of the y-axis is $a = 0$.

The graph of $x = 5$, $x = 0$ and $x = -4$ is shown in the above figure.

(ii) The equation $y = b$ represents a straight line parallel to x-axis and at a distance b from it.

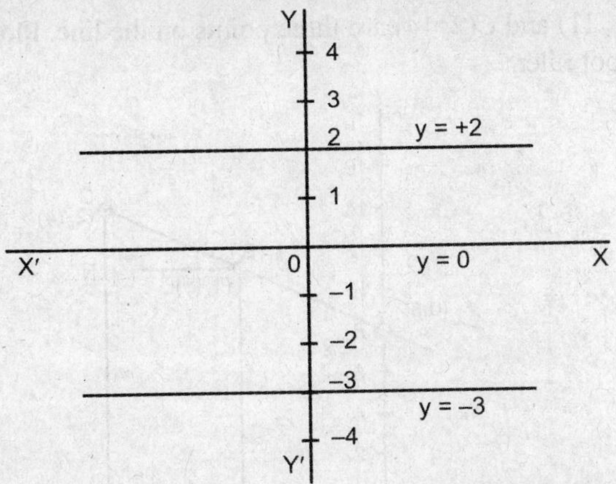

If the line is above x-axis, b is +ve.

If the line is below x-axis, b is –ve.

If the line coincides with x-axis, $b = 0$.

The equation of x-axis is $y = 0$.

The graphs of $y = 2$, $y = 0$ and $y = -3$ are shown in the figure above.

General method to draw the graph of linear equation $ax + bx + c = 0$ and to find the slope of the line.

1. Write the given equation in the form showing one variable in terms of the other variable (generally in the form $y = mx + c$)
2. Now give three, four values to x and find the corresponding values of y.
3. Plot these points named by ordered pairs.
4. Draw the straight line joining these points.

To find slope of line

1. Calculate the change in y over the corresponding change in x. It is the slope of the line

i.e., $\dfrac{\text{Change in } y}{\text{Change in } x}$.

2. If the equation is in the form $y = mx + c$, then m is called the slope of the line.

3. If the equation is of the form $ax + bx + c = 0$, then slope is given by $-\dfrac{\text{Coeff. of } x}{\text{Coeff. of } y} = -\dfrac{a}{b}$.

4. Differentiate the given equation to find $\dfrac{dy}{dx}$. Then $\dfrac{dy}{dx}$ is also the slope of the line.

Example 8: Draw the graph of the function $y = 3x + 8$ and find the slope of the line.

Solution:

The equation of the line is

$$y = 3x + 8.$$

Putting	$x = 0$	we get	$y = 8$
Putting	$x = 1$	we get	$y = 11$
Putting	$x = 2$	we get	$y = 14$

$A(0, 8)$, $B(1, 11)$ and $C(2, 14)$ are three points on the line. Plot these points and join them by a foot ruler.

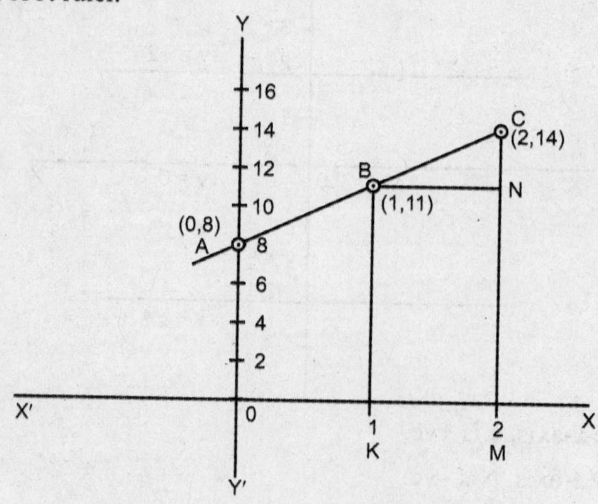

To find the slope draw BK, CM perpendicular to x-axis and BN perpendicular to CM.

The slope is given by $\frac{CN}{BN} = \frac{\text{Change in } y}{\text{Change in } x}$

Now

$$CN = CM - NM = 14 - 11 = 3$$

$$BN = KM = OM - OK = 2 - 1 = 1$$

$$\text{Slope} = \frac{3}{1} = 3.$$ Hence the result.

Solve These

Draw the graphs and find the slopes.

(i) $x + y = 0$

(ii) $2x - y = 3$

(iii) $x - y = 2$

(iv) $4x + y = 3$

Answers

(i)

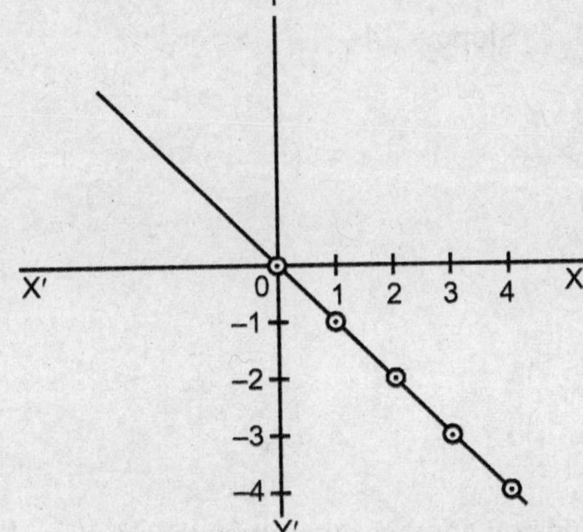

Slope = −1

(ii)

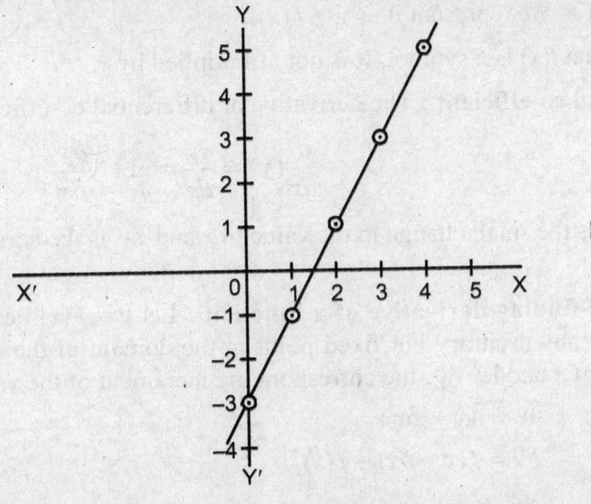

Slope = 2

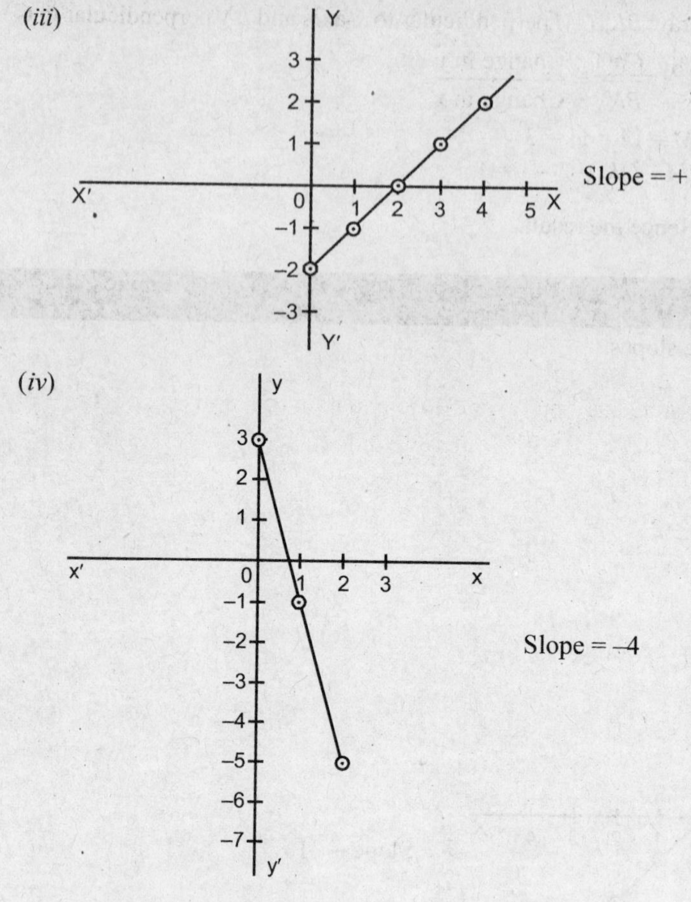

8.5 DIFFERENTIATION

Function. When the value of a quantity y depends on another quantity x, then y is said to be a function of x. We represent it as $y = f(x)$.

Note that $f(x)$ is a symbol. It is not f multiplied by x.

Differential co-efficient : The derivative or differential co-efficient of y w.r.t. x is denoted by

$$\frac{d}{dx}(y) = \frac{dy}{dx} = \underset{\delta x \to 0}{\text{Lt}} \frac{\delta y}{\delta x}$$

where δx is the small change in the value of x and δy is the corresponding small change in the value of y.

Method of finding derivative of a function : Let $y = f(x)$ be a derivable function of x. Let x represent any arbitrary but fixed point in the domain of the function. Let δx be the small increment of x and let δy, the corresponding increment of the value of y.

$$\therefore \quad y + \delta y = f(x + \delta x)$$

$$\Rightarrow \quad \delta y = f(x + \delta x) - f(x)$$

$$\Rightarrow \quad \frac{\delta y}{\delta x} = \frac{f(x+\delta x)-f(x)}{\delta x}$$

By definition

$$f'(x) = \underset{\delta x \to 0}{\text{Lt}} \frac{\delta y}{\delta x} = \underset{\delta x \to 0}{\text{Lt}} \frac{f(x+\delta x)-f(x)}{\delta x}$$

It is worthwhile to note that $\frac{\delta y}{\delta x}$ is the quotient of δy and δx but $\frac{dy}{dx}$ is not the quotient of dy and dx.

Instead, $\frac{dy}{dx}$ is to be interpreted as $\frac{d}{dx}(y)$ i.e., differentiation of y w.r.t. x.

1. Derivative of *kx* w.r.t. *x*

Let $y = kx$ .... (1) where k is any constant.

Let δx be an increment of x and δy, the corresponding increment of y.

$\therefore \quad y + \delta y = k(x + \delta x)$ .... (2)

$$(2)-(1) \Rightarrow = y+\delta y - y = k(x+\delta x)-kx$$

$$\delta y = k\,\delta x$$

$$\Rightarrow = \delta y = k\,\delta x$$

$$\Rightarrow = \frac{\delta y}{\delta x} = k$$

Taking limits $\delta x \to 0$

$$\underset{\delta x \to 0}{\text{Lt}} \frac{\delta y}{\delta x} = \underset{\delta x \to 0}{\text{Lt}}\ k$$

$$\frac{dy}{dx} = \text{k}$$

$$\frac{d}{dx}(kx) = \text{k}$$

2. Derivative of e^x w.r.t. *x*

Let $y = e^x$ .... (1)

Let δx be an increment of x and δy by the corresponding increment of y.

$$y + \delta y = e^{x+\delta x}$$

$$(2)-(1) \Rightarrow \delta y = e^{x+\delta x} - e^x$$

$$\Rightarrow \delta y = e^x.e^{\delta x} - e^x$$

$$\Rightarrow \frac{\delta y}{\delta x} = \frac{e^x \cdot e^{\delta x} - e^x}{\delta x}$$

$$= \frac{e^x(e^{\delta x}-1)}{\delta x}$$

Taking limits $\delta x \to 0$

$$\underset{\delta x \to 0}{\text{Lt}} \frac{\delta y}{\delta x} = \underset{\delta x \to 0}{\text{Lt}} \frac{e^x(e^{\delta x}-1)}{\delta x}$$

$$\frac{dy}{dx} = e^x \log e \qquad \Big| \because \underset{\delta x \to 0}{\text{Lt}} \frac{e^{\delta x}-1}{\delta x} = \log e$$

$$\frac{dy}{dx} = e^x \qquad | \because \log e = 1$$

$$\frac{dy}{dx}(e^x) = e^x$$

3. Derivative of x^n w.r.t. x

Let $y = x^n$ .... (1) where n is any natural number.

Let δx be an increment of x and δy, the corresponding increment of y.

$$y + \delta y = (x + \delta x)^n. \quad ... (2)$$

$$(2)-(1) \Rightarrow \delta y = (x ++ \delta x)^n - x^n$$

$$\Rightarrow \delta y = x^n + {}^nC_1\, x^{n-1}\delta x + {}^nC_2\, x^{n-2}(\delta x)^2 + ... + {}^nC_n\,(\delta x)^n - x^n$$

$$\Rightarrow \delta y = n\,x^{n--1}\delta x ++ \frac{n(n--1)}{\lfloor 2}x^{n--2}(\delta x)^2 ++..... ++ (\delta x)^n$$

$$\Rightarrow \delta y = \delta x\left[nx^{n-1} + \frac{n(n-1)}{\lfloor 2}x^{n-2}\delta x + ... + (\delta x)^{n-1}\right]$$

Dividing both sides by δx

$$\Rightarrow \frac{\delta y}{\delta x} = \frac{\delta x\left[nx^{n-1} + \frac{n(n-1)}{\lfloor 2}x^{n-2}\delta x + ... + (\delta x)^{n-1}\right]}{\delta x}$$

$$\Rightarrow \frac{\delta y}{\delta x} = nx^{n-1} ++ \frac{n(n-1)}{\lfloor 2}x^{n-2}\delta x ++..... ++ (\delta x)^{n-1}$$

$$\Rightarrow \underset{\delta x \to 0}{\text{Lt}} \frac{\delta y}{\delta x} = \underset{\delta x \to 0}{\text{Lt}}\ nx^{n-1} ++ \frac{n(n-1)}{\lfloor 2}x^{n-2}\delta x ++..... ++ (\delta x)^{n-1}$$

$$\frac{\delta y}{\delta x}(x^n) = nx^{n-1}$$

$$\therefore \quad \frac{d}{dx}(x^n) = nx^{n-1}$$

4. Derivative of sin x w.r.t. x

Let $$y = \sin x \quad \text{.... (1)}$$

Let δx be an increment of x and δy, the corresponding increment of y.

$$\therefore \quad y ++ \delta y = \sin(x ++ \delta x) \quad \text{.... (2)}$$

$$(2)-(1) \quad \Rightarrow \quad \delta y = \sin(x ++ \delta x) - \sin x$$

$$= 2\cos\left(x + \frac{1}{2}\delta x\right)\sin\frac{\delta x}{2}$$

$$\frac{\delta y}{\delta x} = \frac{2\cos\left(x+\frac{\delta x}{2}\right)\sin\frac{\delta x}{2}}{\delta x} \quad \left|\ \because \sin C - \sin D = 2\cos\frac{C+D}{2}\sin\frac{C-D}{2}\right.$$

$$\Rightarrow \quad \frac{\delta y}{\delta x} = \frac{\cos\left(x+\frac{\delta x}{2}\right)\sin\frac{\delta x}{2}}{\frac{\delta x}{2}}$$

Taking limits

$$\underset{\delta x \to 0}{\text{Lt}} \frac{\delta y}{\delta x} = \underset{\delta x \to 0}{\text{Lt}} \cos\left(x + \frac{\delta x}{2}\right) \underset{\delta x \to 0}{\text{Lt}} \frac{\sin\frac{\delta x}{2}}{\frac{\delta x}{2}}$$

$$= \cos x \cdot 1 \quad \left|\ \because \underset{x \to 0}{\text{Lt}} \frac{\sin x}{x} = 1\right.$$

$$\therefore \quad \frac{dy}{dx} = \cos x$$

i.e., $$\frac{d}{dx}(\sin x) = \cos x$$

On the lines of sin x we can find the following derivatives:

$$\frac{d}{dx}(\cos x) = -\sin x \quad \frac{d}{dx}(\tan x) = \sec^2 x$$

$$\frac{d}{dx}(\cot x) = -\operatorname{cosec}^2 x \quad \frac{d}{dx}(\sec x) = \sec x \tan x$$

$$\frac{d}{dx}(\text{cosec}) = -\operatorname{cosec} x \cot x \quad \frac{d}{dx}(a^x) = a^x \log a \qquad \text{(on the lines of } e^x\text{)}$$

5. Derivative of log x w.r.t. x

Let $$y = \log x \quad \text{.... (1)}$$

Let δx be the small increment in x, then the corresponding increment in y be δy.

Then $$y + \delta y = \log(x + \delta x) \quad \text{.... (2)}$$

$$(2)-(1) \Rightarrow \quad \delta y = \log(x + \delta x) - \log x$$

$$\Rightarrow \quad \delta y = \log\frac{(x+\delta x)}{x}$$

$$\Rightarrow \quad \frac{\delta y}{\delta x} = \frac{1}{\delta x}\log\left(1+\frac{\delta x}{x}\right)$$

$$\Rightarrow \quad \frac{\delta y}{\delta x} = \frac{1}{x}\cdot\frac{x}{\delta x}\log\left(1+\frac{\delta x}{x}\right)$$

$$\Rightarrow \quad \frac{\delta y}{\delta x} = \frac{1}{x}\cdot\frac{x}{\delta x}\log\left(1+\frac{\delta x}{x}\right)$$

Taking limits

$$\underset{\delta x\to 0}{\mathrm{Lt}}\frac{\delta y}{\delta x} = \underset{\delta x\to 0}{\mathrm{Lt}}\frac{1}{x}\log\left(1+\frac{\delta x}{x}\right)^{\frac{x}{\delta x}}$$

| when $\delta x \to 0$ then $\frac{\delta x}{x} \to 0$

$$\frac{dy}{dx} = \frac{1}{x}\cdot\underset{\delta x\to 0}{\mathrm{Lt}}\log\left(1+\frac{\delta x}{x}\right)^{\frac{x}{\delta x}}$$

| $\Rightarrow \underset{\frac{\delta x}{x}\to 0}{\mathrm{Lt}}\left(1+\frac{\delta x}{x}\right)^{\frac{x}{\delta x}} = e$

$$\Rightarrow \quad \frac{dy}{dx} = \frac{1}{x}\log e$$

$$= \frac{1}{x} \qquad \left|\because \log e = 1\right.$$

$$\Rightarrow \quad \frac{d}{dx}(\log x) = \frac{1}{x}.$$

Derivatives of some functions are given below:

(i) $\frac{d}{dx}(x^7) = 7x^6$ | $\because \frac{d}{x}(x^n) = nx^{n-1}$

(ii) $\frac{d}{dx}\left(\sqrt{x}\right) = \frac{d}{dx}\left(x^{1/2}\right) = \frac{1}{2}x^{1/2-1} = \frac{1}{2}x^{-\frac{1}{2}} = \frac{1}{2}\sqrt{x}$

(iii) $\frac{d}{dx}(x^2+3) = \frac{d}{dx}(x^2) + \frac{d}{dx}(3) = 2x + 0 = 2x$ | $\because \frac{d}{dx}(C) = 0$

(iv) $\frac{d}{dx}(C\cdot v) = C\cdot\frac{d}{dx}(v) = C\cdot\frac{dv}{dx} = C$ | $\because v$ is the function of x

(v) $\frac{d}{dx}(5x^2) = 5\cdot\frac{d}{dx}x^2 = 5\cdot 2x = 10x$

(vi) $\frac{d}{dx}(\sin 7x) = \cos 7x\frac{d}{dx}(7x) = 7\cos 7x$

(vii) $\frac{d}{dx}\left[(2x+3)^5\right] = 5(2x+3)^4\frac{d}{dx}(2x+3) = 5(2x+3)^4\cdot 2 = 10(2x+3)^4$

(viii) $\frac{d}{dx}(\log x^2) = \frac{d}{dx}(2\log x) = 2\frac{d}{dx}\log x = \frac{2}{x}$

(ix) $\frac{d}{dx}(e^{5x}) = e^{5x}\frac{d}{dx}5x = 5e^{5x}$

Solve These

Find the derivative of following functions.

1. (*i*) $x^2 + 2$ (*ii*) $\frac{1}{x^2}$ (*iii*) $x + \frac{1}{x}$

2. (*i*) $x^{3/2}$ (*ii*) $x^{-2} - \frac{x^3}{x^4}$ (*iii*) $(ax + b)^n$

3. (*i*) $a^{\sin x}$ (*ii*) e^{x^2+5} (*iii*) $5x^{2/3}$

4. (*i*) sin 5x (*ii*) tan 5x (*iii*) cos 5x

5. If $x = a(\theta + \sin\theta)$, $y = a(1 - \cos\theta)$

find $\frac{dy}{dx}$. Hint. $\left(\frac{dx}{d\theta} = a(1 + \cos\theta) \quad \frac{dy}{d\theta} = a\sin\theta \quad \frac{dy}{dx} = \frac{\frac{dy}{d\theta}}{\frac{dx}{d\theta}}\right)$

Answers

1. (*i*) 2x (*ii*) $-\frac{2}{x^3}$ (*iii*) $1 - \frac{1}{x^2}$

2. (*i*) $\frac{3}{2}x^{1/2}$ (ii) $-\frac{2}{x^3} + \frac{1}{x^2}$ (*iii*) $an(ax + b)^{n-1}$

3. (*i*) $a^{\sin x}\log a\cos x$ (*ii*) $2x\, e^{x^2+5}$ (*iii*) $5 \times \frac{2}{3}x^{-1/3}$

4. (*i*) 5 cos 5x (ii) 5 $\sec^2 5x$ (*iii*) –5 sin 5x

5. $\tan\frac{\theta}{2}$

Some important results of Trigonometry which are used in differentiation and integration

1. $\sin^2\theta + \cos^2\theta = 1$
2. $\sec^2\theta = 1 + \tan^2\theta$
3. $\operatorname{cosec}^2\theta = 1 + \cot^2\theta$
4. $\sin(A \pm B) = \sin A\cos B \pm \cos A\sin B$ and $\sin 2A = 2\sin A\cos A$
5. $\cos(A \pm B) = \cos A\cos B \mp \sin A\sin B$ and $\cos 2A = \cos^2 A - \sin^2 A$ or $1 - 2\sin^2 A$ or $2\cos^2 A - 1$
6. $\sin C + \sin D = 2\sin\frac{C+D}{2}\cos\frac{C-D}{2}$

7. $\sin C - \sin D = 2\cos\frac{C+D}{2}\sin\frac{C-D}{2}$

8. $\cos C + \cos D = 2\cos\frac{C+D}{2}\cos\frac{C-D}{2}$

9. $\cos C - \cos D = 2\sin\frac{C+D}{2}\sin\frac{D-C}{2}$

10. $1 + \cos A = 2\cos^2\frac{A}{2}$

11. $1 - \cos A = 2\sin^2\frac{A}{2}$

12. $\tan(A + B) = \frac{\tan A + \tan B}{1 - \tan A \tan B}$ and $\tan 2A = \frac{2\tan A}{1 - \tan^2 A}$

θ	0	$\frac{\pi}{6}$	$\frac{\pi}{4}$	$\frac{\pi}{3}$	$\frac{\pi}{2}$
$\sin\theta$	$\sqrt{\frac{0}{4}}$	$\sqrt{\frac{1}{4}} = \frac{1}{2}$	$\sqrt{\frac{2}{4}} = \frac{1}{\sqrt{2}}$	$\sqrt{\frac{3}{4}} = \frac{\sqrt{3}}{2}$	$\sqrt{\frac{4}{4}} = 1$
$\cos\theta$	$\sqrt{\frac{4}{4}} = 1$	$\sqrt{\frac{3}{4}} = \frac{\sqrt{3}}{2}$	$\sqrt{\frac{2}{4}} = \frac{1}{\sqrt{2}}$	$\sqrt{\frac{1}{4}} = \frac{1}{2}$	$\sqrt{\frac{0}{4}} = 0$

$\sin(-\theta) = -\sin\theta$	$\cos(-\theta) = \cos\theta$	$\tan(-\theta) = -\tan\theta$
$\sin(90° + \theta) = \cos\theta$	$\cos(90° + \theta) = -\sin\theta$	$\tan(90° + \theta) = -\cot\theta$
$\sin(90° - \theta) = \cos\theta$	$\cos(90° - \theta) = \sin\theta$	$\tan(90° - \theta) = \cot\theta$
$\sin(180° + \theta) = -\sin\theta$	$\cos(180° + \theta) = -\cos\theta$	$\tan(180° + \theta) = \tan\theta$
$\sin(180° - \theta) = \sin\theta$	$\cos(180° - \theta) = -\cos\theta$	$\tan(180° - \theta) = -\tan\theta$
$\sin(270° + \theta) = -\cos\theta$	$\cos(270° + \theta) = \sin\theta$	$\tan(270° + \theta) = -\cot\theta$
$\sin(270° - \theta) = -\cos\theta$	$\cos(270° - \theta) = -\sin\theta$	$\tan(270° - \theta) = \cot\theta$
$\sin(360° + \theta) = \sin\theta$	$\cos(360° + \theta) = \cos\theta$	$\tan(360° + \theta) = \tan\theta$
$\sin(360° - \theta) = -\sin\theta$	$\cos(360° - \theta) = \cos\theta$	$\tan(360° - \theta) = -\tan\theta$

8.6 MAXIMA AND MINIMA

Neighbourhood of a point. If a is any real number, then any open interval containing a is called a neighbourhood of a. For example (–2, 2), (–2, 1), (–0.6, 0.7) are all neighbourhoods of real number $\frac{1}{2}$.

Local maximum value. A function $f(x)$ is said to have a local maximum value at $x = a$ if $f(a)$ is greatest of all its values of x lying in same neighbourhood of a. A local maximum value is also called a relative maximum or simply a maximum value.

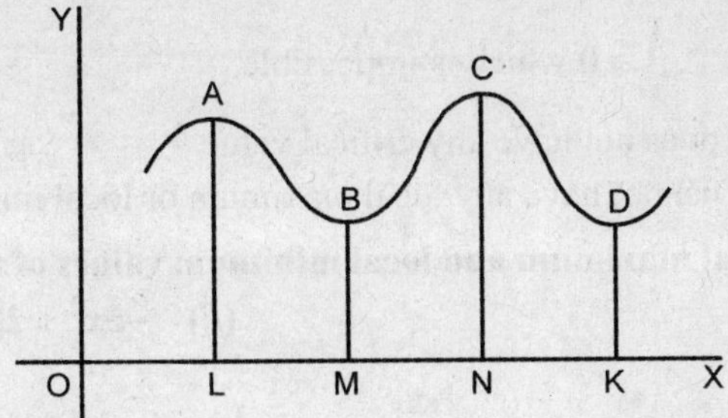

The above figure shows the graph of same function $f(x)$. It is seen that at A and C. The ordinate ceases to increase and if at A, $x = a$, we find that $AL = f(a)$ and it is greater than all other ordinates i.e., values of $f(x)$ in the neighbourhood of A i.e., $x = a$.

Thus from the above definition $f(x)$ is said to have a maximum value of A, C etc.

Local minimum value. A function $f(x)$ is said to have a local minimum value at $x = a$ if $f(a)$ is the smallest of all its values for values of x lying in same neighbourhood of a. A local minimum value is also called a relative minimum value or simply minimum value.

In the above figure B, D are points where the ordinates are less than those in the small neighbourhood of these points and as such we find that $f(x)$ has minimum values at B, D etc.

Local extremum value. A local maximum or a local minimum of a function is called a local extremum value.

Working rule for solving problems

Step I : Differentiate the given function and put $f'(x) = 0$ to get the critical values of $f(x)$.

Step II : Arrange the critical values in the ascending order of magnitude.

Step III : For a particular critical values at $x = a$

(*i*) If $f''(a) < 0 \Rightarrow f(a)$ is a local maximum value.

(*ii*) If $f''(a) > 0 \Rightarrow f(a)$ is a local minimum value.

(*iii*) If $f''(a) = 0 \Rightarrow f'''(a)$ must be studied.

If $f'''(a) \neq 0$ then $(a, f(a))$ is called a point of inflexion. If $f'''(a) = 0$ then $f^{iv}(a)$ is studied at $x = a$.

Example 9: Show that the following functions do not have local maxima or minima.

(*i*) $2x + 7$ **(*ii*) $\log x$**

Solution:

(*i*) Let $f(x) = 2x + 7$

$\therefore$ $f''(x) = 2$

$f''(x) = 0 \Rightarrow 2 = 0$ which is impossible.

$\therefore$ Given function does not have any critical values.

$\therefore$ Given function cannot have any local maximum or minimum value.

(*ii*) Let $f(x) = \log x$

$\therefore$ $f'(x) = \frac{1}{x}$

Put $f'(x) = 0 \quad \Rightarrow \quad \frac{1}{x} = 0$ which is impossible.

$\therefore$ Given function does not have any critical value.

$\therefore$ Given function cannot have any local maximum or local minimum value.

Example 10: Find the local maximum and local minimum values of the following functions.

(i) $2x^2 - 3x + 5$ ***(ii)*** $-5x^2 + 20x + 9$

Solution:

(i) Let $f(x) = 2x^2 - 3x + 5$

$\therefore \quad f'(x) = 4x - 3$ and $f''(x) = 4$

Put $f'(x) = 0 \quad \Rightarrow \quad 4x - 3 = 0 \quad \Rightarrow \quad x = \frac{3}{4}$

The critical value for $f(x)$ is $x = \frac{3}{4}$

$$f''\left(\frac{3}{4}\right) = 4 \text{ which is} > 0$$

$\therefore \quad x = \frac{3}{4}$ is a local minimum and the corresponding local minimum value is

$$f\left(\frac{3}{4}\right) = 2\left(\frac{3}{4}\right)^2 - 3\left(\frac{3}{4}\right) + 5$$

$$= 2\left(\frac{9}{16}\right) - \frac{9}{4} + 5$$

$$= \frac{9}{8} - \frac{9}{4} + 5$$

$$= \frac{31}{8}$$

Local minimum value at $x = \frac{3}{4}$ is $\frac{31}{8}$.

(ii) Let $f(x) = -5x^2 + 20x + 9$

$f'(x) = -10x + 20 \qquad f''(x) = -10$

Put $f'(x) = 0 \quad \Rightarrow \quad -10x + 20 = 0 \quad \Rightarrow \quad x = 2$

The critical value for $f(x)$ is $x = 2$.

Now $f''(x) = -10$ which is < 0

$x = 2$ is a local maximum and the corresponding local maximum value is

$$f(2) = -5\,(2)^2 + 20 \times 2 + 9 = 29$$

$\therefore$ Local maximum value = 29 at $x = 2$.

Example 11: Find the local maxima and local minima, if any, of the function $f(x) = x^3 - 6x^2 + 9x + 15$. Find also the local maximum and local minimum values.

Solution:

We have $f(x) = x^3 - 6x^2 + 9x + 15$

$f'(x) = 3x^2 - 12x + 9 = 3(x^2 - 4x + 3)$

$= 3(x-1)(x-3)$

Put $f'(x) = 0 \Rightarrow 3(x-1)(x-3) = 0$

$\Rightarrow$ $x = 1, 3$

The critical values for $f(x)$ in the ascending order are $x = 1, 3$.

Also $f''(x) = 6x - 12$

Critical value at $x = 1$

$f''(1) = 6(1) - 12 = -6$ which is < 0

$x = 1$ is a local maximum and the corresponding local maximum value is

$$f(1) = (1)^3 - 6(1)^3 + 9(1) + 15 = 19$$

Critical value at $x = 3$

$f''(3) = 6(3) - 12 = 6$ which is > 0

$x = 3$ is a local minimum and the corresponding local minimum value is

$$f(3) = (3)^3 - 6(3)^2 + 9(3) + 15 = 15$$

Hence local maximum value = 19 at $x = 1$

and local minimum value = 15 at $x = 3$.

Solve These

1. Find the critical values for the following functions.

   (*i*) $x^2 - 2x + 4$ (*ii*) $x^3 - 1$

2. Show that the following functions do not have local maxima or minima.

   (*i*) $x + 5$ (*ii*) $\log(x + 4)$

3. Find the points of local maxima and local minima and also find the local maximum and local minimum values of the following functions.

   (*i*) x^2 (*ii*) $2x^3 - 21x^2 + 36x - 20$

Answers

1. (*i*) $x = 1$ (*ii*) $x = 0$

3. (*i*) Local minimum value = 0 at $x = 0$

   (*ii*) Local maximum value = –3 at $x = 1$

   Local minimum value = –128 at $x = 6$

8.7 PARTIAL DIFFERENTIATION

Partial Derivatives of first order : Let $z = f(x, y)$ be a real valued function of two independent variables x and y, then $\underset{\delta x \to 0}{\text{Lt}} \frac{f(x+\delta x, y) - f(x, y)}{\delta x}$, if it exists, is called partial derivative of z (or f) w.r.t. x and it is generally denoted by $\frac{\partial f}{\partial x}$ or $\frac{\partial z}{\partial x}$ or $f\,x(x, y)$ or fx or zx. $\frac{\partial f}{\partial x}$ is read it as curly f by curly x.

Similarly $\underset{\delta x \to 0}{\text{Lt}} \dfrac{f(x, y+\delta y) - f(x, y)}{\delta y}$ if it exists is called partial derivative of z(or f) w.r.t. y and it is generally denoted by $\dfrac{\partial f}{\partial y}$ or $\dfrac{\partial z}{\partial y}$ or $fy(x, y)$ or fy or zy.

From the above definition we conclude that if $\mu = f(x, y)$ is a function of two variables x and y, then the partial derivative of μ w.r.t. x is the differentiation of μ w.r.t. x taking y as constant.

Example 12: Find fx and fy for the function $f(x, y) = y^x$.

Solution:

$$f(x, y) = y^x$$

Differentiating partially w.r.t. x, we get

$$fx = \frac{\partial f}{\partial x} = y^x \log y \qquad \because \frac{d}{dx}(a^x) = a^x \log a$$

Now differentiating partially w.r.t. y we get

$$fy = \frac{\partial f}{\partial y} = xy^{x-1} \qquad \because \frac{d}{dx}(x^n) = nx^{n-1}$$

Example 13: If $f(x, y) = \log(x^2 + y^2)$, find fx and fy.

Solution:

$$f(x, y) = \log(x^2 + y^2)$$

Differentiating partially w.r.t. x we get

$$fx = \frac{\partial f}{\partial x} = \frac{1}{x^2 + y^2} 2x$$

$$= \frac{2x}{x^2 + y^2}$$

Differentiating partially w.r.t. y we get

$$\frac{\partial f}{\partial y} = \frac{1}{x^2 + y^2} \times 2y = \frac{2y}{x^2 + y^2}$$

Solve These

1. Find the first order derivatives of the following functions.

   (*i*) $\dfrac{1}{\sqrt{x^2 + y^2}}$ (*ii*) $ax^2 + 2hxy + by^2$

2. Find $\dfrac{\partial \mu}{\partial x}, \dfrac{\partial \mu}{\partial y}, \dfrac{\partial \mu}{\partial z}$ if it is given that $\mu = x^2y + y^2z + zx$.

ANSWERS

1. (*i*) $\dfrac{-x}{(x^2 + y^2)^{3/2}}; \dfrac{-y}{(x^2 + y^2)^{3/2}}$ (*ii*) $2(ax + hy)$; $2(hx + by)$

2. $\dfrac{\partial \mu}{\partial x} = 2xy + z^2 \quad \dfrac{\partial \mu}{\partial y} = x^2 + 2yz \quad \dfrac{\partial \mu}{\partial z} = y^2 + 2zx$

8.8 PARTIAL DERIVATIVES OF HIGHER ORDER

Since each of the partial derivatives $\frac{\partial f}{\partial x}, \frac{\partial f}{\partial y}$, in general, is a function of x and y, so each of them possesses partial derivatives w.r.t. the independent variables x and y.

(*i*) The partial derivative of $\frac{\partial f}{\partial x}$ w.r.t. x is given by $\frac{\partial}{\partial x}\left(\frac{\partial f}{\partial x}\right) = \frac{\partial^2 f}{\partial x^2}$ or fxx

(*ii*) The partial derivative of $\frac{\partial f}{\partial y}$ w.r.t. y is given by $\frac{\partial}{\partial y}\left(\frac{\partial f}{\partial y}\right) = \frac{\partial^2 f}{\partial y^2} = fyy$

(*iii*) The partial derivative of $\frac{\partial f}{\partial x}$ w.r.t. y is given by $\frac{\partial}{\partial y}\left(\frac{\partial f}{\partial x}\right) = \frac{\partial^2 f}{\partial y \partial x}$ or fyx

(*iv*) The partial derivative of $\frac{\partial f}{\partial y}$ w.r.t. x is given by $\frac{\partial}{\partial x}\left(\frac{\partial f}{\partial y}\right) = \frac{\partial^2 f}{\partial x \partial y}$ or fxy

$\therefore \frac{\partial^2 f}{\partial x^2}, \frac{\partial^2 f}{\partial y^2}, \frac{\partial^2 f}{\partial x \partial y}, \frac{\partial^2 f}{\partial y \partial x}$ are all called second order partial derivatives.

Example 14: Verify that $\frac{\partial^2 f}{\partial x \partial y} = \frac{\partial^2 f}{\partial y \partial x}$ for the function $\log \frac{x^2 + y^2}{xy}$.

Solution.

Let $f(x, y) = \log \frac{x^2 + y^2}{xy} = \log(x^2 + y^2) - \log xy$

$$\frac{\partial f}{\partial x} = \frac{1}{x^2 + y^2} \times 2x - \frac{1}{xy} \times y = \frac{2x}{x^2 + y^2} - \frac{1}{x}$$

$$\frac{\partial^2 f}{\partial y \partial x} = 2x \cdot \frac{-2y}{(x^2 + y^2)^2} - 0 = \frac{-4xy}{(x^2 + y^2)^2} \quad \text{.... } (i)$$

Now $\frac{\partial f}{\partial y} = \frac{1}{x^2 + y^2} \times 2y - \frac{1}{xy} \times x = \frac{2y}{x^2 + y^2} - \frac{1}{y}$

$$\frac{\partial^2 f}{\partial x \partial y} = 2y\left(\frac{-2x}{(x^2 + y^2)^2}\right) - 0 = \frac{-4xy}{(x^2 + y^2)^2} \quad \text{.... } (ii)$$

From (*i*) and (*ii*), we see that

$$\frac{\partial^2 f}{\partial x \partial y} = \frac{\partial^2 f}{\partial y \partial x}.$$ Hence the result.

Example 15: $f = \tan^{-1}\left(\frac{y}{x}\right)$ verify that $\frac{\partial^2 f}{\partial y \partial x} = \frac{\partial^2 f}{\partial x \partial y}$.

Solution:

Given $$f = \tan^{-1}\left(\frac{y}{x}\right) \quad \text{.... }(i)$$

Differentiating (*i*) partially w.r.t. *x*, we get

$$\frac{\partial f}{\partial x} = \frac{1}{1+\left(\frac{y}{x}\right)^2} \times \left(\frac{-y}{x^2}\right) = \frac{-y}{x^2+y^2} \quad \text{.... }(ii)$$

Differentiating (*i*) partially w.r.t. *y*, we get

$$\frac{\partial f}{\partial y} = \frac{1}{1+\left(\frac{y}{x}\right)^2} \cdot \frac{1}{x} = \frac{x}{x^2+y^2} \quad \text{.... }(iii)$$

Differentiating (*ii*) partially w.r.t. *y*, we get

$$\frac{\partial^2 f}{\partial y \partial x} = \frac{\partial}{\partial y}\left(\frac{-y}{x^2+y^2}\right)$$

$$= \frac{(x^2+y^2)(-1)-(-y)(2y)}{(x^2+y^2)^2}$$

$$= \frac{y^2-x^2}{(x^2+y^2)^2} \quad \text{.... }(iv)$$

Differentiating (*iii*) partially w.r.t. *x*, we get

$$\frac{\partial^2 f}{\partial x \partial y} = \frac{\partial}{\partial x}\left(\frac{x}{x^2+y^2}\right) \frac{(x^2+y^2)(1)-x(2x)}{(x^2+y^2)^2}$$

$$= \frac{y^2-x^2}{(x^2+y^2)^2} \quad \text{..... }(v)$$

From (*iv*) and (*v*), we get $\frac{\partial^2 f}{\partial y \partial x} = \frac{\partial^2 f}{\partial x \partial y}$. Hence the result.

Solve These

1. Verify that $\frac{\partial^2 z}{\partial y \partial x} = \frac{\partial^2 z}{\partial x \partial y}$ when $z = \log\frac{x^2+y^2}{xy}$.
2. Verify that $\frac{\partial^2 z}{\partial y \partial x} = \frac{\partial^2 z}{\partial x \partial y}$ when $z = ax^2 + 2hxy + by^2$.

8.9 INTEGRATION

Integration is just the reverse process of differentiation.

The purpose of integration is to find out the function whose differential co-efficient is given.

The symbol $\int dx$ represents the operation of finding integral of the function w.r.t. x. Thus

$$\int \cos x\, dx = \sin x + c \qquad \therefore \frac{d}{dx}(\sin x) = \cos x$$

where c is called the constant of integration.

Important integration formulae

1. $\int x^n dx = \frac{x^{n+1}}{n+1} + C$ provided $n \neq -1$ as $\frac{d}{dx}\left(\frac{x^{n+1}}{n+1}\right) = x^n$

2. $\int 1 dx = x + C$ as $\frac{d}{dx}(x) = 1$

3. $\int (\mu + v) dx = \int \mu dx + \int v dx$

4. $\int \frac{1}{x} dx = \log x + C$ as $\frac{d}{dx}(\log x) \; \frac{1}{x}$

5. $\int a^x dx = \frac{a^x}{\log_e a} + C$ as $\frac{d}{dx}(a^x) = a^x \log a$

6. $\int e^x dx = e^x + C$ as $\frac{d}{dx}(e^x) = e^x$

7. $\int \cos x\, dx = \sin x + C$ as $\frac{d}{dx}(\sin x) = \cos x$

8. $\int \sin x\, dx = -\cos x + C$ as $\frac{d}{dx}(\cos x) = -\sin x$

9. $\int \sec^2 x\, dx = \tan x + C$ as $\frac{d}{dx}(\tan x) = \sec^2 x$

10. $\int \text{cosec}^2 x\, dx = -\cot x + C$ as $\frac{d}{dx}(\cot x) = -\text{cosec}^2 x$

11. $\int \sec x \tan x\, dx = \sec x + C$ as $\frac{d}{dx}(\sec x) = \sec x \tan x$

12. $\int \text{cosec} x \cot x\, dx = -\text{cosec}\, x + C$ as $\frac{d}{dx}(\text{cosec}\, x) = -\text{cosec}\, x \cot x$

8.10 DEFINITE INTEGRAL

A definite integral is one whose lower and upper limits are given.

It is denoted by $\int_a^b f(x)dx$, and is read as integral of $f(x)$ w.r.t. x between $x = a$ and $x = b$.

If $\int f(x)dx = g(x)$

then, $\int_a^b f(x)dx = [g(x)]_a^b = g(b) - g(a)$.

Example 16: Evaluate $\int_1^2 x^2 dx$

Solution:

$$\int_1^2 x^2 dx = \left[\frac{x^3}{3}\right] = \frac{2^3}{3} - \frac{(1)^3}{3} = \frac{8}{3} - \frac{1}{3} = \frac{7}{3}$$

Example 17: $\int_0^{\pi/4} \sin x \cos x \, dx$

Solution: $\int_0^{\pi/4} \sin x \cos x dx = \int_0^{\frac{\pi}{4}} \frac{1}{2}(2\sin x \cos x)dx = \frac{1}{2} \int_0^{\frac{\pi}{4}} \sin 2x \, dx = \frac{1}{2}\left[\frac{-\cos 2x}{2}\right]_0^{\frac{\pi}{4}}$

$$= -\frac{1}{4}[\cos 2x]_0^{\frac{\pi}{4}}$$

$$= -\frac{1}{4}\left[\cos 2\frac{\pi}{4} - \cos 0\right]$$

$$= -\frac{1}{4}\left[\cos\frac{\pi}{2} - \cos 0\right]$$

$$= -\frac{1}{4}[0-1]$$

$$= \frac{1}{4}.$$

Solve These

1. Integrate the following functions w.r.t. x and find within the limits $x = 2$ to $x = 4$.

   (*i*) x^3 (*ii*) $\sqrt{x}$

2. Evaluate the following integrals

   (*i*) $\int_0^{30°} \sin 7x \, dx.$ (*ii*) $\int_{15°}^{30°} \cos(4x-3) \, dx$

3. Evaluate the following integrals

   (*i*) $\int_0^5 \frac{dx}{5^x}$ (*ii*) $\int \sqrt{1+x} dx$

4. Evaluate $\int (1+\cos x)^{1/2} dx$ Hint. $\int (1+\cos x) = 2\cos^2 \frac{x}{2}$

Answers

1. (*i*) 60 (*ii*) 3.448
2. (*i*) 0.2666 (*ii*) $\frac{1}{4}$ [sin 117° – sin 57°]

3. (i) $\frac{1}{5}\log\frac{5}{2}$ (ii) $\frac{2}{3}(1+x)^{3/2}+C$

4. $2\sqrt{2}\cos\frac{x}{2}$

8.11 FACTORIALS

Factorial Notation : The continued product of first n natural numbers i.e., product of all natural numbers beginning with 1 and ending with n is written as $\underline{|n}$ or $n!$ and read as factorial n. Thus

$$n! = 1 \cdot 2 \cdot 3 \cdot .... n$$

or writing the factors in reverse order

$$n! = n(n-1)(n-2) .... 3 \cdot 2 \cdot 1$$

For example $4! = 4 \cdot 3 \cdot 2 \cdot 1 = 24$

$3! = 3 \cdot 2 \cdot 1 = 6$

and $0!$ is always 1 (i.e., $0! = 1$)

A property of factorials :

$$\begin{aligned} 6! &= 6 \cdot 5 \cdot 4 \cdot 3 \cdot 2 \cdot 1 = 6 \cdot 5! \\ &= 6 \cdot 5 \cdot 4! = 6 \cdot 5 \cdot 4 \cdot 3! \\ &= 6 \cdot 5 \cdot 4 \cdot 3 \cdot 2! \end{aligned}$$

Also we know that $n! = n(n-1)(n-2) .... 3 \cdot 2 \cdot 1$

which can be written as $n = n(n-1)!$

or $n = n(n-1)(n-2)!$

or $n = n(n-1)(n-2)(n-3)!$ and so on.

Example 18: Find the value of $\frac{11!}{7!\ 4!}$.

Solution:

$$\frac{11!}{7!\ 4!} = \frac{11 \cdot 10 \cdot 9 \cdot 8 \cdot 7!}{7!\ 4!}$$

$$= \frac{11 \cdot 10 \cdot 9 \cdot 8}{4 \cdot 3 \cdot 2 \cdot 1} = 330$$

Example 19: Prove that $(2n)! = 2^n n! [1 \cdot 3 \cdot 5 \cdot ...... (2n-1)]$.

Solution:

$$\begin{aligned} (2n)! &= 1 \cdot 2 \cdot 3 \cdot 4 \cdot .... (2n-1)\, 2n \\ &= (2 \cdot 4 \cdot 6 \cdot .... 2n)[1 \cdot 3 \cdot 5 \cdot .... (2n-1)] \\ &= 2^n(1 \cdot 2 \cdot 3 \cdot .... n)[1 \cdot 3 \cdot 5 \cdot .... (2n-1)] \\ &= 2^n\ n!\ [1 \cdot 3 \cdot 5 \cdot .... (2n-1)] \end{aligned}$$

Hence the result.

Solve These

1. Find the value of

(a) $\frac{8!}{6!}$ (b) $\frac{10! - 9!}{9!}$

2. Prove that $12! = 2^6 \cdot 6!(1 \cdot 3 \cdot 5 \cdot 7 \cdot 9 \cdot 11)$

3. $\frac{(n+2)!}{n!} = n^2 + 3n + 2$. Prove it.

4. $(2n)!\,(n-1)! = 2(n!)\,(2n-1)!$. Prove it.

Answers

1. (*a*) 56 (*b*) 9

8.12 PERMUTATIONS AND COMBINATIONS

Permutations. The different arrangements that can be made with a given number of things taking some or all of them at a time are called permutations.

The symbol ${}^nP_r$ is used to denote the number of permutations of n things taken r at a time.

To find the value of ${}^nP_r$

The number of permutations of n things taken r at a time is the same as the number of ways in which r places in a row can be filled with n different things.

Suppose that we have n things. The first place can be filled up by any one of these n things. Thus there are n ways of filling up the first place.

When the first place has been filled up by any one of the n ways, we are left with $(n-1)$ things and any one of them can be put in the second place. Therefore the second place can be filled up in $(n-1)$ ways. So by the principle of Association, the number of ways of filling up the first two places is $n(n-1)$.

When the first two places have been filled up in any one of the $n(n-1)$ ways, then we are left with $(n-2)$ things. So the third place can be filled up in $(n-2)$ ways.

By the principle of Association, the number of ways of filling up the first three places is $n(n-1)(n-2)$.

Proceeding in this way, the number of ways in which r places can be filled up is

$$\begin{aligned} {}^nP_r &= n(n-1)(n-2) \,\ldots\ldots\ldots \text{ upto } r \text{ factors} \\ &= n(n-1)(n-2) \,\ldots\ldots\ldots\, (n-(r-1)) \\ &= n(n-1)(n-2) \,\ldots\ldots\ldots\, (n-r+1) \end{aligned}$$

Therefore $\quad {}^nP_r = n(n-1) \,\ldots\ldots\ldots\, (n-r+1)$

For example $\quad {}^7P_4 = 7 \times 6 \times 5 \times 4 = 840$

$${}^5P_4 = 5 \times 4 \times 3 \times 2 = 120$$

When $\quad r = n,\ {}^nP_r = {}^nP_n = n(n-1)(n-2) \,\ldots\ldots\, \text{to } n \text{ factors}$

$$\begin{aligned} &= n(n-1)(n-2) \,\ldots\ldots\, (n-(n-1)) \\ &= n(n-1)(n-2) \,\ldots\ldots\, 1 \\ &= n! \end{aligned}$$

So $\quad {}^nP_n = n!$

Now to prove that $\quad {}^nP_r = n \times {}^{n-1}P_{r-1} = \frac{n!}{(n-r)!}$

$$\begin{aligned} \text{L.H.S.} = {}^nP_r &= n(n-1)(n-2) \,\ldots\ldots\ldots (n-r+1) \\ &= \frac{\{n(n-1)(n-2)\ldots\ldots(n-r+1)\}\{(n-r)(n-r-1)\ldots\ldots3\cdot2\cdot1\}}{(n-r)(n-r-1)\ldots\ldots3\cdot2\cdot1} \end{aligned}$$

$$= \frac{n!}{(n-r)!}$$

$$\text{R.H.S.} = n \times {}^{n-1}P_{r-1}$$

$$= n \times \frac{(n-1)!}{((n-r)\cdot(r-1))!}$$

∵ We have proved above $^{n}P_r = \frac{n!}{(n-r)!}$

$$= \frac{n.(n-1)!}{(n-r)!} = \frac{n!}{(n-r)!}$$

$$\therefore \quad {}^{n}P_r = n \times {}^{n-1}P_{r-1} = \frac{n!}{(n-r)!}$$

Example 20: Find the value of $^{12}P_4$.

Solution:

$$^{12}P_4 = 12 \times 11 \times 10 \times 9$$
$$= 11880$$

Example 41: If $^{n-1}P_3 : {}^{n+1}P_3 = 5 : 12$, find the value of n.

Solution:

$$\frac{^{n-1}P_3}{^{n+1}P_3} = \frac{5}{12}$$

or $$\frac{(n-1)(n-2)(n-3)}{(n+1)\ n(n-1)} = \frac{5}{12}$$

Simplifying $$\frac{(n-2)(n-3)}{(n+1)n} = \frac{5}{12}$$

Cross-multiplying, $12(n^2 - 5n + 6) = 5n\,(n + 1)$

$$\Rightarrow \quad 12n^2 - 60n + 72 = 5n^2 + 5n$$

$$\Rightarrow \quad 7n^2 - 65n + 72 = 0$$

$$\Rightarrow \quad n = \frac{65 \pm \sqrt{(-65)^2 - 4(7)(72)}}{2\times 7}$$

$$= \frac{65 \pm 47}{14} = 8 \quad \text{or} \quad \frac{9}{7}$$

Rejecting $\frac{9}{7}$ as n is a +ve integer.

Hence $n = 8$.

Example 42: In how many ways can the letters of 'Lahore' be arranged ?

Solution:

Total number of letters in the word Lahore = 6

These are all different letters.

∴ Number of arrangements of these letters taken all at a time

$$^{6}P_6 = 6! = 720.$$

Example 21: How many words can be formed from the letters of the word DAUGHTER so that the vowels are never together ?

Solution: Total number of letters in the word DAUGHTER is 8. These 8 letters are all different.

First of all, let us find those arrangements in which vowels are always together.

When the vowels A, E, U are always together, they can be supposed to be put in a bracket and treated as one letter (A, E, U). So the number of letters becomes 6.

i.e., (8 – 3 + 1) (D, G, H, T, R (A, E, U))

These 6 letters can be arranged in $^6P_6$ ways = 6! ways

Now the three letters in the group (A, E, U) can be arranged among themselves in $^3P_3 = 3!$ ways.

∴ Required numbers of such words = 6! 3! = 720 × 6 = 4320.

Now total numbers of arrangements of letters of the word DAUGHTER is 8!

∴ Number of words in which vowels are never together

= Total number of words – Numbers of words in which vowels are always together

= 8! – 4320

= 40320 – 4320 = 36000.

Solve These

1. How many different words can be formed with the letters of the word 'LUCKNOW'?
2. Prove that $^{2n}P_n = 1 \cdot 3 \cdot 5 \cdot .... (2n-1) \cdot 2^n$.
3. Find n if $^{n+3}P_6 : {}^{n+2}P_4 = 14 : 1$.
4. In how many ways 5 books on English and 4 books on Hindi can be placed on a shelf so that the books on the same subject always remain together?
5. How many words can be formed out of the letters of the word 'ORIENTAL' so that no two of the vowels are together?

Answers

1. 7! = 5040
3. 4
4. 5! 4! 2!
5. $4!\ {}^5P_4 = 2880$.

Combinations : The different selections or groups that can be made out of a given number of things taking some or all of them at a time are called combinations.

The symbol ^nC_r is used to denote the number of combinations of n things taken r at a time.

To find the value of ^nC_r

The number of combinations of n things taken r at a time is denoted by ^nC_r. Let these combinations be x. Because each combination contains r things and these r things in any one of the combinations can be arranged among themselves in $r!$ ways (as we know by permutations).

Hence one combination will give rise to $r!$ permutations. So x combinations will give rise to $x \cdot r!$ permutations. But the number of permutation of n things taken r at a time is ${}^nP_r$.

$$ {}^nP_r = x \cdot r! = {}^nC_r \cdot r! $$

$$ {}^nC_r = \frac{{}^nP_r}{r!} = \frac{n!}{(n-r)!\,r!} $$

$$ \therefore \quad {}^nC_r = \frac{n!}{r!(n-r)!} $$

To prove that $\quad {}^nC_r = {}^nC_{n-r}$.

We know that $\quad {}^nC_r = \dfrac{n!}{r!(n-r)!}$

Changing r to $n-r$ we get

$$ {}^nC_{n-r} = \frac{n!}{(n-r)!(n-(n-r))}. $$

$$ = \frac{n!}{(n-r)!\,r!} $$

$\therefore \quad {}^nC_r = {}^nC_{n-r}$. Hence the result.

Example 22: Evaluate ${}^{50}C_{47}$.

Solution:

$$ {}^{50}C_{47} = {}^{50}C_{50-47} = {}^{50}C_3 = \frac{\lfloor 50}{\lfloor 3 \lfloor 47} = \frac{50 \cdot 49 \cdot 48 \cdot \lfloor 47}{\lfloor 3 \cdot \lfloor 47} $$

$$ = \frac{50 \cdot 49 \cdot 48}{3 \cdot 2 \cdot 1} = 19600. $$

Example 23: If ${}^nC_{10} = {}^nC_{15}$, find the value of ${}^{27}C_n$.

Solution:

Given $\quad {}^nC_{10} = {}^nC_{15}$

Either $10 = 15$ or $10 + 15 = n$ $\quad | \because {}^nC_r = {}^nC_{n-r}$

But $10 = 15$ is impossible

So $n = 10 + 15$

$\therefore n = 25$

Now we have to calculate ${}^{27}C_n$ i.e., ${}^{27}C_{25}$ $\quad | \because n = 25$

$$ {}^{27}C_{25} = \frac{27!}{25!\,2!} = \frac{27 \cdot 26 \cdot 25!}{25!\ 2!} $$

$$ = \frac{27 \cdot 26}{2 \cdot 1} = 351 $$

So $\quad {}^{27}C_{25} = 351.$

Example 24: If ${}^{n+1}C_{r+1} : {}^nC_r = 11 : 6$ and ${}^nC_r : {}^{n-1}C_{r-1} = 6 : 3$, find the values of n and r.

Solution:

$$\frac{{}^{n+1}C_{r+1}}{{}^{n}C_{r}} = \frac{11}{6} \text{ and } \frac{{}^{n}C_{r}}{{}^{n-1}C_{r-1}} = \frac{6}{3}$$

$$\Rightarrow \frac{\frac{(n+1)!}{(r+1)!\{(n+1)-(r+1)\}!}}{\frac{n!}{r!(n-r)!}} = \frac{11}{6} \text{ and } \frac{\frac{\lfloor n}{\lfloor r \lfloor n-r}}{\frac{(n-1)!}{(r-1)!\{(n-1)-(r-1)\}!}} = \frac{6}{3} = 2$$

$$\Rightarrow \frac{(n+1)!}{(r+1)!(nr)!} \times \frac{r!(nr)!}{n!} = \frac{11}{6} \text{ and } \frac{\lfloor n}{\lfloor r \lfloor n-r} \times \frac{(r-1)!(n-r)!}{(n-1)!} = 2$$

$$\Rightarrow \frac{(n+1)!\ r!}{(r+1)!\,n!} = \frac{11}{6} \text{ and } \frac{n!\,(r-1)!}{r!\,(n+1)!} = 2$$

$$\Rightarrow \frac{(n+1)n!\ r!}{(r+1)\,r!\,n!} = \frac{11}{6} \text{ and } \frac{n(n-1)!\,(r-1)!}{r(r-1)!\ (n-1)!} = 2$$

$$\Rightarrow \frac{n+1}{r+1} = \frac{11}{6} \text{ and } \frac{n}{r} = 2$$

$\Rightarrow\ 6n + 6 = 11r + 11$ and $n = 2r$

$\Rightarrow\ 6(2r) + 6 = 11r + 11$ $\quad n = 2 \times 5$

$\Rightarrow\ 12r + 6 = 11r + 11$ $\quad = 10$

$r = 5.$

Hence $n = 10,$ $\quad r = 5.$

Solve These

1. Evaluate
   (*i*) ${}^{51}C_{49}$ (*ii*) ${}^{100}C_{96}$
2. If ${}^{n}P_{r} = {}^{n}P_{r+1}$ and ${}^{n}C_{r} = {}^{n}C_{r-1}$, find *n* and *r*.
3. Prove that ${}^{2n}C_{n} = \dfrac{2^n\ 1\cdot 3\cdot 5\cdot......(2n-1)}{n!}$
4. If ${}^{18}C_{r} = {}^{18}C_{r+2}$, evaluate ${}^{r}C_{5}$ and ${}^{11}C_{r}$

Answers

1. (*i*) 1275 (*ii*) 3921225
4. 56, 165

8.13 PROBABILITY

Probability means chance or possibility occurrence of some event.

Experiment. An experiment is defined as a process of well-defined outcomes.

Random experiment. A random experiment is defined as an experiment in which all possible outcomes are known in advance.

For example, If we toss a coin we will either get head or tail.

or, in throwing of a dice there are 6 possibilities 1 or 2 or 3 or 4 or 5 or 6.

Sample space. The sample space of a random experiment is the set of all possible outcomes.

For example,

	Random Experiment	*Sample Experiment*
1.	Throwing of a fair dice	S = {1, 2, 3, 4, 5, 6}
2.	Tossing of a coin	S = {H, T}
3.	Tossing of two coins	S = {HH, HT, TH, TT}
4.	A family of two children	S = {BB, BG, GB, GG]

Event. An event is a subset of sample space. An event is called simple event, if it contains only one sample point. In the experiment of throwing a die, the event A of getting 3 is a simple event.

Equal likely outcomes. The outcomes of a random experiment are called equally likely, if all of these have equal preferences. In the experiment of tossing of a coin, the outcomes head and tail are equally likely.

Exhaustive outcomes. The outcomes of random experiment are called exhaustive if they cover all the possible outcomes of the experiment. In throwing of a dice, the outcomes 1, 2, 3, 4, 5, 6 are exhaustive.

Probability. Suppose in a random experiment there are n equally likely, exhaustive outcomes. Let A be an event and there are m outcomes favourable to the happening of it.

Then the probability $P(A)$ of the happening of the event A is defined as

$$P(A) = \frac{m}{n}$$

or $$P(A) = \frac{\text{Total no. of favourable cases in the happening of } A}{\text{Total no. of equally likely exhaustive cases}}$$

It is clear from the definition that

$$0 \leq m \leq n \Rightarrow 0 \leq \frac{m}{n} \leq 1$$

$$\Rightarrow 0 \leq P(A) \leq 1$$

The number of cases favourable to the non-happening of the event A is $n - m$.

$$\therefore \quad P(\text{not } A) = \frac{n-m}{n}$$

$$= \frac{n}{n} - \frac{m}{n} \quad 1 - \frac{m}{n}$$

$$= 1 - P(A)$$

$$P(\bar{A}) = 1 - P(A) \qquad (\bar{A} = \text{not } A)$$

$$\Rightarrow \quad P(\bar{A}) + P(A) = 1$$

Example 25: What is the probability of getting an even number in the throw of an unbiased dice?

Solution:

In this experiment, there are 6 equally likely possible outcomes, *i.e.*, {1, 2, 3, 4, 5, 6} and let A be the event of getting even number.

$$A = \{2, 4, 6\}$$

Favourable cases $= 3$

Total no. of cases $= 6$

$$P(A) = \frac{3}{6} = \frac{1}{2}$$

Example 26: Find the probability of getting the sum 10 in a single throw of two dice.

Solution:

Here $S = \{(1, 1), (1, 2), (1, 3) \ldots\ldots\ (6, 5), (6, 6)\}$

No. of possible outcomes are $6 \times 6 = 36$

Let A be the event of getting sum 10

$$A = \{(4, 6), (5, 5), (6, 4)\}$$

Favourable cases $= 3$

$$P(A) = \frac{3}{36} \ \frac{1}{12}.$$

Example 27: Find the probability of getting a 'King' or 'Queen' in a single draw from a well shuffled pack of playing cards.

Solution:

Let A be the event of getting a King or a Queen in the draw.

No. of favourable cases for happening of the event A is $4 + 4 = 8$

Total number of cases $= 52$

$$P(A) = \frac{8}{52} = \frac{2}{13}.$$

Solve These

1. Find the probability of getting an odd number in a single throw of a fair dice.
2. Find the probability of getting a number less than 2 in a single throw of a fair dice.
3. In a simultaneous toss of two coins, find the probability of getting exactly two heads.
4. Find the probability of getting no head in a single toss of three coins.
5. A ball is drawn at random from a box containing 4 white, 7 red and 12 black balls. Determine the probability that the ball drawn is red.

Answers

1. $\frac{1}{2}$
2. $\frac{1}{6}$
3. $\frac{1}{4}$
4. $\frac{1}{8}$
5. $\frac{7}{23}$

8.14 MUTUALLY EXCLUSIVE EVENTS

Two events are said to be mutually exclusive events if both cannot occur together with same trial. In experiment of rolling a die, the events $A = \{1, 3\}$ and $B = \{2, 4, 6\}$ are mutually exclusive events. In the same experiment, the events $A = \{1, 3\}$ and $C = \{1, 3, 5, 6\}$ are not mutually exclusive events because if 3 appears on the die it is favourable to both A and C.

Addition Theorem (For mutually exclusive events). If A and B are two mutually exclusive events associated with a random experiment, then

$$P(A \text{ or } B) = P(A) + P(B).$$

Proof: Let n be the total number of exhaustive, equally likely cases of the experiment.

Let m_1 and m_2 be the number of cases favourable to the happening of the events A and B respectively.

$$P(A) = \frac{m_1}{n}$$

and $$P(B) = \frac{m_2}{n}$$

As the events are given to be mutually exclusive, so there will be no sample point common to both events A and B.

$\therefore$ The event A or B can happen in exactly $m_1 + m_2$ ways

$$\therefore \quad P(A \text{ or } B) = \frac{m_1 + m_2}{n} = \frac{m_1}{n} + \frac{m_2}{n} = P(A) + P(B)$$

Hence $$P(A \text{ or } B) = P(A) + P(B)$$

Addition Theorem (For non-mutually events). If A and B are two non-mutually exclusive events associated with a random experiment, then

$$P(A \text{ or } B) = P(A) + P(B) - P(AB)$$

Proof. Let n be the total number of exhaustive and equally likely cases of the experiment.

Let m_1 and m_2 be the number of cases favourable to the happening of the events A and B respectively.

$$\therefore \quad P(A) = \frac{m_1}{n}$$

$$P(B) = \frac{m_2}{n}$$

As the events are given to be non-mutually exclusive, there will be some sample points common to both events A and B.

Let m_3 be the number of common sample points

$$P(AB) = \frac{m_3}{n}$$

These m_3 sample points are also included in the events A and B separately.

Total number of sample points in A or B

$$= m_1 + m_2 - m_3$$

$$P(A \text{ or } B) = \frac{m_1 + m_2 - m_3}{n} = \frac{m_1}{n} + \frac{m_2}{n} - \frac{m_3}{n} = P(A) + P(B) - P(AB)$$

Example 28: The probability that a company executive will travel by bus is $\frac{2}{3}$ and that he will travel by train is $\frac{1}{5}$. Find the probability of his travelling by bus or train.

Solution:

Let A = the event that the company executive travels by bus

$$\therefore \quad P(A) = \frac{2}{3}$$

Let B = the event that the company executive travels by train

$$P(B) = \frac{1}{5}$$

Events in this question are mutually exclusive because either he can travel by bus or by train.

$\therefore$ The probability of his travelling by bus or by train

$$P(A \text{ or } B) = P(A) + P(B) = \frac{2}{3}+\frac{1}{5} = \frac{13}{15}.$$

Example 29: One number is drawn from numbers 1 to 150. Find the probability that it is either divisible by 3 or 5.

Solution:

Here $\quad S = \{1, 2, 3, \ldots\ldots, 149, 150\}$

Let $\quad A$ = the event that number is divisible by 3

$$A = \{3, 6, 9, \ldots\ldots, 147, 150\}$$

$$P(A) = \frac{50}{150}$$

B = The event that the number is divisible by 5

$$B = \{5, 10, 15, \ldots\ldots, 145, 150\}$$

$$P(B) = \frac{30}{150}$$

The events are not mutually exclusive because some points are common to both A and B.

The common points are 15, 30, 45, ..., 150.

So $\quad AB = \{15, 30, 45, \ldots\ldots., 135, 150\}$

$$P(AB) = \frac{10}{150}$$

So by the Addition theorem

$$P(A \text{ or } B) = P(A) + P(B) - P(AB)$$

$$= \frac{50}{150}+\frac{30}{150}-\frac{10}{150} = \frac{70}{150} = \frac{7}{15}$$

Hence the result.

Solve These

1. A bag contains 30 balls numbered from 1 to 30. One ball is drawn at random. Find the probability that number of the ball is a multiple of 5 or 6.

2. Find the probability that a card drawn from a pack of playing cards is either King or Spade.

3. A box contains 4 red balls, 4 green balls and 7 white balls. What is the probability that a ball drawn is either red or white?

Answers

1. $\frac{1}{3}$

2. $\frac{4}{52}+\frac{13}{52}-\frac{1}{52}$

3. $\frac{11}{15}$

Evaluate Yourself

Multiple Choice Questions

1. $\log_a 1$ is equal to
   (*a*) 0 (*b*) 1
   (*c*) ∞ (*d*) 10

2. $\log_a m$ is equal to
   (*a*) $\log_a m \times \log_b a$ (*b*) $\log_b m \times \log_a b$
   (*c*) $\log_m b \times \log_b a$ (*d*) $\log_m b \times \log_a b$

3. Characteristic of log 0.5828 is
   (*a*) –2 (*b*) 1
   (*c*) $\bar{2}$ (*d*) $\bar{1}$

4. For the curve $y = x^3 + 1$, the values of y corresponding to values of x as –2 and 2 are
   (*a*) 7, –9 (*b*) – 3, 6
   (*c*) – 7, 9 (*d*) 6, – 3

5. Slope of the line $2x - y = 3$ is
   (*a*) – 2 (*b*) $-\frac{1}{2}$
   (*c*) $\frac{1}{2}$ (*d*) 2

6. Derivative of $x + \frac{1}{x}$ *w. r. t.* x is
   (*a*) $1-\frac{1}{x^2}$ (*b*) $1+\frac{1}{x^2}$
   (*c*) $-1+\frac{1}{x^2}$ (*d*) $-1-\frac{1}{x^2}$

7. Experssion for sin C – sin D is

(a) $2\cos\frac{C-D}{2}\sin\frac{C+D}{2}$ (b) $2\cos\frac{C+D}{2}\sin\frac{C-D}{2}$

(c) $2\sin\frac{C+D}{2}\sin\frac{C-D}{2}$ (d) $2\cos\frac{C+D}{2}\cos\frac{C-D}{2}$

8. Integration of x^3 w. r. t. x within the limits $x = 2$ to $x = 4$ has the value

(a) 60 (b) 40

(c) 20 (d) 10

9. The value of $\frac{8!}{6!}$ is

(a) 224 (b) 28

(c) 112 (d) 56

10. The number of ways 5 books on English and 4 books on Hindi can be placed on a shelf so that the books on the same subject always remain together, is

(a) 5 ! 4 ! 3 ! (b) 5 ! 4 ! 2 !

(c) 4 ! 3 ! 2 ! (d) 5 ! 3 ! 2 !

Short Answer Questions

1. Simplify the following into a single logarithm

(a) log 5 + log 2 (b) $\log_3 2 + \log_3 2 + \log_3 2$

[Ans. (a) log 10 (b) $\log_3 8$]

2. Convert log(x) to be in the form ln(x)

[Ans. $\log 10(x) = \frac{ln(x)}{ln(10)}$]

3. Rearrange the pH equation, pH = $-\log_{10}[H^+]$ such that $[H^+]$ is the subject of the formula.

[Ans. $[H^+] = 10^{-bh}$]

4. Rearrange the Arrhenius equation

$k = A\ \exp\left(-\frac{E_a}{RT}\right)$ so that Y is the subject of the formula.

[Ans. $T = \frac{E_a}{R\,ln\left(\frac{k}{A}\right)}$]

5. Find the values of x that make $x^2 + 4x - 1 = 0$.

[Ans. $x = -2 \pm \sqrt{5}$]

Show the values of x on the graph

6. Formic acid is a weak acid with a dissociation constant K_a of 1.8×10^{-4}. The K_a rotates the concentration of the H^+ ions denoted $[H^+]$ and the amount of acid dissolved denoted N by the equation

$$K_a = \frac{[H^+]^2}{N\ [H^+]}$$

Given that there is 0.1 mole of formic acid dissolved, calculate the pH of the solution.

[**Ans.** pH = 2.4]

7. Find the lengths *x*, *y*, *z* in the right angled triangles below.

(a)

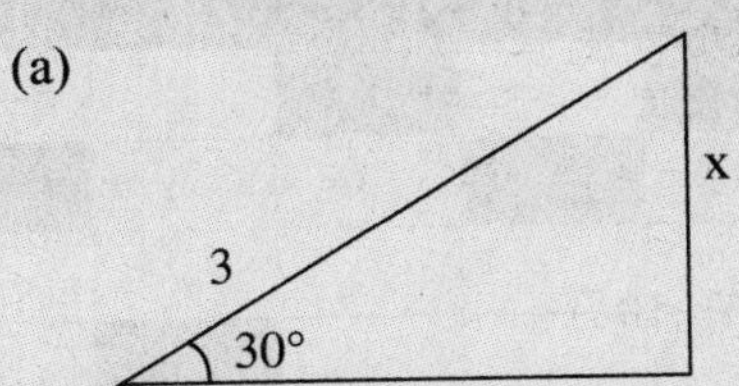

(b)

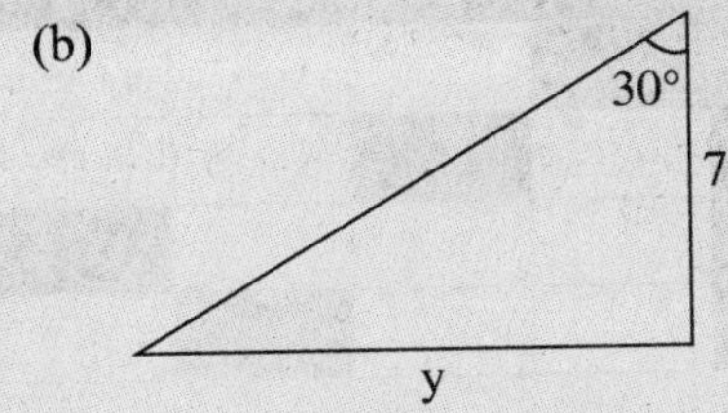

(c)

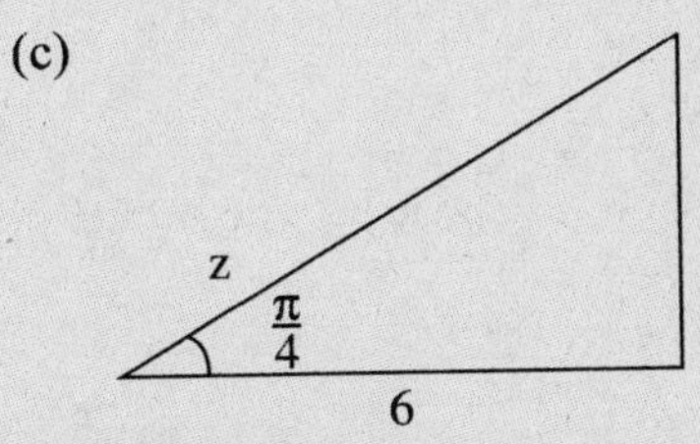

[**Ans.** (a) $\frac{3}{2}$ (b) $\frac{7\sqrt{3}}{3}$ (c) $6\sqrt{2}$]

8. A carbon-carbon bond has a length of 154 pm. If the bond is positioned at an angle of 30° to the surface as shown, what is the projected length of the bond?

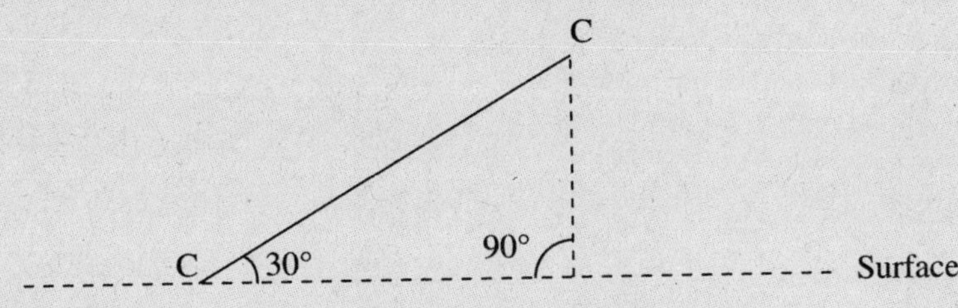

[**Ans.** 133 pm]

9. Coulomb's law states that the magnitude of attractive force ϕ between two charges decays according to the inverse square of the intervening distance r, *i.e.*

$$\phi = \frac{1}{r^2}$$

Suppose we plot a graph of ϕ on the y-axis and r on the x-axis. What is the gradient?

[**Ans.** $\frac{d\phi}{dr^2} = \frac{-2}{r^3}$]

10. In *X*-ray crystallograpgy, the Bragg's equation relates the distance d between successive layers in a crystal, the wavelength of the *X*-rays λ, an integer n and the angle through which the *x*-rays are scattered θ in the equation:

$$\lambda = \frac{2d}{n}\sin\theta$$

What is the rate of change of λ with θ ?

[**Ans.** $\frac{2d}{n}\cos\theta$]

Answers

Multiple Choice Questions

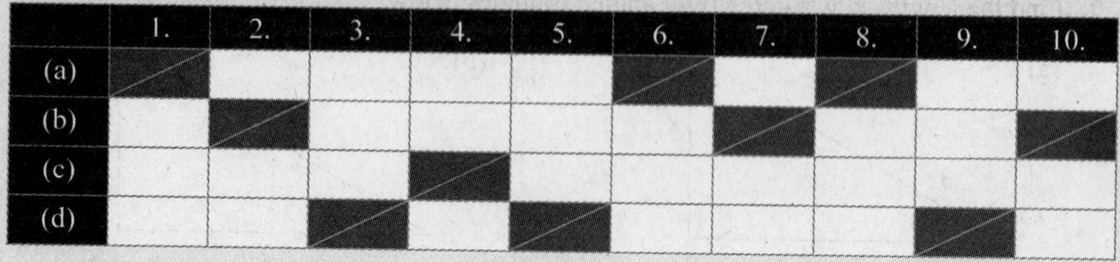

	1.	2.	3.	4.	5.	6.	7.	8.	9.	10.
(a)	■					■		■		
(b)		■					■			■
(c)				■						
(d)			■		■				■	

PAPER II

Quantitative Analysis

1

Water Quality Analysis

1.1 INTRODUCTION

Complexometric titrations are those titrations which involve the reaction of metal ion with a ligand to form a soluble complex. If the titration involves the formation of a chelate, it is known as chelatometric titration.

Schwarzenbach is accepted to be the pioneer in this field of analysis of metal ions. Further contributions to this field were made by other chemists notable among them Flaschka.

There are some essential requirements for a complexation reaction so that it could be used in a titration. These are:

(*i*) The rate of reaction should be fast enough so the titration could be carried out in a reasonable time.

(*ii*) The complex formed should be sufficiently stable.

(*iii*) The complexation reaction should involve minimum steps to ensure a sharp end point.

(*iv*) The complexation reaction should be strictly stoichiometric.

(*v*) No precipitation should occur during titration.

1.2 EDTA

Ethylenediamine tetra acetic acid abbreviated as EDTA is one of the most suitable and widely used chelating ligand.

$$\begin{matrix} HOOC-CH_2 \\ HOOC-CH_2 \end{matrix} \Big> N-CH_2-CH_2-N \Big< \begin{matrix} CH_2COOH \\ CH_2COOH \end{matrix}$$

It is a hexadentate ligand which co-ordinates with a metal ion through two nitrogen atoms and four oxygen atoms as shown below:

$$\begin{matrix} \leftarrow O^- - \overset{\overset{O}{\parallel}}{C}\,CH_2 \\ \leftarrow O^- - \underset{\underset{O}{\parallel}}{C}\,CH_2 \end{matrix} \Big> \overset{\nearrow}{N} - CH_2 - CH_2 - \overset{\nwarrow}{N} \Big< \begin{matrix} CH_2 - \overset{\overset{O}{\parallel}}{C}\,O^- \rightarrow \\ CH_2 - \underset{\underset{O}{\parallel}}{C}\,O^- \rightarrow \end{matrix}$$

EDTA is a versatile complexing agent. It can form complexes with a large no. of metals at proper pH conditions which can be achieved with the help of buffer solutions.

Solutions of EDTA can be used to carry out titrations to estimate the amount of Ca^{2+} and Mg^{2+} present in water in order to determine its hardness. It forms a complex with Mg^{2+} which has the following structure.

EDTA has the following notable properties:

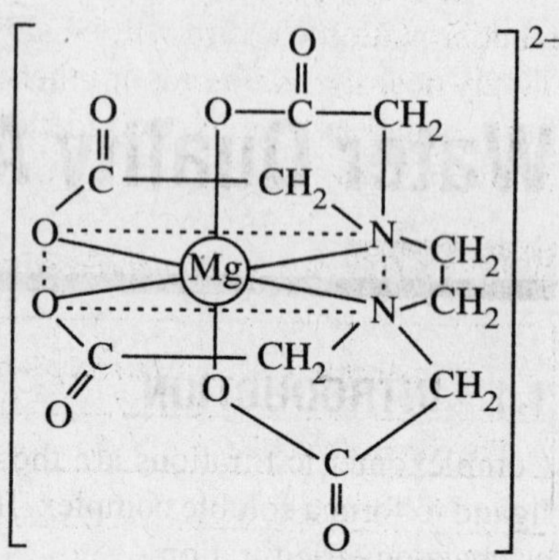

(*i*) It is a white crystalline powder with a limited solubility in water.

(*ii*) It can form complexes instantaneously and stoichiometrically. As such it can be directly employed as a titrant to perform the complexometric titrations for the estimation of calcium, magnesium, zinc and other metals.

(*iii*) The stability of EDTA metal complexes is markedly influenced by pH. It has been found that the complexes of bivalent metals are stable in ammoniacal solution but tend to decompose in acidic medium. However the complexes of trivalent transition metals are stable even in the presence of strong mineral acids.

(*iv*) Almost all such complexes are soluble in water.

It may, however, be pointed out here that these complexometric titrations are highly versatile having their merits as well as demerits. The merit lies in the fact that the same reagent can be used for the estimation of a large number of ions. The demerit is that on account of the high reactivity of the reagent, there is a greater probability of interference by other ions. Consequently, this leads to low selectivity. However, the selectivity can be markedly improved by use of appropriate experimental conditions such as *controlling the pH and by using buffer solutions.*

1.3 STANDARD EDTA SOLUTION

EDTA is usually employed as its sodium salt *viz,* disodium dihydrogen ethylene diamine tetra acetic acid $[Na_2H_2(C_{10}H_{12}O_8N_2).2H_2O]$ commonly known as disodium EDTA or more commonly as EDTA only. The commercially available A.R. reagent may contain some traces of moisture. It is dried at 80°C and the salt can now be directly employed as a primary standard. As such its standard solution can be prepared by weighing the compound directly and dissolving in double distilled water. Generally EDTA solutions having concentrations 0.01 M and 0.05 M are employed. These can be prepared by dissolving respectively 3.72 g and 18.6 g of EDTA (mol. mass = 372) per litre of the solution. 0.01 N and 0.05 N solutions are prepared by dissolving 1.86 g and 9.3 g of EDTA respectively in one litre of the solution.

1.4 INDICATORS IN COMPLEXOMETRIC TITRATION

In general, *metallochromic indicators are employed to determine the end point in* EDTA titrations. These indicators are actually organic dyestuffs which can form intensely coloured complexes with metal ions. Since the indicator colour is markedly influenced by the pH of the solution, therefore, in all EDTA titrations, the pH of the solution must be maintained within some optimum range by the use of buffers. The metallochromic indicator selected, should be one which forms complex with the metal ion to be titrated which is quite stable at the pH employed but sufficiently unstable so as to get readily decomposed by the titrant. The reaction involved at the end point is:

Metal – indicator complex + titrant ⟶ Metal-titrant complex + Indicator.

Thus, the colour observed will actually be the colour of the free indicator.

It may be mentioned here that if the indicator complex is not sufficiently unstable, its reaction with the titrant will be slow. Hence, in such a case the titration should be carried out slowly near the end point, or otherwise, the solution may be warmed to accelerate the reaction. Some commonly employed metallochromic indicators along with their pH range are given below in Table 1.1.

TABLE 1.1 *Some commonly used complexometric indicators.*

Indicator	***Useful pH range***	***Colour at the end point***	***Metal ion for which employed***
Eriochrome black T	8 — 10.5	Sky blue	Mg, Cd, Zn
Murexide	6 – 13	Deep purple	Ca, Cu, Co, Ni
Xylenol orange	1 — 5	Lemon yellow	Pb, Bi, Co, Th

These indicators are briefly described as under:

Eriochrome Black T. It is also known as *Solochrome Black T.* Chemically, it is sodium 1-(1-hydroxy-2 naphthylazo)-6-nitro-2-naphthol-4-sulphonate:

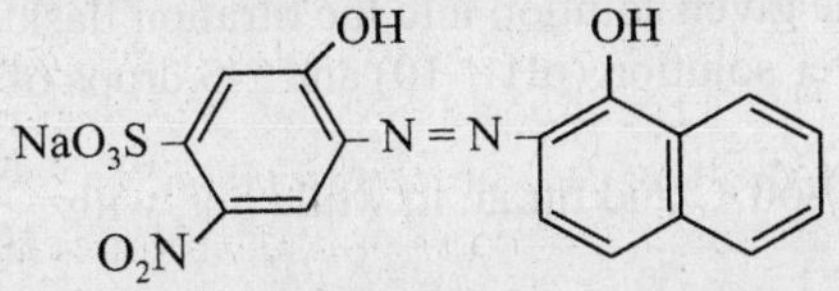

OH OH

NaO_3S – N = N –

O_2N

This indicator has been used successfully in the estimation of Mg, Cd, Hg, Pb, Cu, Zn, Mn, Fe, Al, Co, Ni and Pt metals. It works perfectly in the pH range of 8 – 10.5. Buffer solutions are employed to maintain the pH. The indicator solution is red below pH 5.5, blue in the pH range of 7-11 and yellowish orange above pH 11.5. At the end point in EDTA titrations, the indicator is set free and the colour will change form red to sky blue.

To prepare the indicator solution, dissolve 0.1 g of Eriochrome Black in 7-8 ml of triethylamine and 2-3 ml. of absolute alcohol.

Alternatively, 0.4 per cent solution of Eriochrome Black T in methyl alcohol can also be used.

Murexide. It was probably the first metal indicator to be used in EDTA titrations. It is the ammonium salt of purpuric acid and has the following structure.

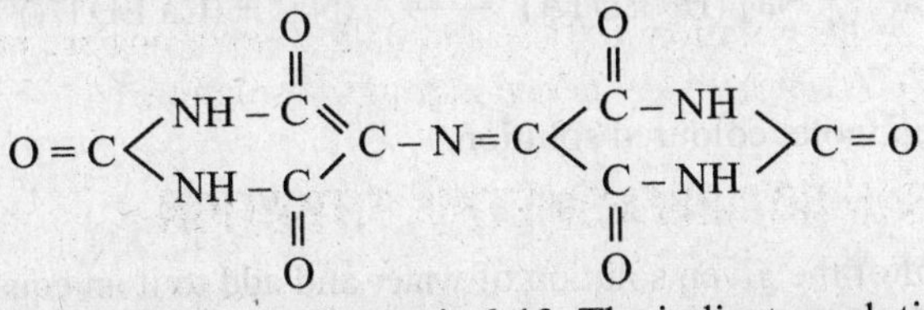

$$O{=}C\begin{matrix} NH-C(=O) \\ NH-C(=O) \end{matrix}\!\!>C-N=C<\!\!\begin{matrix} C(=O)-NH \\ C(=O)-NH \end{matrix}\!\!>C{=}O$$

The optimum pH range of this indicator is 6-13. The indicator solution is red-violet below pH 9; violet in pH range of 9-11 and blue if the pH is above 11. It forms complexes with Ca, Cu, Co, Ni, etc. Freshly prepared saturated (about 1%) aqueous solution of murexide is used as indicator.

Preparation of buffer solution of pH 10

Add 57 ml of concentrated ammonia solution (sp. gravity = 0.88) to 7 g of A.R. of ammonium chloride and then dilute to 100 ml by adding redistilled water.

Experiment 1: Determine the amount of calcium ion present in a given sample of water and estimate its total hardness in ppm.

Requirement: $\frac{M}{100}$ EDTA solution.

Theory. The given solution is first titrated against standard EDTA to determine both Ca^{2+} and Mg^{2+} ions present normally in hard water. It is again titrated, in a strongly alkaline medium (in which Mg gets precipitated as its hydroxide) to determine the Ca^{2+} ions present in it. The difference then leads to the evaluation of Mg^{2+} ions. Different indicators are used for the two titrations.

Procedure. The experiment is carried out in the following steps:

First Titration. *Determination of both Ca^{2+} and Mg^{2+} ions.*

Reactions

$$Ca^{2+} + Na_2\,(H_2\,EDTA) \longrightarrow 2Na^+ + (Ca\,EDTA)^{2-} + 2H^+$$
$$Mg^{2+} + Na_2\,(H_2\,EDTA) \longrightarrow 2Na^+ + (Mg\,EDTA)^{2-} + 2H^+$$

Indicator. Eriochrome Black T.

End point. Red to sky blue coloured solution.

Procedure

1. Pipette out 20 ml of the given solution into the titration flask and add an equal volume of water. Add to it 5 ml. of buffer solution (pH = 10) and 2-3 drops of the indicator.

2. Heat the solution to 50-60°C and titrate it, while hot, with $\frac{M}{100}$ EDTA solution from the burette.

3. Go on adding EDTA until the solution turns purple in colour.

4. Shake the contents of the flask for about half a minute and again add EDTA, drop by drop and with continuous shaking, till the solution turns blue. Repeat titrations to obtain three concordant values.

Observations. Let the values of EDTA solution used = V_1 ml.

Second titration. *Estimation of Ca^{2+} ions.*

Reactions

$$Mg^{2+} + 2NaOH \longrightarrow Mg(OH)_2 \downarrow + 2Na^+$$
$$Ca^{2+} + Na_2\,(H_2\,EDTA) \longrightarrow 2Na^+ + (Ca\,EDTA)^{2-} + 2H^+$$

Indicator. Murexide

End point. Red to deep violet coloured solution.

Procedure

1. Pipette out 20 ml of the given solution of water and add to it an equal amount of distilled water followed by 5 ml. of 2N NaOH solution when Mg^{2+} will get precipitated as $Mg(OH)_2$.

2. Shake the contents of the flask for about two minutes.

3. Rinse down the sides of the flask with a little of distilled water and add 2 ml. of buffer solution. Add 2-3 drops of indicator.

4. Run down the EDTA solution from the burette into the flask till the colour of the solution changes from red to violet. Repeat titrations to obtain three concordant values.

Observations. Let the volume of EDTA solution used = V_2 ml.

General Calculations

(i) To calculate amount of Ca^{2+} and Mg^{2+}

$$1000 \text{ ml. of } 1 \text{ M EDTA} \equiv 1 \text{ mole of EDTA} \equiv 1 \text{ mole of } Ca^{2+}$$

$$\equiv 1 \text{ mole of } Mg^{2+}$$

$$V_1 \text{ ml of } \frac{M}{100} \text{ EDTA} \equiv \frac{V_1}{1000} \times \frac{1}{100} \text{ Mole of EDTA}$$

$$\equiv \frac{V_1}{100000} \text{ mole of EDTA}$$

$$\equiv \frac{V_1}{100000} \text{ mole of } Ca^{2+} \text{ and } Mg^{2+} \text{ ions}$$

Now,

$$V_2 \text{ ml of } \frac{M}{100} \text{ EDTA} = \frac{V_2}{1000} \times \frac{1}{100} \text{ mole of } Ca^{2+}$$

$$= \frac{V_2}{100000} \text{ mole of } Ca^{2+}$$

Thus, 20 ml. of hard water contains $\frac{V_2}{100000}$ moles of Ca^{2+} and

$$\left(\frac{V_1}{100000} - \frac{V_2}{100000}\right) \text{ moles of } Mg^{2+}$$

$$\text{or } \frac{V_1 - V_2}{100000} \text{ moles of } Mg^{2+}$$

$$\text{Strength of } Ca^{2+} \text{ per litre of water} = \frac{V_2}{100000} \times \frac{1000}{20} = \frac{V_2}{2000} \text{ moles}$$

$$= \frac{V_2 \times 40}{2000} \text{ g}$$

Similarly,

$$\text{Strength of } Mg^{2+} \text{ per litre of water} = \frac{(V_1 - V_2) \times 24}{2000}$$

(ii) To calculate total hardness

Total hardness of water is expressed as calcium and magnesium salts taken together and is calculated as milligram of calcium carbonate per litre.

Now 20 ml. of water contains $\frac{V_1}{100000}$ moles of Ca^{2+} or $CaCO_3$ for the purpose of hardness.

(Remember $V_1/10000$ moles of Ca^{2+} and Mg^{2+} can be taken as $V_1/100000$ moles of Ca^{2+})

$$\therefore \ 1000 \text{ ml. of water contains} = \frac{V_1}{2000} \text{ moles of } CaCO_3 = \frac{V_1}{2000} \times 100 \text{ g } CaCO_3$$

$$= \frac{V_1 \times 100 \times 1000}{2000} \text{ mg of } CaCO_3 = 50 \ V_1 \text{ mg of } CaCO_3$$

1 mg per litre means 1 part per million (ppm)

Therefore hardness of water = 50 V_1 mg of $CaCO_3$ = 50 V_1 ppm.

Instructions for Lab. Assistant.

Provide

1. Water containing 0.5 g per litre each of calcium chloride and magnesium chloride
2. $\frac{M}{100}$ EDTA solution (3.72 g EDTA in one litre water)
3. 2N NaOH solution
4. Buffer solution of pH = 10
5. Eriochrome Black T and murexide indicators.

Experiment 2: To determine the chemical oxygen demand (COD) of a sample of water

General

Chemical oxygen demand refers to the quantity of a oxygen required during chemical oxidation of organic matter in water which is formed due to decayed vegetable matter, animal waste and human waste. Results in this investigation can be obtained within a few hours.

Reactions

$$K_2Cr_2O_7 + 4H_2SO_4 \rightarrow K_2SO_4 + Cr_2(So_4)_3 + 4H_2O + 30$$

$$2KI + H_2So_4 \rightarrow K_2So_4 + 2HI] \times 3$$

$$2HI + [O] \rightarrow H_2O + I_2\ ] \times 3$$

$$K_2Cr_2O_7 + 7H_2SO_4 + 6KI \rightarrow 4K_2SO_4 + Cr_2(SO_4)_3 + 7H_2O + 3\,I_2$$

$$I_2 + 2Na_2S_2O_2 \rightarrow Na_2S_4O_6 + 2\,NaI$$

Indicator. Starch solution

End Point. Disappearance of a blue colour

Requirement

1. Polluted water sample
2. Conical flasks fitted with glass stoppers-6
3. Distilled water
4. Water bath
5. K I solution (10%)
6. 4N H_2SO_4
7. 0.2N Na_2SO_3 Solution
8. Starch solution
9. Water blanks

Procedure

1. Take 6 titration flasks fitted with glass stoppers. Label them as sample 1, sample 2, sample 3, Blank 1, Blank 2 and Blank 3.

2. Add 50 mL sample water to each sample flask and 50 mL blank (distilled water) to each blank flask using a pipette.

3. Add 5 mL $K_2Cr_2O_7$ solution to each flask. Shake them thoroughly to mix.

4. Keep all the flasks on a large water bath which can accommodate six flasks. Heat the flasks for about one hour at 100°C and then remove them from the bath and wait for 15 minutes.

5. Perform the titration with each flask by adding 5 ml of K I solution and 10 ml of H_2SO_4 acid solution.

6. Run 0.2N $Na_2S_2O_3$ from the burette into the flask in small lots with shaking until a pale yellow colour is observed in the flask.

7. Now add 1 ml of starch solution. The solution will turn blue. Continue the titration with 0.2N $Na_2S_2O_3$ solution till the blue colour disappears and does not reappear on waiting.

8. Repeat the titration with other sample flasks and blank flasks.

Observations.

Volume of sample water taken each time = 50 ml

Volume of blank (distilled water) taken each time = 50 ml

	With sample water			With blank (distilled water)		
S.No	Initial Burette reading	Final Burette reading	Volume of $Na_2S_2O_3$ consumed	Initial Burette reading	Final Burette reading	Volume of $Na_2S_2O_3$ consumed
1.	-----------	-----------	-----------	-----------	-----------	-----------
2.	-----------	-----------	-----------	-----------	-----------	-----------
3.	-----------	-----------	-----------	-----------	-----------	-----------

Mean volume with sample water = v_1 ml   Mean volume with blank = v_2 ml

Calculations.

Normality of $K_2Cr_2O_7$ solution with blank is obtained by applying normality equal

$$\underset{K_2Cr_2O_7}{N_1 V_1} = \underset{Na_2S_2O_3}{N_2 V_2}$$

Substituting the values,

$$N_1 \times 5 = \frac{N}{50} \times v_2 \text{ or. } N_1 = \frac{N}{50} \times \frac{v_2}{5}$$

Normality of $K_2Cr_2O_7$ solution with the sample solution is given by

$$\underset{K_2Cr_2O_7}{N_1' \times V_1'} = \underset{Na_2S_2O_3}{N_2'' \times V_2''}$$

Substituting the values, we have

$$N_1' \times 5 = \frac{N}{50} \times v_1 \text{ or } N_1' = \frac{N}{50} \times \frac{v_1}{5}$$

N_1 should be greater than N_1'

COD is given by the difference of oxygen is the blank and sample water. Strength/litre of oxygen $= (N_1 - N_1') \times 8$ g/litre from $K_2Cr_2O_7$

$$\text{Strength of oxygen supplied by 5 ml of } K_2Cr_2O_7 = \left(N_1 - N_1'\right) \times 8 \times \frac{5}{1000} \text{ oxygen}$$

This much oxygen was used by 50 mL of the sample water

$$\text{Oxygen used by 1 litre or 1000 mL water} = \left(N_1 - N_1'\right) \times 8 \times \frac{5}{1000} \times \frac{1000}{50}\, g$$

$$= \left(N_1 - N_1'\right) \times \frac{8}{10}\, g$$

$$= \left(N_1 - N_1'\right) \times 0.8\, g$$

$$= \left(N_1 - N_1'\right) \times 0.8 \times 10^3\, mg$$

or $$\text{COD or the sample} = \left(N_1 - N_1'\right) \times 0.8 \times 10^3 \text{ ppm}$$

Provide

1. $K_2Cr_2O_7$ solution (N/20 or 2.45 g/litre)
2. 10% K I solution (10 g dissolved is 100 ml water)
3. $Na_2 S_2O_3$ solution (5 g dissolved in 1 litre, N/50 solution)
4. 4 N H_2SO_4 (conc. H_2SO_4 diluted 10 times)

Caution.

Add a small volume of conc. H_2SO_4 at a time with constant stirring and cooling.

5. Freshly prepared starch solution

Experiment 3: To determine the biological oxygen demand (BOD) of a sample of water.

General

Biological oxygen demand or BOD is the amount of organic compounds in the sewage or polluted water and is measured by the amount or volume of oxygen required by bacteria to metabolise it under aerobic conditions. It gives us an estimate of the organic pollution. We incubate the water sample in dark at 20°C for 5 days. The oxygen consumed by bacteria is estimated titrimetrically used iodine titration

Reactions.

$$K_2CrO_7 + 4H_2SO_4 \rightarrow K_2SO_4 + Cr_2(SO_4)_3 + 4H_2O + 3O$$

$$2KI + H_2SO_4 \rightarrow K_2SO_4 + 2HI] \times 3$$

$$2HI + [O] \rightarrow H_2O + I_2\ ] \times 3$$

$$K_2Cr_2O_7 + 7H_2SO_4 + 6KI \rightarrow 4K_2SO_4 + Cr_2(SO_4)_3 + 7H_2O + 3\,I_2$$

$$I_2 + 2Na_2S_2O_3 \rightarrow Na_2S_4O_6 + 2\text{ Na I}$$

Indicator. Starch solution

End Point. Disappearance of blue colour

Requirement

1. Polluted water sample
2. Conical flasks fitted with glass stoppers
3. Distilled water
4. Water bath
5. KI solution (10 %)
6. 4 N $H_2S_2O_4$
7. 0.2N Na_2SO_3 Solution
8. Starch solution
9. Water blanks
10. Allylthiourea
11. BOD incubator

Procedure

1. Adjust the pH of water sample such that it is neither acidic nor alkaline. This can be done by adding dropwise 1N H_2SO_4 or 1N NaOH using a pH meter. Alternatively, litmus paper may be used to bring about neutrality. Number the flasks 1 to 6.

2. Take 50 ml water sample in a titration flask no. 1, 2 and 3. Add 5 ml $K_2Cr_2O_7$ solution to flask 1, add 5 ml KI solution and 10 ml H_2SO_4 acid solution.

3. Run 0.2N $Na_2S_2O_3$ solution from the burette into the flask in small lots with shaking until a pale yellow colour is observed in the flask

4. Now add 1 ml of starch solution. The solution will turn blue. Continue the titration with 0.2 *N* $Na_2S_2O_3$ solution till the blue colour disappears and does not reappear on waiting. Record the volume of sodium thiosulphate consumed.

5. Repeat the titrations with flask no 2 and 3

6. Add 1 ml allylthiourea to 50 ml sample water each in flask no. 4, 5 and 6. Incubate the flasks at 20°C in dark for 5 days in an incubator

7. Take out the flasks from the incubator one by one. Perform the titration with 0.2N $Na_2S_2O_3$ for each flask as explained above.

8. Record the observations in a table and calculate the result as explained below.

Observations.

Volume of $K_2Cr_2O_7$ solution taken each time = 5 ml

Sample water before incubation Bottle No 1, 2, 3				***Sample water after incubation bottle No 4, 5, 6***		
S.No	***Initial burette reading***	***Final burette reading***	***Volume of $Na_2S_2O_3$ solution used***	***Initial burette reading***	***Final burette reading***	***Volume of $Na_2S_2O_3$ solution used***
1.	------------	------------	------------	------------	------------	------------
2.	------------	------------	------------	------------	------------	------------
3.	------------	------------	------------	------------	------------	------------

Mean volume of $Na_2S_2O_3 = v_1$ ml Used before incubation

Mean volume of $Na_2S_2O_3 = v_2$ ml used after incubation

Calculations.

Normality of $K_2Cr_2O_7$ solution with sample water before incubation can be obtained by the normality equation

$$N_1 V_1 = N_2 V_2$$
$$(K_2Cr_2O_7) \quad (Na_2S_2O_3)$$

Substituting the values, we have

$$N_1 \times 5 = \frac{N}{50} \times v_1 \text{ or } N_1 = \frac{N}{50} \times \frac{v_1}{5}$$

Normality of $K_2Cr_2O_7$ solution with the sample water after incubation is given by using normality equation

$$N_1' \times V_1' = N_2'' \times V_2''$$
$$(K_2Cr_2O_7) \quad (Na_2S_2O_3)$$

Substituting the values, we have

$$N_1' \times 5 = \frac{N}{50} \times v_2 \text{ or } N_1' = \frac{N}{50} \times \frac{v_2}{5}$$

$N_1 > N_1'$. The difference is the two normalities corresponds to biological oxygen demand BOD.

Strength/litre of oxygen supported by $K_2Cr_2O_7 = (N_1 - N_1') \times 8$ g/litre

Strength of oxygen supplied by 5 ml $K_2Cr_2O_7 = (N_1 - N_1') \times 8 \times \frac{5}{1000} g = \frac{(N_1 - N_1')}{25} g$

This much oxygen was used by 50 ml of sample water.

Oxygen used by 1 litre of sample water $= \frac{(N_1 - N_1')}{25} \times \frac{1000}{50} g = (N_1 - N_1') \times \frac{4}{5} g$

Or BOD $= (N_1 - N_1') \times \frac{4}{5}$ g or $(N_1 - N_1') \times \frac{4}{5} \times 10^3$ mg/litre $= (N_1 - N_1') \times \frac{4}{5} \times 10^3$ ppm

Viva-Voice Questions with Answers

Q.1. What do you mean by the term 'ligand' ?

Ans. It is an atom, molecule or ion capable of donating one or more pairs of electrons to the central metal ion.

Q.2. What is a complex ion ?

Ans. A complex ion is a cationic or an anionic species in which a central metal cation is linked to a number of ligands.

Q.3. What are complexometric titrations ?

Ans. Titrations which involve the formation of soluble, undissociated, stoichiometric complex at the equivalence point are called complexometric titrations.

Q.4. What does EDTA stand for and what is its structure ?

Ans. Ethylenediaminetetraacetic acid.

$$\begin{matrix} HOOCH_2C \\ HOOCH_2C \end{matrix} \rangle N - CH_2 - CH_2 - N \langle \begin{matrix} CH_2COOH \\ CH_2COOH \end{matrix}$$

Q.5. Name the most commonly employed indicator in EDTA titration.

Ans. Eriochrome Black T.

Q.6. What is a buffer solution ?

Ans. A solution which can resist the change in its pH on addition of small amount of an acid or a base is called a buffer solution.

Q.7. What are chelating ligands ?

Ans. Polydentate ligands whose structures permit the linkage of two or more donor sites to the same metal ion simultaneously, thereby resulting in formation of a closed ring structure, are called chelating ligands.

Q.8. What do you mean by 'hard water' ?

Ans. Water which does not easily form lather with soap is called hard water.

Q.9. What is the cause of hardness of water?

Ans. It is due to the presence of bicarbonates, chlorides and sulphates of calcium and magnesium in water.

Q.10. What type of ligand is EDTA ?

Ans. It is hexadentate ligand.

Q.11. What is the full form of BOD?

Ans. Biological oxygen demand.

Q.12. What is the full form of COD?

Ans. Chemical oxygen demand.

Q.13. What is the utility of the terms BOD and COD?

Ans. These terms are used in the context of investigating the pollution caused by organic substances in water.

Q.14. Which is greater out of BOD and COD?

Ans. COD is normally higher because more organic compounds can be chemically oxidized than biologically oxidesed.

2

Estimation of Metal Ions

2.1 POTASSIUM DICHROMATE TIRATIONS

Potassium dichromate is a strong oxidising agent in acidic medium and it is used for estimation of many reducing salts, especially ferrous salts.

$$K_2Cr_2O_7 + 4H_2SO_4 \longrightarrow K_2SO_4 + Cr_2(SO_4)_3 + 4H_2O + 3(O)$$

$$Cr_2O_7^{2-} + 14H^+ + 6e^- \longrightarrow 2Cr^{+3} + 7H_2O$$

Unlike potassium permanganate solution, potassium dichromate is available in absolutely pure form and solution of potassium dichromate are very stable and can be stored indefinitely without any change. Moreover, $KMnO_4$ cannot be used with chlorides because it may be used up in oxidising HCl. $K_2Cr_2O_7$ is however, free from this disadvantage and may be used in the presence of HCl or its salts.

2.2 INDICATOR AND END POINT IN POTASSIUM DICHROMATE TITRATIONS

Unlike $KMnO_4$ it does not act as self-indicator, there being no sharp changes in colour during the process of titrations. Moreover, the final product possesses a green colour due to Cr^{3+} ions.

Two kinds of indicators are used in potassium dichromate titrations:

1. *External Indicator*
2. *Internal Indicator*

1. External Indicator

About 1% solution of pure potassium ferricyanide is used as an external indicator. This may be prepared as: Take a crystal of pot. ferricyanide in a clean test tube and wash the crystal twice with a few ml of distilled water to remove any pot. ferrocyanide adhering on the surface. Reject washings. Then, dissolve the crystal in about 2 ml of distilled water.

Use of External Indicator

Place a series of small drops of freshly prepared indicator solution on a dry white tile by means of a thin glass rod. To 20 ml of the solution to be titrated, add half a test tube of dil. H_2SO_4. Run in dichromate solution from the burette in 1 ml lots and after every addition shake the reaction mixture and take out a drop of the reaction mixture from the conical flask with the help of a thin clean glass rod, mix it with one of the drops of ferricyanide on the test-plate (see Fig. 2.1). If a blue colour is produced, it shows the presence of ferrous ions in the solution.

$$3Fe^{2+} + 2[Fe(CN)_6]^{3-} \longrightarrow \underset{\text{Blue complex}}{Fe_3[Fe(CN)_6]_2 \downarrow}$$

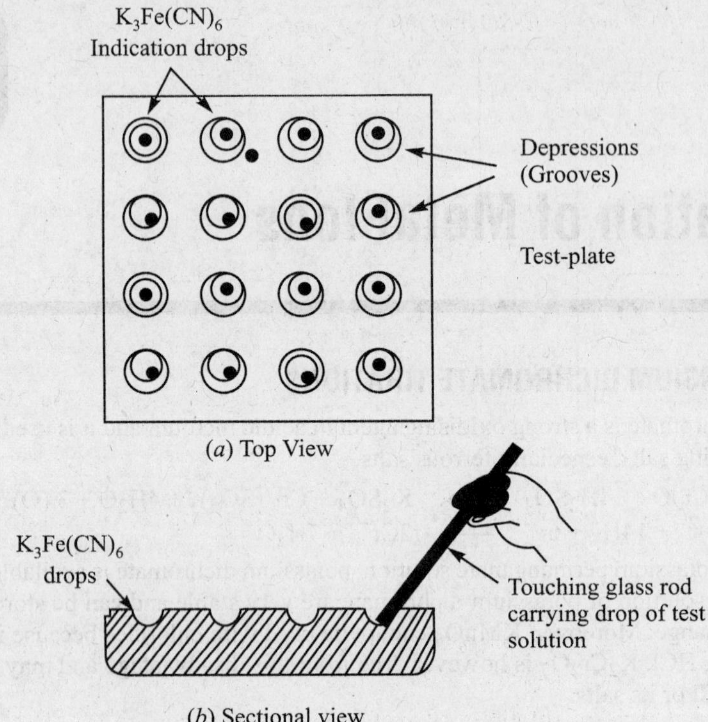

Fig. 2.1: Use of test-plate for external indicator

Continue the addition of the dichromate until a droplet of the reaction mixture from the titration flask ceases to give any blue colour with the indicator drop.

The first titration which is obviously a rough one, gives the rough range in which the true reading lies. In the subsequent titrations, test is carried out after each addition of 0.1 ml.

Notes:

1. The indicator solution of potassium ferricyanide must be free from ferrocyanide radical. Its absence is tested with ferric chloride solution when no blue colour is produced.

2. Drops of the indicator are arranged on a white porcelain tile. They are yellowish coloured. A glass rod wetted with the reaction solution is touched with a drop. After each test, the glass rod is thoroughly washed before performing the next test.

3. Freshly prepared solution of potassium ferricyanide should always be used.

4. Near the end point, the bluish green colour in the indicator develops slowly and it is advisable to allow the test drop on the tile to stand for 3-4 minutes before deciding about the completion of reaction.

5. Potassium ferricyanide indicator is not added into the titration flask containing ferrous salt solution. In that case, a deep bluish colour is produced at once.

6. Frequent testing will lead to inaccurate results.

2. Internal Indicator

There are various internal indicators which are in use. The three commonly employed are:

(*i*) *1% solution (in conc. H_2SO_4) of diphenyl amine.*

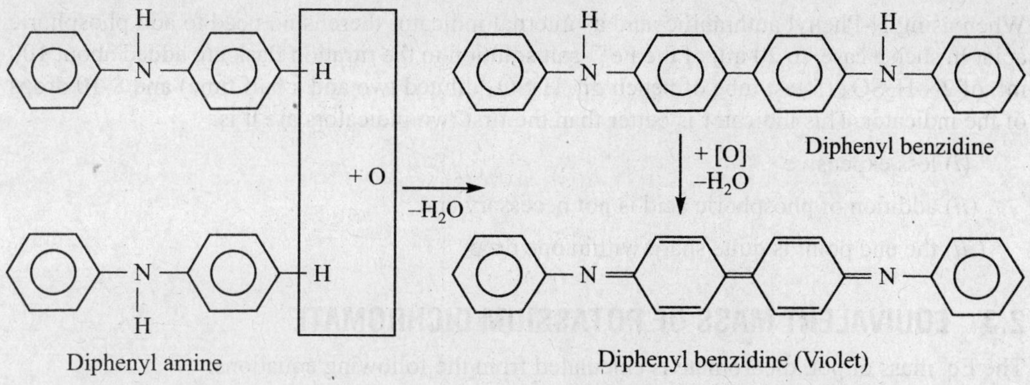

Diphenyl benzidine

+ O

$-H_2O$

+ [O]

$-H_2O$

Diphenyl amine

Diphenyl benzidine (Violet)

This indicator has no influence on the colour of the reaction mixture, but when a slight excess of potassium dichromate is present, the latter oxidises, the indicator producing an intensely blue coloured compound, which indicates the end point. However ferric ions (formed in the course of titration of ferrous salts) are likely to cause the oxidation of the diphenyl amine prematurely *i.e.,* before $K_2Cr_2O_7$ is in excess. In order to prevent this, some syrupy phosphoric acid is added to solution of ferrous salt before titration is carried out. The ferric ions produced by the oxidation are taken up by phosphoric acid giving a ferric phosphate complex which is almost undissociated and thus the ferric ions are prevented from oxidising diphenyl amine.

For titrating 20 ml of solution of ferrous ions, add about 20 ml dil. H_2SO_4, 5-6 drops of indicator and then 5 ml syrupy phosphoric acid, now acid $K_2Cr_2O_7$ sol. from the burette is added until the last drop causes a change from green to blue-violet which persists on shaking. This is the end point.

(*ii*) *1% solution (in Conc. H_2SO_4) of diphenyl benzidine.*

Diphenyl benzidine gets oxidised to violet diphenyl benzidine and hence it can be conveniently used as an indicator in redox titrations involving pot. dichromate as the oxidant. (For reaction refer above). 1% solution of diphenyl benzidine in conc. H_2SO_4 is employed as an indicator. The titration is carried out in the presence of phosphoric acid which helps in lowering the concentration of the ferric ions thus giving a sharp end point (blue violet or purple colouration) 2 or 3 drops of the indicator are used.

Rest of the details are the same as given above in (*i*).

(*iii*) *N-Phenyl anthranilic acid.*

This is found to be a better indicator than the others.

How to prepare this indicator?

(*a*) 0.25 g of the solid N-Phenyl anthranilic acid is dissolved in 12 ml of 0.1 N NaOH solution and the volume is raised to 250 ml by diluting with water and this solution is ready to be used as indicator.

Or

(*a*) 0.25 g of the solid N-Phenyl anthranilic acid is dissolved in 10 ml of 5% Na_2CO_3 solution and the volume is raised to 250 ml by diluting with water.

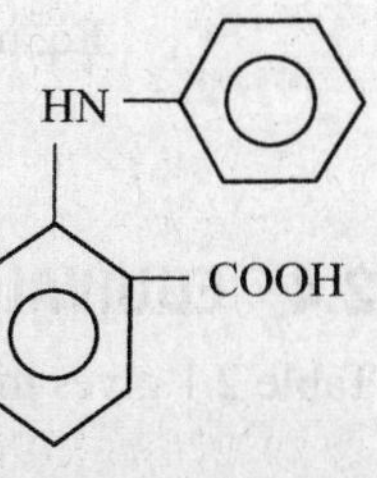

HN

COOH

N-Phenyl anthranilic acid

Use of N-Phenyl anthranilic acid as an indicator

When using N-Phenyl anthranilic acid as internal indicator there is no need to add phosphoric acid. In such a case, to 20 ml. of the Fe^{++} salt solution in the titration flask are added about 100 ml. of 2N H_2SO_4 (5 test tube of bench dil. H_2SO_4 diluted two and a half time) and 8-10 drops of the indicator. This indicator is better than the first two indicators are it is:

(*i*) less expensive

(*ii*) addition of phosphoric acid is not necessary and

(*iii*) the end point is quite sharp within one drop

2.3 EQUIVALENT MASS OF POTASSIUM DICHROMATE

The Eq. mass of pot. dichromate is calculated from the following equations:

(*From molecular equations*):

$$K_2Cr_2O_7 + 4H_2SO_4 \longrightarrow K_2SO_4 + Cr_2(SO_4)_3 + 4H_2O + 3\,(O)$$

$$K_2Cr_2O_7 + 8HCl \longrightarrow 2KCl + 2CrCl_3 + 4H_2O + 3\,[O]$$

i.e.,

$$K_2Cr_2O_7 \equiv 3\,[O]$$

$$(2 \times 39 \times 2 \times 52 \times 7 \times 16) \equiv 3 \times 16$$

$$294 \text{ parts by mass of } K_2Cr_2O_7 \equiv 48 \text{ parts by mass of oxygen}$$

$$\therefore \quad \text{Eq. mass of } K_2Cr_2O_7 = \frac{294}{48} \times 8$$

$$= 49$$

(*From ionic equations*):

A better method for deducing the Eq. mass of pot. dichromate is with the help of the ion -electron equation:

$$Cr_2O_7^{2-} + 6e^- \longrightarrow 2\,Cr^{+++} + 7O^{2-}$$

$$7O^{2} + 14H^{+} \longrightarrow 7H_2O$$

$$Cr_2O_7^{2-} + 14H^+ + 6e^- \longrightarrow 2Cr^{+++} + 7H_2O$$

Since $6e^-$ are used up by dichromate ion, the Eq. mass of the ion is $\frac{1}{6}$th of the ion mass.

$$\therefore \quad \text{Eq. wt.} = \frac{249}{6} = 49.$$

For Dichromate Radical:

$$Cr_2O_7^{2-} \equiv 3[O]$$

$$216 \text{ parts} \equiv 3 \times 16 \text{ parts.}$$

$$\text{Eq. mass of } Cr_2O_7^{2-} \text{ radical} = \frac{216 \times 8}{3 \times 16}$$

$$= 36.$$

2.4 EQUIVALENT MASSES OF REDUCING AGENTS

Table 2.1 gives the equivalent masses of common substances required in $K_2Cr_2O_7$ titrations.

TABLE 2.1 *Equivalent masses of common substances*

Substance	Ion-electron Equation	Eq. mass = Mol. mass./No. of e⁻ lost or gained
1. Potassium dichromate ($K_2Cr_2O_7$)	$Cr_2O_7^{2-} + 14H^+ + 6e^-$	$\frac{392}{1} = 392$
2. Ferrous sulphate ($Fe_5O_4 . 7H_2O$)	$\longrightarrow 2Cr^{3+} + 7H_2O$	$\frac{278}{1} = 278$
3. Ferrous ammonium Sulphate (Mohr salt) ($FeSO_4(NH_4)2SO_4 . 6H_2O$)	$Fe^{2+} \longrightarrow Fe^{3} + + e^-$	$\frac{294}{6} = 49$
4. Feeric sulphate $Fe_2(SO_4)_3$	$FeSO_4 + H_2SO_4 + O \longrightarrow Fe_2(SO_4)_3 + H_2O$	$\frac{400}{2} = 200$

2.5 PRIMARY STANDARDS IN $K_2Cr_2O_7$ TITRATIONS

1. **Potassium dichromate.** It is available in a pure form and is quite stable, so its standard solution can be prepared by dissolving a known mass of it in a given volume of its solution.

2. **Mohr's salt.** [$FeSO_4$. $(NH_4)_2SO_4.6H_2O$]. It is a double salt containing stable ferrous sulphate. Its standard solution is prepared by dissolving a known mass of it (Eq. mass of Mohr's salt is 392) in distilled water to a known volume of the solution.

A few drops of H_2SO_4 are added to make the solution clear and check hydrolysis before diluting it to a known volume.

2.6 GENERAL PROCEDURE FOR POTASSIUM DICHROMATE TITRATIONS

1. Potassium dichromate solution is always taken in the burette and its upper meniscus noted as it is coloured yellowish orange.

2. To a known volume of ferrous salt in the titration flask, an equal volume of dil. H_2SO_4 is added and titration is carried out in cold.

3. In case, diphenyl benzidine is used as internal indicator, then to 20 ml of the Fe^{++} salt solution in the titration flask, an equal volume of dil. H_2SO_4 (5N) (one full test tube of bench dilute acid). About 5 ml of syrupy phosphoric acid and 2 to 3 drops of indicator are added. *Towards the end of titration (when ratio of Fe^{+++} to Fe^{++} ions is high, the ferric ion exerts a slight oxidising action on the indicator. The addition of phosphoric acid reduces the above effect due to the formation of a complex ion.*

4. While using N-Phenyl anthranilic acid as internal indicator, there is no need to add phosphoric acid. In such a case, to 20 ml of the Fe^{++} salt solution in the titration flask are added about 100 ml of 2N H_2SO_4. (5 test tubes of bench dil. H_2SO_4 diluted two and a half times) and 10 drops of the indicator.

Experiment 1: The given solution was prepared by dissolving a mixture of ferrous sulphate crystals $FeSO_4$. $7H_2O$ and anhydrous ferric sulphate $Fe_2(SO_4)_3$. Determine

volumetrically the percentage composition of mixture. Provided N/20 $K_2Cr_2O_7$ solution:

Theory. The strength of ferrous sulphate can be found out by titrating the mixture against $K_2Cr_2O_7$. To calculate the strength of ferric sulphate, the solution is reduced by stannous chloride when ferric sulphate is also reduced to ferrous sulphate. Excess of stannous chloride is destroyed by means of mercuric chloride. The resulting solution is again titrated against $K_2Cr_2O_7$ to get the total normality of both components. By difference, we get the normality of ferric sulphate and then its strength.

Reactions

(*i*) $K_2Cr_2O_7 + 4H_2SO_4 \longrightarrow K_2SO_4 + Cr_2(SO_4)_3 + 4H_2O + 3[O]$

(*ii*) $2FeSO_4 + H_2SO_4 + [O] \longrightarrow Fe_2(SO_4)_3 + H_2O$

(*iii*) $Fe_2(SO_4)_3 + 6HCl \longrightarrow 2FeCl_3 + 3H_2SO_4$

$2FeCl_3 + SnCl_2 \longrightarrow SnCl_4 + 2FeCl_2$

(*iv*) $SnCl_2 + 2HgCl_2 \longrightarrow SnCl_4 + \underset{\text{(ppt.)}}{Hg_2Cl_2 \downarrow}$

(v) $2FeCl_2 + 2HCl + [O] \longrightarrow 2FeCl_3 + H_2O$

Or In the ionic form of equations

(*i*) $2Cr_2O_7^{2+} + 14H^+ + 6e^- \longrightarrow 2Cr^{3+} + 7H_2O$

(*ii*) $Fe^{2+} \longrightarrow Fe^{3+} + e^-$

(*iii*) $2Fe^{3+} + Sn^{2+} \longrightarrow 2Fe^{2+} + Sn^{4+}$

(*iv*) $2Hg^{2+} + Sn^{2+} \longrightarrow Hg_2^{2+} + Sn^{4+}$

(*v*) $Fe^{2+} \longrightarrow Fe^{3+} + e^-$

The exercise involves the following steps:

1. *Titration of mixture against $K_2Cr_2O_7$*

Indicator. N-Phenyl anthranilic acid.

End point. Green to violet red.

Procedure

1. Pipette out 20 ml of the mixture solution into a titration flask.

2. Add about 100 ml of 2N H_2SO_4 and 10 drops of the indicator and titrate against potassium dichromate solution from the burette.

3. Addition of $K_2Cr_2O_7$ solution is continued till the last drop changes the colour of the solution from green to violet red.

4. Repeat the procedure to get the set of three concordant volumes.

2. *Reduction and titration of mixture against $K_2Cr_2O_7$*

(*a*) Reduction.

1. Pipette out 20 ml of the mixture solution in the titration flask and add 2-3 ml of conc. HCl and heat to boil the solution.

2. Now add to it dropwise from a burette stannous chloride solution with shaking till the yellow colour of solution has disappeared.

3. Then add 1-2 drops more. Cool the flask containing solution at once under the tap and then add 10 ml (about half test tube) of a saturated solution of mercuric chloride, rapidly in one lot and with thorough mixing, to remove excess of stannous chloride.

A slight-silky white precipitate of mercurous chloride is obtained.

If (*i*) no precipitate is obtained (due to insufficient quantity of $SnCl_2$), or

(*ii*) a heavy precipitate is obtained, or

(*iii*) a grey or black precipitate is obtained, reject the solution and repeat the reduction

(*b*) Titration. After reduction, add 100 ml of dilute sulphuric acid and titrate against $K_2Cr_2O_7$ using N-Phenyl anthranilic acid as internal indicator by the usual method. Take the mean of three concordant volumes.

Observations.

First titration. (*$K_2Cr_2O_7$ against mixture*)

Vol. of mixture taken each time = 20 ml.

Let the vol. of $K_2Cr_2O_7$ = V_1 ml.

Second titration. (*$K_2Cr_2O_7$ against reduced solution*)

Vol. of mixture used each time for reduction and titration = 20 ml.

Let the vol. of $K_2Cr_2O_7$ used = V_2 ml.

Calculations.

(*a*) *To calculate the normality of mixture due to ferrous sulphate.*

$$20 \text{ ml of } N_1 \; FeSO_4 = V_1 \text{ ml of N/20 } K_2Cr_2O_7$$

$$\therefore \quad N_1 \text{ (Normality of } FeSO_4) = \frac{V_2}{20 \times 20}$$

(*b*) *To calculate the normality due to total ferrous sulphate after reduction*

$$20 \text{ ml of } N_2 \text{ mixture solution after reduction} = V_2 \text{ ml of N/20 } K_2Cr_2O_7$$

$$\therefore \quad N_2 \text{ (Total Normality of } FeSO_4) = \frac{V_2}{20 \times 20}$$

To find out strength of $FeSO_4.7H_2O$ and $Fe_2(SO_4)_3$

(*i*) $FeSO_4.7H_2O$

$$\text{Eq. mass of } FeSO_4.7H_2O = 278$$

$$\text{Strength of } FeSO_4.7H_2O = 278 \times N_1$$

$$= X \text{ g/litre (say)}$$

(*ii*) $Fe_2(SO_4)_3$

$$\text{Eq. mass of ferric sulphate} = \frac{\text{Mol. mass}}{2} = \frac{400}{2} = 200$$

This is clear from the relations:

$$\underset{400}{Fe_2(SO_4)_3} \equiv 2FeCl_3 \equiv 2FeCl_2 \equiv \underset{16}{[O]}$$

or

$$\text{Eq. mass} = \frac{400}{16} \times 8 = 200$$

Normality due to ferric sulphate = Total normality – Normality of ferrous sulphate

$$= N_2 - N_1 = N_3 \text{ (say)}$$

$$\therefore \quad \text{Strength of ferric sulphate} = 200 \times N_3$$

$$= Y \text{ g/litre (say)}$$

(*c*) *To calculate the percentage composition*

$$\text{Total strength} = (X + Y)\ \text{g/litre}$$

$$\text{Percentage of } FeSO_4.7H_2O = \frac{X}{X+Y} \times 100$$

and

$$\text{Percentage of } Fe_2(SO_4)_3 = \frac{Y}{X+Y} \times 100$$

Instructions to the Laboratory assistant

(*i*) A solution by mixing 4.0 litres of N/20 ferrous sulphate and 1.0 litre of N/20 $KMnO_4$. ($KMnO_4$ will oxidise some ferrous sulphate to ferric sulphate)

(*ii*) N/20 $K_2Cr_2O_7$ (to be used twice)

(*iii*) Saturated solution of $HgCl_2$ and

(*iv*) $SnCl_2$ solution.

2.7 IODINE TITRATIONS

Titrations which involve the use of iodine directly or indirectly are called iodine titrations. These titrations can be classified as under:

1. Iodimetric titrations

Iodimetric titrations are *those titrations in which a standard iodine solution is used as an oxidant and is directly titrated with a reducing agent*. Iodimetric procedures are used for determination of reducing agents like thiosulphates, sulphites, arsenites, stannous chloride, etc., by titrating them against standard sol. of iodine run from burette. Some oxidation reduction reactions are given as under:

(*i*) $$2Na_2S_2O_3 + I_2 \longrightarrow Na_2S_4O_6 + 2NaI$$

Ionic equation

$$2S_2O_3^{2-} + I_2 \longrightarrow S_4O_6^{2-} + 2e^-$$

(*ii*) $$SnCl_2 + I_2 + 2HCl \longrightarrow SnCl_4 + 2HI$$

Ionic equation

$$Sn^{2+} + 2H^+ + I_2 \longrightarrow Sn^{4+} + 2HI$$

(*iii*) $$Na_3AsO_3 + I_2 + H_2O \longrightarrow Na_3AsO_4 + 2HI$$

Ionic equation

$$AsO_3^{3-} + I_2 + H_2O \longrightarrow AsO_4^{3-} + 2H^+ + 2I^-$$

(*iv*) $$Sb_2O_3 + 2I_2 + 2H_2O \rightleftharpoons Sb_2O_5 + 4HI$$

Ionic equation

$$Sb^{3+} \rightleftharpoons Sb^{5+} 2e^-$$

and $$2I_2 + 4e^- \longrightarrow 4I^-$$

2. Iodometric titrations

Iodometric titrations are *those titrations in which some oxidising agent liberates iodine from an iodide and the liberated iodine is titrated against standard solution of reducing agent added from a burette*. In such titrations a neutral or an acidic solution of oxidising agent is employed. The amount of iodine liberated from an iodide (*i.e.*, KI) is proportional to the quantity of the oxidising agent present. Iodometric titrations are carried out for determination of $CuSO_4$, $K_2Cr_2O_7$, $KMnO_4$, ferric ions, antimonate ions, H_2O_2, MnO_2, bromine, chlorine, etc. The equations for some of the reactions are as follows:

(*i*)
$$2KMnO_4 + 3H_2SO_4 \longrightarrow K_2SO_4 + 2MnSO_4 + 3H_2O + 5[O]$$
$$2KI + H_2SO_4 \longrightarrow K_2SO_4 + 2HI] \times 5$$
$$2HI + [O] \longrightarrow H_2O + I_2] \times 5$$
$$2KMnO_4 + 8H_2SO_4 + 10KI \longrightarrow 6K_2SO_4 + 2MnSO_4 + 8H_2O + 5I_2$$

Ionic equation
$$2MnO_4^- + 10I^- + 16H^+ \longrightarrow 2Mn^{2+} + 8H_2O + 5I_2$$

(*ii*)
$$K_2Cr_2O_7 + 7H_2SO_4 + 6KI \longrightarrow 4K_2SO_4 + Cr_2(SO_4)_3 + 7H_2O + 3I_2$$

Ionic equation
$$Cr_2O_7^{2-} + 14H^+ + 6I^- \longrightarrow 2Cr^{3+} + 7H_2O + 3I_2$$

(*iii*)
$$CuSO_4 + 2KI \longrightarrow K_2SO_4 + CuI_2] \times 2$$
$$2CuI_2 \longrightarrow Cu_2I_2 + I_2$$

or
$$2CuSO_4 + 4KI \longrightarrow 2K_2SO_4 + \underset{\text{white ppt.}}{Cu_2I_2} + I_2$$

Ionic equation
$$2Cu^{2+} + 2I^- \longrightarrow Cu_2^{2+} + I_2$$

(*iv*)
$$I_2 + 2Na_2S_2O_3 \longrightarrow Na_2S_4O_6 + 2NaI$$

Ionic equation
$$I_2 + 2S_2O_3^{2-} \longrightarrow S_4O_5^{2-} + 2I^-$$

2.8 INDICATOR AND END POINT

In titrations, involving iodine (free or liberated) *1% starch solution* is used as an indicator. Iodine forms a *deep blue complex* with starch.

(*i*) In *Iodimetry*, when iodine is taken in the burette, starch solution is added to the reducing agent taken in the titration flask in the beginning and end point is appearance of blue colour.

(*ii*) In *iodometry*, when the solution of a reducing agent is run from the burette into titration flask containing liberated iodine, starch solution is added just before the approach of end point *i.e.*, when the colour of iodine fades from brown to pale yellow. *The end point in this case is disappearance of blue colour.*

2.9 PREPARATION AND USE OF STARCH SOLUTION

One percent starch solution is prepared by making a paste of 1.0 g of starch with a little water and pouring it in 100 ml of boiling water with vigorous stirring. Solution is boiled for a few minutes, cooled and filtered off.

Note: In iodimetry, it is dangerous to pipette out reducing agents like arsenious oxide, sodium arsenite and tartaremetic as they are poisonous. Hence it is advisable to take these substances in the burette and iodine in the titration flask.

2.10 STANDARD SUBSTANCES

(*i*) **Iodine.** In the preparation of a standard solution of iodine following difficulties arise:

(*a*) Iodine is almost insoluble in water.

(*b*) Iodine is very volatile and its aq. sol. has an appreciable vapour pressure. Both these difficulties are overcome by dissolving iodine in an aq. solution of potassium iodide where dissolution occurs due to the formation of potassium tri-iodide.

$$KI + I_2 \rightleftharpoons KI_3$$

Greater the concentration of iodide solution, more is the solubility of iodine in it. This tri-iodide liberates iodine so readily during titration that the solution behaves as if the dissolved iodine were all free iodine.

From the equation

$$I + e^- \rightleftharpoons I^-$$

It follows that the Eq. wt. of iodine as an oxidising agent is the same as its at. wt. *i.e.,* 127.

(*ii*) **Sodium thiosulphate.** $Na_2S_2O_3.5H_2O$ (Hypo). It is readily available in pure form and its standard solution may be prepared by direct weighing. However, due to efflorescent nature, there is no certainty about its exact water content. *It is, therefore, not suitable as a primary standard.*

(*iii*) **Potassium dichromate.** It is a primary standard and is employed for standardizing sodium thiosulphate (Hypo). It is used in iodometry.

(*iv*) **Arsenious oxide.** It is available in a state of purity (99.9%) and an excellent primary standard for the standardization of iodine solution.

$$H_3As_3O_3 + I_2 + H_2O \rightleftharpoons H_3AsO_4 + 2HI$$

There exists reversible relationship between arsenious oxide and iodine.

In case hydrogen iodide is not removed from the solution, as it is formed, the reaction proceeds in the backward direction. To check this, $NaHCO_3$ is added. Sodium hydroxide and sodium carbonate cannot be used for this purpose since they react with iodine.

2.11 EQUIVALENT MASSES OF COMPOUNDS USED IN IODINE TITRATIONS

1. Iodine. I_2. It acts as a weak oxidizing agent in aqueous solution.

$$I_2 + H_2O \longrightarrow 2HI + [O]$$

$$2I = [O]$$

$$2 \times 127 \quad 16$$

$$\text{Eq. wt.} = \frac{2 \times 127}{16} \times 8 = 127$$

Ionic equation

$$I_2 + 2e^- \rightleftharpoons 2I^-$$

$$\text{Eq. wt.} = \frac{\text{Mol. mass}}{2} = \frac{253}{3} = 127$$

Hence, equivalent mass is the same as atomic mass, *viz* 127.

2. Sodium thiosulphate, $Na_2S_2O_3.5H_2O$. It is a reducing agent and is oxidized by iodine as:

$$2Na_2S_2O_3 + I_2 \longrightarrow Na_2S_4O_6 + 2NaI$$

$$\text{or} \quad 2Na_2S_2O_3.5H_2O \equiv 2I$$
$$2 \times 248 \qquad 2 \times 127$$

$$\text{Eq. mass} = \frac{2 \times 248}{2 \times 127} \times 127 = 248$$

Ionic equation

$$2S_2O_3^{2-} \longrightarrow S_4O_6^{2-} + 2e^-$$

$$\text{Eq. mass} = \frac{2 \times \text{Mol. wt.}}{2} = \frac{2 \times 248}{2} = 248$$

Hence, the equivalent mass of sodium thiosulphate pentahydrate is equal to its molecular mass *i.e.*, 248.

3. **Arsenious oxide, As_2O_3.** It gets oxidized to arsenic oxide As_2O_5 by iodine solutions:

$$As_2O_3 + 2I_2 + 2H_2O \rightleftharpoons As_2O_5 + 4HI$$

$$As_2O_3 \equiv 4I$$
$$198 \qquad 4 \times 127$$

$$\text{Eq. mass} = \frac{198}{4 \times 127} \times 127$$

$$= \frac{198}{4} = 49.5$$

Ionic equation

$$2As^{3+} \longrightarrow 2As^{5+} + 4e^-$$

$$\text{Eq. mass} = \frac{\text{Mol. wt}}{4} = \frac{198}{4} = 49.5$$

Hence, the equivalent mass of arsenious oxide is one-fourth of its molecular mass.

4. **Sodium arsenite, Na_3AsO_3.** It also gets oxidized by iodine solution.

$$Na_3AsO_3 + I_2 + H_2O \rightleftharpoons Na_3AsO_4 + 2HI$$

$$\text{or} \quad Na_3AsO_3 \equiv 2I$$
$$192 \qquad 2 \times 127$$

$$\therefore \quad \text{Eq. mass} = \frac{192}{2 \times 127} \times 127 = \frac{192}{2} = 96$$

Ionic equation

$$AsO_3^{3-} + H_2O \longrightarrow AsO_4^{3-} + 2H^+ + 2e^-$$

$$\therefore \quad \text{Eq. mass} = \frac{\text{Mol. wt.}}{2} = \frac{192}{2} = 96$$

Hence, the equivalent mass of sodium arsenite is one-half of its molecular mass.

5. **Tartaremetic** $\begin{array}{l}\textbf{CHOHCOOK} \\ | \\ \textbf{CHOHCOO(OSb)}\end{array} \cdot \frac{1}{2}\textbf{H}_2\textbf{O}$

It also gets oxidized by iodine solution.

$$2\begin{array}{l}\text{CHOH COOK} \\ | \\ \text{CHOH. COO(OSb)}\end{array} + H_2O \longrightarrow 2\begin{array}{l}\text{CHOH COOK} \\ | \\ \text{CHOH COOH}\end{array} + Sb_2O_3$$

$$Sb_2O_3 + 2I_2 + 2H_2O \longrightarrow Sb_2O_5 + 4HI$$

$$\text{Thus} \quad 2\begin{array}{l}\text{CHOHCOOK}\\ |\\ \text{CHOHCOO (OSb)}\end{array} \equiv 4\text{I}$$

$$2 \times 334 \qquad 4 \times 127$$

$$\therefore \quad \text{Eq. wt.} = \frac{2 \times 334}{4 \times 127} \times 127 = 167$$

Hence, the equivalent mass is one-half of its molecular mass.

$$\text{Eq. wt. of } Sb_2O_3 = \frac{1}{4}\text{Mol. wt} = 73$$

$$\text{Eq. wt. of Sb} = \frac{1}{2}\text{At. wt.} = 61$$

Ionic equation

$$Sb^{3+} \longrightarrow Sb^{5+} + 2e^-$$

$$\therefore \quad \text{Eq. mass of Sb} = \frac{\text{At. mass}}{2} = \frac{122}{2} = 61$$

6. **Potassium dichromate, $K_2Cr_2O_7$.** The equation involved is

$$K_2Cr_2O_7 + 7H_2SO_4 + 6KI \longrightarrow 4K_2SO_4 + Cr_2(SO_4)_3 + 7H_2O + 3I_2$$

$$\text{or} \quad K_2Cr_2O_7 \equiv 6\text{I}$$

$$294 \qquad 6 \times 127$$

$$\therefore \quad \text{Eq. mass} = \frac{\text{Mol. mass}}{6} = \frac{294}{6} = 49$$

Hence, the equivalent mass is one-sixth of its molecular mass.

Ionic equation

$$Cr_2O_7^{2-} + 14H^+ + 6e^- \longrightarrow 2Cr^{3+} + 7H_2O$$

$$\therefore \quad \text{Eq. wt.} = \frac{\text{Mol. wt.}}{6} = \frac{294}{6} = 49$$

7. **Potassium permanganate, $KMnO_4$.** The equation involved is

$$2KMnO_4 + 8H_2SO_4 + 10KI \longrightarrow 6K_2SO_4 + 2MnSO_4 + 8H_2O + 5I_2$$

$$\text{or} \quad KMnO_4 \equiv 10\text{I}$$

$$2 \times 158 \qquad 10 \times 127$$

$$\therefore \quad \text{Eq. mass} = \frac{2 \times 158}{10 \times 127} \times 127 = 31.6$$

Hence, the equivalent mass is one-fourth of its molecular mass.

Ionic equation

$$MnO_4^- + 8H^+ + 5e^- \longrightarrow Mn^{2+} + 4H_2O$$

$$\therefore \quad \text{Eq. wt.} = \frac{\text{Mol. wt.}}{5} = \frac{158}{5} = 31.6$$

8. **Copper sulphate, $CuSO_4.5H_2O$.** The equation involved is

$$2CuSO_4 + 4KI \longrightarrow Cu_2I_2 + I_2 + 2K_2SO_4$$

$$2CuSO_4.5H_2O \equiv 2I$$

$$2 \times 249.5 \qquad 2 \times 127$$

$$\therefore \quad \text{Eq. mass} = \frac{2 \times 249.5}{2 \times 127} \times 127 = 249.5$$

Ionic equation

$$Cu^{2+} + e^- \longrightarrow Cu^+$$

$$\therefore \quad \text{Eq. mass} = \frac{\text{Mol. mass}}{1} = \frac{249.5}{1} = 249.5$$

Hence, the equivalent weight is the same as the molecular weight.

The equivalent masses of some common compounds which find use in iodine titration are grouped in Table 2.2

TABLE 2.2 *Equivalent weights of some common compounds*

	Compound	Mol. mass	Eq. mass = Mol. mass/No. of electrons lost or gained
1.	Iodine, I_2	254	127
2.	Sod. thiosulphate $Na_2S_2O_3.5H_2O$	248	$\frac{\text{Mol. mass}}{1} = 248$
3.	Sodium thiosulphate $Na_2S_2O_3$ (anhy).	158	$\frac{\text{Mol. mass}}{1} = 158$
4.	Sodium arsenite, Na_3AsO_3	192	$\frac{\text{Mol. mass}}{2} = 96$
5.	Arsenious oxide, As_2O_3	198	$\frac{\text{Mol. mass}}{4} = 49.5$
6.	Arsenic, As	75	$\frac{\text{At mass}}{2} = 37.5$
7.	Tartaremetic, CHOH-COOK | CHOH-COO(OSb) $\cdot\frac{1}{2}H_2O$	334	$\frac{\text{Mol. mass}}{2} = 167$
8.	Antimonous oxide, Sb_2O_3	292	$\frac{\text{Mol. mass}}{4} = 73$
9.	Antimony, Sb	122	$\frac{\text{At. mass}}{2} = 61$
10.	Copper sulphate $CuSO_4.5H_2O$	249.5	$\frac{\text{Mol. mass}}{1} = 249.5$
11.	Copper Sulphate $CuSO_4$	159.5	$\frac{\text{Mol. mass}}{1} = 159.5$

Contd...

Contd...

12.	Potassium dichromate, $K_2Cr_2O_7$	294	$\frac{\text{Mol. mass}}{6} = 49$
13.	Potassium permanganate, $KMnO_4$	158	$\frac{\text{Mol. mass}}{5} = 31.6$
14.	Stannous chloride (SnCl2.H2O)	292	$\frac{\text{Mol. mass}}{4} = 73$

In iodometry, iodine is envolved from an iodide by an oxidising agent in acid or neutral medium. Following instructions should be followed in iodometry.

2.12 GENERAL INSTRUCTIONS FOR IODIMETRY

1. Always take iodine solution in the burette.

2. Take a known volume (say 20 ml) of the reducing agent like sodium thiosulphate, sodium arsenite, sodium sulphite, tartaremetic, etc., in the titration flask.

3. Iodine does not dissolve in water. Its aqueous solution is obtained by dissolving a mixture of I_2 and KI in water. Roughly double the quantity of KI is needed to dissolve iodine in water.

4. 1 ml of starch solution is added as indicator in the beginning.

5. Iodine solution is added from the burette in small lots and near the end point in drops with constant shaking of the titration flask.

6. Just appearance of a blue colour is the end point.

2.13 GENERAL INSTRUCTIONS IN IODOMETRY

1. Always take hypo solution in the burette.

2. Take a known volume (say 20 ml) of the oxidising agent in the titration flask.

3. Add a full test tube of dil. H_2SO_4 if the solution in the titration flask is $KMnO_4$ or $K_2Cr_2O_7$.

4. Add half a test tube 10% of KI to the oxidising agent in the flask and shake it well to liberate iodine.

5. Evolution of iodine by interaction between an iodide and the oxidising agent is slow. So, a time of 1-2 minutes should be allowed for the completion of the reaction.

6. The titration flask should be covered with a watch glass to prevent the loss of iodine due to its volatile nature.

7. Run down hypo solution from the burette dropwise while shaking the flask, till the reddish-brown, colour fades to pale yellow (straw colour).

8. HI (from excess of KI and acid) is readily oxidised by air especially in the presence of Cr^{+3} salts. To overcome this difficulty about 1 g solid $NaHCO_3$ should be added to the solution. The CO_2 evolved keeps the atmospheric oxygen off. Keep the flask covered as far as possible.

$$2KI + H_2SO_4 \longrightarrow K_2SO_4 + 2HI$$

$$2HI + (O) \text{ from air} \longrightarrow H_2O + I_2 \uparrow$$

9. The solution should be diluted before titration to check volatility of iodine during the titration.

10. On adding 1-2 ml of *freshly prepared* starch solution a blue colour is obtained.

11. Continue the addition of hypo till the blue colour is discharged which shows the end point.

12. The indicator should be added near the end point otherwise a *stable starch iodide complex* is formed and the blue colour does not disappear on adding more of hypo solution.

13. In titrations between acidified $K_2Cr_2O_7$ containing KI and hypo a green colour persists at the end point due to Cr^{3+} ions.

Experiment 2: Determine volumetrically the strength per litre of the given solution of $CuSO_4.5H_2O$. Provided N/20 potassium dichromate solution. Ask for what you require.

Requirement. Approx. N/20 hypo solution.

Theory. First of all hypo solution is standardised by titrating against N/20 $K_2Cr_2O_7$ solution. The normality of copper sulphate solution is then determined by titrating it against the standardised hypo solution. From this the strength and percentage purity are calculated. The exercise involves double titration.

First Titration. *Titration of hypo against dichromate.*

Equations.

$$K_2Cr_2O_7 + 4H_2SO_4 \longrightarrow K_2SO_4 + Cr_2(SO_4)_3 + 2H_2O + 3\,[O]$$

$$2KI + H_2SO_4 \longrightarrow K_2SO_4 + 2HI$$

$$2HI + [O] \longrightarrow I_2 + H_2O$$

$$2Na_2S_2O_3 + I_2 \longrightarrow Na_2S_4O_6 + 2NaI$$

Indicator. Starch solution.

End point. Blue to light green colour (hypo solution in the burette).

Procedure

1. Pipette out 20 ml of potassium dichromate solution into a titration flask. Add one test tube of dil. H_2SO_4 and half test tube of 10% KI solution and 1-2 g solid sodium bicarbonate.

2. Cover the flask with a watch glass and wait for two minutes. Dilute with 50 ml of water and run the hypo solution from the burette into the titration flask with shaking.

3. Add one ml starch solution when the colour of solution becomes pale yellow.

4. Run hypo solution dropwise till the blue colour changes into light green colour.

5. Repeat the titration to obtain three concordant values.

General Calculations

To calculate the normality of hypo solution.

Let $\quad V_1$ ml of N_1 hypo solution $\equiv$ 20 ml of $\frac{N}{20}$ $K_2Cr_2O_7$

Applying normality equation, we have

$$N_1 \times V_1 = \frac{1}{20} \times 20$$

$$\therefore \quad N_1 \text{ (normality of hypo solution)} = \frac{1}{V_1}$$

Second titration. *Titration of copper sulphate solution against standardised hypo solution.*

Equations.

$$CuSO_4.5H_2O + 2KI \longrightarrow CuI_2 + 2K_2SO_4 + 5H_2O$$
$$2CuI_2 \longrightarrow Cu_2I_2 + I_2$$
$$2Na_2S_2O_3 + I_2 \longrightarrow Na_2S_4O_6 + 2NaI$$

Indicator. Starch solution.

End point. Blue coloured solution to a white ppt. (hypo solution in the burette).

Procedure

1. Pipette out 20 ml copper solution into a titration flask. Add half test tube of 10% KI solution.

2. Cover the flask with a watch glass and wait for 2 minutes. Dilute the solution with 50 ml distilled water.

3. Run the hypo solution from the burette into the flask till a pale yellow colour is obtained. Add 1 ml of starch solution. Blue colour is obtained.

4. Run hypo solution into the flask dropwise till the blue colour disappears and a white precipitate due to the formation of cuprous iodide appears.

General calculations

(*i*) *To calculate the normality of copper sulphate solution.*

Let V_2 ml of N_1 hypo solution = 20 ml of N_2 copper sulphate

Applying normality equation, we get

$$\underset{\text{Hypo}}{N_1 \times V_2} = \underset{CuSO_4}{N_2 \times 20}$$

$\therefore$ N_2 (normality of copper sulphate) $= \dfrac{N_1 \times V_2}{20}$ (where N_1 is the normality of hypo solution from first titration)

(*ii*) *To calculate the strength of copper sulphate.*

Strength/litre of $CuSO_4.5H_2O$ = Normality × Eq. mass of $CuSO_4\ 5H_2O$

Substituting the values,

Strength/litre of $CuSO_4.5H_2O$ = $N_2 \times 249.5$

or $= x$ g

Instructions for laboratory assistant

Provide:

(*i*) A solution containing 12.5 g of $CuSO_4.5H_2O$ per litre

(*ii*) $\dfrac{N}{20}$ hypo solution

(*iii*) $\dfrac{N}{20}$ $K_2Cr_2O_7$ solution

(*iv*) 10% KI solution

(*v*) Freshly prepared starch solution.

Viva-Voice Questions with Answers

Potassium Dichromate Titrations

Q.1. Mention any two internal indicators employed in $K_2Cr_2O_7$ titrations.

Ans. Diphenyl amine and N-Phenyl anthranilic acid.

Q.2. What function does phosphoric acid serve in $K_2Cr_2O_7$ titrations in which diphenylamine is used as internal indicator?

Ans. It helps in minimising the oxidation of diphenyl amine by ferric ions since they form a complex with phosphate ions provided by phosphoric acid.

Q.3. Do you add phosphoric acid in case of N-Phenyl anthranilic acid indicator as well?

Ans. No, in this case the titration can be carried out in the absence of phosphoric acid.

Q.4. What are external indicators?

Ans. Those indicators which are not added to the titration flask containing reagent solution *e.g.*, potassium ferricyanide.

Q.5. Why can't we use potassium ferricyanide solution as internal indicator?

Ans. It produces a deep blue colour with ferrous salt solution taken in the titration flask.

Q.6. Why is it essential to wash the crystals of potassium ferricyanide while preparing the ferricyanide indicator?

Ans. It helps to remove the superficial coating of the ferrocyanide.

Q.7. Can you prepare a standard solution of potassium dichromate?

Ans. Yes, because potassium dichromate can be obtained in pure state.

Iodine Titrations

Q.8. What is iodimetry?

Ans. Titrations which involve the use of iodine solution directly for estimation of reducing agent like sodium thiosulphate, arsenites are known as iodimetry.

Q.9. What is iodometry?

Ans. The estimations of oxidising agents involving the determination of iodine liberated by the action of potassium iodide are referred to as iodometry.

Q.10. What is the use of adding $NaHCO_3$ in iodometric titration?

Ans. To prevent oxidation of HI formed during the titration.

Q.11. Why do we prefer to use freshly prepared starch solution as indicator?

Ans. When kept for long time, starch solution undergoes bacterial action which results in its decomposition and this renders it ineffective as an indicator.

Q.12. During the iodometric titrations of copper sulphate, generally the blue colour of starch iodide reappears after it is discharged by hypo solution at the end point, why?

Ans. It is because traces of iodine absorbed by cuprous iodide (formed during the titration) are set free.

Q.13. What precautions do you take to get a correct end point in the above case?

Ans. In such a case a sharp end point may be obtained by adding a pinch of ammonium or potassium thiocyanate just before the end point. The thiocyanate ion is absorbed by cuprous iodide and displace any absorbed iodine.

Q.14. Why is it necessary to avoid the presence of free mineral acids in iodometric titrations involving copper sulphate?

Ans. It is so since the precipitate of cuprous iodide formed during titration dissolve in mineral acids like H_2SO_4 or HNO_3.

Q.15. In iodometric titrations starch solution is added just near the end point, why?

Ans. It is because if starch is added in the beginning *i.e.,* in high concentration of iodine, it may form a stable starch iodine complex and hence all the iodine would not be titrated.

3

Estimation of Acid and Alkali Content

3.1 COMMERCIAL VINEGAR

Vinegar is prepared by biochemical fermentation of sugars to alcohols and further fermentation to vinegar. The reactions involved in the conversion of sugars to vinegar are:

$$\underset{\text{Glucose}}{C_6H_{12}O_6} \xrightarrow{\text{Yeast}} 2\,C_2H_5OH + 2\,CO_2$$

$$\underset{\text{Ethanol}}{C_2H_5OH} \xrightarrow{\text{Acetobactor}} \underset{\text{Acetic acid}}{CH_3COOH} + H_2O$$

It is possible to prepare vinegar from any fruit or sugary substance. Thus we have malt vinegar which is obtained by fermentation of malt. Similarly we have spirit vinegar which is obtained by fermentation of dilute alcohol. Vinegar has a long shelf life. It is used as a preservative and in the preparation of pickles. Vinegar is a dilute solution of acetic acid and can be estimated volumetrically against a standard solution of sodium hydroxide.

Experiment 1: Determine the strength of acetic acid in the commercial vinegar using NaOH.

Reactions $\underset{\text{Acetic acid}}{CH_3COOH} + NaOH \rightarrow \underset{\text{Sodium acetate}}{CH_3COONa} + H_2O$

Indicator. Phenolphthalein

End Point. Pink to colourless (acetic acid in the burette)

Procedure

1. Clean the burette with water. Rinse and fill the burette with the given solution of vinegar. Note the initial reading.

2. Pipette out 20 ml of N/10 sodium hydroxide after rinsing and drop it into a titration flask.

3. Add 1-2 drops of phenolphthalein indicator to the flask. The colour of the solution in the flask will turn pink.

4. Run the vinegar solution from the burette into the flask with shaking till the pink colour disappears. Note down the burette reading. Calculate the volume of acetic acid required to neutralise sodium hydroxide solution.

5. Repeat the titration tell 3 concordant values of volume of acetic acid used are obtained. Record the observations and calculate the result as follows.

Observations.

Volume of acetic acid taken by pipette each time = 20 ml.

S.No	Initial Burette reading	Final Burette reading	Volume of acetic acid used (ml)
1.	------------	------------	------------
2.	------------	------------	------------
3.	------------	------------	------------

Concordant volume = v_1 ml

Calculations.

Apply normality equation

$$\underset{\substack{\text{Vinegar}\\\text{(Acetic acid)}}}{N_1V_1} = \underset{\text{NaOH}}{N_2V_2}$$

Substituting the values, we have

$$N_1 \times v_1 = \frac{N}{10} \times 20$$

or

$$N_1 = \frac{N}{10} \times \frac{20}{v_1}$$

Where N_1 is the normality of acetic acid in the sample of vinegar.

Strength of vinegar solution = Normality × Eq. mass of acetic acid

= N_1 × 60 g/litre (60 is the equivalent mass of acetic acid)

Provide

1. Glacial acetic acid is 17 N. Dissolve 6 ml of glacial acetic acid is one litre water and label it as vinegar sample

2. $\frac{N}{10}$ NaOH . Dissolve 4 g NaOH pellets is one litre of distilled water.

3. Phenolphthalein indicator

Experiment 2: Determination of alkali content in antacid tablet using HCl.

General

Antacids are substances that remove excess acid from gastric juices and provide relief from indigestion, acidity and gastric ulcers. Antacids change the pH level in the stomach to normal level. Antacids contain substances which are alkaline is nature and thus neutralise acidic substances. Commonly present substances in antacids are aluminium hydroxide Al $(OH)_3$, magnesium hydroxide Mg $(OH)_2$ and sodium hydrogen carbonate $NaHCO_3$. Commonly found antacid tablets available in the market are digene, gelncil, etc. Their content in the tablets are estimated using acid-alkali titration.

Reactions.

$$Al(OH)_3 + 3\,HCl \rightarrow AlCl_3 + 3\,H_2O$$
$$Mg(OH)_2 + 2\,HCl \rightarrow Mg\,Cl_2 + 2\,H_2O$$
$$NaHCO_3 + HCl \rightarrow NaCl + CO_2 + H_2O$$

Indicator. Phenolphthalein

End Point. Pink to colourless (HCl in the burette)

Procedure

1. Rinse and fill the burette with N/10 HCl

2. Dissolve a crushed tablet of the antacid in 20 ml water in a titration flask. Shake and swirl the flask till the tablet goes into water.

3. Add 1-2 drops of phenolphthalein to the titration flask.

4. Note the initial reading of the burette. Run the acid solution from the burette into the titration flask in small lots and with shaking till a permanent pink colour is obtained. First reading is rough reading.

5. Repeat the titration with a new tablet each time till three concordant readings of the volume of acid used, are obtained.

6. Tabulate the readings and calculate the result as explained below.

Observations.

Volume of antacid solution taken each time = 20 ml

S.No	Initial burette reading	Final burette reading	Volume of Hcl used (mL)
1.	----------	----------	----------
2.	----------	----------	----------
3.	----------	----------	----------
4.	----------	----------	----------

Concordant volume = v ml

Calculations.

V mL of *N*/10 HCl neutralises 20 mL of antacid solution

Applying normality equation

$$\underset{\text{Antacid solution}}{N_1V_1} = \underset{\text{HCl}}{N_2V_2}$$

Substituting the values, we have

$$N_1 \times 20 = \frac{N}{10} \times V$$

or

$$= \frac{1}{10} \times \frac{1}{20} \times V = \frac{V}{200} N$$

Thus, normality of antacid solution $= \frac{V}{200} \times N$

Strength per litre of alkali content or OH^- ions = Normality × Eq. wt of OH^-

$$= \frac{V}{200} \times \frac{17}{50} \text{ g / litre}$$

Strength of alkali metal 20 mL of solution or per tablet $= \frac{V}{200} \times \frac{17}{50} g$

Result

The amount of alkali content or $[OH^-]$ per tablet $= \frac{V}{200} \times \frac{17}{50} g$

Provide

1. $\frac{N}{10}$ HCl
2. Gelucil or digene tablets

3.2 POTASSIUM PERMANGANATE TITRATIONS

Potassium permanganate is a powerful oxidising agent and is used in a number of titrations. In the presence of dil. H_2SO_4, it readily oxidises ferrous salts, oxalic acid and oxalates. Nitric acid being a strong oxidising agent cannot be used while hydrochloric acid, react with $KMnO_4$ and evolves CO_2 gas, particularly, in the presence of ferric salts. Therefore, H_2SO_4 is the most suitable acid to get acidified $KMnO_4$, as it has action with permanganate ion.

The key equation for such titration is

$$2KMnO_4 + 3H_2SO_4 \longrightarrow K_2SO_4 + 2MnSO_4 + 3H_2O + 5[O]$$

The reactions with different reducing agents may be represented as under:

(*i*) *With ferrous sulphate*

$$2FeSO_4 + H_2SO_4 + [O] \longrightarrow Fe_2(SO_4)_3 + H_2O$$

(*ii*) *With Mohr's salt*

$$FeSO_4(NH_4)_2SO_4.6H_2O \longrightarrow FeSO_4 + (NH_4)_2SO_4 + 6H_2O$$

$$2FeSO_4 + H_2SO_4 + [O] \longrightarrow Fe_2(SO_4)_3 + H_2O$$

(*iii*) *With oxalic acid*

$$\begin{matrix} COOH \\ | \\ COOH \end{matrix} + [O] \xrightarrow{60\text{-}70°C} 2CO_2 \uparrow + H_2O$$

(*iv*) *With oxalates*

$$\begin{matrix} COOM \\ | \\ COOM \end{matrix} + H_2SO_4 \xrightarrow{60\text{-}70°C} \begin{matrix} COOH \\ | \\ COOH \end{matrix} + M_2SO_4$$

$$\begin{matrix} COOH \\ | \\ COOH \end{matrix} + [O] \longrightarrow 2CO_2 \uparrow + H_2O$$

It must, however, be clearly borne in mind that the above action between potassium permanganate and sulphuric acid takes place only when there is some readily oxidisable substance present in contact. It is not a reaction that would occur when dilute sulphuric acid is added to potassium permanganate alone.

3.3 POTASSIUM PERMANGANATE ACTS AS 'SELF INDICATOR'

No external indicator is required in potassium permanganate titrations because potassium permanganate which possesses a deep pink colour, itself acts as indicator.

When added to a solution of reducing agent, the colour of potassium permanganate is discharged and this continues till the reducing agent is exhausted. The addition of a droplet of potassium permanganate solution in excess produces a persistent pink colour which marks the end of the titration.

3.4 DETERMINATION OF EQUIVALENT MASSES

The eq. wt. of an oxidising agent or a reducing agent may be determined by any one of the following methods:

(*i*) Available oxygen or hydrogen concept

(*ii*) Electron concept

(*iii*) Oxidation number concept

Equivalent mass of oxidising agent

1. Potassium permanganate ($KMnO_4$)

(*i*) *Available oxygen or hydrogen concept*

In acidic medium $KMnO_4$ supplies oxygen according to the following equation:

$$2KMnO_4 + 3H_2SO_4 \longrightarrow K_2SO_4 + 2MnSO_4 + 3H_2O + 5[O]$$

i.e., $2KMnO_4 = 5O = 10H$

$$\therefore \quad \text{Eq. wt. of } KMnO_4 \text{ in acidic medium} = \frac{2 \times \text{Mol. mass of } KMnO_4}{10}$$

$$= \frac{2 \times 158}{10} = \frac{316}{10} = 31.6$$

Also Eq. mass of $KMnO_4$ = No. of parts of $KMnO_4$ which would displace 8 parts of oxygen

$$= \frac{2 \times 158 \times 8}{80}$$

[$\because$ 80 parts [O] = 2 × 158 parts $KMnO_4$]

$$8 \text{ parts [O]} = \frac{2 \times 158 \times 8}{80} \text{ parts} = \frac{158}{5} = 31.6$$

(*ii*) *Electron concept*

In acidic medium permanganate ion (active ion) is reduced according to the following equation:

$$MnO_4^- + 8H^+ + 5e^- \longrightarrow Mn^{++} + 4H_2O$$

Hence no. of electron gained is five.

$$\therefore \quad \text{Eq. mass of } KMnO_4 \text{ in acidic medium} = \frac{\text{Mol. mass of } KMnO_4}{5} = \frac{158}{5} = 31.6$$

(iii) Oxidation number concept

$KMnO_4$ is reduced to colourless manganous ion in the presence of dilute sulphuric acid.

$$\underset{+1}{K} \quad \underset{+7}{Mn} \quad \underset{-8}{O_4} \longrightarrow \underset{+2}{Mn} \quad \underset{+6}{S} \quad \underset{-8}{O_4}$$

The change in oxidation number of Mn = (+7) – (+2) = 5

$$\text{Hence} \quad \text{Eq. mass of } KMnO_4 = \frac{\text{Mol. wt. of } KMnO_4}{5} = \frac{158}{5} = 31.6$$

Equivalent Mass of Reducing Agents

1. Ferrous amm. sulphate [$FeSO_4.(NH_4)_2SO_4.6H_2O$)] *i.e.* Mohr's salt

(i) Available oxygen or hydrogen concept

In acidic solutions ferrous sulphate present in ferrous amm. sulphate is oxidized to ferric sulphate by $KMnO_4$ according to the following equation:

$$2KMnO_4 + 3H_2SO_4 \longrightarrow K_2SO_4 + 2MnSO_4 + 3H_2O + 5[O]$$

$$10[FeSO_4.(NH_4)_2SO_4.6H_2O] + 5H_2SO_4 + 5[O] \longrightarrow 5Fe_2(SO_4)_3 + 10(NH_4)_2SO_4 + 5H_2O + \underset{\text{(water of crystallization)}}{60H_2O}$$

From this equation it is clear that 10 molecules of ferrous amm. sulphate are oxidized by 2 molecules of $KMnO_4$

i.e., $\quad 10[FeSO_4.(NH_4)_2SO_4.6H_2O] \equiv 2KMnO_4 \equiv 5O \equiv 10H$

or $\quad [FeSO_4.(NH_4)_2SO_4.6H_2O] \equiv H$

Hence the equivalent mass of ferrous amm. sulphate is the same as its molecular mass.

i.e., Eq. mass of ferrous amm. sulphate

$$= \frac{\text{Mol. mass of ferrous amm. sulphate}}{1}$$

$$= \frac{392.0}{1} = 392.0$$

(ii) Electron concept

The partial equation for the oxidation of ferrous ion to ferric ion may be written as follows:

$$Fe^{++} \rightleftharpoons Fe^{+++} + e^-$$

∴ The number of electron lost is one.

$$\therefore \quad \text{Eq. mass of ferrous amm. sulphate} = \frac{\text{Mol. mass}}{1} = \frac{392.0}{1} = 392.0$$

(iii) Oxidation number concept

In this case ferrous ion is oxidized into ferric ion.

$$\underset{+2}{2Fe} \quad \underset{-2}{SO_4} \longrightarrow \underset{+6}{Fe_2} \quad \underset{-6}{(SO_4)_3}$$

Hence change in oxidation number per atom of ion is from +2 to +3 *i.e.,* by one unit of oxidation.

Hence, Eq. wt. of ferrous amm. sulphate $= \frac{\text{Mol. wt.}}{1} = \frac{392.0}{1} = 392.0$

2. Oxalic acid [$H_2C_2O_4$. $2H_2O$]

(i) Available oxygen or hydrogen concept

It is oxidized to CO_2 and H_2O by $KMnO_4$ by the following hypothetical equation:

$$H_2C_2O_4 + O \longrightarrow 2CO_2 + H_2O$$

$\therefore$ I mole of oxalic $\equiv$ O

$H_2C_2O_4.\ 2H_2O \equiv O$

126 parts of oxalic acid $\equiv$ 16 parts of oxygen

$\therefore$ Equation mass oxalic acid $= \frac{126 \times 8}{16} = 63$

(ii) Electron concept

Partial oxidation of oxalate ion into CO_2 and H_2O is according to the following equation:

$$C_2O_4^{2-} \rightleftharpoons 2CO_2 + 2e^-$$

$\therefore$ The number of electrons lost 2.

$\therefore$ Equivalent mass of oxalic acid $= \frac{\text{Mol. mass oxalic acid}}{2} = \frac{126}{2} = 63.$

(iii) Oxidation number concept

In the oxidation of oxalic acid into CO_2 and H_2O, following change in oxidation number of oxygen takes place

$$\underset{+2}{H_2}\quad \underset{+6}{C_2}\quad \underset{-8}{O_4} \longrightarrow \underset{+4}{2C}\quad \underset{-4}{O_2}$$

$\therefore$ The change in oxidation number of two atoms of carbon is from +6 to +4 *i.e.*, by two units of oxidation.

$\therefore$ Equation mass of oxalic acid $= \frac{\text{Mol. mass of oxalic acid}}{2}$

$= \frac{126}{2} = 63$

Similarly the equivalent mass of any alkali metal oxalate,

$$\begin{array}{c} COOM \\ | \\ COOM \end{array} = \frac{\text{Mol. wt.}}{2}$$

Some of the common equivalent masses needed in permanganate titration are given in table below. (with ion electron configuration)

Substance	Ion electron equation	Eq. mass = Mol. mass/No. of electrons lost or gained
1. Potassium permanganate ($KMnO_4$)	$MnO_4^- + 8H^+ + 5e^- \longrightarrow Mn^{2+} + 4H_2O$	15/5 = 31.6
2. Oxalic acid ($C_2H_2O_4$ $2H_2O$)	$C_2O_4^{2-} \longrightarrow 2CO_2 + 2e^-$	126/2 = 63
3. Sodium oxalate ($Na_2C_2O_4$)	.........Do..........	134/2 = 67

Contd...

Contd...

4. Ferrous sulphate ($FeSO_4.7H_2O$)	$Fe^{2+} \longrightarrow Fe^{3+} + e^-$	278/1 = 278
5. Mohr's salt Ferrous ammonium sulphate [$FeSO_4(NH_4)_2SO_4.6H_2O$]	$Fe^{2+} \longrightarrow Fe^{3+} + e^-$	392/1 = 392
6. Ferrous oxalate ($FeC_2O_4.2H_2O$)	$Fe^{2+} + C_2O_4^{2-} \longrightarrow Fe^{3+} + 2CO_2 + 3e^-$	180/3 = 60
7. Manganese dioxide [MnO_2]	$MnO_2 + 4H^+ + 2e^- \longrightarrow Mn^{2+} + 2H_2O$	87/2 = 43.5
8. Hydrogen peroxide (H_2O_2)	$H_2O_2 + 2H^+ + 2e^- \longrightarrow 2H_2O$	34/2 = 17

3.5 STANDARD POTASSIUM PERMANGANATE SOLUTION

Potassium permanganate is not primary standard substance. It is always impure and contaminated with manganese dioxide. Ordinary distilled water is associated with organic matter which may reduce potassium permanganate to manganese dioxide. The presence of manganese dioxide (MnO_2) is unwanted because it catalyses the auto decomposition of permanganate solution on standing. Because of these reasons a standard solution of permanganate cannot be prepared by exact weighing directly. Its standard solution is obtained by an indirect method.

The solution of $KMnO_4$ is first prepared, kept for sometime, filtered through purified glass wool and is standardized against a primary standard. The substances which are commonly used to standardize $KMnO_4$ are hydrated oxalic acid, $H_2C_2O_4.2H_2O$, sod. oxalate, $(COONa)_2$ and ferrous ammonium sulphate. $FeSO_4$ $(NH_4)_2$ SO_4. $6H_2O$. They are employed as primary standard as they are available in pure form and are stable. Sodium oxalate is the best of all.

3.6 GENERAL INSTRUCTIONS FOR KMNO$_4$ TITRATIONS

1. $KMnO_4$ solution is always taken in a burette.

2. Avoid the use of burette with a rubber pinch cock as potassium permanganate attacks rubber.

3. If you forget to add dilute sulphuric acid to the solution in the titration flask, a brown precipitate will appear on running $KMnO_4$ solution into it due to formation of MnO_2 which cannot be destroyed by adding the acid now. In such a case throw away the solution and start afresh.

4. No indicator is added since the pot. permanganate acts as self indicator.

5. In case oxalic acid or an oxalate is the reducing agent to be titrated, add dil. Sulphuric acid as directed above and heat the flask to 60-70°C on a tripod stand with a wire gauge before adding permanganate. To ascertain that the solution in the flask has been heated to the desired temperature, heat it for 3-4 minutes, hold with the left hand, touch its bottom with your righthand as shown in Fig. 3.1. If it is unbearable to touch, it is in order, otherwise heat more. May be that you take long to complete the titration and the solution get cold. Heat the titration flask again to the same temperature. Make sure that the reaction mixture is duly hot at the end point.

Fig. 3.1: *Judging the temperature of the flask*

However, heating is not to be done if the solution in the titration flask is $FeSO_4$ solution or Mohr salt.

6. Never run in large amount $KMnO_4$ solution at a time. This may form a brown precipitate of hydrated manganese dioxide in a titration flask and spoil the titration.

7. Unlike oxalic acid and oxalates, the oxidation of ferrous ion proceeds in cold, hence the solutions of ferrous salts are titrated against $KMnO_4$ solution in cold.

8. As $KMnO_4$ solution is run into the hot solution of oxalic acid in the titration flask, the temperature of the latter solution will come down. Therefore, it is advisable to see that the pink colour obtained at the end of the titration does not disappear on re-heating the titration flask.

9. The sulphuric acid used in $KMnO_4$ titration should be chemically pure.

10. One of the solutions must be primary standard *i.e.,* a substance which is available in pure form and is quite stable, $KMnO_4$ is a secondary standard ($FeSO_4$. $(NH_4)_2$ SO_4. $6H_2O$], oxalic acid and oxalates are primary standards.

Experiment 3: Determine the strength per litre of oxalic acid in the given solution. Provided approx. N/20 $KMnO_4$

Theory. This is a double titration. In the first titration, we shall determine the exact normality of $KMnO_4$ by titrating it with a standard solution (say N/20) of Mohr salt. In the second titration, oxalic acid solution is titrated against the $KMnO_4$ solution, whose exact normality has ben evaluated.

First titration (Mohr salt against $KMnO_4$)

Reactions $2\ KMnO_4 + 3\ H_2SO_4 \rightarrow K_2SO_4 + 2MnSO_4 + 3H_2O + 5O$

$2FeSO_4$ (From Mohr Salt) + $H_2SO_4 + O \rightarrow Fe_2(SO_4)_3 + H_2O$

Ammonium sulphate present in Mohr salt does not react.

Indicator: $KMnO_4$ is self-indicator

End point: Appearance of a permanent pink color.

Procedure:

1. Rinse the burette with the given $KMnO_4$ solution and fill the burette with this solution. Note down the initial reading.

2. Pipette out 20 ml of Mohr salt into a titration flask. Add one test tube of dil. H_2SO_4 (5N). **Do not heat the flask.**

3. Add $KMnO_4$ from the burette in small instalments and with shaking till a permanent pink color is obtained in the flask. Note down the final reading on the burette. This is rough titration.

4. Repeat the titrations as explained above till 2 or 3 concordant values of volume of $KMnO_4$ solution used, are obtained.

Observations:

S.No.	Initial burette reading	Final burette reading	Volume of $KMnO_4$ used (ml)
1.	.....	.....	.....
2.	.....	.....	.....
3.	.....	.....	.....
4.	.....	.....	.....

Mean value of volume used = say v_1 ml

Calculation:

From this titration, we shall calculate the exact normality of $KMnO_4$ solution. Apply the normality equation:

$$\underset{(KMnO_4)}{N_1V_1} \equiv \underset{\text{Mohr Salt}}{N_2V_2}$$

Substituting for different quantities, we have

$$N_1 \times v_1 \equiv \frac{N}{20} \times 20$$

or

$$N_1 = \frac{N}{20} \times \frac{20}{v_1}$$

Where N_1 is the exact normality of $KMnO_4$ solution.

Second titration ($KMnO_4$ solution against Oxalic acid solution)

Reactions:

$$2KMnO_4 + 3H_2SO_4 \longrightarrow K_2SO_4 + MnSO_4 + 3H_2O + 5O$$

$$\begin{array}{l} COOH \\ | \\ COOH \end{array} 2H_2O + O \xrightarrow{60\text{-}70°C} 2CO_2 + 3H_2O$$

Indicator: $KMnO_4$ itself

End Point: Appearance of a pink colour

Procedure:

1. Pipette out 20 ml of oxalic acid solution into a titration flask. Add one test tube of dil. H_2SO_4 acid (5N).

2. Heat the flask to 60–70°C or when it is unbearable to touch at the back of the palm.

3. Note down the burette reading and run the $KMnO_4$ solution from the burette into the flask in small lots and with constant shaking till a permanent pink color is obtained. Note down the final reading of the burette.

4. First titration is rough titration. Repeat the titrations 3 or 4 times till the concordant values of volumes of $KMnO_4$ solution used, are obtained.

5. Record the observations and calculate the result as given below:

Observations:

S.No.	Initial burette reading	Final burette reading	Volume of $KMnO_4$ used (ml)
1.	.....	.....	.....
2.	.....	.....	.....
3.	.....	.....	.....
4.	.....	.....	.....

Value of $KMnO_4$ used = v_2 ml (say)

Calculations

From this titration, we shall calculate the normality of oxalic acid solution. Apply the normality equation:

$$\underset{\text{Oxalic acid}}{N'V'} \equiv \underset{KMnO_4}{N''V''}$$

Substituting for various quantities, we have

$$N' \times 20 = N_1 \times v_2 \quad \text{(Value of } N_1 \text{ is obtained from the first titration)}$$

or $$N' = \frac{N_1 \times v_2}{20}$$

Where N′ is the normality of oxalic acid solution.

Strength\litre of oxalic acid = Normality × Eq. weight of oxalic acid

$$= N' \times 63$$

Instructions for the lab staff. Provide

1. Approx. N/20 $KMnO_4$ solution i.e. 1.5 g of $KMnO_4$ dissolved per litre of the solution
2. N/20 Mohr salt solution i.e. 19.6 g Mohr salt dissolved per litre of the solution
3. A solution containing 3 g per litre of oxalic acid

Viva-Voice Questions with Answers

Q.1. What is meant by acidimetry and alkalimetry ?

Ans. Determination of strength of acids and alkalies by titration is called acidimetry and alkalimetry.

Q.2. Which indicators are used for the following titrations ?

(*i*) Strong acid – Weak base

(*ii*) Weak acid – Strong base

Ans. (*i*) Methyl orange

(*ii*) Phenolphthalein

Q.3. Name two weak acids and weak bases.

Ans. *Weak acids* – Acetic acid, oxalic acid

Weak bases – Sodium carbonate, sodium hydrogen carbonate

Q.4. Which indicator is preferred for the titration of strong acid and strong bases ?

Ans. Although both phenolphthalein and methyl orange can be used for strong acid - strong base titrations, phenolphthalein is preferred.

Q.5. How does the colour change when the medium changes from acidic to basic in the case of

(*i*) Methyl orange (*ii*) Phenolphthalein ?

Ans. *Methyl orange* *From red to yellow*

Phenolphthalein *From coloureless to pink*

Q.6. Why does sodium hydroxide not act as primary standard ?

Ans. It is hygroscopic and corrosive.

4

Estimation of Inorganic Salts and Hydrated Water

4.1 ACIDIMETRY AND ALKALIMETRY

We know that an acid on reacting with an alkali produces a salt and water, *e.g.;*

$$HCl + NaOH \longrightarrow NaCl + H_2O$$

$$H_2SO_4 + 2NaOH \longrightarrow Na_2SO_4 + 2H_2O$$

The reaction of an acid with an alkali is called neutralisation and this fact forms the basis of all such titrations. Thus the strength of an unknown base can be determined by titrating it against a standard solution of an acid. *Determination of strengths of acids and alkalies by titration is known as Acidimetry and Alkalimetry.*

4.2 INDICATORS

Indicators are those substance which have one colour in acidic medium and an all together different colour in alkaline medium.

Indicators generally used in the determination of end point in acidimetry and alkalimetry titration are:

(*i*) Phenolphthalein.

(*ii*) Methyl Orange.

The choice of the indicator for a particular titration depends upon the nature of the acid and the alkali to be titrated.

Acid	Base	Indicator
Strong	Strong	Phenolphthalein or methyl orange
Weak	Strong	Phenolphthalein
Strong	Weak	Methyl orange

Strong acids are : HCl, NHO_3.

Strong bases are: NaOH, KOH.

Weak acids are : CH_3COOH, $(COOH)_2.2H_2O$ and succinic acid etc.

Weak bases are : $NaHCO_3$, Na_2CO_3, $KHCO_3$, K_2CO_3.

Note: For titrating a strong acid against a strong base, though both indicators can be used; *Phenolphthalein should be preferred to methyl orange.* It gives a clear indicator of end point.

Colour changes of indicators in acids and alkalies

Indicator	Alkali	Acid
Methyl orange	Yellow	Orange red (or reddish pink)
Phenolphthalein	Pink	Colourless

Standard Substances used for Acid Alkali Titrations. Standard solutions of sodium carbonate and oxalic acid are generally used for determining the strength of solutions of the substances like HCl, NaOH, etc., where standard solutions cannot be prepared directly.

***(i)* Sodium Carbonate.** Its standard solution can be easily made by dissolving a known weight of it in water and making the solution to a known volume.

Eq. wt. of Na_2CO_3 (anhydrous) is 53 and the mol. wt. is 106

$\frac{N}{10}$ solution of Na_2CO_3 can be obtained by dissolving 5.3 g/in one litre of the solution.

$\frac{M}{10}$ solution of Na_2CO_3 would contain 10.6 g/litre.

The standard solution of Na_2CO_3 is used for standardizing the solutions of HCl, H_2SO_4 etc.

***(ii)* Oxalic Acid.** Equivalent weight of hydrated oxalic acid is 63 and the molecular weight is 126 its $\frac{N}{10}$ solution would contain 6.3 g/litre, and $\frac{M}{10}$ solution would contain 12.6 g/litre.

Experiment 1: Estimate a mixture of Na_2CO_3 and $NaHCO_3$ by acid based titration given that 10.0g of it has been dissolved in one litre of the given solution. Provided N/10 HCl.

Theory. The mixture of Na_2CO_3 and $NaHCO_3$ is dissolved in a known volume of water. The solution is first titrated with a standard solution of HCl using methyl orange indicator. This gives us the total normality due to Na_2CO_3 and $NaHCO_3$. Then the mixture solution is titrated with standard solution using phenolphthalein indicator. The neutralization of Na_2CO_3 takes place in two steps.

$$Na_2CO_3 + HCl \rightarrow NaHCO_3 + NaCl$$
$$NaHCO_3 + HCl \rightarrow NaCl + CO_2 + H_2O$$

As soon as CO_2 is evolved, it reacts with phenolphthalein indicator. Phenolphthalein stops working as indicator. However, methyl orange is not affected by the evolution of CO_2.

Thus the normality that we shall obtain with methyl orange indicator will give the total normality due to Na_2CO_3 and $NaHCO_3$. But the normality that we shall obtain with phenolphthalein indicator will be equal to half the normality due to Na_2CO_3 only. By calculation we can determine the amount of Na_2CO_3 and $NaHCO_3$ in the mixture.

First titration

Indicator. Methyl Orange

End point. Appearance of pink color

Procedure

1. Pipette out 20 ml of the given solution into a titration flask. Add 2 drops of methyl orange indicator.

2. After rinsing the burette with N/10 HCl solution, fill it with this solution and note down the initial reading.

3. Add HCl from the burette into the titration flask in small lots with constant shaking till a permanent pink color is obtained. First reading is rough reading.

4. Repeat the titrations three or four times till concordant values of volumes of HCl used are obtained. Add HCl dropwise near the end point.

5. Note down the readings in a table and find the concordant volume of the acid used.

Second titration

Indicator. Phenolphthalein

End Point. Disappearance of pink colour

Procedure

1. Pipette out 20ml of the given solution into a titration falsk. Add 2 drops of phenolphthalein indicator. A pink colour will be obtained.

2. After rinsing the burette with N/10 HCl solution, fill the burette with this solution and note down the initial reading.

3. Add HCl from the burette into the titration flask in small lots with constant shaking till the pink color is just discharged. First reading is rough reading.

4. Repeat the titration three or four times till concordant values of volumes of HCl used are obtained. Add HCl dropwise near the end point.

5. Note down the initial and final readings in a table and find out the concordant volume of acid used.

Observations.

First titration with Methyl orange indicator

S.No.	Initial Reading	Final Reading	Volume of acid used (ml)
1.	.....	.....	.....
2.	.....	.....	.....
3.	.....	.....	.....
4.	.....	.....	.....

Concordant volume = v_1 ml (say)

Second titration with phenolphthalein indicator

S.No.	Initial Reading	Final Reading	Volume of acid used (ml)
1.	.....	.....	.....
2.	.....	.....	.....
3.	.....	.....	.....
4.	.....	.....	.....

Concordant volume = v_2 ml (say)

Calculations.

Let the weight of the mixture per litre be = x g

First titration (Using Methyl orange as indicator). Let the volume of mixture solution taken each time = 20 ml.

Volume of N/10 HCl required for neutralization = v_1 ml

Apply normality equation

$$\underset{\text{Mix}}{N_1V_1} = \underset{\text{HCl}}{N_2V_2}$$

Substituting the values

$$N_1 \times 20 = \frac{N}{10} \times V_2$$

or $$N_1 = \frac{N}{10} \times \frac{v_1}{20} \qquad (\because V_2 = v_1)$$

where N_1 is the total normality due to Na_2CO_3 and $NaHCO_3$

Second Titration (using phenolphthalein as indicator)

Let the volume of mixture solution taken each time = 20 ml.

Volume of N/10 HCl required for neutralisation = v_2 ml

Apply normality equation

$$\underset{\text{Mix}}{N_1'V_1'} = \underset{\text{HCl}}{N_2'V_2'}$$

Substituting the values

$$N_1' \times 20 = \frac{N}{10} \times v_2 \qquad (\because V_2' = v_2)$$

or $$N_1' = \frac{N}{10} \times \frac{v_2}{20}$$

where N_1' is equal to half the normality due to Na_2CO_3

$\therefore$ Normality due to Na_2CO_3 = $2N_1'$

Normality due to $NaHCO_3$ = Total normality – normality due to Na_2CO_3

= $N_1 - 2N_1'$

Strength/litre of Na_2CO_3 = Normality × Eq. weight

= $2N_1' \times 53$ g

Strength/litre of $NaHCO_3$ = Normality × Eq. weight

= $(N_1 - 2N_1') \times 84$ g

After obtaining the weights of Na_2CO_3 and $NaHCO_3$, we can determine the percentage of each in the mixture.

Instructions for the Lab Staff

Provide

1. A solution containing 5.0 g per litre of sodium carbonate and 5.0 g per liter of sodium hydrogen carbonate
2. N/10 HCl
3. Phenolphthalein indicator
4. Methyl orange indicator

Experiment 2: Estimate the calcium content in chalk as calcium oxalate permanganometry. Provided N/20 $KMnO_4$.

Theory chalk contains calcium carbonate which is converted to calcium acetate (soluble) by reaction with acetic acid. The calcium acetate obtained is treated with excess of ammonium oxalate. The precipitate of calcium oxalate is dissolved is in dilute sulphuric acid to form oxalic acid. This oxalic acid is titrated against standard solution of potassium permanganate. From the titration, we obtain the concentration of calcium.

Reactions.

$$CaCO_3 + 2\,CH_3COOH \rightarrow \underset{\text{Calcium acetate}}{(CH_3COO)_2\,Ca} + CO_2 + H_2O$$

$$\underset{\text{Calcium acetate}}{(CH_3COO)_2\,Ca} + \underset{\text{Ammonium Oxalate in excess}}{\begin{matrix} COONH_4 \\ | \\ COONH_4 \end{matrix}} \rightarrow \underset{\text{Calcium oxalate}}{\begin{matrix} COO\,Ca \\ | \\ COO \end{matrix}} + 2CH_3\,COONH_4$$

$$\begin{matrix} COONH_4 \\ | \\ COONH_4 \end{matrix} + H_2SO_4 \rightarrow (NH_4)_2\,SO_4 + \begin{matrix} COOH \\ | \\ COOH \end{matrix}$$

$$2\,KMnO_4 + 3\,H_2SO_4 \rightarrow K_2SO_4 + 2\,MnSO_4 + 3\,H_2O + 5\,[O] \quad .....(1)$$

$$\left.\begin{matrix} COOH \\ | \\ COOH \end{matrix} + [O] \rightarrow 2CO_2 + H_2O\,\right] \times 5 \quad .....(2)$$

Adding eq. (1) and (2)

$$2\,KMnO_4 + 3\,H_2SO_4 + 5\,COOH \rightarrow K_2SO_4 + 2\,MnSO_4 + 10\,CO_2 + 8H_2O$$

Indicator. $KMnO_4$ acts as self indicator

End Point. Colourless to pink ($KMnO_4$ in the burette)

Procedure

A. Preparation of calcium acetate solution.

1. Weigh about 5g but exactly of the given sample of chalk. Crush it and transfer to a 250 mL beaker.
2. Add enough dilute acetic acid to dissolve the chalk sample.
3. Boil it for a few minutes, stir the mixture in the beaker to obtain a clear solution.

B. Precipitation of calcium oxalate

1. Allow the solution to cool. Add ammonium hydroxide to remove excess of acetic acid. This can be done using a litmus paper. When the excess acid had been removed, blue litmus will not turn red.
2. Add ammonium oxalate solution dropwise with stirring till no more precipitate is formed. Allow the solution to stand for an hour.
3. Filter the precipitate and wash it with water 2-3 times to remove excess of ammonium oxalate. This can be done by testing the filtrate for oxalate ions. Pink colour of hot acidified $KMnO_4$ is discharged with oxalic acid.

C. Dissolving the calcium oxalate precipitate

1. Dissolve the precipitate obtained is dil H_2SO_4 and transfer the solution to a 250 ml measuring flask.

2. Give washings to the beaker and transfer to the measuring flask. Add water to complete the volume in the flask. Shake to obtain a homogeneous solution of calcium oxalate

D. Titration with N/20 $KMnO_4$

1. Rinse the burette with $KMnO_4$ and fill it with this solution. Take the initial reading.

2. After rinsing pipette out 20 ml of calcium oxalate solution into a titration flask. Add 1 test tube of 4 N sulphuric acid to the flask.

3. Heat the flask to 60-70°C till it is unbearable to touch.

4. Run down $KMnO_4$ solution to the flask in small lots and shaking of the flask till a permanent pink colour is obtained. First reading is rough reading.

5. Repeat titration till 3 concordant values of volume of $KMnO_4$ solution used, are obtained.

6. Tabulate the readings and calculate the result as follows:

Observations.

Mass of chalk taken = wg

Volume of calcium oxalate = 20 ml

Solution taken each time

S.No.	Initial burette reading	Final burette reading	Volume of $KMNO_4$ used (ml)
1.	------------	------------	------------
2.	------------	------------	------------
3.	------------	------------	------------
4.	------------	------------	------------

Concordant volume = *v* ml

Calculations.

Calculation of strength of calcium oxalate

V ml of *$KMnO_4$* solution is equivalent to 20 ml of calcium oxalate solution

Applying normality equation

$$\underset{\text{Calcium oralate}}{N_1V_1} = \underset{KMnO_4}{N_2V_2}$$

Or $$N_1 \times 20 = \frac{N}{20} \times V$$

Or N₁ (normality of calcium oxalate solution) $= \frac{N}{400} \times V$

Strength of calcium/litre = Normality × Eq. mass

$$= \frac{N}{400} \times V \times 20 \qquad (\text{Eq. mass of Ca} = \frac{40}{2} = 20)$$

$$= \frac{N}{20} \times V \text{ g/litre}$$

Strength of calcium in 250 ml of the solution $= \frac{N}{20} \times \frac{V}{4}$ g/litre

Percentage of calcium in the sample $= \frac{N}{20} \times \frac{V}{4} \times \frac{100}{w}$

Thus substituting the values of V and w, we can obtain the desired result

Provide

1. $\frac{N}{20}$ $KMnO_4$ solution (2.3 g/litre)
2. $\frac{N}{5}$ Ammonium oxalate solution (12.0 g/litre)
3. 4 N H_2SO_4
4. Sample of chalk

Experiment 3: You are provided with a solution of Mohr's salt [$FeSO_4(NH_4)_2SO_4.xH_2O$], 20 g of which have been dissolved per litre. Determine volumetrically the value of 'x'. Provided N/20 (approx.) $KMnO_4$ solution. Ask for what you want.

Requirement. N/20 $FeSO_4$

Theory. Firstly $KMnO_4$ is standardised against standard N/20 $FeSO_4$, then $KMnO_4$ is titrated against Mohr's salt solution to find out the exact normality of Mohr's salt solution. Knowing this, the mol. wt. (same as eq. wt.) is calculated.

Equations.

$$2KMnO_4 + 3H_2SO_4 \rightarrow K_2SO_4 + 2MnSO_4 + 3H_2O + 5[O]$$

$$2FeSO_4 + H_2SO_4 + [O] \rightarrow Fe_2(SO_4)_3 + H_2O$$

$$2FeSO_4.(NH_4)\ 2SO_4 + H_2SO_4 + [O] \rightarrow Fe_2(SO_4)_3 + 2(NH_4)_2SO_4 + H_2O$$

or In the form of ionic equations

$$MnO^-_4 + 8H^+ + 5e^- \rightarrow Mn^{2+} + 4H_2O$$

$$Fe^{2+} \rightarrow Fe^{3+} + e^-$$

Procedure

1. *Titration of $FeSO_4$ against approx. N/20 solution of $KMnO_4$.*

Rinse and fill the burette with $KMnO_4$ solution, Pipette out 20 ml of ferrous sulphate solution into the titration flask and add one test tube full of dil. H_2SO_4. Unlike oxalic acid and oxalates, do not heat. Start titration by adding $KMnO_4$ solution from the burette, little at time with constant shaking. Note the final reading at the reach of the end point i.e. when just appearance of permanent pink colouration takes place. Takes 3 or 4 concordant sets of readings and take the mean.

2. *Titration of $KMnO_4$ against Mohr's salt solution.*

Procedure remains the same as above except that Mohr's salt is taken in place of ferrous sulphate.

Observations.

First titration *($FeSO_4$ against $KMnO_4$)*

Indicator. $KMnO_4$ acts as self indicator.

End point. Just appearance of permanent light pink colouration.

Vol. of N/20 $FeSO_4$ used each time = 20 ml

Let the vol. of $KMnO_4$ used be v_1 ml

Second titration. *[$KMnO_4$ against Mohr's salt solution]*

Indicator and End point. Same as in first titration.

Volume of Mohr's salt solution used each time = 20 ml

Let the volume of $KMnO_4$ solution be v_2 ml.

Calculations.

Step I. *To find out exact normality of $KMnO_4$ solution.*

Using
$$\underset{KMnO_4}{N_1V_1} \equiv \underset{FeSO_4.7H_2O}{N_2V_2}$$

Substituting for different quantities we have,

$$N_1 \times v_1 = \frac{N}{20} \times 20$$

or
$$N_1 \text{ (Normality of } KMnO_4) = \frac{N}{20} \times \frac{20}{v_1} = \frac{N}{v_1}$$

Step II. *To find out normality of Mohr's salt solution.*

$$\underset{\text{Mohr's salt}}{N'V'} \equiv \underset{KMnO_4}{N''V''}$$

Substituting for various quantities we have,

$$N' \times 20 = N_1 \times v_2 \quad \text{or } N' = \frac{N_1 \times v_2}{20}$$

(Put the value of N_1 from step 1)

N′ is the normality of Mohr's salt solution.

Step III. *To calculate the value of 'x' i.e., the no. of water molecule*

Strength/litre of anhydrous salt = Normality × Eq. wt of anhydrous salt

$$= N_2 \times 284$$

Mol. wt. of anhydrous salt is the same as the eq. wt. *i.e.* 284

$$\frac{\text{Mol. wt. of hydrated Mohr's salt}}{\text{Mol. wt. of anhydrous Mohr's salt}} = \frac{\text{Wt. of hydrated salt}}{\text{Wt. of anhyd salt}}$$

$$\frac{284 + 18x}{284} = \frac{20}{N_2 \times 284}$$

From this value *x* can be calculated (Remember '*x*' is always a whole number).

Instructions for the Lab staff. Provide

(*i*) 20 g/litre of Mohr's salt

(*ii*) N/20 $KMnO_4$ (approx. 1.5 g/litre)

(*iii*) N/20 $FeSO_4.7H_2O$ (approx. 14.0 g/litre)